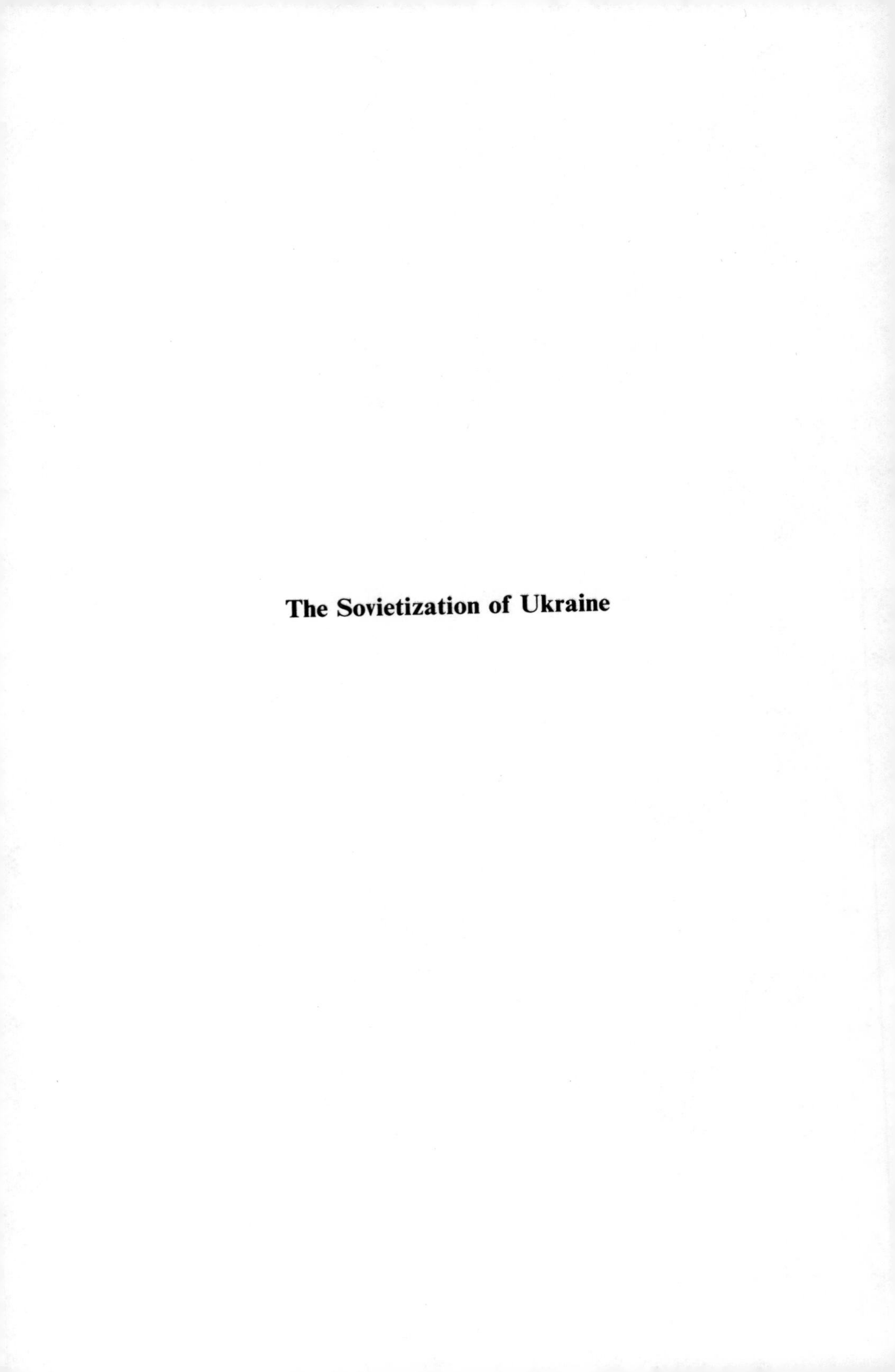

The Sovietization of Ukraine

THE SOVIETIZATION OF UKRAINE 1917–1923

The Communist Doctrine and Practice of National Self-Determination

Revised Edition

Jurij Borys

The Canadian Institute of Ukrainian Studies
Edmonton 1980

THE CANADIAN LIBRARY IN UKRAINIAN STUDIES

Canadian Cataloguing in Publication Data
Borys, Jurij, 1922–
The Sovietization of Ukraine 1917–1923
(Canadian library in Ukrainian studies)

Originally presented as the author's thesis, Stockholm, 1960, under title: The Russian Communist Party and the Sovietization of Ukraine
Bibliography: p.
Includes index.
ISBN 0-920862-01-2 bd.
ISBN 0-920862-03-9 pa.

1. Ukraine—Politics and government—1917– 2. Nationalism—Ukraine. 3. Kommunisticheskaia partiia Sovetskogo Soiuza. 4. Self-determination, National. I. Canadian Institute of Ukrainian Studies. II. Title. III. Series.
JN6599.U4B6 1980 947'.71084'1 C80–091020–6

Cover design: Larisa Sembaliuk

Printed in Canada by Printing Services, University of Alberta
Distributed by the University of Toronto Press
5201 Dufferin St.
Downsview, Ontario
Canada M3H 5T8

To My Sons: Ragnar, Martin,
Stefan, and Philip

Contents

Tables

Foreword to the Second Edition

In very recent years two major emphases have characterized Soviet studies in North America. One is the renewed scrutiny of the formative, "Leninist" period of the Soviet system. Here the emphasis has been on the truth of the vanquished; it is a search for the might-have-beens of Soviet history. The attentive reader will hardly doubt that a major source of this renewed interest has been the belief, so widespread among the generation maturing during the 1960s, that the Russian revolution contains profound lessons for our current predicament, that, if only it had somehow avoided the wrong turning of Stalinism, the Soviet experiment would have presented a solution for the malaise of industrial society. This note sounds clearly in what is probably the most impressive of the revisionist histories of the Soviet formative years, Stephen F. Cohen's *Bukharin and the Bolshevik Revolution* (New York, 1973). Anyone who compares Cohen's respectful treatment of Bukharin to Edward H. Carr's equally distinguished approach twenty years ago to the same general subject will be struck by the very considerable change in viewpoint. Whereas Carr was impressed by the physical strength and the material achievement of the early Soviet regime (and consequently exhibited some sympathy for Stalin), Cohen is not looking for the truth *of* the victors but for truth *for* tomorrow. Yet the fundamental defect of both approaches, I think, is that the vanquished whom Cohen examines as much as the victor whom he rejects were part and parcel of the hyper-centralization of Bolshevism.

The second emphasis in contemporary Soviet studies is the recognition that the Soviet experience is not, and never has been, an experience of Russians alone. At first sight this trend may appear to be unrelated to the first emphasis mentioned above. But the options opened up by the double revolution in the Russian empire were at least as much options for differing national experiences as they were for alternative Communist perspectives. Some of the national options were Marxist, some were not. As early as 1950, when Yugoslavia's break with Soviet orthodoxy had become definitive, specialists began to note the striking parallel between Tito's "national Communism" and the kind of Communism which had been advocated—unsuccessfully—by Bolsheviks in Ukraine. Unfortunately, it has taken nearly three decades for North American political establishments to realize that the national components (both Russian and non-Russian) of Bolshevism constituted, in germ, the complex structure of the Communist bloc as we know it today.

One of the great achievements of Jurij Borys' book is to have recognized, long before the two emphases just noted became fashionable, the significance of the complex relationship between Bolshevism and nationalism in the critical Ukrainian arena. In order to present this recognition in a meaningful way, he had to review the history of the Ukrainian national movement, and he did it very well. But that was only preliminary to his examination of the Marxist political forces operating in Ukraine; on this subject (as I wrote in the *Journal of Modern History* shortly after the book appeared) "the heart of his treatment is comprehensive and original." Since that time monographs and more general treatments have examined various aspects of the relation of Marxism to the Ukrainian national environment, but Borys' work provides a judicious and authoritative introduction.

To put Borys' achievement in full perspective without resorting to hindsight, I must again quote my initial appraisal:

> If this review were to close at this point, one would be justified in concluding that Borys' work is a significant contribution to history. It is, however, somewhat more than that. To a greater extent than any other writer on this period of Ukrainian history (and, with few exceptions, on this period of Soviet history in general), Borys has endeavoured to present the sociological and the economic as well as the purely political aspects of his subject.

Let me spell out briefly just what this concern for sociological and economic factors entails. Borys has used a great deal of quantitative data, including such diverse materials as the elections to the constituent assembly and the distribution of land ownership. In this resort to quantification Borys was years ahead of most political scientists and historians working on Soviet subjects in general, to say nothing of those analysing specific nationality problems. To an extent rare in works completed nearly twenty years ago, his book also fits in the mainstream of historiographical evolution. As Fernand Braudel and other writers of the *Annales* school have urged, history must turn from the *évênementiel* to a more profound and comprehensive examination of social and economic forces. It is, for many, not easy to understand how difficult this turn was in the 1950s, especially for a writer of the Ukrainian emigration, which contained then more than its share of writers over-impressed by the claims of German idealist philosophy and historicism. Today I think one can safely assert that the kind of approach Jurij Borys adopted has been entirely vindicated by the general evolution of historiography and the social sciences. We can therefore acknowledge our gratitude to him for having moved Soviet studies in general and Ukrainian studies in particular one step closer to the mainstream of Western thought. When I wrote the lines quoted earlier, I had never met Jurij Borys. Since that time I have talked with him many times, and have come to appreciate him as a colleague as well as a scholar. It is extremely gratifying to see his pioneering study once again in print.

John A. Armstrong — Epiphany 1978
Madison, Wisconsin

Publisher's Preface to the Second Edition

This work was originally published in Stockholm in 1960, with the title *The Russian Communist Party and the Sovietization of Ukraine: A Study in the Communist Doctrine of the Self-Determination of Nations.* The second edition has been revised stylistically and divided into smaller chapters. Pages 67–99 of the original edition have been replaced by the author's more recent study of political parties in Ukraine on the eve of the 1917 revolution (chapter III of the present edition). The map that appeared in the first edition has been redrawn and illustrations added. The Canadian Institute of Ukrainian Studies would like to thank Professors Richard Pipes and George Luckyj for permission to reprint photographs that originally appeared in their books as well as Hryhory Kostiuk and Melanie Czajkowskyj for providing a portrait from the Vynnychenko archives. The Institute would also like to express gratitude to Geoffrey Lester, cartographer in the Geography Department, University of Alberta, who gave of his time to prepare the map for this edition.

Preface to the Second Edition

A distinct truism of our time is that it is an age of nationalism. The significance of ethnic fragmentation and the demand for national self-determination has become universal. The urge for national identity and self-realization has penetrated all social fabrics, affecting all human relations and destabilizing ethnically pluralist political structures.

When this book was being prepared in the late fifties, nationalism was not a recognized or appreciated force. It had been discredited by Nazism and other extreme nationalisms. Even well-informed scholars had an impression that nationalism and nation-states were anachronistic aberrations. Racism, chauvinism, and irrational behaviour were not part of the free human being they envisaged.

However, with time it became obvious that man's need for group identity and national loyalty was fundamental. In any analysis of social and political conflicts this phenomenon could no longer be ignored. National identity, tribalism, and ethnicity became an integral conceptual framework for social studies. As a result, we are now witnessing an unprecedented upsurge of theoretical and empirical studies dealing with ethnic, cultural, and religious aspects of mankind.

To a large measure this awareness on the part of the scholarly community led to the decision to publish a new edition of this book. The decisive input came from Professor Ivan L. Rudnytsky of the University of Alberta, who may therefore be considered the initiator of this endeavour.

When the Canadian Institute of Ukrainian Studies was created in 1976, its director, Professor Manoly R. Lupul, supported the project and provided financial assistance. He and Professor Rudnytsky deserve special recognition and my gratitude.

I would also like to express my sincere appreciation to several readers who greatly improved the prose of the earlier edition: Virginia Savage, Cambridge, Mass., who read the whole manuscript; Arthur Milne, University of Calgary, who assisted me in rewriting the first chapter; my colleague Professor Frank McKinnon, who edited the conclusions; and Dr. Muriel G. Solomon, who assisted me in the time-consuming proofreading of galleys. Finally, I would like to extend my appreciation to the staff of the Canadian Institute of Ukrainian Studies for editorial and technical assistance, especially to Assya Berezowsky, Olenka Lupul, Theresa Lacousta, and Peter Matilainen, who typed the entire manuscript. Dr. John-Paul Himka deserves much credit for seeing the work through its several editorial stages.

Jurij Borys
Saltsjöbaden

December 1979

Preface to the First Edition

The appearance of this study is due to the generous assistance of many persons and institutions, to whom I wish to express my sincere gratitude. This work was started under the late Professor Elis Håstad, to whom I am deeply indebted for his encouragement and support during my graduate studies and preparatory research work. I also owe very much to his successor at the Department of Political Science at the University of Stockholm, Professor Gunnar Heckscher, for his advice and valuable corrections during the final preparation of the manuscript. I am especially indebted to him for the initiation of a discussion of my work at an early stage at an *ad hoc* seminar arranged by the School of Slavonic and East European Studies at the University of London. In this connection I wish to express my gratitude to Professor Hugh Seton-Watson, Dr. G. H. Bolsover, Dr. Leonard Shapiro, Dr. John Keep, and Mr. M. Mikula for their valuable suggestions during that discussion.

The preparatory research was made possible by a post-graduate fellowship awarded to me by the University of Stockholm during the academic years 1955–58. A grant from the Swedish National Council for Social Research enabled me to spend a year abroad collecting materials from various libraries in Western Europe. Other grants from the same Council made it possible for me to obtain microfilms from foreign libraries and covered the costs of translation of the larger part of the manuscript.

It is impossible, within the scope of this preface, to mention all the institutions and libraries whose generous aid I would like to acknowledge; but the following are outstanding: the Royal Library, Stockholm; the University Library, Uppsala; the University Library, Lund; the Archives of the Labour Movement, Stockholm; the University Library, Helsinki; the New York Public Library; the Harvard College Library, Cambridge, Mass.; the Public Record Office, London; the British Museum, London; the Bibliothèque de documentation internationale contemporaine, Paris; the Institut des études slaves, Paris; the Shevchenko Scientific Society, Sarcelles; the Ècole des languages orientales vivantes, Paris; the private collection of Volodymyr Vynnychenko, Mougins; the Institute for the Study of the USSR, Munich; the University Library, Vienna; the Staatsarchiv, Marburg; the Hamburgisches Weltwirtschaftsarchiv; the Bibliotek des Instituts für Weltwirtschaft, Kiel; the Internationaal Instituut voor Sociale Geschiedenis, Amsterdam; the University Library, Prague; the Library of the Czechoslovak Foreign Ministry; the Lenin Library, Moscow.

The main body of the printed sources, however, is to be found at the Russian Institute of the University of Stockholm, where the substantial part of the manuscript was prepared. I am most obliged to its director, Dr. N.Å Nilson, and to Drs. B. Kalnins and P. R. Vitvickij for their ready assistance.

Furthermore, I wish to express my gratitude to Dr. Nils B. E. Andrén and Dr. Bohdan Kentrschynskyj for their examination of this manuscript and valuable suggestions. To Mr. Victor Swoboda, Lecturer at the School of Slavonic and East European Studies, London, I am immensely indebted for his careful translation.

My wife, Ann Mari, deserves special recognition for her valuable assistance in reading the manuscript and preparing the index, and not least of all for her indefatigable patience during the most difficult phase of this work.

Jurij Borys
Stockholm

November 1959

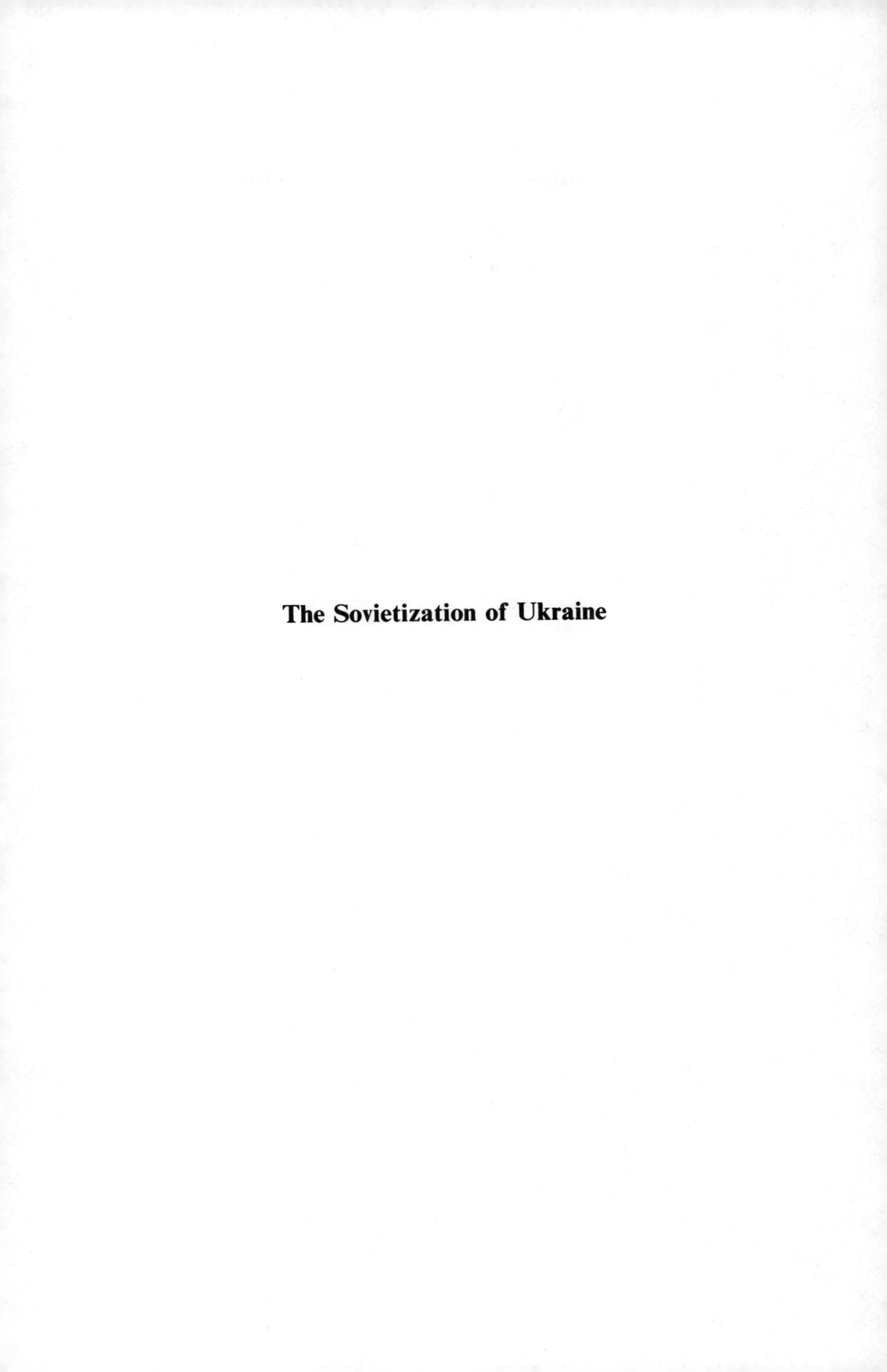

The Sovietization of Ukraine

Introduction

The exploration of Soviet affairs, particularly the question of nationalities, is a complicated and unenviable task, and has rarely been accomplished satisfactorily. There are, of course, many obstacles to surmount. The greatest hindrances are the lack of primary sources, the tendentious approach to the history of the Communist movement taken by non-Communist investigators, and the even more biased presentation of events by Soviet historians.[1] The nationality policy of the Russian Communist party has been treated by Western scholars in several articles and more extended works. But the subject is still far from exhausted.[2]

The subject of this study is the Communist doctrine of the self-determination of nations, as applied by Russian Bolsheviks[3] in Ukraine. The Bolshevik faction of the Russian social democratic party, posing as a protector of the nationalities of Russia, from the very beginning propounded "self-determination of nations" as its slogan. The theoretical aspects of the self-determination issue were defined during the prerevolutionary period, 1903–17. It was mainly Lenin who in 1913–16 formulated the Bolshevik position on national self-determination, although he had to revise his opinion on this issue many times during his political career. However, more than fifty years after the first pronouncements, the national antagonisms within the Soviet orbit continue to exist and are of great concern.[4] The issue was brought to the fore by a series of nationalist upheavals within the Communist bloc: the rebellion of Yugoslav Communists under Tito, the Hungarian revolution in the autumn of 1956, the Czechoslovak crisis of 1968, and, of course, the rift with the Chinese Communists.

Since the Russian Bolsheviks derived their attitude towards the nationality problem, as towards other problems, from Marx's teachings, I include a summary of the views of Marx and his early followers on the question of nationalities. Historically, the situation on the European continent and in the colonies had developed in such a way that even Marx could not entirely ignore the nationality problem. The core of Marx's theory lay, however, in the axiom of class conflict, with the nationality antagonisms playing only a secondary role. While seeking a formula for the solution of this problem, the Russian Bolsheviks, even more than their forerunners, were obliged to include this issue in their political programme, which was more than their Marxist conscience allowed. During the tsarist regime, relations among the different nationalities in Russia had become so strained and those peoples had become so antagonistic to the Russian government that the idea of the self-determination of nations, with the right of secession, was welcomed by most nationalities. Lenin's adoption of the self-determination principle was severely criticized by the Bolshevik left wing (Rosa Luxemburg, Karl Radek, Nikolai Bukharin, Georgii Piatakov, and Evgeniia Bosh), which accused him of bringing the problem of nationalities into false prominence among the proletariat of the subjugated nationalities. A careful analysis of Lenin's declarations and a comparison with those of the "leftists" shows, however, that nothing essential separated them.

The main part of this work concerns Bolshevik policy in Ukraine, as an example of how the Communist doctrine of national self-determination has been applied. For economic as well as strategic reasons, the retention of Ukraine within Russia's orbit was the *conditio sine qua non* for the success of the Communist revolution.

Chapter II explores the social and economic basis for Communism in Ukraine. The question whether conditions for the Communist revolution were less favourable in Ukraine than in Russia is theoretical, but worthy of consideration; it is, for example, generally agreed that industry in the borderlands of Russia, including Ukraine, was at a lower stage of development, and therefore the working class was smaller. Some attention is given, in chapters III and V, to the problem of the national heterogeneity of the social democratic movement in Ukraine and to the Bolshevik attitude towards the national separatism of Ukrainian social democrats. The national feelings among the proletariat of the non-Russian nationalities seem to have been stronger than the social feelings; this explains the existence of the separate national social democratic parties, which defended their independence against the centralist demands of Russian social democracy. Centralism within the party was for Lenin and his followers an axiom that later was to serve as a norm in the relations between Soviet Russia and the borderlands. There is some question about Lenin's position on self-determination for Ukraine, even in a modified form by which self-determination was to be applied only by the proletariat. If he recognized Ukraine's right to self-determination, why then was he opposed to the existence of an independent Ukrainian social democratic party and a separate Ukrainian Communisty party?

Chapter IV describes the Ukrainian national revolution that took place under the aegis of the Ukrainian Central Rada (Council). It covers the period when the so-called Provisional Government was in power in Russia. That government was non-committal on the demands of the nationalities and continually postponed the question of Ukraine's autonomy until the all-Russian constituent assembly should meet. The conflict between the Provisional Government and the non-Russian nationalities proved advantageous to the Bolsheviks, who accused the government of continuing to suppress these nationalities.

The establishment of the Soviet regime in Ukraine is discussed in chapters VII–IX. To demonstrate more clearly the social and political forces upon which the Soviet power in Ukraine relied, I have briefly analysed (in chapter VI) the creation of the Communist party of Ukraine and, in this connection, the left-wing tendencies in the Ukrainian Social Democratic Worker's Party (USDWP) and the Ukrainian Party of Socialist Revolutionaries (UPSR). To what extent did these parties assist in the process of the sovietization of Ukraine? It was imperative for the Russian Bolsheviks to absorb the Ukrainian elements into the party in order to pacify the Ukrainian peasantry, which was hostile to the Soviet regime. The relations between the Ukrainian peasantry and the Russian Communist party were crucial to the survival of the Soviet regime in the Ukrainian countryside.

The growth of national consciousness among the Ukrainian elements of the Russian Communist Party (Bolsheviks) (RCP[B]) is dealt with in the chapter on the creation of the Communist Party (Bolsheviks) of Ukraine (CP[B]U). In that chapter, the friction between the RCP(B) and the CP(B)U over the nationality issue is also discussed.

The sovietization of Ukraine was to serve as a means for maintaining it within the Russian political sphere. The relations between the Soviet Russian republic (RSFSR) and the Ukrainian Soviet republic (UkSSR) between 1919 and 1922 are examined in chapter X to illustrate that sovietization. This work ends with chapters (XI–XII) on the creation of the Soviet Union in 1922–23. These chapters attempt to clarify the attitude of the non-Russian Communists towards the centralist tendencies of the Russian Communists.

In the course of this work, I have kept in mind a number of important questions. How did the Russian Communists develop and apply the Marxist, internationalist (in principle) doctrine to the problem of national self-determination? Was the real aim of the Russian Communists a united and indivisible socialist Russia, and did they advocate the principle of self-determination only as a means towards this end? Did the degree to which the Russian Communists yielded to various nationalities depend on the degree of resistance to the centralist tendencies of the party? Why did Russian Communists before the Bolshevik revolution refuse to recognize the right of self-determination, rejecting even the federative principle for the future socialist Russian state, when eventually they not only admitted the federative principle, but in some cases even recognized the independence of non-Russian nationalities? Why did they not abolish the Ukrainian Soviet republic and other national republics immediately after the establishment of Soviet power in Ukraine and other borderlands?

Sources and Relevant Literature

In the study of the Bolshevik revolution, the chief problem for scholars is without doubt the lack of access to unpublished sources and the unreliability of such printed material as is available. To sift the truth out of this vast and chaotic mass is no easy matter. Verification of documents and of their veracity offers the greatest difficulty. Valuable source material certainly exists in the numerous archives of the Soviet Union, but this is inaccessible to Western students and may be used only by those Soviet scholars considered reliable by the party.

This dearth of source material has been my gravest problem, and I have had to turn to what could be found outside the Soviet Union. The only unpublished materials I have been able to utilize were Trotsky's papers (I received selected copies of these from Harvard University, and I was allowed to consult them in the International Institute for Social History in Amsterdam), and the official German documents at the Public Record Office, London. Of vital importance for my work were rare publications from the library of the Czechoslovak Foreign Ministry.

Soviet official reports and publications; minutes of congresses, conferences, and meetings of the Communist party; the sessions of Soviet congresses and the All-Russian (All-Union) Central Executive Committee (VTsIK); government decrees; and statutory documents are of great importance. Minutes of the Communist party congresses and conferences and the congresses of the CP(B)U are available. There is also a collection of documents entitled *Istoriia KP(b)U v materiialakh ta dokumentakh*, published during the Stalin era; it is a biased collection of the party's resolutions, decisions, and propaganda brochures of lesser value. Of greater interest is *1917 god na Kievshchine* (edited by V. Manilov), a diary of occurrences in Kiev during the days of the Bolshevik revolution. Perhaps the most reliable sources are gathered in the periodical *Letopis revoliutsii* (later *Litopys revoliutsii*), the organ of the Committee for the History of the Ukrainian Revolution and the Communist Party. This journal contains archival documents, memoirs, research material, and bibliographies, making it one of the more important sources on the history of the CP(B)U and the Russian Social Democratic Workers' Party (Bolshevik) (RSDWP[B]) in Ukraine. It was violently criticized for its Ukrainian nationalism, and it closed in 1933 following Mykola Skrypnyk's suicide.[5] Of importance for our knowledge of the party's policy towards Ukraine during the formation of the Soviet Union are the minutes of the meetings of the all-union congress of soviets and the VTsIK, and later of the two chambers, the all-union congress and the council of nationalities, in which discussions on the powers of Soviet republics are recorded.

Official Soviet publications are to a large extent misleading because of the one-sided choice of documents, involving omission of those which might be detrimental to the party. After the inauguration of the "Stalin cult," documents concerning party history were subjected to thorough censorship in which the part played by the "enemies of the people"—among them Trotsky, Zinovev, Kamenev, Bukharin, Skrypnyk, Shumsky, Chubar, Kosior, and Rakovsky—was distorted and denigrated.

Even Lenin's works are not free from this tendency. Some of Lenin's letters to Inessa Armand, written in 1914 and published for the first time in 1950, contain much interesting material showing Lenin's cunning tactics towards the Ukrainian social democratic movement. The same can be said of Lenin's letters written in 1922 to the members of the politburo, which were for many years withheld from the public and were first published in 1956.[6] Lenin's speeches on the Ukrainian question at the conference of the RCP(B) held in December 1919 have never been found among the minutes of the conference.[7]

Bias is most noticeable in official publications from the later part of the Stalin era. Selection of many of the documents dealing with the Bolshevik revolution in Ukraine proceeded according to a certain pattern and with a definite object in view.[8] The aim was to show the so-called "revolutionary unity" of the Russian and Ukrainian peoples and to accentuate the "earnest desire" of the Ukrainians to be reunited with Russia. Evidence of the Ukrainian fight for independence has been left out or tendentiously presented. These deficiencies have subsequently been criticized even by Soviet historians themselves.[9]

The Communist newspapers and brochures present a special problem. The only newspapers available in more or less complete form are the official organ of the RCP(B), *Pravda*, and that of the Soviets of Workers' Deputies of the RSFSR, *Izvestiia*. The remainder, with the exception of certain issues of the Ukrainian soviet organ, *Visti*, printed in Kharkiv, and the paper of the CP(B)U, *Kommunist*, are lost. The theoretical party publications, *Bilshovyk Ukrainy*, published in Kharkiv (1926–35) and in Kiev (1935–52), is available except for the years 1926 and 1927, for which there are only a few issues extant. The Borotbist organ, *Borotba*, and that of the Ukrainian Communist Party (Borotbist), *Chervonyi prapor*, which contain very important material, are, with the exception of a few numbers, unavailable in Europe. The Communist press cannot be used as a source without critical examination since these newspapers were under the strict control of the most orthodox members of the party.

Available memoirs contain valuable material but can hardly be used as source material without careful scrutiny. Moreover, they are tainted with party discipline. As often as not, the author writes according to party orders. Such was the case with the many memoirs published during the twenties in *Letopis revoliutsii*. The writers were Bolsheviks who had been active in Ukraine during the revolution. In their descriptions, the sovietization of Ukraine is presented as the result of a complete and wholehearted uprising of the Ukrainian people. These authors naturally miss no opportunity to defame the Ukrainian national movement and their opponents in other parties, while praising the aims of the Communist party, especially their own achievements.

The writings of Lenin and Stalin contain important material concerning the policy of the RCP(B) towards Ukraine in general and the CP(B)U in particular. Vladimir Antonov-Ovseenko, Commander-in-Chief of the Red Army in Ukraine during 1918–19, however, gives in his memoirs[10] a documentary record and personal evidence of this policy.

The relevant literature, whether memoirs or other edited records, is plentiful but tendentious. Works published before Stalin's regime give a much more realistic picture than those published thereafter. The early works on the history of the Soviet regime in Ukraine, such as M. Popov, *Narys istorii Komunistychnoi partii Ukrainy* (1931), M. Ravich-Cherkassky, *Istoriia KP(b)U* (1923), and M. Iavorsky, "K istorii KP(b)U" (1922), were intended to bring about a change in public opinion in a Ukraine troubled by peasant revolt. Nevertheless, all of them, especially Iavorsky, were rejected by the party at the end of the 1920s. The principal error of both "bourgeois" and "Marxist" historians in Ukraine was that they "considered the history of Ukraine as an independent process."[11] In 1930 Iavorsky was accused of diminishing the role of the proletariat in the revolution in Ukraine, and of presenting this revolution "not as a result of the class relationships of the forces struggling in Ukraine, but as an invasion of the Russian proletariat into Ukraine."[12]

The historiography of the Stalin epoch spent much energy on belittling the Ukrainian national movement, presenting it as a bourgeois invention. The CP(B)U's role in the revolution was also belittled. In the end, the Ukrainian problem was brought up only when it was unavoidable or suited the purpose of the party. "The history of Ukraine was written without history," as one Soviet critic put it, writing of the first volume of *Istoriia Ukrainskoi RSR* (History of the Ukrainian SSR).[13] Soviet authors treat the history of Ukraine in such a way that it becomes not the history of Ukraine but rather all-Russian history in Ukraine. The authors of the draft sketch of the second volume of the history of the Ukrainian SSR were accused, in the lead article of the 1955 issue of *Voprosy istorii*, of having "shortened the material of the history of Ukraine to such an extent that the factual peculiarities of the development of the Ukrainian people disappear almost completely."[14]

The classic Stalinist work on the revolution in Ukraine is A. V. Likholat's *Razgrom natsionalisticheskoi burzhuazii na Ukraine 1917–1922* (1954). The author devotes 640 pages to a representation of Stalin as the great leader of genius; at the same time he degrades and eliminates all "Trotskyites and bourgeois-nationalists" and other "enemies of the people," spring-cleaning history to such an extent that finally only Stalin remains, with Lenin as a shy second. It is difficult to catch even a glimpse of the truth throughout the whole of this large work. According to Likholat, everything connected with the revolution and the establishment of Soviet power in Ukraine was inspired, initiated, and realized by the party and by Stalin in particular. It is therefore not surprising that Likholat's book became the object of post-Stalin criticism. This criticism was directed, however, at the work's isolation of Stalin as the prime mover; the criticism was in no way made in the name of historical objectivity. In *Voprosy istorii*, 1956, Likholat's book was criticized because it "lacks real scientific analysis" and "does not make both ends meet." The reviewer went on to condemn the whole book because of its "fundamental shortcomings" and because "the author departs from historical truth, does not provide a fundamental Marxist-Leninst analysis of events, and lays bare his ignorance concerning many questions." The reviewer came to the conclusion that the book should never have been published at all and that "it has only seen the light of day, and perhaps gained a few champions, thanks to the lack of Bolshevik criticism and independence among the historians."[15]

Of approximately the same value is F. E. Los' book on the 1905 revolution in Ukraine.[16] Its object was to show at all cost the organic unity of the revolution in Russia and Ukraine. The national question was ignored completely, a fact which was later pointed out by post-Stalin critics, again for quite other reasons than a concern for Ukrainian nationalism.[17]

The non-Communist Ukrainian literature is often controversial as well. Written by persons who had taken an active part in the anti-Bolshevik war in Ukraine, it is often highly polemical. But in spite of many errors these works are of great importance, since they contain valuable documentation of the revolutionary events in Ukraine. Thus they can often be used as a check on Soviet records and data. The following works come under this heading: D. Doroshenko, *Istoriia Ukrainy*; P. Khrystiuk, *Zamitky i materiialy do istorii ukrainskoi revoliutsii 1917–1920*; V. Vynnychenko, *Vidrodzhennia natsii*; I. Mazepa, *Ukraina v ohni i buri revoliutsii.* Doroshenko, a member of the socialist federalist party and minister of foreign affairs in Hetman Skoropadsky's government, was a professional historian. He was unable to hide his personal sympathies with Skoropadsky's regime. Khrystiuk, a member of the UPSR and the secretary-general of the Rada government, has published material and documents on the Ukrainian revolution which bear witness to his political leanings. It was during his work on this material that he began wavering between the Soviets and the Ukrainian nationalists, a fact which made possible his return to Ukraine under Soviet rule. Vynnychenko's work, which has a certain source value, is full of contradictions. The book contains authentic records of his term of office as prime minister in the Rada government, but he interpolates obvious insinuations against both the government in which he participated and the persons with whom he cooperated. His book has been widely criticized in different quarters, and by no means least by the Communists. It must be remembered when dealing with Vynnychenko's book that he had been a leftist social democrat, and that after the Directory's setbacks in the war against the Bolsheviks he fled to Vienna, from where he started to court his former enemies, the Bolsheviks, with the aim of returning to Ukraine and joining the Soviet government. After only three months' "cooperation" with the Bolsheviks, Vynnychenko again left Ukraine and settled in France, from where he criticized the Bolsheviks. That certain Western historians call

Vynnychenko "the most honest" of the Ukrainian national leaders can be attributed to their biased approach to the Ukrainian problem. Mazepa's memoirs have no doubt the quietest and most objective tone, notwithstanding his active participation in the revolution as prime minister during the regime of the Directory and also as a member of the Ukrainian social democratic party.

Works by Western historians about the years of the revolution in Ukraine are few and rather sketchy. The most prominent and valuable is John Reshetar's *The Ukrainian Revolution, 1917–1920*, which stresses in particular the development of the Ukrainian national movement, the attitude of the different political parties to Ukrainian independence, and the attitude of the Great Powers. My subject is briefly treated by Basil Dmytryshyn in *Moscow and the Ukraine, 1918–1953*, and by Roman Smal-Stocki's *The Nationality Problem in the Soviet Union and Russian Communist Imperialism*. The study by Iwan Majstrenko, *Borot'bism*, gives a detailed analysis of the left trend within the UPSR and its relation to the Russian Bolsheviks. The book by George Luckyj, *Literary Politics in the Soviet Ukraine*, is among the best works in the field. A well documented but somewhat biased study of the genesis of Soviet rule in Ukraine was made by V. Stakhiv. The Marxist theory of self-determination is briefly dealt with by Edward H. Carr,[18] Stanley Page,[19] and Bertram Wolfe.[20]

Several aspects of the Bolshevik revolution and of the Ukrainian problem have been dealt with by other Western scholars who have written general works on the Soviet Union or Ukraine.[21] E. H. Carr's *The Bolshevik Revolution* has become a recognized standard work on the Soviet Union. He has in some respects given a rather prejudiced evaluation of the relations between the non-Russian nationalities and the Russian Bolsheviks. This can probably be attributed to his scepticism as regards the future of small nations.[22] He emphasizes evidence showing the desire of the non-Russian nationalities for union with Russia, while disregarding facts proving the opposite. The same can be said about George Kennan, an expert on Soviet-American relations.[23] His predilection for the Great Powers has seriously weakened his otherwise impressive analytical ability to present an objective picture. In *The Formation of the Soviet Union*, which deals with my subject in part, Richard Pipes presents a many-faceted study of the Bolshevik policy towards Ukraine as well as towards other non-Russian nationalities. Finally, Seton-Watson's book, *The Pattern of Communist Revolution*, which is mainly an analysis of the Communist movement "on the world scale," incidentally gives a realistic picture of the nationality aspect of the Bolshevik revolution.

CHAPTER I

Bolsheviks and National Self-Determination before the Revolution

Marx and Engels on the Self-Determination of Nations

The Russian Bolsheviks have always held themselves to be the most faithful adherents of Marx and Engels in all spheres, including the nationality question. What determined the theory and practice of the Russian Bolsheviks in this matter is open to conjecture: Was it the ideological legacy of Marxism or the realities of Russian politics? Before interpreting the Russian Bolshevik solution, let us examine classical Marxian thought on the nationality question.[1]

It is generally agreed that neither Marx nor Engels offered a solution to the nationality question, in which they were not especially interested. Nevertheless, it would be wrong to say that they were blind to concrete national problems or failed to cast light upon the relationships among nationalities in the nineteenth century. Marx and Engels considered the nationality question to be the result of the historical development of relations among forces of production which determine man's existence, psychology, and his cultural and national manifestations. Considering nationality from the standpoint of historical materialism, they subordinated it to economic relationships and explained national antagonisms as economic conflicts manifesting themselves in class struggles. For example, the *Communist Manifesto* states that "the worker has no country," that the labour from which capital's profits are derived has deprived the proletariat of its national character. The proletariat, according to the programme of the *Manifesto*, has first to win its political rights through struggle and thus become a nation. But beyond this neither Marx nor Engels analysed the problem of the national character of the proletariat. From Marx's work, it transpires that nationality *per se* would disappear in tandem with the withering away of the state:

> National differences and antagonisms between peoples are daily more and more vanishing, owing to the development of the bourgeoisie, to freedom of commerce, to the world market, to uniformity in the mode of production and in the conditions of life corresponding thereto.
>
> The supremacy of the proletariat will cause them to vanish still faster. United action, of the leading civilized countries at least, is one of the first conditions for the emancipation of the proletariat.
>
> In proportion as the exploitation of one individual by another is put an end to, the exploitation of one nation by another will also be put an end to. In proportion as the antagonism between classes within the nation vanishes, the hostility of one nation to another will come to an end.

Even a cursory glance at present-day relations among nationalities shows how mistaken were Marx's forecasts of more than one hundred years ago. For Marx and Engels, nationality coincided with the state, which, they believed, ought to be large under prevailing historical conditions (which required economic development);[2] hence their unfavourable attitude towards small nationalities. This principle was realized for the first time with the American Declaration of Independence in 1776, which, by invoking the idea of self-determination as a natural right, codified the ideas of Grotius, Locke, and Rousseau. The concept of democracy proclaimed by the French revolution became a spark which ignited the revolutionary waves of 1848 in Central and Western Europe, and these ideas reverberated in the strongholds of autocracy, tsarist Russia and Habsburg Austria. Great Power nationalism in France and Great Britain stimulated the drive towards national unification among the Germans, Italians, Poles, and Hungarians, which in turn set in motion the national aspirations of their neighbours who found themselves within the orbit of the Great Powers, e.g., the Irish in Great Britain, the Danes in Germany, the Czechs, Slovaks, Croats, and Ukrainians in Austria-Hungary, and the Ukrainians in Russia. Everywhere nationalism conflicted with nationalism, and while the smaller, so-called unhistorical nationalities demanded the right of national self-determination, the large, "historical" nations strove towards imperial unity, trying to preserve the *status quo*. The national antagonisms expressed in the events of 1848 and subsequent years must be considered the result of those liberal democratic ideas which gave the right of emancipation and of self-determination not only to the human individual but also to nationalities as organizations of these individuals. It is an open question whether these ideas of nationalism and national self-determination were "destructive, disintegrating, and reactionary."[3]

Liberals such as John Stuart Mill contended that the small nationalities should remain within the orbit of powerful historical nations in the name of civilization and progress, provided that they be justly governed.[4] It is doubtful whether the downtrodden nationalities of Germany (Danes and Poles), of Britain (the Irish), of Austria (Czechs, Poles, Ukrainians, and Italians), of Hungary (the Slovaks, Ukrainians, and Croats), of Russia (Poles, Ukrainians, Finns, Baltic and Caucasian nationalities) and of Turkey (the Caucasians, Arabs, and Balkan nationalities) would benefit from continuing to live within the confines of these empires. The monolithic structure of these great empires was won and maintained at the expense of the freedom of these minor nationalities, which strove to establish their separate identity. In the name of progress and the future success of the proletarian revolution, Marx inveighed against the decrepit Russian and Ottoman empires.

Marx and Engels stood for the creation and consolidation of large political entities, particularly a great and united Germany. They opposed the self-determination of small, "unhistorical" nationalities whose assimilation was an ineluctable law of history, a necessary means of propagating West European civilization. Marx wrote in the *New York Tribune* on the dissolution of the Kroměříž (Kremsier) Diet[5] by the Austrian government and on the role of the Slav deputies in it:

> Scattered remnants of numerous nations, whose nationality and political vitality had long been extinguished, and who in consequence had been obliged, for almost a thousand years, to follow in the wake of a mightier nation, their conqueror, the same as the Welsh in England, the Basques in Spain, the Bas-Bretons in France, and at the more recent period the Spanish and French Creoles in those portions of North America occupied of late by the Anglo-American race—these dying nationalities, the Bohemians, Carinthians, Dalmatians [i.e., the Czechs, Slovenes, Croats], etc., had tried to profit by the universal confusion of 1848, in order to restore their political *status quo* of A.D. 800. The history of a thousand years ought to have shown them that such a retrogression was impossible; that if all the territory east of the Elbe and Saale had at one time been occupied by kindred Slavonians,

> this fact merely proved the historical tendency, and at the same time physical and intellectual power of the German nation to subdue, absorb, and assimilate its ancient eastern neighbours; that this tendency of absorption on the part of the Germans had always been, and still was, one of the mightiest means by which the civilization of Western Europe had been spread in the east of that continent; that it could only cease whenever the process of Germanization had reached the frontier of large, compact, unbroken nations, capable of an independent national life, such as the Hungarians, and in some degree the Poles; and that, therefore, the natural and inevitable fate of these dying nations was to allow this process of dissolution and absorption by their stronger neighbours to complete itself.[6]

Thus the small unhistorical nationalities were to be swept away by the tides of history like so much flotsam on the seas navigated by the great historical nations, particularly Germany. Whether the nationalities Marx and Engels identified as unhistorical were in fact so is open to dispute, since the Czechs, Serbs, Croats, and even the Ruthenians had had their historical past, albeit short and not particularly illustrious. No one could maintain that these nationalities had appeared out of nowhere.[7]

Engels, in the same derisive spirit as Marx, was equally inimical to the unhistorical nationalities, which he considered mere ethnic material suitable for assimilation. The small Slavic nationalities were a fiction or at any rate a tool of Russian pan-Slavic policy: the "numerous small relics of peoples which, after having figured for a longer or shorter period on the stage of history, were finally absorbed as integral portions into one or another of those more powerful nations" deserved no encouragement.[8] Engels expanded his views in the *Neue Rheinische Zeitung*,[9] which began to appear from 1 June 1848 under the editorship of Marx. In the article, "Democratic Pan-Slavism," Engels attacked Bakunin, who in one of his pamphlets had appealed for the "liberty, equality and fraternity of all nations," for the establishment of state boundaries "drawn justly in the spirit of democracy which will be determined by the supreme will of the peoples themselves on the basis of their national peculiarities," for the insurrection of the Slavs against Germany and Austria, and for the creation of a Slav union together with Russia.[10] Bakunin's call for national peace and liberty unleashed a storm of invective from Engels, who called it "an empty pipe dream." The Austrian Slavs, except the Poles, "never had their own history; they are dependent on the Germans and the Hungarians for their history, literature, politics, commerce, and industry; they are already partially Germanized, Magyarized, Italianized." And finally, Engels argued, "neither Hungary nor Germany can tolerate the severing and independent establishment of such buffer states, incapable of life." In Engels' opinion, it was just as well that the Germans and Hungarians "drove together into one great state all those tiny, shrivelled, weak little nations, thus enabling them to participate in the historical development from which they would have been remote if they had been left to their own devices. For without violence, without iron scrupulousness, nothing is achieved in history, and if Alexander the Great, Caesar, and Napoleon had suffered from the same sentimentality to which pan-Slavism now appeals on behalf of its now slothful clients, what would have become of history then!"[11]

Probably Engels was under the combined influence of Germanophilia and Russophobia. In his review article of Bakunin's pamphlet, *Democratic Pan-Slavism*, Engels waxed indignant against the Southern Slavs for being the unwitting tools of Russian reactionary imperialism and accomplices in the suppression of the Italian and Hungarian revolutions in 1848: "Not counting the high nobility, bureaucracy, and the military, the Austrian *camarilla* found support only among the Slavs. The Slavs decided the fall of Italy, the Slavs stormed Vienna, the Slavs march at the present moment from all sides upon the Hungarians." Their spiritual leader is Palacký, a Czech, and in the role of the fighters there are the Croats with General Jelačić.[12]

Ferdinand Lassalle, founder of a non-Marxist faction of German socialism, was also antipathetic towards the "unhistorical" nationalities; Hegel's and Fichte's influence is more evident in Lassalle than in Marx or Engels. While admitting the principle of free independent peoples as the "basis and source, the mother and the root of democracy generally," with the aid of very ingenious dialectics Lassalle arrived at the conclusion that the right to an independent life has in the end certain limits. These limits arise in the competition among peoples through which there emerges the subjugation and assimilation of the weaker by the stronger. In *Der italienische Krieg* (1869), Lassalle wrote:

> The principle of nationalities is rooted in the right of the spirit of the people (*des Volksgeistes*) to its own historical development and self-realization. However, there were and are peoples who by themselves are unable to rise to an historical existence; others, who have attained it, but cannot develop further, and repose like motionless ruins outside history; finally, there are also such who, although they have their own development, remained behind the faster, more powerful development of their neighbours, thus giving the latter in the periods of their own stagnation the opportunity of conquering individual parts of their country.[13]

Lassalle's German patriotism is most clearly evident in his 1863 correspondence with the celebrated German economist, Johann Karl Rodbertus-Jagetzow, in which he agreed completely with the latter's philosophy, hoping to see the day when the Turkish mantle would fall to Germany and when German soldiers or workers' regiments would take up their position on the Bosphorus. Lassalle wrote:

> Very often I advocated just this point of view before my party comrades who allowed themselves to call me for this "a dreamer" .... It seems that in spirit we were born like Siamese twins. No, I am no partisan of the nationality principle .... I recognize the right of nationality only for great civilized nations ... and not for races whose right consists rather in having to be assimilated and developed by the former.[14]

Even these motives do not fully explain why classic Marxism had a negative attitude towards small nationalities. It cannot be attributed to the fact that "the later liberal idealization of the small nation had not yet begun, and there was no reason why Marx and Engels should be affected by this sentiment,"[15] for acknowledgement of the equality of rights of all nations antedated Marx by many years.[16] Nor can it be explained on the grounds that Marx and Engels favoured countries in which bourgeois development was already well advanced and which might therefore provide a promising field for eventual proletarian activities.[17] For neither Austria nor Hungary were more developed than, say, Bohemia, and industrialization was only proceeding rapidly on the empire's periphery. In Hungary the feudal system remained intact for a long time, even into the twentieth century. On the other hand, there are certain scholars who interpret Marx and Engels as "patriotic Germans, aiming at the creation of a nationally united German Republic," and therefore "German jingoism was in Marx linked with a foggy internationalism."[18] Although it is true that Marx and Engels desired the unification of Germany, it is not obvious whether they did so in the name of the proletarian revolution on a world scale or in the name of German nationalism.

Another motive was much more germane to Marx's and Engels' evaluation of national movements. They started with the Manichean premise that, just as there are progressive and reactionary classes, there are also progressive nations which forward the cause of the proletarian revolution (mainly nations with developed capitalist production and a class-conscious proletariat) and reactionary nations which impede the revolution (mainly backward agrarian nations with little capitalist enterprise). In "The Eighteenth Brumaire of Louis Napoleon," Marx claimed that peasant nations are formed "by the simple addition of homologous quantities, much as potatoes in a sack form a sackful of potatoes." In Marx's and Engels' opinion, the "peasant class" is reactionary and therefore doomed to perish. The evidence for this view consisted in the fact that in countries such as Bohemia and even Poland, the indigenous nationalities were agricultural, while trade and manufacturing rested in the hands of Germans and Jews.[19] (Nevertheless, it should be remembered that the Poles also had a class which was undergoing *embourgeoisement.*) In Marx's view, the peasant composition of their nations served as a motive for denying the Czechs and South Slavs the right to independence from Austria. Writing in 1852, Marx held that the Czechs' abortive attempt to recover their national rights in 1848 "was ample proof that Bohemia could only exist henceforth as a part of Germany."[20]

Marx tempered his scepticism towards the "unhistorical" nations in the aftermath of the events of 1848. Thereafter he admitted a future statehood for the Poles while preaching that Poland's renascence would be effected by a new social force, "peasant democracy."[21] This was a revision of his long-standing suspicion of the political role of the peasantry. Marx clung to his negative attitude with regard to the Czechs, and Engels wrote a series of articles justifying the Serbs' aspirations to statehood, but only if they did not interfere with the paramount interest of the West European proletariat.[22] "We must work towards the liberation of the West European proletariat and to this end we must subordinate everything else. And no matter how interesting the Balkan Slavs, etc., might be, if their striving towards liberation comes into collision with the interests of the proletariat, then they interest me very little."[23]

Neither Marx nor Engels were enraptured by Herder's humanist nationalism of equality and fraternity among peoples and the inherent right to existence of both civilized and uncivilized peoples.[24] They were to some extent enchanted by Hegel's ideas of history as a struggle among peoples in which only the great and able nations have a place in the history of mankind; the stateless nations are unhistorical, *geschichtslose Nationen*, who cannot be bearers of the Absolute Spirit. Hegel dismisses the role of the Slavs in history, considering them to be agricultural people and therefore unable to "take part in the rising freedom."[25] While for Hegel war among peoples was the mechanism of history, for Marx the same purpose was fulfilled by the revolutionary class struggle. Marx's view of the Slavs was merely a materialistic reinterpretation of Hegel; Marx, like Hegel, regarded the Slavs as "agricultural people," reduced to a role of stateless vegetation.[26]

Marx's attitude towards small nationalities is marred by inconsistency, which cannot be explained away by his use of the terms "revolutionary" and "civilized" in reference to this or that particular nationality; for he defended the Poles' right to national existence even though they were no less agricultural than the Danes of Schleswig or the Czechs of Austria. The Irish, an agricultural nationality, enjoyed none of Marx's sympathy till 1859, when he wrote that the secession of Ireland from Britain was "inevitable."[27] Marx reached this conclusion after having convinced himself that "the English working class will never accomplish anything before it has got rid of Ireland .... English reaction in England had its roots in the subjugation of Ireland."[28] Lenin did not see Marx's inconsistency on the Irish question, writing on the contrary that "on the Irish question, too, Marx and Engels pursued a consistently proletarian policy, which really educated the masses in the spirit of democracy and socialism."[29] Marx and Engels were also inconsistent on the Polish question. As E. H. Carr has pointed out, "the attitude of Marx and Engels to Poland was also affected by the practical difficulties of reconciling German and Polish claims."[30] On the one hand, they supported the Poles' claims against Russia, but they rejected Polish territorial demands against Germany.[31]

The First International took a stand on the national question antithetical to Marx's earlier position. After the defeat of the Polish revolt in 1863, all liberal opinion in Europe was up in arms against Russian policy, and the Polish question also appeared on the agenda of socialist circles. The Polish question was also broached at the first congress of the First International on 3–9 September 1866. The English report, apparently prepared by Marx, speaks of "the necessity of the elimination of any imperialist influence of Russia in Europe by means of the acknowledgement of the principle of self-determination of nations and the restoration of a social democratic Poland"; for the existence of a democratic Polish regime "will depend on whether Germany will be the vanguard of 'the Holy Alliance' or of republican France."[32] However, at the congress a disagreement between Marx and the French delegation surfaced. The French regarded the Polish question as only of interest to Germany[33] and they also demanded the liberation of peoples both in Russia and in Poland itself.[34]

Marx's resolution was decried as inconsistent and did not in any event have enough support; therefore Johann Becker, editor of the magazine, *Der Vorbote*, proposed a compromise resolution on the rights of all peoples which was finally adopted.[35] Thus the German section of the International also pursued a course diverging from Marx's, and in its organ, *Der Vorbote*, advocated the rights of even the smallest nationalities to independence.[36] While the French accused Marx of German patriotism, Marx accused the French of French chauvinism, alleging that their delegate, Paul Lafargue, "by his denial of nationalities quite unconsciously understood their absorption in a model French nation."[37] In later pronouncements, Engels advocated the independence of Poland because "they [the Poles] are the only anti-pan-Slavic Slavs,"[38] and "so long as national independence is absent, a great people is historically unable even to consider in the slightest degree seriously any of its internal problems." Before 1859, "socialism in Italy was unthinkable, and even republicans were few in number." Also, "the international movement of the proletariat is generally possible only among independent nations." Therefore Engels came to the conclusion that "as long as Poland was divided and oppressed, a strong socialist party could not develop in the country itself," and that "in order to struggle, one must first have some ground under one's feet, some air, some light, and some space. Otherwise everything is but empty talk."[39] Engels allowed the right of existence only to two subject nationalities in Europe, the Irish and the Poles.[40]

Marx's classic pronouncement on the Irish problem had a vital influence on Russian Marxists, particularly Lenin, who expressly referred to this case as an example of proletarian policy.[41] In the letter of the General Council of the First International to the Swiss Romansh council,[42] Marx advocated national liberty for the Irish people in the name of the growth of the social revolution in England. In his view, the revolution there would be accelerated if English landlordism lost its bastion, Ireland. "English landlordism loses not only a large source of its riches, but also the most important source of its moral force as a representative of England's domination over Ireland." Through forced union with Ireland, the English bourgeoisie could separate the proletariat of Ireland from that of England and fan national and religious passions.[43] Engels frankly warned that "the English proletariat becomes in fact more and more bourgeois," that its development leads to a situation in which "this most bourgeois of all nations will in the end have a bourgeois aristocracy and a bourgeois proletariat side by side with the bourgeoisie."[44] This is precisely why Marx in the above-mentioned letter proposed "that, not to mention international justice, a necessary preliminary condition of the liberation of the English working class is the transformation of the present compulsory union, i.e., the slavery of Ireland, into an equal and free union, if such is possible, or into a complete separation, if this is unavoidable."[45]

The Bolshevik specialists on the nationality question such as G. Safarov interpret this attitude as an attempt to promote "the international unity of the proletariat on the principle of democratic centralism."[46] However, our impression is that the Marxists were in principle Great-Power chauvinists. This seems to be implicit in their appraisal of Germany's role in a future proletarian revolution and of the pre-eminence of German social democracy in the international proletarian movement. This led Marx and Engels up "Hegelian byways." Hegel had insisted that the Absolute Spirit had ultimately embodied itself in Germany; he therefore idealized the

Prussian *status quo* under Friedrich Wilhelm III and recognized only the ethics and rights of the German people who had become its bearer.

In much the same way Marx and Engels believed that after the Franco-Prussian War the centre of gravity of the international workers' movement had shifted to Germany, where the powerful development of the forces of production would hasten the advent of the socialist millennium. So entranced were they by the theory of the preeminence of the German proletariat that they subordinated the whole European workers' movement and the course of history to it. For this reason they looked forward to Prussia's defeat of France.[47]

Engels was undoubtedly in favour of preserving existing great states and treated the self-determination of small, "unhistorical" nations with open disdain. The Poles, Danes, and Czechs would have to wait until the coming of the socialist revolution in Germany to fulfil their national aims. Any opposition to this order of things was chauvinistic and reactionary. One can readily understand in what an awkward position this placed the proletariat and social democratic parties of the subject nations. The German social democrats were exalted as a model to be imitated by other socialist organizations, particularly the Russian Bolsheviks who contemplated the world-historical role of the Russian proletariat, impelling them to the excesses of imperialist chauvinism. This in turn elicited a justifiable protest from socialists of the nations subject to Russia.

The étatist principle advanced by Marx and Engels was officially sanctioned by the Second International, in which the socialist parties of the subjugated nationalities did not have direct representation but could express their opinions only through the party organizations of their respective states.[48] In the era of the Second International, Western Europe had already been remade to conform to the nationality principle. West European capitalism was already mature and undergoing a transformation into imperialism, the highest stage of capitalism. Meanwhile, Eastern Europe—Austria, Russia, and Turkey—remained nationally heterogeneous with capitalism only in its embryonic stages. The Second International's stand on the nationality question was even more diffident than its predecessor's, owing to Russian and German domination.[49] Russian social democrats—both Mensheviks and Bolsheviks—proved to be no less centralist than their German mentors. The sole resolution adopted by the Second International at its London congress of 1896 stated:

> The congress advocates the full right to self-determination of all nations. It expresses its sympathy with the workers of any country suffering till now under the yoke of a military, national, and any other despotism; the congress appeals to the workers of all these countries to enter into the ranks of

> conscious workers of the whole world, in order to struggle together with them for the overcoming of international capitalism and for the realization of the aims of international social democracy.[50]

The Marxists of the Great Powers were irritated by the persistence of the nationality question and tried to confine its discussion to specific cases. Neither at Paris (1900), Amsterdam (1904), nor Stuttgart (1907) did the congresses pass any decision on the self-determination of nations, though they did protest national oppression. The majority of the parties of the Second International endeavoured to resolve the national question by conferring mere cultural autonomy on the nationalities, leaving their political status unchanged. Austrian social democrats, led by Otto Bauer and Karl Renner, were in the forefront of those advocating cultural autonomy. To its very grave, the Second International failed to resolve the nationality question in a satisfactory way, though ideological discussion by the Austrians and Russians continued unabated.[51]

Russian Social Democracy and the National Question

The Russian Social Democratic Workers' Party's (RSDWP) concern with the nationality problem developed very gradually. Russian socialists' initial preoccupation with the overthrow of the tsarist political and social order, reflected in their pronouncements during the 1880s and 1890s, overshadowed the nationality question. By the turn of the century, however, the national problem had become vexing enough to draw the attention even of the tsarist regime. Henceforth, the nationality question became increasingly important also for Russian social democrats.[52]

The remainder of this chapter examines the RSDWP's position on the nationality question during the pre-October-1917 period. Much of the party's internal debate on this matter was convoluted and highly theoretical. Only after the Bolshevik revolution were the party's theses on the nationality question brought to bear on the problem. Several interesting questions about this prerevolutionary period arise. With what premises about the small nationalities in Russia did the party enter the October revolution? Did the party arrive at a general solution to the nationality question, or did it have a more flexible set of principles whose application depended on the stage of development of each nation's social formation in a given epoch? Was the general solution or set of principles of purely Marxian provenance, or was it conditioned by the multinational composition of Russia? Here we relate Bolshevik doctrine on nationality prior to the October revolution to the concrete case of Ukraine. Although the works of Lenin and Stalin during this period furnish the answer to some of these questions, there is reason to doubt Soviet historiography's claim that Lenin and Stalin perfected a theory for the solution of the nationality question.

The Russian labour movement that preceded the RSDWP completely omitted the nationality question from its programme. Early labour organizations such as the South Russian Workers' League in Odessa (founded in 1875) and the North Russian Workers' League (founded in St. Petersburg in 1878) also neglected the nationality question. This may be attributed to several factors: the early Russian labour movement was strongly influenced by the currents of utopian internationalism and national nihilism, and many of the leaders of the movement felt more Russian than internationalist. Georgii Plekhanov, for example, inclined strongly towards Russian patriotism.[53] Marx and Engels' predilection for large states frequently served as a justification for the *status quo* in national relationships in Russia.

The nationality question was first broached at the first RSDWP congress in Minsk in 1898. The congress adopted a resolution which stipulated the "right of nations to self-determination."[54] It did not, however, contain any specific proposal about how this right would be enacted; indeed, the text merely restated a section from a resolution of the international socialist congress of 1896 by which "all socialist parties were enjoined to work for the right of self-determination of all nations."[55] Also for the first time, the nationality question began to impinge on the internal organization of the party: the congress decided to exclude the minority social democratic organizations from the RSDWP organization. It was decided instead to organize a single social democratic workers' party embracing all the workers of the Russian empire, without regard to nationality.[56] The Jewish Bund, by way of exception, enjoyed an autonomous status within the RSDWP.[57] The Lithuanian social democratic party organization boycotted the congress and refrained from joining the RSDWP because it was dissatisfied with mere autonomous status as conferred on the Bund; it insisted on both the federal organization of the RSDWP and the recognition of the territorial autonomy of Lithuania.[58] The national composition of the congress was almost uniformly Russian, with a few Jewish delegates, a fact which explains the centralist tendency of the congress' decisions.[59]

The nationality question surfaced again at the party's second congress (held in Brussels and later in London, 1903) in the guise of a dispute about the autonomous status of the Jewish Bund within the RSDWP. This issue led to a general debate on the question of national self-determination.[60] It should be noted that there were numerous minority social democratic parties in the Russian borderlands that advocated federal reorganization of the Russian empire and whose influence on the RSDWP was obvious.

The discussions on party statutes at the second congress provide a wealth of material for assessing the various points of view with respect to nationality and party organization. The congress accepted paragraph 3, postulating "a broad local self-government; regional self-government for those borderlands which are distinctive in regard to their peculiar forms of life and the composition of their population." Paragraph 9 guaranteed "the right of self-determination to all nations in the state."[61] This paragraph sparked a heated controversy within the ranks of the RSDWP. The party's left wing, including Georgii Piatakov, Evgeniia Bosh, and Bukharin, opposed Lenin's concept of self-determination. Of the minority social democratic organizations, only the Polish branch, headed by Rosa Luxemburg, opposed this paragraph, preferring the *Iskra* thesis that social democracy supports the self-determination of the *proletariat* of every nation and *not* the categorical self-determination of nations. The Polish social democrats opposed the rebirth of an independent Poland on the grounds that this would further the nationalistic aims of the rival Polish Socialist Party (PPS). The Polish social democrats held that the solution of the national question lay in the democratization of the institutions of historically existing states. They therefore insisted that paragraph 7 of the RSDWP statutes allow the creation of "institutions that guarantee complete freedom for the cultural development of all nationalities living within the state."[62] This proposal, akin to the cultural autonomy thesis put forward by the Austrian social democrats, gained wide currency among minority social democrats in Russia, who were attracted by its flexibility; for although the Polish social democrats intended to use it to limit the autonomist aspirations of the minority nationalities, the proposal in fact produced quite the opposite effect. For this reason Lenin and his followers vigorously combatted the Polish programme.

Discussion on the nationality question at the second congress was confined to the search for ways to preserve the integrity of the Russian empire in a form acceptable to the minority nationalities; it did not touch the more basic question of whether the empire itself ought to be dismembered into its national elements. None of the leading party figures, centralist or cultural autonomist, upheld a strong position on the right of national self-determination. There was, however, a significant disparity between the centralists and cultural autonomists on how the minority nationalities might best be preserved and developed within the framework of the Russian empire. The Bund insisted on guarantees for the cultural development of nationalities, while the centralists led by Lenin opposed the inclusion of such provisions in the party programme, preferring merely a protest against the inequalities and suppression of national minorities. They could not grasp why the Bund insisted that social democracy protect even apparently moribund nationalities.[63] Debate on this issue grew so heated and confused that some speakers, in an effort to paper over the differences, tried to reduce the concept of national self-determination to an innocuous form, by which it would mean only "the right to form a distinct political unit, but not at all the right to local self-government."[64]

Paragraph 9 of the party programme was therefore mainly intended as propaganda to appease nationally-minded social democrats such as the Jewish Bund, PPS, and USDWP. It should be noted that the attitude of the Leninist faction of the party towards the Jewish Bund differed from its general nationality policy in that the Jews were not considered a nation equal in stature to the Poles or the Ukrainians. A typical sample of Lenin's views on the Jewish nationality problem is his article, "The Bund's Position within the Party":

> The Bund's third argument, which consists of invoking the idea of a Jewish nation, indubitably raises a question of principle. Unfortunately, however, this Zionist idea is entirely false and reactionary in its essence. "The Jews ceased to be a nation, for a nation is inconceivable without a territory," says one of the most outstanding Marxist theoreticians, Karl Kautsky .... The idea of a separate Jewish people, which is utterly untenable scientifically, is reactionary in its political implications. The incontrovertible, empirical proof is furnished by well-known facts of history and of the political reality of today. Everywhere in Europe the downfall of medievalism and the development of political freedom went hand in hand with the political emancipation of the Jews, their substituting for Yiddish the language of the people among whom they lived, and in general their indubitably progressive assimilation by the surrounding population ....
>
> This is precisely what the Jewish question amounts to: assimilation or isolation? And the idea of Jewish "nationality" is manifestly reactionary, not only when put forward by its consistent partisans (the Zionists), but also when put forward by those who try to make it agree with the ideas of social democracy (the Bundists). The idea of a Jewish nationality is in conflict with the interests of the Jewish proletariat, for, directly or indirectly, it engenders in its ranks a mood hostile to assimilation, a "ghetto" mood.[65]

S. M. Schwarz rightly remarks that this thesis "came close to being Bolshevik gospel."[66] With the active support of several influential European Marxists such as Karl Kautsky and Alfred Naquet (a French Jewish radical), not to mention the authority of Marx himself, Lenin concluded that assimilation was the only solution to the Jewish problem:[67] the Bund's demand for federalism within the party was its main heresy.[68]

The leaders of the Bund, however, "had never even thought of forming a Jewish political unit on Russian soil."[69] The Bund's attitude is best expressed by its leading theoretician, Medem (Grinburg), who distinguished two variants of the nationality question. The first referred to a territorially compact nation artificially united with a larger and stronger nation to form a state, e.g., the Ukrainians, Finns, and Poles within the Russian empire; having preserved its political and social traditions, such a nation begins a struggle for independence which can result in a new state. The second variant concerned nationalities dispersed over a common territory but closely interrelated politically and economically. These nations, e.g., the Jews in Russia, Ukraine, and Poland, were not struggling for independence. Medem insisted that national independence was no solution to the nationality problem because of the impossibility of creating nationally homogeneous states out of so many *disjecta membra.* Poles would remain in Ukraine, Ukrainians in Poland, Poles in Belorussia, Belorussians in Poland, Russians in Ukraine, Ukrainians in Russia, etc. National independence for the Poles, Ukrainians, and Finns would only liberate the national majority in Poland, Ukraine, and Finland; it would not remedy the national plight of the Jews in Poland, Ukraine, or Finland, for whom a national state would only be a matter of changing masters.[70]

Other nationalities, such as the Poles, Ukrainians, and Finns, were dissatisfied with mere cultural autonomy. As noted above, the PPS refused to cooperate with the RSDWP and combatted the Polish social democrats[71] because neither would recognize an independent Poland.

Lenin's wing of the RSDWP opposed the dismemberment of the Russian empire into its national constituents and even decentralization of the government. Lenin himself spared no effort in subduing the federalist demands raised by the national organizations. The first serious rift between Lenin and the federalists was occasioned by the manifesto issued by the Armenian Social Democratic Union, which stated: "Taking into consideration the fact that the Russian state is composed of many different nationalities, living at different stages of cultural development, and assuming that only a broad development of local self-government can guarantee the interests of these heterogeneous elements, we consider it necessary to constitute a *federative* republic in the free Russia of the future."[72] Replying to the Armenian comrades, Lenin told them to "exclude from their programme the demand for a federative republic and to limit [themselves] to a demand for a democratic republic in general .... It is no business of the proletariat to *propagate* federalism and national autonomy ... which will inevitably result in the demand for on autonomous *class* state."[73] The proletariat had to strive towards closer bonds among larger groups of the working masses, possibly on a larger territory. This was the first time Lenin declared that the proletariat would not strive towards the self-determination of nations and nationalities *per se*, but rather towards the self-determination of the *proletariat* within every nation.

One of Lenin's early contributions on self-determination was his dispute with the PPS on the Polish demand for independence.[74] Citing Marx,[75] Kautsky,[76] and Franz Mehring as authorities, he argued that the Polish demand for independence was anachronistic, since by the turn of the century St. Petersburg had superseded Warsaw as the focus of revolutionary activity in Europe. The Polish proletariat's demanding an independent state was nothing but a "facetious comedy."[77] Lenin could accept neither the PPS' plan that Poland secede from Russia after the fall of the tsarist regime, nor its claim that Polish secession would hasten the regime's demise. On the contrary, he alleged that by its separatist policy the PPS caused the "disintegration of the power of the proletariat" and led to the consolidation of despotism in Russia. According to Lenin, "we subordinate our support of national demands, of national independence, to the interests of the proletarian struggle," while the PPS does the opposite.[78] In this dispute, Lenin adhered to the classical Marxian view that history is nothing but class struggle, that class antagonism in society is stronger than any other force, and that the proletariat has no fatherland, hence no national consciousness. Just as the property-owning classes of different nations were solidly united by their common material interest, the workers, Lenin said, were united on the basis of class struggle.

Lenin's antipathy towards Polish independence was incompatible with the literal meaning of paragraph 9 of the party programme. While antagonizing the Polish social democrats (who insisted on the deletion of paragraph 9), he also alienated the PPS[79] by limiting the right of national self-determination to the *proletariat* of every nation. He used every instrument at his disposal to centralize the party.

The RSDWP(B)'s third congress, held in London in 1905, left intact the party's earlier theses on the national question. (It should be noted in passing that there was a parallel conference of the RSDWP[M] in Geneva at which the nationality question was of little importance.) The one resolution bearing directly on the nationality question urged the central committee of the party and the local CCs to "make every effort to come to an agreement with the national social democratic organizations," with the aim of uniting all social democratic organizations into the federal

RSDWP.[80] Even the party's fourth congress in Stockholm, April 1906, in which the national social democratic organizations such as the Bund and the Polish and Lithuanian parties took part, neglected the nationality question;[81] it was raised only in connection with the status of the nationality parties within the RSDWP organization. The congress was not prepared to take a stand on this complicated issue because it lacked urgency.[82] A vocal minority maintained that it was of the utmost importance that the congress reached a decision or the nationality parties would solve it independently.[83] Mark Liber (Mikhail I. Goldman) told the congress that "to this day the party has no general directive for the solution of the nationality question, hence there is a squabble every time it faces new aspects of this question."[84]

The fifth congress of the RSDWP(B) met in London, May–June 1907, during the period of reaction in Russia. This congress, like that in Stockholm in 1906, paid little heed to the nationality question; indeed, had it not been for the Bund's representatives, who criticized the RSDWP's deputies in the Duma for neglecting the national question, it may have been altogether forgotten.[85] Liber told the congress that the party had omitted this question because it "has not liberated itself from the academic attitude towards the national question."[86] The congress adopted a resolution moved by the Bund in which the social democratic deputies in the Duma were reprimanded for missing the opportunity to criticize the tsarist government on nationality policy.[87]

The active period of the RSDWP came to an end with the London conference. The Stolypin reaction decimated the party's representation from sixty in the second Duma to fifteen in the third Duma.[88] As a result of this repression, the central committee left Russia, settling temporarily in Helsinki and finally in Zurich. Even the party's organ, *Sotsial-demokrat*, emigrated. Both the Bolshevik and Menshevik wings fell into decline. Even Lenin despaired:

> Tsarism is victorious. All the revolutionary and opposition parties are smashed. Decay, demoralization, dispersion, desertion, pornography instead of politics. Increased gravitation towards philosophical idealism; mysticism as a cloak for a counter-revolutionary disposition.[89]

Lenin took advantage of his respite in exile to formulate his basic theses on the nationality question, which remained virtually unchanged during the decisive years of the revolution until 1918. Though not a prime concern of the party during this interlude, Russian chauvinism among the ruling classes of tsarist Russia and the nationalism of the oppressed nationalities' bourgeoisie forced him to pay attention to the nationality question.[90]

The Austrian social democrats' liberal attitude towards the national question undoubtedly made the issue more urgent within the ranks of the RSDWP. The Austrian programme of personal cultural autonomy appealed strongly to groups such as the Bund and Armenian social democracy. Equally influential was the Mensheviks' liberal stance, adopted after their August 1912 conference, which attracted many minority organizations. The Mensheviks conceded for the first time that the non-Russian nationalities' demand for national cultural autonomy was in accordance with the party's programme.[91]

Lenin concentrated on the nationality question during 1912 and 1913;[92] never before or after did he devote himself so wholeheartedly to this question as during this period.[93] He criticized two divergent approaches to the national question: on the one hand, that of overt enemies of national self-determination such as the Luxemburgists and the Russian nationalists, and on the other, that of national organizations such as the PPS and USDWP which demanded federalism or the independence of their countries. Lenin often vented his hostility to the separatists and federalists in the party, but his position was ambivalent, since it upheld both national self-determination and the unity of proletarians of all nations irrespective of national barriers. For example, in the "Project of the Platform for the Fourth Congress of the Social Democracy of the Latvian Region," Lenin emphasized that "only the proletariat in our time defends the real freedom of nations and the unity of workers of all nations,"[94] and that the workers "stand for complete unity among the working masses of all nations" in all educational, political, and other workers' organizations. He meant that the proletarians should ignore national feelings and devote themselves fully to proletarian solidarity in their class struggle. According to Lenin, the question of self-determination for nationalities should be decided solely by the proletariat which, eschewing national rivalries, would force the nationalities to live together within the Russian empire. For this reason, Lenin directed his ideological propaganda at the proletariat of the subjugated nationalities.

While affirming the abstract right of all nations to self-determination, he did not allow the proletariat of these nationalities to participate in the national liberation movement. Moreover, self-determination was made to depend on the interests of the proletariat, i.e., on the suitability of secession for the proletariat.[95] In the "Theses on the National Question," Lenin wrote that the secession of the borderlands should be decided by their entire population.[96] This remarkably liberal doctrine was never again mentioned by Lenin.

Of much greater importance was the question of national cultural autonomy, i.e., the creation of national schools and other institutions that would secure national development. This demand was raised in the Duma by the non-Russian deputies and supported by the Kadets and Trudoviks. The Bolsheviks' attitude, expressed in the resolution at the August conference in Poronin, was completely negative. They declared that the "division of the school system within a single state according to nationalities is undoubtedly harmful from the point of view of democracy generally and especially from the point of view of the interest of the class struggle of the proletariat."[97] The resolution held further that the cultural autonomy demanded both by Jewish bourgeois parties and by petty bourgeois opportunist elements of certain nationalities aimed at a kind of cultural separatism. It was stressed that the Austrian example proved this idea damaging, because it fragmented workers of different nationalities into separate organizations.[98] As noted above, the Austrian Social Democratic Party did not hold the classical Marxist position on the nationality question. Its ideologists, Otto Bauer and Karl Renner, formulated a principle for the solution of the national question in Austria that left the state intact and at the same time perpetuated national diversity. The Austrian pattern was national cultural self-government for every nationality living in the state. According to Bauer and Renner, the political and economic integrity of Austria could best be preserved by satisfying the cultural aspirations of all its nationalities. Special institutions had to be created to guarantee these cultural rights. Even the Austrian Social Democratic Party and the trade unions had to be organized according to the nationality principle.[99]

Medem, speaking for the Bund, advocated a similar solution for the Russian party. The RSDWP should not be content merely to declare all nationalities free and equal. It should take positive steps, i.e., accept the demand for constitutional guarantees for nationalities and the creation of special institutions to promote their cultural development. "To declare the right of small nationalities to national education," said Medem, "and to leave the realization of this right in the hands of the ruling bourgeoisie, means that we promise all, but give nothing."[100] Medem opposed Lenin's idea of territorial autonomy because it did not guarantee the rights of the minorities of any given territory. Therefore he proposed that cultural questions should be decided by national minority organs elected by the minorities and not restricted to any one territory.

The worst crime of cultural autonomy, according to Lenin, was that it led to the separation of citizens by nationality, making small national communities into special juridical personalities, with their own taxation, assembly, and government. It also inflamed national hostility and enmity within the working class. Lenin stressed that

> Marxism is incompatible with nationalism, even the most "just," "pure," refined, and civilized nationalism. Marxism puts forward, in the place of nationalism of any kind, internationalism, the fusion of all nations in a higher unity that grows up visibly with every kilometre of railway, with each international trust, with every ... workers' union.[101]

Lenin considered the assimilation of the Jews in Europe and of other nationalities in America the supreme historical process destroying national backwardness. He maintained that all Marxists who accused other Marxists of being assimilationists were, in reality, "nationalist petty bourgeois."[102] As soon as some minority socialist stressed his national position and defended his national viewpoint, Lenin accused him of nationalism.

Lenin maintained that the nationality principle was historically inevitable in bourgeois society, but he warned Marxists of all nationalities that, by recognizing this reality, they must not turn into apologists of nationalism. Proletarian consciousness must not be obscured by bourgeois ideology. He warned the proletariat not to go further in the nationality question than condemnation of national oppression. The proletariat had no business supporting a positive nationality programme that would preserve national barriers. He was against all national oppression, but simultaneously he was opposed to independent national development. In contrast to the Austrian social democrats, Lenin supported every force leading to the eradication of national distinctions. "The proletariat," he wrote, "not only declines to undertake the defence of the national development of any nation, but, on the contrary, warns the masses against such illusions, defends the fullest freedom of capitalist circulation, welcomes any assimilation of nations except what is forced or based on privilege."[103]

Since the educational system was a very important tool in the development of national ideology, Lenin was wary of surrendering it to national institutions, as the Bund advocated. Lenin thought that the "separation of educational and similar matters would preserve, intensify, and strengthen 'pure' clericalism and 'pure' bourgeois chauvinism."[104] Like many other Russian social democrats who had never experienced national oppression, Lenin could not understand the Marxists of the oppressed nationalities. It is difficult to believe that he was so naive as not to see the advantages in the standardization of the school system for the Russian empire and nation. He could not allow that the process of national fusion attendant upon the country's economic development should be weakened. Lenin buttressed his point of view by the unsuitable example of Switzerland, where a three-language system was practised, and where, as Lenin's opponent Libman (P. L. Girsh) stressed, decentralism and federalism were already in effect.[105] (Lenin, of course, was against both federalism and state decentralization.)

Analysing Lenin's position with regard to the self-determination of nations, one must always bear in mind his hostility towards the real separation of the nationalities from Russia. Lenin's defence of the RSDWP's programme against Rosa Luxemburg and other "nihilists" is of very little significance. Nevertheless, it explains why Lenin supported national movements in some cases. He claimed that the bourgeoisie initially leads every national movement, aiming at secession and the creation of an independent state: "The working class supports the bourgeoisie only in order to secure national peace, ... in order to secure equal rights and to create the best conditions for the class struggle ... while supporting the bourgeoisie only conditionally." Lenin inveighed against the "practicality" of the "secession of every nation" because "in reality it is absurd; it is metaphysical in theory, and in practice it leads to the subordination of the proletariat to the policy of the bourgeoisie."[106] "The whole task of the proletariat in the national question is 'impractical' from the standpoint of the nationalist bourgeoisie of every nation, because, being opposed to all nationalism, the proletariat demands 'abstract' equality."[107]

Even the non-Russian socialists were reluctant to accept Lenin's "abstract" position, which would effectively legitimize the *status quo*. Great nations that had long ago secured their national independence and therefore their national culture could easily accept Lenin's "abstract" formula, because it did not imply the further de-Russification of non-Russian nationalities. It was difficult to reconcile Lenin's standpoint with that of the nationality socialists; while the nationality socialists aimed at the liberation and development of their respective nationalities, Lenin and his followers urged the assimilation and fusion of small nationalities with large ones. For Lenin, the preservation of the Russian empire was a necessary condition for the success of the revolution: "In our fight we take the given state as our basis; we unite the workers of all nations in the given state; we cannot vouch for any particular path of national development; we are marching to our class goal by all possible means."[108]

Lenin analysed self-determination from the perspective of the proletarian revolution, dividing every nation into two camps with conflicting interests: the bourgeoisie and proletariat. Lenin supported the national movements only in so far as they opposed the Russian autocratic regime, i.e., in so far as they had a general democratic content. Lenin wrote: "It is this content that we support *unconditionally*." But he emphasized that the proletariat could not support the trend towards national particularism, i.e., national separatism, because this counteracted the proletariat's struggle for solidarity and unity of interests. Lenin thus never supported any concrete demand for the secession of any nationality in Russia. One of his theoretical justifications of the principle of national self-determination was elaborated in 1915:

> The proletariat of Russia cannot lead the people to a victorious democratic revolution ... without already and "*rückhaltlos*" demanding the complete freedom of secession of all nations of Russia oppressed by tsarism. We demand this not independently from our revolutionary struggle for socialism, but because this latter struggle will become an empty word if it is not closely connected with the revolutionary way of dealing with all democratic problems, including the national one. We demand the freedom of self-determination, i.e., independence, i.e., the freedom of secession of oppressed nations, not because we dream of economic dismemberment and of the ideal of small states, but, on the contrary, because we want large states and the drawing together, even merging, of nations, but on a genuinely democratic, genuinely internationalist basis which is unthinkable without the freedom of secession.[109]

This is very reminiscent of Marx's reasoning in favour of the self-determination of Ireland. But already as early as 1913 Lenin declared himself against the *de facto* separation of the nationalities of Russia. In a letter to the Armenian Bolshevik Stepan Shaumian, Lenin wrote:

> We stand for the autonomy of *all* parts; we are for the *right* of secession (but not for the *secession* of all!). Autonomy is *our* plan for the establishment of a democratic state. Secession is not our plan at all. We in no way preach secession. On the whole we are against secession. But we are in favour of the *right* to secession in view of Black-Hundred Great Russian nationalism which has soiled the matter of national cohabitation to such an extent that sometimes stronger ties will result after a free secession!
>
> The right to self-determination is an exception from our general premise of centralism. This exception is absolutely necessary in face of Black-Hundred Great Russian nationalism, and the slightest renunciation of this exception is opportunism (as with Rosa Luxemburg), a silly little game that suits Black-Hundred Great Russian nationalism. But an exception must not be interpreted expansively. There is and there must be nothing, absolutely nothing, apart from the *right* to *secession*.[110]

It is noteworthy that Lenin here admitted openly that the Bolsheviks, far from planning the disintegration of the Russian empire, sought to forestall it. At least one recent writer contends that Lenin's support only for the *abstract* right to secession proves his "Great-Power chauvinism" (*velikoderzhavnichestvo*) and "Russian jingoism" (*rusotiapstvo*): "the policy of centralization from below justified on account of 'all-powerful economic ties,' though camouflaged by various 'rights'—'self-determination,' 'secession,' freedom to leave the Union."[111] There was little difference between Lenin and Shaumian on the nationality question. Shaumian opposed self-determination and even autonomy or federation, advocating merely provincial self-government. Lenin attacked this point of view as being "of advantage to the blasted coppers." Fearing the ultimate effects of self-determination as well as secession, Shaumian wrote that "the right to national self-determination does not only mean the right to secession, but also to federative ties and autonomy." Lenin could not agree with Shaumian's interpretation and refused to recognize that the right to self-determination involved a right to federation. "A federation is a union of equals, a union which requires *general* agreement .... In principle we are against federation: it weakens economic ties; it is an unsuitable type [of order] for a single state."[112] As we shall see, by 1916 Lenin was forced by the opposition of the national movements to recognize the principle of federalism; he included it in the first constitution of the RSFSR in 1918. In his article, "The Socialist Revolution and the Right of Nations to Self-Determination," published in *Der Vorbote* in April 1916, Lenin wrote: "The recognition of self-determination is not equivalent to the recognition of federation as a principle." But he stressed that circumstances could make social democracy "prefer federation, which is the only road to complete democratic centralism."[113]

Lenin's obviously negative attitude towards the secession of the Russian nationalities is difficult to reconcile with the claim that his proclamations on the principle of self-determination elicited the symphathy of the nationalities against the Russian non-Communist regime.[114] As we shall see, the nationality leaders grasped quite early the intentions of Lenin and his friends within the RSDWP. Lenin either ignored or underestimated the vitality of national awareness among the nationalities, while overestimating their class consciousness. Whatever Lenin's assessment, he acted against the intentions of the social democrats of the nationalities, not to mention their bourgeoisie. The dispute between Lenin and the Ukrainian social democrat Iurkevych is only one illustration.[115] Any attempt by the Bolsheviks to organize a united Russian social democratic party and to claim the hegemony of Russian social democracy over the workers' movement throughout the empire was vigorously opposed by the nationality social democrats, who suspected Lenin of being a genuine Russian chauvinist.

Certainly Lenin's opponents on the nationality question, the Russian liberals and especially the Russian nationalists, and even such party stalwarts as Rosa Luxemburg and Piatakov, misinterpreted Lenin, accusing him of favouring the disintegration of the Russian empire. Rosa Luxemburg categorically opposed national self-determination in the form advocated by Lenin:

> Instead of striving towards the greatest unity of the revolutionary forces in the whole territory of the state in the spirit of purely international class policy, ... instead of defending tooth and nail the indivisibility of the Russian state as the territory of the revolution, instead of opposing ... to all nationalist separatist strivings the inseparable unity of the proletarians of all nations throughout the territory of the Russian revolution, the Bolsheviks, on the contrary, with their shrieking nationalistic phraseology about "the right of nations to self-determination including secession" supplied the bourgeoisie of the borderlands ... a splendid pretext, nay, even a banner for its counter-revolutionary struggle. Instead of warning the proletariat of the borderlands against any separatism as being a purely bourgeois snare, they confused the proletarian masses of the borderlands by their slogan and made them a prey to the demagogy of the bourgeois classes. By this nationalistic demand they themselves were the cause of the disintegration of Russia.[116]

Lenin, however, made it clear that the Bolsheviks stopped short of supporting *actual* secession, recognizing only the *right* to secession.[117] The Bolsheviks proved this by applying self-determination only in a few special cases; the Bolsheviks acceded to the independence of the Baltic republics, Finland, and Poland not because of their convictions on the principle of national self-determination, but because they lacked the military might to unite these peoples with Russia.[118]

Lenin was no doubt hazy on the matter of self-determination. His articles and pamphlets are written ambiguously and one readily gets the impression that he was in favour of the liberation of nationalities. He was more frank about the party's objectives in letters to his party comrades, where it is clear that national self-determination is nothing but a slogan, a propaganda device to incite the nationalities against the tsarist government and its allies. It is characteristic that Lenin's position before the First World War was developed in discussions with the social democrats of the nationalities, such as the Bund, and the Polish, Latvian, Armenian, and Ukrainian social democratic parties. During this period, he emphasized the unity of the RSDWP and strongly opposed decentralization within the party.

After the outbreak of hostilities in August 1914, Lenin's principal antagonist changed from the minority social democrats within Russia to the social democrats of the warring nations. Discussion turned to the sphere of war and socialist revolution. Interestingly enough, Lenin neglected the ideas of national self-determination propagated by the representatives of the Great Powers, especially Woodrow Wilson. Liberation of small nationalities became a weapon used by both sides to incite the masses to support irredentism on the territory of the enemy. In this manner, the German government promised to liberate Poland, the Baltic peoples, Finland, and Ukraine from the yoke of Russia, and Persia, the Muslim peoples, and Ireland from the yoke of England. The Entente, on the other hand, tried to stir up the Slavic minorities of Austria-Hungary and to incite the Arabs against the Turks. The Russian government also set forth as one of its war aims the liberation of the Slavic peoples from German, Austro-Hungarian, and Turkish oppression. The self-determination of nations thus became another weapon in the arsenal of the Great Powers.

During the war the national question became the main object of dispute between the Zimmerwald Left, led by Lenin, and the other socialist groups and parties of the belligerent nations. As is well known, the majority of socialist parliamentary representatives of the belligerent nations voted in support of their respective governments on the general grounds of self-defence.[119] The support given by the German Majority Social Democrats to the German war measures was a crushing blow to the socialists of such countries as France and Belgium, which were victims of German aggression.[120]

The German social democrats were guided by the thought of Heinrich Cunow, Edward David, and Paul Lensch. Cunow gave a pluralistic account of the genesis of the working classes, contending that national consciousness to the same extent as class consciousness is a socio-historical reality. He did not support the self-determination of small nationalities, because their demands did not correspond to historical development. The course of history was, according to Cunow, against national differentiation and for the assimilation of small nationalities by larger, culturally superior nations. Like Lenin, he argued that the right to self-determination could not be applied indiscriminately to all nationalities.[121] Another German social democrat, Edward David, defended the integrity of the state borders of Germany against French designs on Alsace-Lorraine and Danish claims on northern Schleswig, despite the national composition and aims of the majority of the populations of these areas. He advocated an expansionist policy for Germany in the economic field, holding that it was Germany's duty to master the world.[122] Lensch completely accepted Engels' theory that the unhistorical nations were doomed to eventual assimilation into larger nations in the name of progress.[123] For Lensch, the right to national self-determination was nothing more than "*geistige Rückstände der kleinbürgerlichen Demokratie von Anno Tobak*,"[124] and in practice it was just a "dictatorship of the illiterates."[125] In the Habsburg monarchy the social democratic party folded under the government's war measures. In Great Britain the majority of the parliamentary Labour party supported the government, which led to MacDonald's resignation from the chairmanship of the Labour parliamentary group. The Russian social democrats (five Bolsheviks and six Mensheviks) refused to vote in favour of war measures in the Duma. The socialist revolutionaries and Trudoviks refused to support the war measures of the government, but within the RSDWP there were groups that eventually supported the government and thus earned the nickname "defencists."

Lenin opened a broadside against the socialist defencists, castigating them in innumerable letters and articles. He bitterly assailed Kautsky and other centrists as well as the Mensheviks for refusing to break with their national governments. He condemned the leaders of the Second International for the "betrayal of socialism." They had prepared the collapse of the Second International

> by renouncing class struggle, with its transformation into civil war, which is necessary at certain moments; by preaching bourgeois chauvinism under the guise of patriotism and the defence of the fatherland and by ignoring or renouncing the ABC truth of socialism ... that workers have no fatherland; by confining themselves in the struggle against militarism to a sentimental philistine point of view instead of recognizing the necessity of a revolutionary war of the proletarians of all countries against the bourgeoisie of all countries.[126]

In the manifesto of the central committee of the RSDWP, 1 November 1914, Lenin unmasked the war aims of the English and French bourgeoisie:

> ... to seize the German colonies and to destroy a rival nation distinguished by a more rapid economic development. For this noble purpose the "advanced democratic" nations assist ruthless tsarism, to strangle still further Poland, Ukraine, etc., and to repress still more the revolution in Russia .... The leaders of the International have committed treason against socialism by voting for the war credits, by repeating the chauvinist ("patriotic") slogans of the bourgeoisie of "their own" countries in justification and defence of war, and by entering the bourgeois cabinets of the belligerent countries.[127]

Thus Lenin condemned all participants in the war measures. He set the aim of European social democrats as "the transformation of the contemporary imperialist war into a civil war."[128] The immediate aim of the social democrats in more backward Russia, which had not yet undergone its bourgeois revolution, was "the establishment of three fundamental conditions of a consistent democratic reconstruction: a democratic republic (with complete equality of rights and with self-determination for all nations); confiscation of the landowners' lands; and an eight-hour working day."[129] Thus Lenin considered the defeat of Russian tsarism to be the lesser of two evils. He wrote: "The lesser evil would be the defeat of the tsarist monarchy, the most reactionary and barbarous government which had oppressed the largest number of nationalities and the largest mass of the population of Europe and Asia."[130]

This provoked great dissension within Bolshevik ranks abroad, particularly on the formulation of national self-determination. This theoretical dispute nearly caused a new split in the ranks of the left. As Gankin and Fisher pointed out: "The questions of self-determination, disarmament and the arming of peoples separated the Dutch, Swedish, Norwegian, and Polish lefts from the Bolsheviks. Division relating to these and other controversial matters developed among the Bolsheviks, and embroiled Lenin in a hot dispute with the Bolsheviks of the former *Vpered* group [Anatolii Lunacharsky, Dmytro Manuilsky] on the national question, and with the Bukharin-Piatakov group on the defeat of one's own government, the right to self-determination, and the minimum programme in general."[131]

As to the Polish left, there was a long-standing controversy on the matter of self-determination. The world war gave fresh impetus to the discussion on self-determination. From the start, Rosa Luxemburg had no real understanding of Lenin's theses on the national question; her position was influenced by the question of Polish independence, for long a point of controversy within the Polish socialist movement. The crux of Rosa Luxemburg's argument was that the slogan of the independence of Poland was incompatible with the general struggle of Polish and Russian workers to overthrow tsarism and carry out a social revolution. The Polish left mainly stressed the assumption that, under imperialism, finance capital tended "*to outgrow the limits of national states* . . . and to form, *in Europe also, larger state units* by combining adjacent territories that complement each other economically, regardless of the nationality of the inhabitants." The starting point for the social democrats' opposition to annexation was "*the renunciation of any defence of the fatherland.*" The Polish left declared that social democracy "*does not advocate either an erection of new boundary posts in Europe or the re-erection of those which have been torn down by imperialism.*" Only a socialist society would eliminate all national oppression.

Polish social democracy would not agree to the formula of the self-determination of nations for a number of reasons. "*The right of national self-determination is impracticable in capitalist society*," it argued; "on the basis of capitalist society it is totally impossible to make the will of nations the deciding factor in questions concerning the changing of boundaries as the so-called right of self-determination demands." Self-determination interpreted so that "a single section of a nation should decide whether it wishes to belong to one or another state" was also "particularistic and undemocratic," because "such an issue would have to be passed throughout the entire state and not in one province." "*The right of self-determination is not applicable to socialist society*." Socialism would abolish all national oppression because it abolished all class interests. There was no assumption that in a socialist society a nation would acquire the character of an economic and political unit. "In all probability it would possess only the character of a cultural and linguistic unit, since the territorial subdivision of the socialist cultural sphere, in so far as the latter might exist, can result only from the demands of production, and then, of course, instead of individual nations having to decide separately about the subdivision of the basis of their own supremacy (as '*the right of self-determination*' demands) all citizens concerned would *participate in that decision*." Polish social democracy further stressed that the slogan of self-determination had undesirable consequences in that it "spreads false conceptions regarding the character of both a capitalist and a socialist society, and misleads the proletariat." "In the programme of the proletariat of the *oppressed nations*, the slogan of the right of self-determination may serve as a bridge to social patriotism. As the experience of the Polish, Ruthenian [Ukrainian], and Alsatian labour movements indicates, this slogan serves as an argument for the nationalist movement within the labouring class and as an argument for the hopes built on the success of one of the belligerent nations, thus disrupting the international front of the proletariat." On the other hand, "this slogan could arouse in the proletariat of the oppressing nation the illusion that . . . it is already able to determine its own destiny and is, therefore, obliged to protect, together with other parts of the nation, their 'common' interests and their will."[132]

It is difficult to see the reason for Lenin's former opposition to these theses since they were in fact identical with his own theory as explained in his letters to Shaumian. At least the assumption that the nations in a socialist society would not possess any political or social character, but only a cultural and linguistic one, was quite close to his view. The principles advanced by the Polish social democrats were in some instances supported by Bukharin, Piatakov, and Evgenia Bosh. In defining national self-determination, Bukharin stated that the imperialist epoch is an epoch of the absorption of small states by large states, and of a constant reshuffling of the political map of the world by large states to form a more unified type of state structure. As for the slogan of self-determination, Bukharin saw only two cases for its application: "1) the case where in the course of the imperialist war a 'foreign' territory is annexed; 2) the case of the 'disintegration' of an existing state organism." In both cases Bukharin saw simply different forms of the slogan, "*defence of the fatherland.*" He stressed, furthermore, that "the deflection of the proletariat's attention towards the settling of 'national' problems has become particularly harmful, especially now that the question of mobilizing the proletarian forces on the world scale ... has been raised in a *practical* manner." Bukharin declared that "in no case and under no circumstances will we support the government of a Great Power that suppresses the uprising and revolt of the oppressed nation; neither will we mobilize the proletarian forces under the slogan, 'the right of nations to self-determination.'" The task of social democracy at that time was to be "*a propaganda of indifference*" with respect to the "fatherland" and the "nation."[133]

Bukharin's theses were very unrealistic on a number of counts. No doubt they were wrong with respect to the tendency of imperialism towards the absorption of small state units by large state units. As is well known, there is evidence of the opposite tendency, of the disintegration of the larger states and the creation of small independent states in Europe and Asia. Despite Bukharin's prophesies, a number of states such as Poland, Czechoslovakia, Finland, and the Baltic states were created in postwar Europe. Bukharin's theses could hardly be accepted by small, subjugated nations or even by some of the belligerent nations, because it meant capitulation before the enemy. Lenin correctly interpreted this conception, saying that it would "in practice signify rendering involuntary support to the most dangerous opportunism and chauvinism of the Great-Power nations."[134]

Lenin criticized Piatakov, Bukharin, and Bosh, whose views on self-determination resembled those of Rosa Luxemburg and Karl Radek, in a number of articles and letters. Replying to Piatakov, who used the pseudonym P. Kievsky, Lenin criticized this trio for "peculiar errors of logic." They had misunderstood the Marxian position on the problem of democracy in general: "The Marxian solution of the question of democracy consists in the *utilization* against the *bourgeoisie* of *all* democratic institutions and tendencies, by the entire proletariat .... Marxism teaches that 'the struggle against opportunism,' by refusing to participate in the democratic institutions of a particular democratic society, ... is a *complete capitulation* before opportunism."[135] By denying the principle of self-determination, Piatakov was opposing the principles of Marxian tactics. Lenin stressed that the right of nations to self-determination must figure for some time in the programme even of a socialist society.

The principal characteristic of the controversies between Lenin and the leftists on the national question was that the latter did not understand Lenin's intention of winning over the nationalities as "future allies of the proletariat." As Baevsky remarked, "to accept the position of Rosa Luxemburg meant to lose these allies."[136] From the point of view of revolutionary Marxism, Lenin was correct: recognition of the right of nationalities to secession could assure mutual assistance between the proletariat and the subject nationalities against the tsarist regime. But as we have already noted, Lenin did not intend to proceed directly towards this goal, because he refused to support the nationalities in developing or maintaining their national identities.

Lenin might have ignored the opinion of nationalities after the Bolsheviks seized power, but he could not do so while the tsarist regime was in power. He was ready to support the nationalities only in so far as their movement was "democratic," i.e., capable of being directed against the tsarist regime. Drawing a parallel with the interpretation of national liberation offered by Marx, who opposed the independence of the Czechs and South Slavs but supported the independence of Poland in the interests of "European democracy," Lenin also subordinated the self-determination of nations to the interests of a future "proletarian revolution." Drawing from the wisdom of Marxism, Lenin declared that "1) the interests of the liberation of several of the largest peoples of Europe are above the interests of the liberation movement of small nations; 2) that the demands of democracy must be understood on the all-European scale—one must now say: world-scale—and not in isolation," for, declared Lenin, "the individual demands of democracy, including self-determination, are not the absolute, but a *small part* of the common democratic—now: common socialist—*world* movement. It is possible that in individual concrete cases the small part contradicts the whole; then it [the small part] must be rejected."[137]

The *crux* of Lenin's solution to the nationality problem was "the closest drawing together and the subsequent *merging of all* nations." All his literary and propaganda activity was directed to this end. According to Lenin, there was only one road: "a real internationalist education of the masses, i.e., educating the members of the oppressing nation to be 'indifferent' to the problem of whether small nationalities would belong to their state or to the neighbouring state or would be granted independence." The social democrats of the oppressed nations had to stress the "voluntary union" of nations.[138] Lenin himself admitted that there might be "people who have not gone deeply into the question" who would find this conception "contradictory."[139] This formula was not clear even to some of Lenin's leftist opponents among the Bolsheviks; Piatakov, for instance, criticized Lenin's formula as inconsistent. It was not clear to Piatakov "what the worker will think when, asking the propagandist how the proletarian has to treat the question of independence (i.e., the political independence of Ukraine), he gets the answer: a socialist strives for the right of secession but is conducting propaganda against secession." Piatakov wrote that proletarians would call such a dialectic "jugglery."[140] Lenin, in his reply to Piatakov, wrote that "every sensible worker will think that P. Kievsky [Piatakov] *cannot think*," because the proletariat demanded the real right to self-determination from the present government, and "when we ourselves become a government we will do this *not at all* to 'recommend' secession, but on the contrary, to facilitate and hasten a democratic *rapprochement* and fusion of nations."[141]

The so-called democratic revolution, the period between the February and October revolutions, brought no serious changes in the Bolshevik party's theory of the self-determination of nations. Old slogans and old premises of "the unity of the party" were still predominant in party doctrine. Even though conditions in Russia had changed (there was relative freedom of speech and assembly), the Bolsheviks remained an opposition party. The Provisional Government could not solve the nationality problem because of the deeply conflicting attitudes of the parties concerned. The government was unwilling to recognize the principle of self-determination; but by postponing the solution of the nationality problem, the Provisional Government left itself open to attack by the Bolsheviks. At the seventh (April) conference of the RSDWP(B) in 1917, the first conference held at home under legal conditions, the nationality question was used as a weapon against the democratic regime of the Provisional Government.

Stalin, at that time Lenin's disciple in this matter, was the main speaker on the nationality question. Stalin pointed out the inability of the Provisional Government to solve the nationality problem, especially Finland's and Ukraine's demands for autonomy. He stressed that the oppression of the nationalities in Russia was due to the highly undemocratic character of its regime. "The more democratic a country, the less the national oppression," declared Stalin. He recalled the party slogan on the self-determination of nations, stating that "the oppressed nations forming parts of Russia must be allowed the right to decide for themselves whether they wish to remain part of the Russian state or to secede and form independent states."[142] At the same time, he pointed out that self-determination "must not be confused with the expediency of secession in any given circumstances." "When we recognize the right of oppressed peoples to secede, the *right* to determine their political destiny, we do not thereby settle the question of whether particular nations should secede from the Russian state at a given moment .... Thus we are at liberty to agitate for or against secession, according to the interests of the proletariat, of the proletarian revolution." Stalin expressed the hope that after the overthrow of the autocratic tsarist regime, the mistrust felt by the nationalities towards Russia would diminish and their solidarity with Russia would increase. He believed that after the overthrow of tsarism, "nine-tenths of the peoples will not desire secession." For those peoples who would not secede from Russia but were distinguished by peculiarities of social life and language, Stalin proposed regional autonomy.[143]

Both Lenin and Stalin in their speeches supported the demands of Finland, Ukraine, and Poland. Lenin in his polemics with the Polish social democrats, who rejected Poland's right to secession, declared: "Why must we, the Great Russians, who oppress a greater number of nations than any other people, renounce the recognition of the right to secession of Poland, Ukraine, Finland? The suggestion is made to us to become chauvinists because thus we would ease the position of the social democrats in Poland." Lenin was convinced that "freedom of union presupposes freedom of secession. We, the Russians, must stress freedom of secession, and in Poland [social democrats must stress] the freedom of union."[144]

Lenin and Stalin were contradicted at the conference by Piatakov, Feliks Dzerzhinsky, and Filip Makharadze (a Georgian social democrat). In his speech, Piatakov stressed that Stalin's conception was anachronistic because he was applying a nationality problem from the feudal period to the present situation. Piatakov pointed out that from the point of view of the social and economic interrelations, which "established close and indissoluble ties between all nations," the "independence of nations is obsolete, needless, and archaic." Dating as it did from another historical epoch, the demand for independence was reactionary because it would put history into reverse.[145] He accused Stalin of being metaphysical because his thesis spoke of the will of the nation as a whole and not of the will of the class. He was against the "separatist movement" because, as a movement at odds with socialist revolution, it was counter-revolutionary. In accord with his own anti-separatist attitude he correctly interpreted the position of the party as being against the secession of nationalities, against the slogan of national states. "If we say that the realization of these rights is pernicious, then it is unintelligible why these rights are declared," said Piatakov.[146] Citing empirical facts in support of his thesis, he pointed out that it was easier to formulate the principle of self-determination in Petersburg where there were no nationality movements or immediate conflicts than in the borderlands. He stressed that his experience in Ukraine, where the Ukrainian social democrats interpreted the formula of self-determination in their own way, was adequate evidence of these difficulties. Since there was no general line on the application of self-determination, every party functionary had to decide the question of the secession of his province on his own.

Lenin, replying to Piatakov, remarked that everything that Piatakov had said was "an unimaginable muddle," and that Piatakov, thanks to his attitudes, was playing into the hands of Russian chauvinism. "We are indifferent and neutral towards the separatist movement. If Finland, if Poland, [and if] Ukraine secede from Russia, there is nothing bad in this. What is there that is bad? Whoever says there is something bad is a chauvinist. One would have to be crazy to continue Tsar Nicholas' policy."[147] He went on to point out that Norway had separated from Sweden, improving relations and confidence between the Norwegian and Swedish proletariat. Lenin was convinced that the declaration of Finland's and Ukraine's freedom to secede would actually prevent secession. He was so obsessed by this theory that he simply could not admit any contrary assumption. The actual course of relations between Soviet Russia and Ukraine must have disillusioned Lenin, for the Ukrainians separated from Russia in spite of the Soviet regime there. But at the seventh conference Lenin was probably not referring to the concept of a nation that Stalin had advanced in 1912–13.[148] Stalin's "strictly objectivist definition of nation" was not imperative for the Bolsheviks at the time of the April conference.[149] It was another more revolutionary definition based on class division that prevailed. According to this conception, the principle of self-determination was applicable to the proletariat of every nation and not to the nation as a whole.

The resolution adopted by the conference stressed that even the current regime suppressed the nationalities and that "only under the consistently democratic-republican organization and administration of the state" was the elimination of the suppression of nationalities possible. The denial of the right to secession was identical with the policy of annexation. Only recognition of this right would secure complete solidarity among the workers of different nationalities and contribute to the real democratic *rapprochement* of nations. The resolution once again stressed that the right to secession had to be decided by the proletariat in each case independently, taking into account existing circumstances and striving to maintain proletarian unity.[150] It did not answer the question of whether the party was for or against self-determination. Judging by Stalin's declaration, the party was against the secession of the nationalities.

An intermediate position on self-determination was taken by Trotsky, who at that time was moving closer to Bolshevism. In his article, "The Peace Programme," written in May 1917,[151] he spoke of the national community as a living focus of culture and of the national language as its vital organ. This role of the nation would be preserved for an indefinite period of history. Therefore social democracy must and would in the interests of this material and spiritual culture secure freedom of development for the national community. On the other hand, Trotsky pointed out that the national principle could not pretend to have *absolute* meaning, for it could not stand in the way of the tendency of modern economies to organize the political and economic centralization of Europe and the world. From the point of view of historical development and in the interests of social democracy, the centralizing tendency of the contemporary economy was "the *predominant* one, and it must be guaranteed the complete possibility of fulfilling its genuinely liberating historical mission: *the construction of a united world economy*, independent of national boundaries and state customs barriers." He, like Piatakov, advocated the slogan "away with frontiers," but he formulated it in the context of a "democratically united Europe." Small nations in Europe, as Trotsky saw it, had to abstain from creating economic units antagonistic to each other. In other words, "in order to enable the Poles, Serbs, Romanians, and others, to create really unconstricted national associations, it is necessary to have the state borders that divide them destroyed; it is necessary for the borders of *the state as an economic, and not national, organization* to be broken asunder, [thus] embracing the whole of capitalist Europe .... The prerequisite of the self-determination of Europe's large and small nations is the union of Europe itself." He pointed out that the self-determination of weak nationalities was dependent on the European revolution. Trotsky directed this thesis against the German "social patriots," David and Landsberg, who rejected self-determination as reactionary romanticism, and against Luxemburg, Piatakov, and others who simplified this problem, making it dependent on the socialist revolution.[152]

There is no need to stress that Trotsky's attitude was more consistent with classical Marxism than was Lenin's. It is possible that Lenin had the same thing in mind when he spoke about the fusion of nationalities, but he was adroit enough not to say openly that he was against the independence of small nationalities. However, Lenin was more determined than Trotsky with regard both to the fusion of the national differences and to the role of national culture in future development. Lenin accused Trotsky of eclecticism and of objectively supporting Russian "social imperialism."[153] The Bolsheviks wanted the national movement in the borderlands to be a double weapon: on the one hand, they wanted to turn national antagonism, provoked by the ruthless suppression of the nationalities, against the tsarist regime; and on the other, they sought to stop the increase of national antagonism which might, if it spread among the proletariat, endanger the fusion of the proletariat of different nationalities. The proletariat had to be separated from its national bourgeoisie, which, according to Lenin, had in the past deceived the proletariat and led it into the embraces of the reigning classes of Russia.[154] The Bolsheviks, therefore, when the principle of national self-determination was incorporated into the party programme, simultaneously reserved the right to agitate for the union of the proletariat of all nationalities. This, of course, presupposed that the will of the proletariat would not express itself in the direction condemned by party doctrine.

On the Unity of the Bolshevik Party

The theoretical argument for the integrity of the Russian social democratic party within the territory of the Russian empire was provided by the Bolshevik wing of the RSDWP, led by Lenin, at the very beginning of its existence. Lenin's premise was that the proletariat of all the nationalities in the Russian empire should be organized in a single, unified party organization. This evoked suspicion and opposition among the nationality organizations; they felt that the principle of self-determination implied the existence of separate national parties. The Bolsheviks, however, rejected not only the independent existence of the nationality parties but also their autonomy within the Russian party. A decentralized social democratic party was not intended by the Bolshevik solution of the nationality problem.

During the debates on the organizational structure of the RSDWP at the second congress, Lenin condemned the request for federalism in intra-party relations as injurious to the party and contradictory to the principles of social democracy under Russian conditions. He denounced all thought of federalism and democracy within the party as something noxious. Democracy and especially the election of party leaders were described by Lenin as a "utopia," as "an empty and harmful joke"; his principle was "no democracy, no elective status, but instead the organization of the party from above."[155] Another prominent party leader, Plekhanov, also declared himself against democracy and federalism in the party as being "harmful and bringing death and destruction."[156] Federalism, in Lenin's opinion, was harmful because it would legitimize dissension and estrangement within the proletariat.[157]

Is it possible to find any ideological influence of Marx on the Russian Bolsheviks in this respect? While the *Communist Manifesto* recognized "communists of various nationalities," it seems that Lenin interpreted the *Manifesto*'s concern for "the common interest of the entire proletariat, independently of all nationality" as the prohibition of nationality parties in Russia, their subjugation to a unified Russian party. Lenin's argument was the following: "In questions of the struggle with the autocracy, of the struggle with the bourgeoisie of the whole of Russia, we must act as a single, centralized, fighting organization, we must lean upon the whole proletariat without distinguishing language and nationality .... [We must] not create organizations that would go separately, each along its own path, nor weaken the strength of our thrust by splitting up into numerous independent political parties."[158] Thus Lenin presupposed that the success of the proletarian revolution depended upon a united and centralized party. He could not accept the idea of mere solidarity of the different national parties, believing that national parties would split the common front. Whether the national elements in the party did in fact play any important role during the Bolshevik revolution is questionable.

The Bolshevik majority at the second congress ultimately recognized organizations based on territorial, not national, principles. Thus Poland, Finland, and the Caucasus were each to organize a local organization to include all workers living within their territory. But the Bolsheviks would not recognize the autonomy of the nationality-based Jewish Bund. The Bund demanded the exclusive right to represent the Jewish working masses, regardless of territorial considerations; all Jewish workers were to have separate organizations joined to the Bund, which in turn would enter the RSDWP on the federative principle.[159] The Bund's demands reflected the Austrian solution of the organizational problem of the social democratic party, which admitted the nationality principle. Liber, the Bund's representative, found nothing ridiculous or incompatible in the existence of the federative principle in the programme of social democracy.[160] The Bolshevik "integralists" condemned this as an anti-socialist, nationalistic attempt to create a kind of state within the state.[161]

The intention of the "integralists" was to subordinate the national organizations to the Russian party bureaucracy. During debates on the status of the party, Rusov recommended that the congress accept a form of organization that would prevent the possibility of a local organization "growing up into either a separatist or parochial (*kustarnicheskaia*) local organization."[162] The party could more easily command a small district organization than a large one, which after getting large enough might incline towards separatism. The evidence for such a possibility, according to B. M. Knuniants (Rusov),[163] was the experience with a strong Bund.[164] The RSDWP ideologist, Aleksandr Martynov, formulated the Marxist attitude towards party unity, against federalism and inefficient local organization: "If contemporary socialism synthesizes the various forms of the proletarian movement and reflects only its general historical tendency, then it is obvious that from this point of view the organization of a social democratic party ought to be so constructed that the predominance of common social democratic interests over local interests is on the whole secured."[165] In other words, Russian social democratic interests were to receive priority over those of the national organizations.

However, circumstances compelled the Russian Bolsheviks to compromise in many respects with the national demands of the local parties. The first example of this was the recognition of the autonomy of the Bund and some independence for other organizations, principles introduced into the party statutes.[166] This very limited autonomy, with a very unclear formulation, did not satisfy the Bund, which left the congress before the sessions were over, giving as its reason the obvious intention of the congress to liquidate it.[167] The removal of the Bundist opposition did not close the issue. In connection with the debates on the status of district and national organizations the question arose of organizations for those borderlands that differed ethnically from Russia proper. This question was undoubtedly more important since it affected the problem of the integration or disintegration of the Russian empire; the dispute with the Bund did not raise this kind of controversy. It is remarkable that on this issue no leading party chief such as Lenin, Plekhanov, Martov, or Trotsky participated in the debates. It can be assumed that deaf-mute tactics were practised in this difficult problem.

In his argument for the existence of separate organizations for the borderlands, Noi Zhordaniia,[168] a leader of the Georgian social democrats (Mensheviks), stressed the necessity of party organs for those borderlands differing ethnically from Russia proper. "Like the Russian social democrats who have their own central organization, we, the Georgian and Armenian social democrats, also want to have such an organization."[169] Knuniants, another representative of the Caucasian social democrats, protested against certain orators who identified the Caucasian Union with the Bund, for the Bund was a nationalist organization and the Caucasian Union a district, territorial organization.[170] The opponents of the Caucasians argued that their demand was in contradiction to party centralism and that there was no need to create any intermediate organization whose existence might stimulate nationalist dissension; but they nevertheless admitted that such unions were bound to exist until the day that the central committee was strong and authoritative.[171]

Aleksandr Egorov (Levin) warned the congress of a "new Bundism" on the rise in the Caucasus. There were similarities between the Bund's arguments and the Caucasian argument. Both stressed social, local, and linguistic peculiarities and also special national traits. If the Caucasian representatives were modest and quiet, it was because their power and organization in comparison with those of the Bund were insignificant.[172] As a result of the debates, the congress adopted the following resolution presented by D. A. Topuridze (Karsky): "The congress recognizes the establishment of district (*raionnye*) organizations as unions of the committees acceptable in the parts of Russia that are distinguished by great peculiarities in language, composition of the population, etc. The approval of such organizations is entrusted to the party's central committee."[173] This resolution was adopted by twenty-eight votes to two, with seven abstentions. There is evidence that the centralist trend within the RSDWP was advocated by the Russian social democrats, while social democrats in the borderlands fought for autonomy.

The third congress of the RSDWP left unchanged the decisions of the previous congresses. The fact of the separate existence of a number of nationality-based parties and organizations compelled the RSDWP to take radical measures for a clarification of the issue. The third congress thus enjoined local committees "to make every effort to achieve agreement with the national social democratic organizations" and thus prepare for the "union of all social democratic parties in a single RSDWP."[174] The decisions of the fourth congress were also in the same spirit.[175]

The rejection of a separate existence for the nationality social democratic parties by the RSDWP had no effect upon the actual existence of such parties. Their independent existence was especially odious to the Bolshevik faction because the majority of the national parties were adherents of Menshevism. There is much evidence that the national parties used the split within the RSDWP to strengthen their own position. At the Prague conference of the RSDWP no national organizations were represented, although they had been invited several times,[176] a fact noted in the resolution of the conference.[177] Relations between the RSDWP (Bolsheviks) and the national organizations did not improve after this conference; on the contrary, separatism became more deeply rooted. The fact that the national organizations did not participate in the "February conference" (1913) was again registered in the resolution.[178] On the eve of the First

World War the national organizations were completely in the Menshevik camp, which was at that time improving its position on the international socialist arena. The Second International took the path of moderate socialism and rejected the revolutionary slogans of the Bolsheviks and their centralist attitude within the party. On the nationality question, the Austrian concept of "personal cultural autonomy" prevailed, and thus the social democratic party in Austria was organized on federalist principles. Since the Russian Mensheviks had accepted this principle, the national organizations inclined towards Menshevism.[179]

Meanwhile, the Bolsheviks continued their policy of strict party centralism against national separatism within the party. After the complete schism with the Mensheviks in 1912, they reiterated their disapproval of separatism. At the party's seventh conference in April 1917 an integralist formula *vis-à-vis* the national parties was adopted. "The interests of the working class demand the amalgamation of the workers of all the nationalities of Russia into common proletarian organizations, political, trade union, co-operative, cultural, and so forth."[180] It was stated that the proletariat of all the nationalities of a given state had to be organized in "a single and indivisible proletarian collective body, a single party."[181] The proposal that workers should be organized according to nationality, i.e., "so many nations, so many parties," was rejected on the grounds that it led to the disintegration of the idea of class solidarity. At the conference no opposition to the official party position emerged. The conference was almost wholly Bolshevik with only a handful of Mensheviks attending.[182]

The question of the status of the national minorities within the party was raised again at the sixth party congress in August 1917 by the Lithuanian Bolsheviks, Vinkentii Mitskevich-Kapsukas and Zigmas Angaretis (Aleksa). In a very carefully worded statement they demanded that the national minorities in the party organizations be allowed to organize their sections for the purpose of propaganda and agitation and also to issue their own papers and literature. These sections were to carry out their activities on their own but were to be ultimately subject and responsible to the control of the party. Kapsukas justified this demand by pointing out that the rejection of such sections could lead those organizations into an illegal position within the party. The majority of the congress opposed this amendment.[183]

The eighth party congress held in March 1919 was decisive with respect to the definition of the unity of the party. As a result of a report made by Grigorii Zinovev, the congress adopted a resolution stating: "At the present time Ukraine, Latvia, Lithuania, and Belorussia exist as separate Soviet republics. Thus, at the given moment, the problem of the forms of *statehood* is solved. But this does not mean that the RCP ought, in its turn, to organize itself on the basis of a federation of independent Communist parties." Accordingly, the congress decided that "*one* centralized Communist party with one central committee guiding all the work of the party in all parts of the RSFSR is imperative. All decisions of the RCP and its leading organs are unconditionally compulsory for all branches of the party, irrespective of their national composition. The central committees of the Ukrainian, Latvian, and Lithuanian Communists have the rights of district committees (*oblastnye komitety*) of the party and are completely subordinated to the CC RCP."[184] There was no opposition to this very odd resolution, which even Zinovev found somewhat peculiar. He wondered how long it would be possible to uphold the contradiction of "one single centralized party beside a federation of states." He assumed that in this case one would have to yield, that the federative principle for the state would give way to the centralist principle prevailing in the party. He also assured the conference that if, after the Austrian revolution, an attempt were made to organize independent Czech, German, Ruthenian (Ukrainian), and Polish Communist organizations, Russian Communists would tell them that they were in error.[185] Thus Zinovev predicted the unity of the Communist party in future Soviet states, but, of course, he did not say which nations were to be Soviet states.

The *Leitmotiv* of the Russian Bolsheviks was undoubtedly prevention of the disintegration of the political and territorial arena of their activity. If the federative principle were to be introduced into the party, then the scope of the Russian Communist party would be limited to Russian ethnic territory. Preservation of a unitary party would have far-reaching consequences for federative relations between Soviet Russia and the national Soviet republics, since Bolsheviks believed in the hegemony of the Communist party in state affairs.[186]

CHAPTER II

Ukraine: The Socio-Economic Environment

Territory and Population

Because of its geographical position, natural resources, and economic development, Ukraine played an important role in prerevolutionary Russia. It was no exaggeration on the part of many Russians of rank when they considered Ukraine one source of Russia's greatness.[1] Any government of Russia, even Bolshevik, was obliged to continue the expansionist policies Peter I and Catherine II took towards Ukraine. Russian rulers spared no effort to instil the conviction abroad that Ukraine was just a province of Russia, integrated with Russia not only politically but also with respect to religion, language, and culture. As a result, Ukraine was obliterated from the political map of Europe. It became officially just the southern part of Russia, sometimes called *Malorossiia* (Little Russia) and its population *malorosy* (Little Russians).

The territory later known as Ukraine was initially undefined. It was situated between Romania, Poland, the Kursk province of Russia, the river Don, and the Black Sea. Russia, Poland (up to 1795), and Austria-Hungary (after 1772) all laid claim to parts of this area. The provinces considered Russian Ukraine before the First World War, and later forming the Ukrainian Soviet republic, amounted to 445,000 square kilometres. The territory of the Ukrainian republic after the Second World War was 576,600 square kilometres[2] and is now, after the incorporation of the Crimean peninsula, 602,600 square kilometres.[3] The ethnic territory claimed by the Ukrainians themselves was much larger, 729,000 square kilometres, extending to the territory known as the Kuban in Cis-Caucasia and to a part of Voronezh province.[4] This territory amounted to only about 3 per cent of the territory of Russia, but its geographical position made it very important, both strategically and with regard to communications. Through Ukraine, Russia was linked with the Balkans, Central Europe, Poland, and the Black Sea. The Russians argued that without Ukraine, Russia would revert to the status of an Asiatic country, deprived of her position in European affairs.

Demographically, Ukraine was of much greater importance than its size would suggest. At the time of the revolution, it comprised about 17 per cent of the whole population, and after the secession of Poland, Finland, and the Baltic states this proportion rose to 21 per cent. The nationality figures for the whole of Russia, according to the census figures of 1897 and 1926, are shown in Table 1.

These figures show that the Ukrainians were the second largest nationality in Russia, making up together with other non-Russians a majority of the population of Russia. Only after the secession of Poland and the Baltic states did Russians gain a slight majority. For the same reason the proportion of Ukrainians increased to 21.6 per cent.

Natural Resources of Ukraine

The great significance of Ukraine lay in its natural resources and economy. The following account of the economic importance of Ukraine for Russia is only a short survey intended to enable the reader to see the Ukrainian problem in a wider perspective.[5] Russian industrial potential before the revolution and afterwards was based mainly on the raw materials from the borderlands, primarily Ukraine. Official Russian statistics show that the importance of Ukrainian iron production increased rapidly after 1893; Table 2, comparing Ukraine's production of cast iron (in thousands of poods) with other regions of Russia, bears this out.

In iron production, Ukraine equalled all other regions put together at the end of the nineteenth century, and it outstripped them by the beginning of the twentieth century. The importance of Ukrainian cast iron increased even after the revolution. Table 3 gives the share of Ukraine in

Table 1. Nationalities of the Russian Empire and USSR, 1897-1926

Nationality	1897	Per cent	1926	Per cent
Russians	55,667,500	44.5	77,732,200	54.0
Ukrainians	22,380,600	17.9	31,189,500	21.6
Poles	7,931,300	6.3	781,700	0.5
Belorussians	5,885,500	4.7	4,738,200	3.3
Jews	5,063,200	4.0	2,597,400	1.8
Kazakhs and Kirghiz	4,285,800	3.4	4,578,600	3.2
Turkic peoples and Tatars	3,767,500	3.0	4,898,800	3.4
Germans	1,790,500	1.4	1,237,900	0.8
Uzbeks, Sarts, Kurama	1,702,800	1.4	2,440,900	1.7
Lithuanians	1,658,500	1.3	51,100	0.0
Bashkirs, Mishars, Tepters	1,493,000	1.2	983,100	0.7
Latvians	1,435,900	1.1	141,400	0.1
Georgians	1,352,500	1.0	1,820,900	1.2
Armenians	1,173,100	0.9	1,565,800	1.1
Moldavians and Romanians	1,121,700	0.9	283,500	0.2
Mordvins	1,023,800	0.8	1,339,900	0.9
Estonians	1,002,700	0.8	154,600	0.1
Chuvash	843,800	0.6	1,117,300	0.8
Tadzhik group	350,400	0.3	376,400	0.3
Turkmens	281,400	0.2	427,600	0.3
Smaller nationalities	5,455,000	4.3	5,870,900	4.0
Total	125,666,500	100.0	144,327,700	100.0

SOURCE: *Narodnost i rodnoi iazyk naseleniia SSSR* (Moscow, 1928), pp. xxiv-xxvii. For 1897, see also P. N. Miliukov, *Rossiia na perelome,* 2 vols. (Paris, 1927), Vol. I, pp. 205-06, and K. Fortunatov, *Natsionalnye oblasti Rossii,* p. 4.

the production of cast iron (in tons) in the Soviet Union. Ukrainian production of iron ore on the eve of the First World War, in 1913, was 57 per cent of total Russian production.[6]

Table 4 shows the development of production of Ukrainian coal (in thousands of poods).

As table 5 demonstrates, from 1913 to 1938 Ukrainian coal (in tons) remained important.

Table 2. Regional Iron Production in the Russian Empire, 1893-1906

Year	1893	1900	1906
Ukraine	19,868 (29.2%)	82,573 (50.0%)	102,006 (62.2%)
Urals	30,919 (45.5%)	50,212 (30.4%)	38,214 (23.3%)
Poland (Russian)	10,062 (14.8%)	18,219 (11.0%)	18,452 (11.3%)
Central Russia	7,172 (10.5%)	14,011 (8.5%)	5,253 (3.2%)

SOURCE: *Zheleznaia promyshlennost Iuzhnoi Rossii,* p. 79, quoted in M. Iavorsky, *Ukraina v epokhu kapitalizmu* (Kharkiv, 1924), pp. 27-28.
NOTE: One pood equals 16.38 kilograms.

Table 3. Iron Production in the Soviet Union and Ukrainian SSR, 1913-38

	1913	1927-28	1938
Soviet Union	4,216,000[a]	3,282,300	14,487,400
Ukrainian SSR	2,882,500 (68.4%)	2,361,300 (71.9%)	8,800,800 (60.7%)

SOURCE: *Sotsialisticheskoe stroitelstvo Soiuza SSR (1933-1938 gg.)* (Moscow-Leningrad, 1939), p. 56. Cf. also P. I. Liashchenko, *Istoriia russkogo narodnogo khoziaistva* (Moscow, 1927), pp. 380 ff.
[a]Excludes Poland, Finland, and the Baltic provinces.

Table 4. Coal Production in the Russian Empire and Ukraine, 1860-1913

Year	All Russia	Share of Ukraine
1860	18,290	6,000 (32.8%)
1900	986,327	671,811 (68.1%)
1906	1,326,454	1,060,530 (80.0%)
1913	2,199,952	1,683,780 (76.5%)

SOURCE: M. Iavorsky, *Ukraina v epokhu kapitalizmu* (Kharkiv, 1924), p. 37. Cf. also B. L. Lychkov, *Rudnye i nerudnye bogatstva Ukrainy*, Vol. I (Kiev, 1926), p. 9.

However, the economic importance of Ukraine consisted not only in the production of coal and iron. Especially during the Bolshevik revolution, the agricultural importance of Ukraine, rightly called "the granary of Europe," was very great. Even before the First World War a large proportion of Russia's grain was produced in Ukraine. Between 1909 and 1913, Ukraine produced 98 per cent of Russia's wheat, 75 per cent of its rye, and 27 per cent of its oats.[7] Still greater was the share of Ukraine in the production of sugar, estimated by Soviet sources as shown in Table 6 (production of raw sugar, in quintals [100 kilograms]).

Table 5. Coal Production in the Soviet Union and Donets Basin, 1913-38

	1913	1929	1933	1938
Soviet Union	29,117,000	40,067,000	76,333,000	132,888,000
Donets Basin	25,288,000	30,980,000	51,060,000	80,733,000
(Ukrainian SSR)	86.8%	77.3%	67%	61%

SOURCE: *Sotsialisticheskoe stroitelstvo Soiuza SSR (1933-1938 gg.)* (Moscow-Leningrad, 1939), pp. 47-48.

Table 6. Sugar Production in the Soviet Union and Ukrainian SSR, 1913-37

	1913-14	1927-28	1937
Soviet Union	13,468,000	13,331,000	24,211,000
Ukrainian SSR	11,048,000	10,864,000	17,898,000
	82.0%	81.5%	73.9%

SOURCE: *Sotsialisticheskoe stroitelstvo Soiuza SSR (1933-1938 gg.)* (Moscow-Leningrad, 1939), p. 79.

The economic importance of Ukraine to a great extent determined Bolshevik policy towards Ukraine. In general, one can find some degree of correlation between the economic importance of any given province of Russia and its attraction for the Russian Bolsheviks. This dependence was recognized by the Bolshevik leaders during the revolution.[8]

Social and Economic Conditions in Ukraine on the Eve of the Revolution

Among the neglected issues in the study of the Bolshevik revolution in the borderlands and in Ukraine in particular is the consideration of social and economic conditions. The question of whether the preconditions for this revolution were identical in all parts of the Russian empire has not been approached at all by historians outside the Soviet Union or at most has been treated summarily, using uncritical generalizations.[9]

According to the classical Marxian view, the success of a Communist revolution is determined by the stage of capitalist development and by the extent of industrialization. Where there is no industry there is no proletarian class, hence the conditions for a proletarian revolution, let alone for Communism, are absent. Therefore, when studying the potentiality for Communism in any given country, it is necessary to study its industrial development. (Of course, the mere industrialization of a country does not necessarily lead to its Bolshevization; the emergence of this radical movement is usually determined by a combination of factors.)

Bolshevik historians agreed that prerevolutionary Russia was a colonial power very much like Britain or France, with a similar relationship between the mother country and its colonies. Lenin, in his analysis of Russian economic conditions, concluded that the borderlands of Russia after the reform of 1861 (the abolition of serfdom) were in a dependent colonial position. While in Russia proper industries were in rapid growth, the borderlands remained agricultural, supplying Russia with raw materials. The industrial regions of Russia proper received food from the borderlands, used the borderlands as a market for their factory-made products, and supplied the borderlands with labour and artisans.[10] "Ukraine," wrote Naumov, "was one of the chief supply bases of the tsarist mother country. The agriculture of Ukraine developed in a capitalist direction chiefly for the satisfaction of the export needs of tsarist Russia."[11]

Mid-nineteenth century Ukraine was considered very backward industrially, even as compared with Russia, i.e., the St. Petersburg, Ural, and Moscow provinces. With the influx of foreign capital (mainly French and Belgian),[12] there was rapid industrial development in Ukraine's eastern provinces, but this did not substantially change the social and political face of Ukraine. In spite of its expanding mining industry, Ukraine remained an agricultural country because industrial growth was confined primarily to metallurgy and mining, industries localized in the southern part of Left-Bank Ukraine.[13] Other branches of industry, mainly light industry and handicrafts, lagged behind their counterparts in Russia. Matvii Iavorsky blamed the stunted growth of these industries on Russian industrialists, who jealously guarded their privileges in Ukraine, and on foreign investment, which was not yet interested in these fields of production.[14]

At the end of the nineteenth century the mining industry in Ukraine grew very rapidly. In 1860 the Donets basin produced 6 million poods of coal, and in 1900 the output increased to 183 million poods. Similar increases occurred in the production of iron ore and steel. But Ukraine remained a backward province of Russia, relegated to supplying the industries of the metropolis with raw materials. Soviet writers emphasize that Ukraine for a long period "lived a common economic and political life with Russia," and that "the development of communal manufacture created in Russia and in Ukraine the necessary material prerequisites for the victory of socialism [and] made the socialist revolution a completely inevitable result of their historical process in conformity with [social] laws."[15]

A slower tempo of industrialization meant a slower increase in the number of workers and consequently a less revolutionary proletariat. The problem of the development of the working class in Ukraine has been investigated mainly by Soviet writers.[16] Most writers agree that the ratio of proletarians to non-proletarians was higher in Russia than in Ukraine. In Russia in 1879 there were 326,754 workers, while in Ukraine there were only 13,451 or about 3.9 per cent of the total proletariat in the Russian empire.[17] According to Soviet sources, at the beginning of the twentieth century there were 2,792,000 persons employed in large enterprises, the mining industry, and the railways in Russia. In Ukraine, at the same time, there were about 360,200 workers of this kind.[18] Lenin estimated that the number of mining workers increased as shown in Table 7.

Table 7. Miners in the Russian Empire, Urals, and Ukraine, 1877-1902

Year	All Russia	Urals	South (Ukraine)
1877	256,919	145,455 (56.6%)	13,865 (5.4%)
1893	444,646	238,630 (53.7%)	54,670 (12.3%)
1902	604,972	249,805 (41.3%)	145,280 (24.0%)

SOURCE: V. I. Lenin, "Razvitie gornoi promyshlennosti," *Sochineniia*, 4th ed., 35 vols. (Moscow, 1941-50), Vol. III, p. 429.

In 1912 the tsarist government compiled detailed data on the distribution of the mining industry and other enterprises. The data demonstrates clearly that the characteristic feature of the industrialization of Ukraine was that Ukraine was a source of raw materials and unfinished products for the Russian heavy and light industries.

The situation in heavy and light industry during this period is reflected in Table 8, which shows the distribution of enterprises and the number of workers employed in them. Heavy industry in the whole of Ukraine did not exceed that of the Moscow region alone. The textile and paper industries were exclusively concentrated in the Central Russian regions: Moscow, St. Petersburg, and Vladimir. In all the above-mentioned industries, Ukraine's share, as measured by the number of workers employed, was only 14.3 per cent. The Moscow region alone concentrated 17 per cent of all industrial workers. The growth of industry and the labour force in Ukraine is illustrated in Table 9, compiled from pre-Soviet and Soviet sources.

Table 9. Enterprises and Workers in Ukraine, 1904-08

Year	Enterprises	Workers
1904	3,012	249,527
1905	2,947	236,855
1906	2,920	242,879
1907	2,895	249,934
1908	3,318	301,700

SOURCE: Aleksynsky, "Chy zaderzhala revoliutsiia rozvytok kapitalizmu na Ukraini," *Dzvin,* 1913, No. 1, pp. 31-36. D. Shlosberg, "Profesiinyi rukh 1905-1907 rr. na Ukraini," *Litopys revoliutsii,* 1930, No. 6, pp. 478-80. P. I. Liashchenko, *Istoriia narodnogo khoziaistva SSSR,* 2 vols. (Moscow, 1956), Vol. II, p. 483.

NOTE: According to Aleksynsky, p. 36, in 1908 there were 3,039 enterprises and 261,769 workers in Ukraine.

For comparison, the figures for Poland and the Baltic provinces (1908) are given in Table 10.

In Ukraine the enterprises and workers were distributed as shown in Table 11.

The agricultural provinces (Podillia, Volhynia, Kiev, Poltava) had more small enterprises, but the provinces with metallurgical and mining industries, such as Katerynoslav and Kharkiv, had a larger number of workers.

This geographical distribution of industry in Ukraine had very

Table 8. Industrial Enterprises in Ukraine by Provinces and by Branches of Industry, 1912

Provinces	Cotton		Wool		Silk		Flax, hemp, and jute		Mixed industries manufacturing fibrous substances	
	Enterprises	Workers	Enterprises	Workers	Enterprises	Workers	Enterprises	Workers	Enterprises	Workers
Chernihiv	1	8	10	4,797	—	—	30	2,241	—	—
Katerynoslav	—	—	1	125	—	—	—	—	1	14
Kharkiv	3	130	2	426	—	—	2	2,701	—	—
Kherson	6	47	1	7	—	—	3	1,921	7	122
Kiev	—	—	4	196	—	—	—	—	4	342
Podillia	—	—	17	563	—	—	—	—	—	—
Poltava	—	—	—	—	—	—	1	108	—	—
Tavria	2	52	—	—	—	—	3	80	—	—
Volhynia	—	—	5	78	—	—	—	—	—	—
Ukraine total	12	237	40	6,192	—	—	39	7,051	12	478
Russia total	850	550,762	1,205	155,094	174	33,176	258	100,154	429	42,527
Share of Ukraine in %	1.4	0.04	3.3	4.0	—	—	15.1	7.0	2.8	1.1

Continued

Provinces	Paper, paper goods, printing		Woodworking		Metal, manufacture of machinery apparatus and tools		Mineral substances		Animal products	
	Enter-prises	Workers	Enter-prises	Workers	Enter-prises	Workers	Enter-prises	Workers	Enter-prises	Workers
Chernihiv	2	386	59	2,442	7	380	7	236	9	173
Katerynoslav	22	430	28	1,360	88	18,282	86	9,248	6	211
Kharkiv	44	2,443	10	814	43	7,614	69	8,783	6	110
Kherson	84	2,623	55	2,949	149	17,293	51	2,613	25	888
Kiev	38	2,786	67	2,239	56	6,675	67	5,598	9	774
Podillia	3	146	7	137	9	406	12	599	1	9
Poltava	27	763	16	532	20	586	24	936	5	74
Tavria	17	425	12	290	62	5,737	27	1,225	—	—
Volhynia	16	1,716	109	4,069	22	556	45	6,049	8	247
Ukraine total	253	11,720	363	14,832	456	57,529	388	35,287	69	2,486
Russia total	1,436	99,676	2,358	124,159	2,328	338,449	1,811	197,941	803	51,350
Share of Ukraine in %	17.6	11.8	15.4	11.9	19.6	17.0	21.4	17.8	8.6	4.8

Continued

Provinces	Food		Chemical		Mining		Other industries not included in the preceding categories		Total	
	Enterprises	Workers	Enterprises	Workers	Enterprises	Workers	Enterprises	Workers	Enterprises	Workers
Chernihiv	200	11,142	10	4,633	—	—	1	34	336	26,472
Katerynoslav	140	2,931	5	2,087	—	—	2	146	379	34,834
Kharkiv	157	24,421	12	1,348	—	—	1	120	349	48,910
Kherson	234	10,991	30	542	—	—	19	1,608	664	41,604
Kiev	291	53,118	4	1,061	—	—	7	1,956	547	74,745
Podillia	230	28,531	2	135	—	—	2	158	283	30,684
Poltava	185	9,395	3	145	—	—	1	60	282	12,599
Tavria	91	4,158	—	—	—	—	6	86	220	12,053
Volhynia	99	12,729	3	89	—	—	1	178	308	25,711
Ukraine total	1,627	157,416	69	10,040	—	—	40	4,346	3,368	307,612
Russia total	4,719	341,137	550	77,529	276	30,455	159	8,782	17,356	2,151,191
Share of Ukraine in %	34.5	46.1	12.5	12.9	—	—	25.2	49.5	19.4	14.3

SOURCE: *Statisticheskii ezhegodnik na 1914 g.* (St. Petersburg, 1914), pp. 204-13.
NOTE: In the source, Ukraine figures as the South of Russia *(Iug Rossii)*.

Table 10. Enterprises and Workers in Poland and the Baltic Provinces, 1908

	Enterprises	Workers
Poland (Russian)	3,172	270,200
Baltic provinces	1,179	97,800

SOURCE: P. I. Liashchenko, *Istoriia narodnogo khoziaistva SSSR,* 2 vols. (Moscow, 1956), Vol. II, pp. 494-98.

Table 11. Enterprises and Workers in Ukrainian Provinces, 1908-11

Province	Enterprises	1908 Workers	1911 Workers
Chernihiv	336	23,300	18,563
Katerynoslav	362	70,300	31,964
Kharkiv	329	43,700	36,104
Kherson	612	35,700	28,422
Kiev	595	63,900	58,869
Podillia	339	31,800	28,065
Poltava	274	11,000	8,847
Volhynia	471	22,000	19,272
Total	3,318	301,700	230,106

SOURCE: P. I. Liashchenko, *Istoriia narodnogo khoziaistva SSSR,* 2 vols. (Moscow, 1956), Vol. II, p. 483 (1908). K. Myrhorodsky, "Z robitnychoho zhyttia," *Dzvin,* 1913, No. 2, p. 130 (1911).

well-defined borders. Almost the whole of the mining and metal industry was located in the southern steppe region of Ukraine (Katerynoslav and Kherson provinces), while the remaining provinces (Kiev, Poltava, Chernihiv, Volhynia, Podillia) were central to the food industry. This is borne out in Table 12.

In the southwestern provinces of Ukraine the unskilled workers of breweries and sugar refineries predominated; connected as they were with the countryside, they had no such revolutionary tendencies as the workers of the mining and metal industries in the southern steppes of Ukraine. The towns in the southwestern provinces were predominantly administrative centres or trade intermediaries between the countryside and the industrial towns of other provinces. The workers of the southwestern towns consisted almost exclusively of craftsmen.

Table 12. Mining and Metal Industry in Ukraine, 1912

	Southern steppe provinces		Other provinces	
	Absolute figures	% of total for Ukraine	Absolute figures	% of total for Ukraine
Number of enterprises	571	17.2	167	4.8
Number of workers	247,809	53.7	17,181	3.7
Value of enterprises in roubles	3,183,619,000	32.8	34,223,900	2.8

SOURCE: Mikhels, "Promyshlennye raiony Ukrainy," in *Materialy po raionirovaniiu Ukrainy* (Kharkiv: Gosplan SSSR, 1923), p. 136.

Another peculiarity of Ukraine, apart from the above-mentioned backwardness with respect to both industrialization and the development of a large industrial working class, was the *national* heterogeneity of the population in general and of the working classes in particular. This fact deserves emphasis because there was a correlation between a given social class and its attitude towards Ukrainian national self-determination. In Ukraine, as a result of the development of industry, the immigration of Russian workers, and the policy of Russification, the working masses in heavy industry were predominantly Russian by nationality and more so by culture. The artisans and the professional classes were mostly of Jewish origin, although in their cultural and political orientation they were more Russian than Jewish.

The Ukrainian masses, predominantly agricultural, comprised smaller strata within the middle class. Ukrainians also made up the lowest strata in the cities. According to the census of 1897, seven of the nine Ukrainian provinces contained nearly twenty million people altogether. Their distribution by nationality is given in Table 13.

The statistics for 1926 for all nine Ukrainian provinces set the population of Ukraine at 29,018,187, distributed among the nationalities as shown in Table 14.

Another demographic characteristic of Ukraine was the domination of its cities by national minorities, mainly Russians and Jews. The national composition of the urban population of the seven provinces in the 1897 census is shown in Table 15.

Table 13. Nationalities in Ukrainian Provinces, 1897

Province	Ukrainians	Russians	Jews	Total
Katerynoslav	1,456,000	365,000	99,000	2,113,000
Kharkiv	2,009,000	441,000	13,000	2,492,000
Kherson	1,462,000	575,000	322,000	2,733,000
Kiev	2,819,000	209,000	430,000	3,559,000
Podillia	2,442,000	99,000	369,000	3,018,000
Poltava	2,583,000	73,000	110,000	2,778,000
Volhynia	2,096,000	105,000	395,000	2,989,000
Total	14,867,000	1,867,000	1,738,000	19,682,000
Percentage	75.5	9.5	8.8	

SOURCE: *Entsiklopedicheskii slovar,* Vol. XXVII (St. Petersburg, 1899), pp. 76-77. V. Stankevich, *Sudby narodov Rossii* (Berlin, 1921), p. 49.

NOTE: P. N. Miliukov estimated the number of Ukrainians in Russia in 1897 at 22,045,000. *Rossiia na perelome,* 2 vols. (Paris, 1927), Vol. I, p. 205.

Table 14. Nationalities in Ukraine, 1926

Nationality	Number	Per cent
Ukrainians	23,218,860	80.0
Russians	2,677,166	9.2
Jews	1,574,391	5.4
Poles	476,435	1.6
Germans	393,924	1.4
Moldavians	257,794	0.9
Other nationalities	419,627	1.5
Total	29,018,187	100.0

SOURCE: *Natsionalnaia politika VKP(b) v tsifrakh,* ed. S. M. Velikovsky and I. Levin (Moscow, 1931), p. 46. Cf. also *Statisticheskii spravochnik SSSR, za 1928 god* (Moscow, 1929), pp. 32-35.

The towns, then, were largely non-Ukrainian, with the exception of those in the provinces of Poltava and Kharkiv, which were always regarded as bastions of Ukrainian nationalism. Although ethnic Russians (and Russified Ukrainians) did not predominate by themselves, together with the Jews, who were always more Russian than Ukrainian, they made up

Table 15. Nationalities in Ukrainian Cities, 1897

Province	Ukrainians	Russians	Jews	Total
Katerynoslav	65,000	98,000	62,000	241,000
Kharkiv	199,000	145,000	12,000	367,000
Kherson	136,000	355,000	224,000	789,000
Kiev	129,000	152,000	142,000	459,000
Podillia	72,000	33,000	103,000	222,000
Poltava	157,000	30,000	80,000	274,000
Volhynia	46,000	44,000	119,000	234,000
Total	804,000	857,000	742,000	2,586,000
Percentage	31.1	33.1	28.7	

SOURCE: V. Stankevich, *Sudby narodov Rossii* (Berlin, 1921), p. 49.

what was in effect a Russian majority in most of the cities. We may infer that a similar situation prevailed at the time of the Bolshevik revolution, since in the postrevolutionary period, according to the census of 1926, the national composition of the main Ukrainian cities was (in percentages) as shown in Table 16.

Table 16. National Composition of Ukrainian Cities, 1926

City	Ukrainians	Russians	Jews	Poles	Others
Dnipropetrovsk	35.9	31.5	26.7	1.8	4.1
Kharkiv	38.3	37.0	19.5	1.3	3.9
Kiev	42.1	24.1	27.2	2.7	3.9
Luhansk	26.1	56.2	10.7	1.3	5.7
Odessa	17.4	38.7	36.5	0.3	7.1

SOURCE: *Entsyklopediia ukrainoznavstva,* Vol. I (Munich-New York, 1949), p. 158.

From Table 16 it is evident that the Ukrainians, even two years after the so-called "Ukrainianization," were not in the majority in any large Ukrainian city. In all the cities the majority was made up of the non-Ukrainian minorities. The Ukrainians were the smallest national group (not counting the Poles) in Odessa and Luhansk; in the other three cities, though they were the largest single national group, they did not form an absolute majority. The statistics for the growth of the population of Kiev between 1874 and 1926 (in percentages) provide further evidence of the Russification of the Ukrainian city (Table 17).

Table 17. National Composition of Kiev, 1874-1926

Year	Ukrainians	Russians	Jews	Poles	Others
1874	59.8	15.1	10.2	6.1	8.8
1897	22.2	54.2	12.1	6.7	4.8
1917	16.4	49.5	18.7	9.2	6.2
1919	25.3	42.9	21.2	6.8	3.8
1920	14.3	46.6	31.9	3.7	3.5
1923	27.1	35.6	31.1	3.0	3.2
1926	42.1	24.5	27.4	2.6	3.4

SOURCE: I. Vikul, "Liudnist mista Kyiva," in *Demografichnyi zbirnyk*, ed. Ptukha (Kiev, 1930), p. 221.

There was a clear tendency towards de-Ukrainianization in Kiev up to 1917, after which, probably as a result of the national independence of Ukraine in 1918–19, the Ukrainian population increased rapidly to 25.3 per cent, only to fall to 14.3 per cent in 1920 under Bolshevik rule. As a result of the Ukrainianization, by 1926 the Ukrainian element increased again to 42.1 per cent.

As these statistics make clear, the population of Ukraine on the eve of the Bolshevik revolution was heterogeneous, and the cities were non-Ukrainian in composition and character. Among the proletariat, the non-Ukrainian element was even more predominant. At the time of the revolution the industrial proletariat of Ukraine was, for the most part, Russian, Jewish, and Russified Ukrainian. This was a result of the way the industrialization of Ukraine had developed with foreign capital and foreign manpower. According to the Soviet historian, A. M. Pankratova, "there was a rush of peasants from all the provinces into Ukraine, into the agricultural steppe country and the coal mines of the Donets basin."[19]

The industrial population of Ukraine in 1897 numbered, according to Los, 753,454,[20] of which 290,587 or 38.7 per cent spoke the Ukrainian language.[21] Of the total industrial population in Katerynoslav province, only 29 per cent were Ukrainian, while in Kherson province 17 per cent were Ukrainian. Los estimated that 73.3 per cent of the workers in the Donets basin had immigrated from Russia and other provinces, while only 26.7 per cent had come from the Ukrainian provinces.[22] Later Soviet historians refuse to accept this and claim that the Russians in the working class of Ukraine made up only a very insignificant proportion.[23] In determining nationality, however, a distinction must be made between national origin and language. Many workers of Ukrainian origin could not speak Ukrainian. According to a report of Radchenko, the president of the Ukrainian trade unions, Ukrainians made up 49 per cent of the membership of Ukrainian trade unions, but only 17 per cent of them could speak Ukrainian.[24]

In the early 1930s Soviet scholars published statistics bearing on the question of nationality and the industrial proletariat. According to L. Zinger, on 1 October 1932 there were 22,598,600 workers in the Soviet Union, distributed among the Soviet republics as shown in Table 18.

Table 18. Workers in Soviet Republics, 1932

Republic	Number of workers	Per cent
RSFSR	16,171,700	73.5
Ukraine	4,380,000	19.9
Belorussia	507,000	2.5
Uzbekistan	475,700	2.1
Azerbaidzhan	395,300	1.7
Georgia	343,700	1.5
Armenia	115,300	0.5
Turkmenistan	111,800	0.5
Tadzhikistan	96,400	0.4

SOURCE: L. Zinger, *Natsionalnyi sostav proletariata SSSR* (Moscow, 1934), p. 9.

An overwhelming proportion of the workers in industry was concentrated in the Russian federation and Ukraine.

The territorial distribution of the workers among the Soviet republics has little relevance to the problem of the distribution of the workers among the nationalities in the Soviet Union. As has been shown in the case of Ukraine, the greater part of the workers can be of Russian origin or of Russian national orientation. More relevant, then, are the statistics on the representation of the titular nationalities among the workers of the national republics (Table 19). It is necessary to point out that these figures relate to a time after the so-called *korenizatsiia*, which was an effort to make the republics more indigenous in administration and economy. Consequently, they are less relevant for the period of the revolution. Still, these figures do show that the most underrepresented were the Kirghiz, who in 1926 made up 66.6 per cent of the total population of their republic but only 16.5 per cent of the republic's proletariat. The Ukrainians were also underrepresented. Although they constituted 80 per cent of the total population of the Ukrainian SSR in 1926, they accounted for only 58 per cent of Ukraine's proletariat. The same can be said of the Turkic peoples

Table 19. Nationality of Workers in Soviet Republics, 1931

Republic	Nationality	Per cent of the total number of workers
Armenian SSR	Armenians	85.1
Azerbaidzhan SSR	Turkic peoples	27.6
Bashkiria	Bashkirs	14.4
Belorussian SSR	Belorussians	62.6
Crimean ASSR	Crimean Tatars	8.9
Georgian SSR	Georgians	59.3
Kirghiz ASSR	Kirghiz	16.5
Tatar ASSR	Tatars	23.3
Ukrainian SSR	Ukrainians	58.1

SOURCE: L. Zinger, *Natsionalnyi sostav proletariata SSSR* (Moscow, 1934), p. 11.

in Azerbaidzhan who formed 71.7 per cent of the total population.[25]

The national composition of the Ukrainian trade unions as registered in 1931 (Table 20) shows that Ukrainians were underrepresented among the members of the trade unions. Both the Russians and the Jews were overrepresented, more than double their percentage of the total population. This phenomenon reflects the overwhelmingly agricultural character of the Ukrainian nation.

The national composition of wage-earning workers in the trade unions in Ukraine in 1931 is given (in percentages) in Table 21.

Although the Ukrainians were in the majority in all walks of life, they nevertheless were concentrated in agriculture and transport, while the Russians were employed mainly in industry and administration, and the Jews mainly in industry, administration, and intellectual work. This emerges more clearly from Table 22, which gives the nationality and occupation of the Ukrainian SSR's working population in 1926 (in percentages). According to these figures, the proportion of Ukrainians in industry was still lower in 1926 than in 1931. This indicates that by 1931 more of the Ukrainian population, as a result of the Ukrainianization and the growth of industry in the late twenties, had moved into urban industries. Nevertheless, the Ukrainians remained predominantly employed in agriculture and transport.

The Ukrainian demographer Kubiiovych, analysing the census of 1926, arrived at an occupational distribution of the total population of Ukraine (Table 23, in percentages), which differs from that of Table 22. While the

Table 20. National Composition of Ukrainian Trade Unions, 1931

Nationality	Members of trade unions	Per cent	Nationality of the total population (in percentage)
Ukrainians	1,116,397	58.1	80
Russians	479,356	25.0	9.2
Jews	240,372	12.4	5.4
Poles	32,652	1.7	1.6
Germans	10,891	0.6	1.3
Belorussians	7,097	0.4	0.3
Tatars	5,522	0.3	—
Greeks	2,023	0.2	0.4
Moldavians	1,903	0.1	0.9
Latvians	1,399	0.1	—
Others	23,656	1.1	—

SOURCE: L. Zinger, *Natsionalnyi sostav proletariata SSSR* (Moscow, 1934), p. 78. *Natsionalnaia politika VKP(b) v tsifrakh*, ed. S. M. Velikovsky and I. Levin (Moscow, 1931), p. 46.

Table 21. National Composition of Wage-Earning Workers in Ukrainian Trade Unions, 1931

Trade unions	Ukrainians	Russians	Jews	Others
Agriculture	75.4	11.5	8.4	4.7
Industry	51.9	31.1	12.4	4.6
Transport	73.9	19.3	3.5	3.3
Intellectuals	55.5	15.6	24.3	4.6
Others	60.3	23.7	11.4	4.6
Total	58.1	25.0	12.4	4.5

SOURCE: L. Zinger, *Natsionalnyi sostav proletariata SSSR* (Moscow, 1934), p. 79.

Ukrainians constituted about 80 per cent of the total population and the Russians 9.2 per cent and the Jews 5.4 per cent, 90.7 per cent of the Ukrainians were employed in agriculture, with only 3.8 per cent in industry and 2.6 per cent in the public services. Of all the industrial workers, even in 1926 only 42.9 per cent were of Ukrainian nationality, while the

Table 22. National and Occupational Structure of Workers in Ukraine, 1926

Nationality	Total number of workers	Agriculture	Manufacturing industry	Handicrafts	Transport
Ukrainians	54.64	81.33	42.90	41.53	70.00
Russians	29.17	9.57	41.02	13.59	23.53
Jews	8.69	1.06	7.89	38.42	1.10
Others	7.5	8.04	8.19	6.56	5.37

SOURCE: *Natsionalnaia politika VKP(b) v tsifrakh,* ed. S. M. Velikovsky and I. Levin (Moscow, 1931), p. 126.

NOTE: V. Zatonsky gave somewhat different figures; he estimated the number of Ukrainians who were industrial workers at 41.6 per cent and transport workers at 64.6 per cent. "Materiialy do ukrainskoho natsionalnoho pytannia," *Bilshovyk Ukrainy,* 1927, No. 6, p. 24.

Table 23. National and Social Composition of Ukrainian Population, 1926

	Ukrainians	Russians	Jews
Agriculture	90.7	51.8	8.9
Industry	3.8	20.0	40.0
Commerce	0.8	3.3	14.9
Administration	2.6	12.2	20.7
Others	2.1	12.7	15.5

SOURCE: *Entsyklopediia ukrainoznavstva,* Vol. I (Munich-New York, 1949), p. 138.

majority of the industrial workers, mainly Russian and Jewish, belonged to the national minorities.[26]

The consequence of the national diversity in Ukraine was that the proletarian organizations and political parties were organized, not only according to their political and professional interests and ideas, but often according to their national identity. Thus there existed a number of social democratic parties (Ukrainian, Russian, Jewish, Polish) and later also a number of Communist parties. As a result, before the revolution national antagonism often coincided with social and political cleavages. Because of the peculiar distribution of economic, social, and political power, a tendency towards de-Ukrainianization of the upper social class could be observed. Owing to the Russifying policy of the Russian government, high offices in Ukraine were distributed among the Russians or other nationalities loyal to the idea of one, indivisible Russian nation.

On the basis of the socio-economic survey presented in this chapter, it is fair to conclude that the Ukrainians were not well suited for a proletarian socialist revolution. First, compared with Russia proper, the proletariat in Ukraine was too small and undeveloped to take a leading role in the revolution; second, the proletariat in Ukraine did not represent the majority nationality of the territory, since it was largely non-Ukrainian; and third, national cleavages would make a united social democratic movement difficult, if not impossible.

CHAPTER III

Political Parties in Ukraine

Nationalism was the most important movement in Central and Eastern Europe during the late nineteenth and early twentieth centuries.[1] However, national identity was not necessarily acquired by birth or citizenship, for individuals usually determined their own nationality. For instance, one might be a citizen of the Russian or Austro-Hungarian empires but be of Russian, Ukrainian, Armenian, or Czech nationality.

A similar situation existed with regard to political affiliation. Thus a Ukrainian or Polish worker with radical political leanings had to decide, on the one hand, whether he would support a social democratic or socialist revolutionary party, and, on the other, whether it would be a Russian, Ukrainian, or Polish social democratic or socialist revolutionary party. The electoral campaign was therefore two-dimensional, divided between different political parties and different ethnic affiliations within the same political party. As will be seen later, it was partly the prospect of fighting against the fraternal Ukrainian or Georgian parties that prompted Lenin to demand an integrated and united social democratic party for the whole of Russia. Of course, this ideal was valid as long as the Russian empire remained intact; as soon as non-Russian areas separated and created *de facto* independent states, or whenever the Russian state became a federation of republics, the existence of distinct national parties of any kind was inevitable.

The national differentiation of political life was possible only under a political system that recognized freedom of assembly and organization. Neither the tsarist nor the Soviet government was favourably disposed to political pluralism. Thus nationality parties flourished only during the short liberal period after the Russian revolution of 1905 and from the February revolution of 1917 to the final victory of Bolshevism in Russia and its borderlands. Ukrainian political parties should be classified as revolutionary parties during the first period and as semi-governing parties during the second. After the final establishment of the Bolshevik government in Ukraine, Ukrainian national parties were abolished. They continued to exist only in exile, where they indulged in forceful ideological and propagandistic campaigns against each other and especially against the Russian political parties.

Another characteristic of parties in Ukraine and in such other regions of the Russian empire as Finland and the Baltic region was that nationality often coincided with social stratification. In Ukraine the majority of the Ukrainian ethnic population belonged to the lower strata of society and was composed not only of poor and middle-class peasants and dispossessed agricultural workers, but also the lower strata of the rural intelligentsia—clerks, school teachers, and priests. In the urban areas the Ukrainian element was found among industrial workers, servants, police, and military officers of lower rank. There were very few Ukrainians among the higher echelons of society. Such individuals as Tereshchenko, a sugar magnate and later foreign minister in the Russian Provisional Government, and Savenko, the Russian chauvinist from the newspaper, *Kievlianin*, can hardly be considered Ukrainians.

Consequently, rightist or conservative Ukrainian parties were a rarity, and most political groups bearing the epithet Ukrainian were—in fact or in name—socialist. Some were more socialist than nationalist, others expressed a nationalistic zeal that in most cases took precedence over class solidarity. Because these two aspects of Ukrainian politics were so closely interwoven, most parties had to navigate carefully between nationalism and socialism. Non-socialist political parties in Ukraine were not common.

Political parties active in Ukraine between 1917 and 1920 were influenced by the Ukrainian national movement as formulated in the late nineteenth and early twentieth centuries. This had been a protest movement, struggling not so much for political power within the framework of existing institutions as against national oppression. In positive terms, the goal was self-determination for the Ukrainian nation. The abolition of national autonomy, guaranteed in 1654 by the Treaty of Pereiaslav, forced the Ukrainian political movement to concern itself largely with problems of cultural renascence and the re-emergence of national consciousness. In a sense, the Ukrainophile movement remained apolitical and indifferent to social reform. Beyond protest against Russification, the Ukrainophiles raised no objections to the tsarist regime[2] and continued to flourish long after the Russian revolution of 1905. Their organization, the *Stara hromada* (Old Society), attracted most of the moderate intellectuals, who cherished a strong sentiment for the country's romantic past but never advocated anti-Russian separatist action. Their maximal political demand was confined to autonomy for Ukraine. The *Stara hromada*, together with the *Zahalna ukrainska organizatsiia*, had an important influence on the future national struggle, fostering national feeling among the masses and educating the national cadres that played such an important role in the Ukrainian movement of 1917. These organizations also influenced Russian liberals to take a more positive attitude towards the Ukrainian question in the Duma and in the press.[3]

In opposition to this "non-political" movement, a more radical political party came into being, the Ukrainian Radical Democratic Party (URDP). Ideologically, this party was influenced by Mykhailo Drahomanov, a learned historian and sociologist from the University of Kiev. Like his contemporaries, Mykola Ziber and Serhii Podolynsky, Drahomanov was a moderate socialist who was influenced by Proudhon and Saint-Simon as well as by Bakunin. Most of his thought was given to economic and social reforms and to the education of the masses. His ideology was a mixture of syndicalist socialism and conventional liberalism. With regard to Ukraine, Drahomanov claimed political freedom and the re-emergence of the Ukrainian nation as a member of the family of civilized nations.[4]

The URDP, in many respects the most influential party in Ukraine, was a non-socialist, liberal party that resembled the Russian constitutional democrats (Kadets). The middle peasants, the lower and middle bourgeoisie of the cities, and a significant number of the intelligentsia provided the social basis for the Ukrainian radicals. They demanded a constitutional monarchy in Russia, a federalist structure for the empire, and autonomy for Ukraine. In the second Imperial Duma more than thirty of the forty Ukrainian deputies represented this party.

In 1908 a moderate element of the URDP formed a non-party organization, the Ukrainian Progressist Association (TUP—*Tovarystvo ukrainskykh postupovtsiv*). Most prominent among its leaders were Mykhailo Hrushevsky, the historian and later president of the Ukrainian republic, Serhii Iefremov, and Ievhen Chykalenko. The TUP demanded autonomy for Ukraine and concentrated mainly on combatting aggressive Russian nationalism.[5]

The Revolutionary Ukrainian Party (RUP), founded in Kharkiv in

1900, was the embryonic organization of the future socialist party. Most of the social democratic leaders of 1917 received their political training in this party, which, ideologically, was a conglomeration of Ukrainian nationalism, Drahomanovism, and Marxism. Originally, it was a "bloc of very heterogeneous elements" with members of "different political shades, from liberals and nationalists to socialists." One contemporary, Natalia Romanovych-Tkachenko, described how the RUP was, on the one hand, composed of intelligentsia, students, and peasants urging that "the workers of the world unite," while, on the other, it included also a right wing that dreamed of purely nationalist goals.[6]

After the right wing broke away, the RUP inclined towards social-democratic ideals. In 1903 the Kievan committee of the RUP adopted a radical Marxist programme that appeared as a kind of Ukrainian variant of the Russian social democratic party. However, this programme was bitterly criticized by the nationalist and non-Marxist factions of the party. Although the RUP was obviously inclined towards Marxism, its national aspirations antagonized the Russian social democrats. This antagonism became more acute when the RUP claimed to represent not only the Ukrainian agricultural proletariat, but also the industrial workers. The most prominent leaders in the RUP were Mykhailo Rusov, Dmytro Antonovych, Petro Kanivets, Vlodymyr Vynnychenko, Mykhailo Tkachenko, Oleksander Skoropys-Ioltukhovsky, and Mykola Porsh. Many subsequently became leaders of the Ukrainian social democratic party.[7]

Very soon the RUP was split into different factions. Its right wing, under the leadership and ideological influence of Mykola Mikhnovsky, formed in 1902 the Ukrainian People's Party (*Ukrainska narodna partiia*). This new party adopted Mikhnovsky's nationalistic programme, slightly camouflaged by a small dose of socialism. It became the most nationalistic of all Ukrainian parties, demanding an independent, though socialist, Ukraine. During the period of the Ukrainian republic, 1917–19, it adopted the label of socialism, renaming itself the Ukrainian Party of the Socialist-Independentists.[8]

The leftist elements of the RUP formed the Ukrainian Social Democratic Union, generally known as the *Spilka*, which accepted the Russian social democratic platform *vis-à-vis* the nationalities and the unity of the movement for the whole of Russia. The *Spilka* entered the Russian social democratic party as an autonomous organization, accepted *Iskra*'s principle that in the provinces there should be unified organizations without regard for national differences, and recognized the Russian party programme of "complete equality for all citizens regardless of sex, religion, race, and nationality."[9] The nihilistic approach of certain Russian social democrats towards the nationality question forced many members of *Spilka* (Tkachenko, Vikul, V. Dovzhenko) to return "to the bosom of the national-socialistic Ukrainian Social Democratic Workers' Party."[10]

In 1908 members of the *Spilka*, under the leadership of M. Basok-Melenevsky, started the newspaper, *Pravda*, in which Leon Trotsky cooperated. At first, *Pravda* was published in the name of the *Spilka* and in Ukrainian, but soon it became the organ of the Trotsky group and appeared in Russian. The editorial board consisted of Trotsky, Basok-Melenevsky, Matvei Skobelev, Semen Semkovsky, and Adolf Ioffe.[11] The *Spilka* was one of the strongest organizations in the social-democratic movement. In the 1907 elections to the second Imperial Duma, it won fourteen seats, while the Ukrainian social democratic party received only one. At the London congress of the Russian social democratic party in 1907, the *Spilka* was represented by ten delegates, who sided with the Menshevik faction and were quite hostile towards Lenin's Bolsheviks. That same year the organization ceased to exist. Its decline was due mainly to the fact that it was unable to compete with the Russian party for hegemony in the large urban areas, where the Russians had firm control. Thus, isolated from the peasants and unable to win over the industrial workers, the *Spilka* lost the social basis of its existence.[12]

The Ukrainian Social Democratic Workers' Party (USDWP) was formally constituted at a congress of the Revolutionary Ukrainian Party held in 1905. The party represented a kind of synthesis embodying the varying demands put forth by Ukrainian socialists. They wanted their Russian colleagues to recognize them as the sole representatives of the Ukrainian proletariat, either as an independent section of the international socialist movement or as an autonomous section of the Russian party. But their demand to receive a status similar to that of the Jewish Bund, Latvian social democracy, or Polish social democracy was rejected.[13]

In principle, the Ukrainian social democrats supported the idea of an independent Ukrainian state, but they had for tactical reasons temporarily accepted autonomy within the Russian federation as their minimum demand. Ideologically, the party stood close to the Russian Mensheviks and adopted a Ukrainian variant of the Erfurt programme of German social democracy. Its short-term objectives were the education of the Ukrainian workers in the spirit of class solidarity and national consciousness, and the creation of a strong Ukrainian socialist movement as a counterpoise to Russian centralist ambitions.

The USDWP differed from the Russian party on two main points: it rejected the dictatorship of the proletariat and it demanded recognition of the nationality principle in the organization of socialist parties. After the reactionary government of Stolypin was installed, some of the social democratic leaders emigrated to Galicia, where under Austro-Hungarian rule the Ukrainian national movement developed freely. The party published a monthly journal, *Our Voice*, which served as the organ of Ukrainian social democrats from Russia and Austria. In exile, they waged a severe struggle against attempts by Russian and Polish socialists to monopolize activity and ignore a separate Ukrainian socialist movement.[14] A heated dialogue developed between Lenin and Lev Iurkevych, a Ukrainian social democrat who accused the Russian socialists of "nationalistic intolerance" and demanded "complete organizational freedom for the labour movement of the subjugated nations."[15] Lenin, on the other hand, accused Iurkevych of all sins, fighting him because "this scabby, foul, nationalistic bourgeois . . . , under the banner of Marxism, had prophesized the division of the workers according to nationality, [and] a *separate* national organization of the Ukrainian workers."[16] Lenin was disturbed by the activity of the Ukrainian socialists, who intruded into his revolutionary plans for Russia and only complicated the entire problem by adding unpleasant, disintegrative elements to the general confusion. But the Ukrainian social democratic party persisted, writing to the Second International congress in Stuttgart in 1907, and again to the Kienthal conference, appealing to the international proletariat to support its demand for Ukrainian national autonomy.[17] Among its leaders were Porsh, Valeriian Sadovsky, Simon Petliura, Tkachenko, and Vynnychenko, all of whom played important roles in the Ukrainian republic, 1917–20.[18]

When Russian armies captured Galicia during the First World War, most of the Ukrainian social democrats fled to the West. Some of them, like Iurkevych, continued propaganda activity from Switzerland. There Iurkevych published a newspaper, *Borotba* (Struggle), criticizing both pro-Russian elements and other organizations like the Union for the Liberation of the Ukraine, which acted on the assumption that the defeat of the tsarist armies was the only hope for Ukrainian liberation.

The Ukrainian socialist revolutionary party was one of the last to emancipate itself from association with its Russian counterpart. Several semi-independent organizations of Ukrainian socialist revolutionaries (SRs) existed, but not until 1907 was an all-Ukrainian party founded. During the First World War, Ukrainian SRs published an illegal journal in Kiev, *Borotba*, which, even after the liberation of Russia from tsarist rule, continued to exist as an official organ of the party. Ukrainian SRs ideologically resembled their Russian equivalent, but differed in their commitment to the national movement. They supported the idea of a federal Russian republic and free development for the Ukrainian language.[19]

Ukrainian political parties in the period before the fall of the tsarist regime could be characterized as revolutionary parties proposing different political ideologies but representing, nevertheless, a single national liberation movement. Only after assuming *de facto* political power in the middle of 1917 did they begin to transform themselves into national governmental parties. However, the abnormal circumstances caused by the social and political struggle in the Russian empire affected both the character and the structure of the parties.

On the eve of the Russian revolution of 1917 the Russian government, political organizations, and public opinion persistently neglected to recognize openly the Ukrainian question. Most reactionary circles ascribed the Ukrainian movement to a German-Austrian intrigue against Russia, while more liberal Russians attributed it to the fanatic activity of a small number of intellectuals. Only the tenacity and energy of individual political and cultural leaders kept the movement alive. The reaction after the 1905 revolution had driven most Ukrainian national parties and organizations either underground or into exile, and, until the Russian occupation of Galicia in 1914, Lviv remained the principal centre of Ukrainian political and cultural life.

Only after the fall of the tsarist regime did a more favourable perspective open for free political activities among the non-Russian nationalities. The Provisional Government, having abolished the restrictive legislation, also opened the avenue for national self-assertion to Ukrainians. Numerous cultural and political organizations, which began to organize soon after the change in the regime, manifested in different ways the basic national aspirations of their people. Ukrainian self-determination was complicated by the fact that almost 25 per cent of its population belonged to non-Ukrainian minorities—predominantly Russian, Polish, and Jewish. These national groups exhibited more political influence than might have been expected from their number. Being predominantly urbanites on a higher level of social stratification and having, further, the support of official policy and governmental bureaucracy, they exercised an enormous challenge to any radical movement that proclaimed liberation for Ukraine.

A specific phenomenon of the political life in Ukraine was that, as a rule, parties organized not only according to ideological or socio-economic criteria but also according to nationality.

Ukrainian political parties, representing the largest nationality in Ukraine (approximately 75 to 80 per cent of the entire population), exhibited solid political power, both individually and as a bloc. They received 75 per cent of all votes cast in Ukraine during the elections to the all-Russian constituent assembly in December 1917. As in the Russian part of the empire, the socialist revolutionaries proved to be the strongest party, while the Ukrainian social democrats and other socialist groups received far fewer votes.[20]

The following review embraces all political parties and organizations of some significance in the period between the February revolution and the final victory of Bolshevism.

The Ukrainian Party of Socialist Revolutionaries (SRs) was founded in April 1917. There was very little ideological difference between them and the Russian socialist revolutionaries. They were a kind of agrarian socialist party, similar to the Russian *narodnik* movement in the late nineteenth century. The socialization of land and its distribution among the peasants solely for their own use represented in reality the abolition of private ownership. Nevertheless, this prospect attracted more peasants than any other political programme available at that time. In a resolution, the SRs called for the creation of a Ukrainian land fund, which was to carry out the distribution of land to the peasants. At this early stage, they demanded autonomy for Ukraine, called for the immediate convocation of a territorial Ukrainian constituent council, and proposed that a federal-democratic republic would be the best form of state for Russia. By the end of 1917, their policy regarding the nationality question had gradually evolved from the demand for limited autonomy to that of complete independence for Ukraine.

The Ukrainian SRs derived their support from lower- and middle-class peasants and partly from the rural proletariat. Urban elements were a rarity. In a bloc with the Ukrainian Peasants' Union (*Selianska spilka*), the SRs carried over 60 per cent of all votes in Ukraine in the election to the all-Russian constituent assembly. The weight of the party was felt in all spheres of political life during the entire period of the Ukrainian People's Republic. In the Rada they played an important role, especially after the president of the republic, Hrushevsky, joined them. The Ukrainian SRs formed the first government in January 1918, when their representative, Vsevolod Holubovych, formed a cabinet. This cabinet was shortlived, however, for the German military authorities soon initiated a *coup d'ètat*, and authority was transferred to the conservative Hetman Pavlo Skoropadsky. The Ukrainian SRs remained opposed to the Russian Provisional Government as it tried to postpone recognition of Ukrainian autonomy, and they were also helpful during the critical period in January 1918, when the Rada proclaimed the independence of Ukraine. With regard to independent statehood, they expressed the old socialist dream of federation for all countries. The party organ, *Narodna volia*, emphasized that "[by] satisfying the demand for independence, Ukrainian democracy has not deviated an inch from the idea of world brotherhood, from plans for a free union of all countries."[21]

During the rule of the Directory, the Ukrainian SRs joined the opposition, though for a short period they did form a cabinet. The party's influence over the policy of the Directory gradually declined, however, because of a split within its ranks. Already in January 1918 there were signs of internal conflict,[22] and by April the party suffered its first split. The left internationalist faction, later called the Borotbists, unexpectedly took over the party's central committee, while the right wing formed its own faction, the so-called Centre. Since the right wing continued to support the Directory in its struggle against the Bolsheviks, the left wing refused to do so. The leaders of the right and centre wings went into exile in 1920, where they continued to split into factions while simultaneously waging a propaganda war against the Soviet system in Ukraine. Subsequently, most of its leaders, including Professor Hrushevsky, Pavlo Khrystiuk, Mykola Shrah, and Mykhailo Chechel, returned to Soviet Ukraine. There they continued literary or scholarly activities until the beginning of the Stalin era, when they were tried for anti-Communist and nationalist activity and liquidated. Other Ukrainian SR leaders included Mykola Kovalevsky, Oleksander Sevriuk, Mykyta Shapoval, and Mykhailo Zalizniak.

The left wing of the party, the Borotbists, occupied an uncertain position between the Rada and Soviet power, moving to the left or the right according to the mood of the peasantry. Fundamentally leftist, they disagreed basically with Bolshevism on the peasant issue and, being a peasant party, they could not become one-hundred-per-cent Communist. On the other hand, their "nationalism" antagonized Lenin's party. They also refused the dictatorship of the proletariat, which from the Bolshevik point of view was a horrible sin. The Borotbists, as well as other leftist parties standing on the Soviet platform, were disillusioned with the irreconcilable attitude of the Bolsheviks in the matter of sharing power. In the end, they were driven into open conflict with the Bolsheviks. Their partisans, under the command of Otaman Hryhoriiv, seized Odessa from the French occupation forces. However, increased pressure from General Anton Denikin's anti-Communist Volunteer Army drew the Borotbists "on this [the Soviet] side of the barricades."[23]

As the ninth congress of the Russian Communist party declared in March 1920, the main reason for the antagonism of the Bolsheviks towards the Borotbists was that the latter "had not broken with their chauvinist past"—in other words, with their defence of Ukrainian independence.[24] The Borotbists made several attempts to receive recognition from the executive committee of the Comintern, as the only representatives of the Ukrainian working masses, the only real Communist party. The Comintern cynically proposed that the Borotbists liquidate their party and join the Communist Party (Bolsheviks) of Ukraine (CP[B]U).[25] After the consolidation of Soviet power in Russia and Ukraine, the Borotbists decided to amalgamate with the CP(B)U and perhaps even nursed the idea of taking over its leadership from within.[26] The influence of the Borotbists upon the CP(B)U was recognized even by the chairman of the Council of People's Commissars of Soviet Ukraine, Khristiian Rakovsky: "The two parties, the CPU and UCP . . . met each other half way, the one rectifying its Communist line, the other adapting itself to the pecularities and specific conditions of the social, economic, national, and cultural life in Ukraine."[27]

Although the dreams of the Borotbists did not materialize, their activity did pressure the centralist Bolsheviks into making considerable concessions to Ukrainian national aspirations, at least in the cultural field. Without the existence of this party and the Ukrainian Communist Party (Independentists), about whom more will be said below, it may be doubted whether the Bolsheviks would have recognized even the formal existence of the Ukrainian Soviet republic. Most of the leaders of the Borotbists, such as Mykhailo Poloz, Mykola Liubchenko, Vasyl Blakytny (Ellan), and Ivan Lyzanivsky, continued their "nationalistic" activity within the CP(B)U and the Russian Communist party until they disappeared as victims of Stalin's terrorist activities.

The Ukrainian Social Democratic Workers' Party was a continuation of the party with the same name discussed above. Ideologically, it was similar to the Russian Mensheviks or any other West European socialist party that advocated democratic processes and moderate revolutionary activites. In principle, it was a Marxist party, but it was very different from the Communist variant of Marxism. It adhered to the parliamentary system of government and rejected the principle of the dictatorship of the proletariat and especially of its party. Its agrarian policy was similar to that of the SRs, advocating the expropriation of the large estates and the distribution of land among the poor peasants.[28]

In one respect the Ukrainian social democrats differed from the Mensheviks, and that was on the nationality question. The Mensheviks did not extend their liberalism beyond the recognition of limited autonomy to non-Russian nationalities, and this included Ukraine. The Ukrainian social democrats progressively adopted the idea of an independent Ukrainian state. The party, under the leadership of the successful writer,

Vynnychenko, and a devoted Ukrainian patriot, Petliura, had an enormous influence on the development of the Rada. While in March 1917 the social democrats expressed Ukrainian national ambitions in only a very limited form, by January 1918 the party assumed the role of a fully independent government within the framework of the Ukrainian People's Republic. As Vynnychenko has indicated, the Ukrainian social democratic party was prepared to "abandon its social democratic purity" for the sake of national unity. National liberation became the first priority, while "the solution of social problems had been postponed until the future."[29] It was never a popular mass party, but it did have talented leaders, among whom were Vynnychenko, Petliura, Porsh, Sadovsky, Isak Mazepa, Volodymyr Chekhivsky, Borys Martos, Dmytro Antonovych, and Panas Fedenko.

The social base of the organization was a conglomeration of Ukrainian workers and radically-minded intelligentsia. It was not as successful as the SRs at the elections, and it elected only two deputies to the all-Russian constituent assembly. Its official organ was *Robitnycha hazeta* (Workers' Newspaper). After the defeat of Ukrainian independence in 1920, the majority of leaders as well as many of the rank-and-file members went into exile—first to Poland, then to Czechoslovakia—where they pursued propaganda activity and organized émigré workers and youth into the socialist movement. The former premier, Vynnychenko, made an attempt to collaborate with the Ukrainian Soviet regime and was even appointed to that government in 1920, but he soon became disillusioned by the hegemonistic attitude of Russian leadership, returned to Vienna, and engaged in energetic criticism of Soviet rule in Ukraine.[30]

The Ukrainian social democratic party, however, was affected by radical waverings within its own leadership. As early as January 1918 its left wing had pronounced itself in favour of the Soviet system. Its local leader in Kharkiv, Medvediev, even became the chairman of the Central Executive Committee of Ukraine for a short period. Another left-wing social democrat, Ievhen Neronovych, became for a short time people's secretary (minister) for war in the Soviet Ukrainian government. At the first congress of the CP(B)U in 1918, this group brought for a time the first truly Ukrainian contingent into the Communist party. One of them, Opanas Butsenko, was even elected to the central committee of the CP(B)U.

However, the real split in the Ukrainian social democratic party did not occur until the end of 1918, during the war between the Directory and Soviet Russia.[31] A new organization was founded with an entirely "independent" position on most questions. The issue of disagreement between the moderate and right wing of the party and the independentists was concerned with the system of government in the Ukrainian republic and the relationship with the Russian Soviet government. The independentists believed that Ukraine could survive as an independent state only under a Soviet system. This was obviously a mere stratagem which, they thought, would have deprived the Russian Bolsheviks of the claim that they were fighting for a Soviet Ukraine; such a government would already have been in existence.[32] Apart from this argument, an important influence on the evolution of the Ukrainian social democrats towards Communism resulted from the general drift to the left in Europe, especially in Germany and Hungary.

The right wing argued that the introduction of the dictatorship of the proletariat in Ukraine, where a Ukrainian working class was weak, would mean dictatorship by the Russian Bolsheviks. As Vynnychenko put it: "We shall have here the dictatorship of the Piatakovs, Antonovs, etc."[33] The independentists tried their programme, but it did not prove successful; neither the Russian Bolsheviks, their emissaries in Ukraine, nor the Soviet Premier, Rakovsky, was willing to recognize the "bourgeois nationalist" elements in their government. At the end of the Civil War, when the Russian Bolsheviks made their third attempt to sovietize Ukraine, the independentists cooperated with the Soviet authorities and soon changed their name to the Ukrainian Communist Party or Ukapists. The organization was legally recognized, but after the consolidation of Bolshevik power the Ukapists were ordered to disband and join the CP(B)U. The Ukapists applied for membership in the Comintern, but membership was refused and they were branded as typical Ukrainian "nationalist-separatists."[34] The independentists published a newspaper, *Chervonyi prapor* (Red Banner), and their most prominent leaders included Mykhailo Tkachenko, Iurii Mazurenko, Ievhen Neronovych, and Mykhailo Drahomyretsky.

The Ukrainian Party of Socialist Federalists[35] was formed in March 1917 by members of the Ukrainian Progressist Association (TUP). In composition as well as in ideology the socialist federalists resembled the Russian Kadets, although they stressed the need for Ukrainian cultural autonomy. The party was socialist in name only. In fact, it was a typical petty-bourgeois, liberal party advocating the transformation of Russia into a federation of free states with Ukraine as an equal member. As a long-range goal, the socialist federalists advocated the formation of a world federation. However, after the decline of democratic government in Russia they supported the Rada's claims for independence.

During the Skoropadsky regime the Ukrainian socialist federalists progressed rapidly towards the idea of an independent Ukraine. When leftist, pro-Soviet tendencies arose among other Ukrainian parties in 1919, this party stood firmly for the preservation of liberal democracy. As a party, it did not attract any mass membership nor did it collect a considerable number of votes in the 1917 elections. Nevertheless, the party played a very important political role, supplying a large number of highly qualified functionaries to the Rada as well as to the Skoropadsky government and the Directory. The leading socialist federalists were Andrii Nikovsky, Serhii Iefremov, Volodymyr Leontovych, Dmytro Doroshenko, Volodymyr Prokopovych, and Oleksander Shulhyn. They were influential figures within the Ukrainian national movement, men with polished manners and rather "civilized," moderate inclinations—perhaps too moderate to be useful in the political situation that developed in Ukraine and elsewhere in Eastern Europe after the First World War.

The Ukrainian Party of Socialist Independentists[36] was composed mainly of Ukrainian patriots who either had a military background or who were still in active service. Genetically, this was a direct continuation of the Ukrainian People's Party, and it should not be confused with the independentists who formed a left-wing faction of the Ukrainian social democrats. The socialist independentists were determined separatists, the only party that worked from the beginning for an independent, sovereign Ukrainian state. Mykola Mikhnovsky exercised a decisive influence over this little group of fanatical nationalists, and his pamphlet, *Independent Ukraine*, became a kind of bible for the increasing number of nationalistic youth. In spite of its "socialist" label, the party had very few socialist ideas in its programme, being almost exclusively a petty-bourgeois nationalist party. It placed its policy priorities on the formation of a strong patriotic Ukrainian army, the only effective instrument for the implementation of national sovereignty. The stubborn opposition of most Russian parties and the Provisional Government to Ukrainian national demands provided a favourable atmosphere for the socialist independentists. The socialist independentist political programme almost totally neglected the social and agrarian issues, and its influence on the electorate was minimal. In addition to Mikhnovsky, other active leaders were Andrii Makarenko, Panas Andriievsky, Oleksander Stepanenko, and Ivan Lutsenko.

The Ukrainian Democratic Agrarian Party[37] was perhaps the most conservative of all Ukrainian parties. It was founded in the summer of 1917 at Lubny, in connection with a congress of landowners in Poltava. In a sense, it adhered to the well-known thesis of Petr Stolypin, who initiated a programme to support strong, independent farmers and thus stabilize the countryside. Its programme was written by the well-known historian, Viacheslav Lypynsky, whose ideal was a Ukraine dominated by the landed

Cossack aristocracy. According to Lypynsky, Ukraine should be organized as an independent monarchy ruled by a hetman. His and the party's position regarding the minorities was determined by the latters' attitude towards Ukrainian independence: "Every alien that recognizes our right to full independence is our ally, even if he has a different view on other political questions."[38] The "separatist" position distinguished the democratic agrarians from the Union of Landowners, which contributed much to the successful *coup d'ètat* that in April 1918 elevated General Skoropadsky to the position of hetman. Dmytro Dontsov, the brothers Serhii and Volodymyr Shemet, and M. Boiarsky were the most important party members.

The Ukrainian Federalist Democratic Party was founded in December 1917 by such moderate Ukrainian intellectuals as B. Berenkovych, V. Naumenko, I. Kviatkovsky, and Professor Ivan Luchytsky. It was another conservative party with a very cautious social programme that sought to transform Russia into a federal state. The federalist democrats played a minimal role in Ukrainian political life.

Several Russian political parties existed in Ukraine during the period under consideration. Indeed, there were fundamental differences in the motivations of the Russian and the non-Russian political organizations. The Russian elements did not have any national liberation goals; on the contrary, they represented political objectives that conflicted with those of the Ukrainian parties. Most important was their tendency to keep Ukraine within the orbit of the Russian empire. As central power disintegrated in Moscow, the Russian parties assumed a watchdog function and became the sole representatives of centripetal, integrative tendencies in Ukraine. Regardless of ideological and social differences, the Russian parties that still functioned after the declaration of an independent Ukrainian state acted in unison on one particular issue—opposition to Ukrainian self-determination.

On the extreme left was *the Communist Party (Bolsheviks) of Ukraine* (CP[B]U). Lumping it together with other Russian parties may raise justifiable objections, for there are indeed methodological difficulties in classification. From the structural and organizational point of view, it may well be called Russian. The same may be said about its composition during the period under study. In spite of the seemingly positive attitude of the Bolsheviks, and of Lenin in particular, towards the self-determination of nationalities, their position concerning national parties was strictly negative.

Lenin held that the proletariat of all nationalities in the Russian empire should be organized into a single united party organization. The Bolsheviks not only rejected the independent existence of nationality parties but even refused to recognize the autonomous existence of any nationality organization.[39] It is interesting to note that Lenin's animosity towards the prospect of independent existence for national parties was far more categorical *vis-à-vis* Ukrainian social democracy than, for instance, the Jewish Bund; he did not question the latter's existence but merely fought its demand for autonomy within the Russian party, a move that would have created a precedent for other national parties. Favouring a strictly centralized party, Lenin demanded the complete subordination of local organizations. This principle was reiterated in a resolution adopted by the eighth party congress in March 1919: "At the present time, Ukraine, Latvia, Lithuania, and Belorussia exist as separate Soviet republics ... but this does not mean that the Russian Communist party ought, in its turn, to organize itself on the basis of a federation of independent Communist parties." On the contrary, "*one* centralized Communist party with one central committee guiding all the work of the party in all parts of the RSFSR is imperative .... Central committees of the Ukrainian, Latvian, and Lithuanian Communists have the rights of regional committees of the party and are completely subordinated to the CC RCP."[40]

In accordance with the attitude of the Russian Bolshevik leadership, the social democratic organizations of the Bolshevik faction did not, at the beginning, attempt to organize a separate party or a separate centre for its organizations on Ukrainian territory. Although the first Soviet government in Ukraine was established in December 1917, the Communist party of Ukraine was officially created only in July 1918—i.e., only after the end of that regime, when most of its leaders went into exile in Moscow. Its relationship with the Russian centre in Moscow caused a great deal of friction among the leaders of CP(B)U, which divided into two factions, the integralists and the independentists.

Apparently, the more nationalistic members of the Bolshevik faction in Ukraine approached the idea of a separate organization soon after it became evident that this territory was achieving a kind of autonomous status within the Russian empire. These attempts were hampered by two forces—the Bolsheviks in Ukraine with centralist tendencies, such as Evgeniia Bosh and Georgii Piatakov, and, naturally, the Russian Communist party (RCP) in Moscow. On behalf of the politburo, Iakov Sverdlov wrote: "*The creation of a separate, Ukrainian party,* whatever it might be called, whatever programme it might adopt, *is considered undesirable.*"[41] Soon, however, more positive voices were heard from Moscow, and in late December 1917 an independent social democratic organization "with the same rights as an independent region" was recognized.[42] The Communist party of Ukraine was created at a congress held in Moscow in July 1918. It was independent in name though actually subordinate to Moscow, a status that reflected the position of the centralist elements in the CP(B)U (the so-called "Katerynoslavians"). It also reflected the general position of the RCP regarding Ukraine, which considered it an integral part of Russia and the CP(B)U "part of a single Russian Communist party." After stormy debates, the resolution presented by the "nationalist" Skrypnyk, demanding the creation of "a separate Communist Party (Bolshevik) of Ukraine [to be] formally tied with the Russian Communist party through the international commission of the Third International," was rejected.[43]

In brief, the position of the two different factions of the CP(B)U regarding its status reflected the ethnic composition of the party. The Russian and Russified elements were inclined towards a centralized party for all of Russia, while the Ukrainian elements defended the idea of an autonomous or independent existence. The creation of the CP(B)U was, however, the result of general political circumstances, and it was considered a kind of necessary compromise with growing Ukrainian nationalism. From the very beginning, the Russian Communist leadership adopted a negative position based on the decisions of the congresses and the rules of the party. Even after the creation of the CP(B)U, Moscow exercised close control of the Ukrainian organization, and special emissaries of the central committee were sent to every congress of the CP(B)U in order to protect the interests of the centre. Such a role was played by Kamenev at the second congress, Sverdlov at the third, Stalin at the fourth, and Zinovev at the fifth. In addition, the central offices of the CP(B)U were consistently occupied by faithful centralists, for the most part Russians. Thus Piatakov, Kviring, Molotov, and later Kosior, Kaganovich, and Postyshev, all non-Ukrainians, held the position of first secretary of the party. Even the central committee was predominantly non-Ukrainian.[44]

There are no reliable statistics on the ethnic composition of the CP(B)U for the early period. However, the figures from 1922 and 1926 are quite illustrative. The composition of the CP(B)U according to nationality is shown in Table 24.

Only after nine years of the existence of the Ukrainian Soviet republic did the Ukrainian elements constitute the largest group in the party. Small wonder that Bukharin, at the twelfth party congress in 1925, admitted that "in Ukraine ... the composition of the party is Russian-Jewish."

The figures published by Lenin and Radkey reveal the precarious position of the Bolsheviks. At the elections to the Kiev city council on

Table 24. National Composition of the CP(B)U, 1922-26 (Percentage)

	1922	1926
Russians	53.6	37.4
Ukrainians	23.3	43.9
Jews	13.6	11.2
Others	9.5	7.5

SOURCE: M. Ravich-Cherkassky, *Istoriia Kommunisticheskoi partii (b-kov) Ukrainy* (Kharkiv, 1923), pp. 241-42. *VKP(b) v tsifrakh*, 5th ed. (Moscow, 1926), pp. 26-27.

7 August 1917, they received six seats out of a total of ninety-eight, and in the elections to the all-Russian constituent assembly held at the end of the year, they received only 10 per cent of the vote in Ukraine. With regard to party membership, the picture was even less encouraging. Bolshevik sources reveal that in Kiev their organization had by March 1917 about two hundred members, and these chiefly craftsmen.[45] At the sixth congress of the Russian Bolshevik party in August 1917, the Bolsheviks of Ukraine represented about 23,000 members, while the Petrograd organization alone had 40,095 members.[46] There is much evidence of the weakness of the Bolsheviks in Ukraine during the struggle against the Rada and later during the Directory.

The party's final success must be attributed to the external conditions in Eastern Europe, the general disintegration of anti-Bolshevik forces, and the indecisiveness of the Western powers, conditions in which such organizational geniuses as Lenin and Trotsky most certainly prospered. Had it not been for the Russian military intervention in Ukraine, the local Bolsheviks would have had to wait for better times. However, they constituted a compact, determined organization and a considerable propagandist instrument in the struggle against the idea of an independent Ukrainian state. This movement, assisted by the gigantic force concentrated in Soviet Russia, succeeded in neutralizing, for the time being, the national aspirations of the Ukrainian people.

The Russian Party of Socialist Revolutionaries (SRs)[47] ideologically resembled its Ukrainian counterpart and in most cases was identical to the SRs in Russia proper. It was separated from the mother organization merely by political or administrative borders. The relationship between the Russian and the Ukrainian SRs was not clarified until the Provisional Government made its first concessions on the Ukrainian question, accepting *de facto* the autonomous government of the Rada. Subsequently, the minority parties accepted the idea of participating in the autonomous Ukrainian government. The minorities (Russian, Jewish, and Polish) asked for 40 per cent of the seats in the provisional representative council (the Rada), but they were allotted only 30 per cent. The Russian SRs received four seats in the *Little Rada*, and one of its leaders, A. M. Zarubin, was appointed minister for post and telegraph. After the declaration of the independence of the Ukrainian republic on 25 January 1918, Zarubin resigned. The SRs supported the idea of an autonomous Ukraine within the Russian federation, but they were negatively disposed towards the idea of an independent Ukraine. In the competition against their Ukrainian counterparts the Russian SRs lost most of their influence among the electorate during the elections to the all-Russian constituent assembly. The party disappeared from the Ukrainian political scene at the end of 1919, partly because members emigrated to Russia or abroad and partly because of transfers to the Russian Communist party. The most prominent leaders among the Russian SRs in Ukraine were Zarubin, Sklovsky, Sukhovych, and Zaluzhny.[48]

The Russian Social Democratic Workers' Party (Mensheviks)[49] formed the Ukrainian section of the all-Russian Menshevik party, competing, on the one side, against the Russian Bolsheviks and, on the other, against the Ukrainian social democrats. During the first period of liberalism in Russia after the March revolution, the Mensheviks predominated among the industrial workers and radical intelligentsia. In the elections of 1917 the party obtained an insignificant number of votes, 2.5 per cent in the whole of Russia and less than 1 per cent in Ukraine. By the end of 1918 many of their supporters had joined the Bolshevik party. The Menshevik attitude towards Ukrainian national aspirations resembled that of the Bund. Without much enthusiasm, they accepted the autonomous status of Ukraine, but they voted against the Fourth Universal. They participated in the Rada government with the prime intention of averting the tendency towards separation of Ukraine from Russia. A joint resolution of the Mensheviks and the Bund ridiculed the idea of a separate Ukrainian state, which "assists the plans of the Austro-German imperialists . . . , the independence of Ukraine . . . means victory not for the revolution, but for imperialism, and is bound to weaken Russia and international democracy." They voted against the Universal in order to "show the international proletariat its loyalty to the proletarian ideal."[50] One could hardly expect a more absurd motivation than the one provided in this resolution. Mikhail Balabanov and Konstantyn Kononenko were among the foremost leaders of the Mensheviks in Ukraine.

The Russian People's Socialists,[51] together with its left wing, the Trudoviks, represented petty-bourgeois groups that leaned towards a liberal democratic ideology. In many cases they cooperated with the Ukrainian Party of Socialist-Federalists and other bourgeois groups. With regard to Ukrainian national demands, this party was favourably inclined; it did not call for the creation of a fully sovereign, independent state, but rather envisioned a federalist Russia. It was one of the marginal political organizations with very little influence and hardly any power. In the elections of 1917 it was unable to elect a single representative from Ukraine and it elected only four from the whole of Russia. Its leaders, A. S. Zarudny and Arnold Margolin, played a significant role in bringing Ukrainian and minority interests together.

The Russian constitutional democrats,[52] widely known as the Kadets, did not differ ideologically or socially from the all-Russian party led by Pavel Miliukov. This rather conservative liberal party, which defended human rights and fought for constitutional rule in Russia, categorically denied the demands for Ukrainian national self-determination, going so far as to reject autonomy even within the Russian federation. Instead, it recommended a kind of local autonomy with some concessions in cultural matters. In this respect, the Ukrainian branch of the Kadets resembled the party's metropolitan leadership. It should be remembered that the Kadets caused a major crisis in Moscow in July 1917, when they withdrew their ministers from the coalition in protest against the Provisional Government's recognition of the Ukrainian General Secretariat as the *de facto* government of Ukraine. During the elections of 1917 the Kadets collected 2.4 per cent of the votes in Ukraine, which roughly corresponded to its strength on the all-Russian scale. The following year some Kadets participated in Hetman Skoropadsky's government. The leading Kadets in Ukraine were S. G. Krupnov, Fedor Shteingel, Mykola Vasylenko, A. Rzhepetsky, and S. M. Hutnyk.

The Russian monarchists in Ukraine[53] often appeared under the designation *The Bloc of the Non-Partisan Russians*, representing extreme Russian chauvinism and reaction. They flocked around the well-known newspaper, *Kievlianin*, which was published by the Russian nationalist and Ukrainophobe, Vasilii Shulgin. This political group was highly inimical to the idea of a Ukrainian state, opposing even moderate demands for cultural autonomy. They even refused to recognize the existence of a Ukrainian nationality, maintaining that there existed only one Russian nation from the Carpathian Mountains to Vladivostok. Consequently, the monarchists and reactionary Russian nationalists did everything to obstruct the realization of Ukrainian national emancipation. During the

Skoropadsky regime they attempted to turn Ukraine into a base for restoring the unity of the Russian empire, and during the Civil War they supported such reactionary military leaders as Denikin, Petr Vrangel, and Iudenich.

Besides the above-mentioned local groups, there were a number of reactionary groups organized largely by Russians who fled to Ukraine after the Bolshevik seizure of power in Russia. Their common interest was to fight against the Bolshevik regime and to restore a one and indivisible Russia. Among the most important was *the Conference of the Members of the Legislative Chamber*, a pro-German monarchist group headed by Baron V. V. Meller-Zakomelsky, V. Gurko, and Krzhizhanovsky. Even the Kadet Professor Pavel Miliukov participated for a time in this organization. The group was later reorganized and renamed *the Council of State Union* (*Sovet gosudarstvennogo obedineniia*) and included men like Aleksandr Krivoshein and S. N. Tretiakov. The struggle against Ukrainian independence was one of its political priorities.

At the same time, *the Kiev National Centre* was organized, whose aim was to unite the "representatives of all non-socialist parties, except for the extreme right, as well as representatives of all citizens' groups and organizations under a slogan [stressing] 'the need to reinstate one, indivisible Russia, fight against Bolshevism, fight against Germany, and keep faith with the Entente.'" The foremost duty of the National Centre was to "fight against Ukrainian independence," since the Ukrainians were not a nation but rather "a political party organized by Austria and Germany." The major personalities in this group were M. Fedorov, Volkov, Salazkin, Shulgin, and Professor Novgorodtsev.[54]

If the existence of Russian political parties in Ukraine can be considered unique, the existence of Jewish and Polish political organizations was typical for ethnically diverse countries that recognized personal national autonomy. The theory, which was advocated by the Austrian socialists Otto Bauer and Karl Renner, proposed cultural autonomy not only for nationalities occupying a distinct territory, but even for those scattered through the country. In order to guarantee this right, special institutions had to be created. Even political parties, including social-democratic ones, should be organized according to nationality principles. The Ukrainian republic can be considered the first state in modern times to have implemented these principles, admitting the representatives of the minority parties to its parliament, the Rada, as well as to its government, the General Secretariat.

The Jewish political community took advantage of the situation and missed no opportunity to have its voice heard and its influence felt. There was a slight tactical difference between the Jewish parties in Ukraine and those in other parts of Russia. The dilemma faced by Jewish parties was twofold: on the one hand, they were heavily involved in the struggle for the emancipation of their fellowmen from national, religious, and social suppression; on the other hand, they opposed in principle the idea of the disintegration of the empire and the creation of a number of independent national states. In this sense, they seem to have contradicted their own political purpose. The Jews were unique in that they did not inhabit any specific territory. Hence, they had no desire to have any particular lands separated from the rest of the empire. On the whole, the Jews in Ukraine, as in the other borderlands, sided with the dominant nation, first with the Poles and then with the Russians, and, tending to consider themselves superior to the surrounding peasants, they "continued to speak their German dialect ... or adopted the superior, dominant culture of ruling Great-Russia."[55] Bertram Wolfe concludes that "almost unconsciously, most of the Jews of the cities of Poland, Lithuania and the Ukraine tended to become opponents of the national separation movements that arose during the break-up of the empire in 1917."[56]

In principle, Jewish political parties sought a solution to the nationality problem within the framework of a general liberal democratic system that would guarantee the greatest personal and group freedom in economic, cultural, and religious activity. Even an extreme Jewish nationalist organization like the Zionists did not aspire to more than the right of the Jews to preserve their national traditions. Thus it was not the principle of national self-determination that they professed, but rather general humanitarian emancipation and the establishment of individual freedoms and social justice. This tendency can partly explain why only a segment of the Jewish political community organized in their own national parties. In most cases, Jewish elements were found in all parties, but especially in radical ones like the Menshevik and the Bolshevik factions of the Russian social democratic party.

The General Jewish Workers' League, the Bund, was originally organized to represent the Jewish radical intelligentsia, artisans, and semi-proletariat in the territories of Lithuania, Poland, and Russia. The Bund was the first social democratic organization on Russian soil with a definite programme and organization. It had a great impact not only on the Jewish community in Eastern Europe, but also on the Russian social democratic movement as a whole.[57] At the time of the February revolution, the Ukrainian branch of the Bund had 175 local organizations. The Ukrainian section was subordinated to the all-Russian Bund, which in turn was closely allied to the Russian social democratic party, the Mensheviks.

In Ukraine the Bund fought for the national autonomy of the Jews and consequently supported Ukrainian demands for autonomy. On the other hand, it strongly opposed the creation of an independent Ukrainian state.[58] However, it was the only minority party that, during the entire period, cooperated with the Ukrainian parties and took an active part in the Rada government.

As Ukrainian nationalism gained in strength and anti-Semitic outbreaks took place, the Bund showed strong pro-Communist leanings, a sign of drastic political wavering. There soon appeared an inner conflict within the Bund leadership, leading to a split, from which three factions emerged: a right wing, led by Mark Liber; a centre, headed by Moisei Rafes; and a left wing, under Haifets. The Haifets group joined the Russian Communist party, and shortly thereafter the centre followed in its footsteps. In May 1918 the Bund, together with the United Jewish Socialist Party, formed a Jewish Communist Union, which soon joined the Russian Communist party.[59]

The Jewish People's Party[60] was a petty-bourgeois group without the slightest trace of the socialism that was so popular at the time. It had no great influence and drew its support mainly from Jewish intellectuals and professionals.

The United Jewish Socialist Party[61] belonged to the bloc of socialist revolutionaries, but it soon came into conflict with the Russian SRs, basically because of the great emphasis that the Jewish section placed on the nationality question. That circumstance, however, drew this party closer to the Ukrainian SRs. The Jewish SRs supported the Ukrainian demand for autonomy and participated in the Rada. After a split in 1918, its left wing, together with the Bund, formed the above-mentioned Jewish Communist Union. Among leaders of the Jewish SRs were Moisei Litvakov, Gutman, Dubinsky, Moisei Zilberfarb, M. Shats-Anin, and Chugrin.

The Jewish Social Democratic Workers' Party (*Paolei-Zion*)[62] stood farthest to the right of all the socialist groups. It did not have a great number of adherents, since the radical Jewish elements as a rule joined the Bund or the Mensheviks; and though it was close to the Ukrainian Social Democratic Party, it did not favour Ukrainian independence or separation from Russia. Like other political parties, the *Paolei-Zion* split during the Civil War, whereupon its left wing formed a new organization called the Social Democratic Party, *Paolei-Zion.* The party's leading figures included Solomon Goldelman, P. I. Mentskovsky, and Avram Revutsky.

The Zionist Party[63] in Ukraine was perhaps the most conservative and nationalistic of all Jewish parties, and it devoted much energy to promoting the idea of a separate autonomous Jewish unit. Therefore it understood, more than any other minority party, Ukrainian political aspirations, and, because of its position on the national question, it could cooperate with the Rada. The Zionists energetically propagated the use of Hebrew and the preservation of orthodox Judaism. The leading figures in Ukraine were Zangwil, Mandelstam, Paperin, M. Sirkin, and Sheltman.

The Polish minority resembled, in a sense, the Russians, except that their continued imperialist ambitions deprived them of a sense of reality. This was especially evident among the more conservative elements of the landowning class, which had difficulty accepting the idea that the *chłopi*, as they customarily called the Ukrainian peasants, could raise themselves to the level of an independent nation equal to the Polish one. More moderate Polish elements approached the problem realistically, considering Ukrainians a natural ally against Russian imperialism and in most cases cooperating with the Ukrainian national movement. There were only two significant political parties in Ukraine that represented Poles.

The Polish Socialist Party (PPS-Centre)[64] was the Polish equivalent of the Russian Mensheviks or the Ukrainian social democrats. On the nationality issue, it was similar to those Ukrainian socialists who supported the declaration of an independent Ukrainian republic. During the Piłsudski-Petliura alliance against Soviet Russia in 1920, the party was closely associated with the Ukrainian social democrats. Its leaders were K. Domosławski, Wł. Korsak and Jan Libkind. In 1919 the latter formed a pro-Bolshevik wing.

The Polish Socialist Party (PPS-Left)[65] stood close to the Russian social democratic party, differing from it only on the nationality question. The PPS-Left agitated for an independent Polish republic and consequently supported the Ukrainian demand for independence. However, when the Bolsheviks entered Ukraine early in 1918, the majority of its leaders went over to their camp. Among its most prominent leaders were Witold Matuszewski and Bolesław Iwiński.

The Polish Democratic Centre Party[66] represented Polish landowners in the Ukrainian countryside and inevitably was opposed to the more radical agrarian policy of the Rada. The party avidly promoted the idea of an independent Poland, but was indecisive with regard to Ukrainian self-determination. When the Third Universal was adopted, the Polish representative in the Rada, Walery Rudnicki, declared that its political content was implicitly directed against the interests of the Polish minority. On the other hand, he expressed joy that "the Ukrainians were entering the European community of nations." Besides Rudnicki, who served as under-secretary for Polish affairs in the Rada cabinet, the party leadership included M. Mickiewicz, Stanisław Stempkowski, Roman Knoll, J. Ursyn-Zamarajew, and M. Baraniecki.

The Polish Executive Committee[67] was a conservative Polish organization that provided moral and material support for the liberation movement in Poland and that claimed to be a non-partisan organ for all Poles residing in Ukraine. These pretensions were energetically challenged by other Polish political parties. The committee was favourably disposed towards the idea of an independent Ukrainian state. Its president was Joachim Bartoszewicz, and among other leaders were M. Baraniecki and Zygmunt Chojecki.

Political parties in Ukraine, and the diversity of their political orientation, reflected the complexity of social and ethnic problems. The four major nationalities (Ukrainians, Russians, Poles, and Jews) organized their own national political groups. The pre-eminence of the national idea and the consequent fragmentation of political life was reflected even in the working class, which, contradicting Marx's thesis about class solidarity, formed political parties according to national divisions. Thus in Ukraine there were Ukrainian, Russian, Polish, and Jewish social democratic parties.

However, the major distinction between the Ukrainian and minority parties was in their attitude towards self-determination. Whereas the Ukrainian parties emphasized national liberation as the first step towards the solution of other problems, the minority parties were decidedly more cautious. The Russian parties, being merely remnants of the national Russian parties before the *de facto* separation of Ukraine, became the principal custodians of Russian imperial interests and strove to prevent Ukrainian self-determination. The Polish political parties recognized in principle the demand for an independent Ukrainian state; however, in matters concerning Ukrainian-Polish borders they adhered. to the traditional Polish position. Almost all Jewish political parties and some of the Russian socialist parties (Mensheviks, SRs, and Trudoviks) agreed to the demand for Ukrainian autonomy within a federal Russian empire but categorically rejected the idea of Ukrainian independence. On the other hand, the bourgeois and reactionary Russian parties adopted a firm, integralist position, considering the Ukrainian liberation movement a German invention.

The Russian Bolsheviks in Moscow and their agent, the CP(B)U, were very ambiguous; they recognized the "abstract right of the Ukrainian people to self-determination," but they still considered it the duty of the Russian state to neutralize this right. The creation of the Soviet Ukrainian state, headed by Rakovsky's puppet government, reflected this political line. The intense struggle of the Ukrainian political parties, the national liberation government, and the army, and the continuing activity of the Ukrainian leftist parties, the Ukapists and the Borotbists, after the defeat of the Directory, all contributed immensely to the Bolsheviks' recognition of Ukrainian pseudo-statehood.

CHAPTER IV

Ukraine's Struggle for Statehood

The assimilatory and centralizing policy of the tsarist government in Ukraine, which lasted more than 250 years, left a deep psychological impact on the Ukrainian people.[1] It inhibited the ideological groundwork of the Ukrainian national movement, and when the revolution broke out in 1917, the Ukrainians were politically naive and unprepared to present effectively and realize their national demands. The leaders of the Ukrainian movement, wrote Vynnychenko, "at once and without hesitation or bargaining put their faith in the revolution" and rejected any other method of winning freedom, including reliance on foreign powers hostile to Russia. "The Ukrainians now put their faith wholeheartedly in the all-Russian revolution, in the triumph of justice, the restoration of the rights of the oppressed peoples. After 250 years of alienation the Ukrainians now for the first time felt themselves at home in Russia; for the first time they could regard the interests of their former prison as something which concerned themselves, as their own interests."[2]

Only a few months after the outbreak of the revolution, when the first wave of enthusiasm had subsided and was replaced by disillusionment with "the love of liberty and the honesty" of Russian democracy, the Ukrainian leaders began to consider concrete measures for achieving their national demands. Since the oppression to which the Ukrainian people had been subjected was chiefly cultural and national, it was largely national, rather than—as in Russia—social, concerns that characterized the Ukrainian revolution. The social struggle broke out only later, during the process of reconstructing the Ukrainian state. It is remarkable that even within occupational and class organizations, national political questions were pre-eminent; teachers, doctors, lawyers, members of cooperatives, students, workers, peasants, soldiers, and other such groups emphasized their national awareness in establishing their organizations. Most of the political parties, too, agreed that "without national liberation the attainment of social liberation is impossible."[3]

It was in this atmosphere that the first Ukrainian governmental body was formed in March 1917. This was the Ukrainian Central Rada or Council (*Ukrainska Tsentralna rada*). The initiative to form the Rada was taken by the society of Ukrainian progressists ([TUP], later renamed the Ukrainian Party of Socialist Federalists), but the Rada was conceived as an all-Ukrainian political centre. It drew up its programme only after the national congress was held in Kiev in April 1917. The work of the Rada was directed by Professor Mykhailo Hrushevsky, who had recently returned from exile; he was assisted by Volodymyr Koval, Fedir Kryzhanivsky (representing the cooperative movement), Dmytro Antonovych (USDWP), and Mrs. O. Skrypnyk (representing the students).[4] Before long, the Rada became the authentic national representative organization of the Ukrainian people, encompassing all Ukrainian political parties and influential organizations. It became a centre in which, to use the words of Vynnychenko, "every expression of the awakened national energy" was assembled.[5]

The Rada's first tasks were "to master all the forces at the disposal of the Ukrainian people, to use these forces to rouse the Ukrainian people to national consciousness, to secure national gains, and finally, on the basis of this achievement, to carry out a social transformation in accordance with our own national pattern."[6] In the beginning, the Rada "consciously and deliberately adopted the attitude of being the national representative of the Ukrainian people alone." This led to frequent charges of chauvinism,[7] and the political organizations of the non-Ukrainian minorities supported the Rada only at a later stage.

Simultaneously with the establishment of the Rada, the political parties reorganized to meet the requirements of the new situation in Ukraine. Their congresses drafted the principles for national policy in Ukraine, which in turn were reflected in the Rada, whose activity was largely determined by the political parties. The social democrats (USDWP) under the leadership of Vynnychenko had the greatest influence in the Rada. At first the USDWP was even prepared to "abandon its social democratic purity" for the sake of national unity. The party's foremost concern was to "secure the national unity of the Ukrainian front, postponing the solution of social problems to the future."[8] This inevitably caused complications, since the Ukrainian social democrats were affiliated with the international working-class movement through their ideological union with Russian "revolutionary democracy." But Russian democracy was prepared to use every method at its disposal to break the united Ukrainian front. The Russian social democrats offered their Ukrainian comrades every kind of cooperation, but only provided the latter withdrew from the Central Rada.[9] This Russian pressure was reflected in the decisions taken at the USDWP conference in May 1917; national demands concerning the reorganization of Russia were cautiously formulated, going no further than the demand for "a federation of autonomous national or provincial units." However, the party's long-standing demand for Ukrainian autonomy was expressed in unambiguous terms.[10] At this time the separatist movement in Ukraine was not strong enough to make itself felt as forcefully as was possible only a few months later. It is characteristic of this period that only a handful of votes at the conference supported independence for Ukraine. The idea of separatism was considered dangerous because it could weaken the revolutionary movement through the whole of Russia. The supporters of separatism were generally regarded as "scholastics, pure theorists, fanatical adherents of independence, or as neurotics hypersensitive on the question of nationality."[11]

From the very beginning the Ukrainian socialist revolutionaries were less cautious in this respect. As early as their party congress on 17–18 April 1917, they put forward fairly radical demands, although they did not go so far as to call unequivocally for independence. They maintained that "the most important requirement of the Ukrainian people is the implementation of a broad national territorial autonomy for Ukraine, in which the rights of the national minorities are guaranteed. A territorial Ukrainian constituent council should be summoned without delay with the task of working out the basis and structure of this autonomy." The congress also expressed its opinion concerning the future form of the Russian state, which it hoped would become a "democratic federal republic."[12]

At the same time, the third influential party in the Rada, the socialist federalists, demanded that Ukrainian autonomy be made a reality "at once, all forces and means being mustered to this end"; the ultimate sanction should rest with the all-Russian constituent assembly.[13] Since many of its leading members were in Petrograd, this party assumed the task of forcing through the Ukrainian demands in the Russian capital, and it was called upon to wage several battles with the Russian Provisional

Government.[14]

In order to "rally and demonstrate the Ukrainian forces throughout the country" and to determine the course of the national liberation struggle, the Rada summoned a national congress on 18–20 April 1917 in Kiev. This step was enthusiastically welcomed by the population at large, from workers and peasants to the intelligentsia and soldiers at the front. Nine hundred delegates arrived in Kiev, representing Ukrainian military, cultural, financial, peasant, and working-class organizations as well as the political parties. The congress signalled the close of the preparatory stage of the Ukrainian revolution, called the "national-cultural period." The period of the "national-political struggle" now began; the congress demanded wide autonomy for Ukraine.[15]

Concomitantly with the formation of the Rada, Ukrainian professional and class organizations began to assume more definite shape, especially those of the peasants, who had hitherto been part of the all-Russian peasant organization. An all-Ukrainian peasant congress, held 23–29 June 1917, demanded that Russia be transformed into a federal union in which an autonomous Ukraine would have an independent parliament and army.[16] The congress was arranged at the initiative of the powerful *Selianska spilka* (Peasant Union) led by Mykola Stasiuk and strongly influenced by the Ukrainian socialist revolutionaries.[17] At the same time, the Ukrainian trade unions held their constituent congress in Kiev. This was dominated by the Ukrainian social democrats and voiced the opinions of Vynnychenko. It is therefore not suprising that it also supported the Rada and its General Secretariat in its struggle for autonomy.[18]

From the beginning, a question of great importance for the national movement was the Ukrainianization of military units belonging to the Russian army. This meant that Ukrainian soldiers in the Russian army should be brought together in special Ukrainian units. The chairman of the Rada's General Secretariat, Vynnychenko, declared that the "task of the Secretariat in military questions is to give the army a national Ukrainian character both at home and, as far as possible, at the front itself."[19] As early as April 1917 the Hetman Bohdan Khmelnytsky regiment formed spontaneously in Kiev, and the commander on the western front, General Aleksei Brusilov, sanctioned it. In a conversation with General Brusilov and Colonel Konstantin Oberuchev, Aleksandr Kerensky, then minister of war, admitted that the government had no choice but to recognize the Ukrainian military formations that had been arbitrarily established.[20] The Russian Provisional Government, which otherwise consistently opposed Ukrainian demands, was in this case compelled to accept accomplished facts. Further steps in this direction, however, were not to be taken "before the end of the war, and then only in accordance with the decision of an assembly which could give its sanction."[21]

The first Ukrainian military congress was held in Kiev on 18–21 May 1917. More than 700 delegates represented 900,000 "armed, nationally-conscious, revolutionary-minded, and, to some extent, organized Ukrainian soldiers at the front, in the fleet, and behind the front."[22] The military congress called for decisive measures to bring about an autonomous Ukraine.[23] It displayed, in fact, a most radical nationalism.

Even though the first Ukrainian military units were being formed and the national movement was becoming progressively better organized, the Russian Provisional Government continued to behave as though the Ukrainian question did not exist. In spite of this, the Ukrainians were anxious to achieve their demands in conformity with the existing legal order. The Rada therefore decided to send a delegation led by Vynnychenko to Petrograd to persuade the Provisional Government to recognize the Rada as the autonomous organ of Ukraine and to recognize in principle Ukraine's right to autonomy. A memorandum that the delegation took with it also demanded that the Ukrainian question be taken up at the future peace conference and the Ukrainian delegates be allowed to attend such a conference. The Rada urged the Provisional Government to set up a special commissariat for Ukrainian affairs and requested government financial allocations.[24]

The delegation found its demands categorically rejected on the grounds that the Ukrainian question could only be settled by the all-Russian constituent assembly.[25] The Ukrainian delegates were even more disappointed when "Russian democracy" also turned its back on them: the democratic Russian newspapers in Petrograd refused to support the Ukrainian delegation or even to publish the text of the Ukrainian memorandum.

The failure of the delegation in Petrograd generated great bitterness in Ukraine and sharpened rather than blunted the national demands. Prior to the delegation the majority of the Rada adhered to quite moderate positions on the question of autonomy; when, for example, the socialist revolutionary Arkadii Stepanenko urged that the Rada be proclaimed the provisional government of Ukraine and immediately sever bonds with Russia to form an independent state, he was supported by only a handful of delegates—and even his own party colleagues spoke against him.[26] But the situation changed when the Rada delegation returned from Petrograd empty-handed. On 16 June 1917 the Rada adopted a resolution accusing the Provisional Government of "deliberately flouting the interests of the

Ukrainian working people and the principle of self-determination, to which the Provisional Government had itself declared its adherence."[27]

At the same time, as the news of the stubbornness of the Provisional Government reached Ukraine, the second Ukrainian military congress was held, although it had been forbidden by the war minister, Kerensky.[28] The delegates declared that they would not return to their units until the autonomy of Ukraine had been achieved. They urged the Rada "not to negotiate further with the Provisional Government on this question but to take the necessary steps for the definite organization of the country in consultation with the national minorities."[29] The Ukrainian peasant congress also criticized the Rada for its accommodating attitude towards the Provisional Government; the Rada should "demand, and not politely request," autonomy.[30] At this congress the demand for an independent Ukraine was much stronger than ever before. The leaders of the Rada, however, were hesitant, since the national movement was weak in the cities. As Vynnychenko pointed out, it was out of the question to provoke an open conflict with the Provisional Government because the Ukrainian towns were hostile to the notion of an independent Ukraine.[31]

Further efforts to influence the Provisional Government were without avail, and the pressure of public opinion compelled the Rada to settle the question of autonomy on its own. On 23 June 1917 the Rada issued its First Universal to the Ukrainian people, which proclaimed the autonomy of Ukraine. Without separating from Russia, Ukraine was henceforth to be a free country with its own parliament and legislature. The Rada decreed that the population, beginning 1 July, pay a special tax to aid the national cause.[32] The reaction to the First Universal was spontaneous and solemn. Numerous delegations from the entire country poured into Kiev to deliver the population's greetings to the Rada and often to make a vow of loyalty to it, regarded now as the provisional Ukrainian government.[33]

After much hesitation, the Rada decided to form the first Ukrainian government in mid-June 1917. This was the General Secretariat, a coalition government dominated by the social democrats and headed by Vynnychenko, who also assumed responsibility for internal affairs, while other secretaries were responsible for nationality affairs, finances, agriculture, food, war, justice, and education.[34] Authority was invested in a legislative organ, the Rada, whose task was to "guard the freedom and rights" of Ukraine and to "build a new order in free Ukraine," and in an executive, the General Secretariat.[35] Ukraine now possessed the three prerequisites for statehood: territory, population, and authority. In forming the General Secretariat, the Rada laid the cornerstone for the restoration of the Ukrainian state.

The First Universal and the formation of the General Secretariat provoked a strident reaction among Russian and other minority groups in Ukraine. The Russian newspaper, *Birzhovye vedomosti*, branded the Universal a crime against the Russian state and urged Petrograd to take the strongest measures to frustrate the Rada's intentions. The Russian social democratic newspaper, *Kievskaia mysl*, accused the Rada of "entering upon a path that endangered the Russian revolution."[36] The chairman of the Russian workers' soviet in Kiev, Nezlobin, charged the Rada with "petty-bourgeois nationalism," while the Russian socialist revolutionary Friumin prophesied that the Rada's actions would lead to anarchy and harmful consequences for both the Russian revolution and Ukrainian autonomy.[37]

The Jews, however, seem to have been impressed by the rising tide of the Ukrainian movement and to have drawn their own conclusions. On 12 July the Jewish social democratic party in Ukraine discussed the Ukrainian national question and adopted a resolution greeting "the stubborn struggle of the Ukrainian people for self-organization in accordance with autonomous democratic principles." The resolution urged the Provisional Government to recognize the Rada and the General Secretariat as "the autonomous central organ of the Ukrainian nation."[38] The Jewish Bund still refused to recognize the Rada as the legal authority in the country, but it went so far as to urge the Provisional Government to establish a special territorial organ—in which the Rada would also be represented—to "determine the forms in which and the means by which autonomy could be introduced in Ukraine."[39]

The Rada sought an understanding with the minorities. It had from the first reserved places for the minority representatives, but these had not been filled because of differences of opinion on the question of Ukrainian autonomy and on the competence of the Rada to bring this about. On 7 July the Rada appointed a special committee to draw up statutes for Ukrainian autonomy. The committee was to consist of a total of ninety-eight deputies, of which the Ukrainians should provide seventy-one, the Russians eleven, the Jews eight, the Belorussians two, and the Tatars, Moldavians, Czechs, Greeks, and Bulgarians one each.[40] The minorities, however, took their places only at a later date.

Even within the Rada itself there were some doubts about the competence of this body, because relations with the Provisional Government in Petrograd were still undefined. While the socialist revolutionary Kovalevsky declared that his party regarded the Rada as "the supreme legal organ of the Ukrainian people and the supreme authority" and the General Secretariat as empowered to prepare a national budget,[41] the socialist federalist Oleksander Shulhyn maintained that the General Secretariat could not be regarded as a government since "this would violate the rights of those national minorities which did not participate in the election of the Central Rada. We would be able to form our government if we had an independent Ukrainian state or at least if federation were a reality, but we are as yet only in the process of achieving autonomy."[42]

The General Secretariat listed the completion of the following tasks as its immediate programme: a) reorganization of local and central administrative bodies; b) establishing the principles of an economic policy that would make Ukraine an economically viable state; c) reorganization of the system of justice; d) convocation of a congress of representatives of all the peoples and provinces of Russia; e) agreement with the national minorities in Ukraine; f) reorganization of education to give it a Ukrainian character; g) regulation of the agrarian question and drafting laws for agrarian reform; and h) Ukrainianization of the army.[43]

When it became evident that the Ukrainians were determined to achieve their autonomy with or without its consent, the Provisional Government found itself obliged to open negotiations with the Rada. To this end three ministers of the Provisional Government, Kerensky, Iraklii Tsereteli, and Mikhail Tereshchenko, arrived in Kiev on 11 July 1917 and began negotiations with the Little Rada and the General Secretariat at the Rada's headquarters.[44] On 13 July a "proposal concerning the national and political status of Ukraine" was drawn up; so, too, were the basic principles of the Universal that the Rada was to publish simultaneously. According to Hrushevsky, who took part in the negotiations, the three Petrograd ministers declared that the Provisional Government recognized the General Secretariat as the supreme organ of government in Ukraine, responsible to the Rada. Thus the Rada, too, was recognized as the highest revolutionary organ of power in the country. The Rada in turn promised not to take any further steps towards autonomy beyond what the Provisional Government had already recognized. The ministers from Petrograd firmly rejected the Rada's request for a department of war.[45]

Apparently, however, the three ministers made greater concessions than the Provisional Government had intended; their report on what occurred in Kiev occasioned a stormy meeting of the government. Although the general lines of the agreement with the Rada were accepted, they nevertheless led to a new government crisis and the withdrawal of the Kadet ministers from the government.[46] The Kadets claimed that "the decision on the Ukrainian question has brought chaos in the relations of the government with a provincial organ and opens an almost legal path for the Rada to bring about Ukrainian autonomy arbitrarily."[47]

On 16 July the Provisional Government sent Vynnychenko a telegram signed by Kerensky, Tsereteli, and Tereshchenko recognizing the General Secretariat as the supreme organ of power in Ukraine. The composition of the General Secretariat was to be decided by the Russian government acting in harmony with the Rada, which was to admit representatives of the democratic organizations of the minorities.[48] On the same day the Rada published its Second Universal, in which it announced the result of its negotiations with the Provisional Government.[49] When Vynnychenko presented this document and the government's telegram to the Rada he was greeted by the delegates with the cry of "Long live our prime minister."[50]

The agreement with the Provisional Government and the Second Universal were viewed by the deputies as the first sign that Russian democracy was at last prepared to meet Ukrainian demands for autonomy. After the Universal was read aloud, Hrushevsky declared: "We are now passing to a higher stage and are obtaining real autonomy for Ukraine with a legislative and an executive organ—the Rada and the General Secretariat."[51]

The compromise agreement between Petrograd and Kiev provoked not only a crisis in the Provisional Government, but also serious differences of opinion inside the Rada. The agreement was approved by the Rada, 247 to 36, with 70 abstentions. It was chiefly the socialist revolutionaries and the soldiers' deputies who considered the Russian terms unsatisfactory.[52] There is no doubt that the Second Universal was a compromise, accepted by both sides because they were unable to realize their aims by force. Neither the Provisional Government in Petrograd nor the Rada in Kiev had at their disposal the forces required for an open conflict.

The attitude of the minorities to the Rada changed radically when the Provisional Government made its first concessions on the Ukrainian question. Now they also began to accept the Rada and its General Secretariat. After some deliberation it was agreed that representatives of the minorities should take their place in both the Rada and the Little Rada as well as in the General Secretariat. The Ukrainians offered the minorities 30 per cent of all the places, while they themselves demanded 40 per cent. Finally, the minorities accepted the Ukrainian terms, and on 25 July the Rada met for the first time with the representatives of the minorities participating. At the same time, the number of deputies in the Rada was increased to 822, distributed as follows:

All-Ukrainian council of peasants' deputies — 212
All-Ukrainian council of soldiers' deputies — 158
All-Ukrainian council of workers' deputies — 100
Councils of [non-Ukrainian] soldiers' and workers' deputies — 50
Ukrainian socialist parties — 20
Russian socialist parties — 40
Jewish socialist parties — 35
Polish socialist parties — 15
Representatives of towns and counties — 84
Representatives of professional, cultural, financial, and citizen organizations and national parties — 108[53]

The composition of the Rada was unique in parliamentary history. It consisted of representatives of the political parties and economic and cultural organizations as well as the trade unions. But its composition corresponded to the spirit of the time and was similar to that of the Provisional Government in Petrograd.

The Little Rada comprised fourteen Ukrainian socialist revolutionaries, fourteen Ukrainian social democrats, five Ukrainian socialist federalists, six representatives of the Jewish Workers' Party, four from the Bund, four Russian socialist revolutionaries, three Mensheviks, three Zionists, two representatives of *Paolei-Zion,* two from the Polish Democratic Centre, three Polish left-wing socialists, one Russian popular socialist, one Kadet, and one representative of the Ukrainian peasant association *Selianska spilka.*[54]

The General Secretariat was re-formed as follows: Vynnychenko (USDWP), chairman and secretary for internal affairs; Martos (USDWP), agriculture; Sadovsky (USDWP), justice; Petliura (USDWP), war; Ivan Steshenko (USDWP), education; Vsevolod Holubovych (UPSR), communications; Stasiuk (UPSR), food; Khrystofor Baranovsky (non-party), finance; Aleksandr Zarubin (RPSR), post office and telegraph; Shulhyn (SF), nationality affairs; Zilberfarb (Jewish Workers' Party), vice-secretary for Jewish affairs; Rafes (Bund), comptroller general; Khrystiuk (UPSR), secretary of state; M. Mickiewicz (Polish Democratic Centre), vice-secretary for Polish affairs.

The secretariat for trade and industry was reserved for the Russian Mensheviks, who at this time had not yet decided whether or not they would take part in the Rada. Petro Stebnytsky (SF) was appointed commissar of the General Secretariat to the Provisional Government in Petrograd, with the rank of secretary of state.[55]

On 29 July, after heated discussions with representatives of the minorities, the Rada agreed on the statutes for Ukrainian autonomy. The Rada was proclaimed the supreme legislative organ in Ukraine. Executive power was to be exercised by the General Secretariat of the Rada, which was to be formed by and be responsible to the Rada. The Provisional Government was only to confirm the composition of the General Secretariat, which should comprise fourteen secretarial posts and exercise its power through all the organs of authority in Ukraine. The General Secretariat should pass on to the Provisional Government for sanction all the suggested laws adopted by the Rada.[56]

A delegation consisting of Vynnychenko, Rafes, and Baranovsky now left for Petrograd with these statutes to obtain the approval of the Provisional Government.[57] Once again the delegation of the Rada met with a serious reverse in Petrograd. The statutes were completely rejected, and instead the Ukrainian delegates were presented with the so-called "Provisional Instruction for the Provisional Government's General Secretariat in Ukraine." According to this instruction, the General Secretariat was to be made into a body subordinate to the Petrograd government. On the proposal of the Rada, it was to be appointed by the Provisional Government and be responsible to it. The question of Ukrainian autonomy was once again to be postponed to the all-Russian constituent assembly. The authority of the General Secretariat was confined to five Ukrainian provinces—Kiev, Poltava, Volhynia, Podillia, and Chernihiv. The number of secretarial posts was reduced from fourteen to nine, of which minorities were to be given four.[58]

After the delegation returned to Kiev, Vynnychenko said that the policy of the government in Petrograd was clearly to provoke the Rada to take hasty measures that could then serve as a pretext for liquidating the Ukrainian movement.[59] Rafes, who was a member of the delegation and represented the Jewish Bund, insisted that the instruction was not the result of an agreement and did not correspond to the wishes of the delegation, and that therefore the Rada need not consider it binding.[60] The socialist revolutionaries urged that the instruction be ignored and that Ukrainian autonomy be brought about in a revolutionary manner, without reference to Petrograd. The social democrats called the instruction a miserable scrap of paper, the work of the Kadets.[61] Most other representatives of the Ukrainian parties took the same point of view. One of them castigated the document as "a bastard, conceived by the Russian socialist revolutionaries in their illegitimate intercourse with the Kadets."[62]

Despite all this criticism the Rada finally agreed not to reject the instruction outright. Vynnychenko was afraid that rejection might provoke a full-scale war with Petrograd and warned against this.[63] The socialist federalist Shulhyn saw, in spite of everything, certain possibilities in the instruction for continuing to work for the realization of Ukrainian autonomy by legal means.[64] The representatives of the minorities, especially Rafes, shared this point of view. Rafes asserted that "the positive side of the instruction is its flexibility, which allows a loose interpretation."[65] The Russian representatives defended themselves against accusations decrying the "imperialistic tendencies" of Petrograd and tried to calm the Ukrainians with the argument that the success of the revolution was dependent on social as well as national factors. They recommended accepting the instruction for the sake of the revolution.[66] *Paolei-Zion* declared that the Provisional Government had clearly aimed the instruction at the sympathies of the minorities, since it assigned them four of the nine posts in the General Secretariat.[67]

The Polish representative Rudnicki considered it impossible to negotiate with the "undemocratic government," though it would nonetheless be advisable to make use of its instruction. He advised keeping all fourteen secretarial posts: "The General Secretariat in its entirety will be sanctioned by the Rada, and nine secretaries will be approved by the Provisional Government."[68] The eagerness with which the Rada worked for the admission of the minority representatives into the Rada is evidence of its desire that the Petrograd government recognize it as the representative and government of all of Ukraine and its population.

After debate, the Rada adopted a resolution on 22 August declaring that the instruction of the Provisional Government was attributable to the imperialistic designs of the Russian bourgeoisie on Ukraine; that it rendered void the agreement with the Provisional Government of 3 July; that it satisfied neither the requirements of the Ukrainian population nor those of the minorities; and that it exacerbated the situation. The resolution promised that the Rada would mobilize all the working masses of Ukraine to fight for their interests and to rally round the Rada.[69] The Rada had emerged from this lengthy crisis as the victor. As one of the secretaries wrote: "The unfortunate instruction of 4 August helped to popularize the Central Rada and the General Secretariat. Thus the struggle started, and forces began to be mobilized."[70]

The new General Secretariat, formed by Vynnychenko and approved by the government in Petrograd, faced the difficult task of promoting Ukrainian autonomy while hampered by official relations with Petrograd. The new relationship did not achieve a relaxation of tension. The Provisional Government tolerated the Rada only because it was compelled to do so.

The Provisional Government, however, was growing weaker with every passing day. Not only in Ukraine but also in other parts of the former Russian empire new national states were emerging and showing no respect whatsoever for Petrograd.[71] Moreover, the Bolsheviks were steadily gaining in strength; the Provisional Government had a foretaste of the danger they embodied in the unsuccessful July revolt that the Bolsheviks organized. In the local elections held in September 1917, the Bolshevik share of the votes in Petrograd rose from 11 to 51 per cent.[72] Symptoms of disintegration began to appear in the army, the administration, and the security system.[73] To make matters worse, the Provisional Government was now faced with the Kornilov revolt, which, though suppressed, still had momentous consequences for the struggle with the Bolsheviks. In panic Kerensky mobilized all "revolutionary" forces against Kornilov and released all the Bolshevik leaders who had been arrested during the attempted *coup d'état*. The Bolsheviks used this opportunity to mobilize their forces for the decisive rising in November.

It was from this period onwards that the Rada and its General Secretariat gradually proceeded to take power into their own hands in Ukraine. The authority of the Rada increased in direct ratio to the mounting anarchy in Russia.[74]

Symptoms of weakness in Petrograd began to arouse concern in Kiev that the state of anarchy might spread from Russia to Ukraine. In reaction to this, the idea of independence began to take an increasingly concrete form. A declaration of the General Secretariat on 10 October 1917 clearly indicates the Rada's intention to take action that in practice would amount to a complete separation from Petrograd. This declaration concerned preparations for summoning a Ukrainian constituent assembly (Petrograd insisted that this should not be summoned before the all-Russian constituent assembly had been held), agricultural reforms, and a reorganization of banking, taxation, and education. In addition, the scope of the General Secretariat was widened, contrary to the directives of the Petrograd government, to cover nine Ukrainian administrative areas; and the secretariats responsible for food, communications, post office and telegraph, justice, and war were re-established.[75]

The declaration caused a great stir among the minorities in the Rada, especially because during the discussions the term "sovereignty" began to crop up. When the Kadet representative Krupnov asked Vynnychenko what the General Secretariat had meant by a Ukrainian constituent assembly, he replied that this term "meant the same in Ukrainian as in Russian or French." Krupnov then demanded on behalf of his party that these words be included in the minutes of the Rada. Some days later the Kadets withdrew their representatives from the Rada, since they could not accept the declaration of the General Secretariat, especially the summoning of the Ukrainian constituent assembly and the demand for separate Ukrainian representation at future peace negotiations.[76]

The other minorities, though they supported the declaration, reacted vehemently to the far-reaching interpretations that the Ukrainian party representatives put upon it. When the word "sovereignty" was mentioned, the representative of the Bund, Rafes, said that this word had not been used in the declaration, otherwise it would not have been accepted by the minorities. "Unless you are for an indivisible Russia you ought not to speak about sovereignty. You feed the masses with slogans, which can give rise to all kinds of utopian dreams. We regard the break with the Russian constituent assembly as a counter-revolutionary action and we shall fight against it."[77] The Mensheviks warned the Ukrainians not to overestimate their strength, and the Russian socialist revolutionaries declared they were "for federation, but not the kind of federation demanded by the Ukrainians."[78]

The Ukrainians' answer to the objections of the minorities reflects how far the idea of autonomy had progressed since the March revolution. Even Vynnychenko, in spite of his official recognition by the Provisional Government, now thought it possible to proclaim himself an adherent of Ukrainian sovereignty. "The Russian government promises much but gives little. We [Ukrainian social democrats] do not now put forward any demand for independence. But we cannot swear that we shall not change our opinions as circumstances change, especially since Ukraine has never promised not to secede from the Russian state."[79] The socialist revolutionary Shapoval said: "We need not be afraid of a civil war. Our main enemy is Russian centralism. In the struggle against this enemy we shall not shy from any methods."[80] Another socialist revolutionary, I. Maievsky, declared: "If there are moral, economic, and political ties between Ukraine and Moscow, Ukraine will never secede; but if there are no such ties, then there is no force that can prevent secession. If the Ukrainians in Russia are to be treated the way they have been for the last six months, then this will inevitably lead to complete separation."[81]

The Provisional Government, however, in spite of its powerlessness even in purely Russian affairs, apparently had no intention of changing its intractable policy towards Ukraine. It replied to the Ukrainian declaration by ordering an investigation of the activity of the General Secretariat and threatening to bring it to trial.[82] The secretaries Vynnychenko, Zarubin, and Steshenko were ordered to Petrograd to give an explanation. The Provisional Government also allegedly stopped payment on the 300,000 roubles it had granted the General Secretariat two months earlier.[83]

The harsh actions of the Provisional Government helped repair relations between the Ukrainians and the minorities in the Rada. On 21 October both the Ukrainians and the minorities in the Little Rada unanimously passed a resolution declaring that "the wishes of the people who live in Ukraine for self-determination can only find expression through the Ukrainian constituent assembly."[84] The Bund in particular now began to support the Ukrainians with fewer reservations.[85]

In early November 1917 the most important and representative congress of the autonomist period was held in Kiev. This was the third all-Ukrainian military congress, attended by nearly 3,000 delegates as well as foreign observers representing French, Belgian, and Romanian military units.[86] The congress disapproved of the measures the Provisional Government had taken against the Rada and the General Secretariat and urged the representatives of the Rada present at the congress to make a definite break with Petrograd.[87] The congress demanded that the Rada "immediately, at its next session, proclaim the establishment of the Ukrainian republic" and summon the Ukrainian constituent assembly, which should determine the "principles of Ukraine's federal ties with other peoples."[88]

The congress called upon Vynnychenko to ignore the orders of the Provisional Government to go to Petrograd, but Vynnychenko replied that the journey would still take place as a final attempt to satisfy Ukrainian demands by legal means. At the same time, Vynnychenko firmly declared that the General Secretariat did not consist of officials of the Provisional Government; it was responsible not to the Provisional Government but to the Rada. He predicted, moreover, that the Provisional Government would not succeed in maintaining a centralized Russia and that "a federation of free republics" would soon be established.[89]

The Provisional Government never had the opportunity of even attempting to carry out its planned reprisals against the General Secretariat. When Vynnychenko, together with Zarubin and Steshenko, arrived in Petrograd, the Provisional Government was no more. The Bolsheviks had seized power on 7 November, ushering in a new and momentous era in the history of Russia. Their *coup d'état* also had fateful consequences for Ukraine.

As soon as the news of the Bolshevik *coup* reached Kiev, the Little Rada formed a "Committee for the Defence of the Revolution in Ukraine," responsible to the Rada. All the socialist parties in Ukraine were represented on the committee, including the Bolsheviks. Its chief purpose was "to fight in all ways against the enemies of the revolution, to preserve law and order in the country, and to defend the gains of the revolution in cooperation with the General Secretariat."[90] However, the situation in Kiev was more complex than the formation of this committee might indicate, because the *coup d'état* in Petrograd had brought to the fore three mutually hostile groups: the Rada, the military staff in Kiev (adherents of the Provisional Government), and the Bolsheviks.

As early as 8 November, the Little Rada condemned the Bolshevik *coup* in a resolution containing the following passage: "Since the Ukrainian Central Rada recognizes that power both in the realm and its constituent parts should pass into the hands of revolutionary democracy as a whole, the Rada considers it impermissible that this power be taken by the council of workers' and soldiers' deputies, which is only a part of revolutionary democracy, and [the Rada] declares that it is against the *coup* in Petrograd and will energetically resist every attempt to support a revolt in Ukraine."[91]

Since there was no longer a central power in Petrograd, the Rada in Kiev exercised in practice all functions of authority.[92] Contact with Petrograd was broken, and a new central government recognized by the Rada had not been formed. Political leaders in Ukraine now had to make important decisions to carry forward the national movement and save Ukraine from the disintegration and anarchy that characterized Russia.

On 20 November 1917 the Rada issued its Third Universal, which proclaimed the Ukrainian People's Republic. The Universal pointed out that the central government no longer existed, and that lawlessness and ruin were engulfing Russia. "Our land too is in danger. Without a strong, uniform, national governmental authority in Ukraine, it too can be plunged into the abyss of conflict, civil war, and ruin. ... Without separating from the Russian republic, and preserving our unity, we shall entrench ourselves in our country to help Russia as a whole transform the Russian republic into a federation of free and equal peoples." Until the Ukrainian constituent assembly had been summoned, the Rada with its General Secretariat was to exercise all legislative and executive power in the country.

The Universal proposed that the territory of the Ukrainian People's Republic embrace those provinces "in which Ukrainians comprise a majority of the population": Kiev, Podillia, Volhynia, Chernihiv, Poltava, Kharkiv, Katerynoslav, Kherson, and Tavrida (excluding the Crimea). The final delimitation of the Kursk, Kholm, and Voronezh regions as well as of neighbouring areas was to be carried out later in accordance with the "organized wishes of the people." The Universal went on to proclaim the expropriation, without compensation, of large landholdings belonging to private persons, the state, and the church. The land was to be owned by all the working people. A labour law was to be introduced without delay, and an eight-hour working day was established immediately. Capital punishment was abolished and an amnesty for political prisoners proclaimed. Freedom of religion, of thought, and of the press was guaranteed, as well as the right to strike, to form associations, and to demonstrate. Russians, Jews, Poles, and other minorities in Ukraine were guaranteed national and personal autonomy. The elections to the Ukrainian constituent assembly were to be held on 9 January 1918, and an electoral law was to be drawn up at once.[93]

Both before and after its proclamation the programme of the Third Universal provoked lively exchanges of opinion, especially between the minorities and the Ukrainian party representatives. These discussions had played a part in the formulation of the Universal. It was to satisfy the demands of the minorities that the Universal so forcibly stressed that Ukraine should remain in federation with Russia.[94] When the text of the Third Universal went before the Little Council, the representatives of the minorities raised strong objections; some of them abstained from voting.[95] Although the Jewish representatives voted for the Universal, they expressed fears that the proclamation of the Ukrainian People's Republic would weaken the all-Russian revolutionary front. According to Rafes, the Bund during this period took the line that, while it would vote for the Third Universal, it would also "push the Rada to a position as close as possible to the Council of People's Commissars in Petrograd."[96] The Mensheviks also expressed the fear that "the unity of the revolutionary front can suffer from the Universal."[97] The representative of the Polish Democratic Centre, Rudnicki, objected that the Universal was directed against the interests of the Polish minority. He had in mind, no doubt, the provisions for the expropriation of private estates. He professed joy that "the Ukrainians were entering the European community of peoples," but declared that he would abstain from voting and relinquish his post as vice-secretary for Polish affairs in the General Secretariat. Later, however, his party decided to remain in the General Secretariat.[98]

Ukrainians greeted the Third Universal with enthusiasm. The all-Ukrainian council of peasant deputies, whose congress took place at the end of November, called the Universal "an act of great historical importance" and affirmed that the planned political, social, and economic reforms were calculated to secure peace and order in Ukraine.[99] The newspaper of the socialist revolutionaries, *Narodna volia*, wrote that common action with those peoples in Russia "who have not yet been wholly abandoned to anarchy and are still capable of self-defence" is the only way to "save Ukraine and the revolution in Russia."[100] The other

Ukrainian socialist revolutionary organ, *Borotba*, wrote in reference to the Third Universal: "What the Ukrainian intelligentsia and the Ukrainian people for whole generations have dreamt of and fought for for centuries has become a fact .... The act of the Central Rada has restored ... the tradition of the Ukrainian state." But, the newspaper went on to say, the Ukrainian socialist revolutionaries "never regarded the idea of the Ukrainian state ... as sufficient in itself, an idea to which all else should be subordinated." They demanded a Ukrainian state because this was in the interest of the working people and its achievement was a precondition for realizing the goals of the socialist revolutionary party in its class struggle. But the Ukrainian People's Republic should endeavour to establish federal ties with other free republics, because "federation is a higher form of international collaboration than the existence of separate states."[101]

The social democrats continued to hold a federalist line. This seems to have been at the time a particularly convenient way of justifying the concrete progress towards achieving Ukrainian independence. In their newspaper, *Robitnycha hazeta* (No. 179), they expressed their theses as follows: "Let us prepare the path for federation. By our work for this cause we preserve the unity of the Russian realm, strengthen the unity of the entire Russian proletariat and the striking power of the Russian revolution .... Either the complete dissection of Russia—its disintegration into separate independent states—or federation. There is no other way." The newspaper of the socialist federalists, *Nova rada* (No. 180), announced that "the Third Universal has laid firm foundations for the national and social reconstruction of Ukraine in union with the other countries of Russia."

The Bolshevik newspaper in Kiev dissented: "The entire Universal consists of the usual bourgeois-democratic melodrama, which can be interpreted in many different ways. Workers and peasants can be persuaded that the Universal is directed against landlords and capitalists, while these in turn can be calmed by explanations that it was necessary to pacify workers and peasants by certain concessions." Naturally, the newspaper asked the question: Why did the Rada not support the Bolshevik government in Petrograd?[102]

While these exchanges continued, the Rada further consolidated its hold over Ukraine. The General Secretariat now took over all government funds, and even the commander on the southwestern front, General Volodchenko, accepted the authority of the Ukrainian government.[103]

The peace question had also come to the fore in Ukraine, and in its Third Universal, as well as in various proclamations of the General

Secretariat, the Ukrainian government urged both the Central Powers and the Entente to make peace, stressing, of course, that the Ukrainian people should also have representatives at the peace negotiations. However, on 22 December 1917 the Bolsheviks arranged a cease-fire with the Central Powers in the name of all of prewar Russia, without taking into account the new states that had arisen on the ruins of the Russian empire.[104] In view of the break with Petrograd and the difficult situation that the burdens of the long war had brought about in Ukraine, the Rada was compelled to take steps at once to win peace also for Ukraine. The impulse for this came from the commander on the Romanian front, who reported in a telegram to the Rada that, after discussion with the Romanian government, he felt "obliged to open peace negotiations with the enemy." He asked the Rada to "send its representative to these negotiations."[105]

During the ensuing debate, the representatives of the Ukrainian parties said that the negotiations with the Central Powers should be opened in the name of the Ukrainian republic, while representatives of the minorities opposed a separate peace. The Ukrainian social democrats maintained that "the Ukrainian People's Republic should take the cause of peace into its own hands, since it is an independent state. It should inform the Russian government, the Council of People's Commissars, of this, as well as the Central Powers and the Entente. We previously stressed the ties of Ukraine with Russia. But the changes that have taken place have freed our hands, and Ukraine should now regard itself as an independent state and should once and for all consummate its national self-determination. Better to die than to fail to achieve this goal."[106] Another social democrat added that the Ukrainians had always desired peace, "but the Russian government stood in our way. This barrier no longer exists."[107] The Ukrainian socialist revolutionaries took the same line, while the socialist federalists hesitated over a separate peace and instead recommended appealing to the West European democracies to hasten a general peace. The minorities were undecided. They wanted peace, but were afraid that a separate Ukrainian peace would reduce the chances of federation with Russia for which they still hoped. But on the whole, sentiment in the Little Rada was such that the chairman of the General Secretariat, Vynnychenko, could state with satisfaction that the leading parties of the Rada shared the same opinion as the General Secretariat, namely, that the "question of peace will not tolerate any delay."[108] By twenty-nine votes to eight the Little Rada decided to send representatives to the truce negotiations in Brest Litovsk.[109]

On 24 December the General Secretariat sent a note to the belligerent and neutral powers announcing Ukraine's intention to take part in the cease-fire and peace negotiations. The note pointed out that the authority of the People's Commissars did not extend to all of prewar Russia and did not include the Ukrainian republic. The General Secretariat contended that a peace made by the People's Commissars would not bind the Ukrainian People's Republic.[110]

The Central Powers were interested in Ukraine's endeavours to make peace, and they encouraged the Ukrainian government to take the decisive step. The Entente also tried to entice the Ukrainians, but their approach to the Ukrainian government took, of course, a different direction. In the middle of December 1917 both France and England appointed official representatives to Kiev, which the Ukrainians interpreted as *de facto* recognition of the Ukrainian People's Republic.[111] The sympathies of the Rada were obviously on the side of the Entente, but to decline a separate peace meant continuing the war. This prospect would be so immensely unpopular among the wearied populace that the choice was either to make a separate peace or to lose the support of the masses. This was the decisive consideration; the Rada chose to accept the proposals of the Central Powers and make a separate peace with them. Peace became more urgent as the danger of war with Russia, against whom the Rada would need military help, became ever more threatening.

With the dispatch of the Ukrainian peace delegation to Brest Litovsk, the time was ripe to declare the Ukrainian People's Republic completely independent of Russia, formally as well as practically. This was done on 22 January 1918, when the Rada proclaimed its Fourth Universal: "From today the Ukrainian People's Republic is the independent, free sovereign state of the Ukrainian people, subject to none." The Universal gave an account of the development of relations with the People's Commissars in Petrograd, which had now "declared war on Ukraine and is sending troops to our country, Red Army soldiers and Bolsheviks, who rob our peasants of their bread and without any compensation whatsoever take it with them to Russia, ... murder innocent people, and spread lawlessness, theft, and destruction." The Rada announced that it had decided "quite independently" to open peace negotiations with the Central Powers. It promised demobilization of the army in the near future. As in the Third Universal, a number of concrete social and agrarian reforms were promulgated; the Fourth Universal also stated that "all democratic freedoms proclaimed in the Third Universal of the Ukrainian Central Rada are confirmed." The Fourth Universal guaranteed all nations in the independent Ukrainian People's Republic the right of national and political autonomy.[112]

The Fourth Universal represented the culmination in the development of the concept of Ukrainian statehood during the Russian revolution. For the first time in centuries Ukraine was formally free of political ties with Russia. It was difficult for Ukrainian politicians to get used to this, especially since not only did the strong and influential minority groups remain suspicious of Ukrainian sovereignty, but certain Ukrainian political circles also had grave doubts whether the rupture of federal ties with Russia was politically advisable.

Vynnychenko, in memoirs written two years later, used various arguments to justify the severance of formal, and in practice non-existent, federal ties with Russia. In one passage he remarked: "The fact that Russia declared war on Ukraine was the chief reason for breaking federal ties. The Ukrainian government had both the formal and the moral right to consider itself no longer bound by any ties to a state that was at war with Ukraine. In reality independence was already a fact. We already had independent international connections, our own separate army, our own front, our own complete state apparatus."[113]

During the debates in the Rada after the adoption of the Fourth Universal, Vynnychenko said: "I am convinced that the basic ideas of this Universal will lead us to a federation of socialist republics throughout the world."[114] The Ukrainian socialist federalists at this time put forward the slogan, "Through independence to federation."[115] It was no longer a question of federation with Russia alone, but of a world-wide federation of socialist states.

The Ukrainian socialist revolutionaries, who made up the largest party in the Rada and who were in reality responsible together with the social democrats for the achievement of sovereignty, declared in their newspaper, *Narodna volia*, 22 January 1918, that "the proclamation of independence did not in itself represent the final goal of the Ukrainian re-emergence. On the contrary, the slogan of independence by itself had never been an attraction for true socialists .... The proclamation of independence was brought about by circumstances .... By satisfying the demand for independence Ukrainian democracy has not deviated an inch from the idea of world brotherhood, from plans for a free union of all countries."[116] The socialist revolutionary president of the Rada, Hrushevsky, also wrote in the same spirit and gave assurances that the federalist tradition would remain "our guiding national-political idea" in the future.[117] The socialist federalists took the same position.[118] In the Rada only the socialist independentists repeatedly stressed the necessity of declaring an independent Ukraine, arguing that this would raise the patriotic spirit of the army and preserve it from Bolshevism.[119]

The attitude of the minorities was different. The Mensheviks and the Bund worked out a joint declaration (quite an interesting document) that accused the Bolsheviks of plunging Russia into the abyss of anarchy by their "treacherous policy." Bolshevik policies had been "preparing the ground for the development of separatist tendencies .... These separatist tendencies assist the plans of the Austro-German imperialists, plans that include not only open annexation but also the establishment of states that are only superficially independent and are intended as a buffer between Europe and Russia. The independence of Ukraine, which has come about in such circumstances, ... means victory, not for the revolution, but for imperialism, and it is a result of the weakening of Russian and international democracy .... Ukrainian democracy is loosening its ties with Russian democracy at a tragic moment for the Russian revolution." The document concluded that the two factions had voted against the Fourth Universal to "show the international proletariat their loyalty to the proletarian ideal."[120] The other minority groups also had a negative attitude to separatism, although several of their representatives had agreed to the proclamation of the Ukrainian People's Republic on 20 November 1917. Their misgivings about the Fourth Universal were reflected in how they voted in the Little Rada on 22 January 1918. Of forty-nine votes, thirty-nine supported the Fourth Universal, four opposed it, and there were six abstentions. All Ukrainian parties and factions voted for the Universal, as did the Polish Socialist Party. Three Mensheviks and a Bund representative voted against it. Those who abstained were the Russian socialist revolutionaries and representatives of *Paolei-Zion*, the United Jewish Socialist Party, the Jewish Democratic Union, and the Polish Democratic Centre.[121] These, especially the Jewish political parties, maintained their hostile attitude to Ukrainian independence even later.[122]

The Ukrainian struggle for statehood in 1917–18 passed through three clearly defined stages: the struggle for autonomy from March to November 1917, the struggle for federation from November 1917 to January 1918, and independence from 22 January 1918.

After the collapse of Russian despotism in March 1917, the Ukrainian people became conscious of its national existence and, heartened by the breakdown of the old regime in Russia, began making concrete national demands. The Ukrainians did not at first demand independence in the same categorical manner as did, for example, the Poles. On the contrary, they requested only a limited form of autonomy, an autonomy that was cultural rather than political.

This moderation at the beginning of the revolution and the failure of the struggle for independence in 1919–20 has often led to speculation whether the idea of Ukrainian statehood really existed or whether it was still immature during this period. Here, of course, there is confusion between the concept itself and the unsuccessful attempt to make of it a reality. The realization of an idea is to a large extent dependent upon a combination of internal and external factors.

It is apparent from such political acts as the formation of the Rada in April 1917 that the Ukrainian people, after only a few weeks of half-hearted requests for cultural autonomy, passed over to demands for political autonomy. In its First Universal, the Rada proclaimed the will of the people for political autonomy and recognition as a nation. This declaration won the spontaneous support of the broad masses of the Ukrainian people.

The next step reflecting the political development of the Ukrainian people was the proclamation of the Ukrainian People's Republic in November 1917. Although it pledged to remain within the framework of the Russian democratic republic as one of its federal constituents, the formation of the Ukrainian People's Republic was a clear indication that the Ukrainian people were marching towards national independence. It was also at this time that the Entente and the Central Powers began their attempts to involve Ukraine in the European conflict, which led to the recognition of Ukraine as an independent state by a number of countries. The inflexible chauvinism that almost all Russian groups displayed in regard to the Ukrainian movement only succeeded in making the idea of federal ties with Russia less popular in Ukraine. The Ukrainian national leaders soon realized that only the complete independence of the Ukrainian state could ensure the normal development of the Ukrainian people.

The proclamation of Ukrainian independence in January 1918 was but a formal confirmation of a situation that had existed in reality ever since Ukraine broke its bonds with Petrograd after the overthrow of the Provisional Government. The level of political development of the Ukrainians at this time was reflected in the unanimity with which Ukrainian parties in the Rada voted for the Fourth Universal. The question of relations with Bolshevik Russia and with anti-Bolshevik Russian forces was to be decided by power struggles. The Bolshevik victory over other Russian forces did not in itself make any significant difference for the Ukrainian national movement: its significance lay in Lenin's negation in practice of the doctrine of self-determination. The future of the Ukrainian liberation movement was to be determined less by the success of the Bolshevik revolution than by the success of a fixed idea about a greater Russia, White or Red, among Russians of all political denominations.

CHAPTER V

The Russian Bolsheviks and the Ukrainian Question: To October 1917

Before the February Revolution

By the time of the first Russian revolution of 1905–06, the Ukrainian problem had already become acute.[1] During the short period of *lzhekonstitutsionalizm* (sham constitutionalism), as Miliukov[2] referred to it, Ukrainians as well as other nationalities within Russia had the opportunity of raising their voices against national oppression. The Imperial Duma became the forum for these discussions.[3] At the first Duma there were forty-four deputies in the Ukrainian group, elected by the Polish-Ukrainian-Jewish bloc.[4] These deputies, supported by some Kadets and Trudoviks, brought up for discussion the prohibition of the Ukrainian language and the question of self-government for Ukraine.[5] At the second Duma the Ukrainian deputies tried in vain to persuade the Duma to intervene in the Ukrainian question.[6] During the Stolypin reaction that followed the first wave of constitutionalism, there was no discussion of the Ukrainian problem, and it was not raised again until the fourth Duma reconvened in 1915. In the Duma this time the Russian Kadets and Trudoviks spoke for the Ukrainian nationality. One of the characteristic gestures of assistance made by the Kadets was the address delivered by their leader, Pavel Miliukov, in February 1915. He protested against the persecution of the Ukrainians and declared that the Ukrainian movement existed, and that one could neither suppress it nor alter its significance. The sole question was whether this movement would be hostile or friendly towards Russia. Miliukov assured the Duma that there was as yet no separatist movement in Ukraine, but that such a movement could develop if inquisitorial methods continued to be applied to Ukrainian culture by Russian nationalists like Savenko and his political friends.[7] The Kadets, however, did not intend to support unconditionally the national demands of Ukraine. They had never recognized the right of self-determination for the nationalities of Russia.

What was the reaction of the Bolsheviks to the debate in the press and the Duma over the suppression of the Ukrainians? Did Lenin, as Soviet historians have often emphasized, really defend Ukraine from national extinction?[8]

During the first Russian revolution, Lenin and his followers, as well as their organizations working in Ukraine, ignored the Ukrainian question, presumably because they wanted to wait and see whether Ukrainian nationalism would survive the struggle against the Russian nationalism of Vladimir Purishkevich and A. I. Savenko. Why otherwise should Lenin have employed so much intrigue and stratagem as he did later in his arguments against Iurkevych and other Ukrainian social democrats who claimed to represent the Ukrainian-speaking proletariat? It was during the émigré period of Lenin's activity that he formulated his conception of nationality in general and his attitude towards Ukrainian social democracy in particular.[9] The Russian social democrats made every effort to isolate their Ukrainian counterparts.

During the Stolypin reaction the attempts of the Russian government to silence the Ukrainians forced the Russian social democrats to take a stand on the Ukrainian question. Lenin was aware of the threat to the proletarian unity of all nationalities posed by repressive Russian nationalism. While protesting against national oppression, he never ceased to caution the social democrats of the nationalities against bringing national antagonism into the proletarian sphere. He warned against this the first time the Bolsheviks became involved in the Ukrainian question, at the Duma session on 2 May 1913. Having been criticized at the fifth RSDWP congress for the party's neglect of the opportunity to take up the Duma's debates on the nationality question, Lenin prepared a speech for the Bolshevik deputy Hryhorii Petrovsky,[10] in which he criticized the government for suppressing the Ukrainian nation. Lenin repeatedly stressed that Russia was nationally heterogeneous, having 57 per cent (more than a hundred million) non-Russian inhabitants, and that therefore a minority in the empire were suppressing a majority. The peculiarity of the national problem in Russia, Lenin noted, was that the national minorities inhabited the borderlands of the empire and that their suppression was much more ruthless than in any other country. He also noted that on the other side of the borders the kinsmen of the suppressed nationalities enjoyed greater national freedom.[11]

Lenin declared that it was not the business of social democrats to suppress Ukraine or any other country. The tsarist government, Lenin wrote, "is not only economically suppressing nine-tenths of the population but is also demoralizing [the Great Russians], humiliating, dishonouring, prostituting them, by teaching them to oppress other nations and to cover up their shame with hypocritical and quasi-patriotic phrases."[12]

Petrovsky made his appearance on the tribune of the Duma to deliver Lenin's speech at the time when Ukrainians were arguing with the government to lift its prohibition against the public commemoration of Shevchenko's birthday. Petrovsky enumerated all the injuries the government had done Ukraine and concluded by saying that the Russian government kept the enslaved peasants in a state of greater backwardness than the Negroes in America. The country had been exploited materially and repressed culturally, with the result that illiteracy in Ukraine was the highest in the Russian Empire.[13]

In spite of his opposition to the development of national cultures, Lenin supported the right of the Ukrainians to use their own language in the schools and administration. This is curious, since, as is clear from his critique of Bishop Nikon,[14] Lenin did not mean to defend Ukrainian culture from Russification. National culture was to him a "clerical or bourgeois fraud"; "only clerics and bourgeois can speak about national culture, and the working masses can speak only about the international ... culture of a worldwide labour movement. Only such a culture can mean complete, real, sincere equality of nations," because this culture held no element of national oppression.[15] On the one hand, Lenin protested against badgering the Ukrainians for "separatism," but, on the other, he fought against "national socialists like Dontsov."[16]

In the same period, Lenin made some characteristic pronouncements on the future of the Ukrainian nation. Although admitting the existence of a separate Ukrainian nationality (something he was never to do with regard to the Jews), he nevertheless contended that the proletarians of the leading nation, in this case the Great Russians, should "unite the workers of all nations in any given state," and that they "cannot vouch for any particular path of national development." Thus he went on to say that the question "whether Ukraine . . . is destined to form an independent state will be determined by a thousand factors that cannot be foreseen. Without attempting idle guesswork, we firmly uphold what is beyond doubt, namely, the right of Ukraine to form such a state. We respect this right; we do not uphold the privileges of the Great Russians over the Ukrainians; we educate the masses in the spirit of recognition of that right, in the spirit of rejecting the state privileges of any nation."[17] But Lenin did not intend to wait and see how the Ukrainian right to independence would develop. He hoped to keep Ukraine as well as other nations within the Russian empire. This emerges clearly even from his criticism of Russian nationalists like Savenko, who had fiercely attacked the Ukrainian "Mazepists"[18] because they "threaten to weaken ties between Ukraine and Russia" and were supported by the Austrians. Lenin advised the Russian nationalists to use the same methods as the Austrians to strengthen their position in Ukraine, "granting the Ukrainians freedom to use their language, self-government, and autonomous Diet, etc. . . . Is it not clear," wrote Lenin, "that the more liberty the Ukrainian nationality enjoys in any particular country, the firmer will its ties with that country be?"[19]

Lenin did not openly advocate the assimilation of the Ukrainians as he did of the Jews. But he maintained that everybody "who was not wrapped in nationalistic prejudices" must admit the great progress in the assimilation of nationalities under capitalism. The unity of the Ukrainian and Great Russian proletariat was axiomatic in Lenin's view:

> Take for instance Russia, and the relation of the Great Russians to the Ukrainians. Undoubtedly every democrat, not to mention the Marxist, will readily fight against the enormous humiliation of the Ukrainians and demand their complete equality. But to threaten the present ties and unity of the Ukrainian and Great Russian proletariat would be real treachery to socialism and a foolish policy even from the point of view of the bourgeois "national task" of the Ukrainians.[20]

Lenin considered progressive the infiltration of Great Russian workers into Ukrainian industries and the assimilation of the Ukrainian workers. "For some decades," wrote Lenin, "there has been clear evidence of rapid economic development in the south, e.g., in Ukraine, which attracted hundreds of thousands of peasants and workers from Great Russia into capitalistic estates, mines, and towns. In these areas, the assimiliation of the Great Russian and the Ukrainian proletariat is obvious and is undoubtedly progressive." According to Lenin, it was capitalism and not the backward, sluggish, Ukrainian or Great Russian *muzhik* that produced the spirited proletarian whose way of life cures any specific national short-sightedness. The Ukrainian Marxists had to strengthen the influence of the Russian "proletarian culture" on the Ukrainian working masses. Lenin wanted to present the Russian social democrats as free from every sort of national chauvinism.

> If a Ukrainian Marxist be so saturated with a *fully rightful* and *natural* detestation of the Great Russian oppressors that he transfer ever so small a part of this detestation, be it only disinclination, to the proletarian culture and cause of the Great Russian workers, then such a Marxist falls into the sordidness of bourgeois nationalism. The same would characterize the Great Russian Marxist if he only for a moment forgets the demands of full equality for the Ukrainians or their right to create an independent state.[21]

As long as the Great Russian and Ukrainian workers lived side by side, they had to work together in close organizational unity. Therefore Lenin declared war on any separatism of the proletarians of subjugated nationalities: "Every utterance about the separation of the workers of one nation from another, every attack on Marxist assimilation, every opposition on questions concerning the proletariat of one national culture as a whole as against another national culture as a whole, etc., is bourgeois nationalism, against which a merciless struggle is imperative."[22]

Much evidence supports the conclusion that Lenin was in favour of a centralized and indivisible Russian empire.[23] He criticized the Russian government and nationalists, not because he preferred to see Russia divided into small states, but for the opposite reason—because they antagonized the Ukrainians, thus rendering impossible fusion with the Great Russians.[24]

Lenin's struggle with the Ukrainian social democrats affords valuable insights into his Ukrainian policy. To understand his antagonism towards the Ukrainian social democrats, we must remember that they had exposed Lenin as a Great Russian chauvinist and regarded the RSDWP as an instrument for the Russification of non-Russian workers.

The most merciless critic of the Russian social democrats, especially of Lenin, was the Ukrainian left-wing social democrat Lev Iurkevych (Rybalka), whom Lenin honoured with epithets like "ragamuffin," "Ukrainian national chauvinist," "nationalistic bourgeois," and "crook." Iurkevych saw through Lenin's slogan, "the self-determination of nations," and asserted that this principle as understood by Russian Marxists was "an empty and needless phrase."[25] He pointed out that the Russian Marxists, in spite of their public declarations, had consistently and continually opposed any independence for Poland. He stressed that authentic national self-determination "is a very deep social process," and he asked: "How can a nation exercise self-determination if it is politically and culturally dead?"

According to Iurkevych, the national movements claimed only national political rights within the state to which they belonged, and the formulation of the slogan of independence at the moment would be the same as trying "to examine the sun with a lantern." "The root of the present national question," wrote Iurkevych, "lies in the right of nations to cultural and political self-determination, but the Russian Marxists are blind to this and prefer to juggle with the term the 'state self-determination of the subjugated nations.'"[26]

Iurkevych dated the animosity of Russian Marxists towards the Bund from the beginning of the Bund's activity in Ukraine. He thought that Russian Marxists were afraid of the "bad influence of the Bund on the Ukrainian workers." He based his assumption on the declarations of the old *Zoria*, which recognized the existence of the Bund "among the Poles and Latvians" but opposed its existence in "the South (i.e., Ukraine)," because the Bund's principle of the independence of the Jewish proletariat could "exercise a disorganizing influence on the working groups of South Russia."[27] Even Martov stressed that the separation of the Jewish workers from the RSDWP could bring about a split in the local organizations and, even worse, could tremendously weaken the movement, since the Jewish artisans "were often the avant-garde of a local movement, formed the leading workers' cells, and produced the best agitators."[28] In view of the Bund's support of the Ukrainian social democrats against the persecution by the RSDWP, the fears of the Russian Marxists were not groundless. Both the Bund and the USDWP championed national cultural autonomy, and both demanded federal principles in the RSDWP. Iurkevych advocated the independence of the Ukrainian labour movement, organized in an independent social democratic party federated with RSDWP.

In an article, "On the Ukrainian Workers' Newspaper," Iurkevych launched a campaign against the Russian Marxists' influence in Ukraine. "The millions of Ukrainian workers awakening to a nationally-conscious life," he wrote, could no longer be satisfied by the Russian Marxists, "because these cannot use Russian there to make their appeal." The Ukrainian Marxists, on the other hand, had to break with old "peasant" traditions because "with only peasant sympathies we, as well as the whole Ukrainian renascence, shall never be able to escape and shall never transcend an ethnographic-zoological existence." He urged the Ukrainian Marxists to work for the harmony of the urban and rural movements. Iurkevych exhorted Ukrainian Marxists to turn their attention to the cities, to the heavy-industrial workers, "among whom, despite a low standard of living, there is evidence of the awakening not only of class, but also of national, consciousness."[29]

Iurkevych composed the USDWP petition for recognition as an independent organization: "We, the Ukrainian Marxists, also demand the organizational separation of our workers' movement, and if we are to be consistent we must request it not only in political, but also in professional (trade) and cooperative, form."[30] Earlier Iurkevych had classified Lenin's argument against independent national organizations—that they would participate in national movements "together with all bourgeois parties and groups"— as nonsense. "Can we condemn the Marxists," he asked, "on the grounds that they, together with the bourgeois parties, are in favour of democratic political reform?"[31] He noted that the Austrian example had not convinced the Russian Marxists; on the contrary, they called this method of solving the national problem "an entirely non-Russian way." Neither Stalin's arguments against the Austrian reformist solution to the national question nor the way Russian Marxists linked the "freedom of nationalities" with "probable radical change" satisfied Iurkevych. He believed that the problem was not in the "*tempo* of our political movements." However the Marxists were to act, they must, according to Iurkevych, strive for such state reform "as will give the maximum guarantee of the free development of nations, and therefore the division of the labour movement by nationalities is inevitable in all circumstances."[32]

The democratization of the Russian empire did not necessarily imply a solution to the problems of nationality. "A state that is inhabited by many nationalities, no matter how democratic it is, can never rid itself of ... national oppression and struggle if it is centrally organized." "National autonomy and political decentralization corresponding to the national division of the state are inevitable, but such reform is not organically bound to political democratization. A national renascence has its own peculiar national and political aims, which, quite naturally, are closely associated with general democratic political endeavour."[33] "As long as the nation has no political rights, there can be no national freedom. To win these rights, a nation has to be recognized as a political organization by the state."[34]

He admitted that under capitalism it was impossible to eradicate completely national oppression and struggle, but Marxists had to strive nonetheless for international solidarity and fraternity among workers. "There is only one road to this end: the recognition of complete organizational freedom for the labour movements of the subjugated nations."[35]

Iurkevych complained that among the Russian Marxists, especially the Bolshevik faction, a strongly centralist disposition predominated, and that they considered Ukrainian cities their monopoly. "Naturally we are going to fight against this nationalistic intolerance of our Russian comrades, and we shall continue to do so until they recognize all our rights, until they begin to look on us as the representatives of the Ukrainian workers."[36]

Iurkevych and his political companions had reason to suspect Lenin and his followers of animosity. Two sources show Lenin's hostility towards the Ukrainian socialists, Iurkevych in particular. In the Bolshevik theoretical paper, *Prosveshchenie*,[37] Lenin openly attacked the "national cultural autonomy" advocated by the Bund and other national social democrats, including Iurkevych; and in his letters to Inessa Armand[38] Lenin conspired against Iurkevych because of his separatism.[39]

In a letter dated 1 April 1914, Lenin, then in Cracow, asked Inessa Armand to publish an address he had written to the Ukrainian workers. He preferred not to have it published under his own name or that of Armand, because she too was "Russian"; better that it appear under the signature Oksen Lola "and a few other Ukrainians." Lenin placed great importance on organizing "at least a small group of anti-separatists" among the Ukrainian social democrats. "It is of vital importance," he wrote, "that a voice from among the Ukrainian SDs should call for unity and oppose the division of the workers by nationality." Armand was to copy Lenin's address and then give it to the Ukrainian Lola to translate into Ukrainian and send to *Put pravdy*. He recommended that it be signed by Lola or "(better) in the name of a group (at least two or three persons) of the Ukrainian Marxists (still better: the Ukrainian workers)." This, he added, had to be done "tactfully, quickly, against Iurkevych and *without his knowledge*, because this crook will bungle." He referred to Iurkevych as "this scabby, foul, nationalistic bourgeois, who under the banner of Marxism had prophesied the *division* of the workers according to nationality, and a *separate* national organization of the Ukrainian workers."[40]

Lenin not only prepared the "Address to the Ukrainian Workers," arranged for its translation into Ukrainian, and planted some Ukrainian names under it, but he also commented on it in *Trudovaia pravda*. "With pleasure," he wrote, "do we publish the address of our comrade the Ukrainian Marxist." He went on to emphasize the great importance to Russia of workers' unity and regretted that the "misleaders" of the workers, "the petty bourgeois from *Dzvin*, are doing their utmost to turn the Ukrainian SD workers away from the Great Russian."[41] (Later, Lenin discharged Lola from his position of trust because "Lola is naive" or "obviously evasive," but "anyway, by means of him, we took a little *step* forward."[42])

Lenin's hostility to the Ukrainian socialists was greater than his hostility to Jewish or Latvian socialists; it was only matched in fact by his enmity to the Polish Socialist Party (PPS). Lenin fought the Bund's demand for federalism but not the Bund's very existence. However, with regard to the Ukrainian social democratic organization, Lenin refused to recognize its separate existence. He required the Ukrainian Marxists not only to cease opposing the Russification of the Ukrainian nation, especially of the proletariat, but even to assist the process. When Lenin mentioned assimilation of Russian and Ukrainian workers, it was clear that he referred only to the assimilation of the Ukrainian masses by the Russian. Such assimilation would not produce a pure proletarian nation, composed of all nationalities, but would strengthen the Russian nation. He tried to convince the Ukrainian Marxists that the creation of an independent Ukrainian social democratic organization was harmful. Lenin was probably afraid to see his political, especially his revolutionary, activity restricted to Russian ethnic territory. He was encouraged by the weakness of Ukrainian social democracy and still more by the small size of the Ukrainian nationally-conscious proletariat. He must have been unsettled by the ideas of the Ukrainian national-minded social democrats like Iurkevych and alarmed by the possibility of a rising national consciousness among Ukrainian workers.

From February to October 1917

During the period of the Provisional Government, the Bolsheviks aggravated the antagonism between the government and the nationalities. Siding with the nationalities time after time, they posed as defenders of national rights against Russian imperialism. And Kerensky's Provisional Government, as we have seen, did not accede to immediate national self-determination, declaring the issue irrelevant; it even rejected the modest demands for national autonomy for Ukraine and Finland. The Provisional Government kept referring this problem to the constituent assembly, whose fate in those stormy days was very uncertain.

The policy of the Russian Bolsheviks on the Ukrainian question manoeuvred between Russian nationalism, which aimed at complete and forcible Russification of the Ukrainians, and Ukrainian nationalism, which aimed at Ukraine's separation from Russia. In Lenin's opinion, the more freedom given to the nationalities, the more trust they would have towards Russia. With this maxim Lenin argued that Ukraine and Finland would not separate from Russia; it was sufficient for the Soviet regime to be installed in Russia to prevent it: "If the Ukrainians see that we have a Soviet republic, they will not separate, but if we have Miliukov's republic, they will separate."[43] In the case of Ukraine, it was apparent immediately after the Bolshevik revolution how overly optimistic and bold Lenin's forecasts had been. It must be acknowledged, however, that Lenin recognized (and opposed) the oppression of the nationalities in Russia as one of the chief causes of antagonism between the Russian and non-Russian proletariat. In his article, "Finland and Russia," Lenin appealed to the workers and peasants not to follow the annexationist policy of the Russian capitalists, Aleksandr Guchkov and Miliukov, and the Provisional Government towards Finland, Kurland, and Ukraine. "Do not be afraid to admit the freedom to secede of all these nations. It is not by force that other peoples are to be attracted to union with the Great Russians, but only by a truly voluntary, a truly free agreement, which is impossible without the freedom to secede. ... The freer Russia is and the more decisively our republic recognizes the freedom of secession of non-Russian nations, the more strongly will other nations strive towards union with us, the less friction will there be, the rarer will be actual cases of secession, the shorter will be the time for which some of the nations will secede."[44]

Lenin let no opportunity slip to attack the Provisional Government for its nationality policy. When in June 1917 the minister of war, Kerensky, banned the Ukrainian military congress, Lenin attacked him in the article, "It Is Not Democratic, Citizen Kerensky." "The minister of war considers the congress of the Ukrainians 'inopportune' and by his authority he bans this congress! Quite recently citizen Kerensky 'pulled up' Finland, now he has decided to 'pull up' the Ukrainians. And all this is done in the name of 'democracy!'" Lenin stressed that "by his imperialist nationalist policy citizen Kerensky only strengthens, only inflames, just those separatist strivings against which the Kerenskys and the Lvovs want to struggle."[45]

On the occasion of the First Universal and the reaction to it from the Provisional Government and Russian political circles, Lenin wrote two short articles, "Ukraine" and "Ukraine and the Defeat of the Ruling Parties in Russia," in which he criticized the government's Ukrainian policy: "No democrat, not to mention a socialist, will dare deny the full validity of the Ukrainian demands. Likewise, no democrat can deny the *right* of Ukraine to free secession from Russia: it is the unconditional recognition of this right that alone permits agitation for a free union of the Ukrainians and the Great Russians, for a *voluntary* uniting into one state of two peoples." He believed that only the recognition of this right was able to break "in fact, irrevocably, finally, with the accursed tsarist past which did *everything* for the *mutual alienation* of peoples that are so near, both in language and in place of habitation, in character, and in history. ... Accursed tsarism transformed the Great Russians into the hangmen of the Ukrainian people, in every way nourished in it hatred for those who forbade Ukrainian children even to speak and learn their native language." Lenin therefore appealed to Russian democracy to break with that past and "regain for itself, for the workers and peasants of Russia, the fraternal trust of the workers and peasants of Ukraine. This cannot be done without the full recognition of the rights of Ukraine, including the *right* to free secession." Lenin also repeated that the Bolsheviks were "no supporters of small states," that they were for a close union of the workers of all countries against the capitalists of their own and of all countries in general, that the Russian worker must not force his friendship on the Ukrainian worker but must win it, "*conquering it* by an attitude as to an equal, as to an ally and a brother in the struggle for socialism."[46] In another article Lenin stated that the government parties, the SRs and the Mensheviks, had suffered defeat on the Ukrainian question, since they had succumbed to counter-revolutionary intimidation by the Kadets. He defended the demand of the Rada to have one representative in the central Russian government, noting that the demand was very modest, since "in 1897 the Great Russians numbered 43 per cent of Russia's population, while the Ukrainians numbered 17 per cent, i.e., the Ukrainians could demand, instead of one minister in sixteen, six!!" The government had demanded from the Ukrainians the "guarantee of correctness"; this Lenin termed "arrant shamelessness," for "nowhere in Russia, *neither in the central government* nor in a single local office ... is there any guarantee of correctness, nor is there, as is common knowledge, any correctness .... Only for Ukraine 'we' demand 'guarantees of correctness!'" He advised the SRs and the Mensheviks to meet "the very legitimate and very modest demands" of the Ukrainians. "Give in to the Ukrainians—this is the voice of reason, for otherwise it will be worse; the Ukrainians cannot be kept by force, they will only be embittered. Give in to the Ukrainians—then you will open the road to trust between both nations, to their brotherly union as equals!"[47]

It must be conceded that Lenin, more than any other Russian revolutionary, possessed the courage to face the truth squarely and admit the responsibility of Russian society for the oppression of the nationalities. He saw that terror could not stop the Ukrainian national movement, and therefore he proposed different tactics to retain Ukraine within Russia's orbit. No doubt one motive for Lenin's criticism of the government was to appear to Ukrainians as a defender of the rights of nations subjugated by Russia and thus to gain allies for the party against Kerensky's Provisional Government. This, however, does not mean that the Ukrainians did not see the duplicity of Lenin and his party. Of this they had too many proofs and incriminating statements from Lenin himself. However, external forces drove the Bolsheviks and the nationalists of the subjugated nations into the same camp. As Popov wrote, the Rada's conflict with the Provisional Government was very advantageous for the Bolsheviks and their plans.[48]

With these two articles Lenin concluded his intervention in the Ukrainian question in the pre-October period, in the period when the RCP was an opposition party. However, the Bolsheviks had other opportunities to appear as protectors of Ukrainian national liberation. When the first all-Russian congress of soviets of the workers' and soldiers' deputies met between 3 June and 7 July, the Bolshevik deputies—Lev Kamenev, Aleksandra Kollontai, Grigorii Zinovev, Evgenii Preobrazhensky—evinced the same hostile attitude towards the government's Ukrainian policy as did Lenin. Thus, at the 30 June session, in discussing the creation of a separate Ukrainian socialist faction to be composed of twenty Ukrainian SRs and SDs, Kamenev stated that in "normal circumstances" the Bolsheviks would not have supported the Ukrainians, for "we, the SD Bolsheviks, consider it absurd to separate different parties on a national basis," but "now something unheard of and inadmissible in any democratic country is happening with the Ukrainian problem"; the refusal of the soviets to have two or three Ukrainian representatives "could be interpreted as a demonstration in the same direction as that which the Provisional Government is now making against the demands of the Ukrainian people."[49] Preobrazhensky then proposed that the congress dissociate itself from and condemn the nationality policy of the Provisional Government "as anti-democratic and counter-revolutionary, delaying till this day the solution of vital and urgent problems connected with the realization of the national rights of the oppressed nationalities of Russia; and [the congress should] disclaim any responsibility for the consequences of this policy, which has led to the conflicts with Finland and Ukraine."[50] The Bolsheviks were influenced primarily by the advantages to be gained for proletarian unity. Preobrazhenksy argued that the Bolshevik position would "enable the Ukrainian proletariat to develop its class struggle within the Ukrainian people against every chauvinism, against every nationalist demagogy."[51] The Bolsheviks considered their best tactical move to be condemnation of the government's policy so far and immediate recognition "of the Ukrainians' right to full autonomy and to the creation of an independent state."[52]

The Bolshevik resolution was rejected by the congress, which adopted the resolution of the governmental faction of the SRs and SDs. Another view on the government's policy in the Ukrainian question was expressed by the Russian social democrat Plekhanov, who during the war had opposed Lenin's faction on the issue of "the defence of the fatherland." Plekhanov reacted to the First Universal in the spirit of an adherent of the unity and indivisibility of the Russian empire. In place of self-determination, he somewhat vaguely recognized "the right to self-defence," i.e., "the right of every people to remove from its path those obstacles that have been erected there by the unjust claims of other peoples." But this was not to say that he wanted to see the decentralization of Russia in the form of a federation of nationalities. "We, the social democrats, the vast majority of us, are by no means the adherents of an extreme federalism." He was against Ukrainianization and state subsidies for Ukrainian national and cultural needs and also against the appointment of a special commissar for Ukrainian affairs within the Provisional Government. He opposed also the Rada's demand to participate in the peace conference. In Plekhanov's opinion all these, if granted, "could entail considerable practical difficulties."[53] Plekhanov attributed the conflict between the Provisional Government and the Rada to the Provisional Government, which "did not treat the demands of the Ukrainians with sufficient attention" and so "aroused among them very dangerous discontent." But he also held that the Central Rada should not have "had recourse to extreme measures"; it should have exercised "*a lawful pressure upon the government*" and "*appealed to the Great Russian people.*" The conflict, he said, served German imperialism, which aimed at detaching Ukraine; Great Russia would thus be "thrown back perhaps to the times of Tsar Aleksei Mikhailovich. This would be for her the equivalent of a death sentence."[54] Plekhanov more than once defended the territorial integrity of Russia; this placed him among the "social patriots."

The Bolsheviks also discussed the nationality question at the so-called Moscow conference (*Moskovskoe soveshchanie*). At the meeting of the inner circle of the party CC on 19 August, they accused the Provisional Government of "fanning violence towards Finland and Ukraine."[55] And in the declaration of the CC RCP(B) of 13 September, they demanded "the realization in actual fact of the right to self-determination of nations living in Russia, in the first place the satisfaction of the demands of Finland and Ukraine."[56] The party raised the same demand on the occasion of the democratic conference (*demokraticheskoe soveshchanie*) in September 1917.[57]

Before October, the party's policy towards the subjugated nationalities, including the Ukrainians, was limited, it seems, to these declarations—propaganda to discredit the Provisional Government in the eyes of the masses, especially those of the subject nations. This was the period of the war for the masses, of preparation for the Bolshevik revolution. The national movements, which in this period stood on the same side of the barricades as the Bolsheviks, were for the Bolsheviks an auxiliary revolutionary force.[58] The Bolsheviks unquestionably had much better chances than other Russian socialists, if not to gain the sympathy, at least to neutralize the hostility of the Ukrainian masses. But it is probable that the Rada saw through the contradictions of the Bolshevik declarations, since the Ukrainian leaders understood that the Bolsheviks opposed the cultural development of nations and thus also their actual self-determination.

The Local Bolsheviks and the Ukrainian Question

Bolsheviks were also active in Ukraine itself. Often the local Bolsheviks pursued a somewhat different policy towards the Rada and the Ukrainian national movement than did their all-Russian counterparts. This was so, first, because the Ukrainian Bolsheviks[59] did not constitute a single organizational unit, with an independent party centre; rather, they were divided into local Bolshevik organizations, unconnected among themselves, each subordinated separately to the RSDWP(B) and therefore unable to unify political tactics, especially since the directives from the party centre in Petrograd seldom arrived in time. Furthermore, as a Bolshevik historian wrote, "the central directives were not always able to hit the nail on the head, because the CC of the [Russian] Bolsheviks was not familiar with the state of affairs here .... For Petrograd, the struggle against the Central Rada was a matter of secondary importance."[60] Against the Ukrainian national movement, organized and united in Kiev, there stood a weak and lonely Bolshevik organization in Kiev, led by such pillars of "Luxemburgism" in the national question as Piatakov and Bosh.

The Kiev organization, though characterized above all by Luxemburgism, also comprised some adherents of Lenin's theses and even *samostiinyky*—protagonists of Ukrainian independence. At the very beginning of the revolution, the Bolsheviks in Ukraine were generally little interested in the question of nationalities, and they either ignored the Ukrainian question or considered it of secondary importance; they concentrated instead on discrediting the government parties and gaining the sympathy of the masses.[61]

"It seemed to us then," wrote Iurii Lapchynsky, "that the question of nationalities only made the task more complicated, only distracted the workers' attention from the main issue: from the revolutionary work of destruction .... And we, the Bolsheviks of the older generation, ... subjectively were extremely ill-prepared to embrace the idea of an all-Ukrainian unity and to understand that as a result of the great revolution, Ukraine would be regenerated as a great independent country .... Our previous party practice taught us ... that there were 'three provinces' in the 'South of Russia': Kiev, ... Odessa, ... and Kharkiv .... The idea that Ukraine was something continuous could be held only by those who at some time had worked in the *Spilka*, the USDP, or the RUP, but very few such people were among us. And although the petty-bourgeois national movement made itself felt among us from the very first days after the revolution, ... the attitude of most of us to the national cause was as to one that did not concern us, the revolutionary workers."[62]

Popov attributed this to "bourgeois and philistine imperialist nationalist superstitions influencing certain elements of the working class and the party."[63] Needless to say, the negative attitude of the Ukrainian Bolsheviks to Ukrainian national aspirations played into the hands of the Central Rada, which could declare with confidence that all Russian parties without exception were the protagonists of a single, united, and indivisible Russian empire. Evgeniia Bosh, a leader of the Kiev organization, wrote unambiguously on this weak point of party policy:

> The prolonged preparatory work of the social chauvinists [i.e., the Ukrainian social democrats and socialist revolutionaries], of the bourgeois nationalists of Ukraine and their cunning and skilful policy were not unmasked before the masses. The soviet and party workers in Ukraine were plunged up to the neck in the struggle within the soviets with Russian conciliators (*soglashateli*), in the unmasking of Kerensky's policy ... ; for the struggle with the Ukrainian chauvinists there was neither time nor inclination left. And it must be admitted that our totally erroneous and inadmissible attitude to the work of the chauvinists promoted their growth and strengthened them, so that now they are in our way.[64]

Elsewhere Bosh confessed that the Bolsheviks did not struggle with the Rada until the October revolution itself: "And only then, at what for us was the decisive moment, did our mistake assume shape and appear in its full magnitude; but time was lost."[65] That some Bolsheviks in Ukraine had no interest at all in the Ukrainian problem is confirmed in the writings of other participants in the revolution. Considering the national composition of the Bolshevik organizations in Ukraine,[66] the position of the party is understandable.

In areas of Ukraine where the workers were either Russian or largely Russified, as in the Donets basin, the party's attitude to the Ukrainian question was less friendly than in areas where the Russian element was not dominant, as on the Right Bank of the Dnieper. Popov wrote on this:

> As far as the organizations of the Donets basin led by Kharkiv and

> Katerynoslav were concerned, which relied upon the Russian, Russified, or semi-Russified masses of the proletariat, they were prepared to ignore the national question even more, to dodge it, taking as a pretext the argument that it was absolutely necessary to preserve and strengthen the united front and liaison with the Russian proletariat .... The leading groups of our party workers, especially in Left-Bank Ukraine, when elaborating the political line, *used to forget, or not take fully into account, the very special characteristics of Ukraine and the importance of the Ukrainian national movement.*[67]

It is noteworthy that the Ukrainian Bolsheviks had a more negative position on the Ukrainian question and a more aggressive posture *vis-à-vis* the Rada than did the central RCP(B). While the Russian Bolsheviks attacked the Provisional Government and its Ukrainian policy, the local Bolsheviks in Ukraine were hostile to the Ukrainian national struggle. The leader of the Kiev organization, G. Piatakov, assumed the position, as it were, of a Russian imperialist;[68] he regarded Ukraine as an inseparable part of the Russian empire and of the Russian economic entity, and Kiev "as one of Russia's large cities and not as the centre of Ukraine."[69] He felt, simply, that Russia's economic existence would be impossible without Ukrainian coal, sugar, and grain. He defended this position at the meeting of the Kiev committee of the RSDWP(B) on 17 June 1917:

> We support the Ukrainians in their protests against all kinds of bureaucratic prohibitions by the government, such as the prohibition of the Ukrainian military congress. But generally we should not support the Ukrainians, for this movement is not advantageous to the proletariat. Russia cannot exist without the Ukrainian sugar industry, the same can be said about coal (the Donets basin), grain (the black earth belt), etc. These branches of industry are closely connected with all the rest of Russia's industry. Moreover, Ukraine does not form a distinct economic region, for it does not possess banking centres, as Finland does. If Ukraine separates itself by a customs barrier from the rest of Russia, then the industry of the Kharkiv, Chernihiv, Poltava, and other districts, which still bears a handicraft character, will successfully compete with the backward local factory industry ... which represents a retrograde step and is extremely undesirable for the proletariat.

For Piatakov, the Ukrainian national movement was counter-revolutionary, because it opposed the social revolution and because it "tries to bind the revolutionary movement with national fetters and turn backwards the wheel of history." The task of the Bolsheviks, in his opinion, was twofold: to protest against the policies of Kerensky's government and "to fight the chauvinist aspirations of the Ukrainians."[70]

This position, at least at that time, differed from that of Lenin, who had not yet begun calling the Ukrainian national movement counter-revolutionary. Lenin also was, in principle, against the secession of nationalities from Russia, but at that time he had made no pronouncement to that effect. Piatakov referred the solution of the Ukrainian question to the all-Russian constituent assembly: "While advocating broad regional autonomy we will nevertheless oppose a Diet, for a Diet can also establish customs barriers and thus become dangerous to the proletariat. But to convene a Ukrainian constituent assembly at the demand of the Central Rada alone without a general territorial vote is unthinkable and technically unfeasible."[71] Another Kievan Bolshevik, A. Gorovits, regarded even the nationalization of land, which the Ukrainian peasants' congress discussed at that time, as a threat to Russia, because "the Ukrainian lands are most fertile, and if the Ukrainian peasants, in view of the repressive measures the government applies against them, refuse to contribute grain, then the population of the northern provinces will be left without bread."[72]

For a long time the Kiev organization rejected Lenin's formula of self-determination. Piatakov argued, not without foundation, that this principle made the Bolsheviks look ridiculous: "We cannot rely upon this formula alone, for by saying to the oppressed nationalities, 'you have the right to secede, but we do not recommend it,' we place ourselves in a ridiculous position."[73] Another Kievan Bolshevik said that "the nation is an anachronism, the ideology of the past, ... one of those 'sacred things' that the proletariat must sweep away." He appealed for an outright condemnation of self-determination; the Bolsheviks should not fear being called imperialists.[74] Lenin's view did find some support, however; in Ukraine at that time M. Zarnytsin and Isaak Kreisberg backed Lenin. Speaking of self-determination, Zarnytsin contended that "there is only the question of the right to secession." "We agitate, not for secession, but only for the right to secession, but in every individual case the question must be considered separately, not from the point of view of national interests, but from the point of view of the international struggle of the working class for socialism." With respect to the secession of Ukraine the Bolsheviks at the time demanded a referendum in which both the Ukrainians and the national minorities would take part.[75]

The Kievan Bolsheviks came out against the First Universal. The Rada, they explained, was "soaked in chauvinism" and "relies on the kulaks," and in the Universal "there is no class position, only national aspirations are clearly expressed"; "the whole tone of the Universal is chauvinist, bourgeois."[76] They considered the self-determination of Ukraine possible only after "consistent democratization of the state," meaning "the transfer of power into the hands of the workers and the poorer peasantry."[77] On one point all Kievan Bolsheviks agreed—on the segregation of the proletariat from the bourgeoisie. Zarnytsin in his resolution stressed that "national emancipation is indissolubly connected with class emancipation; we appeal to the proletarians and the semi-proletarians of Ukraine to renounce cooperation with their national bourgeoisie."[78]

CHAPTER VI

The Formation of the Communist Party of Ukraine (CP[B]U)

Although the first Soviet government in Ukraine was established in December 1917, the Communist party of Ukraine was not created officially until July 1918—only after the first attempt to sovietize Ukraine had failed. In spite of the party's recognition of the right of nations to self-determination, including secession, and the recognition of formally independent Soviet republics in the borderlands, the RCP advocated a single centralized Communist party for the whole of former Russia. Only after the collapse of the first Soviet regime in Ukraine was a local party created with a delimited territory for its activity, but it was totally subordinated to the Russian party. The policy of the RCP towards the Communist parties in the borderlands reflected the party's genuine feeling on self-determination: if the RCP had espoused secession for the nationalities, it would have accepted the existence of separate parties for each nationality, just as it did in regard to other European nations. The independent existence of a nation without its own government (which the Communist parties in fact were) was an absurdity.

Soviet historiography has neglected the history of the Communist parties in the borderlands; during the Stalin period this topic was seldom even mentioned. There were attempts in the twenties to write the history of the Communist Party (Bolsheviks) of Ukraine, but the requirements of scholarship were subordinated to "the struggle with the Ukrainian nationalist deviation within the CP(B)U" as well as to an assault on that "manifestation of imperialist Russian chauvinism" that failed to distinguish between Ukraine and the districts of Penza and Tambov.[1] Every attempt of Soviet historians to separate the history of the CP(B)U from the history of the RCP or even to see differences between the revolutions in Ukraine and Russia met with merciless criticism from the RCP. Soviet historiography on the Ukrainian party passed through three stages: 1) the Skrypnyk period in Ukraine and the pre-Stalinist period in the Soviet Union (1922–33), when relative freedom of scholarship existed, and—thanks to the Ukrainianization process—the national aspect of Soviet rule in Ukraine was emphasized in historiography;[2] 2) the Postyshev period in Ukraine and the Stalin period in the USSR (1933–54), when a rigidly doctrinaire interpretation of history was inculcated, to the complete exclusion of the national factor;[3] 3) the Khrushchev period, from 1955 to the mid–1960s, when national factors and separate Communist parties in the republics were revived.[4] This last period may be characterized as a synthesis of the preceding trends. While stressing the indestructible ties of the Russian and the Ukrainian proletariats and the subordination of the Communist party of Ukraine to the RCP, the historiography of the Khrushchev period distorted the history of the CP(B)U less than did that of the Stalin period.

The historians of the CP(B)U are known to have suffered a great deal at the hands of the higher party organs. Moisei Ravich-Cherkassky was censured immediately after the publication of his work "not only for the errors and mistakes of this history, but also for having attempted to write it at all."[5] He was also criticized for his allegedly erroneous theory of the dual roots of the CP(B)U, for considering the CP(B)U a revolutionary union of the Russian and Ukrainian proletariats organized in the Russian and Ukrainian social democratic movements.[6] Matvii Iavorsky was liquidated in the thirties, and his works fell under anathema; he had dared to emphasize the "special characteristics" of Ukrainian Bolshevism.[7]

The roots of the Communist party in Ukraine must be sought in the original organizations of Russian social democracy that had existed in Ukraine. These organizations were far less numerous than in central Russia and were, to a greater degree than in Russia proper, under Menshevik influence. On the eve of the October revolution, the social democratic movement in Ukraine had three national trends. In one trend, represented by the USDWP, Ukrainian national aspirations were foremost; the RSDWP, with its Bolshevik and Menshevik factions represented the Russian trend; the Jews were represented by the Bund.

The Bolsheviks were so weak numerically in the first months of the revolution (March–July) that they were unable to set up their own organizations and had to share the organizational framework of the Mensheviks.[8] Sentiment in Bolshevik circles at that time ran against the independence of Ukraine and therefore against a distinct Ukrainian social democratic organization. The separation of Ukraine was considered a betrayal of the revolution, as was the separation of the Ukrainian party organization.[9] In consequence, the Bolshevik groups in Ukraine did not form a cohesive organization; they each had independent connections with the party CC in Petrograd. They never thought of themselves as something apart from the RSDWP; as one contemporary wrote: "The Bolsheviks were Russian social democrats who originated from the Russian Social Democratic Workers' Party."[10] The absence of a local political and organizational centre, however, made the activity of the Ukrainian Bolsheviks very clumsy, especially when they came into contact with a rather well-organized Ukrainian political centre, the Central Rada.

According to a Soviet historian of the CP(B)U, until the overthrow of the tsarist regime a Bolshevik centre was unnecessary in Ukraine, which had the same political task as the rest of Russia—the struggle against autocracy. This also justified the existence of a single, centralized RSDWP(B), which sought to "keep revolutionary Russian Marxism pure from Menshevik and national deviations." But after the February revolution, circumstances were supposed to have changed, and therefore the tactics of the party were supposed to change as well. Henceforward the differentiation of interests in Ukraine proceeded rapidly. In the same historian's opinion, circumstances compelled the party to create in Ukraine a separate Bolshevik centre to lead the struggle against the Russian and Ukrainian national bourgeoisie. Without breaking with the centre in Russia, "which supplied the general direction of the revolutionary struggle," the Ukrainian centre was to assume leadership with regard to "the Ukrainian realities." Thus the struggle "could not be simply transferred as a pattern from the north to the south."[11]

The First Attempt to Organize a Ukrainian Party

Bolshevik efforts towards unity within the region must not be equated with striving to create a Ukrainian Communist organization, let alone an independent Ukrainian Communist party. Very few Bolsheviks thought in these terms in the summer of 1917; some Bolsheviks came round to these ideas only under the pressure of events during the evacuation of Ukraine in March 1918. Generally, the Bolsheviks feared that the formation of a Ukrainian party organization would automatically lead down nationalist bypaths. In principle, if the Bolsheviks in Ukraine were to be true followers of Lenin, the creation of a separate party was incompatible with party statutes and therefore inadmissible. A centre for the Bolsheviks of Ukraine could be created only as a regional association, whose powers would be the same as those of, say, Tambov. The Bolsheviks arrived at even such innocent "separatism" very slowly and reluctantly.

The regional conference of the RSDWP(B) of the southwestern region, which took place on 23 July 1917, may be regarded as the first attempt to form such an association.[12] A resolution of this conference set up a regional committee of nine members.[13] "For convenience in work," national sections were to be formed and publications issued in the languages of the nationalities that populated the "southwestern region." *Golos sotsial-demokrata* was to become the organ of the Kiev committee and of the regional committee of the southwestern region.

At the same time, a regional conference of the Donets and Kryvyi Rih basins elected a regional committee headed by Fedor Sergeev (Artem). This committee directed the activities of the Bolshevik organizations on the Left Bank of the Dnieper.[14] Thus already at this time two Bolshevik centres came into existence in Ukraine, and the Ukrainian Bolsheviks were long to remain divided into two opposing camps.[15] The Kiev committee had far fewer members than the Donets and Kryvyi Rih committee;[16] moreover, its activity in the predominantly agrarian part of Ukraine influenced its character and reduced its effectiveness. This may help explain the partial cooperation of the Kiev Bolsheviks with the Central Rada.

Unification of the Bolsheviks continued to be a burning question, because the committees proved ineffective and the Central Rada was increasingly assuming leadership in Ukraine. On 9 November the newspaper, *Proletarskaia mysl*, wrote that all Bolshevik organizations in Ukraine should unite in a regional organization that would enter the RSDWP(B) as one of its sections. "This centre," the paper said, "will bring uniformity into the actions of organizations that are at present disunited and will conduct a resolute struggle against the policy of nationalism and chauvinism." Agitation and propaganda were to be adapted to local peculiarities and conducted in the vernacular.[17] A letter from the regional committee of the southwestern region to the central committee of the RSDWP(B) announced that the committee had decided to convoke a regional party congress to solve the questions of government in Ukraine, the attitude towards the Central Rada, and especially the creation of a centre in Ukraine for all party organizations in the region. The letter said this was necessary because of the chauvinism and the corrupting influence of the Ukrainian socialist parties and the Central

Rada; a single party centre in Ukraine was required to counterbalance "the bourgeois nationalist Ukrainian social democratic party. We ask for your approval and directives in connection with the forthcoming congress."[18] Thus the main motive for creating a party centre was the struggle against the Central Rada.

The demands of the party organizations in Ukraine for the creation of a single centre were discussed at the meeting of the central committee of the RSDWP(B) on 12 December 1917. The Ukrainian Bolsheviks had requested "permission to call themselves the SD Workers' Party of Ukraine, since the *Rosiiska* SDWP means in Ukrainian 'Russian.'"[19] The central committee resolved, "in view of the need to discuss all data 'for' and 'against,' and because of the lack of time," to refer this question to the bureau of the CC comprising Stalin, Lenin, Trotsky, and Sverdlov.[20] Speaking for the bureau, Sverdlov professed no objection to the convocation of a regional congress of party organizations for the elaboration of common tactics. But as to a separate party, Sverdlov wrote: "*The creation of a separate, Ukrainian party*, whatever it might be called, whatever programme it might adopt, *we consider undesirable*. Therefore we suggest that activities in this direction not be pursued. A different matter is the convocation of a regional congress or conference that we would regard as an ordinary regional congress of our party. There can be no objection against calling the region not southwestern, but Ukrainian."[21] This was the same old theory of the indivisibility of the RSDWP(B) that had been proclaimed, against the wishes of the Bund, even before the revolution. As to replacing "southwestern region" with "Ukraine," even many Russian nationalists at that time were making the same change in terminology.

The central committee of the RSDWP(B) long vetoed a separate regional party for Ukraine. Only after a Soviet government was set up in Kharkiv to counterbalance the Central Rada did the CC agree to "an independent SD organization." A letter of the CC RSDWP(B) of 18 December 1917 to the Poltava committee[22] of the party said: "We did not reply to your question about Ukraine, for up to now no final decision has been passed by the CC. Now the question has been resolved as follows: Ukraine as an independent *unit* may have its independent SD organization, and for this reason it may call itself the Social Democratic Workers' Party of Ukraine, but since they [the Bolsheviks of Ukraine] do not wish to secede from the common party, they exist with the same rights as an independent region."[23] According to this letter, the Bolsheviks of Ukraine "do not *wish* to secede from the common party"; but the letter of the secretary of the CC RSDWP(B), Elena Stasova, dated 26 December 1917, said that the Ukrainian organization "*must* be included in our party" and "it *must* exist with the rights of local organization."[24] The CC did not agree to the organization of an independent party in Ukraine, since its attitude towards the self-determination of the Ukrainians and other nationalities precluded this. A Soviet scholar writes that the independence of the party organization in Ukraine was "a new and complicated question for our party, since it was closely connected with the question of the state organization of the peoples of Russia .... The creation of the Communist party of Ukraine could not be separated from the problem of the self-determination of the Ukrainian people, of the creation of Ukrainian Soviet statehood."[25] In spite of the opposition of the centralists, however, the Bolsheviks of Ukraine slowly approached territorial unity of the party organizations.

The Kiev Conference

An important step towards the creation of a separate Communist party in Ukraine was the regional conference of the southwestern region, the so-called Kiev conference, which took place on 16–19 December 1917. Present were forty-seven delegates, representing twenty-four organizations of seven districts (Kiev, Katerynoslav, Kherson, Podillia, Chernihiv, Poltava, and Volhynia) and two military organizations, which together represented 18,021 members.[26] Since the Kharkiv and Donets basin organizations, the most numerous and the most revolutionary ones, were not represented at the conference, it did not have an all-Ukrainian significance and was not binding for the whole of Ukraine. One of the early historians of the CP(B)U explained that "Kiev and its district, being populated predominantly by the Ukrainian peasantry, were in the grip of the nationalist madness (*ugar*), while Katerynoslav felt it practically not at all, and Kharkiv and the Donets basin still less."[27]

The conference engaged in a heated debate over the creation of a single centre for Ukraine. One group, led by Evgeniia Bosh and Vladimir Aussem, defended the *edinaia i nedelimaia* position and opposed a single centre or changing the name of the existing organization. Some delegates considered the very idea of changing the name "heretical." Others considered changing the name of the organization to "Ukrainian" impossible, "because it is chauvinism" and because the Bolsheviks "could be confused with other Ukrainian parties." Moreover, if the name "Russian party" was harmful, "it will be of no help to us if we add to the heading 'RSDWP' the subheading 'SD of Ukraine.'" Bosh opposed establishing a separate party when the Bolsheviks were marching towards socialism, towards "a real uniting of the proletariat." At this time it was "ridiculous to speak of a national party." Volodymyr Zatonsky, Leonid Piatakov, and Vasyl Shakhrai, however, favoured the change of name. In view of the growth of Ukrainian nationalism, they argued, a separate party was imperative. Shakhrai, who read a report on organizational matters, said that because Ukraine had separated as a federated republic, the party had to adapt to this circumstance and organize a regional centre to direct the party's work in Ukraine. But he stressed that the organizational principle was territorial, not national. Shakhrai proposed to call the party the "RSDWP of the Bolsheviks in Ukraine." Its publications should be in Ukrainian; the party organ, he said, should adapt itself to the peasantry and be written "in simple language." L. Piatakov supported Shakhrai. The old name, RSDWP, he said "hinders our work. It is very difficult to work under the name of the Russian Bolsheviks; it repels the masses from us. If we stay under our former name we shall always be the Russians." He therefore proposed calling the Bolshevik organization in Ukraine, at least temporarily, "the Social Democracy of Ukraine," and if Ukraine declared itself independent—"the USDWP." Zatonsky likewise felt that "the name 'Russian' must be thrown out." Gorovits, arguing with Bosh and her followers, explained that "nobody has mentioned the organization of a national party. It is a matter of a territorial organization on the pattern of the Latvian, Polish SD, etc .... The SD of Ukraine will be a regional organization of the RSDWP .... It will not be an independent party."[28]

The conference elected a "chief committee" consisting of Aussem, Shakhrai, Lapchynsky, Bosh, Zatonsky, V. M. Aleksandrov, Ivan Kulyk, A. Grinevich, and A. Gorovits; V. S. Liuksemburg, Ian Hamarnyk, L. E. Galperin, and Leonid Piatakov were elected as candidates to the committee.[29] The composition of this committee did not strengthen the idea of a separate party, since those opposed held half the seats. Although the conference adopted Shakhrai's proposal to rename the organization, its relationship to the CC RSDWP(B) remained unchanged. At that time Shakhrai and Lapchynsky alone were in favour of the federative principle, in respect to both the state and the party.

The majority of the Bolsheviks in Ukraine were then advocating one indivisible Russian Soviet republic and a single Communist party. This was in harmony with the CC RSDWP(B), which defended the party's indivisibility. Only after the bitter experience of the overthrow of Soviet power in Ukraine in April 1918 did the majority of the Bolsheviks from the Right Bank force through a separate party.

The Taganrog Conference

During the evacuation of the Bolshevik government and party functionaries from Ukraine in April 1918, a conference of the Central Executive Committee of Ukraine (TsIKU) took place in Taganrog (Katerynoslav province). This conference dissolved the TsIKU and the People's Secretariat and formed the "insurgence nine." It also decided to form an independent Communist party of Ukraine.[30] There were about seventy[31] participants at the conference, representing the Bolshevik organizations of Kiev, Kharkiv, Katerynoslav, the Donets basin, Vinnytsia, Chernihiv, Poltava, Kherson, and Ielysavethrad. As Ravich-Cherkassky later wrote, the conference gathered "by chance," without previous preparation, in connection with the arrival of the TsIKU and the People's Secretariat. Its decision to create an independent Communist party for Ukraine was not unexpected: "Historical necessity impelled the Communists of Ukraine towards the creation of a single party centre."[32] Disagreeing with Erde,[33] who regarded even the creation of the Kiev chief committee as premature, Ravich-Cherkassky argued that since there existed in Ukraine the government of the People's Secretariat, there was no reason why there should not also exist a party centre to direct that government. Only a blind man could not see, he continued, the necessity of an independent Communist party in a Ukraine that had proclaimed its independence.[34] The historian Iavorsky likewise contended that under the special circumstances that had arisen in Ukraine the formation "of a single centre and a single organization ... now became obvious and indisputable for all the participants of the conference."[35] As the records of the conference show, however, the creation of a separate party aroused dissension and provoked the Katerynoslav delegation into leaving the conference.[36] In the view of this delegation, the Ukrainian proletariat had no exceptional tasks differing from those of the Russian proletariat. Ukraine was simply one sector in the counter-revolutionary front and war had to be waged in alliance with the proletariat of Petrograd and Moscow. The Katerynoslav delegation therefore proposed: "To create an autonomous party with its own central committee and congresses, but subordinated to the common central committee and to the congresses of the Russian Communist party."[37] This motion, made by Kviring, was in the spirit of the "one and indivisible Russia." It was rejected even though, according to Ravich-Cherkassky, it represented the views of more than four-fifths of all party members in Ukraine, including most proletarian members.[38]

An entirely opposite position characterized a section of the Kievans, the so-called Poltavians, represented, among others, by Mykola Skrypnyk and

Vasyl Shakhrai. They proposed creating an independent Communist party with its own central committee and congresses, but connected with the Russian Communist party through the International Commission (the Third International).[39] The conference adopted this motion, twenty-six votes against twenty-one.[40] This was, in the eyes of the Russian Bolsheviks, an entirely "nationalistic" position. More moderate Soviet historians have explained that its representatives had considered the peasantry the mainstay of the revolution, and that the motion had been adopted under pressure from the Ukrainian social democrats-independentists.[41] Kviring considered this position not only a manifestation "of the Ukrainian deviation, but also an attempt of the 'Kievans,' i.e., of the left Communists (the Bukharinite, anti-Brest [Litovsk] Communism) to secure themselves organizationally against the Leninist majority of the RCP."[42] It is obvious, however, that nationalism did not cause the Kiev delegates, led by Piatakov, to vote for an independent Ukrainian organization; this had never been their policy. Skrypnyk tried to moderate the impression of separatism and nationalism by proposing the name "the Communist Party (Bolsheviks) of Ukraine." This, however, did not spare him attacks from the Russian Bolsheviks or accusations of nationalism.[43] The resolution to establish an independent party, then, was supported chiefly by two groups who found a common language on that question: the leftists or Kievans and those Ukrainian elements in the party inclined to nationalism, such as Shakhrai. According to Skrypnyk, the resolution about the independence of the CP(B)U was also approved by the RCP itself, a fact which came to light only in 1936.[44]

The conference elected an organizational bureau with seven members: Skrypnyk, Piatakov, Zatonsky, Hamarnyk, Kreisberg, Andrei Bubnov, and Stanislav Kosior, only two of whom were Ukrainians. Its tasks were to convoke a party congress in Moscow on 20 June 1918, to begin negotiations with the Ukrainian left SDs-independentists on the subject of unification, and to elaborate the party statutes.[45] The bureau consisted mostly of the Kievans who determined party policy towards Ukraine until the second congress, when the Katerynoslavians gained the upper hand. The resolution of the Taganrog conference completely contradicted party doctrine about unity on the territory of former Russia. The sixth conference of the RSDWP(B) pointed this out, expressly stating that only regional organizations, subordinated directly to the CC RSDWP(B), could exist in the borderlands.

The First Congress of the CP(B)U

In the spring of 1918 events in Ukraine developed unfavourably for the Bolsheviks. Both the party and the government took refuge in Russia; only insignificant illegal organizations, unable to generate much political activity, remained in Ukraine. Skoropadsky's regime took control in April, and Ukraine was recognized, both *de facto* and *de jure*, even by the Council of People's Commissars, as an independent state. Ukrainian Bolsheviks in exile suffered from internal discord, chiefly between "leftists" and "rightists." The former felt it necessary to continue a revolutionary struggle against the Central Powers and Skoropadsky's regime in Ukraine, while the rightists, accepting Lenin's position that Soviet Russia needed a respite from war, felt that without Russian military assistance any attempt at revolution in Ukraine was mere adventure.[46]

As to a separate party for Ukraine, the first congress retreated to the old line, and the CP(B)U now became dependent on the CC RCP. Two factions emerged both over the question of a separate party and over the relationship between Ukraine and Russia, although in the latter question the division between the two groups was not clearly defined. As for the independence of the party, the Taganrog resolution had been completely revised. Skrypnyk's proposal, in which he again defended the independence of the CP(B)U, was rejected. His motion had run as follows: "The Communist organizations of Ukraine are uniting in a separate Communist Party (Bolshevik) of Ukraine, with its own central committee and congress, formally tied with the Russian Communist party through the International Commission of the Third International."[47] Later, after Skrypnyk's suicide, when these documents were being published, the editors accused Skrypnyk of "errors of a nationalist character ... which later took the form of an open, clearly defined nationalist deviation."[48] Kviring's counter-motion was adopted instead. It said that because the struggle of the proletariat in Ukraine was inseparably connected with the struggle of the Russian proletariat and because not one of the concrete questions before the Communists of Ukraine could be solved correctly "without reference to the tactics of the Russian party, ... the all-Ukrainian congress of the party has resolved: 1) To unite the Communist party organizations of Ukraine in an autonomous (as regards local matters) Communist party of Ukraine, with its own central committee and congresses; it shall, however, form part of a single Russian Communist party, subordinated in matters of programme to the general congresses of the Russian Communist party, and in general political matters to the CC RCP(B). 2) To charge the CC RCP(B) to put the CP(B)U organizationally and tactically into touch with the Communist parties of Germany, Austria, and the occupied countries."[49] This resolution was adopted at a closed session after stormy debates. According to Popov: "The Katerynoslavians, relying on the support of the CC RCP(B), demanded, as an ultimatum, the adoption of this resolution. The leaders of the Kievans were compelled to give in after prolonged resistance."[50]

The question of the independence of the CP(B)U was at that time of prime importance for the Katerynoslavians. It would determine whether the Ukrainian party would pursue an independent revolutionary policy in Ukraine or whether the Ukrainian revolution would be part of the Russian one, led by a Ukrainian organization under the immediate leadership of the RCP. It would determine, in other words, whether the CP(B)U was to be guided by the Leninist majority of the RCP or by the left Communists,[51] a question connected with the problem of the Brest Litovsk peace and with the attitude of the Ukrainian Bolsheviks towards the "respite." For this reason, at the first congress of the CP(B)U, Lenin supported the Katerynoslavians who, besides, held a position more favourable for party unity.[52] The question of peace thinned the ranks of the Kievans considerably, since Skrypnyk and his adherents proposed a separate, Leninist resolution,[53] which collected the most votes (forty-three in favour and six against, with three abstentions).[54] The split among the Ukrainian Bolsheviks was not connected with the split in the RCP. The leftists in Ukraine advocated a separate party for various reasons. Some of them, like Skrypnyk and Zatonsky, seriously considered an independent Soviet Ukrainian state, with a separate party making use of the revolutionary mood of the peasantry. Bubnov, Piatakov, and other leftists opposed Lenin on the question of the Brest Litovsk peace. The rightists shared Lenin's view of a separate party, but their mood was one of discouragement; they had lost confidence in their own Ukrainian Bolshevik forces and relied only on the forces of the Red Army, so that now their attitude was pro-Russian and extremely anti-Ukrainian. Because they feared the national spirit reigning among the Ukrainian peasantry, they stood apart from that class. Thanks to the intervention of the RCP and of Lenin himself, the rightists, who had been outvoted on the question of the revolution, did not leave the congress.[55] The Russophile proclivities of the Katerynoslavians and their underestimation of the peasant and national questions derived, according to Popov, from the social basis of their organization. He wrote that the Katerynoslavians relied mainly upon the organizations of the Donets basin and Katerynoslav, where the Russian proletariat predominated, and hence they were detached from the Ukrainian peasantry.[56] The attitude of the Katerynoslavians or rightists created a gulf for a long time to come between the Bolsheviks and the Ukrainian peasant masses.

The first congress elected a central committee of the CP(B)U comprising I. K. Amosov (Tochilin), Andrei Bubnov, Opanas Butsenko, R. B. Farbman (Rafail), Sh. A. Gruzman (Aleksandr), L. I. Kartvelishvili (Lavrentii), Stanislav Kosior, Isaak Kreisberg (Isaakov), Emmanuil Kviring, Iurii Lutovinov, Georgii Piatakov, P. L. Rovner (Akim), Isaak Shvarts (Semen), L. L. Tarsky, and Volodymyr Zatonsky, with the candidates Petro Slynko (a former Ukrainian SD independentist) and Mykhail Maiorov (Maior-Biberman); out of fifteen members, three were Ukrainians.[57] The majority of the CC were leftists. Significantly, such pillars of the Bolsheviks of Ukraine as Skrypnyk[58] and Ia. A. Epshtein (Iakovlev) were not elected to the CC. The CP(B)U thus found itself under the leadership of the Kievans, and Piatakov was elected party secretary.[59] Another Kievan, Bubnov, was elected chairman of the military revolutionary committee, which was supposed to have been created to replace the "insurgence nine" and the People's Secretariat.[60]

The policy of the CC of the CP(B)U was to urge an insurrection against the German forces. A rising was in fact attempted in August 1918, but ended in a fiasco. Only the northern parts of Chernihiv province reacted to the order of the CC CP(B)U of 5 August, calling for a general rising, while the rest of Ukraine ignored the order.[61] The Bolsheviks of the Kievan group overestimated both the strength of the insurgent movement and the sympathy the party enjoyed among the peasantry. The strategem of making use of the Ukrainian peasantry's discontent with the German occupation and with Skoropadsky's regime did not succeed. Because of the uprising, the party cells throughout Ukraine were completely routed; this issue supplied the Katerynoslavians with ammunition to criticize the existing CC at the second congress.

The Second Congress of the CP(B)U

The second congress of the CP(B)U, like the first, took place in Moscow, in exile. It was at a time when the Hetmanate felt secure under the reliable protection of the German forces. The workers' movement had been disarmed politically and had in many instances taken the political line of the Mensheviks. "The proletariat still did not believe in its powers; it waited for salvation from Soviet Russia and looked askance at the Ukrainian countryside which had so recently betrayed the revolution, remaining neutral in the unequal struggle of the revolutionary working class with ... German imperialism."[62] The congress met from 17 to 22 October 1918. One hundred twenty-five delegates represented over five thousand party members.[63] The Katerynoslavians retaliated at this congress by condemning the policy and tactics of the preceding CC CP(B)U led by Piatakov and Bubnov. The main target of criticism was the unsuccessful uprising in Ukraine. The Katerynoslavians were supported by Kamenev, who represented the CC RCP at the congress as a mediator (or more correctly as a supervisor). He condemned the insurgent tactics of the Kievans and their attitude in favour of the Ukrainian peasantry, warning that such an attitude caused the party to deviate from the genuine road of class struggle to the road of Ukrainian nationalism and the petty bourgeoisie. He asserted, in the style of the Katerynoslavians, that the road to a Soviet Kiev lay not over Starodub but over Rostov.[64] In a word, all hopes lay in the Red Army of Russia. "The internal forces of the Ukrainian revolution," remarked Popov, "had gotten lost somewhere."[65] To accuse the party of Ukrainian chauvinism, while the party and almost all its leaders stood on the imperialist Russian platform, was hypocritical.[66] The critics of Piatakov and Kamenev admit that, on the whole, the second congress "did not, after all, devote enough attention to the national question, did not work out any concrete measures for the realization of the Leninist national policy in Ukraine."[67] However, since the Russophile elements, i.e., Katerynoslavians like Kviring and Epshtein, were supported by the CC RCP, Lenin shares in the responsibility for these deviations of the CP(B)U. The subsequent policy of the CP(B)U, guided by the new CC CP(B)U, was completely in keeping with the spirit of the resolutions of the congress. In the opinion of the Bolsheviks themselves the task of the new leadership of the party was "to prepare the advance of the Russian Soviet army into Ukraine"; and therefore the work of the party was concentrated in large industrial centres, in order that, having taken them, "the Soviet army could immediately lean on the support of the masses of the workers."[68]

The new CC CP(B)U comprised Stalin, Sergeev (Artem), Shvarts (Semen), Epshtein, Kviring, Ia. N. Drobnis (Samuil), O. I. Zimak, L. L. Tarsky, Sh. A. Gruzman, Samuil Zaks (Gladnev), and N. I. Bezchetvertnoi (Nikolai). All except Stalin belonged to the Katerynoslavian faction. The Kievans withdrew their candidates and took no part in the elections of the CC; some were nonetheless also elected to the CC on Kviring's motion: Piatakov, Zatonsky, M. V. Reut, Petro Slynko. Only two of the fifteen members were Ukrainians. The following were elected as candidates: Rovner, A. M. Zharko, Skrypnyk, M. Borisov (Zhuk), Morshin, Kashko, Zolotov, T. I. Kharechko, Lazar, A. O. Blyznychenko, Hamarnyk, Kosior, Vinokur, Luhovy.[69] Stalin possibly owed his election to the CC to his recent appointment by the CC RCP as permanent liaison officer for Ukraine. Somewhat later he also entered the revolutionary committee of Ukraine. Thus the leadership of the CP(B)U passed into the hands of the Russophiles. All resolutions adopted by the congress had a Katerynoslavian colouring. One resolution said: "The chief tasks of the CP(B)U are uniting Ukraine with Russia, deepening and broadening the party machinery, transferring the centre of gravity of party operations to the territory of Ukraine itself, and concentrating party forces primarily in the working class centres. In all its prepatory work the party must lean upon the force of proletarian Russia, coordinate its measures with, and subordinate them to, the CC RCP, and choose the moment for a general offensive solely in agreement with it [the CC RCP]."[70]

The new CC introduced certain innovations in organization. Its activities were divided into "abroad and underground." The former department was to be conducted by the foreign bureau, comprising Stalin, Kviring, and Artem, which at the same time directed the general work of the party in Ukraine; it was thus the highest authority in the CP(B)U. For underground work an executive bureau was elected: Gladnev, Epshtein, and Tarsky. Agitation and propaganda were to be directed by Piatakov. The central revolutionary committee was led by Aussem, Bubnov, and Piatakov.[71]

Relations between the CP(B)U and the RCP were not discussed at the congress. This question was decided solely on the authority of the representative of the CC RCP, Sverdlov, who unambiguously let it be understood that the CC RCP would tolerate no changes in the existing relationship. He said that "if at present we are still going to insist on the preservation of formal independence for the Communist party of Ukraine, at the same time every one of us must be clearly aware that this is the formal side of the matter. In essence, we have been and are a single Russian Communist party .... Of whatever parts this party may be composed, the centre regards these disjointed parts as those of a single organism."[72] In a word, the CP(B)U was presented with no alternative but to become a cog in the RCP machinery, subordinated in political and organizational questions to the CC RCP. Sverdlov, when formulating the status of the CP(B)U, acted in obedience to the instructions of Lenin and the CC RCP. After this, the CP(B)U remained an autonomous part of the RCP with the rights of a regional organization.

The Third Congress of the CP(B)U

The leadership of the CP(B)U that was elected at the second congress actively helped the Red Army during the winter of 1918–19 to install the Soviet regime in Ukraine. However, only from January 1919 did the forces of Soviet Russia begin to advance successfully on Ukraine. Kharkiv was taken on 3 January and Kiev on 4 February. In the spring of 1919 the whole of Eastern Ukraine, including the Kiev district, was in Bolshevik hands. The Soviet regime was introduced with a government led at first by Piatakov, and then by Rakovsky. These Red Army successes permitted the convocation of the third congress of the CP(B)U on 1 March in Kharkiv. As at its predecessors, here too prevailed a tense atmosphere of struggle between the leftists and rightists, which was again to be solved by the representative of the CC RCP, Sverdlov. Now he too sided with the Katerynoslavians, reiterating the need for the subordination of the CP(B)U to the CC RCP. He divided the programme of the CP(B)U into organizational and political activity. "When it is a matter of the political line of the CC of the Communists of Ukraine," Sverdlov said, "it is necessary to connect it in the closest possible way with the work of the central committee of the Russian Communist party." Everyone knew, he continued, "that a whole series of basic principles and directives are not being introduced by the local [committees] nor by the central committee of the party of Ukraine, but by the common central committee of the party. Nor could it have been otherwise not only in Ukraine, but also in Latvia, Lithuania, and Estonia; in all places and everywhere that we have created independent Soviet republics, we have left our sole Communist party; we have preserved its unity, [while] the general political leadership has been in the hands of the central committee of the party."[73] The status of the CP(B)U remained the same. Rakovsky, who was now a member of the CP(B)U and the head of the Soviet Ukrainian government, said: "The Communist party of Ukraine regards itself as a member of a single Communist International. It maintains close organizational ties with the Communist party of Russia, whose southern detachment is the CP(B)U."[74] Manoeuvering for status among the CP(B)U and other parties ended at the eighth congress of the RCP, which took place a few weeks after the congress of the CP(B)U.[75] The CC CP(B)U elected at the third congress was even more Russophile than the one elected by the second. It comprised Piatakov, Bubnov, V. Meshcheriakov, Kliment Voroshilov, Khristian Rakovsky, Hamarnyk, Oleksander Khmelnytsky, Kviring, Farbman (Rafail), Andrei Ivanov, Zatonsky, Kharechko, Rovner, Drobnis, and Stanislav Kosior (three Ukrainians out of fifteen members).[76] Neither Slynko nor Skrypnyk, who were Ukrainians not only by ethnic origin, but also by conscious choice,[77] were included. This congress was marked by the decline of the old factional struggle. The policy of the CC was completely subordinated to the CC RCP and was determined chiefly by opposition to Ukrainian peasant risings and to the Directory. The military command of the Red Army made the CC CP(B)U completely subordinate to itself. At the end of the summer (1919) the CP(B)U again left the territory of Ukraine.

The Homel Conference

The fall of the second Soviet republic in Ukraine at the end of the summer of 1919 had far-reaching repercussions for the CP(B)U. In accordance with a directive of the CC RCP, the CC CP(B)U was dissolved and its members sent to other work.[78] It was replaced by the Moscow-based "rear bureau," consisting of Kosior, Farbman, and Drobnis.[79] According to Lapchynsky, the Ukrainian Communists were very despondent and defeatist because of "the difficulty of operations in Ukraine amidst the conflagration of *kulak* risings everywhere, under the ever-growing pressure of the White offensive." Now the so-called federalists, led by Slynko and Lapchynsky, began to oppose the official policy of the party in Ukraine and convoked a party conference in Homel, in Chernihiv province, in the last days of November. They felt that "it is impossible to pursue the policy of *edinaia i nedelimaia*; that the Soviet Ukrainian republic, while remaining in the closest contact with Russia, must exist as a separate state unit, corresponding to the particular, specific needs of the country; that the Ukrainian party, while united in a single Communist organization with the party of other union republics on the principles of democratic centralism, must have the possibility of pursuing independent work within the boundaries of Ukraine under the leadership of its own CC, as applicable to its peculiarities."[80] The conference was mainly attended by the Communists of Volhynia and Chernihiv provinces, as well as Manuilsky, Zatonsky, Kosior,[81] Iurii Kotsiubynsky, Musulbas, Vasyl Poraiko, S. Odintsov, and others.[82] This meeting did not have the character of an official party conference, but rather of a semi-private meeting. But it helped clarify the position of the federalists towards party policy in Ukraine and the relationship between the RCP and the CP(B)U. Lapchynsky's theses on party structure said that for the success of the struggle for Soviet power in Ukraine it was necessary to unite all Communist forces in one party, "the Ukrainian Communist Party of Bolsheviks," a completely independent section of the International. Its supreme organ was to be the all-party congress. The UCP(B) was to have at its disposal all party workers within the boundaries of Ukraine and was to unite all Communists working there, irrespective of nationality; it was also to unite all parties that worked in Ukraine and shared the principles of the Communist International. Lapchynsky felt that the CC had to convoke a broad party conference in the near future.[83] This was similar to the resolution of the Taganrog conference. There were also other parallels between the Homel and the Taganrog conferences. Both conferences took place in periods of the Soviet regime's decline, at times of despondency among the Communists. Both conferences reflected some reconsideration of the Ukrainian national movement. Both conferences gave voice to separatist tendencies.

After the Homel conference, the Communists of Ukraine never again seriously raised the question of the CP(B)U's independence. After the third congress, a series of conferences—not congresses—began, since regional organizations like the CP(B)U had no right to convoke congresses.

The Fourth Conference of the CP(B)U

The fourth conference of the CP(B)U took place on 16 March 1920, that is, after the self-criticism of the Communists on the Ukrainian question.[84] It was directed by a presidium consisting of Stalin, Petrovsky, Rakovsky, Drobnis, Farbman, Feliks Kon, Ivanov, Dorogan, and Vladimir Kosior[85]—almost exclusively former Katerynoslavians, with an admixture of ordinary advocates of *edinaia i nedelimaia*. Only one, Petrovsky, was a Ukrainian. The conference began in a tense atmosphere. The work of the preceding CC was criticized again, especially its dissolution during the offensive of Denikin and Petliura. According to Ravich-Cherkassky, the meetings of the conference "were turned into a continuous uproar." Lifshits criticized the former CC for having dissolved itself in obedience to a directive from Moscow, which had not appointed it; the members of the former CC "had been appointed by the third all-Ukrainian congress, to whom they had to submit their report, and nobody could dissolve them."[86] Another delegate to the conference remarked that "the CC CP(B)U was merely a fiction, it is merely a signboard," since "the composition of the CC has been changed just as some cavilling lady changes her maid"; he demanded that the party be freed from advocates of "cringing and servility."[87] Another speaker charged that "the northern [Russian party] workers have ruined our Ukrainian revolution."[88] On the other hand, D. Kin, Sinev, Rachkovsky, and others defended the policy of the CC, because the party in Ukraine was too weak to be an independent factor in the revolution. Rachkovsky called an independent CC "a luxury," since in any case "all political activity is determined in Moscow by the CC RCP." Bosh also spoke against the criticism directed at the centre.[89] Kosior complained that over Ukraine hovered "some curse" "that does not permit working in agreement"; local organizations not only failed to support the CC but even worked against it. He recalled "the harmful activity of the federalists in the Volhynian organization" who were of the opinion that "Soviet Russia grows fat at the expense of the hungry workers of Ukraine" and Ukraine was falling "into the role of an occupied country."[90] Rakovsky said: "We have no proletarian party in Ukraine; we have an intelligentsia and petty-bourgeois (*meshchanskaia*) party that is afraid of Communist tasks."[91] This most dramatic of conferences was also the most antagonistic to the RCP.

The CP(B)U showed such resistance at this conference because an opposition to "democratic centralism" had emerged in Ukraine. The opposition consisted of such functionaries sent to Ukraine from Russia as Timofei Sapronov, Lev Sosnovsky, Kharechko, and Nikolaev. They opposed centralism in the party, administration, and factories.[92] The principle of centralism was advocated at the conference by Stalin, who spoke on behalf of the CC RCP.[93] He proposed the creation of a "labour army" to raise the productivity of the Donets basin and other industrial regions in Ukraine. According to this plan joint direction of enterprises would be replaced by one-man management (*edinonachalie*).[94] Sapronov protested against this principle, since this "will create a whole army of 'bureaucrats by appointment,'" who would oust the trade unions from control over production. "Only the collegiate principle will enable the working class, while taking part in industry, to exercise control over the specialists."[95]

The opposition mastered the situation completely and not only condemned the activity of the old CC but elected the new CC CP(B)U almost exclusively from its own ranks: Piatakov, Petrovsky, Ivanov (Aleksei), Zatonsky, Hamarnyk, Drobnis, Farbman (Rafail), Sapronov, Voroshilov, Kviring, Sergei Minin, Ganzei, Vladimir Kosior, Kharechko, Blakytny, Oleksander Shumsky, and Vlas Chubar (six Ukrainians out of seventeen members).[96] Popov stressed later that Petrovsky, Chubar, and the former Borotbists, Blakytny and Shumsky, withdrew their candidatures to protest the factional character of the election.[97] It is interesting that the most prominent leaders of the party in Ukraine—Rakovsky, Manuilsky, S. Kosior, and Iakovlev (Epshtein)—were not elected to the new CC. Ravich-Cherkassky later wrote that it was in fact difficult to tell whether the opposition was directed against the old CC or merely against the above-mentioned "central figures."[98]

The CC RCP opposed the decisions of the fourth conference. The conflict within the CP(B)U was exposed at the ninth congress of the RCP (29 March – 5 April 1920). At the congress the representatives of the CP(B)U, Iakovlev and Bubnov, criticized the policy of the CC RCP towards Ukraine and particularly towards the CP(B)U. Iakovlev stressed that the CC RCP had disbanded the CC CP(B)U in a rather clumsy fashion, and that instead of creating a strong organization, Moscow used Ukraine as a post for Communists who for one reason or another the CC RCP found unsuitable. "Ukraine," he complained, "is being turned into a place of deportation." Bubnov also criticized the CC RCP's policy towards Ukraine, remarking that the CC RCP had dispersed the Ukrainian CC and sent its members to subordinate positions in the interior of Russia. Thus "the CC [RCP(B)] continues its policy of disbanding the central institutions and of weakening Communism in Ukraine."[99]

Lenin, replying to this criticism and referring generally to the character of the fourth conference of the CP(B)U, declared that the RCP did not recognize the resolutions of the Ukrainian conference which "criticized comrade Rakovsky and baited him in a completely inadmissible fashion." He accused the leaders of that conference of having disruptive elements hiding behind them, "elements of the petty bourgeoisie (*meshchanstvo*) and otamanism, which are still very strong in Ukraine."[100]

At this ninth congress of the RCP Lenin proposed creating a "temporary organ," which was to comprise two members of the old CC CP(B)U, two of the new CC, and Shumsky from the Borotbists.[101] However, the CC RCP decided on 5 April 1920 to dissolve the CC CP(B)U that the conference had elected and "to create a temporary CC CPU of such a composition as may reflect the will of the overwhelming majority of the RCP as it has been expressed at the last congress of the party." This "temporary" CC CPU comprised Sergeev (Artem), Blakytny, Zatonsky, Zalutsky, Stanislav Kosior, Feliks Kon, Manuilsky, Minin, Petrov, Rakovsky, Chubar, Shumsky, and Iakovlev.[102] Of thirteen CC members only five were Ukrainians. By this decision the CC RCP hoped "to put an end to the squabble that is demoralizing Communist circles, and to secure unity and consistency in the pursuit of the Soviet and party policy in Ukraine."[103] The temporary CC was given a directive to purge the party ranks of "petty-bourgeois, intelligentsia, and semi-intelligentsia elements," and to carry out within a month the re-registration of all members of "the regional Ukrainian organization."[104] The purge that took place after this directive resulted in the exclusion from the CP(B)U of 21,430 members, i.e., 22 per cent of all party members.[105] To secure a free field of action for the new CC, the CC RCP decided "to transfer from

Ukraine for work in Great Russia those responsible party workers whose active participation in the struggle, which is as yet new (*svezhaia*), would inevitably render more difficult their harmonious and concerted work within the party and Soviet institutions on the basis of decisions passed by the ninth congress of the party."[106]

To obliterate the bad impression created by this radical intervention in the CP(B)U's internal affairs, the CC RCP sent Zinovev to Ukraine, who "explained" to the local Bolsheviks that the CP(B)U was merely a regional organization of the RCP, and Ukraine was merely one of "the largest regions of our federative republic." Zinovev's declaration was characteristic not only of his own views on Ukraine but also of the views of most leaders of the RCP. Zinovev, in his speech at the fourth all-Ukrainian congress of soviets (May 1920), sharply attacked the "decentralizers" in the "democratic opposition" for their exaggerated complaints of centralism in Ukraine. In Ukraine, as opposed to Russia, where at times there actually was too much centralism and *glavkokratiia* (red tape), the trouble lay in "excessive decentralism." "Here, in Ukraine, the old slogan 'power in the provinces,' which has now become reactionary, is still alive."[107] Trotsky, Kamenev, and Ioffe were also sent to Ukraine for the same purpose as Zinovev had been: to smooth away the disputes within the CP(B)U and stamp out "otamanism." This delegation of the CC RCP held a joint meeting with the CC CP(B)U on 19 May, at which "these disagreements were liquidated by the authority of the CC RCP."[108]

These measures thoroughly tamed the party in Ukraine. The fourth conference marks the end of the period of armed struggle for Soviet power. Of course, the struggle on the internal and ideological fronts still continued. Ukraine continued to be the weak spot of Communism in Eastern Europe. Peasant risings against Soviet rule and nationalist deviations within the party itself continued long after the final establishment of Soviet power.

The Fifth Conference of the CP(B)U

The fifth conference of the CP(B)U (November 1920) inaugurated the period of the consolidation of Soviet rule. Reviewing the past, factions criticizing the former CC again arose. There now appeared a new, so-called workers' opposition that accused the party of fawning upon the peasantry and alleged that the party had sold the interests of the proletariat to the peasants "for a mess of pottage."[109] This workers' opposition, as Ravich-Cherkassky rightly noted, was as devoid of Ukrainian background as had been the opposition to centralism. "Both democratic centralism and the workers' opposition," wrote Ravich-Cherkassky, "were flowers transplanted into Ukraine from another and foreign political climate."[110]

The autonomist faction also reappeared with Blakytny as its spokesman. The autonomists also included Skrypnyk, who criticized party policy towards the nationalities, especially the relationship between the Ukrainian SSR and the RSFSR.[111]

This conference was, as none of its predecessors had been, entirely a manifestation of the will of the CC RCP, apparently because party members from outside Ukraine dominated the conference. Over half of the delegates were Red Army men who had arrived from Russia to fight against the offensive of Piłsudski and Petliura on Kiev in May 1920.[112]

The fifth conference brought no essential changes into the relationship between the CP(B)U and the RCP, which had been determined by the preceding conferences and congresses. The CC elected at this conference was very similar in its composition to the one appointed by the CC RCP after the fourth conference.[113] Represented in it were chiefly the old Bolsheviks of the former left and right factions. No representatives of the workers' opposition nor of the autonomists were elected to the CC. Viacheslav Molotov became first secretary of the CP(B)U, a position he held until the tenth congress of the RCP, when he was elected secretary of the RCP. On the whole, after its fifth conference the CP(B)U was to become an obedient agency of the CC RCP. The subsequent history of the CP(B)U, however, shows that the struggle between it and the RCP over their mutual relationship long continued unabated.

In sum, although among the local Bolsheviks there were adherents of a separate Communist party in Ukraine, the origin of the CP(B)U was in fact due neither to them nor to the organizational principles of the RCP(B). The CP(B)U was created in response to circumstances, as a kind of necessary compromise with the forces of Ukrainian nationalism, which, owing to the creation of a separate Ukrainian state under the leadership of the Central Rada, were able to put pressure on the party. The issue of the CP(B)U divided leading party circles into two factions. In the first were the centralists, who defended the hegemony of the Russian Communist party (originally the RSDWP[B]) and perceived the workers' movement in Ukraine as an integral part of the all-Russian workers' movement, with no special tasks and needs; it therefore needed no separate party, and everything had to be left as before, with the district organizations in Ukraine subordinated directly, and each independently, to the CC RCP. This was the attitude of the Katerynoslavians led by Kviring and Epshtein (Iakovlev), and of a number of the Kievans, particularly Evgeniia Bosh.

The other group consisted of the federalists and independentists (*samostiinyky*), who demanded a separate Communist party for Ukraine. During the struggle against the Central Rada and through to the Taganrog conference, they demanded a separate party, though closely connected with the RCP. After the Taganrog conference, they demanded an independent party connected with the RCP only through the Communist International. They also defended this position at the first congress of the CP(B)U, but afterwards they limited their demands to autonomy.[114] This group was represented by Shakhrai, Skrypnyk, and Lapchynsky, and by the former Borotbists—Slynko, Butsenko, M. Vrublevsky, and Shumsky.

From the very beginning the CC RCP was hostile to the very idea of a separate party in Ukraine; this is evident in the decisions of all RCP congresses and the statutes of the party. Only once, after the Taganrog conference, does the CC seem to have recognized, for tactical reasons, the existence of a separate party in Ukraine. But from the first congress of the CP(B)U, the CC RCP adopted the Katerynoslavian position, which considered the CP(B)U an ordinary regional organization, completely subordinate to the RCP. Control of the Ukrainian organization was exercised through the emissaries of the CC sent to every congress and conference of the CP(B)U. This was Kamenev at the second congress, Iakov Sverdlov at the third, Stalin at the fourth, and Zinovev at the fifth. The CC CP(B)U was allocated a very limited field of activity, primarily of a technical character. The main political line was determined by the CC RCP.

The National Composition of the RCP(B) and the CP(B)U

The nationalities represented in the RCP(B) can be illustrated by data from the congresses of the Russian Communist party during the first five years of the revolution, provided in Table 25. The figures in Table 25 are not complete. Those for the seventh, eleventh, and twelfth congresses are not available, and even the existing statistics are incomplete. At the ninth party congress, for example, the Georgians are omitted, but we know that Stalin and many other Georgians attended. The same can be said about the Ukrainians. Analysing the list of participants in the tenth congress, we find that sixty delegates from the Communist party of Ukraine were present, of whom at least one-third were Ukrainians.[115] Ukrainians might have figured under the rubric "Russians," but this very seldom happened.

As is evident, Russians dominated the congresses, controlling more than two-thirds of the delegates. Jews and Latvians, in relation to their share in

Table 25. Nationalities at the Congresses of the RCP(B)

	Number of Delegates				
Nationality	Sixth congress	Eighth congress	Ninth congress	Tenth congress	Thirteenth congress
Russians	92	190	372	494	(65.2%)
Jews	29	49	77	94	(8.7%)
Latvians	17	21	32	35	(6.1%)[a]
Ukrainians	6	11	16	—	(4.4%)
Poles	8	10	8	—	—
Belorussians	—	2	10	—	—
Lithuanians	4	5	1	—	(1.9%)
Estonians	3	3	3	—	—
Armenians	1	4	2	8	(2.3%)
Georgians	6	3	—	4	(1.9%)
Finns	2	3	—	—	—
French	—	1	—	—	—
Germans	—	1	1	—	—
Tatars	—	1	4	18[b]	(1.6%)[c]
Moldavians	2	—	1	—	—
Zyrians	—	1	—	—	—
Kirghiz	—	—	—	9	—
Persians	1	—	1	—	—
Chuvash	—	—	1	—	—
Greeks	—	—	1	—	—
Meshcheriakians	—	—	1	—	—
Others	—	—	—	28	—
Total	171[d]	305[d]	530[d]	690[d]	

SOURCE: *Shestoi sezd RSDRP(b). Avgust 1917 g.* (Moscow, 1934), p. 274. *Vosmoi sezd Rossiiskoi kommunisticheskoi partii (bolshevikov). 18-23 marta 1919 goda. Stenograficheskii otchet* (Moscow, 1919), p. 411. *Deviatyi sezd RKP(b). Mart-aprel 1920 g.* (Moscow, 1934), p. 551. *Desiatyi sezd RKP(b). Mart 1921* (Moscow, 1933), p. 807. *Trinadtsatyi sezd Rossiiskoi kommunisticheskoi partii (bolshevikov). Stenograficheskii otchet. 23-31 maia 1924 g.* (Moscow, 1924), p. 558.

[a]The source refers to "Latvians and Estonians."

[b]Of which fifteen were Turkestan Tatars and three Russian Tatars.

[c]This rubric is called *"tiurko-tatary."*

[d]Number of delegates who filled out the questionnaire.

the total population, were overrepresented. The Ukrainians did not amount to more than 5 per cent at the congresses, although they were about 20 per cent of the total population of the Russian empire.

This situation changed dramatically during the period of the so-called *korenizatsiia*[116] of the Communist parties in the non-Russian republics during the early twenties. In 1927 the principal nationalities in the party were represented as shown in Table 26.

Table 26. Nationalities in the All-Union Communist Party, 1922-27

Members and candidates	1922 (percentage)	1927	1927 (percentage)
Russians	72.00	743,167	65.00
Ukrainians	5.88	134,030	11.72
Jews	3.20	49,511	4.33
Belorussians	1.47	36,420	3.19
Armenians	1.02	19,019	1.66
Georgians	1.98	16,985	1.49
Tatars	1.05	15,646	1.37
Uzbeks	0.54	13,585	1.19
Latvians	2.53	13,336	1.17
Kazakhs	—	12,041	1.05
Poles	1.50	11,941	1.05
Turkic peoples	0.65	11,237	0.98
Total		1,144,053	

SOURCE: M. Fainsod, *How Russia Is Ruled* (Cambridge, Mass., 1953), p. 218 (1922). *Itogi desiatiletiia sovetskoi vlasti v tsifrakh, 1917-1927* (Moscow, 1928), pp. 26-27 (1927).

Although the Russians kept their absolute majority in the Communist party, a significant change took place with respect to the Jews and the Ukrainians. While the Jews increased from 3.20 per cent at the time of the tenth party congress (1922) to 4.33 per cent in 1927, the Ukrainians increased from 5.88 per cent to 11.72 per cent. As to the Latvians, their decline in the party reflected the secession of their country from Russia.

Table 27 illustrates the strength of the Communist party of Ukraine in the postrevolutionary years.

In 1922 (1 April) the Communist party of Ukraine had 54,818 members, distributed according to nationality and social strata as shown in Table 28.

In 1922, then, the Russians dominated the Communist party of

Table 27. Membership and National Composition of the CP(B)U, 1917-24

	Total	Ukrainians	Russians	Jews
1917	18,021	—	—	—
1918	5,014	—	—	—
1919	16,363	—	—	—
1920	25,247	—	—	—
1921	75,000[a]	—	—	—
1922	54,000	23.3%[b]	53.6%	13.6%
1923	50,000	24.0%[c]	—	—
1924	105,000[c]	33.0%[b]	—	—

SOURCE: *Ezhegodnik Kominterna,* 1923, pp. 476-77.

NOTE: Somewhat different figures are given by other Soviet sources. Cf. M. Ravich-Cherkassky, *Istoriia Kommunisticheskoi partii (b-kov) Ukrainy* (Kharkiv, 1923), pp. 82, 90.

[a]An official party source gives 68,092 as the total membership of the CP(B)U at the sixth conference. *Biuleten VI vseukrainskoi konferentsii Kommunisticheskoi partii (bolshevikov) Ukrainy,* No. 2 (Kharkiv, 1922), p. 62.

[b]*Budivnytstvo radianskoi Ukrainy. Zbirnyk* (Kharkiv, 1929), Vol. II, p. 164.

[c]N. Popov, *Narys istorii Kommunistychnoi partii (bilshovykiv) Ukrainy,* 5th ed. (Kharkiv, 1931), pp. 267, 270, 282, 290.

Table 28. National and Social Composition of the CP(B)U, 1922

Nationality	Total	Percentage	Towns (percentage)	Country (percentage)	Army (percentage)	Workers (percentage)	Officials (percentage)
Ukrainians	11,920	23.3	21.1	54.1	14.0	20.0	20.5
Russians	27,490	53.6	51.1	36.6	64.5	57.7	46.5
Jews	6,981	13.6	—	—	—	13.1	22.3
Poles	1,241	2.6	—	—	—	2.7	2.6
Others	3,604	7.1	—	—	—	—	—

SOURCE: M. Ravich-Cherkassky, *Istoriia Kommunisticheskoi partii (b-kov) Ukrainy* (Kharkiv, 1923), pp. 241-42.

Ukraine. This situation changed remarkably after the "Ukrainianization" of the party, so that in 1926 the 151,939 members of the CP(B)U were divided according to nationality as shown in Table 29.

In spite of their predominance in the total population of Ukraine, the

Table 29. National Composition of the CP(B)U, 1926

	Total	Percentage
Ukrainians	66,455	43.9
Russians	57,004	37.4
Jews	16,988	11.2
Poles	2,806	1.9
Belorussians	1,808	1.2
Latvians	1,190	0.8
Others	5,688	3.6

SOURCE: *VKP(b) v tsifrakh,* 5th ed. (Moscow, 1926), pp. 26-27.

Ukrainians were still a minority in the Communist party. In the leadership of the party they played an even lesser role.

On the Genesis of the CP(B)U

There is no doubt that the Communist Party (Bolshevik) of Ukraine grew out of purely Russian social democratic organizations which, as has already been pointed out, comprised some Jewish and Ukrainian elements. Ideologically these organizations stood for all-Russian principles and showed no sympathy for the Ukrainian national renascence. That part of the CP(B)U which was of Ukrainian origin often showed its national sympathies. However, it is possible to speak of the presence of Ukrainian elements in the party only after the amalgamation of the UCP and of the Borotbists with the CP(B)U. The entrance of the Borotbists especially influenced the national character of the CP(B)U.[117]

Soviet historiography of the twenties offered various theories on the roots of the CP(B)U. The first historian of the Communist party in Ukraine, Ravich-Cherkassky, asserted that the CP(B)U derived from the Ukrainian and Russian proletariats in Ukraine, which came together into one stream only after the proletarian revolution, thus uniting the industrial and the rural proletariat. The former, nationally and linguistically almost exclusively Russian, carried on its struggle under the leadership of the local organizations of the Bolshevik party. The rural proletarians and semi-proletarians, Ukrainian by nationality, were organized and led by the Ukrainian socialist parties (at first by the RUP, then by the USDWP). The Bolshevik organizations of the industrial proletariat, according to

Ravich-Cherkassky, had a correct attitude towards the class struggle but ignored the Ukrainian national question. The Ukrainian social democratic party, by contrast, while ideologically correct *vis-à-vis* the national question and the Ukrainian question, took an erroneous position in the class question. Only after the proletarian revolution did these two currents unite, forming the CP(B)U. In Ravich-Cherkassky's opinion, "the history of the CP(B)U is the sum of two histories: that of the Ukrainian proletariat and that of the Russian proletariat in Ukraine."[118]

According to another theory, there was no history of the CP(B)U separate from that of the RCP(B); there was only the history of the activities of the RCP(B) on the territory of Ukraine. The notion of a separate history of the CP(B)U was regarded as a sign of nationalism. Historical studies had to avoid dealing with party history in terms of nationalities; events in the borderlands had to be presented as particular problems forced into the framework of an all-Russian history. This theory, which is actually less of a theory than a directive of the CC RCP(B), began to be introduced without fanfare in the mid–1930s.[119]

Skrypnyk, the chief ideologist of the CP(B)U in the twenties, opposed both these views. He reproached Ravich-Cherkassky for "hushing up the petty-bourgeois character ... of the RUP and of the Menshevik Ukrainian social democratic party" and trying "to carry out a kind of 'Ukrainianization' of the history of our party."[120] In opposition to the dualistic theory there was a monistic theory, which treated the amalgamation of the CP(B)U with elements of the UCP (Borotbists), of the Bund, and of the Communist Jewish Ferband as an assimilation by the CP(B)U of these latter groups. In the thirties it was emphasized that the CP(B)U "derives its origin from the social democratic Bolshevik organizations ... [and] if the former Borotbists, Ukapists, and Bundists entered the CP(B)U, they did so not with their old petty-bourgeois views, but after having condemned [and] rejected them."[121]

How Strong Were the Communists in Ukraine?

What were the conditions under which the Soviet regime in Ukraine was installed during the period of the October rising of the Bolsheviks? Did any noticeable differentiation of Ukrainian society take place, and was there any trend towards Bolshevization of the masses in Ukraine immediately before the October revolution? Data concerning the results of the elections that took place during November and December 1917 and testimonies of contemporaries are of great interest for studying this problem.

In Ukraine's capital itself, Kiev, the Bolsheviks were very weak. Their organization (the RSDWP[B]) had in March 1917, according to Soviet sources, about "two hundred members, chiefly craftsmen."[122] The situation was no better in the provinces; at the April conference of the district organizations of the Kiev province it was said that "organizations are everywhere insignificant in the majority of cases, they have few organizers of their own, and they all expect help from the Kiev organization."[123] A similar situation prevailed throughout Ukraine. At the beginning of the February revolution, independent Bolshevik organizations existed only in Kharkiv, Katerynoslav, Kiev, and Luhansk, while in such cities as Odessa, Mykolaiv, Kherson, Vinnytsia, Zhytomyr, Poltava, and Ielysavethrad, and in many places in the Donets basin, there existed united organizations which in fact were under the "Menshevik-'defencist' leadership."[124]

It was these independent Bolshevik organizations, having at that time, "apart from Kiev, 7,000 organized workers," that were represented at the all-Russian April conference of the RSDWP(B). As Popov himself stressed, this was a very small number; from the Urals organizations alone 14,000 workers were represented at the conference and from the central industrial region—23,000.[125] At the sixth congress of the RSDWP(B) in August 1917 the Bolsheviks of Ukraine represented about 23,000 members,[126] while the Petrograd organization alone had 40,095 members.[127]

The weakness of the Bolsheviks showed up in various municipal and Duma elections in 1917. In the elections to the Kiev City Duma on 7 August 1917 the Bolsheviks obtained six seats out of the total of ninety-eight. The strength of the various parties and organizations that took part in these elections may be seen in Table 30. It is also apparent from this table that the Bolsheviks did not enjoy much support from the voters of Kiev, since they drew only some 5–6 per cent of the total vote.

That the course of events immediately after the October revolution and the Bolshevization of Russia did not have any great influence on Ukraine is borne out by the results of the elections to the all-Russian constituent assembly in November and December 1917. The results show the relative strength of the political parties before the October revolution. Although these elections took place under extremely complicated and abnormal political conditions, and were the first elections of their kind in the history of Russia, they are generally considered to reflect the relatively freely expressed will of the population. The elections took place in a transitional period between the democratic regime of the Provisional Government and the Bolshevik regime of the Soviet of People's Commissars. They were announced by the Provisional Government for 25–27 November, but they took place under the Bolshevik regime and with its consent.[128] They were

Table 30. Elections to Kiev City Duma, 1917

Parties and organizations	Votcs	Percentage	Seats	Percentage
Bloc of Mensheviks, SRs, and the Bund	63,586	39.6	37	37.7
Bloc of Ukrainian social democrats and SRs	35,238	22.6	20	24.8
Bloc of Russian voters	23,032	14.3	15	15.3
Kadets	15,078	9.3	9	9.0
Bolsheviks	9,520	5.9	6	6.0
Bloc of Polish voters	8,893	5.5	5	5.0
Jewish democratic bloc	6,741	4.0	4	4.0
Jewish socialist bloc	4,223	2.6	2	2.0
Polish socialist parties	1,622	1.0	—	—
Ukrainian socialist federalists	1,060	0.6	—	—
Bloc of land leaseholders	552	0.3	—	—
Total	169,545		98	

SOURCE: *1917 god na Kievshchine. Khronika sobytii,* ed. V. Manilov (Kiev, 1928), p. 179.

held without the direct intervention of the government and in accordance with the "four-adjective" principle, i.e., they were secret, general, equal, and direct. A student of these elections, Radkey, wrote that "the vote in November 1917 was an authentic expression of the will of the Russian people."[129]

On the all-Russian scale, the results of these elections show that the Russian SRs were then the strongest party, having collected 15,848,004 votes or 39 per cent from the total of 41,686,876; the Bolsheviks obtained 9,844,637 votes or 24.5 per cent; the Mensheviks received 1,364,826 votes or 3.2 per cent. The Ukrainian parties, considered together, obtained 4,957,067 votes or 12.2 per cent.[130] Table 31 shows the party distribution of the 703 deputies to the Duma, from 66 electoral districts.

Lenin, in an article on the elections from the standpoints of geography and nationality, cited some interesting data, which showed the Bolshevik vote distributed as shown in Table 32.

Significantly, the Bolshevik vote came from the central industrial region and from the army. The lowest percentage of the Bolshevik vote was in Ukraine, Siberia, and the eastern Urals region, followed by the Volga region. In Ukraine the Bolsheviks obtained only 10 per cent of all the

Table 31. Elections to the All-Russian Constituent Assembly, 1917

	Seats	Percentage
Right SRs	299	42.7
Bolsheviks	168	23.0
Ukrainian SRs	81	11.5
Left SRs	39	5.5
Moslems, Bahkirs, Kirghiz	28	4.0
SR groups from nationalities (Moslems, Chuvash, Moldavians, Buriats)	19	2.7
Mensheviks	18	2.5
Kadets	15	2.2
Armenians	10	1.4
Cossacks	9	1.2
Jews, Poles, Estonians	9	1.2
People's socialists	4	0.5
Ukrainian SDs	2	0.2
Rightists	2	0.2
Total	703	

SOURCE: O. H. Radkey, *The Election to the Russian Constituent Assembly of 1917* (Cambridge, 1950), p. 21. N. Rubinshtein, *Bolsheviki i uchreditelnoe sobranie* (Moscow, 1938), p. 54.

Table 32. Geographical Distribution of Bolshevik Vote in Elections to the All-Russian Constituent Assembly, 1917

Regions	Total vote	Bolsheviks	Percentage
Central industrial	5,242,500	2,305,600	44
Western	2,961,000	1,282,200	44
Northern	2,975,100	1,177,200	40
Army and navy	4,363,600	1,671,300	38
Volga black earth	6,764,300	1,115,600	16
Eastern Urals	3,583,500	443,900	12
Ukraine	7,581,300	754,000	10
Siberia	2,786,700	273,900	10
Total	36,258,000	9,023,700	

SOURCE: V. I. Lenin, "Vybory v uchreditelnoe sobranie i diktatura proletariata," *Sochineniia,* 4th ed., 35 vols. (Moscow, 1941-50), Vol. XXX, pp. 232-33.

votes, while in central regions of Russia they received about 40 per cent. This feature of the elections was cited by Lenin in his polemics against the Luxemburgists, who accused him of "exaggerating the national question in Ukraine." Lenin argued that it was risky to ignore the Ukrainian question.[131]

The correlation of forces against the background of the elections in Ukraine shows even more clearly the weakness of the Bolsheviks and the strength of the Ukrainian parties. According to data (Table 33) collected by Radkey and verified by other sources, the Ukrainian parties obtained in independent ballots 4.3 million votes or 53 per cent; apart from this the Ukrainian SRs collected 1.2 million votes in joint ballots with the Russian SRs. The Bolsheviks, as mentioned above, obtained 754,000 votes or 10 per cent.[132] Lenin, commenting on these figures, correlated the results of these elections with the tempo of the revolution in given regions of Russia. In those places where the Bolshevik revolution was victorious early and without great complications, for instance in the northern provinces of Russia including Petrograd and the central industrial region including Moscow, the Bolsheviks obtained a majority of votes in the elections: in the Petrograd province 50 per cent were cast for the Bolsheviks and 26 per cent for the SRs, while the city of Petrograd gave 45 per cent for the Bolsheviks and 16 per cent for the SRs; the Livonian province—72 per cent for the Bolsheviks; the central industrial region—56 per cent for the Bolsheviks and 8 per cent for the SRs; Tver province—54 per cent for the Bolsheviks and 39 per cent for the SRs; Vladimir province—56 per cent for the Bolsheviks and 32 per cent for the SRs.[133]

The Bolshevik vote in Ukraine came from the industrial centres of Katerynoslav, Kharkiv, and Chernihiv provinces. Chernihiv province cannot be included in the industrial region, and it is difficult to say to what the comparatively high percentage of the Bolshevik vote could be attributed. In Right-Bank Ukraine the Bolsheviks obtained only 3–4 per cent of the votes cast.

Table 33. Elections to the All-Russian Constituent Assembly in Ukraine by Districts and Military Fronts, 1917

Districts	Ukrainian parties	SD Bolsheviks	Russian SRs	SD Mensheviks	Minor socialist parties	Constitutional democrats	Other non-soc. parties	Other nationality parties	Unclassified	Total votes
Chernihiv	484,456	271,174	105,565	10,813	10,089	28,864	30,658	31,116	911	973,646
Katerynoslav	556,012	213,163	231,717	26,909	16,859	27,551	34,665	86,173[a]	—	1,193,049
Kharkiv	(see Russian SRs)	110,844	650,386[b]	17,775	48,983	59,509	28,013	13,014	—	928,526
Kherson[c]	72,504	77,122	354,312[b]	14,936	—	54,493	—	(43,608)	77,416	649,391
Kiev	1,256,271	59,413	19,201	11,532	—	28,630	48,641	(153,276)[d]	50,763	1,627,727
Podillia[c]	656,116	27,540	10,170	4,028	852	7,951	284	123,319[e]	—	830,260
Poltava	760,022	64,460	198,437[b]	5,993	4,391	18,105	61,115	34,631	2,102	1,149,256
Volhynia	569,044	35,612	27,575	16,947	—	22,397	—	55,967[f]	76,666	804,208
Total	4,354,425	859,330	1,507,463	108,933	81,174	247,500	203,376	441,104	227,858	8,201,063
Percentage	53.0	10.0	18.3	1.3	0.9	3.0	2.4	5.3	2.8	
Baltic fleet	—	43,053	15,947	—	9,736	—	28	—	—	68,764
Black Sea fleet	12,895	10,771	12,251	1,943	—	—	—	—	4,769	52,629
Northern front	88,956	471,828	249,832	10,420	5,868	13,687	—	—	—	840,591
Romanian front	180,576	167,000	679,471	33,858	—	21,438	—	—	46,257	1,128,600
Southwestern front	168,354	300,112	402,930	79,630	—	13,724	—	—	42,673	1,007,423
Western front	85,062	653,430	180,582	8,000	(2,429)	16,750	(3,055)	(3,510)	8,069	976,000
Total	535,843	1,646,194	1,541,013	133,851	18,033	65,599	3,083	3,510	101,768	4,074,007

SOURCE: O. H. Radkey, *The Election to the Russian Constituent Assembly of 1917* (Cambridge, 1950), Appendix.

NOTE: Figures in parentheses taken from earlier, less complete tabulation.

[a] Jewish nationalists, 37,032; Jewish socialists, 14,021; German, 25,977; Greek, 9,143.

[b] Joint list, Ukrainian SRs and Russian SRs.

[c] Known to be substantially incomplete (one *uezd* or more missing).

[d] Jewish nationalists, 86,943; Jewish socialists, 35,443; Polish, 30,890.

[e] Jewish nationalists, 62,547; other Jewish, 13,860; Polish, 46,912.

[f] Two Jewish lists.

CHAPTER VII

The First Attempt to Sovietize Ukraine

Self-determination through the Soviets

The policy of the RCP(B) towards the Central Rada after the October revolution was determined less by ideological principles than by practical circumstances. The economic situation of Bolshevik Russia and the disintegration of the empire had a great influence on the party's attitude to the borderlands. Stalin admitted later that Russia could not have lasted long without the periphery's raw materials. The party was thus conscious that it could not permit the slightest disintegration of the Russian state. In its first phase the Bolshevik revolution was confined to the territory of Central Russia, to the ethnographic limits of the Great Russian people. On the peripheries power passed into the hands of national governments that neither ideologically nor ethnically had much in common with the Soviet regime in Petrograd. Almost all the borderlands of Russia, from Finland to the Caucasus, dissociated themselves from the Bolshevik revolution, regarding the Soviet regime as the government of Great Russia alone; but even as such the regime was not treated seriously, since very few prophesied a long life for it. This situation confronted the Soviet government with very gloomy prospects, both strategically and economically. The position of Ukraine was in many respects a special one, both for economic reasons (the dependence of Russia on Ukrainian coal, iron, grain, and sugar) as well as for strategic reasons. Moreover, near its borders, on the Don, Russian anti-Bolshevik forces began organizing under the leadership of Lavr Kornilov and Mikhail Alekseev, with the connivance of General Aleksei Kaledin of the Don Army. General Kaledin even initiated measures for the creation of a "south-eastern alliance" with the Astrakhan, Kuban, and Terek Cossacks. The task of this alliance was to furnish opposition to a Bolshevik revolution in these regions and eventually to provide aid for the restoration of prerevolutionary Russia. The Don and Kuban territories were rich in grain, which was then very scarce in Russia. After the Ukrainian Rada refused to send grain north to Russia, the Bolsheviks made efforts to keep at least the Don district within their orbit.

The relations between the Ukrainian Central Rada and the Council of People's Commissars in Moscow had become strained since the Rada's refusal to recognize the sovereignty of the Soviet government in Ukraine. Moreoever, the General Secretariat of the Rada began immediately after the Bolshevik revolution to work towards the creation of a federative government for the whole Russian empire. As early as September 1917, a congress of the peoples of Russia was convened in Kiev on the Rada's initiative. The congress passed a resolution on the transformation of Russia into a federative republic: "In view of the fact that Russia comprises a multitude of peoples with more or less clearly expressed national consciousnesses and with varied national cultures and historical pasts, and because in economic respects it forms characteristic self-contained economic regions, the only acceptable form of federation is one built upon the national principle .... In view of the aforesaid considerations, the congress of peoples has unanimously adopted [the resolution] that: Russia must be a federative democratic republic."[1] The Bolsheviks found the resolution unacceptable. After the Third Universal of the Rada, the Ukrainian government addressed a note to all newly created governments in the territory of former Russia, including the Council of People's Commissars (CPC), in which it was proposed that immediate steps be taken towards the creation of a "homogeneous socialist government" for the whole of Russia.[2] These proposals led nowhere, since only the Don government replied to the note.[3]

In the actions of the Ukrainian Rada the Russian Bolsheviks saw a threat to their regime and an attempt to restore the Kerensky regime.[4] The Rada's initiative was one of the immediate causes for the conflict, which flared up at the end of December 1917, between the Rada and the Council of People's Commissars in Moscow. In connection with the proposed formation of an all-Russian government, the Rada explored the possibility of convening the constituent assembly in Kiev in case the Bolsheviks should not allow it in Moscow. This prospect worried the Bolsheviks and was probably why they finally did allow the constituent assembly to meet in Moscow.[5] It may be assumed that the Bolsheviks were afraid lest the constituent assembly meet outside their territory and condemn the Soviet regime. It was apparently always their intention to discredit and dissolve it; otherwise it is difficult to imagine why they permitted it to convene at all in January 1918, only to dissolve it immediately thereafter.

At that time the only forces that could oppose Bolshevism were in the Don area and Ukraine. These borderlands were the least Bolshevized; both had their own governments and neither recognized the sovereignty of the CPC in their territories. Bolshevik sources show that what mattered most for the CPC was, first, the Donets basin, where almost all Russia's fuel was concentrated, and, second, Ukraine and the Don, which supplied most of the grain. Trotsky, in his talk with the commander-in-chief, Nikolai Krylenko, expressed the opinion that "the whole army, including the Ukrainians, must know that securing the Donets basin against Kaledin's anarchy is a matter of life and death for the revolution."[6] Another prominent Bolshevik military commander, Vladimir Antonov-Ovseenko,[7] later wrote that it was clear to the Bolsheviks "that if we had allowed this counter-revolutionary movement to gather strength in the favourable surroundings of the Cossack regions, it could have cut us off completely from the Caucasus and the oil of Baku, thus depriving the Soviet centre of the coal of the Donets basin, of the manganese of Kryvyi Rih, of the grain of Ukraine." And he further remarked that actually "the whole future of our country [i.e., of Soviet Russia] depended on whether Kaledin's adventure would succeed or not."[8]

These motives made the Bolsheviks turn their main attention to the Don and Ukraine, where their prime task was evidently the immediate liquidation of these hostile governments. To apply the principle of self-determination to these two countries, which appeared to have such hostile governments, was, in Stalin's words, "a mockery of self-determination and of the elementary principles of democracy."[9] In other words, any government that did not recognize Soviet power and the supremacy of the CPC was faced with the Bolsheviks' wrath. From the standpoint of the success of the Bolshevik revolution, self-determination for Ukraine, the Don, and the Caucasus was unthinkable because of the importance the Bolsheviks attached to keeping these territories within their orbit. But Bolshevik conduct was, in spite of what Stalin said, contrary to the principle of self-determination of nations and to the principles of democracy.

The proclamation of Ukraine's neutrality in the struggle of the CPC with Kaledin, and more so any indirect support given to him by the Ukrainians, was a matter of grave concern for the People's Commissars. The struggle against Kaledin was impossible without the cooperation of Ukraine, if only because the military formations loyal to the CPC were situated on the western and southern fronts and had to be transported via Ukraine. The Rada not only refused to permit the transport of the Bolshevik troops over its territory to fight in the Don area, but it also disarmed Soviet troops in Ukraine on the grounds that no government in the world would tolerate the presence of hostile troops on its territory. The mere fact that the Rada did not recognize the People's Commissars as the government of the whole Russian empire, and in any case did not recognize its sovereignty on the territory of Ukraine, gave the Bolsheviks a pretext for considering the Rada their enemy and including it in the camp of counter-revolutionaries of Kornilov's and Kaledin's stamp. It seemed impossible to settle the conflict between the People's Commissars and the Rada peacefully. Although the hostility of the Bolsheviks towards the Rada was of long standing, the immediate causes of open hostility were the Rada's disarming of Bolshevik units in Kiev and their deportation to Russia in trainloads during the night of 12 December 1917, as well as the arrest of Bolshevik leaders in Kiev who were in charge of the planned rising against the Rada. From then on the Bolsheviks systematically attacked the Rada and all parties that supported it. Stalin, the commissar for nationalities, was the main party strategist on nationality questions, including the Ukrainian question. He formulated the party's policy towards the Rada, shaped public opinion in the matter, and reported to the government and to the soviets on the Rada and the situation in Ukraine. He also was a co-editor of the famous "ultimatum" by which the People's Commissars declared war on the Rada.

Stalin's main intention was both to eliminate the Rada's influence on the Ukrainian masses and to prepare the Russian masses to accept a war against the Ukrainian government as a war against the bourgeoisie, a war against an enemy of the revolution, and particularly as a war for the grain and coal that the Rada had refused to send to Russia. Therefore Stalin wrote in *Pravda* that "the conflict with the Ukrainian Rada is the continuation of the struggle of the proletarians of all the nationalities populating Russia, the continuation of the struggle of the soviets against the united organizations of the bourgeoisie and the landowners." He represented the conflict between the CPC and the Rada as a conflict "of the proletariat and poorer peasantry of Great Russia and Ukraine" with "the landowners and the bourgeois of both countries." "Who," Stalin asked, "goes along with the Rada? Big landowners in Ukraine, then Kaledin and his 'military government' on the Don, i.e., Cossack landowners, and behind both lurks the Great Russian bourgeoisie which used to be a furious enemy of all demands of the Ukrainian people, but which now supports the Rada only because the Rada supports Kaledin." Stalin intentionally confused the Russian bourgeoisie with the Rada in order to represent the latter as a defender of the old order against which the Russian masses were certain to be united in opposition. Further, Stalin generalized in an equally nebulous fashion that the Rada was opposed "in the first place by the Ukrainian workers and the poorest section of the peasantry."[10] Yet it is known that by no means all the workers and even fewer of "the poorest section of the peasantry" were then against the Rada.[11]

However, the main effort of Bolshevik propaganda against the Rada was the so-called ultimatum to the Rada of 17 December 1917. This document has so far been quoted in Soviet and other works only in its official version. The very important drafts written by Lenin, Stalin's amendments, and the whole process of editing the ultimatum have so far been completely ignored, although analysis of these variants, it seems, would reveal most clearly the intentions of the CPC against the Rada.[12] To edit the ultimatum a commission comprising Lenin, Stalin, and Trotsky was established.[13] In the final text of the ultimatum the Rada was accused of such crimes as "the non-recognition by the Rada of Soviet power in Ukraine (among other things, the Rada refused to convene immediately the regional congress of the Ukrainian soviets on the demand of the soviets of Ukraine)." This was an ambiguous policy making it impossible for the CPC to recognize the Rada "as a plenipotentiary representative of the working and exploited masses of the Ukrainian republic." The Rada was then confronted with the following demands: "1) Does the Rada undertake to renounce all attempts at disorganizing the common front? 2) Does the Rada undertake henceforth not to let through without the permission of the commander-in-chief any military units proceeding to the Don, the Urals, or elsewhere? 3) Does the Rada undertake to render assistance to the cause of the revolutionary troops in their struggle with the counter-revolutionary uprising of the Kadets under Kaledin? 4) Does the Rada undertake to stop all its attempts at disarming the Soviet regiments and the workers' Red Guards in Ukraine and to return immediately weapons to those deprived of them? In the event that a satisfactory answer to these questions is not received within forty-eight hours, the Soviet of the People's Commissars shall consider the Rada in a state of open war against Soviet power in Russia and in Ukraine."[14] The tone and the content of the ultimatum bear witness that the People's Commissars by no means considered the Rada an independent government of an independent state, but instead regarded it as some subordinate organ to which they could issue directives and decrees. The People's Commissars could not dictate the form of government to a state which it recognized as independent. This is mentioned in the same document in respect to Finland, whose government was in fact "bourgeois." The last phrase of the ultimatum is nonsensical, because there was as yet no Soviet power in Ukraine. But this is explained by Lenin's first draft, which said that "at the present time," i.e., on 17 December 1917 (nine days before the proclamation of Soviet power in Ukraine), the People's Commissars recognize "the Ukrainian soviets as the representatives of the Ukrainian people and of the free Ukrainian republic, and as the organizations for the revolutionary struggle of the Ukrainian workers and exploited masses against the exploiters," i.e., not the Central Rada. This point in Lenin's draft was removed from the published ultimatum.

In the first draft Lenin also accused the Rada of "an ambiguous bourgeois policy towards the peace: non-participation in the armistice and peace talks *despite* our invitation."[15] The Rada was, of course, conducting talks with the military missions of the Entente who tried to dissuade it from signing a peace treaty with the Central Powers. For a time they were successful, and the Rada long hesitated to conclude an armistice. It agreed only after the Bolsheviks signed the armistice and this disorganized the front, an action which also affected the Ukrainian units. From Lenin's draft it appears that the CPC also intended to reproach the Rada for its land policy, for allegedly conducting "an ambiguous bourgeois-landowner policy in respect to the confiscation of landowners' land."[16] Further, the unpublished draft has it that the Rada disarmed not Soviet forces generally, as is claimed in the ultimatum, but "Russian Soviet forces situated in Ukraine."[17] The word "Russian" was deleted by Stalin from the ultimatum, perhaps to convince the Ukrainians that the Rada had disarmed all Soviet forces, including the Ukrainian ones. While the first versions of the ultimatum are clear evidence of CPC interference in the internal affairs of Ukraine, by dictating to it, among other things, its form of government, land policy, and policy towards the peace treaties, the published version of the ultimatum stresses mostly the "bourgeois" character of the Rada and its connections with the counter-revolutionary Kaledin. Many facts corroborate that the People's Commissars declared war on the Ukrainian Rada both because it had sympathies for or aided Kaledin and because it was not willing to help the CPC in its war against Kaledin. A week before the ultimatum Trotsky and Krylenko discussed moving the Bolshevik forces to the Don through the territory of Ukraine. Krylenko stated that this would involve a territorial violation of the borders of Ukraine. In reply, Trotsky ordered Krylenko to ask the Rada whether it "considers itself obliged to render *assistance* in the struggle against Kaledin."[18]

From Stalin's writings it is clear that another source of hostility to the Rada was its diplomatic relations with the Entente, which held the prospect of Ukraine's recognition as an independent state. Stalin touched upon this problem more than once in his campaign against the Rada. In his article "What is the Rada?" he wrote that in Kiev "some alliance has already been arranged between the French mission and the Rada" with the aim of "maintaining an apearance of a Russian front until February or March and of delaying a final conclusion of the armistice until the spring." Therefore, Stalin concluded, "the Rada or, more precisely, its General Secretariat is a bourgeois government, fighting in alliance with the Anglo-French capitalists against the peace."[19] An important motive for such charges was probably the Central Rada's ability to bring about self-determination for Ukraine and to cut off the supply of grain and coal to Russia, much against the wishes of the People's Commissars.

The party conference in Kiev on 17 December 1917 completely rejected self-determination for Ukraine. The majority of delegates opposed the idea of a Ukrainian republic, considering Ukrainian national aspirations a bourgeois vestige. They would all have liked to overthrow the Central Rada or at least re-elect it so as to secure a majority for themselves. At the conference two attitudes towards Ukrainian statehood crystallized. Some, among them Bosh, Aleksandrov, Aussem, and Vasyl Valiavko, occupied the Luxemburgist position[20] on the Ukrainian question; others such as Zatonsky, Shakhrai, and Lapchynsky attempted to approach Lenin's position (they were far from the "nationalism" of which they were later accused). Bosh seized the opportunity to speak against Lenin's theses, arguing that to raise the national question at this time was anti-revolutionary and anti-Soviet. "We must indicate in each individual instance which mode of self-determination is more in the interests of the proletariat." As to the liberation of Ukraine, she considered it possible only with the victory of Soviet rule in Russia and Ukraine. If in Ukraine the bourgeoisie, which for her included the Central Rada, should be victorious then "here will remain political oppression of national minorities." She was somewhat ambiguous about relations between Ukraine and Russia, admitting that "federation is the best form," but failing to mention whether she would admit federation for Ukraine. She rejected the full secession of Ukraine, because allegedly "Ukraine will not be able to exist as a separate state under a capitalist regime."[21] According to Aleksandrov, national self-determination had to be adapted to the class struggle and federation had to be an instrument of control over Ukraine. Or, as he put it, "we tolerate the federation as an adaptation of the state administration of Ukraine to the all-Russian state administration."[22] Hylynsky considered the slogan of self-determination out of date; "we recognize political federation, but are not going to advertise this." "We do not recognize the economic separation of Ukraine."[23]

A more moderate tone concerning the Central Rada and a more favourable attitude towards the Ukrainian national renascence was adopted by Zatonsky, Lapchynsky, and Shakhrai,[24] who, although they condemned the Rada, did not consider it possible or advisable to overthrow it by force, but rather wished to change its composition through new elections. Zatonsky, who was the main speaker on the Rada, said that it was "a typically petty-bourgeois institution," that it had "detached itself from the landowners, but cannot detach itself from the principle of private property." He admitted that the Bolsheviks aimed at establishing Soviet power, yet even then it was not possible to ignore the question of nationalities.[25] This group defended the view that the Rada was backed by the majority of the Ukrainian people and that it was in control of the situation with regard to the question of nationalities. Shakhrai, for instance, said that "the Rada was composed in accordance with the national principle, and the Bolsheviks missed the opportunity of influencing its composition"; therefore he proposed a resolution stating that the Bolsheviks struggled not against the Rada generally, "but against the present Central Rada with its reactionary composition."[26] Shakhrai, Lapchynsky, and to some degree Zatonsky held the view that relations between Ukraine and Russia had to be based on federative principles.

There was no agreement among the Bolsheviks in Ukraine on the matter of the ultimatum issued by the Petrograd government. The document surprised the Ukrainian Bolsheviks, who did not know about it until the very day of its publication.[27] While some, for instance Shakhrai, regarded it as "a misunderstanding,"[28] others, such as Piatakov and Aleksandrov, approved of it. Zatonsky remarked that the crux of the matter was to evaluate the situation correctly and that it was important to know what attitude would be adopted towards the People's Commissars' measures by revolutionary democracy in Ukraine.

> If it had been only the matter of the passage of troops to the Don, I would have had nothing against the ultimatum, but in it attention is drawn to the fact that the Central Rada does not convene a congress of soviets and does not recognize the authority of the People's Commissars. If the order concerning the soviets proceeds from above, from outside, this constitutes a

> foreign intervention in local affairs, and a national struggle will result .... The Ukrainian masses will throw themselves into the arms of the chauvinists. If war comes, Russia will not be able to wage it [simultaneously] with the Don, with Siberia, with Ukraine, and with others. So far, there is no split among the Ukrainians, and there are no prospects of one; therefore the war would be carried on against the Ukrainian people, and there are only a handful of Bolsheviks.

Therefore the Bolsheviks, in Zatonsky's opinion, had to recommend the CPC to "reconsider this step well. I believe the ultimatum to be the result of misinformation in Petrograd." Zatonsky said that "some points are unhappily worded and were designed for effect, the very thing they have not achieved."[29]

This misinformation had been supplied to Petrograd by Piatakov, who had reported to the CC of the RCP(B) on Ukrainian matters.[30] He, together with other Luxemburgists, outvoted Zatonsky and adopted a resolution sanctioning the ultimatum. Piatakov declared in the discussion that in Kiev they were "defeated, but this does not mean that the cause is lost. The ultimatum is inevitable—there is and can be no other way out. The step of the People's Commissars is correct and logically inevitable. War is obviously a hard course, but it cannot be delayed."[31] Among Piatakov's supporters were Nikolai Tarnogrodsky, Liuksemburg, Kulyk, and Bosh. Fedor Zaitsev admitted that war against the Rada was inevitable, but "it was inconvenient for Piter [Petrograd] to wage war" against Ukraine; therefore he proposed to organize a revolutionary centre in Kiev.[32]

The ultimatum was a signal for an attack on the Rada by the Bolshevik press in Ukraine, chiefly by *Proletarskaia mysl* published in Kiev. The Bolshevik press constantly baited the Rada for its "betrayal of the revolution," for its bourgeois attitudes, and mainly for its cooperation with Kaledin.[33] Propaganda was aimed at discrediting the Rada and its socialism and showing that Rada policy was playing into the hands of counter-revolutionaries. "The Ukrainian SRs and social democrats conduct the same bourgeois policy as the Russian right SRs and Mensheviks, while in Russia the government of workers and poorest peasants sharply breaks up the framework of bourgeois society, while in Russia all the land together with stock and implements passes into the hands of peasant committees, not in words, but in fact; control by the workers is introduced, large industrial concerns are nationalized, capital is taxed, and a merciless struggle with the bourgeoisie is waged."[34] So ran in part the resolution of the congress of the southwestern regional organizations.

The Bolsheviks in their propaganda against the Rada represented themselves as defenders of the national rights of the Ukrainian people, pointing out that the Russian bourgeois parties always refused this right. The Central Rada was accused of having sent delegations to Kerensky and Nikolai Nekrasov in Petrograd and of "having patiently borne the indignities to which they were submitted by these counter-revolutionary rulers." The Central Rada "did not take a single step towards entering into an agreement with the government of the workers and peasants which had opened for all peoples of Russia the road to freedom and happiness." Further, the Ukrainian peasants were told that they would never see either land or freedom if they separated from the workers and peasants of Russia.[35] The conflict between the Rada and the CPC was represented, in this propaganda, not as a conflict between Russia and Ukraine, not as a struggle over the suppression of Ukrainian national aspirations that went beyond autonomy and the limits set by the Bolsheviks, but as a conflict between the workers and the poorer peasantry of Ukraine and Russia, on the one hand, and the bourgeoisie of these countries, on the other.

The main arguments were concentrated on one problem: the form of government in Ukraine. Behind all the slander and complaints about the Rada was hidden the Bolsheviks' fundamental desire—to install a Soviet regime in Ukraine. This was the so-called self-determination of nations through the soviets, as promulgated by Stalin.[36] What this amounted to was the capitulation of the Rada and the installation of a Soviet regime.

The sovietization of Ukraine was on the agenda from the first attempt at a Bolshevik uprising in the summer of 1917, but in view of the weakness of their forces and certain all-Russian considerations it was postponed. The first serious Bolshevik attempt to seize power was the armed encounter between Bolshevik detachments and the detachments of the Provisional Government in Kiev immediately after the October uprising in Petrograd. Although it was Bolshevik detachments that overpowered the Kiev garrison of the Provisional Government, authority passed into the hands of the Central Rada.[37] The unsuccessful October in Ukraine was the Bolsheviks' trial of strength. This attempt convinced the Bolsheviks that it was impossible to install the power of the soviets by the force of local Bolsheviks alone. Therefore they began a propaganda campaign in favour of new elections or of the "sovietization" of the Rada, so as to insure a majority in it for the workers' and soldiers' soviets. These new tactics were initiated by the Russian Communist party and propagated by the local Bolsheviks. In December *Pravda* published a discussion between Stalin and Serhii Bakynsky[38] on Ukrainian matters. Stalin felt that "power in the region, as well as in other districts, must belong conjointly to all workers', soldiers', and peasants' deputies," and that "in the matter of Soviet power, both central and local, no concessions can be made." He even offered a plan to introduce Soviet power. In his opinion, "the inhabitants of Kiev, Odessa, Kharkiv, Katerynoslav, and other cities have to set about convening" a congress of soviets, "of course in conjunction with the Rada." Feigning simplicity, Stalin doubted whether the Rada would refuse to cooperate with a congress that would pass the Rada's death sentence. "'Power to the local soviets' is that revolutionary commandment which we cannot abandon, and we do not understand how the Rada can argue against axioms."[39] Guided by the instructions of the RCP(B),[40] the Bolsheviks in Ukraine now began their campaign for convening a congress of soviets. To camouflage their real intentions, they put forward the idea of "new elections" to the Central Rada. Only two days after the publication of Stalin's interview with Bakynsky, the "organizing committee" issued a notice on an all-Ukrainian congress of soviets to be convened in Kiev on 16 December 1917.

The quotas of representation to the congress reflected the Bolshevik method of seizing power by ensuring that the workers' and soldiers' soviets would outnumber those of the peasants.[41] Favouring the workers and soldiers, the quotas of representation ignored proportionalism. The working class in Ukraine comprised not more than 3 per cent of the whole population, while the peasantry comprised over 80 per cent. In the Bolshevik quota system the majority nationality, the Ukrainians, who were predominantly peasants, were deprived of political influence. The most numerous Ukrainian organizations—the workers', soldiers', and peasants' unions—were allotted only three delegates each; this is not surprising considering their anti-Bolshevik character. The General Secretariat continually pointed out this anomaly of the proletariat's preferential treatment. The question of representation at the congress of the soviets was tantamount to a disagreement in principle between the Rada and the Bolsheviks over the form of government. The Rada, i.e., the parties which supported it, stood for parliamentary democracy. Hence all parties (except the monarchists) and trade unions and other organizations were represented in the Rada. The Bolsheviks, on the other hand, based their power on the soviets of workers' and soldiers' deputies, which were elected according to special quotas, but which were mostly designated from above by party committees and completely dominated by the Communist party. It was this "dictatorship of the proletariat" which the Rada refused to recognize in Ukraine. Stalin, in his report on relations with the Rada at the session of the central executive committee on 27 December 1917, explained it this way: "To understand the origin of this conflict it is necessary to pose the question about the political physiognomy of the Rada. The Rada proceeds from the principle of sharing power between the bourgeoisie, on the one hand, and the proletariat and peasantry, on the other, while the Soviets deny such sharing, giving all power to the people without the bourgeoisie. This is why the Rada replaces the slogan 'all power to the soviets' (i.e., to the people) by its slogan 'all power to the town and country self-governing bodies' (i.e., to the people and the bourgeoisie)."[42]

The Congress of Soviets in Kiev on 17 December 1917

In order to "put an end to the Rada's bossing about," as an old Bolshevik in Ukraine, Petrovsky, described it,[43] and to install a Soviet regime in Ukraine, the congress of soviets of workers', soldiers', and peasants' deputies convened in Kiev on 17 December 1917. This congress was to express the will of the Communist party, manifested in the soviets, which were to elect representatives in accordance with quotas favourable to the Bolsheviks. However, the congress assumed a completely different aspect from that desired by the Bolsheviks, because just before the congress the Central Rada had sent out a circular in which it invited to the congress representatives of peasants' and workers' organizations. Thus some 2,500 delegates assembled, among whom, according to some sources,[44] the Bolsheviks had 60 delegates, and according to others,[45] 130 delegates, while the rest were adherents of the Rada. The Ukrainian SRs, who had done so well in the constituent assembly elections, also held a majority at the congress.[46] The number of Bolshevik delegates was so small partly because the proletarian centres of the Donets basin, Katerynoslav, and Kharkiv ignored the congress.[47]

The legality and correctness of the congress' representation could hardly be disputed in those revolutionary times, for neither the Soviets nor the Rada were elected in normal democratic elections. But from the point of view of the Bolsheviks, the arrival of the delegates from the peasants' union was a breach of the representation quota. Later, Soviet historians wrote that "the congress was packed with thousands of the Rada's adherents ... although they had not received any mandates from their localities."[48] Elsewhere it was stated that "the kulak representatives, making use of their numbers and the armed support of the Central Rada, dispersed the mandate commission, took possession of seals and forms, and issued themselves with mandates for the congress."[49] Considering the Bolshevik attitude to democracy, parliaments, and elections in general, and also considering the question of the hegemony of the proletariat in the revolution, the Bolshevik accusations against the Rada seem ridiculous. A non-Soviet Ukrainian source, refuting Bolshevik accusations, asserts that "the elections for the congress were conducted quite freely, without any pressure from the Ukrainian authorities."[50]

After some incidents, the congress passed a vote of confidence in the Central Rada and condemned the ultimatum of the People's Commissars. The Bolshevik faction then left the congress and moved to Kharkiv, "where it was possible to count upon more favourable soil for the establishment of Soviet power,"[51] and where at that time the third regional congress of the soviets of the Donets and Kryvyi Rih basins was in session. By transferring to Kharkiv the Bolsheviks admitted their complete helplessness in the struggle with the Rada. Realizing that the whole Right Bank of the Dnieper and a part of the Left Bank did not offer favourable ground for the Bolshevik revolution, they transferred their activity to a place where the revolutionary proletariat was much more numerous, and where there was already "a revolutionary army which had arrived from Petrograd under the command of comrade Sivers."[52] The reasons for leaving Kiev were very characteristically described by Skrypnyk, one of the leaders of the first Soviet regime in Ukraine:

> The main mass of the proletariat of Ukraine is in its eastern part, in the Donets basin. In all other parts and cities of Ukraine, the proletariat is rather weak in numbers and organization. The first congress of soviets of Ukraine, convened in Kiev, was drowned in a sea of representatives of the kulak peasants' unions, who were summoned there by the Central Rada. At that time even the workers in towns, district centres, and villages to a large extent still followed the yellow and blue flag of Ukrainian nationalism. There were two possibilities: either to recognize the Central Rada and to try within it to detach the proletariat and the proletarianized strata of peasantry, or to place immediately the conscious proletariat in opposition to the nationalist kulak Central Rada .... For the first road to be followed, the working class of the Dnieper region was much too weak, both numerically and organizationally, and was also only slightly class conscious. It only remained for us to look for a place in that part where the proletariat formed a more numerous, more concentrated, more conscious nucleus. And the delegates from the workers at the first all-Ukrainian congress moved to Kharkiv.[53]

Zatonsky likewise admitted later that the Bolsheviks in Kiev were just "a knot of people," that

> ... it was completely clear that on the all-Ukrainian or even on the district scale the workers of Kiev could not take power, that here it would be necessary to go through the Rada and expect either the collapse of petty-bourgeois illusions in the struggle with the soviets ... or to attempt the sovietization of the Rada by peaceful means, as the Menshevik-SR soviets were sovietized .... Kharkiv with its working-class population had to become a base for the struggle with Kaledin as well as with the Central Rada.[54]

In Popov's opinion, the Bolsheviks in Ukraine before the seizure of power were badly off both quantitatively and qualitatively. In November 1917, in his opinion, the party "relied only on the *proletariat*, and moreover even this proletariat was much less controlled by it than in the north and the centre. *The party's influence on the army was much less, and there was almost no influence on the peasantry.* That was all we had on the eve of the 'October' in Ukraine." Popov wrote that "there were no strong Ukrainian cadres in the ranks of the party," and that "the historical peculiarity of our party is that it has a weak connection with the masses of Ukrainian nationality."[55] Elsewhere he wrote that "in 1917 the Bolshevik party conquered the working masses.[56] But it had not yet started to conquer the peasantry and the village proletariat,"[57] so that "*the active base of the Bolsheviks during their struggle was still only the working class.*"[58] Popov acknowledges that the party had against it "a united front of Ukrainian nationalist socialist parties that depended on compact masses of the Ukrainian petty bourgeoisie, chiefly the *peasantry.*"[59] And elsewhere he admits that the government of the Central Rada "no doubt depended for support on numerous peasant masses and had under its command rather *large military forces*; moreover, extending its struggle with the Bolsheviks, it had every reason for expecting whole-hearted assistance from the non-Ukrainian local bourgeoisie."[60] To this Kulyk adds that the Bolsheviks had support only in large cities, while the periphery was dominated by the Ukrainian "chauvinists."[61] Even Trotsky later admitted that during the initial years of the Soviet regime Bolshevism in Ukraine was weak.[62]

These testimonies, plus the fact that the Central Rada mastered the situation and became the *de facto* government of Ukraine, while the Bolsheviks were compelled to move to the periphery of Ukraine nearest to Russia, refute the assertions of later Soviet historiography that the establishment of the Soviet regime in Ukraine was the result of the struggle of the Ukrainian proletariat itself under the leadership of the Communist party of Ukraine.[63] That the united Ukrainian national front was not broken is regarded by Soviet historians as the Bolsheviks' worst mistake in the "October" period in Ukraine.

The Military Action of Soviet Russia against the Rada

Having failed to sovietize Ukraine through the soviets, the Russian Bolsheviks decided to carry out their plans by military force. That the Soviet government was formed in Kharkiv and not elsewhere reflected not only the proletarian character of that region, but chiefly Kharkiv's occupation by the Red Guards under Antonov. This occupation was the immediate link in the chain of the RCP's policy against the Rada. As is known, the reply of the General Secretariat to the People's Commissars' ultimatum of 17 December was considered at the meeting of the CPC on 18 December, when it resolved "to regard the Rada's reply as unsatisfactory, to consider the Rada in a state of war with us."[64] In their resolution of 1 January 1918 the People's Commissars declared that "only the soviets of the Ukrainian poor peasantry, workers, and soldiers can create in Ukraine a government under which any disagreements between fraternal nations will be impossible."[65] This intention of the RCP was later repeated by Krylenko, the commander-in-chief, on 25 January 1918, in an interview with a delegation of Ukrainian soldiers: "We fight against the Rada for the establishment of the government of soviets of workers', soldiers', and peasants' deputies over the entire territory of the Russian federative republic .... As soon as the government in Ukraine is transferred to the Ukrainian soviet of workers', soldiers', and peasants' deputies, all military operations against Ukraine will cease."[66] This meant that as long as the Rada did not recognize Soviet power, the CPC considered itself in a state of war with the Rada. This policy was a distortion of the principle of the self-determination of nations. That is why the General Secretariat of the Rada wrote in its reply to the ultimatum: "It is impossible to recognize the right to self-determination to the point of secession and at the same time to make a crude attempt upon this right, imposing its forms of political order, as does the Council of People's Commissars of Great Russia in respect of the Ukrainian People's Republic."[67]

It is manifest from Bolshevik sources themselves that at the same time as the People's Commissars made declarations on the right of national self-determination and also on the right of Ukraine to secession, it was also working out a plan to overthrow the Rada by force. According to the testimony of Antonov himself, several days before the ultimatum, on 8 December, Lenin appointed Antonov "to be in direct charge of operations against Kaledin[68] and his 'helpers'" ("by 'helpers'," writes Antonov, "were meant counter-revolutionary Ukrainians supporting Kaledin").[69] After this, Antonov left for general headquarters where, together with Krylenko, he worked out the plan of the offensive against Ukraine that was later approved by Lenin.[70] Antonov concentrated forces and prepared a wide "'encircling' of Ukraine by the units of the southwestern and Romanian fronts."[71] On 14 December, the general staff, led by Krylenko, had already made a number of decisions on this matter.

Sivers with his unit was sent to Kharkiv. On 15 December the general staff appointed Ian Berzin commander of the first Minsk detachment, with orders to "concentrate troops in Kharkiv"; but, as Antonov points out, "there were many soldiers within the nineteenth column who considered themselves Ukrainians, and there were very few conscious revolutionary elements who understood the Rada's counter-revolutionary nature."[72] Therefore the general staff's demands that Berzin take "most decisive measures against the Rada" were of no avail. It was necessary to reorganize the column, so that each regiment was assigned a detachment of 200 "reliable men," reinforced by five hundred sailors.[73]

Antonov arrived on 24 December in Kharkiv, where the revolutionary mood was not at a high pitch. Even the local Bolsheviks led by Sergeev (Artem) were opposed to the struggle against the local adherents of the Rada. Antonov attributed this to special national conditions in Ukraine. "In the city there is a strong Ukrainian influence. The twenty-eighth regiment is Ukrainianized .... It comprises up to 3,000 soldiers, 427 officers, 40 machine-guns." These regiments "are for the Central Rada, but hesitate."[74]

The initial phase of the Russian Soviet government's attack on Ukraine was limited to Kharkiv and several cities in the Donets basin, and amounted to the Soviet army "disarming units of the Central Rada while helping the local workers to introduce Soviet power."[75] But for some reason, from about 10 January 1918, the Bolshevik offensive in the direction of the Don ceased, and peace began to reign there.[76] In January "considerable forces were already diverted against the Ukrainian Rada," and "active operations directed towards Kiev began on 18 January."[77] Thus although the CPC declared Kaledin the main enemy of the revolution and a whole army was amassed for his overthrow, the CPC decided to finish with the Rada first. Soviet sources say nothing about the reasons for this change of target. Probably the Bolsheviks could not stand by and watch the implementation of the Rada's aspirations to secede from Russia, for which purpose it had issued orders to detach the southwestern and Romanian fronts and combine them into one Ukrainian front subordinated to itself. Furthermore, talks had been conducted with emissaries of the Entente on the matter of Ukraine's recognition by those powers. Likewise, the peace talks at Brest Litovsk, which were resumed on 9 January and in which the Ukrainian delegation took part independently and entertained the idea of a separate peace, were extremely alarming to the Russian Bolsheviks and evoked the opposition of the CPC.[78]

The overthrow of the Rada began with an offensive from Kharkiv, and the command "of all troops in action against the Ukrainian Rada" was entrusted to Mikhail Muravev, formerly a colonel in the tsarist army.[79] At the same time Egorov was appointed leader of the Red Guards in the action against Katerynoslav, where a struggle between Rada troops and local Bolshevik detachments took place. It was also planned to send troops from the southwestern front into action against the Rada, chiefly the second guards corps, in which Evgeniia Bosh was the political leader. Faierabend was appointed chief of the western detachment. However, as Antonov remarks, this action did not succeed, since many units refused to fight the Rada.[80] All that could have been done from that direction was to divert the Rada's attention westwards; the general staff had to deliver the main blow at it from Homel in the north.[81] On 19 January Muravev's troops occupied Poltava; on 24 January Romodan was occupied and, after stubborn fighting in which many Ukrainian high school students and cadets perished, Kruty was occupied on 30 January.[82] This opened the road to Kiev. On 5 February Muravev ordered a general offensive against Kiev. The uprising of local Bolsheviks in Kiev, which began simultaneously, was soon suppressed by the Rada's troops. On 9 February Kiev was occupied by Muravev's army, which then proceeded in the direction of Romania with the approval of Lenin and Antonov.[83]

There is a dispute between Soviet and non-Soviet historians about the character of the Red Army. There is no doubt that the troops led by Antonov were Russian and not local Ukrainian, since this was stated by the participants in those events themselves. Thus Muravev wrote in his report to Antonov after the battle at Kruty: "The Petrograd Red Guards, the Viborg and Moscow Guards have shouldered the burden of the whole battle almost alone."[84] In his telegram to Lenin, Muravev wrote that "all hope lies in the Red Guards, therefore please send me in Ukraine several thousand Red Guardists."[85] And on the battles for Kiev an official Soviet source wrote that "on 8 February the workers of Kiev, with the aid of Petrograd and Moscow Red Guards, expelled the Rada from Kiev."[86] Earlier, the commander-in-chief, Krylenko, wrote that "the workers and peasants of Russia were able to form revolutionary detachments and deal a deadly blow to the bourgeois Rada. Our troops are within some ten versts of Kiev."[87] Antonov also supplied many relevant details on the capture of Kiev. Popov wrote that "*the real help of Soviet Russia* was of no small importance," and that even in Kharkiv and Katerynoslav "the local Bolsheviks did not have sufficient strength or courage to put power into the hands of the soviets." He admitted that Soviet power in Ukraine was installed with the energetic participation of Antonov's military units and detachments, which arrived from the north, chiefly from the Petrograd and Moscow garrisons.[88]

If it had not been for the army of Antonov, if it had not been for all those Bolshevik Russian detachments of Mikhail Muravev, Iurii Sablin, Ian Berzin, Rudolf Sivers, Vitalii Primakov, Aleksandr Egorov, and others, who conducted military operations against the Central Rada in accordance with the directives of the CPC and the CC RCP, the creation of a Soviet regime in Ukraine would have ended in failure.[89]

Creation of the First Soviet Government in Ukraine

The Soviet government of Ukraine was formed in Kharkiv at a congress of soviets held simultaneously with the congress of soviets in Kiev that the Bolsheviks had to leave. The Bolsheviks from Kiev joined this congress (of soviets of the Donets and Kryvyi Rih basins) and declared it the first congress of soviets of Ukraine. This congress elected a Central Executive Committee of Ukraine and a People's Secretariat, i.e., the first Soviet government of Ukraine.[90] The representatives of the Donets basin only participated formally in the elections of the TsIKU, while "the Katerynoslav 'sceptics' abstained and took no part in them."[91] It is interesting that the Bolsheviks hesitated to adopt for their government the name "Council of People's Commissars," assuming one similar to that of the government of the Central Rada: "the People's Secretariat." Like the Rada also, the Soviets named their state "the Ukrainian People's Republic."[92] It is likewise interesting that the left Ukrainian social democrat E. G. Medvedev was elected chairman of the TsIKU, and not the leader of the Bolsheviks, the Russophile Piatakov. The People's Secretariat comprised Bosh (internal affairs), Skrypnyk (labour),[93] Sergeev (commerce and industry), Bakynsky (nationalities and foreign affairs), Kulyk (Bakynsky's deputy), Ia. Martianov (post office and telegraph), Ie. P. Terletsky (agriculture), Aussem (finance), Liuksemburg (justice), Shakhrai (military affairs), Iurii Kotsiubynsky (Shakhrai's deputy), Duhanovsky (food), Lapchynsky (general secretary).[94] Even though this government was predominantly Russian by national composition, its policy did not conform entirely to the Russian imperialist pattern. Many of its secretaries opposed the façade of the Secretariat, which was what centralists like Bosh had in mind. It is true that the CPC and the CC RCP did not assign any task to this government other than camouflaging the occupation of Ukraine. A participant in the revolution, Khrystiuk,[95] wrote that the role of the Ukrainian Soviet government was to lend "its name and its banner for the covering up of the occupation policy of Soviet Russia in Ukraine." The minister for internal affairs was the Ukrainophobe and adherent of "*edinaia i nedelimaia*" (one and indivisible

Russia), Bosh; but Skrypnyk and particularly Shakhrai were protagonists of an almost independent Ukraine,[96] while Lapchynsky stood for truly federalist principles. However, the personal composition of the Secretariat mattered little, since the military government of Antonov and Muravev did not allow the Secretariat to exercise its ministerial functions. According to a Soviet source, during its first (Kharkiv) period the Ukrainian Soviet government was "a centre without a periphery, a staff without an army; ... it had neither a territory, nor a population subject to it, nor any armed forces."[97]

The Bolsheviks in Ukraine were not unanimously agreed upon the creation of a Ukrainian Soviet centre. The so-called "Kievans," Piatakov, Bosh, and Kreisberg, and "Katerynoslavians," Kviring and Epshtein, considered Ukraine part of Russia, reasoning that although the Ukrainians were a separate people, from the point of view of the proletarian revolution as well as from the point of view of economic resources and the strength of Russia, the secession of Ukraine would mean the downfall of the revolution. Some Kievans would allow a political federation for Ukraine, but demanded centralism in the economic sphere.[98] Another current was formed by the federalists, who agreed that Ukraine had to be a part of the RSFSR, but in a federal relationship with its own government and also its own Communist party. To this group belonged Skrypnyk, Lapchynsky, and Zatonsky. The third group considered Ukraine an independent, though Soviet, republic, which had to align politically with Soviet Russia, but as an equal. Representatives of this view included Shakhrai, Serhii Mazlakh, and Neronovych. Neronovych belonged then to the Ukrainian social democratic *nezalezhnyky* (independentists), who tended to support the Soviets.

The Kievans held the most power within Soviet Ukraine, which indicates the CC RCP's support for their principles. The federalists and proponents of independence figured in the Secretariat in very insignificant and subordinate positions. Such ministries as foreign affairs, internal affairs, finance, commerce and industry, justice, and food fell to the first group, while the second occupied the ministry of labour and the general secretariat. The independence-oriented Shakhrai held the very important defence portfolio, but he had no ministry and no army—the only Bolshevik army was under the command of Antonov, who neither belonged to the Secretariat nor was subordinate to it.

The tactics of the military authorities were guided by centralist principles, and military circles completely ignored the existence of a Ukrainian Soviet government. Naturally, this soon led to friction between the local Bolsheviks and Antonov, who was unwilling to recognize the

People's Secretariat or any other organ of local government as a *de facto* government. Friction also developed with Muravev, who was unable to come to an understanding with the local soviets of Poltava after its occupation by the Red Army. The soviets of workers', soldiers', and peasants' deputies requested Muravev to withdraw his army from Poltava, because Poltava wished to be neutral towards both the Central Rada and the Kharkiv TsIKU, neither of which they recognized. Muravev replied that he had come to restore "the suppressed Soviet power in Ukraine [and] we shall not leave until you recognize the genuine Kharkiv people's Rada." Antonov supported Muravev and advised him to tell the Poltava soviets that Poltava had to be the base for the struggle with "Kaledin's allies," and that, besides, "we shall try to extract from the Poltava region grain for the hungry central regions of the north and for the front."[99] However, even Antonov himself had to admit that Muravev in Poltava "adopted a definitely sharp tone, the tone of a conqueror, and entered into a sharp conflict with the local soviet and roused all Ukrainians against him."

With the taking of Kiev, Muravev's tone became even sharper, for "his laurels began to be reaped by *Kotsiubynsky* ... who had been appointed the leader of the Ukrainian troops."[100] In obedience to the TsIKU, at a meeting of which Antonov heard complaints about Muravev and other Red Army leaders, Antonov advised Muravev "not to make any political declarations, but to allow a representative of the Ukrainian administration to speak, and to declare yourself the instrument of his will."[101] Antonov had promised the Ukrainian TsIK, he told Muravev, that "we shall keep politically in the background, leaving them the political scene, but keeping to ourselves the strategic position."[102]

Lenin, who had learned of the antagonism between the military and political authorities, wrote to Antonov: "In view of the complaints of the People's Secretariat about friction that arose between you and the TsIK of Ukraine, please inform me, from your side, what is actually the matter; obviously our intervention in the internal affairs of Ukraine, inasmuch as it is not the result of military necessity, is undesirable. It is more convenient to take any necessary measures through the organs of local government, and generally it would be best of all if any misunderstandings were settled locally."[103] As Antonov himself wrote later, his relations with the People's Secretariat of Ukraine from the very beginning "were not particularly firm," and they deteriorated even more after he appointed, without the Secretariat's knowledge, his own commissars[104] at the stations and in some towns of the Donets basin. The people's secretary for internal affairs, Bosh, dismissed those commissars without consulting Antonov and, moreover, reported to Lenin on Antonov's "*samoupravstvo*" (taking the law into his own hands).[105] It was for this reason that Lenin had to turn to Antonov again and implore him "*to eliminate each and every friction with the [Kharkiv] TsIK. This is extremely important for the interests of state.* For God's sake, make peace with them and acknowledge them to possess every sovereignty. I earnestly implore you to remove the commissars you have appointed. I hope very, very much that you will comply with this request and will achieve *absolute* peace with the Kharkiv TsIK. Here an *extremely great national tact* is necessary."[106]

These entreaties of Lenin evidently were not designed to induce Antonov to make peace with Ukrainian independentists from the Bolshevik camp, but to prevent him from spoiling his relations with the "Kharkovians," whom Lenin secretly supported in their desire to separate the Donets basin from the rest of Ukraine. It seems that at that time Lenin did not believe in the success of a Ukrainian Bolshevik revolution and banked on the "Kharkovians" to keep the Donets basin, which was necessary for the Russian state. Meanwhile, relations between the People's Commissars in Petrograd and the People's Secretariat were not very harmonious. Although the People's Commissars recognized the People's Secretariat as the government of Ukraine,[107] it never recognized its satellite in Ukraine as having sovereignty in military and high policy matters. Only in internal affairs was relative freedom of action admitted. However, whenever the situation demanded it, the People's Commissars bypassed even the formal rights of the Ukrainian Soviet government. The food emergency in Russia made the People's Commissars impatient. After Katerynoslav was taken, the RCP(B) sent Grigorii Ordzhonikidze (Sergo) and other "[party] workers from Moscow and Petrograd" to organize the shipment of food to Russia. At the same time, perhaps with the agreement of Trotsky, the people's commissar for food, Kudynsky was appointed chief food commissar in Ukraine. People's secretary E. V. Luhanovsky protested this appointment.[108] Similarly, the TsIKU cancelled Antonov's appointment of Innokentii Kozhevnikov to "the post of special plenipotentiary for the Donets basin," which had been sanctioned by Lenin.[109] The People's Secretariat protested against Muravev's appointment by Lenin as commander of the Romanian front.[110] It is obvious that in view of the confusion existing in the relations between the People's Commissars and the People's Secretariat, and also in view of the subordinate position of the Bolsheviks in Ukraine in relation to the CC RCP, it was impossible to take seriously the sovereignty of Ukrainian Soviet power.

During the combined German and Rada offensive, the Bolsheviks with their People's Secretariat moved to Katerynoslav, where on 17–18 March the second congress of soviets took place. The composition of the congress was indicative of the weakness of the Bolsheviks in the Ukrainian countryside. The participants were the Communist faction and their sympathisers, 428 (including the left USDWP's 27); the united Russian and Ukrainian SRs and their sympathizers, 414; the Ukrainian SDs (*obiedynentsi*), 6; the Bund, 2; the Russian and Ukrainian SRs (the centre and right wing), 4; the anarchists, 3; the maximalists, 4; the independentists, 82; and undetermined, 8.[111] According to one of the delegates, Mazepa, later the Directory's prime minister, the congress divided into halves, approximately 400 Bolsheviks and 380 non-Bolsheviks.[112] Five Bolsheviks were elected to the presidium of the congress: Skrypnyk, Kviring, Hamarnyk, Medvedev, and Ivanov; and five left SRs: A. Sivero-Odoievsky, Kachynsky, Terletsky, Boichenko, and M. Serdiuk.[113] At the same time, a new TsIK was elected; headed by Zatonsky, the TsIK consisted of forty-nine SRs, forty-seven Bolsheviks, five members of the USDWP left, and one representative of the PPS-Left.[114] At the very first meeting conflicts emerged among the delegates concerning the party's policy towards the Central Rada and the peace. The people's secretary for military affairs, Neronovych,[115] argued the hopelessness and harmfulness of struggle with its troops. Neronovych together with Kviring proposed "to give up military operations against the Central Rada and to agree to compromise with it."[116] According to Khrystiuk, Neronovych's thesis, which had been adopted at the meeting of the People's Secretariat[117] and which he was now to submit to the congress, consisted of the following points:

> 1) Soviet power in Ukraine has been established with the aid of an armed revolutionary proletariat, mainly the Great Russian one, and there are almost no local forces as a backing for the existence of Soviet power;
> 2) A further struggle with the army of the Central Rada will inevitably lead to the weakening of the democratic position of the Central Rada and may create a situation in which the Fourth Universal will be lost;
> 3) In view of this it is necessary to conclude a peace with the Central Rada and to reorganize it immediately, uniting its existing composition with the Central Executive Committee of Ukraine elected at the second all-Ukrainian congress of soviets, and with these common forces to realize the principles set out in the Fourth Universal.[118]

This line of reconciliation with the Rada did not, however, appeal to the majority, and it failed.

The congress also discussed the peace question and divided into two groups parallel to the division on the issue in Moscow. The left SRs defended the idea of continuing the war to a victorious end. The Bolsheviks (of Lenin's faction) advocated recognizing the Brest Litovsk peace in order to have a "respite." Skrypnyk, who was the main speaker on the peace, took up Lenin's position. He argued that in Ukraine conditions had arisen for the Bolsheviks which were completely unlike those in Soviet Russia. The international bourgeoisie, he said, did not wish to recognize "the power of the Ukrainian workers and peasants," and the Germans, together with the "Ukrainian bourgeoisie," wanted to destroy Soviet power in Ukraine.[119] The left SRs succeeded in forcing through their resolution against signing the Brest Litovsk peace treaty, but on a second vote the Bolsheviks got their amendments through, so that the resolution did not touch upon the peace at all.[120]

Regarding relations between Ukraine and Russia, the following resolution was passed: "At the present moment the peace treaty that has been forced upon the Russian federation formally breaks the federative ties of Ukraine with the whole Soviet federation. Ukraine has become an independent Soviet republic. But in essence the relationships of Soviet republics remain as before. The toiling masses of Ukraine believe that in the very near future these formal federative ties must be renewed, and all Soviet republics will unite into one world socialist federation."[121] The proclamation of Ukraine's independence was conditional and tactical. In Skrypnyk's words, it was done to achieve independence from "the petty-bourgeois Central Rada and from the power of German and world imperialism."[122] Kulyk, a Bolshevik functionary in Ukraine, wrote that "the proclamation of independence was only a tactical move made in order to have a free hand in the struggle against the invaders, for if Ukraine were to remain a part of Russia, according to the Brest Litovsk conditions, it would not have had the right to bear arms against the German army; for in such an event any responsibility would have fallen upon Russia."[123] It is not surprising that the Bolsheviks achieved the passage of such a resolution, obviously directed against Ukraine's independence, at a congress where Russified elements predominated.

But the resolutions of the congress had little influence on the course of events, because the Bolsheviks and their People's Secretariat soon found themselves beyond the borders of Ukraine, in Taganrog, where the TsIKU and the People's Secretariat were formally dissolved. At its last meeting, the TsIKU resolved to disband itself and to dissolve the People's Secretariat. They were to be replaced by an organizational insurgence centre, the so-called "insurgence nine," which consisted of four Bolsheviks (Skrypnyk,[124] Piatakov, Bubnov, and Zatonsky, with S. Kosior, Kotsiubynsky, Hamarnyk, and Farbman as candidates), four left SRs, and one left SD.[125] The "insurgence nine" were to direct the struggle for the liberation of Ukraine's proletariat. This revolutionary committee issued a demagogic manifesto replete with obvious distortions of fact. The manifesto declared that the recently dissolved Soviet government in Ukraine was the only lawful government, "established by the people and confirmed by the people's will," while the Rada, with the aid of the German army, was establishing in Ukraine a regime "worse than that of Nicholas." Therefore the manifesto appealed to the workers and peasants of Ukraine "to resist with all their might the illegal pseudo-government called the Rada of Ministers and the Central Rada."[126] It was very characteristic that the manifesto did not contain the usual *edinaia i nedelimaia* phraseology that pervaded almost all the declarations and manifestos of the Ukrainian Bolsheviks at that time, especially such leaders as Kviring, Iakovlev, and particularly the manifesto's editor, Piatakov. This was, it seems, an effort to improve their reputation in the eyes of the Ukrainian masses, who by then had almost completely turned away from the Bolsheviks.

However, the government of the Ukrainian Soviet republic went on "being born" and "dying" in exile. Thus when "the nine" moved from Taganrog to Moscow, the workers' and peasants' government again returned to life, and as early as May it took part in talks in Moscow with the CPC on relations between Ukraine and Russia. Then at the first congress of the Communist party of Ukraine, which took place in July 1918 in Moscow, it was resolved to dissolve the People's Secretariat of Ukraine. Thus the Soviet government in Ukraine was dissolved for the second time. In its place a central military-revolutionary committee was organized. In August of the same year, this committee again organized a "Workers' and Peasants' Government of Ukraine." This "government," however, was dissolved at the second congress of the CP(B)U, after an unsuccessful attempt at an uprising in Ukraine. The Bolsheviks themselves called this "the TsIKU playing at government."[127] These attempts at forming a government reflected the unstable and often chaotic policy of the Russian Bolsheviks on the question of nationalities, particularly in the case of Ukraine.

Loss of confidence in their own strength was largely due to the negative attitude of the Ukrainian people towards the Bolsheviks. Almost all participants in the first Soviet regime in Ukraine agree that this regime was maintained only because of the presence of the Red Army and that during the Bolsheviks' struggle against the Rada, the masses were either indifferent or hostile. Bosh wrote that during the German offensive in Ukraine, "the sympathies [of "workers' and peasants' masses"] were not on the side of the Soviet detachments. Almost everywhere the retreating detachments were shot at by local White Guardists .... The Red Army men were not sure that they would not be met with fire from the rear. Apart from the apathy of the masses, which reached the point of hostility, the situation was made worse by the instability of the soviets and by general disorganization in the rear .... The population was not hospitable."[128] Antonov wrote that while the German troops were advancing, "a tide of anti-Soviet uprising swept Ukraine."[129] Muravev reported in a telegram to Antonov:

> I have attempted to rouse the whole south, but it is not the north—the proletariat of Odessa has not given me a single battalion .... Regular troops have refused to fight, and I have at my disposal only several hundred Red Guards .... Treason is everywhere.[130]

The causes of the early fall of the first Soviet government in Ukraine were many. It is true that it was driven out by the German army, but the question remains: Why did the masses not support the Bolsheviks in their struggle against the German and Ukrainian armies? The Bolsheviks themselves recognized that the masses were against them. The population's enmity can be ascribed, first, to the Soviet food policy, the removal of grain and other foods from Ukraine to Russia, and second, to the party's national policy, which ignored and even fought the Ukrainian national movement and which included frequent reprisals against Ukrainians as such, not only against counter-revolutionaries. The hostility towards the Bolsheviks had deep roots; and in 1917 they were not taken seriously.

The Brest Litovsk Treaty and the Policy of the Russian Communist Party in Ukraine

An analysis of Soviet Russia's internal situation and attitude towards the Central Powers in December 1917 and January-February 1918 shows the importance of the Ukrainian question in the Brest Litovsk negotiations, which in turn influenced party policy against Ukraine. Lenin advocated, "before a small private meeting of party workers"[131] on 8 January 1918, the immediate signing of a separate peace. He depicted the situation of Soviet power in Russia as if without "a certain span of time, at least several months" the consolidation and stabilization of the revolution would be impossible. Lenin advocated signing a treaty with the Central Powers mainly because "the probable moment of the outbreak of revolution and the overthrow of any of the European imperialist governments (including the German one) is completely beyond calculation." For Russia itself to wage a revolutionary war in Europe was impossible. Lenin pointed out that the Russian army at that time was unable even to withstand the German offensive, and that "at the present moment the peasant majority of our army would no doubt speak in favour of an annexation with peace, and not of an immediate revolutionary war." Lenin made the success of a "revolutionary war" depend on the victory of a revolution in Germany. "If a German revolution does not take place within the next few months, then the course of events, if the war continues, will unavoidably be such that most serious defeats will compel Russia to conclude an even less advantageous separate peace, and, moreover, the Soviet regime in Russia will probably be overthrown by a peasant army."[132]

The appearance in Brest Litovsk of a delegation from the Central Rada even further weakened the Soviet delegation's position. It is quite possible that the separate peace with Ukraine saved the Central Powers from collapsing as the result of internal revolution, which threatened these states. Perhaps the speculations of a Soviet historian about this crucial point in the negotiations are very near the truth. "The fact that German imperialism was confronted by the forces of Soviet Russia and of Ukraine, which were not united but were fighting between themselves, was of immense importance. If, on the contrary, both Soviet Russia and Ukraine had presented a united front in Brest Litovsk, ... it is questionable how rapidly the revolutionary tide in Germany and Austria-Hungary would have receded ... or whether the Brest Litovsk talks would not have become the starting point for an immediate revolution in Central Europe."[133] However, Ukrainian grain was seen as salvation not only by the Central Powers, but also by the Russian Bolsheviks themselves.[134] For instance, Commander-in-Chief Krylenko, in his order of 22 January 1918, announced that "with the fall of the Rada and with the capture of Kiev we shall again have the possibility of getting grain from Ukraine."[135] Therefore the Bolsheviks sought at any price "not to allow the Central Rada to break up the peace talks that have begun with the Germans." They intended to prevent the Rada from signing a separate peace with the Central Powers, but instead "to support the cause of the Ukrainian poorer classes with military force and to strengthen the Soviet government in Ukraine, into whose hands should pass the conduct, in close alliance with Soviet Russia, of the peace talks with the Germans."[136]

From the very beginning, the tactics of the RCP were to sign a peace in the name of the whole of Russia. When the Rada sent its own delegation, efforts were made to include it in the Russian delegation. The efforts failed because the Rada delegation recognized the CPC as the government of Great Russia alone; so long as there was no socialist government for the whole of Russia, Ukraine had to be represented independently in the peace talks. At first Trotsky recognized the Rada delegation, but when it took an independent course, he began to deny the Rada's competence and claimed that the Ukrainian Soviet government was the sole representative of Ukraine. Therefore a delegation of the People's Secretariat was sent from Kharkiv to Brest Litovsk, headed by the chairman of the TsIKU, Medvedev, and by the secretary for military affairs, Shakhrai.[137] Before the Rada signed the peace with the Central Powers, the Russian Bolsheviks tried to persuade the Germans to sign a peace, not with it, but with the Kharkiv government, the People's Secretariat. They argued that the Rada no longer existed, and that the Ukrainian workers themselves had driven it out. Trotsky also stated that, with the People's Secretariat now controlling Ukraine, the signature of the Rada representatives would be invalid.[138] In another declaration, he argued that "even apart from the position of Ukraine in international law as a constituent part of the Russian federation, there remains in full force the fact that Ukraine is not separated from Russia territorially, and therefore no treaties with Ukraine can be valid without their being recognized by the Russian delegation."[139]

With the aim of preventing the Central Rada from signing the peace, Lenin and particularly Stalin bombarded their delegation with telegrams about the Rada's feebleness. As early as 15 January Lenin wired by private line to the delegation in Brest Litovsk: "Today the delegation of the Kharkiv Ukrainian TsIK is leaving to join you; [the delegation] has convinced me that the Kiev Rada is moribund."[140] On 3 February he announced by radio "to everyone, to the peace delegation in Brest Litovsk particularly," that "the Kiev Rada has fallen."[141] The following day it was announced, again "to everyone," that "Kiev is in the hands of Ukrainian Soviet power. The bourgeois Kiev Rada has fallen and is dispersed. The power of the Kharkiv Ukrainian Soviet regime has been completely recognized."[142] Apparently, these wild exaggerations were calculated to convince the Germans that they were signing peace with a non-existent government.[143]

After the Rada signed the peace, the Bolsheviks tried another tack. They began nursing the hope that the Germans in practice would carry out the treaty with the Kharkiv government instead of with the Rada. The People's Commissars now persuaded the People's Secretariat of Ukraine to take over the obligations of the Brest Litovsk peace. Stalin assumed that the Germans signed the treaty with the Rada not to restore the Rada's regime, but to obtain needed grain. On 24 February Stalin informed the People's Secretariat of the Ukrainian Soviet republic about the conditions of the Brest Litovsk peace treaty, expressing at the same time his own opinions. "It seems to us that the section about Ukraine means not the restoration of Vynnychenko's power, which in itself is of no value to the

Germans, but a very real pressure on us, calculated to make you and us accept the treaty of the old Rada with Austria-Hungary; for the Germans need—not Vynnychenko—but the exchange of manufactured goods for grain and ore." Stalin reported that the CC RCP was of the opinion that the People's Secretariat ought to "send its delegation to Brest Litovsk and declare there that if Vynnychenko's adventure is not supported by the Austro-Hungarians, the People's Secretariat will not raise any objection against the principles of the treaty with the old Kiev Rada."[144]

As subsequent events showed, the Germans rejected the Bolsheviks' proposals and rendered military assistance to the Rada for the removal of the Red Guards from Ukraine. When the Rada, accompanied by German troops, returned to Kiev, the Bolsheviks were surprised; they had considered its overthrow to have settled the matter.[145] Bolshevik naivety is clear from a proclamation of the People's Secretariat, signed by Skrypnyk, which stated that "after our peace delegation signed the peace with Austria-Germany in Brest Litovsk, the regiments of the German bourgeoisie will have to withdraw, and the former Kiev Rada will be gone with the gangs of *haidamaky*."[146]

The treaty of Brest Litovsk had immense consequences for the subsequent relations between Soviet Russia and Ukraine. In accordance with the terms of the Brest Litovsk peace signed on 3 March 1918 by Grigorii Sokolnikov on behalf of the government of Russia, the CPC not only had to evacuate Ukraine but also sign a peace treaty with it, which meant recognizing it as an independent state. Article 5 of the peace treaty declared, in part: "Russia is pledged to conclude immediately a peace with the Ukrainian People's Republic and to recognize the peace treaty between this state and the powers of the Quadruple Alliance. The territory of Ukraine is [to be] forthwith freed from Russian troops, the Russian Red Guards. Russia [must] cease any agitation directed against the government and public institutions of the Ukrainian People's Republic."[147] In spite of this, the CPC continually postponed the talks, which began only after the German government exerted pressure. The question of peace with Ukraine was sharply debated at the seventh congress of the RCP where the opponents of the peace demanded from Lenin an assurance that no peace with the Rada would be signed. At the session of 7 March Moisei Uritsky asked Lenin: "Is it possible that we will betray Ukraine and conclude peace with Petliura?" Uritsky said that to make peace with Vynnychenko would mean "to let the same soviets which have been created with the help of our working class blood be torn to pieces."[148] Bukharin denied that peace would bring the revolution any respite, because, with the loss of Ukraine and the Donets basin, Russia would be deprived of essentials for the consolidation of its forces.[149] Trotsky declared that even if the Germans should demand that the People's Commissars sign a peace with the Rada, it would be necessary to refuse, for otherwise it would be "treason in the full sense of the word"; the Central Rada, he said, "fights against a part of our own proletarian army. ... We cannot conclude peace with the Kievan Rada, which considers the Ukrainian workers class enemies 'number one.'"[150] Lenin gave an explanation and a lesson in the dialectics of revolution to all opponents of peace with the Central Powers and the Rada. He argued that to promise not to conclude peace with Vynnychenko would mean "instead of a clear line of manoeuvring—retreating, advancing when possible—instead of this, binding oneself again by a formal decision. In a war, one must never tie oneself by formal considerations. It is ridiculous not to know military history, not to know that a treaty is a means of gathering strength."[151] The leftists opposed peace with the Rada partly because of their belief in world revolution and their dogmatic opposition to everything bourgeois and particularly to everything "nationalist." The leftists always and openly opposed dividing the Russian empire into small states; Trotsky had been hostile to everything Ukrainian from the very beginning of his political career,[152] and Radek was very much influenced by Rosa Luxemburg on the national and particularly on the Ukrainian question. From the standpoint of the success of the Russian revolution, Lenin's tactics were much more serviceable than the straightforward revolutionary dogmatism of the leftists.

The Ukrainian policy of the RCP after the treaty of Brest Litovsk and the capitulation of the Central Powers was marked by "manoeuvring" tactics, as defined by Lenin.[153] At Brest Litovsk, Soviet Russia had promised both to conclude a formal peace with Ukraine and to cease hostile, subversive activities on Ukrainian territory. In fact, the Bolsheviks adhered to neither condition. The peace talks themselves amounted to little more than an occasion for espionage and subversive activities.

The government of the Ukrainian People's Republic took the initiative with respect to peace talks. On 30 March 1918 the Ukrainian government sent a note to the People's Commissars proposing "to enter immediately into discussions" on the cessation of hostilities and the signing "of a democratic peace."[154] Only after the intervention of the German government[155] did the People's Commissars send a delegation to Smolensk, but apparently without the knowledge of the Ukrainian government, which replied to a note on 14 April proposing Kursk as the meeting place. On 27 April the People's Commissars appointed Dzhugashvili-Stalin "plenipotentiary representative of the Russian Federative Socialist Republic for the conducting of talks on the conclusion of a treaty with the

Ukrainian People's Republic."[156] While notes were exchanged about the site of the talks, a change of regime took place in Kiev. The Soviet delegation arrived in Kiev, where Hetman Skoropadsky received it on 10 May. The head of the Russian delegation was Rakovsky, with Manuilsky as his deputy. The Ukrainian delegation was headed by the attorney general, Senator Serhii Shelukhyn.[157]

The Bolsheviks in Ukraine did not quite share the policy of the RCP on the peace question and the liquidation of the Soviet regime in Ukraine. Rakovsky sharply censured the Soviet commander-in-chief, Antonov, for sabotaging the peace talks. "We must end the business with Ukraine, at least for the time being, and wait for a more favourable historical situation." He further stressed the necessity to cease hostilities in Ukraine; otherwise Soviet Russia would not have peace, but German troops might advance even deeper into Russia.[158] Lenin likewise ordered Antonov to do everything possible to facilitate "the speediest possible cessation of hostilities."[159]

The talks began on 23 May in Kiev. The instructions of the Russian delegation stated that the representatives of Soviet Russia were empowered "to conclude a peace treaty between the Russian Socialist Federative Soviet Republic and the Ukrainian state and to sign both the records of the talks and the peace treaty."[160] On 12 June a treaty was signed concerning the cessation of hostilities between the "two sovereign states," the establishment of railway communications between them, and the setting up of consulates for the duration of the talks.[161] However, the talks soon reached a deadlock, chiefly because of disputes over boundaries and the division of state property. The Russian delegation tried at all costs to push the borders of Ukraine to the west in order to obtain at least part of the Donets basin and its coal for Russia.[162] The border question gave rise to endless discussion. Lenin declared at the joint session of the VTsIK and the Moscow soviet on 14 May 1918 that the difficulties of peace talks with the Ukrainians stemmed from the fact that it was not clear "according to which Universal they wish to determine the boundaries of Ukraine .... The Rada which signed the Universal is deposed" and in its place "the landowner hetman is installed. On the basis of this uncertainty a whole series of questions emerged which show that the questions of war and peace remain where they were."[163] The economic crisis in Russia made peace urgent. As Rakovsky pointed out in an interview in *Pravda*, a very important question for Russia at that time was "the exchange of goods." "The Ukrainian delegation has already expressed the wish to give us both coal and iron, and other goods in certain quantities, but we demand grain first of all, and we count on getting it."[164] But from the whole course of the talks it is obvious that the Bolsheviks had absolutely no intention of bringing them to a fruitful conclusion; rather, they used their stay in Kiev for subversive activites and for the preparation of an uprising against the hetman's regime.[165] It seems that all the delaying tactics and ardent speeches about borders were ways of playing for time and, of course, getting grain from Ukraine in accordance with the treaty. Georgii Chicherin, the people's commissar for foreign affairs of Soviet Russia, told a session of the VTsIK on 2 September 1918 that the main cause of the protraction of talks was the Ukrainian government's "immoderate territorial claims," which left Russia with only 12 per cent of the production of the Donets basin. "The chief difficulty lies in those external obstacles that prevent Ukraine from giving us grain in exchange for the textiles it needs. A final obstacle to any political settlement whatsoever with Ukraine was that the hetman's government made a deal with the so-called Don government of Krasnov and refused to determine the eastern boundary of Ukraine with the Don region."[166] Chicherin's declaration underscores how important it was for the Bolsheviks to obtain grain and coal from Ukraine[167] and also to strike a diplomatic blow against the Don government which then had friendly relations with Ukraine. With the passage of time the international situation, chiefly the balance of forces on the western front, developed more and more in the Bolsheviks' favour. The collapse of the Central Powers opened Ukraine to the Bolsheviks. By 3 November the talks in Kiev were broken off, and Manuilsky was recalled to Moscow. After the departure of the Russian delegation, relations between the Ukrainian and the Soviet Russian governments were suspicious and hostile. The international situation was not at all conducive to releasing tension on the Russo-Ukrainian front. The policy of the Russian Bolsheviks thereafter was marked by agitation for a Bolshevik uprising in Ukraine. For this purpose the Communist party of Ukraine was formally created in Moscow and invested with the full puppet role in the future occupation, the so-called sovietization, of Ukraine.

The first attempt of the Bosheviks to seize power in Ukraine succeeded mainly because of the military intervention of Soviet Russia. This regime, after several weeks in power, was overthrown with the active aid of another external force, Germany.

From the standpoint of the principle, "the right of nations to self-determination," then so much in the air, the struggle for Ukraine assumes a different aspect. In this respect, the chief role was played by the attitude of the Ukrainian population towards whether Ukraine should belong to this or that Great Power or enjoy complete independence. The majority of Ukrainian political parties and other social organizations supported, during the Brest Litovsk peace, the complete independence of Ukraine. In this connection, the provisional parliament of Ukraine, the Central Rada, issued the Fourth Universal proclaiming Ukraine's independence. In the period between the fall of the Russian Provisional government and the military invasion of Ukraine by Soviet troops, power passed into the hands of the Central Rada. The Ukrainian Bolsheviks did not consider themselves able to seize power by force, but tried to sovietize the Rada by means of a new election of deputies to it in accordance with a special Bolshevik system of representation. This attempt failed.

The only hope of the Bosheviks lay in the military intervention of Soviet Russia. With considerable Russian assistance, the Ukrainian Bolsheviks established Soviet power after the Russian model and subordinated Ukraine to Moscow.

The Rada's proclamation of Ukrainian independence coincided with the political plans of the leading statesmen of the Central Powers, which offered Ukraine peace and military aid against the Bolsheviks. The Bolsheviks, once they realized that their hostility to the Rada would result in Ukraine's separation from Russia, changed their tactics and proposed to the Central Powers that they sign a peace not with the Rada, but with the Soviet government of Ukraine with all the obligations this implied. Thus they were prepared to deliver to the Central Powers the same quantities of grain and other produce as the Rada, if only the Central Powers recognized Soviet power in Ukraine. When these measures failed to win over the Central Powers, the Russian Bolsheviks tried to detach Ukraine's industrial regions, the Donets basin and the entire south, in an attempt to save for the revolution whatever could be saved. These attempts too ended in failure, for the Central Powers recognized Ukraine's borders as defined by the Third Universal.

During this period, the policy of the party on the Ukrainian national question was Luxemburgist. Ukrainian national demands were ignored, and after Soviet rule was installed the Ukrainian movement was suppressed. By such methods the Bolsheviks did not gain the sympathies of the Ukrainian masses; on the contrary, these acts destroyed whatever illusions Bolshevik propaganda had inspired in the populace.

Volodymyr Vynnychenko

Pavlo Skoropadsky

Symon Petliura

Mykhailo Hrushevsky

Oleksander Shumsky

Mykola Skrypnyk

Vasyl Shakhrai

Volodymyr Zatonsky

Vladimir Antonov-Ovseenko

Khristian Rakovsky

Evgeniia Bosh

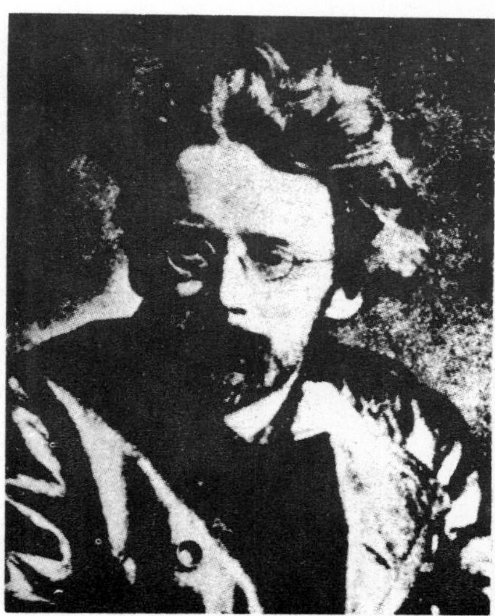

Georgii Piatakov

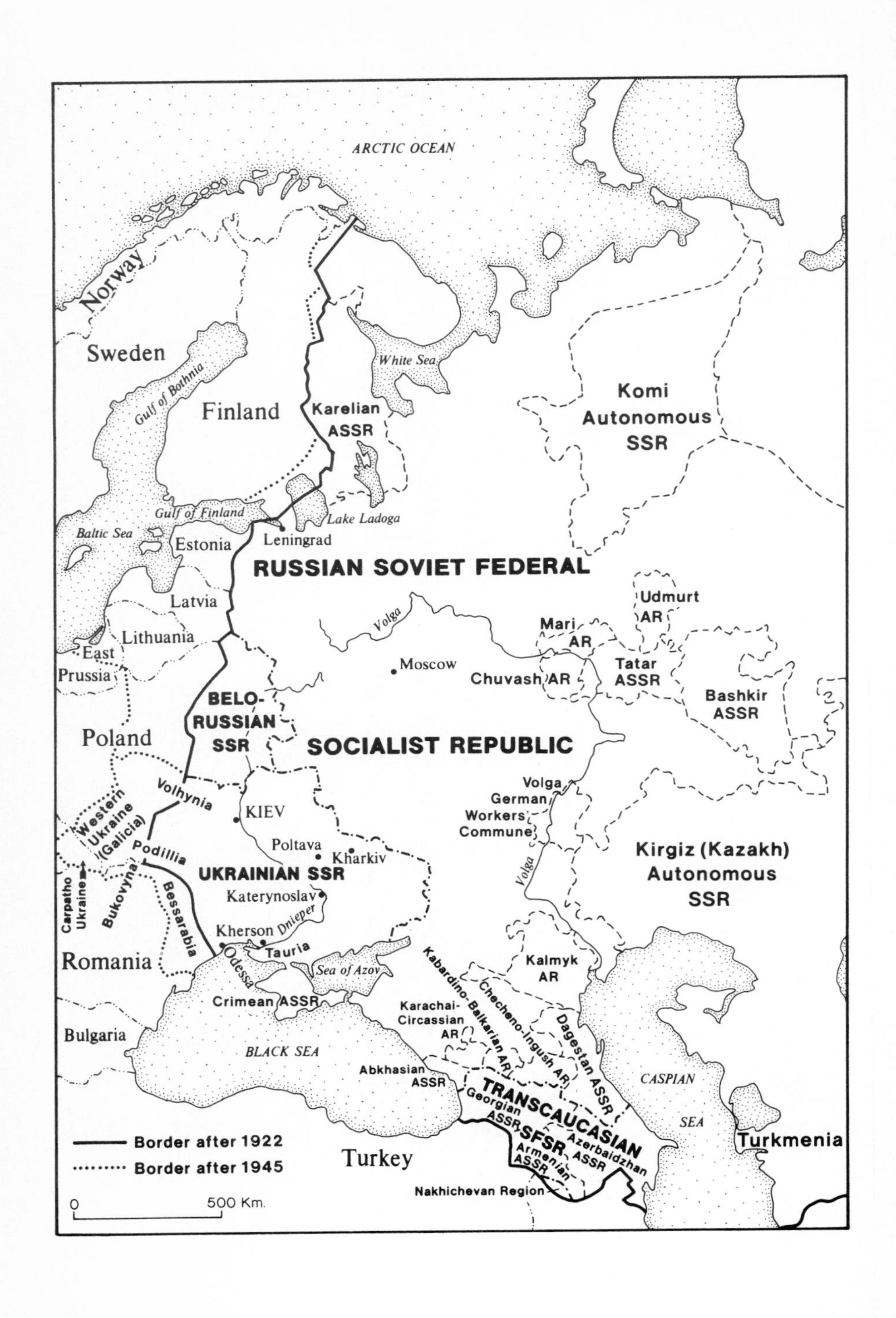

ARCTIC OCEAN
Norway
Sweden
Gulf of Bothnia
Finland
White Sea
Karelian ASSR
Komi Autonomous SSR
Gulf of Finland
Lake Ladoga
Baltic Sea
Leningrad
Estonia
RUSSIAN SOVIET FEDERAL
Latvia
Volga
Udmurt AR
Mari AR
Lithuania
East Prussia
Moscow
Chuvash AR
Tatar ASSR
Bashkir ASSR
BELO-RUSSIAN SSR
Poland
SOCIALIST REPUBLIC
Volga German Workers' Commune
Volhynia
KIEV
Western Ukraine (Galicia)
Podillia
Poltava
Kharkiv
Kirgiz (Kazakh) Autonomous SSR
UKRAINIAN SSR
Carpatho Ukraine
Bukovyna
Bessarabia
Katerynoslav
Kherson
Dnieper
Tauria
Romania
Odessa
Sea of Azov
Kalmyk AR
Kabardino-Balkarian AR
Checheno-Ingush AR
Dagestan ASSR
Crimean ASSR
Karachai-Circassian AR
Bulgaria
BLACK SEA
Abkhasian ASSR
TRANSCAUCASIAN SFSR
Georgian ASSR
Armenian ASSR
Azerbaidzhan ASSR
CASPIAN SEA
Turkmenia
Turkey
Nakhichevan Region
Border after 1922
Border after 1945
0
500 Km.

CHAPTER VIII

The Second Attempt to Sovietize Ukraine

The Prospects of the Sovietization of Ukraine against the Background of the Fall of the Central Powers

Soviet Russia's international position at the end of the First World War very largely determined the subsequent policy of the RCP towards the borderlands, including Ukraine. As early as the beginning of the second half of 1918 it became obvious that the fortunes of war increasingly favoured the Allies. And by then also the Quadruple Alliance existed only on paper. September 1918 brought a crucial turning point in the war. Mutinies broke out in Bulgaria, which was soon compelled to sue for peace. It was followed by Austria-Hungary and Germany itself. In Germany revolution broke out on 9 November; Kaiser Wilhelm II was dethroned and a social democratic government came to power in Berlin. On 11 November the German government was compelled by the armistice to annul the Brest Litovsk treaty. Two days later the Russian Bolsheviks also annulled the treaty.

How did the Russian Bolsheviks view the international situation at that time? Lenin's report of 22 October 1918 indicated that the Bolsheviks hoped for a revolution not in Europe alone, but in the world at large. As Lenin said, "we have never been so near to an international proletarian revolution as we are now." Bolshevism, he said, had become an international phenomenon with an unprecedented influence on the working masses of all countries. He was certain that "the Russian proletariat has established its might, and it is clear that we will be followed by millions and tens of millions of the international proletariat."[1] But Lenin was also aware that Bolshevik power in Russia itself had never been in such a critical state as it was then, and that as soon as the war ended the imperialists of all countries would join in a united campaign against Soviet Russia. The revolutions in Germany and other European countries had a twofold influence on the Bolshevik position in Russia.[2] Lenin was primarily afraid that the Allies would intervene in Ukraine, thus frustrating its sovietization.[3] He accused the German bourgeoisie of being eager to help the Allies "rob" Russia in order to retrieve for itself a share in the spoils. He said that the Anglo-French imperialists had made their objective the overthrow of the Soviet regime in Russia at all costs. They were preparing to attack Russia from the south, through the Dardanelles and the Black Sea or via Bulgaria and Romania, while "at least a part of the Anglo-French imperialists apparently hope that the German government will, by direct or tacit agreement with them, withdraw its troops from Ukraine only gradually in the same stages as the latter is occupied by the Anglo-French troops, to prevent the otherwise inevitable victory of the Ukrainian workers and peasants and the creation by them of a Ukrainian workers' and peasants' government."[4] This was unquestionably propaganda, intended to rouse Russia's masses to patriotic fervour. It follows from Lenin's speech that he never even considered recognizing Ukraine as a separate state. Otherwise, how could the "Anglo-French imperialists" attack Russia through Bulgaria and Romania, which, at least in 1918, had no borders with Russia? Ukraine he regarded as a part of Russia temporarily held by German imperialism. This was why he considered the separation of Ukraine after the Brest Litovsk treaty "the greatest national sacrifice" for Russia.[5] Not without a trace of demagogy, Lenin accused "the bourgeoisie of all the occupied countries: Finland, Ukraine, and Poland" of being venal; they knew of their inability "to hold the ground for a single day if the German occupation forces leave," and now they were selling themselves to the Entente just as they did before to the Germans.[6] Lenin apparently meant that the bourgeois governments of the borderlands would be unable to withstand the armed intervention of Soviet Russia.[7] But the governments of Finland and Ukraine had appealed to foreign troops for aid against the equally foreign troops of Russia. The story of Russian

Bolshevik intervention in the internal affairs of the borderlands is also the story of the genesis of the Soviet regime in Ukraine.

The sovietization of Ukraine was of the greatest importance to the Russian Bolsheviks, not least because Ukraine was their "road to the European revolution."[8] At the second congress of the CP(B)U in Moscow on 20 October 1918 the RCP propaganda mouthpiece, Radek, said that the roads to Romania, Hungary, Austria, and Germany led through Ukraine; the road through Lithuania and Poland was difficult because no revolutionary peasantry existed there. But in Ukraine, although the revolutionary movement was not strong, there was "no element of order." "Therefore our road to aid the workers of the Central Powers lies precisely over Ukraine, over Romania, over Eastern Galicia, and over Hungary."[9]

Thus on the eve of the collapse of the Central Powers, Ukraine for the Russian Bolsheviks was a "vacuum" that had to be filled—at any price—in the wake of the German evacuation. By the occupation of Ukraine the Bolsheviks would redeem themselves in the eyes of Russian patriots, who accused them of dismembering Russia. Such is the sense of Trotsky's declaration at the meeting of the All-Russian Central Executive Committee on 30 October 1918, in which he apologized for signing the Brest Litovsk treaty legalizing the secession of Ukraine. "It was one of our gravest moments when it was necessary to sign the treaty that separated Ukraine and subjected it to Germany and Austria-Hungary .... Soviet Russia has been dismembered. But it developed in the course of events the strongest power of revolutionary attraction."[10]

However, Ukraine remained low on the party agenda. First, Krasnov and Denikin had to be smashed on the Don and Kuban. "Therefore the Soviet government has decided for the time being not to go over to an offensive in Ukraine."[11]

Lenin outlined a simple plan with regard to Ukraine[12] and other borderlands. The Red Army would enter first, followed by the Bolsheviks, who would create Soviet governments for camouflaging the occupation. Lenin's plan is outlined in a telegram of 29 November 1918 to Commander-in-Chief Ioakim Vatsetis. The telegram, containing instructions on how to behave in occupied countries, was first published in 1942. Because of this document's importance and because it is little known, it is quoted here *in extenso*:[13]

> Telegram to the C. in C.
> In Serpukhov
> 29/11
> With the advance of our troops to the west and into Ukraine, regional provisional Soviet governments are created whose task it is to strengthen the

> local soviets. This circumstance has the advantage of taking away from the chauvinists of Ukraine, Lithuania, Latvia, and Estonia the possibility of regarding the advance of our detachments as occupation and creates a favourable atmosphere for a further advance of our troops. Without this condition, our troops would be put into an impossible position in the occupied regions, and the population would not meet them as liberators. In view of this we request that the commanding personnel of corresponding military units be issued instructions that our troops must in every way support the provisional Soviet governments of Latvia, Estonia, Ukraine, and Lithuania, but, of course, only the Soviet governments.
>
> Lenin.

It is hardly surprising that this document was kept under lock and key for twenty-four years: it unmasks the duplicity of Lenin's policy towards those nationalities of Russia that had seceded.

The first attempt to sovietize Ukraine in the beginning of 1918, which was conducted very unceremoniously under the slogan of "one and indivisible Soviet Russia," had taught the Bolsheviks that it was impossible to restore the former empire against the will of the nationalities. However, even now there was no substantial change in the party's Ukrainian policy. Ukraine was once again being "liberated" in the name of the same objectives.

Antonov's Controversy with Vatsetis

In his memoirs, Antonov gives an account of the RCP's plans for the invasion of Ukraine. According to him, the Council of People's Commissars resolved on 11 November 1918 "to issue the following directive to the revolutionary military council [*revvoensovet*] of the republic: within ten days to start an offensive in support of the workers and peasants of Ukraine who have risen against the hetman."[14] On the same day, the *revvoensovet* met with the "Ukrainian Communists." Present were: Commander-in-Chief Vatsetis, Stalin, Skrypnyk, Epshtein (A. Iakovlev), Zatonsky, and Antonov. It became clear at the meeting that the troops of the Central Powers in Ukraine did not represent a serious treat, since after the capitulation their one concern was to go home. Skoropadsky had about 60,000 of his own troops, but they were ill-prepared to fight and half-prepared to act against Skoropadsky in support of the "*radovtsy*," i.e., the Directory, the successor to the Central Rada. The Bolshevik forces comprised two insurgent divisions in the "neutral zone" near Kursk, 3,500 soldiers in all, ill-clad and lacking artillery. According to Epshtein, "there is absolutely no discipline in these detachments. In Ukraine itself ... we have no appreciable forces at our disposal .... Although the workers and many peasants, especially in the Chernihiv region, are on our side, without the transfer of considerable Red Army forces it is quite impossible to count not only upon the success of the revolutionary movement in Ukraine, but even upon its actual onset."[15] It became clear, too, that the Allies were planning to land their troops in the south of Ukraine and support Skoropadsky.[16] Without this, the Soviet regime in Russia was already besieged by three hostile armies: in the south were Krasnov and the Volunteers, in the east the White armies, in the north the Whites and the British landing. To open a fourth, Ukrainian, front, was a step the Bolsheviks could not contemplate. On the contrary, the situation of the Soviet regime in Russia was then so critical that the People's Commissars were attempting to attract the German armies to their side, giving them the task of protecting Soviet Russia in the north against the Anglo-White armies and in the south against Krasnov and chiefly against the White General Alekseev.[17] It is therefore not surprising that Vatsetis was unwilling at the time to commence operations against Ukraine. However, as Antonov points out, the directive of the People's Commissars to the *revvoensovet* was unambiguous: to create a "Ukrainian revolutionary staff." Antonov was appointed commander of the Ukrainian revolutionary committee, in spite of the protest of "Ukrainian officials, led by comrade Artem." As Antonov pointed out, only after Stalin's and Sverdlov's intervention "did my appointment take place."[18] Then Antonov presented his plan of operations in Ukraine, portrayed in very rosy hues and with his characteristic optimism. In his opinion, both the forces of Skoropadsky and of Denikin and Krasnov on the Don were negligible, while the Bolshevik forces were "sufficient for the most active operations." On 17 November the "Ukrainian revolutionary council" was formed, comprising Stalin,[19] Piatakov, Zatonsky, and Antonov, who on 19 November moved to Kursk to direct operations. However, neither the directives of Vatsetis nor the forces at Antonov's disposal were conducive to any further offensive on Ukraine. Antonov and his "Ukrainian officials" began a frenzied campaign against Vatsetis and his staff, suspecting them almost of sabotage.[20] Antonov even went so far as to castigate Vatsetis' actions as contradictory to Lenin's directives.[21] It will be seen later that this was not true. On 22 November Antonov sent Lenin a letter with complaints about Vatsetis. He stressed that, in accordance with the instruction of the People's Commissars, the *revvoensovet* had had to begin active operations immediately in Ukraine, but that nothing had come of that because the commander-in-chief had sabotaged the decision, primarily by not supplying troops.

> I have exhausted all the proper channels and now am troubling you. Help me. Vladimir Ilich, they are calling us in Ukraine. The workers everywhere salute the Bolsheviks and curse the *radovtsy* [the supporters of the Rada]. The latter rejoice over our inactivity and are hastily organizing themselves. Meanwhile, the Germans approach Kiev, the "Volunteers" (according to rumours) have settled in Katerynoslav, and the Cossacks are moving into the Donets basin. Under such conditions, I have decided to advance. Now it is possible to take with bare hands that which later we shall have to go at head down.[22]

Lenin, it seems, was unimpressed by these obviously exaggerated forecasts. Instead, Vatsetis ordered Antonov not to advance towards Kharkiv but to proceed with "the reorganization of Ukrainian detachments."[23] Stalin, however, reassured Antonov in his telegram: "We fully appreciate your anxiety, and I assure you that both Lenin and I will do everything possible .... As yet it is impossible to send large forces to your front, for understandable reasons."[24] Antonov, however, acted in accordance with the first directive, and such detachments as he had at his disposal began to advance on Ukraine; but he was outstripped by the Directory, which overthrew Skoropadsky on 14 December and occupied Kiev and, a few days later, Kharkiv. The controversy between Vatsetis and Antonov continued mainly because Antonov, supported by the Bolsheviks of Ukraine (who were far more eager than the Russian Bolsheviks to get to Ukraine), could not understand Vatsetis' strategy and wanted to give priority to Ukraine. Vatsetis stated this very clearly in his telegram of 4 January 1919. In his opinion a "Ukrainian army" had not yet been established, and consequently it had not been assigned any strategic task. "Strategic tasks in Ukraine," he wrote, "are so enormous that several armies are needed for their solution, and to these demands only the strength of the armies of the RSFSR will be equal; therefore those three or four regiments, the formation of which you have not yet completed, were never given strategic tasks, but only purely tactical ones." He explained once more to Antonov that "so far there is no Ukrainian fighting front." Vatsetis stressed that the Bolsheviks' road to Ukraine lay over the Don, "which means that when the time comes, all forces of the Red Army which are necessary for the task will take part in the solution of the Ukrainian problem." Then Vatsetis reproached Antonov for having begun his unauthorized offensive on Belgorod-Kharkiv-Katerynoslav.[25]

The Impatience of the Ukrainian Bolsheviks

The Ukrainian Bolsheviks were less moderate and in more of a hurry to conquer Ukraine. They were aware that the question of Soviet power in Ukraine hung by a thread and depended on their seizing the right moment. If it were missed, the Central Rada, which had reappeared under the new name of the Directory, would lead the peasant masses against Hetman Skoropadsky and would remain masters of the situation for a long time to come. They were so preoccupied with their struggle against the Ukrainian nationalist parties that the general pattern of the Bolshevik revolution was forgotten. Lenin and particularly Vatsetis apparently had a better understanding of the situation and tried to restrain the CP(B)U. The documents quoted below clearly demonstrate this narrowness of outlook on the part of the Ukrainian Bolsheviks.

Since they were members of the "group of the Kursk direction" and of the "Provisional Revolutionary Government of Ukraine," Piatakov and Zatonsky did everything they could to hasten the military offensive on Ukraine, but, as Zatonsky wrote later, "the Directory started first. It became clear that the initiative was lost and that we would no longer have to fight the hetmanites but the Petliurites."[26] Within a few days, however, the situation in Ukraine changed so much that the CC RCP had to revoke the directive issued earlier regarding a military offensive against Ukraine. There were several reasons for this. One was that the Directory was now in control of the situation, with support from the popular masses, chiefly the peasantry.[27] As Zatonsky remarked, in Moscow the CC of the RCP(B) began to believe that "the masses of the peasantry follow Petliura not because he was first to go against the hetman, but because Petliura himself is to them the dearest and best of all."[28] The Red Army, on the other hand, suffered setbacks on all fronts—on the Don, in Estonia, and in Latvia. This compelled the CC RCP to follow "an extremely cautious policy."[29] Although the group of armies of the Kursk direction and a government for Ukraine had been created, official announcement of these measures was postponed. Moscow even approached the Directory to discuss peace and an alliance. The impatience of the Ukrainian Bolsheviks provoked Lenin's anger, and he tried to restrain them.[30]

It is doubtful that one of the chief political reasons for Lenin's "ambivalence" was that he "neither controlled nor trusted the Ukrainian Communist group, of which Piatakov and Zatonsky were the leaders."[31] Neither Piatakov nor Zatonsky, after all, were separatists; on the contrary, they had always envisaged Ukraine's union with, or rather subordination to, Russia. It was because the "Kievans" favoured an immediate uprising, tried to lead the party on to more radically revolutionary paths, and sought ways to gain influence over the Ukrainian peasant masses that Lenin placed the "Kievans" at the head of the group of armies of the Kursk direction and of the government for Ukraine. It must also be stressed that the Ukrainian Bolsheviks were united at the time. In regard to the question of immediate measures against the Ukrainian Directory, there were no factional disagreements.[32] It is true that disunity in Ukraine was, in some cases, imported from the Russian area. This was so, for instance, in the Tsaritsyn intrigue, when Stalin and Trotsky struggled behind the scenes. When the question of the army leadership in Ukraine arose, both Stalin and Trotsky tried to get their own men in. Trotsky wrote to Sverdlov on 10 January 1919 that in Ukraine it was "necessary to support the authority of the central committee, since among the Ukrainians there is discord and the struggle of cliques in the absence of responsible and authoritative leaders." Trotsky warned against Stalin's men.[33]

There is no doubt that the CC RCP controlled the Bolsheviks of Ukraine. This is borne out by the resolutions of the first and second congresses of the CP(B)U, which decided to abolish the "independence" of the CP(B)U proclaimed—with the CC RCP's blessing—at the Taganrog conference.[34] If Lenin had felt that the Ukrainian Communists could not be trusted, he would have placed the "Katerynoslavians," whom he surely trusted, and not the "Kievans," at the head of the government and of the "group." In view of Piatakov's completely negative attitude towards the Ukrainian national renascence, which fully corresponded with the general intentions of the CC RCP, Lenin had no reason to mistrust Piatakov. Lenin's fear and mistrust of the leftists (Kievans) applied chiefly to the period of the Brest Litovsk peace. After the Central Powers capitulated, Lenin could not have feared being drawn into a war against Germany. Piatakov could at least make an effort not to be hotheaded and was able to listen to instructions from Moscow. Lenin, Vatsetis, and Trotsky knew better than Piatakov what was and was not advantageous for the revolution. Be that as it may, Piatakov's attitude had a certain influence on the policy of the CC RCP on the Ukrainian question. To convince Lenin of the necessity of an offensive against Ukraine, Piatakov and his group not only exaggerated the potential of a Bolshevik revolution in Ukraine, but also threatened independent action.

First, they asserted that the "centre" (CC RCP) had created complete chaos and muddle by its contradictory resolutions and directives and that therefore "instead of the centralization of work which we expected, under the general leadership of the CC RCP a complete muddle has resulted."[35] Secondly, they said that while the political situation looked very promising for the Bolsheviks, a centre was required to direct the struggle and to lead the masses in the fight for Soviet power. The legalization of the Soviet Ukrainian provisional government would, in their opinion, have facilitated the sovietization of Ukraine, for it would have centralized Soviet operations there. This was the same motive the Bolsheviks propounded in December 1917 when they proposed the creation of a regional party centre and government to counterbalance the Central Rada. For the successful sovietization of Ukraine, they considered it necessary: first, that they be given permission to declare themselves the Provisional Workers' and Peasants' Government of Ukraine, to issue a manifesto, and to act as a real government of Ukraine; second, to concentrate all political work in the liberated regions in the hands of the provisional government; third, to establish unity of military command by handing control over to the military council of the Kursk direction (in future to the military council of the Ukrainian army); fourth, to subordinate all military forces operating on the Ukrainain front to the military centre of the Kursk direction; fifth, to suggest to Vatsetis that he undertake no military dispositions on the Ukrainian front without consulting them; sixth, in accordance with this, to separate all military units operating on that front into an independent army, named the Army of Soviet Ukraine, under the command of general headquarters only. Should these wishes not be complied with, they threatened "to renounce any responsibility for further work on this front."[36]

In an exchange of messages on a private line between Zatonsky and Stalin, the centre was again reprimanded for the muddle. Zatonsky stressed also that it was necessary to prevent "repetition of the past," hinting apparently at the absence of a single leading party and government centre during the period of the first Soviet regime. He further stressed that "Ukraine is not simply a theatre of war for the deployment of armies, but a most intricate imbroglio in which are fighting the hetman's and the Rada's centres and our illegal centreless organizations, and the Germans are sitting there into the bargain," and that "it is absolutely impossible to solve the question as simply as the military command tries to do." They had to fight in Ukraine "not so much with machine guns and artillery as with leaflets and martial music, with the brave look of detachments, and naturally with good organization .... The local organization is being impeded by the absence of a leadership centre, by the absence of a 'trade name' and the presence of countless pretenders."[37] A little later, Zatonsky implored Stalin to come "immediately and without fail, or else we shall have either to give up the cause or to decide on undesirable independent undertakings." This appeal resulted from the attempt to withdraw partisan detachments from the Ukrainian front and to transfer them to the Voronezh front against Krasnov.[38] Stalin replied:

> Tell comrade Zatonsky that I cannot come. An all-Russian defence council has been organized, of which I have been elected a member. I am very busy and cannot leave. I have already sent Antonov to you. Belenkovich, whose coming has been insisted upon by Artem, will come. Also some Ukrainians will come, and among them there are some experienced commanders from the Tsaritsyn front. I shall give you more details by letter. If there are any disagreements, resolve them for yourselves together with Antonov. All rights are in your hands.
>
> STALIN[39]

It is not clear from Stalin's message whether the CC RCP decided to leave the decision on action against the Directory to the Ukrainian Bolsheviks themselves, granting them all rights, or whether this applied only to the question of internal disagreement. This answer did not satisfy the Bolsheviks of Ukraine, and Zatonsky intervened again.[40]

Zatonsky stresses that the text of Stalin's reply is not extant, but judging from the minutes of the meeting of the provisional government of Ukraine on 28 November 1918 (at which Antonov, Artem, Zatonsky, Kviring, and Piatakov were present), it was a positive one, for the provisional government decided to declare the formation of a government and thus to come out into the open.[41] This is also confirmed by the fact that Stalin began a press campaign against the Directory and for the support of the Soviet government.[42]

Trotsky Helps the Ukrainian Bolsheviks

At the beginning of January 1919 Trotsky, too, began to exercise an influence upon Lenin in this direction, asserting that the situation in Ukraine had changed so much that there was a good chance of success. He based his arguments on an intercepted telegram sent by Palii, a colonel of the Directory and commander of troops in the Chernihiv region, in which he complained to his government about the Bolshevik leanings of the population and the impossibility of holding the front against the Red Army. In light of this, Trotsky assured Lenin in a telegram (2 January) of "the necessity of a decisive offensive which can bring success with small forces" and asked for "corresponding decisions of the government in this connection."[43] Lenin was unconvinced and reproached Trotsky: "I am very worried lest you have become too enthusiastic about Ukraine to the detriment of the overall strategic task that is insisted upon by Vatsetis .... Vatsetis is in favour of a speedy general offensive on Krasnov, but Vatsetis is apparently unable to overcome the procrastination and separatism of the Ukrainians and other regional peoples."[44] Thus Lenin defended Vatsetis against Antonov and other "Ukrainian" Bolsheviks. In calling them "separatists" he was apparently not castigating them for national separatism but rather for their independent actions in Ukraine. After this, Trotsky sent the defence council a memorandum on "the situation in Ukraine and our tasks," dated 4 January 1919. In view of the plans of the Entente to land a force of 100 to 150 thousand soldiers in Ukraine, Trotsky considered it impossible to leave Ukrainian affairs to take their own spontaneous course. One of the possible variants of policy for Ukraine was to seek agreement with the Ukrainian Directory, which "was inclined to seek support and aid in Soviet Russia." Trotsky rejected this alternative:

> Such a decision would appear extremely sudden. First of all, our alliance with the Petliurites would confuse the Ukrainian working masses and delay the development of the Ukrainian revolution. In the military respect, such an agreement would give us nothing. Petliura's "army" is weak, negligible, its soldiers go over to our side. It does not present any barrier against the Anglo-French landing. In case of a serious thrust of the Anglo-French, Petliura may betray all and everyone and throw himself into their embraces.

Therefore Trotsky proposed as soon as possible to shift "a possible Ukraine-Entente front" further to the south, "as far from Moscow as possible. ... It would be most advantageous for us to establish our line on the left bank of the Dnieper and to destroy all bridges and roads on the right bank. For this, we must proceed to the Dnieper at greater speed. This task is now easily realizable, as was shown by the fate of Kharkiv." He advocated:

> 1) the necessity of the creation of a Ukrainian front with a single command, not against Petliura's detachments, but against regular Anglo-French troops; 2) a decisive policy of an offensive against Ukraine with the aim of reaching at least the line of the Dnieper in the course of the next few weeks; 3) in this connection, a speedy and short blow on Kiev, with the aim of seizing the political centre of Ukraine, which would give us a great moral advantage and weaken our enemies, seems extremely important. In the military respect such a task is realizable with the aid of insurgent detachments and those nearest reserves, which we in any case have to place along the Ukrainian border in order to protect the flanks of our southern army and to cover the roads from Kiev to Kursk and Moscow. With a further advance to the south there may be no doubt that the reinforcement of our detachments would take care of itself from the Ukrainian population and from supplies in its possession.

Trotsky requested approval of this plan of action; the open proclamation of the Ukrainian front; and the conclusion of a formal agreement with the provisional Soviet Ukrainian government to form a single command, which should be made known to the masses of the people of Russia and Ukraine.[45] In analysing this document it is impossible not to see the influence of the Ukrainian Bolsheviks, and chiefly Antonov himself, upon Trotsky. His plan is very similar to those Antonov presented to Vatsetis and the *revvoensovet*.[46] As for Trotsky's attitude to the Ukrainian national movement, he adopted almost completely the standpoint of the Ukrainian Bolsheviks, who, apparently for tactical reasons, treated the Ukrainian Directory as a farcical body with no influence upon the masses. Trotsky was very well informed about the Allies' attitude to the Directory, and therefore he prophesied, not without good reason, that the Entente did not intend "to build its policy upon the Ukrainian Kerenskys and Chernovs," i.e., on the Ukrainian SRs who then predominated in the government of the Ukrainian People's Republic. Of course, the Allies never seriously considered the recognition of Ukraine as an independent state, but rather formulated their plans on the basis of advice from Russian proponents of a one and indivisible Russia, the likes of Denikin and Kolchak. This policy pushed the Ukrainian socialist parties into the embrace of the Bolsheviks. Even the Directory tried to reach an understanding with Soviet Russia, which failed when the Bolsheviks would hear nothing of such a peace.

Creation of the Second Ukrainian Soviet Government

After lengthy debates, on 20 November 1918, following a directive of the CC RCP in Moscow, the Provisional Revolutionary Government of Ukraine was created. Headed by Piatakov, this government consisted of Voroshilov, Sergeev (Artem), Kviring, V. Averin, Zatonsky, and Kotsiubynsky.[47] The CC CP(B)U only learned of this after the event,[48] which means that the CP(B)U had a very limited role, rather like that of a puppet. This provisional government settled in Kursk, or more precisely in a railway carriage in the Kursk station[49] near the Ukrainian border. From there, this government carriage began to make slow progress to Belgorod, and then in the direction of Kharkiv, in the wake of the Red Army. On 29 November 1918 this government issued a manifesto declaring the governments of Hetman Skoropadsky and the Central Rada "dissolved and outlawed." All laws and orders of these governments were revoked. The Bolsheviks termed their own government provisional; after the establishment of Soviet power in Ukraine, an all-Ukrainian congress of soviets would succeed it.

The manifesto said nothing about relations with Russia. The only reference to this was the declaration that the government would strive towards "the establishment of the regular exchange of grain for textiles from Soviet Russia."[50] In its subsequent declaration this government spoke about the solidarity of Ukraine with Soviet Russia. Federative ties between these republics were to be decided upon by the third all-Ukrainian congress of soviets. This declaration mentioned the famine in Russia and appealed to the peasantry to supply grain. "We must help the Russian proletariat, the Red strongholds Moscow and Petrograd, which suffer from hunger."[51] This declaration also revealed the new composition of the government: the leftist Piatakov had been replaced by Rakovsky, a move which stemmed not only from the CC RCP's intention to eliminate factions in the CP(B)U, as Soviet historians claim, but also from the desire to remove the "separatist" danger. Rakovsky was a typically cosmopolitan Bolshevik,[52] almost pathologically ambitious.[53] He was hostile to the Ukrainian national movement, which he considered an invention of the Ukrainian intelligentsia.[54] Rakovsky demonstrated his anti-Ukrainian inclinations more than once and thus antagonized the nationally conscious part of the CP(B)U. Rakovsky declared the demand to make Ukrainian the official language reactionary and absolutely superfluous.[55] Similarly, after Kiev was taken by the Red Army, Rakovsky made a speech there in which he warned that the national problem had to be treated with circumspection; those who reduced the question to language were treating it very superficially. Demands that Ukrainian should be made the official language were "injurious to the Ukrainian revolution," he insisted.[56]

Rakovsky's "cabinet" was so reorganized that Russians and other non-Ukrainians predominated.[57] There was a great deal of reshuffling. In March 1919 Rakovsky's government consisted of Rakovsky himself as head of government and foreign minister; Piatakov, Kviring, Moisei Rukhimovich, commissars for national economy; Sergeev (Artem), commissar for Soviet propaganda; Mykola Podvoisky and Valerii Mezhlauk, commissars for military affairs; Averin and Voroshilov, internal affairs; Zatonsky, education; Andrei Kolegaev, agriculture; Khmelnytsky, justice; B. Mogilev, labour; Aleksandr Shlikhter and Bubnov, food; Zemit, finance; Zharko, communications; Skrypnyk, state control; Antonov-Ovseenko, commander-in-chief; Antonov-Ovseenko, Kotsiubynsky, and Efim Shchadenko, members of the revolutionary military council.[58] This "cabinet," which was appointed from above, satisfied the requirements of party policy towards Ukraine. Its primary task was to help Soviet Russia with grain and other produce necessary for its armies. It is interesting that the more important posts were again occupied by Russians who were almost without exception anti-Ukrainian. Rakovsky himself was Bulgaro-Romanian, and military, internal affairs, and propaganda portfolios were in the hands of Russians. The Ukrainians—Zatonsky, Khmelnytsky, Skrypnyk, Zharko, Kotsiubynsky, and Shchadenko—were given subordinate positions: education (at that time it was impossible even to think of any schools), justice, communications, state control, and the revolutionary military council. In the latter the Ukrainians played an entirely decorative role, for all decisions were made by the military regime led by Antonov, whose activities were controlled by the supreme military inspectorate attached to the Ukrainian government.[59]

The government's inaugural declaration laid stress on the sovereignty of the Ukrainian Soviet republic and its desire for peaceful coexistence with other states. "The government ... invites the peoples and the governments of all countries to establish regular diplomatic relations with the Ukrainian Socialist Soviet Republic and addresses itself in writing in particular to the Soviet socialist governments of Russia, Latvia, Belorussia, Estonia, Lithuania, appealing to them to conclude a close defensive alliance against all attempts to overthrow the established ... power of the workers and peasants."[60] The government no longer announced, as it had always before, its "unbreakable ties" with Soviet Russia. However, these were mere words behind which lay the bitter reality of the occupation.

Legal relations between Ukraine and Russia were formulated somewhat later at the third congress of soviets of Ukraine, which took into consideration those prerogatives delegated to Ukraine by Moscow. It could be seen from Sverdlov's declaration at the third congress of the CP(B)U that "the general political leadership belonged to the central committee of the party," i.e., to the RCP. When the third congress of soviets of Ukraine met, between 6 and 10 March 1919, it had a detailed directive concerning all questions, including the Russian-Ukrainian relationship. The Bolsheviks predominated at this congress, with 1,369 delegates out of 1,721. The remainder belonged to other socialist parties that accepted the Soviet platform.[61] Without inquiring into such matters as the legality of this congress of soviets and the election of deputies, it is nonetheless necessary to point out that at the congress only that part of Ukraine was represented which then belonged to the sphere of the Soviet government of Ukraine. The greater part of the right-bank region, that is, almost half of Ukraine, was then controlled by the Directory; Western Ukraine, of course, had no representation at all at this congress.[62] On the question of the republic's independence and its relations with Soviet Russia, the congress divided into two groups: in opposition to the Bolshevik majority were the Ukrainian left parties, the social democrats, the socialist revolutionary Borotbists, and the Jewish Bund.

In accordance with the CC RCP directive, all major questions of party and government policy in Ukraine were decided in obedience to instructions from Moscow. The RCP(B) aimed at a close union of the Soviet republics with the Russian republic, restraining every indiscretion of the national parties. At the third congress of the CP(B)U, the question of the constitution of the Ukrainian republic was raised, and it was decided that this had to be based in any case on the constitution of the RSFSR, minus its shortcomings.[63] Sverdlov, in the name of the CC RCP, advised against a separate constitution for Ukraine, because, as he said, the constitution of the RSFSR had been adopted by the fifth congress of soviets and "then became, instead of a Russian constitution, an international constitution."[64] Obviously the provinces were not to have separate constitutions.

In spite of what Sverdlov said, the third congress of soviets of Ukraine adopted the first constitution of the Ukrainian Soviet Socialist Republic,[65] which, however, closely resembled the constitution of the Russian republic.[66] In it, just as in the constitution of the RSFSR, the power of "the proletarian dictatorship," in the shape of soviets, was confirmed as the basis for the government of the republic. Section 3 assured participation in the government "exclusively for the working masses, completely removing the ruling classes from such participation." The same applied also to the enjoyment of "the freedom of speech, press, meetings, and unions," which was reserved exclusively for "the working masses." "The ruling classes and the social groups close to them in their political position" did not enjoy these freedoms. Although this constitution literally copied many points from the constitution of the RSFSR, it established all the attributes of sovereignty for Ukraine. The supreme organ of the republic, the congress of soviets, decided all republican legislation. The constitution confirmed the independence and the sovereignty of the Ukrainian SSR. The central organs had the right to fix and alter the borders of the republic, to decide relations with other states, to declare war and to conclude peace, and to decide on military affairs, the monetary system, and domestic policy. The organs of the Ukrainian Soviet government, modelled after the Russian constitution, were the all-Ukrainian congress of soviets of workers', peasants', and Red Army deputies, which was to be the supreme authority in the Ukrainian SSR; and in the interval between two congresses authority was to reside in the all-Ukrainian central executive committee of soviets. The latter, however, was not empowered to deal with questions of "accepting, changing, and adding to the constitution"; on questions of war and peace[67] it could decide only in cases of "urgency, when the convocation of a congress of soviets is not possible in time." The VTsIKS alone was empowered to carry out "the election and deposing of people's commissars and of the president of the Council of People's Commissars; the distribution of the national income and taxes between the central and local government; as well as decisions on the terms and the order of election of the local organs of Soviet government, of the quotas of representation and general regulations." The right to vote and be elected was possessed by all citizens of the Ukrainian SSR eighteen years of age on election day,[68] irrespective of religion, nationality, and sex. In sections 20a, b, and v, "the working masses" were defined. It is noteworthy that the constitution also enfranchised foreigners "belonging to the working class and to the working peasantry." Thus the possibility of voting was ensured for the numerous Russian seasonal workers and above all for the numerous armies that were in Ukraine, as well as for foreigners like Ukraine's premier, Rakovsky.[69]

The members of the Council of People's Commissars were elected by the VTsIKS, which could dismiss them at any time. The Council of People's Commissars also had legislative rights, which were subject to confirmation by the VTsIKS.

The relationship of the Ukrainian SSR to other Soviet republics was left vague. Section 4 stated only that "the Ukrainian Soviet Socialist Republic declares its firm determination to join a single international socialist Soviet republic as soon as the conditions for its formation should arise .... At the same time, the Ukrainian Soviet Socialist Republic declares its complete solidarity with the now existing Soviet republics and its decision to enter into the closest political union with them for the purpose of a common struggle for the triumph of the world Communist revolution and into the closest cooperation in the sphere of Communist construction, which is conceivable only on an international scale." It is unknown why a union (or rather a federation) with the RSFSR was not specifically mentioned, since Ukraine actually was in such a federation. However, it may be supposed that a resolution on this subject would have narrowed down the constitution to a political declaration of the government.[70] The muted tone on federation reflected the pressure of the Ukrainian socialist parties (the Borotbists and independentists) who were represented at the congress[71] and were very influential among the Ukrainian peasantry. At that time it was actually impossible to declare openly a federation with, or rather a dependence upon, Russia. In the declarations of the provisional government of Ukraine this question was then only hinted at very cautiously. The manifesto of the provisional workers' and peasants' government of Ukraine of 1 December 1918 mentioned only "a revolutionary alliance of Russia with Ukraine."[72] The declaration of the same government of 2 February 1919 mentioned "a union of the Ukrainian Soviet Socialist Republic with Soviet Russia on the principle of a socialist federation," but "the forms of this union will be fixed by the third plenipotentiary all-Ukrainian congress of soviets."[73] It is unknown what resolution was passed by the congress on this question, but, according to Soviet sources, the congress issued a directive "to define the relationships of Soviet Ukraine to the RSFSR and to other Soviet republics."[74]

The third congress of soviets of Ukraine elected an all-Ukrainian central executive committee of one hundred members (ninety Communists and ten representatives of the Ukrainian left SRs-Borotbists). The congress also confirmed the composition of Rakovsky's government.[75]

The Elimination of the Ukrainian Directory

The antagonism between the Soviet Russian government and the Directory turned mainly on three points: the Directory's non-recognition of the Soviet regime in Ukraine; its insistence on Ukrainian independence; and its alleged servility and venality towards the Entente. It recognized the soviets of workers' deputies only as a proletarian organization dealing with social questions. The Directory opposed the soviets' claims to authority and resented their attacks on the Ukrainian People's Republic and the Directory, holding that "all questions of the political structure of Ukraine belong to the competence ... of the labour congress of Ukraine."[76] As *Pravda* wrote in its lead article of 4 January 1919, "the Petliurites do not wish to hand over power to the soviets. They admit their existence, but declare that the soviets must be merely trade and professional organs."

The Bolsheviks could not agree to leave the decision on the form of Ukraine's government to the labour congress, in which peasants were assigned over half the seats, the workers less than one third, and the soldiers ("Petliurites") the rest. Moreover, delegates to the congress were elected not by the soviets, but by the peasants in their districts, by the workers in their factories, and by the soldiers in their regiments. "Vynnychenko and Petliura want to create something intermediate between a soviet and a 'democratic' republic: the country will be governed by a parliament, Dumas, and zemstvos, but they will be elected by class vote." On the other hand, *Pravda* objected to the fact that "the Petliurites are not only against any federation with the rest of Russia, but even promise to persecute severely all counter-revolutionaries who defend federation .... They wish to separate Ukraine from the common stream of the revolutionary struggle of the proletariat, to declare their neutrality towards the imperialism of the Entente." *Pravda* summed up by saying that, even if this policy had been sincere, "all the same it would have been definitely a petty-bourgeois policy, leading in the final analysis to the weakening and defeat of the revolution." Therefore *Pravda* proposed not to have "a disdainful attitude to those obviously petty-bourgeois strata who would have wished to come to terms with the revolutionary proletariat ... not in words but in deeds." The Ukrainian republic must be first of all a Soviet republic. "The question of independence is of little importance, but any Soviet republic naturally concludes an *alliance* with Soviet Russia."[77] The tone of the article is comparatively mild; in any case, it is far from that of the notorious attacks on the Directory and particularly of those on Petliura. Undoubtedly, this moderate tone was motivated to a great extent by the semi-official peace talks then beginning in Moscow between the Directory and the Russian Soviet government.

The history of these talks has its peculiarities. As is well known, there were divergencies within the Directory and among Ukrainian parties on the question of relations with the Soviet government of Russia. One sector, comprising the left wings of the socialist parties (the Ukrainian social democrats [independentists] and the left Ukrainian SRs), was in favour of talks with Soviet Russia. The other sector, led by the right wings of the Ukrainian SDs, SRs, and other parties, opposed the talks, because it felt that the Bolsheviks would not agree to any compromise on the form of government in Ukraine. As early as the eve of the collapse of the Central Powers and coincident with that of the Hetmanate, the future president of the Directory, Vynnychenko, entered into secret talks with the Russian Soviet delegation in Kiev, i.e., Rakovsky and Manuilsky, "for the coordination of our actions during the rising." As Vynnychenko wrote later, the Bolsheviks agreed to support the Ukrainian insurgents led by the Directory, "not actively but by strengthening their reconnoitering activities on the fronts, in order to attract the attention of the German-Hetmanate armies." The Bolsheviks seemed to have agreed to recognize that mode of government which was to be established by the new Ukrainian regime and not to interfere at all in the internal affairs of the Ukrainian independent people's republic. "For our part," wrote Vynnychenko, "we promised the legalization of the Communist party in Ukraine." Manuilsky apparently even proposed financial help to Vynnychenko, but the latter did not accept the money.[78] That the Bolshevik promises were merely a tactical manoeuvre was obvious from the preparations the Bolsheviks were making against Ukraine as early as October 1918. After Soviet troops began their offensive on Ukraine in December, the Directory sent several notes to the Soviet government of Russia, asking why the Russian Soviet army was advancing on the territory of the Ukrainian People's Republic.[79] The people's commissar for foreign affairs, Chicherin, cynically replied on 6 January 1919: "The military action on Ukrainian territory is being conducted at this time between the army of the Directory and the army of the Ukrainian Soviet government, which is completely independent." Further, Chicherin reminded the Directory that it was in fact in a state of conflict with "the working masses of Ukraine, who are fighting for the establishment of the Soviet regime," and who would struggle against the Directory so long as it continued to oppose them with force—in other words, to resist the establishment of the Soviet regime. The note mentioned, however, that the government of Soviet Russia would "gladly receive in Moscow" a representative of the Directory.[80]

If it expected Chicherin's declarations to be taken seriously, Moscow must have thought the Directory extremely naive. It was clear to Ukrainians that both the Communist party of Ukraine and the provisional government of Ukraine had been formed in Moscow and sent to Ukraine with military support. The Directory also knew upon what kind of support Ukrainian Soviet power depended. The Directory, in its note of 9 January 1919, told the Russian Soviet government that the allegation that it was not a Russian army which was advancing on Ukraine was a misrepresentation of the facts or ignorance stemming from misinformation given to the commissar for foreign affairs. "In the Kharkiv district a regular force of the Russian army is operating. It consists chiefly of Chinese, Latvians, and Hungarians, and partly of Russians." The Directory protested against the attempts of the People's Commissars to interfere in the internal affairs of the Ukrainian state by dictating to it the Soviet form of government:

> The Russian government lays down, as a condition of the truce, the surrender of power in Ukraine to the soviets of workers' deputies; that is, in other words, to submit the whole working Ukrainian people to the power of the urban working class, and only to that part of this class which is called "the Bolsheviks," which comprises not more than 4 per cent of all the population, while the working class of Ukraine in the main consists of Russian immigrants, strangers, who came here during the war. Thus the creation of so-called Bolshevik soviets, which is insisted upon by the Russian government, would submit the whole Ukrainian peasantry and proletarian intelligentsia to the dictatorship of the factory proletariat, which is numerically insignificant, and would subordinate the statehood of Ukraine to the will of the immigrant element.
>
> The note asked the People's Commissars to reply within forty-eight hours to the following questions:
>
> 1) Does the government of the Russian republic agree to cease military operations against the Ukrainian republic and its working people? 2) If it does agree, does it undertake to withdraw its forces immediately from the territory of Ukraine?

In the event of a positive reply, the Directory undertook "to begin peace talks and the exchange of goods." A negative reply or silence would be considered an official declaration of war by the Russian government upon the Ukrainian republic. This note was signed by the president of the Directory, Vynnychenko, and by members of the Directory—Petliura, Panas Andriievsky, Andrii Makarenko, and Fedir Shvets—and the minister of foreign affairs, Volodymyr Chekhivsky.[81]

The Russian government replied with a note denying the Directory's allegation of an offensive of Latvians, Hungarians, and Chinese hired by the Russian government. It maintained that this was a Ukrainian civil war, not the work of "some agents of the Soviet power," but a product of class antagonisms between "the workers and the poorer peasantry, on the one hand, and the Ukrainian bourgeoisie, on the other." The note protested against depicting the urban and industrial proletariat of Ukraine, "by whose work all Ukrainian industry has been created, as a gathering of strangers and immigrants, who struggle not for their political and economic emancipation, but as the leaders of Russian imperialism." At the same time, the note protested against the Directory's attempt to represent Soviet power in Ukraine as the dictatorship of an insignificant number of the urban proletariat, "since Soviet power represents not only the industrial proletariat but also the whole working peasantry." The Russian government again stressed its readiness to receive representatives of the Directory for talks in Moscow, guaranteeing them safe conduct and extraterritoriality.[82]

After a few days, the Directory sent to Moscow an extraordinary diplomatic mission led by the Ukrainian social democrat (independentist), S. Mazurenko. This mission brought with it the Directory's instructions that the latter agreed to the system of soviets in Ukraine in the form of soviets of working people, in which a proper representation for the Ukrainian peasantry would be assured; and that the Directory would agree to sign an economic treaty and a military alliance with Soviet Russia in its struggle against the Russian "Volunteers" and the forces of the Entente, if Russia recognized the independence of the Ukrainian republic under that form of government which would be established by the labour congress.[83] In its talks with Mazurenko, the Russian delegation insisted on the establishment of a common foreign policy for Russia and Ukraine. As for the form of government, they proposed to solve this question at a congress of soviets constituted on the same principle as the soviets in Russia.[84] Some Ukrainian leaders believed that the mission did in fact have some chance of success, but there was a divergence of views in Ukrainian governmental and party circles. The left Ukrainian socialists thought that the internal and external situation of Soviet Russia was going to compel the Bolsheviks to make peace with Ukraine on any terms.[85] This would give Ukraine a chance to preserve its state independence.

Vynnychenko, speculating after the event, thought that both the Directory and the Council of People's Commissars "had sincere intentions of coming to some understanding and of settling the matter peacefully," but that this was prevented by two evil forces: "Piatakovism," by which he meant the Communists of Ukraine under the leadership of Piatakov, and "otamanism," by which he meant the military forces of the Ukrainian People's Republic under the leadership of Petliura, the chief otaman. In Vynnychenko's opinion, both these forces worked against peace and understanding and attempted to break up at any price the talks that had been initiated. The proponents of "Piatakovism" not only aimed in general to prevent peace, but, according to him, attempted to falsify the peace conditions so that the Directory would not be able to accept them.[86] Vynnychenko accused the proponents of "otamanism" of resisting peace with the Bolsheviks because they wanted to be on good terms with the Entente and to prove to it that the Directory was not made up of Bolsheviks.[87] It must be stressed that Vynnychenko's allegations are largely an attempt to settle personal scores with his rival Petliura, who, in the thick of the struggle, pushed Vynnychenko into a subordinate position in the Ukrainian revolution. Actually, at that time the majority of the Directory were aware that the Russian Bolsheviks were not thinking of concluding peace with the Directory at all, but were merely attempting to discredit it in order to overthrow it in the end. This factor in the talks was mentioned by Vynnychenko himself, as well as by Khrystiuk.[88] The left Ukrainian social democrats and SRs hoped that by proclaiming Soviet power in Ukraine and conducting talks with the Council of People's Commissars, it would be possible to take the masses with them, since the masses were inclining more and more towards the Soviet programme. They felt, too, that by accepting the Soviet system, the grievances of the Russian Bolsheviks against the Directory would disappear.[89]

The talks were soon interrupted, and Mazurenko's mission came to nothing. After this the advance of Soviet forces on Ukraine proceeded rapidly, accompanied by an unscrupulous campaign against the Directory. Did the Russian Bolsheviks actually want to achieve an understanding with the Directory or was this merely flirtation, aimed at lulling resistance in Ukraine and splitting the Directory from within? In any case, it can be asserted that the Ukrainian Bolsheviks, as well as Antonov, Stalin, and finally also Trotsky, were against an understanding with the Directory. We have already seen that Trotsky, in his capacity as chairman of the Russian

RVS, was not in favour of an understanding because "an alliance with the Petliurites would confuse the Ukrainian working masses and retard the development of the Ukrainian revolution." Furthermore, the alliance would bring no advantage, since "Petliura's army is weak and negligible."[90] The Ukrainian Soviet government, led by Rakovsky, opposed the talks from the very beginning. On 1 March 1919, Rakovsky wrote a note, entirely in Trotsky's spirit, to the people's commissar for foreign affairs of the RSFSR, Chicherin; in it he stated that since the Directory had shown "its real counter-revolutionary nature," "we regard not only as useless, but also as harmful for the common revolutionary cause, conducting any talks whatsoever with the Directory."[91] As Antonov points out, after the news that the Entente was seriously contemplating intervention in Russian affairs, even the commander-in-chief himself changed his attitude towards the offensive against Ukraine. He agreed to advance Soviet troops to the Dnieper in accordance with Trotsky's proposal.[92] For these operations, the commander-in-chief promised to provide eight "regular divisions of the Red Army," according to the maximum estimate, or, according to the minimum estimate, four divisions.[93] This overt Russian military intervention provoked "serious doubts of its expediency" among "a section of responsible Ukrainian functionaries."[94] On the other hand, the Bolsheviks greatly exaggerated the significance of the Directory's attempts to conclude a treaty with, and to receive aid from, the Entente.

The Directory also conducted talks with the French expeditionary force in Odessa, where a first contingent of 1,800 men had landed on 18 December 1918. The Directory discussed the Entente's attitude to the Directory and to Ukrainian independence, concentrating chiefly on technical military aid. These talks did not benefit the Directory; on the contrary, they gave the Bolsheviks a pretext to pillory the Directory for having sold itself to the imperialists, drawing parallels with the German military intervention in February 1918.

The Directory was beginning to look towards the all-powerful Entente more and more, while dreams of a peace with the Bolsheviks faded altogether. At that time nobody would have believed that a month later the forces of the Entente would be in flight from Odessa, haunted by the Ukrainian insurgents of Hryhoriiv. The French command, which represented the Entente "in the south of Russia," proposed extremely difficult conditions for the Directory as a basis of understanding with the Entente:

1) The Directory and government were to be reorganized so as to exclude Vynnychenko, Petliura, and Chekhivsky.

2) For a common struggle against the Bolsheviks, the Ukrainian government was to form an army of 300,000, subordinate to the supreme command of the Entente.

3) The Ukrainian army had to be formed within three months; and, in case of a shortage of Ukrainian officers, officers from Russian volunteers would be accepted.

4) For the duration of the struggle against the Bolsheviks, railways and finances were to be under French control.

5) The question of the state independence of Ukraine was to be decided at a peace conference in Paris.

6) The Directory was to appeal to France to accept Ukraine under its protectorate.[95]

It is not known whether the French command took these talks seriously and whether it had real authority from the powers of the Entente, but it is evident that the French hardly desired to come to an agreement with the Directory; otherwise they would not have proposed such "colonialist" conditions.[96] It is no wonder that these were rejected outright. The Directory's mission to the French[97] proposed the following conditions for an agreement:

1) Recognition by the Entente of Ukraine's independence and the admission of a Ukrainian delegation to the peace conference in Paris.

2) The sovereignty of the Directory.

3) The guarantee of a people's regime and of social reforms in Ukraine.

4) The guarantee of cultural freedom to Ukrainian colonies in Siberia.

5) The return to Ukraine of the Black Sea fleet.

6) The recognition of the autonomy of the Ukrainian army, with a right to its own representative in the supreme command.

7) The exclusion from the Ukrainian army of all Russian officers.[98]

The representatives of the Directory met with Colonel Freydenberg at Birzula station, near Odessa. During the talks Freydenberg made it clear that he regarded the removal of Vynnychenko, Petliura, and Chekhivsky as a *conditio sine qua non*. He reproached Vynnychenko and Chekhivsky with Bolshevism, while he objected to Petliura for being the leader of "banditism." Freydenberg declared that generally any changes in the Directory's composition could only take place with French consent. A participant in the talks, Mazepa, pointed out in his memoirs that only the catastrophic position of the Ukrainian armies on the Bolshevik front compelled the delegation to "preserve its equanimity" and continue the talks.[99] It is unknown what instructions in respect to the talks the French command received from its government and what the Entente's attitude was in general to the Directory. In any case, French policy towards Ukraine was very unclear, and the military leadership had instructions to "faire cause commune avec les patriotes russes";[100] but as Reshetar aptly remarks, such instructions were "of little use because there were so many species of patriotism."[101] The French military command in fact sided with the Russian patriots and adopted a hostile attitude towards the Ukrainians.[102]

At the same time as the Ukrainian delegation was listening to the humiliating demands of Colonel Freydenberg in Birzula, Moscow (on 5 March 1919) sent the following telegram to the Directory, signed by the commissar for foreign affairs, Chicherin:[103]

> After the Ukrainian-Russian conference on 2 March, the possibility became clear of an understanding concerning the basis on which the Russian Soviet government can offer its services to the Ukrainian Soviet government and to the Directory so as to reach an agreement for the purposes of struggle against the counter-revolution. This basis would include the Directory's recognition of Soviet power in Ukraine and the recognition of Ukraine's neutrality, with an active defence against the forces of the Entente, of Denikin and Krasnov, and of the Poles. In accordance with this, the Russian Soviet government offers its services, with the above-mentioned aim, to the Ukrainian Soviet government and to the Directory.

This amounted to liquidation of the Directory by diplomacy and was an attempt to prevent it from agreeing with the Entente. While in its previous notes to the Directory the Soviet government of Russia had offered to recognize without any reservations the Soviet power embodied in the provisional workers' and peasants' government, a hint was now dropped that the Directory itself might become such a Soviet government. However, this vagueness was dispersed by a telegram from Kharkiv, signed by the president of the Soviet government of Ukraine, Rakovsky:[104]

> The Ukrainian workers' and peasants' government agrees, on its part, to continue the talks with the Directory in Kharkiv on the basis mentioned by Moscow and promises a guarantee of safe conduct to a delegation of the Directory, as well as personal safety to the members of the government of the Directory, providing that the Directory recognize the workers' and peasants' government of Ukraine.

This provoked indignation even among such advocates of an understanding with Soviet Russia as Chekhivsky and Vynnychenko. The Directory recalled its mission from Moscow on the same day.[105] The results of the diplomatic failure were very soon reflected in the military situation, and the Directory withdrew from Kiev by 5 February 1919 and moved to Vinnytsia. No better fortune befell the "invincible" Entente forces in Odessa. The insurgents of Otaman Matvii Hryhoriiv, a Ukrainian SR, drove the French out of Odessa on 6 March, and this was the end of the Entente's unsuccessful intervention in Ukraine.[106]

After the change in the Directory's government, Serhii Ostapenko became prime minister, Vynnychenko went abroad, and talks with the French were resumed. These talks boiled down to demands that Petliura and Andriievsky leave the Directory, apparently because of their *samostiinytstvo* (independentism). These demands irritated the Ukrainian delegation very much and undermined the authority of the Directory among the people.[107] The French command now began without ceremony to dictate to the Directory the conditions for an understanding. A Captain Langeron sent to Ostapenko, in General Henri Berthelot's name, a prepared draft of the Directory's declaration, which had been dictated by Berthelot, and in which the Directory, having admitted its "mistakes," begged "noble" France and the powers of the Entente for help against the Bolsheviks.[108] The Directory was then supposed to send a manifesto to the powers of the Entente, expressing its happiness because it was "able to come to an understanding with the representatives of the Entente in the matter of aid to Ukraine for repelling the invasion by Russian Bolshevism and for stopping Bolshevism on Ukrainian territory."[109] This document continued with a description of the Ukrainian people's struggle for liberation against the Bolsheviks and the Germans. The whole tone of the manifesto was submissive; it stressed the Directory's inability to master the situation and even less to withstand the Soviet invasion without assistance from the powerful Entente. The talks between the Directory and the military command of the Entente produced no concrete results. Instead, they considerably undermined the authority of the Directory.

At the same time, in February 1919, the people's commissar for foreign affairs of Soviet Ukraine, Rakovsky, in strongly worded telegrams and notes, was protesting against France's intervention in the internal affairs of the Ukrainian state. Rakovsky's note of 6 February to the French foreign minister, Stephen Pichon, was a protest against the presence of French troops on the territory of Ukraine. The Allied command had taken the whole military fleet of Soviet Ukraine and Soviet Russia and was removing grain, sugar, and other produce "necessary for the Ukrainian workers and peasants and for hungry Soviet Russia." Moreover, the actions of the Allies contradicted Wilson's principles "concerning granting the peoples of former Russia the right to decide their own future." The same note agreed that the workers' and peasants' government of Ukraine would send a delegation to the conference on Prince's Islands, but the proposed date of 15 February was considered too near; the note also proposed that the conference take place in Paris.[110] On 26 February a note was sent to the Greek foreign ministry, protesting the intervention of Greek troops in Ukraine.[111] On the same day another note was sent to Pichon, in which France was warned against signing any treaties with the Directory, which was "a fictitious government"; the Directory allegedly no longer had any territory and lacked support from peasants and workers. Moreover, the Directory was also "deprived of any support from national Ukrainian parties," since the Ukrainian SRs concluded an agreement with the CP(B)U and most of the Ukrainian social democrats, while "the majority of the Jewish organizations," i.e., the Bund, decided to reorganize themselves into a Jewish Communist party. It was further asserted that the Russian parties in Ukraine, the SRs and the Mensheviks, did not support the Directory either. Therefore "talks and agreements with the Directory have neither legal nor political significance." In spite of this, Rakovsky said it was the desire of the Soviet government of Ukraine "to conclude peace with all governments, but on the condition *that the French government shall cease considering Ukraine a future colony for French capital, as a new Madagascar, Morocco, or Indo-China*. Any agreement that does not take into consideration the complete independence of the Ukrainian Socialist Soviet Republic is condemned in advance to failure."[112]

Thus while the Directory displayed extreme submissiveness before the French command and the Entente powers in general, while it agreed to all possible concessions, including banning its own president and prime minister, the Soviet government of Ukraine showed a keen sense of national honour, defending Ukraine's interests against external intervention. However, this was merely a pretence. As we have seen,

Rakovsky was neither a Ukrainian patriot nor a defender of Ukrainian independence. With the support of Soviet Russia, the naturally aggressive Rakovsky adopted a very sharp and obdurate tone in his polemic with the French foreign minister. The Directory hardly had the option of assuming such a tone. Pressed on all sides—from the north by Soviet Russia, from the west by Poland, and from the south by Russian volunteers and the French—it had to show maximal patience and conciliation towards the representatives of the Entente, the only force not overtly opposed to the Ukrainian liberation struggle.

Bolshevik Contacts with the West Ukrainian Government

At the same time, the Soviet Ukrainian government took measures to conclude peace with the West Ukrainian government of Sydir Holubovych in order to weaken the Directory, which at that time counted for support on certain considerable forces of that republic. With this in view, Rakovsky sent a note to the government of the West Ukrainian republic, declaring that the problem of the political organization of Eastern Galicia was a matter for the Galician workers and peasants themselves to decide.[113]

This note reminds one in some of its details of the ultimatum of the CPC to the Central Rada (December 1917). On the one hand, it recognizes the right of the West Ukrainian people (of course, only the workers and peasants) to establish freely their own form of government on their own territory, but it stipulates that that form shall be the Soviet form. The note uses very confused terminology; the West Ukrainian People's Republic is called "Eastern Galicia" and "the Eastern Galician People's Republic," while the Ukrainian people on its territory are referred to as "Galician workers and peasants."

The government of Holubovych completely ignored the note, but as it turned out this did not prevent Polish diplomats from using it against the Ukrainians in Paris, where the peace conference was then discussing the Polish-Ukrainian conflict. It was said in Paris that Holubovych's government had conducted talks "in a provocative manner" on the matter of permitting the passage of Soviet troops to Hungary.[114]

On 5 May 1919 Rakovsky sent an almost identical note, though somewhat abbreviated.[115] On 9 May the TsIKU passed a special appeal "to the working masses of Galicia and to the workers of the whole world," which again stressed that the army of Soviet Ukraine had no aggressive intentions against Western Ukraine and that even if its armies crossed the border they would do so only with the aim of finally destroying the army of the Directory. As can be seen from the passages quoted by Antonov, this appeal was issued with a purely propagandistic aim.[116] However, Antonov, in his role of commander of the Ukrainian front, made further attempts to conduct talks with the military command of Western Ukraine. The Bolshevik command, following Lenin's directives, was then making a great effort to make contact with Soviet Hungary; and for this it needed some agreement with the Holubovych government. The latter was under pressure from Polish forces which, in spite of apparent discouragement from the Entente, were waging war against it with the aid of Romania and had succeeded in pushing it eastwards. The government of Western Ukraine tried to make peace with the Poles through the Entente's mediation, but this gave no results and the West Ukrainian government became desperate. Holubovych's government maintained friendly relations with the Hungarian Communist government of Béla Kun just as it had with the former government of Mihály Karolyi. A treaty was even signed for the exchange of goods between the governments of Béla Kun and Holubovych.[117] According to Mykhailo Lozynsky, a participant in the events in Western Ukraine and at that time secretary for foreign affairs, the situation was so utterly hopeless and the government so isolated from the outside world that the mood in government circles was such that "from whatever side a ray of hope had shone, everyone would have rushed there."[118]

In this situation the Bolsheviks offered less and less acceptable conditions for an agreement with Holubovych's government. The defence council of the Ukrainian Soviet republic passed a motion that the commander of the Ukrainian front, together with Zatonsky and Shumsky, should try to conduct talks with the "Galicians." The Soviet army should provide the Galician army with arms, while the Galicians should undertake in return: 1) to break completely with Petliura and to help in his liquidation, 2) to reorganize the Galician army and to dismiss "counter-revolutionary officers," 3) to hand over material evacuated to Galicia by the Petliurites, and 4) to permit the passage of Soviet troops on their way to fight the Romanians.[119] However, this, too, produced no results, for Ievhen Petrushevych, who was then the president of the National Council of the West Ukrainian People's Republic, did not believe in the strength of the Bolsheviks and "considered the Bolsheviks a momentary fire that would not burn for long."[120] The Galician army soon crossed the borders of the Ukrainian republic and launched, together with the army of the Directory, a successful offensive on Kiev, which they captured on 30 August 1919.

The position taken by the West Ukrainian government against the Bolsheviks was influenced by its alliance with the Directory; the whole

West Ukrainian republic, after all, was constitutionally a part of the Ukrainian People's Republic, in accordance with the act of union of 22 January 1919. However, the political situation of the two governments differed to such an extent that they were quite unable to find common ground for international political tactics: they were each threatened by different enemies. While the West Ukrainian republic had always been in a state of war with, and under a constant threat from, Poland, the Ukrainian Directory was in mortal combat with the Bolshevik and anti-Bolshevik Russians, both of which were opposed to Ukraine's independence. It seemed to the Galicians that the Ukrainians should agree with the anti-Bolshevik Russians, on the premise that the latter would undoubtedly oust the Bolsheviks and establish a democratic republic, and as democrats would not deny the Ukrainians their right to an independent state. Yet it was obvious that Denikin, who was then in the closest contact with the Ukrainian problem, would not even hear of an autonomous Ukraine, much less an independent one.[121] The Russophile point of view among the Galicians was propagated chiefly by Vasyl Paneiko and Stepan Tomashivsky, the delegates of the West Ukrainian government in Paris,[122] and to some degree by Kost Levytsky.[123] But it was the helpless situation of the Galician army, rather than its pro-Russian sentiment, that eventually led, in the autumn of 1919, to its alliance with Denikin's forces. The chairman of the Directory was then Petliura who was supported by the rightist factions of the Ukrainian social democrats and social revolutionaries as well as by the Galician social democrats; Petliura was oriented at that time towards Poland, through which he hoped to obtain the Entente's recognition. Petliura and his followers considered an alliance with the White Russian forces unthinkable, if only because what Denikin and his political advisers meant by an alliance with the Directory was the capitulation of the Directory and the renunciation by the Ukrainians of any ambitions for national independence. They pointed to the Russian nationalist policy of Denikin and other White generals towards all borderlands, and rejected the Galicians' attempts to bring about an orientation on Denikin. At that time Petliura cherished the idea of an alliance with Piłsudski against the Bolsheviks, thus neutralizing Denikin. As it turned out, however, no neutralization resulted, since the Entente supported Denikin on the one hand and Poland and Romania on the other.[124]

The internal dissension, caused mostly by outside factors, was exploited by the Bolsheviks, who emphasized to the Ukrainian masses that only they defended Ukrainian national independence. In their policy towards the Galicians the Bolsheviks stressed their desire to help the Ukrainian people of the West Ukrainian republic against the Poles, but, as Antonov said, this help had to be rendered in such a way that the Galicians "would feel their dependence on us," i.e., the Bolsheviks.[125]

A Bread Crusade

The conquest of Ukraine had great significance for the subsequent fate of the Communist revolution, both in Russia and in Europe. This was so not only for strategic reasons, but also chiefly for economic ones. Before the Red Army's decisive offensive against Ukraine of 26 January 1919, Lenin wrote in *Pravda* that "the capture of Ufa and Orenburg, the victories in the south, then the victory of the Soviet rising in Ukraine, open up most favourable perspectives. Now we are able to get sufficient quantities of grain and even more than is necessary for the half-yearly food supply .... Finally, the surplus of grain in Ukraine is really enormous, and the Soviet government of Ukraine offers to help us." Lenin affirmed that, even according to the most pessimistic calculations, there would now be a complete turn "towards the improvement of the whole economic situation, since the bonds with Ukraine and Tashkent mean we need no longer worry about the shortage of raw materials." He therefore appealed to the workers of Russia to set out on a "new crusade" for grain; he proposed to substitute female for male labour in factories, to send every tenth or fifth "man from our midst, from our group, from our factory, etc., into a food-foraging army."[126] Hunger, and economic hardship generally, influenced the Russian Bolsheviks to such an extent during the installation of the second Soviet regime in Ukraine that they completely forgot the lessons of history and again went looting.

In Ukraine the whole attention of the party during January–May 1919 was concentrated on grain. At the plenary meeting of the Moscow soviet on 3 April 1919, Lenin declared that the situation of the Soviet republic had improved, since "in Ukraine we have 258 million poods of grain, out of which 100 million are already under *razverstka*."[127] However, he warned that it was not very easy to get grain from Ukraine, because the peasants there "are intimidated by the Germans and German looting."[128] Elsewhere Lenin said that in Ukraine there were "enormous supplies of grain," but "everything cannot be taken at once," because "there are no men, there is nobody to build Soviet power, there is no machinery, there is no proletarian centre like Petrograd or Moscow, while the Ukrainian proletarian centres are in the enemies' hands." He assured the Bolsheviks of the north that they could and "must help the Ukrainian comrades." The central committee of the RCP(B) proposed the following: "first, to do everything possible to set up machinery in Ukraine and to start work when we have both arms and machinery, and thus to obtain 50 million poods of grain by 1 June."[129] The Bolsheviks saw their immediate salvation in the successful occupation of Ukraine and the Don. Without coal and grain, which Russia obtained chiefly from Ukraine, Soviet Russia "was perishing." Lenin said that "because of the lack of coal the railways and factories are stopping, because of the lack of grain the workers in cities, and in non-agricultural localities generally, experience the pangs of hunger."[130] Lenin demanded that Trotsky himself go to Ukraine "to improve the organization of food supplies." Only after the assurances of the head of the government of Ukraine that matters would proceed satisfactorily and that Trotsky would not be required was his visit called off.[131] Just as the Brest Litovsk peace with the Central Powers was "the grain peace," so the invasion of Ukraine by the Red Army was the "grain expedition." However, as history has shown, neither the Germans nor the Russian Bolsheviks obtained the desired quantity of grain, because the Ukrainian peasants refused to surrender it voluntarily. The rosy prospects depicted by Lenin at the first congress of the Communist International on 2 March 1919 and subsequently at the eighth congress of the RCP on 18–23 March 1919 were followed by a fiasco, since the Ukrainian peasantry, provoked by Red Army and cheka looting, revolted against the Soviet authorities.

The period of the third congress of soviets was the summit of power attained by the second Soviet regime in Ukraine. At that time Soviet authority extended practically over the whole territory of Ukraine, since the Directory troops led by Petliura had been pushed out onto the territory of the West Ukrainian republic. But just when the tide of the Communist revolution swept over much of Europe and disrupted even the ranks of the Entente itself, when the troops of Soviet Russia stood near the Hungarian border ready to cross the Carpathians to aid Béla Kun, and when Communism had broken out in Central Europe—Soviet power collapsed in Ukraine itself, in the country that was to be the bridgehead for Communism's invasion of Europe. Now the power of the Soviets was opposed by the same Ukrainian left-wing socialist parties, the Borotbists and independentists, who during the struggle between the Directory and the Bolsheviks had sided with the Bolsheviks. Everywhere behind the front line of the Bolshevik troops, where the power was in the hands of local soviets, the population rose against Soviet power. The requisitioning of food from Ukraine, as well as the Soviet government's policy of Russification, provoked hostility towards Soviet power, not only among Ukrainian parties that had accepted the Soviet platform but also from the

Ukrainian peasantry.

The Bolsheviks recognized that Rakovsky's power during this period (from January until June) did not extend beyond the boundaries of large towns and the vicinity of the railways. "The victory of Soviet power," Ravich-Cherkassky wrote later, "was a victory over the Ukrainian town, while the village remained untouched by these wars."[132] Commander-in-Chief Antonov likewise wrote in his report to Lenin about the "almost complete absence of Soviet power in the provinces."[133] The Kiev province committee reported that in districts occupied by Soviet troops "armed gangs were roaming, for whose liquidation there has been so far neither time nor strength." Another report said that "the position of Soviet power in the Kiev district is far from good" and that under such conditions there could be no mention of mobilization.[134] Another district reported: "There is complete disorganization in the provinces. The attitude to Soviet power is most negative .... Order is completely absent. Real 'Petliurites' sit in the district soviet. At the district congress a resolution was passed protesting the seizure of power by 'Great Russia and demanding the end of the war and the opening of the front.'"[135] As has been mentioned, the main reason for peasant uprisings against Soviet power in the second period was the party's land policy. Following the decisions of the third congress of the CP(B)U, the party quickly began to implement land reform, the foundation of which was the immediate introduction of sovkhozes, communes, and artels.[136] Only later, at the ninth congress of the RCP, did the land and national policy of the CP(B)U encounter much criticism. Bubnov pointed out that the eighth congress of the RCP had clearly laid down that in Ukraine one should not interfere with the kulak, that there it was necessary to have not only "national tact, but also social tact." But in spite of this the party pursued a completely contrary policy in Ukraine, provoking great discontent not only among the Ukrainian kulaks, but, what was more important, among the middle peasantry as well.[137]

RCP policy towards the nationalities, particularly the Ukrainians, was influenced in the early months of 1919 by the victory of the Red Army on all fronts and by the impetus of the Communist revolution in Central Europe. During the period of the second Soviet regime in Ukraine, Lenin also ignored Ukrainian national demands. He asserted, in complete harmony with the Luxemburgists, that the national movement in Ukraine had no deep roots and that even if it had, the national movement had been "knocked out by the Germans." He claimed that in Ukraine "the language question is such that one does not even know whether Ukrainian is a mass language or not."[138] Evidently under the influence of an economic emergency, Lenin looked at Ukraine almost exclusively as a source of grain. At every mention of Ukraine Lenin added how many poods of grain there were, how many could be taken from there, or how many had already been taken.

It goes without saying that, if the party wished to take grain and fuel from Ukraine, strength was necessary, as well as a compliant Soviet regime that would acquiesce in such a policy. An independent, albeit Soviet, power in Ukraine might have complicated things by demanding a correct exchange of goods between Russia and Ukraine. Therefore the RCP supported in Ukraine that Bolshevik trend which occupied the *edinaia i nedelimaia* position with regard to both party organization and mode of government. Independentists and federalists were not admitted to positions of power in the party and the government. A further proof of this was the RCP's attitude to the Ukrainian Borotbists and social democrats (independentists) who accepted the Soviet platform but, when it came to the relationship between Ukraine and Russia, took a stand for the independence of Ukraine.

During this high tide of the attempted sovietization of Central Europe, the RCP adopted a very peremptory tone towards Ukraine and its Communist party, assigning it all sorts of tasks. The Ukrainian Soviet republic was merely a link in the chain of world revolution, and in party terms the CP(B)U was merely a branch of the RCP(B). It has already been pointed out that both the creation of the provisional government of Ukraine and the delegation of its political tasks were done by permission of the RCP(B). The RCP was even more peremptory in respect to the military tasks of the so-called Ukrainian front, which was under a double command: the commander-in-chief of the RSFSR and the people's commissar for war in Ukraine. However, questions of both strategy and ordinary military routine were under the immediate control of the commander-in-chief. On the other hand, the people's commissar for war of the Ukrainian SSR (at that time, Podvoisky) very often issued completely contradictory instructions to the Ukrainian front, which it considered subordinate to the Ukrainian government. This duality of power led to conflicts between the chief Russian command and the command of the Ukrainian front. However, the "Ukrainian" Bolsheviks together with Antonov considered the questions of strategy and tactics on the Ukrainian front in a somewhat different light. For them, apart from the general international strategic factors, there were also special local tasks. The main thing, however, was that they looked at the revolutionary situation in Ukraine with somewhat patriotic eyes. They realized the weakness of the Bolshevik forces in Ukraine, due mainly to the resistance of the Ukrainian peasantry. But they looked with different eyes at Galicia, which was then at war with Poland. They tried to fan the Ukrainian-Polish antagonism in Galicia lest a Ukrainian-Polish front form against the Bolsheviks.[139]

The Council of People's Commissars of the RSFSR then initiated measures to make peace with the Polish government and the government of the West Ukrainian republic.[140] It could be seen from Lenin's telegram to Vatsetis (22 April 1919) that the Bolsheviks had no intention of occupying the Ukrainian lands of Galicia and Bukovyna, but wanted only to establish a railway connection with Soviet Hungary. The Bolsheviks were not at the time in a state of open war with Poland, but as they approached Polish troop positions conflict became possible. Having no intention at that time of engaging in an open war with the Poles as well, they attempted to settle peacefully any conflict that might arise in connection with the establishment of state boundaries. On 13 April Rakovsky sent a telegram to Chicherin in the name of the Soviet government of Ukraine, requesting his mediation in the talks with Poland on the matter of "a peaceful resolution [on the basis] of the organized expression of the will of the working masses in the disputed territories."[141] Rakovsky's *dêmarche* was a matter of ordinary routine practised by Moscow in regard to Soviet republics on the periphery. On the surface it looked as though the Ukrainian Soviet government was completely sovereign and had nothing in common with the government of Russia apart from friendship. In fact, Moscow treated the government of Soviet Ukraine as an organ of local government without any competence in international affairs. Although formally Rakovsky often acted as prime minister and foreign minister of Ukraine, his actions were completely aligned with Moscow and subordinated to its directives.

The RCP Dilemma: World Revolution or the Preservation of the Communist Regime in Russia?

Whether they acted of their own accord and without directives from the RCP is unknown, but the Ukrainian Bolsheviks undertook an offensive against Romania and Bukovyna in order to establish contact with Soviet Hungary, long before official orders came from Moscow.[142] The hurried storming of Odessa was only a link in the chain of aid to the Hungarian republic. On 6 April, only a day after Odessa was taken, Antonov worked out a plan for an offensive against Romania.[143] On 13 April he issued an order: "Establish contact with Soviet Hungary by a march through Bukovyna and Hungary."[144] The order of the commander of the third army, Khudiakov, of 24 April was even bolder. It said that the task of the

Ukrainian front was "to free Bessarabia and to make energetic preparations for an offensive against Romania with the river Seret as an objective, in order to establish in Romania the power of the proletariat, with the cooperation of the insurgents in the northwest and of the Dobrudja, which sympathizes with us."[145] Commander Antonov himself hoped "to agitate Bulgaria."[146] This was no doubt an exaggeration of the possibilities in the west and, at the same time, an underestimation of the danger from Denikin.[147]

In principle these measures of the Ukrainian Bolsheviks met with Moscow's approval. Trotsky's recently discovered papers[148] enable us to trace the attitude of the CC RCP towards the CP(B)U and towards the strategic tasks of the Ukrainian front. On 18 April 1919 a coded telegram was sent, signed by Lenin and Trotsky, to the chairman of the Council of people's Commissars of Ukraine, Rakovsky; to the People's commissar for war, Podvoisky; and to the commander of the Ukrainian front, Antonov:

> We consider it necessary *to concentrate the main forces of the Ukrainian army in the direction of the Donets and Bukovyna, on the side of Chernivtsi. In the direction of the Donets*, it is a matter of the liquidation of *a very great danger. In the Chernivtsi direction* it is a matter of *relieving Hungary*. It is the duty of the Ukrainian comrades to make every effort for the double task indicated, as we concentrate all our strengh for the eastern front [against Kolchak].[149]

This directive restricted the activities of the Ukrainian Bolsheviks on the western sector to "the matter of relief to Hungary." The action in Romania and Bulgaria, as planned by the Ukrainian Bolsheviks, was not mentioned in the directive. Lenin's and Trotsky's instructions were very general. To clarify in detail the purpose and breadth of the western offensive, the commander-in-chief, Vatsetis, sent a coded telegram "for Lenin only" on 21 April:

> According to today's communique from the Ukrainian front, Ukrainian armies have occupied Husiatyn, in Galician territory. In connection with our movement westward in Galicia and Bukovyna it is necessary for the government to give instructions on the questions: 1) to what extent is that advance permissible from a general political viewpoint? 2) what task is assigned for that advance? 3) what final borders should be occupied by the army and with whom and through whom should connection be sought on the territories in case of advance towards Budapest?[150]

Lenin replied to Vatsetis in a coded telegram of 22 April:

> Advance into part of Galicia and Bukovyna is necessary for connections with Soviet Hungary. This task must be settled more quickly and with more

> decision. But within the limits of that task no occupation of Galicia or Bukovyna is necessary, for the Ukrainian army in absolutely no case should be distracted from its two main tasks, the first, most important, and most pressing of which is aid to the Donets basin. This aid must be achieved quickly and on a large scale .... Communicate your directives to Antonov and your measures to effect their execution.[151]

Thus Lenin gave a clear directive to the Ukrainian Bolsheviks: to aid the Donets basin against the White armies and to secure a railway link with Soviet Hungary. The latter task, however, quickly receded into the background. On the same day, Lenin, in one of his numerous telegrams to Vatsetis, sounded alarmed, since the danger had increased from the Donets basin, where Denikin's units were advancing: "The danger is enormous. Ukraine must recognize the Donets basin front unconditionally as the most important Ukrainian front." For this reason he demanded that large forces be organized.[152]

On 24 April 1919 he said in his telegram to Rakovsky, Antonov, Podvoisky, and Sergei Kamenev: "[It is necessary] at any price and exerting all strength to help us to destroy the [Don] Cossacks as soon as possible, and to take Rostov, even at the price of a temporary weakening in the west of Ukraine; for otherwise there is a threat of ruin."[153]

The RCP's imperious policy towards the Ukrainian Soviet government and party as well as towards the tasks of the army, which was subordinated to the Ukrainian commissar for war, soon brought about a conflict between Moscow and Kiev. The Ukrainian Bolsheviks were often compelled to rely on relatively undisciplined military units consisting of insurgent peasant bands that had gone over to the Soviet side. These insurgents, who were guided politically by the Ukrainian social democrats (independentists) and Ukrainian SRs (Borotbists), had their own specific inclinations and political colouring. In the first place, they were peasants, for whom Soviet power was politically acceptable and in practice bearable only so long as it did not encroach upon their land. In the second place, this was a nationally Ukrainian army, antagonistic to the centralism of the Russian Bolsheviks and their Ukrainian followers. It was precisely these forces, on which hopes were so frequently placed, that constituted the regime's weakest link. Antonov and Podvoisky received directives to subject the insurgent units to ordinary military discipline in order to put an end to the election of commanding personnel and to the "endless meetings," both of which had actually been introduced into the army by the Bolsheviks themselves with the aim of destroying the military discipline of the old army. Now these elections and "endless meetings" were actually working against the party's intentions.

In this respect, Trotsky's memorandum to the CC RCP of 1 May 1919 is very characteristic. Trotsky wrote that the development of military forces in Ukraine was in such a critical state that "a decisive and firm hand on the helm is necessary." "If the stormy explosion of the Ukrainian revolution facilitated to an extraordinary extent the advance of the revolutionary units, on the other hand it also made it more difficult (or rather impossible) for a time to create regular formations." Reproaching Antonov for his tolerance of partisan detachments, Trotsky stressed that "the revolution took everything it could from the improvised insurgent units; any further and these units become not only dangerous, but simply ruinous to the cause of the revolution. ... Comrade Antonov seems to me to be saturated with opportunism in his conciliatory attitude towards this sort of thing." Trotsky proposed "the harshest measures—shootings, transfer to the rear, supplementary labour battalions, imprisonment in concentration camps; once and for all a decisive struggle with the endless-meeting type of commander. Firm measures in one or two cases will immediately make others pull themselves together .... Since this work has ... a decisive significance for the fate of the Ukrainian Soviet republic, I think that the Ukrainian party should concentrate its main efforts in the field of the reorganization and training of the Ukrainian army."[154] Lenin also attacked Antonov for insubordination and separatism. When Antonov raised the problem of the centralization of the military machinery in Ukraine and created the revolutionary military council of Ukraine, under the chairmanship of the people's commissar for war of Ukraine,[155] Lenin opposed this categorically. In his telegram to Antonov (with copies to Rakovsky, Podvoisky, and Sergei Kamenev) of 25 April 1919, Lenin ironically said:

> I have received your coded [telegram] and likewise your project for the division of the southern front and the Ukrainian front. For the first I thank you, for the second I reprimand you for playing at independence. Throwing the Ukrainian armies into the drive on Taganrog is obligatory, immediate, and unconditional.[156]

Complaints about—and dissatisfaction with—Antonov's activities continued. Lenin, as well as Trotsky and Vatsetis, tried to remove him from the Ukrainian front. Thus Trotsky notified Lenin and Efraim Skliansky on 13 May 1919: "I doubt in advance whether the revolutionary military council of Ukraine, comprising Bubnov, Shchadenko, and Antonov, will be able to assume the necessary leadership."[157] Trotsky notified the CC in his next telegram that he, on the basis of his talks with Mezhlauk and Sergei Kamenev, "finally made clear the necessity of removing Antonov, Podvoisky, and Bubnov from military work." He proposed these alternatives: either creating a new revolutionary military council of Ukraine with Sergei Kamenev, Vasilii Glagolev, or Anatolii Gekker in command and with Mezhlauk and Voroshilov as members; or "abolishing the Ukrainian front, subordinating the eastern part of it to the southern front and introducing into the revolutionary military council of the southern front (*revvoensovetiuzh*) one or two Ukrainians." In addition, a separate army of "the Hungarian direction" was to be created. As far as Hryhoriiv was concerned, Trotsky proposed a relentless struggle against him, liquidating with the same blow the other insurgents.[158]

The correspondence between Lenin and Trotsky concerning the reorganization (or rather liquidation) of the Ukrainian front went on. The greatest error of Antonov and Podvoisky[159] was considered to be the neglect of the Donets front, especially their failure to come to its aid with military forces. In another telegram to Rakovsky, Lenin regarded "every minute of delay in bringing military aid from Ukraine to the southern front ... as a crime for which Antonov and Podvoisky are responsible."[160] On 26 May Lenin again emphasized to Rakovsky the necessity to help in the Donets basin and to fight against Hryhoriiv. "Do not miss the moment for the victory over Hryhoriiv, do not permit a single soldier to leave of those who fight against Hryhoriiv. Issue and implement an order for the complete disarming of the population. *Shoot mercilessly on the spot for every concealed rifle.* The whole issue of the moment is a speedy victory in the Donets basin, the collection of all rifles from the villages, the creation of a firm army. Concentrate all strength on this effort, mobilize every single worker."[161]

Lenin did not have to encourage the Bolsheviks to use terror, since they acted indiscriminately in any case. For instance, the sixth regiment of the second division destroyed the village of Hermanivka for giving active aid to the insurgents (the destruction, according to Antonov, had even "upset" Rakovsky himself).[162] Antonov replied to all these threats and entreaties that "uprisings are continual throughout Right-Bank Ukraine. Hryhoriiv operates with his partisan detachments. All railway junctions must be occupied by strong units and also by manoeuvring groups. Therefore, fully conscious of my responsibility for the defence of Soviet power in Ukraine, I declare: I cannot carry out your orders. I am doing everything I can. I need no urging. Either trust or resignation."[163]

The emergency was to a certain extent caused by the lack of banknotes. In spite of the constitution of the Ukrainian SSR according to which Ukraine, as an independent country, had the right to deal with all monetary matters, the CC RCP did not permit the Ukrainian government to mint its own currency. A telegram of 22 May to Rakovsky, signed by

Lenin, Nikolai Krestinsky, and Mikhail Kalinin, said: "The CC RCP suggests to the CC CPU not to put forward for discussion by the Ukrainian Council of People's Commissars any important financial decisions, like the issue of new notes or the exchange of *karbovantsi*,[164] without a previous enquiry to the CC RCP, since such measures may be taken only on the all-Russian scale."[165] However, the main obstacles to aid for the Donets basin were the rebellions in the rear of the Soviet troops, chiefly that of Hryhoriiv on the southern front and those of Zeleny, Struk, and other insurgents in the region of Kiev. Antonov was, by conviction, a devoted Communist who carried out the directives of the party. But actual conditions in Ukraine paralysed all his efforts for the establishment and consolidation of the Soviet regime. Even if he was relatively conciliatory towards the Ukrainian insurgent detachments, as Lenin and Trotsky accused him of being, he was so only in the interests of the revolution, only because he believed that an all-out struggle against the insurgents was impossible at that time. Antonov repeatedly stressed in his reports to the party and to Lenin himself the mistakes of the Soviet organs in their dealings with the peasantry and with the Ukrainian national movement. On the whole, in a situation in which Soviet power was almost exclusively confined to large towns, it was not easy for Antonov to carry out the orders of Moscow and Serpukhov. In his memorandum to Lenin of 17 April 1919, Antonov reported that Rakovsky's policy was erroneous. He felt that especially the "land and national policy in Ukraine cuts at the roots of all the efforts of the military leadership to overcome these disintegrating influences."[166]

Antonov proposed the following measures:

1) introduce into the Ukrainian government the representatives of parties connected with the middling and small-holding peasantry (independentist SDs and Ukrainian SRs);

2) modify the land policy in the spirit of agreement with the middling peasantry;

3) make the people's commissariat for internal affairs work for the organization of local Soviet power;

4) make the "Great Russian" newcomers behave with the greatest tact towards the local population and local peculiarities;

5) stop the rapacious policy towards the grain and coal of Ukraine;

6) urge the party to send two-thirds of its force into the countryside and into the army;

7) reduce by two-thirds all Soviet administrative offices, transferring the functionaries into the provinces for practical work;

8) move the Donets workers into the ranks of our army, which consists of peasants;

9) pursue in the food policy not a requisitional, but a productive, dictatorship.[167]

Even more characteristic for the policy of the Communists in Ukraine were Antonov's complaints of 8 May 1919 to the defence council of Ukraine:

1) The local power has not at all been established and to a certain degree has been imposed upon the majority of the population (for instance, in Aleksandriia an executive committee consisting of Muscovites has been imposed upon the former district congress).

2) Food officers not of local origin, and acting without an understanding of the situation, have set the countryside against the central Soviet power to an extreme degree.

3) The *chrezvychaiki*, which are becoming a state within the state, are almost universally disliked and almost everywhere create complications for the Soviet power . . . .

8) A complete disregard of the prejudices of the local population against the Jews.

9) A tactless attitude of the central authorities towards the national feelings of Ukraine (for instance, sending food consignments to Moscow addressed there directly, especially

> such scarcities as tea and coffee). The orders from Moscow to the Ukrainian railwaymen; the order of the ZRK Arnoldov from Moscow to Hryhoriiv's brigade to detrain, etc., without end, ... organized "bag expeditions" for the food supplies of Ukraine.

The government's land policy was vague and it only upset the peasantry by stressing communes as the first priority. Antonov again proposed to take decisive measures to improve relations with the population. Among other things, he proposed "to abolish the VUChK," subordinating the local chekas to the provincial and district executive committees, and, on the front, to "the special departments." "No agents from Moscow must be allowed to work locally in the name of Moscow, but only in the name of the corresponding organs of Ukraine and under their strict control." He also stressed the importance of "attracting to the central power representatives of the middle and small-holding peasantry."[168] Antonov's reports and proposals were tantamount to flagrant heresy in the eyes of the leaders of the Communist party in Ukraine and of the RCP of that time. In fact, it was none other than Lenin himself who mobilized "bag expeditions" from Russia and organized a "crusade" for bread from Ukraine. Antonov's criticism coincided completely with the criticism of party policy made by the Ukrainian parties from the Directory's camp as well as by Ukrainian left socialist parties, the independentists and Borotbists. Recruiting peasants to the administration was nothing less than a departure from the principle of the dictatorship of the proletariat.

The actual decentralization of the army in Ukraine and disregard for the orders of the CC RCP gradually brought about the abolition of even a formal separateness for the army of the Ukrainian SSR. In May 1919 the CC RCP adopted the draft directive on the military unity of all the Soviet republics. The draft directive stated that "the RSFSR must, in an alliance with the fraternal Soviet republics of Ukraine, Latvia, Estonia, Lithuania, and Belorussia, conduct a defensive struggle against the common enemy" and that "a necessary condition of success in this war is a single command for all detachments of the Red Army and the strictest centralization in the disposal of all forces and resources of the socialist republics." The CC RCP therefore resolved:

> 1) To recognize as absolutely necessary for the whole duration of the socialist defensive war the unification of the entire Red Army supply system under a single leadership subordinate to

the defence council and other central administrative bodies of the RSFSR;

2) to recognize as absolutely necessary for the whole duration of the socialist defensive war the uniting of railway transport and railway network management throughout the area of the fraternal socialist republics under the leadership and management of the people's commissariat of communication of the RSFSR;

3) to recognize as incompatible with the interests of defence the existence in the fraternal Soviet republics of separate organs for the supply of the Red Army and of separate commissariats of communication, and to insist on the transformation of these for the duration of the war into the departments of ... the Red Army of the RSFSR and of the people's commissariat of communication of the RSFSR ... ;

4) to revoke all decrees relating to the supply of the Red Army and to railway transport or to the management of the railway network unless they are not in contradiction with the orders and decrees ... of the RSFSR.[169]

This directive, signed by Lenin and Stalin, made a beginning in that centralizing process which was carried out by all administrative organs of the RSFSR towards other republics and chiefly towards Ukraine. This directive came to be interpreted as a decision of the supreme administration to strive towards a "united Russia." Lenin wrote to Trotsky and Skliansky that the directive of the central committee was "the beginning of a new period in the course of the Great Russian revolution, since apart from the unification of the command of the armed forces there also took place the unification of other branches of the state affairs of the aforesaid *republics.*" He stressed that the army of the united republics should now be called "the all-Russian republican Soviet army" as "a symbol of a single state order which has now been firmly established in Russia."[170] In accordance with this, Lenin wrote in his coded telegram to Trotsky on 2 June that he was "extremely astonished and, to put it mildly, down-hearted" because Trotsky had not carried out the directive of the central committee and had "not removed Podvoisky and Antonov. ... Now it is absolutely necessary to put an end to it; [there must be] no people's commissar for war in Ukraine"; it would be enough to have two districts there, Kharkiv and Kiev, and Antonov was to be transferred to another front.[171]

Trotsky argued with Lenin: "The complaints are unfounded .... In order to abolish the Ukrainian front it would be necessary to have a corresponding preliminary resolution of the TsIK RSFSR .... It would be necessary to put something new in place of the Ukrainian command." But there was not adequate personnel for this purpose.[172] Two days later Trotsky wrote again to Lenin: "Therefore the liquidation of the Ukrainian front, decided upon in principle, cannot be carried out in practice. The so-called carrying out to the ultimate conclusion requires functionaries whom I do not possess at all."[173] The Ukrainian front was, however, liquidated. On 4 June the revolutionary military council (RVSR) issued an order, signed by Trotsky and Vatsetis, to disband the Ukrainian front,[174] and on 14 June it was liquidated. In his last order, Antonov pointed out that "the new tasks which are before the Ukrainian armies coincide with the tasks of the armies of the Russian front and require a simplification of their command and a concentration of military will."[175] This obviously did not save the situation, because the southern front was collapsing with catastrophic speed under Denikin's pressure, while the troops of the Directory, supported by the forces of the West Ukrainian republic, mounted an offensive from the west.

The Red troops retreated in haste and chaos before Denikin's offensive, leaving a poor impression on the population. In this situation of general chaos and disorganization, Lenin and the CC RCP began on the whole to issue unceremonious and peremptory orders to their step-children in the CP(B)U. While Rakovsky's government had been relatively stable, the CC RCP exercised its supremacy over that government and the CP(B)U only in the form of directives on larger political issues. But during Denikin's offensive, beginning in August 1919, the CC RCP treated the leaders of the CP(B)U as native notables. In a coded telegram of 13 August 1919, addressed to Rakovsky with copies to Trotsky and Kosior, Lenin wrote in the name of the politburo: "I urge [you] seriously to close all commissariats except those of war, communications, food supply, and to mobilize everyone to a man for military work, and to assume the task of holding out at least several weeks, since the Council of People's Commissars, the defence council, the TsIK and the central committee of the CP(B)U have been amalgamated."[176] Thus they were "urged" to cease their independent activities and to subordinate themselves to the Moscow centre. For this purpose, the emissaries of the CC RCP, Trotsky, Kamenev, and Ioffe, liquidated the government of Ukraine at a meeting of the TsIK and replaced it with a council for the defence of the republic, led by Rakovsky, with Petrovsky and Ioffe as members (later to be joined by Voroshilov, Bubnov, and Ignatii Dzevaltovsky).[177] After the departure from Kiev, this council settled down in Chernihiv. Here, together with the rear bureau (*zafrontovoe biuro*) set up at the same time in place of the CC CP(B)U, it began its propaganda activities against Denikin and Petliura. They quickly began to publish the *Izvestiia raboche-krestianskoi oborony Ukrainy* and the organ of the CC CP(B)U, *Kommunist*. These organs printed several appeals to the workers and peasants of Ukraine as well as the soldiers of the Petliurite and Galician armies. The appeals played upon the patriotic anti-Polish sentiments of the Galicians and the independentist moods of the Petliurite soldiers. They said that the struggle of these soldiers against the Red Army was conducted not at all for the sake of the independence of Ukraine, but "only for the sake of the triumph of tsarist generals and the Polish nobility."[178]

In exile, all the party and government institutions of the Ukrainian SSR showed no signs of separateness from those of the RSFSR. The personnel of this government was at the CC RCP's free disposal, and a complete liquidation of the all-Ukrainian Soviet power followed. For instance, the head of the government of the Ukrainian SSR, Rakovsky, was appointed the head of the political board of the (Russian) republic. Petrovsky was intended to be the chairman of the Moscow district executive committee; the secretary of the VUTsIK, Mikhail Boguslavsky, was to be the secretary of the political board of the republic; and a whole series of other members of the TsIK of Ukraine were to receive appointments in various district executive committees of the RSFSR. At that time a commission was set up in Moscow for the liquidation of Ukrainian Soviet institutions (administrative organizations).[179]

The collapse of Soviet power in Ukraine was the result primarily of Denikin's offensive from the Don, coupled with that of the Directory's armies from the west. However, the Bolsheviks themselves admit that without the countless peasant uprisings that engulfed the whole of Ukraine, Denikin and Petliura would not have been so successful. Popov was right in stressing that the blow of "international and internal counter-revolutionary forces" coincided in time with the rejection of Soviet power by the masses of peasantry, and that these changes greatly influenced the attitude of the Soviet forces, which largely consisted of peasants. Popov listed the land policy and the food policy among the causes of the peasantry's hostility to Soviet power, thanks to "a certain national isolation of the party and of the Soviet set-up, including the food supply organs, from the Ukrainian peasantry."[180] He pointed out that although the party succeeded in taking only a very insignificant amount of grain out of Ukraine, the circumstances were such that "the smallest trifles suggested to the peasantry, and fanned the idea, that here Moscow was actually robbing Ukraine."[181] Another source of hostility, in his view, was the party's national policy in Ukraine, which amounted to ignoring the national needs of the Ukrainian population. An example of this was the negative attitude of the president of the government of Ukraine himself, Rakovsky.[182] This negation of the national aspirations of Ukraine antagonized the Ukrainian left socialist parties, who by early May 1919 openly began organizing a popular uprising against Soviet power.

CHAPTER IX

The Victory of the Bolsheviks

The final act in the Sovietization of Ukraine was a result of the Soviet military victory over Denikin and the Directory in December 1919 and early 1920. This was the period of military successes for Soviet Russia on all fronts: in Siberia (against Kolchak), on the southern front (against Denikin), and on the northern one. During this period the anti-Bolshevik front suffered its final defeat. The Entente, which supplied the armaments of the anti-Bolshevik forces, could not decide on any consistent policy in "Russian affairs," a problem due in no small measure to the heterogeneity of the anti-Bolshevik forces. Antagonism between the "White" generals and the governments of the newly-created states in the borderlands of Russia was so strong that the creation of a single common alliance was a task to which even the powerful Entente, on whom all these generals and governments depended, was not equal. This created a favourable situation for the Bolsheviks, who exploited the moment very adroitly.[1] Only a few months after Communist Moscow itself had been threatened by Denikin, mere pitiful remnants were left of his armies. The Bolsheviks occupied Ukraine and a part of Siberia; and soon they had so stabilized their international position that the powers of the Entente contemplated peace with them.[2]

A Revaluation of the Nationality Policy in Ukraine

In their Ukrainian policy, the Bolsheviks made considerable adjustments. Having burned their fingers in Ukraine a year earlier on the land and national questions, they now sought a *modus vivendi*. During this period the party also cured itself of its illusions about "world revolution," which had persisted on the eve of the second Soviet regime in Ukraine. Now they considered Ukraine in a more sober light, through the prism of those countless peasant risings which had been the undoing of previous Soviet rule. For this revision of its Ukrainian policy, the party was much indebted to its Ukrainian elements, who pointed out the errors and weaknesses of previous policy. In any case, the thought of a pure and uncamouflaged conquest of Ukraine now seemed more than absurd. The idea had spread among the Bolsheviks of Ukraine that it would even be necessary to grant far-reaching concessions to the Ukrainian national movement and to the peasantry. But there were also among them adherents of the old line on the Ukrainian question. In general, attitudes on the question crystallized along two main lines: on the one hand were the adherents of an independent Ukrainian Soviet republic with its own government and independent Communist party which would independently solve all questions of Ukraine's internal and external policy; on the other hand were those who supported maximal subordination of Ukraine to the Russian federation, with the CP(B)U merely an ordinary regional organization of the RCP. As far as the rank-and-file of the RCP were concerned, there was complete ignorance of the Ukrainian problem. They saw no difference between Ukraine and "the south of Russia"; they did not see that it was a separate state, a separate nation. The Bolsheviks of Ukraine, during their exile until December 1919, represented two different views on the future tactics of the party in Ukraine: federalist and centralist. Federalists such as Lapchynsky, Slynko, and Pavlo Popov very sharply criticized previous party policy in Ukraine, blaming it for the defeat of the second Soviet regime. The federalists' memorandum to the CC RCP, probably written by Popov, indicted the party for its failure in Ukraine:

> The main fault in the policy of the CP(B)U was the absence of a centre of leadership that would have been organically connected with the revolutionary masses of Ukraine and could have given an answer to any question offered by life .... That centre which exists has not been able to master this task not because of the composition of its personnel, but because ... it has considered everything from the viewpoint of narrow centralism, completely disregarding the fact that the course of the revolution in Russia has not been at all uniform, that Ukraine cannot accept as ready-made the forms of life which

> have been worked out in Russia during a year and a half of Soviet construction in circumstances completely different from those in Ukraine .... The *Leitmotiv* of the whole policy of the CP(B)U is a mistrust of the Ukrainian Communist groups and an orientation towards those groups which are, even if not Communist, at least not contaminated by "separatism" ....
> It has come about that, as a rule, the party has also had no influence in the countryside, which is Ukrainian in its composition; it has done nothing to attract the poorer elements to its side, but instead it has gladly admitted to its membership the petty-bourgeois elements from among the Russian and Jewish craftsmen, whose attitude is more or less Russophile .... Ukraine has been regarded merely as an object from which to extract material resources, and, moreover, the interests of the class struggle in Ukraine have been completely ignored.[3]

The memorandum stressed the need for an immediate merger of the two Communist parties in Ukraine, the Bolsheviks and the Borotbists, and emphasized that the leading role in the struggle for the re-establishment of the power of the soviets in Ukraine was not to belong to the Moscow centre, but to the Ukrainian one.[4]

Similar suggestions concerning the revision of party policy in Ukraine were presented by Pavlo Popov in his report to the rear bureau *(zafrontbiuro)* of the CC CP(B)U on 21 October 1919. Popov was one of the party's agents who were left in the territory of the Directory after the Bolsheviks evacuated Ukraine. In his report he suggested the need for an agreement with the Directory against Denikin, since these tactics would have taken away from the Directory its weapon of national antagonism, which was its life-blood, and therefore an alliance with the Directory would mean its disintegration from within.[5]

Popov's theses are permeated by the ideas of the federalists, but they also show very clearly that he had succumbed to the Ukrainian national idea, thanks to the time he had spent in the surroundings of the UNR, where Ukrainian nationalism reached its climax. Popov's theses completely opposed previous party tactics, chiefly those of Trotsky, who had expounded his policy in the CC RCP at the beginning of the second period of Soviet rule in Ukraine, and according to whom there was no possibility of an understanding with the Directory. Popov remarked after the event that nobody in the party had at that time opposed his theses, but, on the contrary, the CC RCP had even tried to come to an agreement with the Directory through Fritz Platten.[6]

The most radical change in the policy of the party was proposed by the federalists at the so-called Homel conference in November 1919. The theses, introduced by Lapchynsky, proposed:

1) Ukraine throughout the whole extent of its territory must be a Soviet socialist republic, ruled exclusively by its own Soviet power, the supreme organ of which is the all-Ukrainian congress of soviets.

2) The uniting of Ukraine with other socialist republics, *independently of whether they have been or will be created on the territory of the former Russian empire or outside this territory*, may take place only on genuinely federative principles, namely, so that the organs of administration common to all federated states should consist of representatives of all members of the federation, and that within Ukraine such organs should function through the local Ukrainian organs of Soviet power.

3) In particular, when certain branches of the administration and of the economy of Ukraine are united with those of Russia and other Soviet republics, the common federative organs controlling these branches must not on any account be identical with the corresponding administrative organs of Great Russia proper.[7]

With regard to party organization Lapchynsky proposed uniting all Communist forces in Ukraine into a single Ukrainian Communist Party (Bolsheviks) which was to be "an entirely independent section of the International." It was said further that the party "must remember that 90 per cent of the population is of Ukrainian nationality, that the whole peasantry of the country is homogeneous in this respect, and that a real education and elevation of the cultural level of the masses and their enlistment for the active construction of Communist society is imaginable only through the restoration of rights to the language of the people .... Therefore the members of the party must definitely break with the contempt inherited from tsarist times for everything local and national and with the habit of regarding Ukraine not as an independent country, populated by one of the numerically largest European peoples, but as an appendage of Russia, of which it actually was a colony all the time."[8]

These considerations of the federalists coincided almost exactly with the criticism of the policy of the party in Ukraine by the Ukrainian left socialists, Borotbists and independentists. When such a position was taken by prominent members of the CP(B)U, it can be imagined that all was not well with party policy in Ukraine.[9] How much truth there was in the criticism offered by all these groups is shown by the subsequent tactics of the RCP in Ukraine, planned by Lenin himself and his adherents at the December conference of the RCP. As will be seen, Lenin took into consideration the arguments of the above-mentioned groups when planning his new tactics in Ukraine.[10]

Prominent leaders of the RCP also insisted on the change of tactics in

Ukraine. Ordzhonikidze (Sergo) wrote to Lenin from Briansk on 19 November 1919 that, when entering "a district of insurgent partisans ... it is necessary to adhere to an extremely flexible policy." It was necessary to master the insurgent movement, sending some of the "chieftains" ("*batko*") to kingdom come and subduing others. "But all this is nothing compared with the tremendously important question of our actual relations with the Ukrainian peasant. Here it is my deep conviction that the policy of dragging him into the commune is senseless and disastrous. This time we must find a common language with the Ukrainian peasant at all costs .... Many of the functionaries of Ukraine must not be returned there. Best of all, the greatest possible number of local personnel is to be attracted; those who are most responsible are to be sent from the centre, and with them a great number of workers from Petrograd and Moscow."[11]

On the eve of the Soviet offensive against Ukraine, Lenin outlined the party's tactics for Ukraine, which were discussed at the meeting of the politburo of the CC RCP(B) on 21 November. This "draft resolution of the CC RCP(B) on Soviet power in Ukraine" was accepted and handed over to the commission for final editing. The draft resolution was adopted with the commission's amendments by the plenary meeting of the CC RCP(B) on 29 November 1919 and then published. On 3 December 1919 this resolution was approved by the eighth all-Russian conference of the RCP(B).[12]

Only in some points was Lenin's draft changed by the commission of the CC RCP; its main trend was faithfully preserved. In the resolution adopted by the eighth all-Russian conference the first point of the draft is absent. Further, Lenin's draft said that the RCP "will strive towards the establishment of federative ties between the RSFSR and the Ukrainian SSR," while the resolution as adopted implies that such federative ties already exist between these two republics. However, the resolution also says that the form of the federation "will be decided finally by the Ukrainian workers and toiling peasants themselves."[13] Even a cursory analysis of this document shows how much Lenin changed his attitude to the Ukrainian national movement, having now recognized its strength. In his draft, Lenin completely revised his earlier underestimation of the Ukrainian national movement and of national consciousness among the population. Now not only the Ukrainian language and Ukrainian culture were recognized, but the Bolsheviks were called upon to be conciliatory towards the "national feelings" which existed "in the backward sectors of the Ukrainian masses." Lenin even went so far as to accept the principle of the Ukrainian socialist parties that there be a preponderance of peasantry in the "revolutionary committees and soviets," although on the condition that the deciding voice in them was to be reserved for the poorer peasantry. Of very great importance was the adoption and application of the paragraph concerning the equality of languages, which meant that the population was able to use Ukrainian in administrative offices and in the army without fear of repression.[14]

The concessions to the peasantry represented a consistent attempt to win over the middle peasant, who had in the past been against Soviet power. The resolution saw its task to be to persuade the Ukrainian peasant that requisitioning grain was to satisfy the needs, not of Russia, but of the Ukrainian Red Army and working class. The disarming of the peasants was supported by the argument that weapons in the hands of the peasantry secured the dictatorship of the "kulak bandits" and not the "dictatorship of the workers." Compulsory introduction of communes and collective farms was likewise abandoned. The communes could be organized only with the agreement of the local peasantry. Of course, on all questions (and chiefly on the question of the middle peasant and his role in the political life of the country and on the national question) Lenin was making temporary tactical concessions which could be withdrawn again after the establishment of the Soviet system in Russia and Ukraine.[15] His resolution was a concession to Ukrainian nationalism and to peasant anti-Communism. Lenin now understood that Ukraine could be sovietized only gradually, by manoeuvring. The recently published speech of Lenin at the eighth conference of the RCP(B) sheds some light on the intentions the resolution expressed. Polemizing with Rakovsky about Soviet state farms, Lenin pointed out that the moderate line was necessary, because "otherwise we shall not achieve a bloc with the small peasantry, and we need this bloc." Lenin said the same to Manuilsky, Drobnis, and Bubnov, who took him to task for his concessions to the Borotbists. "My answer," Lenin said, "consists precisely in pointing out that we need a bloc with the peasantry of Ukraine, and in order to make this bloc we must polemize with the Borotbists, not in the way that it is being done."[16]

On the national question, Lenin did not depart from the basic position, i.e., maintaining close ties between Ukraine and Soviet Russia and restricting the independence of the CP(B)U. Ukrainian, like the language of any other nationality, served merely as a weapon to achieve Communism. Lenin therefore demanded that the Borotbists dissolve the union of Ukrainian teachers, "even if in Ukrainian, even if under the Ukrainian state seal, but in the name of the same principles of the proletarian Communist policy."[17]

The existence of opposition within the party to the revision of Lenin's Ukrainian policy is borne out by Lenin's repeated need to defend the revision. To justify his line he wrote an article, "Elections to the Constituent Assembly and the Dictatorship of the Proletariat" (published in December 1919), which argued that national feeling was very strong among the Ukrainian masses. Lenin indicated that he had been accused by some comrades "at the recent conferences on the Ukrainian question . . . of giving excessive prominence to the national question in Ukraine." Quoting the figures of the 1917 election results, which showed that the Ukrainian parties (chiefly the SRs) obtained the majority of the votes in Ukraine, he defended his position:

> In such a state of affairs, to ignore the importance of the national question in Ukraine, of which the Great Russians are very frequently guilty (and probably the Jews are guilty of it only a little less frequently than the Great Russians), means committing a profound and dangerous error. The division between the Russian and Ukrainian SRs in Ukraine as early as 1917 cannot be a mere accident. Being internationalists, we must first struggle especially energetically against remnants (sometimes subconscious ones) of Great Russian imperialism and chauvinism among the "Russian" Communists; secondly, we must make concessions only on the national question, as it is one of relatively little importance (for an internationalist, the question of state boundaries is of secondary, if not denary, importance). Other questions are important; the basic interests of the proletarian dictatorship are important, the interests of the unity and discipline of the Red Army which is struggling with Denikin are important, the leading role of the proletariat towards the peasantry is important; the question whether Ukraine will be a separate state or not is much less important. We must not be at all astonished or frightened, even by the prospect that Ukrainian workers and peasants will try out various systems and that within several years, say, they will test in practice both amalgamation with the RSFSR and separation from it into a special independent Ukrainian SSR, as well as various forms of close union, etc., etc. To try to solve this question in advance, once and for all, "firmly" and "irrevocably," would have meant a narrowness of outlook or simply stupidity, for the wavering of the non-proletarian working masses in such a question is quite natural, even inevitable, but is not at all alarming to the proletariat.[18]

In a word, Lenin was convinced, on the basis of the experience of two attempts to establish Soviet power in Ukraine, that to be successful this power had to assume Ukrainian national forms. Lenin reminded his comrades who were diehards about "Ukraine as an integral part of Russia" that a compromise in questions of little importance could safeguard the pursuit of his purpose in questions of principle. These tactics of Lenin are set forth even more clearly in another document of that time on the Ukrainian question, his letter "to the workers and peasants of Ukraine on the occasion of the victory over Denikin," 28 December 1919:

> Great Russian Communists must be willing to make concessions in their disagreements with the Ukrainian Communists, the Bolsheviks and the Borotbists, if the disagreements concern the state independence of Ukraine, the forms of its union with Russia, and the national question generally. All of us, both the Great Russian and Ukrainian Communists, and those of any other nation whatsoever, must be unyielding and irreconcilable in regard to the basic, fundamental questions of the proletarian dictatorship, which are the same for all nations, in regard to the prevention of a reconciliation with the bourgeoisie and the prevention of the splitting of the forces which defend us against Denikin.

However, after this "ceremonial" declaration of the self-determination of Ukraine, Lenin went on to say that "in any decision concerning the question of state independence or state boundaries, the Great Russian and the Ukrainian workers of necessity need a close military and economic alliance, for otherwise the capitalists of the Entente, i.e., of the alliance of the richest capitalist countries . . . will crush and strangle us one by one." Forgetting his previous promises, Lenin wrote that "he who breaks the unity and the closest alliance of the Great Russian and the Ukrainian workers and peasants, helps the Kolchaks, Denikins, and the capitalist brigands of all countries."[19] This was not a simple hint at an alliance, but a direct threat to all those who might oppose one.

To implement this line and establish control over the Ukrainian Soviet machinery, the RCP sent to Ukraine many experienced party workers. As a Soviet historian wrote: "From December 1919 until April 1920 more than one thousand political workers were sent to Ukraine from the [Red] Army, in accordance with the transfer orders of the CC RCP(B). This assistance had enormous importance for the restoration of Soviet power in Ukraine."[20]

However, the main task of the Soviet machinery in Ukraine was of an economic character. To facilitate the economic exploitation of Ukraine, Stalin was sent there and "elected" a member of the CC CP(B)U and chairman of the soviet of the labour army, the task of which was "the maximum increase in the output of food, fuel, and raw materials, the establishment of labour discipline in enterprises, and the supply of a labour force to the enterprises."[21] As Prokopenko points out, "that V. I. Lenin and the CC RCP(B) entrusted the leadership of the Ukrainian soviet of the labour army to comrade Stalin indicates the importance attributed to the economic and military policy in Ukraine on the eve of the interventionists' new campaign against the Soviet republic."[22] The main task of the labour army was not to raise the economic strength of Ukraine in general, but to increase production of those raw materials necessary for Russia. In his letter to Stalin of 18 February 1920 Lenin wrote plainly that it was necessary "to assess the work of the Ukrainian labour army (*ukrtrudarm*) daily by the quantity of grain and fuel supplied."[23]

By the end of February 1920 the military and international situation of Soviet Russia had improved enough for Lenin again to modify his line on the national question (in the direction of centralism) and to condemn as counter-revolutionary all attempts to make the borderlands independent. In his report at the first session of the all-Russian TsIK on 2 February 1920, Lenin pointed out that the policy of the Entente was becoming less implacable and interventionist with regard to Soviet power in Russia. He said that the supreme council of the Allies had adopted a resolution on 16 January 1920 to stop the blockade of Soviet Russia. The peace treaty with Estonia had broken the ice in the international arena. Lenin called this treaty, not without foundation, an act "of worldwide historical importance." Lenin announced a policy of close alliance with the eastern borderlands and the Caucasus. As for Ukraine, Lenin said that the separation of Ukraine from Russia "cannot be advantageous in the circumstances of the struggle against imperialism" and that the demand for separation "is a crime."[24] This statement of Lenin's became to a certain extent the directive for party policy in Ukraine.

The offcial CP(B)U had no policy of its own and merely implemented RCP resolutions, translated into Ukrainian the declarations sent from Moscow, and disseminated them. Contemporary documents of the CP(B)U and the all-Ukrainian revolutionary committee repeated the theses of the resolution of the eighth all-Russian conference. A proclamation of the all-Ukrainian revolutionary committee "to the workers and peasants of Ukraine" (21 December 1919), signed by Petrovsky, Zatonsky, and Manuilsky, said that "the free and independent Ukrainian Socialist Soviet Republic again rises from the dead .... At last, in the third year, thanks to the mighty help of the Red Army of the workers' and peasants' Russia, into which merged also the Ukrainian Red Army, the workers of Ukraine gained the possibility of establishing their working class power on Ukrainian soil firmly and forever." Further, the hostile attitude of the tsarist general, Denikin, to the Ukrainian national liberation was emphasized, as were "the attempts of Petliura and similar agents of the Entente, Polish landlords, and Romanian boyars to separate the Ukrainian workers from the Russian ones and to deliver both the former and the latter up to the capitals of Europe and America to be devoured." In reference to the land question the slogans of the resolution of the eighth all-Russian conference were repeated almost word for word. The proclamation also stressed that "the all-Ukrainian revolutionary committee will sharply cut short any intervention in the life of the peasantry which pursues as its aim the forcing upon the peasants of economic organizations which are not the result of their own initiative." This proclamation, unlike the resolution of 3 December 1919, made no mention of the majority in the soviet belonging to the "toiling peasantry."[25]

The all-Ukrainian revolutionary committee functioned as the government of Ukraine as late as mid-February 1920. Then the Council of People's Commissars was created, led by Rakovsky, who was also in charge of the commissariat for foreign affairs. Manuilsky became commissar for agriculture; Hryhorii Hrynko (Borotbist), education; Miron Vladimirov, food; Terletsky (Borbist), justice; Paderin, social insurance; Nikolai Kost, health; Chubar, the plenipotentiary of the supreme federal soviet of national economy; Zatonsky, the people's commissar without portfolio.[26] This government was composed of the representatives "of the Bolshevik Communists of Ukraine, of the Ukrainian Communist Party of the Borotbists, and of the Ukrainian Party of the Left Socialist Revolutionaries (Borotbists)."[27] Notifying the peoples and governments of the whole world of its formation, the declaration of the government proclaimed its firm determination "to defend the independence and integrity of the socialist Soviet republic of Ukraine and its desire to live in peace with all peoples and states, inviting them to enter into economic and diplomatic relations with Ukraine."[28] The declaration concerning the "independence and integrity" of the Ukrainian republic in particular sounds more than ridiculous in view of the party's attitude towards the unity of the Soviet republics.

Ukrainian Left Socialists and Soviet Power

The Ukrainian Social Democrats (Independentists) - Ukapists

In the period of the October revolution a process of differentiation had begun within the two Ukrainian socialist parties, the social democrats and the SRs. During the first conflict of the RCP with the Central Rada a noticeable pro-Soviet trend emerged among some prominent social democrats and SRs. The president of the General Secretariat, Vynnychenko, was himself inclined to the idea that only the introduction of a soviet system would save Ukraine from the Russian Bolshevik invasion.[29] At that time M. Porsh and M. Tkachenko belonged to the left group of the party. However, this group did not dare to go over openly to the Soviet platform, and it continued its uncompromising struggle against the Bolsheviks. The left faction of the USDWP in Kharkiv became much more radical; there Medvedev began cooperating with the Soviet regime and even became the chairman of the TsIKU. Another left social democrat, Neronovych, became for a very short time people's secretary for war in the Soviet government. Among these radical leftists were also Slynko, Butsenko, Vrublevsky, Ievhen Kasianenko (Laryk), and Kokoshko.[30] These leftists took part in the second congress of soviets in Katerynoslav and in the Taganrog conference of the CP(B)U, and their representative joined the insurgent revolutionary committee after the dissolution of the People's Secretariat. At the first congress of the CP(B)U this group united with the CP(B)U, thus introducing the first truly Ukrainian contingent into the Communist party. This merging was considered a great achievement for the party, for it strengthened the party by adding Ukrainian elements "which it had lacked, and from this point of view it was of great political importance, although the group in itself was rather small."[31] The importance of this amalgamation is borne out also by the first congress' election of a left Ukrainian social democrat (Butsenko) to the CC CP(B)U, while another (Slynko) was elected a candidate to the CC, becoming, from September 1918, a member of the CC CP(B)U.[32] As early as December 1918—that is, at the beginning of the war between the Directory and the CPC—an organizational committee of the faction of independentist social democrats was created in Kharkiv. This committee occupied distinct independentist positions and was against the policy of the Russian Bolsheviks in Ukraine. A resolution of the committee of the independentists stated that its faction would struggle with the CP(B)U as an opponent of the national and political rights of the Ukrainian people.[33] They soon moderated their hostile tone towards the CP(B)U and began cooperating with Rakovsky's government, but not for long.

During the second Soviet regime, the USDWP experienced another split. At that time a group of left social democrats broke away and formed a separate party, the Ukrainian Social Democrats (Independentists), led by Tkachenko, Mazurenko, and Mykhailo Drahomyretsky. This final split took place at the sixth conference of the USDWP on 10–12 January 1919. Disagreement arose concerning the mode of government of the Ukrainian People's Republic and of relations with the RSFSR. The question was whether Ukraine was to keep the system of democratic parliamentarianism or whether it was to go over to the Soviet Russian type. While the right wing of the congress under the leadership of Petliura and Vynnychenko were in favour of the parliamentary system, the independentists held the view that Ukraine would be able to keep its national independence only under a Soviet system, which was the only weapon likely to steal the thunder of the Russian Bolsheviks, who would have no pretext for waging war against a similar Soviet government of Ukraine. They hoped that as soon as there was the same authority in Ukraine as in Russia, the Russian Bolsheviks would be deprived of their *casus belli* and would be compelled to recognize Soviet Ukraine as independent.[34] Apart from these arguments, an important role in the leftward drift of the social democrats was played by the general trend in Europe. The revolutions in Germany and Austria and the coming to power of socialists in some countries of Central Europe created the illusion that a world revolution was beginning in which Ukraine, too, had to join.[35] The independentists also pointed out that many insurgent detachments (those of Zeleny, Hryhoriiv, and others) had accepted the Soviet platform.[36] Even the prime minister, Chekhivsky, although he did not belong to the faction of the independentists, supported at this conference the idea of "pure soviets" in Ukraine. Ukraine, he said, did not need a parliament based on universal suffrage, for this was advantageous only to the bourgeoisie; it needed the soviets "without terror and violence." He said that it was necessary to wipe out the difference between the urban and rural proletariat; then the working forces would be united and not divided as they were under the Bolshevik system. In other words, Chekhivsky was in favour of a revised form of soviets, which the RCP would obviously never have accepted. He concluded by saying that their way was neither with the Entente nor with the imperialist "world revolution," which was carried forward on the bayonets of the Chinese.[37]

The adherents of parliamentarianism pointed out the anomaly of the Soviet system in the Ukrainian environment, since in Ukraine the dictatorship of the proletariat, in the absence of a Ukrainian working class, would mean the dictatorship of the Russian Bolsheviks.[38] Vynnychenko stressed that in Ukraine socialism according to the Russian method was impossible, since 80 per cent of the population were peasants; it was impossible to introduce a system of representation such as the Bolsheviks proposed (one worker for every fourteen cooks and fifty peasants), because this would have been a dictatorship over the peasantry and a provocation to civil war. Socialism was not necessarily to be constructed by means of the *sovdepy* system. He called upon the party "to be oriented towards the highly industrialized proletariat of the West and of the whole world, but in any case not towards the backward Russian one, for if we get entangled with it, the Russian Bolsheviks will split us, crush us, oust our forces from the leadership. Then we shall have here the dictatorship of the Piatakovs, Antonovs, etc."[39]

On the question of the independence of the Ukrainian state, the right and left Ukrainian social democrats were in agreement. Both factions defended the independence of the Ukrainian People's Republic, and their attitude to Soviet Russia differed only for tactical reasons. While the rightists considered talks with the Council of People's Commissars to be nothing less than capitulation before the Russian Bolsheviks, the leftists felt that it would only be possible to preserve the independence of Ukraine through an understanding with the CPC.

As early as the first months of 1919 the independentist social democrats found themselves in conflict with the government of Rakovsky, chiefly on the national question. The independentists could tolerate neither the "Russophile" trend of that government nor its Russian composition. On the eve of the capture of Kiev by the Russian troops the independentist social democrats wrote in their organ, *Chervonyi prapor*: "Now a new force approaches Kiev, it comes as an invader, as a conqueror, whose origin is Russia .... Coming to us, under the slogan of a struggle for the power of the soviets, is a government that calls itself Ukrainian, but which cannot be regarded as such by us."[40] Elsewhere in the same paper it was said that the independentist social democrats agreed to enter Rakovsky's government on condition that "1) all official organs of supreme authority, not only Ukrainian but also Russian, recognize the independence of the Ukrainian socialist republic; and 2) a firm national as well as social course is pursued in Ukraine, and Ukrainian alone is the official language."[41] However, Rakovsky's government would not even think at that time of legalizing Ukrainian as the state language and of the separation of Ukraine from Russia. The governmental and party circles began instead an indiscriminate campaign against the independentists for their "nationalism." A Bolshevik remarked at the time that an obstacle in the way of an understanding between the Bolshviks and the independentists was their defence of "*independentist views of the form of government of Ukraine*." He pointed out that only if the independentists renounced this point of their programme and "come nearer to the true Soviet platform, *their participation in the government will undoubtedly be possible*."[42] Government circles began instead to bait the independentists for their independentism and to instruct the cheka not to waste time and to begin their liquidation.[43] *Chervonyi prapor* in January-May 1919 is full of protests against the Russification of Ukraine and particularly of the administrative organs.[44]

When in the spring of 1919 the Ukrainian countryside began to stir and a wave of peasant revolts began to undermine the foundations of the Soviet regime in Ukraine, the Ukrainian social democrats (independentists) began an open struggle against the government of Rakovsky. They often declared that they were not struggling against Soviet power as such or against the

Communist party, but only against Rakovsky's government, because of its anti-Ukrainian character.[45] In fact, this struggle was directed also against the Communist party and Soviet power.

In April 1919 the independentists, together with the Ukrainian SRs of the "centre" and the right wing of the USDWP, signed an agreement for "a common struggle against the occupation government of Rakovsky." It planned to replace the Directory with a "council of the republic" comprising nine persons, three from each of the parties. With an eye to international factors, the council preserved the name Directory. The task of this new Directory was to free the whole of Ukraine from the Russian Bolshevik occupation forces, to overthrow the existing Russian Communist regime in Ukraine, and to defend the sovereignty and independence of the Ukrainian republic. For the organization and leadership of the uprising a revolutionary central committee was to be created.[46] However, various causes (for instance, the absence of the Ukrainian SRs of the "centre" and of the social democrats, who were at that time on the territory occupied by the Directory and participated in its government) aborted this agreement.[47] Instead an all-Ukrainian revolutionary committee was formed, led by the chief otaman, Iurii Mazurenko. On 25 June he sent Rakovsky an ultimatum which said:

> In the name of the insurgent Ukrainian working people I declare to you that the workers and peasants of Ukraine have risen against you as a power of the Russian conquerors which—under cover of slogans that are sacred to us: 1) the power of the soviets of workers and peasants, 2) the self-determination of nations to the point of secession, and 3) struggle against the imperialists, conquerors, and robbers of working masses—not only corrupts these sacred slogans and destroys the genuine power of workers and independent peasants of a neighbouring state, but also exploits them for the sake of aims which are far from those of any socialist system.

Finally, Mazurenko demanded that Rakovsky lay down his authority within twenty-four hours, hand it over to the insurgent revolutionary committees, and withdraw the Muscovite Soviet force from Ukraine.[48]

Apart from this insurgent revolutionary committee, the following otamans of anti-Bolshevik uprisings were also independentists: Zeleny, Sokolovsky, Anhel, Iurii Tiutiunnyk.[49] All these insurgents, together with Hryhoriiv, seriously undermined the Soviet regime in Ukraine in the summer of 1919. The effect of their uprisings was described by a Soviet historian: "The insurrection, led by the independentists, which broke out in May and involved rather numerous partisan military detachments, which to a certain extent found a response among the masses of the peasantry, was a serious blow for the second Ukrainain regime and, strictly speaking, the *beginning of its end.*"[50] In practice these risings prepared the ground for the successes of Denikin and the Directory; but these successes were very short-lived, owing to the lack of coordination and to the mutual hostility which prevailed among various anti-Soviet forces.

Differing attitudes to Rakovsky's government caused a split among the independentists, and their left wing (the left independentists), together with the Borotbists, formed the Ukrainian Communist Party (Borotbists).[51]

During the Bolsheviks' third offensive against Ukraine the independentists reverted to a policy of cooperation with the Soviet authorities. A representative of the independentists, Hrynko, served on the all-Ukrainian military revolutionary committee, which was created in Moscow in December 1919 under the chairmanship of Petrovsky.[52] At their constituent conference on 22–25 January 1920 the independentists changed their name to the Ukrainian Communist Party (UCP), from the Ukrainian initials of which they came to be known as the "Ukapists." They sent a delegation, led by Tkachenko,[53] to Moscow for talks on the legalization of their party. The UCP was legalized, but it remained in opposition to the CP(B)U, chiefly on the national question.[54]

After the final stabilization of the Soviet regime in Ukraine, the fate of the UCP became unenviable. The regime persecuted its members and eliminated them from any government work. Although a legal party, its position was in fact illegal. It continued to advocate the independence of Ukraine, arguing that the status of the Ukrainian SSR differed little from that of Ukraine before the revolution and that Ukraine continued to be economically exploited. The absence of prospects for this party caused pessimism among its members, and it began to split up, while individual members or even groups began to go over to the government party, the CP(B)U. At the end of 1921 a group of CC UCP members (Mazurenko and Iavorsky among them) broke away from the UCP. In 1923 a left faction was formed which subsequently joined the CP(B)U.[55]

The UCP also attempted to legalize its international position and in the autumn of 1924 it applied to the Comintern for membership.[56] These efforts, however, were without success. The internal political situation in Ukraine and the Russian Bolsheviks' domination of the Comintern, which was headed by the staunch Ukrainophobe Zinovev, eliminated the possibility of the UCP being admitted to membership. The Comintern's executive committee not only did not recognize the UCP as an independent member, but condemned the very existence of the UCP, ordering it to dissolve and amalgamate with the CP(B)U.

The executive committee of the Comintern also followed the RCP's line on relations between Ukraine and Russia in general. The Comintern thus rejected the UCP's charge that the RCP pursued a colonial policy towards Ukraine and accused the UCP of nationalism and separatism. The most serious sin of the UCP in the Comintern's eyes, as in the eyes of the Russian Communists, was the proposal for the "separation of the Ukrainian state apparatus, the Ukrainian army, and the Ukrainian workers' movement."[57]

The UCP had no alternative but to disband. The Ukapists joined the CP(B)U to influence its Ukrainian policy from within. According to the secretary of the Kiev district commissar, Petro Kyianytsia, who after the liquidation of the UCP entered the CP(B)U, the Ukapists entered the CP(B)U "with the aim of subversive nationalist work."[58] However, the UCP did not have sufficient membership to play a prominent role in the political life of Ukraine or to influence CP(B)U policy.

The Ukrainian Socialist Revolutionaries (Borotbists)

Simultaneously two factions arose within the Ukrainian Party of Socialist Revolutionaries. The first symptoms of the cleavage became apparent as early as the Central Rada period and particularly during the conflict of the Rada with Soviet Russia. At that time a left-wing faction, the so-called internationalists, emerged in the UPSR, and it criticized party policy at the UPSR third congress.[59] The left wing tried to come to an understanding with the Russian Bolsheviks with a view to establishing Soviet power in Ukraine. According to Vynnychenko, after the Bolsheviks had dissolved the Russian constituent assembly, the left Ukrainian SR members of this assembly reached an understanding with the Soviet government of Russia on the introduction of Soviet power into Ukraine by means of a revolution.[60] However, this plan was unsuccessful and the conspirators were arrested by the troops of the Rada. After the overthrow of the Bolshevik government in Ukraine the left SRs resumed their cooperation with the Rada. The Ukrainian left SRs occupied a mercurial position between the Rada and the Soviet power,[61] moving to the left or the right in accordance with the moods of the peasantry. During the Hetmanate, the left SRs moved increasingly to the left, apparently driven in that direction by the hetman's regime, which terrorized small peasants and inclined towards a one and indivisible Russia. It must be pointed out that the left SRs occupied a nationalist position in respect to Ukraine, which made their coooperation with the Bolsheviks very conditional. Also, as a peasant party, they could not really become one-hundred-per-cent Communist party. Their rural character, and particularly their pro-peasant land policy, did not permit them to become completely Bolshevik. Under the Central Rada, the SRs opposed the Rada's land policy, especially the land bill proposed by Martos (USD). Obviously, the "forty desiatinas" land reform of the Rada was in the interests of the middle class farmer; it was directed against the latifundia and magnates, and not the poor peasantry as Popov tries to prove.[62]

In April 1918 wealthy landowners, with the cooperation of the German troops, overthrew the Rada in an improvised *coup d'ětat* and installed the hetman, whose most important bases of support were the rich landowners and industrialists. By that time the Ukrainian SRs were completely split into factions: the right, the so-called central stream, and the left (the Borotbists). This split came about at the fourth congress of the party, which was held illegally on 13–16 May 1918 in the Sviatoshynskyi forest near Kiev. The right wing of the party advocated a moderate line and, as chief party tactics, the strengthening of the party's position among the masses and its organization on a long-term view. This faction subscribed to the programme of the Ukrainian constituent assembly, which was elected in Janaury 1918, in considering that "the most urgent task of the whole democracy of Ukraine, including the Ukrainian Party of Socialist Revolutionaries, is a resolute struggle for the convocation of the Ukrainian constitutent assembly in the most immediate future."[63] They recognized "the national liberation of the Ukrainian people—through the creation of an independent Ukrainian state—as unavoidable and the indispensable prerequisite for the success of their struggle for their political and social liberation."[64]

The left faction, on the other hand, was in favour of the immediate revolutionary introduction of social reforms and of the overthrow of the hetman's regime by means of rebellion. If one looks for analogies, the right current approached the position then held by European socialism, while the left group approached that of the Russian Bolsheviks. The left faction did not at that time give any priority to the cause of national liberation. The congress adopted the right-wing resolution by a narrow majority, but "because of the unstable composition of the congress" left-wing members only, with the exception of Shrah, were elected into the new CC of the party.[65]

The organ of the left faction was the weekly *Borotba* (Struggle), from which the faction took the name "Borotbists." However, the left SRs were still far from the Bolshevik programme. In the programme of the CC of the party they criticized the policy of the Central Rada for being exclusively national and attacked the Bolsheviks because they ignored nationality. "*The destructive Bolshevik campaign against Ukraine* broke up and demoralized the working strata of the population, causing by its lack of understanding of national matters chauvinism among the masses, making [favourable] ground for national separatism." As for the form of government, the programme of the CC said that "handing over power to the working people in the form of soviets of workers' and peasants' deputies is possible only for the short periods of time of revolutionary upsurge .... Preparations must be made for the transfer of formal power to the organs of local self-government, elected in accordance with the 'five-adjective' formula, and to the parliament in the centre, the first of which must be the Ukrainian constituent assembly."[66] This policy statement proves that the left Ukrainian SRs had a long way to go to reach Bolshevism. They not only condemned the campaign of the Russian Bolsheviks against Ukraine, but they also disagreed with them ideologically on the form of government for Ukraine, advocating parliamentarianism.[67]

One of the experts on the Borotbists, Iwan Majstrenko, rightly remarks that the attitude towards statehood as such in the platform was negative, which shows the influence of the Russian left SRs, the anarchists, and possibly also Drahomanov.[68] During the rising of the Directory against Hetman Skoropadsky, the Borotbists did not join the insurgents organized by the national union but organized their own uprisings. Majstrenko remarks that, while the insurgents who were led by the national union carried yellow and blue flags, the Borotbist insurgents marched under red banners.[69] However, the rising organized by the national union under the leadership of such prominent national figures as Vynnychenko and Petliura played a decisive role in the overthrow of Skoropadsky. A very important role in the struggle against the Hetmanate was played by the well-to-do peasants, who supported the Directory for social and ideological reasons, while regarding the left SRs almost as Bolsheviks who encroached upon their interests. It is difficult to agree with Majstrenko, who on the basis of certain peasants' congresses and the declarations of Vynnychenko, Rafes, and Khrystiuk arrives at the conclusion that "the influence of the Borotbists' programme was manifest in nearly all the resolutions passed by peasant congresses."[70] On the contrary, some resolutions quoted by Majstrenko approved the policy of the Directory and on the land question even demanded a return to the land law of Martos, which had been passed by the Central Rada in January 1918.[71] Majstrenko himself admits that the influence of the Borotbists on the peasant risings was negligible, since "they were unable to profit from their position," and also that the majority of the insurgents followed an otaman not because they agreed with his political platform, which they did not understand, "but because of his personality."[72] From what Majstrenko says, it seems that the Bolshevik Trotsky, and even Antonov, better understood the way of thinking of the Ukrainian village[73] than did the Borotbists. As the party of the rural proletariat, the Borotbists were bound to clash with the well-to-do peasantry that dominated the Ukrainian village politically and economically. The peasants followed the otaman not because he had beautiful eyes and not because he was an otaman, but because he personified the desires and ideas of the peasants of that village or district. All otamans agreed that they must struggle against the confiscation of their grain and land and against the oppression of their faith and nationality; these motives figure in the statements and declarations of all insurgents in Ukraine.

The Borotbists, like other left socialist parties, were extremely disillusioned by the Bolsheviks' irreconcilable attitudes and monopolistic position in the Soviet government. According to one of the Bund's leaders, who by that time had adopted the Soviet platform, the creation of a homogeneous Bolshevik government led by Piatakov "caused great anxiety" among the leaders of the Soviet parties, as this was an attempt to ignore all other groups. He rightly remarks that this stratagem of the Bolsheviks ran the risk of coming into conflict "with that part of the peasantry which keeps step with the revolution and is grouped around the Borotbists."[74]

By mid-January 1919 the Borotbists had formed their own government, parallel with that of Piatakov's. As Rafes wrote later, "this was not simply a gesture, for the Borotbists conducted a great operation and collected large partisan detachments."[75] In the Borotbist government were Mykola Shynkar, Hnat Mykhailychenko, Blakytny, Shumsky, M. Lytvynenko, and Lashkevych. This government issued a leaflet accusing the Directory of "driving the Ukrainian revolution into the dead-end of national petty-bourgeois counter-revolution." The aim of this government was to create a Ukrainian socialist federative republic of peasants' and workers' deputies in union with other socialist republics, including Russia, and the establishment of a dictatorship of peasants', workers', and soldiers' soviets.[76] This government, which had its seat on the right bank of the Dnieper, conducted talks with the Kharkiv government concerning the formation of a common government.[77] At the same time talks went on between the insurgent command of the Borotbists and the command of the Red Army concerning their amalgamation. Rakovsky's telegram to Chicherin indicates that an agreement was reached on 1 February between the command of the Red Army and the otaman Hryhoriiv, "a Ukrainian SR who commands considerable partisan forces and is operating in Kherson province on a continuous front as far as Nikopol." It says further that Hryhoriiv recognized the supremacy of the Kharkiv government and the military command of the RVS, "leaving it to the Ukrainian SR government, established on the right bank of the Dnieper, to negotiate a political agreement with us."[78] However, among the Bolsheviks, especially among their command, the idea predominated that Hryhoriiv could not be trusted and that he should be liquidated. Antonov himself soon became convinced that Hryhoriiv's partisans could be used against the French in Odessa. Antonov's hopes were not fanciful, since, as he admitted, "the main task of the offensive on Odessa fell upon Hryhoriiv's detachments."[79] However, the official declarations of Rakovsky's government and of the RVS of the Ukrainian front said at the time that Odessa had been taken "by Ukrainian Soviet troops"[80] or "by detachments of the Red Army."[81]

A political agreement with the Borotbist government never did come about although the Borotbists joined the Bolsheviks against the Directory. The Bolsheviks, glowing with their victory over the Directory and victories on other fronts and exultant over the progress of the revolutionary tide in Europe, saw no point in entering into an alliance with a party that stood for the independence of Ukraine. Thus at the very time when the Borotbists and other socialist parties of Soviet orientation, like the Ukrainian social democrats (independentists) and the Bund, were making every effort to reach an understanding with the Bolsheviks, the latter completely refused to cooperate. The third congress of the CP(B)U, which took place early in March 1919, rejected the offer of the Borotbists and other pro-Soviet parties. Its resolution "on the attitude towards petty-bourgeois parties" stated that

> despite their acceptance of Soviet rule, these parties are incapable of accepting the programme of the dictatorship of the proletariat with all its consequences, and therefore *their representatives must not be given any responsible posts in the councils.* The congress particularly emphasizes that it is inadmissible to include them in the government of Ukraine, which should consist *solely of representatives of the Communist party*, the only leader of the toiling revolutionary masses.
>
> Concerning attempts of the petty-bourgeois parties (the left Bund, Ukrainian SRs [Borotbists]) to unite with our party, the third congress of the CP(B)U has decided not to admit any groups to the ranks of our party and to accept [new members] only in accordance with the ordinary procedure as laid down in the [party] statute.[82]

This monopolistic attitude of the Bolsheviks precipitated a break with the Borotbists, who soon opposed them openly. It was chiefly the rising of the otaman Hryhoriiv against Soviet rule that worried the Bolsheviks. The commander of the Ukrainian front, Antonov, asked the Russian CPC and the Ukrainian government to admit the Ukrainian socialist revolutionaries and independentist social democrats into Rakovsky's government "to the detriment of Communism, but for the pacification of certain elements of the peasantry."[83] All this had some influence on the CC CP(B)U, which passed a resolution admitting the Borotbists to the government and of the Communist section of the Bund to the VUTsIK. The Borotbists received the portfolios of people's commissars for education, finance, and justice, of deputy commissars for food, internal affairs, and communications, and of deputy chairmen of the economic council (*sovnarkhoz*) and the VUTsIK. The Communist Bund received one place in the VUTsIK, in the person of Rafes.[84] This caused a rupture between the Borotbists and Hryhoriiv, who began his anti-Soviet activities as early as April and was probably in contact with the independentists.[85] The Bolsheviks did everything possible to settle their conflict with Hryhoriiv peacefully, since by his actions he destroyed all their plans to aid Hungary and the Donets basin. Antonov himself had a long telephone conversation with Hryhoriiv after the latter had proclaimed a universal which declared Rakovsky's government overthrown and called upon the people of Ukraine to struggle against "the commune, the chekas, and the commissars from the Muscovite eating place (*obzhorka*)"; the universal also proclaimed the rule of genuine people's soviets without "dictatorship by persons and parties."[86] Antonov besought Hryhoriiv not to take up arms and not to provide opportunities for "foreign invaders," but was unable to pacify him.[87] Even a member of the Ukrainian SRs (Borotbists), Blakytny, achieved nothing. Blakytny tried to persuade Hryhoriiv that the Borotbists' relations with the Communists were "good" and that negotiations were underway for their entering the Council of People's Commissars.[88] Immediately after this, Hryhoriiv was outlawed, which meant that any citizen of Soviet Ukraine, particularly any Red Army man, could shoot Hryhoriiv and his collaborators on sight. Anyone helping Hryhoriiv was to be severely punished, even to the extent of execution by firing squad. The Red terror was declared against the active left SRs and active independentists. The resolution to this effect was signed by the chairman of the VUTsIK, Petrovsky, by Rakovsky, and by the members of the defence council: Bubnov, Zharkov, Ioffe, Podvoisky, and Piatakov.[89]

During Hryhoriiv's conflict with the Bolsheviks, the Borotbists, apart from one group of the so-called active SRs, went over to the Bolsheviks and condemned the uprising. For them it was very important not to permit Denikin and Petliura to make use of the internal situation. A Soviet historian remarks that from the beginning of 1919 the Borotbists moved very far to the left, so that they found themselves "on this side of the barricades," i.e., on the Bolshevik side. He admits, however, that there were misunderstandings between the Borotbists and the Bolsheviks and that the Borotbists "conducted a struggle on many matters with the government and with the Communist party."[90] The main reason for the antagonism of the Bolsheviks towards the Borotbists was that the latter "have not broken with their chauvinist past," as it was put at the ninth congress of the RCP in March 1920.[91]

In view of the retreat of the Soviet government of Ukraine and of the CP(B)U during the offensive of Denikin and Petliura, and impressed by the CP(B)U's lack of any independent attitude towards the RCP, the Borotbists began to nurse the idea of finally taking the helm of the communist revolution in Ukraine into their own hands. Possibly it was with this motive that the Borotbists, together with the left independentists, created a new party—the Ukrainian Communist Party (Borotbists). This was announced in a common letter of the central committees of the UPSR (Communists) and the USDWP (left independentists), addressed to the executive committee of the Comintern and dated 28 August 1919.

Saying that the UCP (Borotbists) "has assumed the leadership of the Ukrainian Communist movement and its representation in the ranks of the Third International," the Borotbists intended to present the executive committee of the Comintern with a *fait accompli*. They wanted to make it appear that the CP(B)U had compromised itself and had ignominiously left the battlefield of its own free will, while they had remained behind Denikin's lines and thus become the leaders of the Communist revolution in Ukraine.[92] In the memorandum of the UCP (Borotbists), the social, political, and national situation in Ukraine and the political development of the revolution were treated in detail; and the factors necessitating the creation of a united Communist party in Ukraine were described as "organically growing out of the complex social and economic conditions and peculiarities of Ukraine." The CP(B)U was represented as an occupying force with no social and political basis.[93] To connect the Soviet regime in Ukraine more organically with conditions there, it was demanded that the UCP (Borotbists) be recognized as the sole authentic Communist party.[94]

The executive committee of the Comintern ignored this declaration in the hope that the UCP (Borotbists), impressed by the victory of the Bolshevik revolution, would yet recognize the hegemony of the CP(B)U. However, events in the summer and autumn of 1919 did not justify this hope. The defeat of the Soviet regime in Ukraine and the centralist attitude of the CC RCP towards the Ukrainian Bolsheviks stimulated sharp criticism even within the CP(B)U and resulted in the formation of factions within the latter party. At the same time there appeared a group of so-called federalists, who criticized the party's policy in Ukraine and agitated for the creation of an independent Ukrainian Communist party.

However, when the military situation soon changed in favour of the Bolsheviks, the federalists became silent.

On the eve of the Red Army's offensive in Ukraine, on 17 December 1919, an agreement was signed in Moscow between the CP(B)U and the UCP (Borotbists) by which the Borotbists "pledged themselves to support with all their might the Russo-Ukrainian Red Army" against the "united forces of Russian and international counter-revolution."[95] In spite of this agreement, the Borotbists did not abandon their hopes of leading the Ukrainian revolution, and to this end they began to form an independent Ukrainian Red Army. This Ukrainian Red Army was to have a Ukrainian character and Ukrainian command and use the Ukrainian language. As Majstrenko points out, their aim was not to split the revolutionary forces; they wanted an alliance of the Ukrainian and Russian armies, which would stay separate ethnically and culturally.[96] With this aim in view they attempted to lure to their side the army of the Ukrainian otamans, Nestor Makhno and Omelian Volokh, but these attempts were unsuccessful. The Borotbists were thus steadily losing ground, and soon they lost all confidence. As the Red Army went from success to success, the Borotbists, with the exception of the smaller otaman detachments, began to collaborate with the Bolsheviks. When, in December, the revolutionary committee of Ukraine was formed under Bolshevik leadership, the Borotbists joined it, thus renouncing their intention of creating their own government. They did not, however, abandon the intention of creating a truly independent Soviet republic with a separate Red Army and independent administration. After the completion of the Bolshevik conquest of Ukraine, the Borotbists undertook to consolidate their forces. They began to publish their papers: *Proletarska pravda*[97] in Kharkiv, *Chervonyi stiah* in Kiev, *Ukrainskyi proletar* in Katerynoslav, and *Borotba*, the official party organ, in Kiev.[98]

At the beginning of 1920 the UCP (Borotbists) again applied for recognition from the Comintern, which proposed instead that they should dissolve their party and join the CP(B)U. To solve the problem of the UCP (Borotbists), the Communist international now created a Ukrainian commission, consisting of the representatives of both parties, the CP(B)U and the UCP(B), under the chairmanship of Zinovev, the president of the International. The session of the International on 22 December 1919 was devoted to the Ukrainian problem; it passed a resolution to the effect that "Ukraine was represented at the first congress of the Communist international solely by the CP(B)U, which the congress recognized as the legal representative of the Ukrainian proletariat." It went on to point out that the UCP (Borotbists) "adheres in its activities to the principles of the

Third International and accepts completely the programme of the RCP (Bolsheviks), but because of its recent formation it does not yet have sufficiently strong support among the urban and rural proletariat of Ukraine and has not yet succeeded in making itself sufficiently known nor in applying correctly the principles of the Third International."[99]

This resolution brought to nought the efforts of the UCP (Borotbists) to be admitted to the International. The resolution is full of distortions and vituperations. The International must have known, for instance, that the Borotbists, more than any other party in Ukraine, represented the interests and the will of at least the rural proletariat and was also "sufficiently known." That it did not always correctly apply the principles of the International, i.e., in reality of the RCP(B), was a different matter.

After the UCP (Borotbists) made one more application to the International, the latter's executive committee decided on 29 February 1920 "to refuse admission of the party of the Borotbists into the Communist International" on the grounds that

> the party of the Borotbists which calls itself a Communist party, in reality departs from the principles of Communism in several extremely important points; in its demand for the immediate formation of a separate national army, and in its open agitation against Communists of other nationalities, in particular Russian Communists who worked in Ukraine .... The executive committee of the Communist International considers that the closest brotherly alliance should exist among those republics in which Soviet rule prevails. The executive committee of the Communist International is aware that the RSFSR at the seventh all-Russian congress of soviets ... recognized unconditionally the independence of Soviet Ukraine and expressed its readiness to join in the closest brotherly association with the Ukrainian Soviet republic. The central committee of the Communist International is convinced that Ukraine can withstand the pressure of the imperialists and their hirelings only by the closest economic and military alliance with Soviet Russia.[100]

The last phrase in particular was taken almost literally from the lexicon of the RCP. This resolution finally decided the question of hegemony in the proletarian revolution in Ukraine. The only alternatives left for the Borotbists were either to abide by the decision of the International or to join the Ukrainian parties of the Directory's camp in an open struggle against the Bolsheviks. The Borotbists chose the first alternative. The UCP(B) decided to amalgamate with the CP(B)U only after a fierce internal struggle. The Borotbists who joined the CP(B)U had their party membership back-dated to 1918, and two representatives of the Borotbists were admitted to the CC CP(B)U. The admission of the Borotbists into the CP(B)U took place only after the intervention of Lenin himself at the ninth congress of the RCP. In joining the CP(B)U the Borotbists brought Ukrainian national elements into the Communist party. Soviet historians also admit that by this step "the CP(B)U acquired a considerable nucleus of functionaries who not only had a command of Ukrainian, but also had ties with the Ukrainian masses. Most of them were particularly closely connected with the countryside."[101] A number of the right-wing Borotbists did not agree with the amalgamation and instead joined the UCP, which had been formed by the independentists and was at that time a legal party in Ukraine.

It is difficult to say why the Borotbists capitulated after their extremely fierce struggle with the CP(B)U for power in Ukraine. Majstrenko concludes that "patriotism and a desire to avoid further downfall of the Soviet government in Ukraine motivated the Borotbist decision." Both their open struggle against the Bolsheviks and their underground activity placed the Borotbists in the camp of the Ukrainian People's Republic, where they did not feel they belonged. The only correct course, in their opinion, was to resist the CP(B)U within the existing Soviet conditions, relying on the support they enjoyed among the Ukrainian people. The Borotbists, Majstrenko continues, held fast to their Communist principles, convinced that a sovereign Ukrainian state was possible only on the Communist side of the barricade.[102] The Borotbists did not criticize the Bolsheviks' social programme, of which they entirely approved; they criticized only the national aspect of the Bolshevik programme. In light of this, it is interesting that the International in its resolutions did not at all stress this nationalist deviation of the Borotbists, but on the contrary accused them of displaying a petty-bourgeois mentality and counter-revolutionary orientation. These tactics were recommended by Lenin himself in his "Remarks on the Draft Resolution of the Executive Committee of the Comintern" of 22 February 1920: "I emphatically insist that the Borotbists be accused, not of nationalism, but of counter-revolutionary and petty-bourgeois mentality."[103] Yet everybody knew at that time that the Borotbists were liquidated not for being counter-revolutionary but for nationalism. Their nationalist deviation is obvious from the criticism they expressed from within the ranks of the CP(B)U. One of the most characteristic actions was Blakytny's article published immediately before the fifth conference of the CP(B)U in the summer of 1920.[104]

The Bolsheviks themselves admitted that much of this criticism was justified (e.g., in the resolution of the eighth all-Russian conference of December 1919). However, from the lips of the Borotbists this criticism sounded particularly unpleasant to the Bolsheviks.

The UCP (Borotbists), like the UCP of the independentists, had considerable influence on the formation of the Ukrainian policy of the CP(B)U and the RCP. Rakovsky rightly points out the reciprocal influence of the two Communist parties:

> The CP(B)U itself did not remain uninfluenced by the UCP. To a great extent under the influence of the UCP the Bolsheviks evolved from "the RCP in Ukraine" (the proposal of the Kviring group at the Taganrog conference) into a genuine Communist party of Ukraine. The federalist trend in the CPU was a wedge that had been driven in by the hands of the Borotbists inside the CPU .... The two parties, the CPU and the UCP ... after violent discussions, met each other half way, the one rectifying its Communist line, the other adapting itself to the peculiarities and specific conditions of the social, economic, national, and cultural life in Ukraine.[105]

It may be assumed that the Borotbists, who as long as they existed never abandoned the "nationalist" platform, joined the CP(B)U with the intention of influencing the CP(B)U from within and even nursed the idea of taking over its leadership. In the words of a former leading member of the Borotbists, Mykhailo Poloz, a former people's commissar for finance of the Ukrainian SSR, the Borotbists joined the CP(B)U under the slogan: "We will join, spread among, and flood over" the Bolsheviks.[106] After the executive committee of the Comintern rejected the Borotbists' application for recognition as the only Communist party in Ukraine, the main mass of the Borotbists and their CC decided to enter the CP(B)U, convinced that from within they might achieve what was impossible to do from without, to take power in Ukraine and thereby tear Ukraine out of the hands of the Bolsheviks.[107] These statements, which were probably fabricated by Pavel Postyshev, must be treated with caution, though they represent correctly the essence of the Borotbists' tactics. There is no doubt that the Borotbists were a Communist party, though of a special kind.[108]

RCP policy towards the Borotbists and other Soviet parties was determined primarily by ideological considerations of the unity of the Communist party and the hegemony of the Bolsheviks in the proletarian revolution. Proceeding from this fundamental principle, the Russian Communists did not wish to recognize the existence of separate national Communist parties in the borderlands of Russia. Therefore the CP(B)U was reduced to the status of an ordinary regional organization. By recognizing the UCP (Borotbists), the party would have had to revise its attitude towards party unity, since the Borotbists demanded not a regional status, but that of a separate, independent Ukrainian party. The Bolsheviks considered it useful to utilize these unorthodox adepts of Communism. However, the CC RCP was more unyielding to the Borotbists than was the CP(B)U, which had to confront the Borotbists in practical life and struggle for power against them.

After the fall of the second Soviet regime in Ukraine, the CP(B)U attempted to unite with the Borotbists, but the CC RCP was unwilling to agree to this. Criticizing the attitude of the RCP in this respect, Bubnov at the ninth congress of the RCP said that during the second Soviet regime in Ukraine (March to July 1919), there existed within the Communist Party (Bolsheviks) of Ukraine a strong trend in favour of amalgamation with the Borotbists, while at the third congress (March 1919) the party spoke against the admission of the Borotbists into the central Soviet institutions of Ukraine. The CC RCP then instructed the CC CP(B)U to include the Borotbists in the Ukrainian Council of People's Commissars; this instruction was, of course, carried out. By this action, the CC RCP strengthened the Borotbists and contributed to the marked increase of their influence among the urban proletariat after the defeat of Denikin.[109]

What instruction was issued by the CC RCP to the CP(B)U concerning the Borotbists was long unknown. The only thing available is Bubnov's declaration after the event. However, there exists a draft resolution by Trotsky, dated May 1919, outlined probably by Lenin, which refers to the liquidation of the Borotbists. The document pointed out that experience had shown that the Borotbists had fallen into the counter-revolutionary camp, mainly because of their struggle for the creation of an independent Ukrainian army; therefore they should be liquidated.[110] An appendix to this resolution recommended:

> To consider the Borotbists a party which contravenes the basic principles of Communism by its propaganda in favour of a division of military forces and by its support of banditism .... Their struggle against the slogan of a close union [of Ukraine] with the RSFSR likewise contradicts the interests of the proletariat. The whole policy must be systematically and unwaveringly directed towards the liquidation of the Borotbists in the near future. Hence not a single error of the Borotbists must be allowed to pass without immediate and severe punishment. In particular, data must be collected concerning the non-proletarian and most unreliable character of the majority of the members of their party. The time for liquidation must be fixed soon; this will be settled by the politburo and communicated to the Ukrainian revolutionary committee.

Trotsky and Rakovsky were assigned "to edit this resolution more precisely by not later than tomorrow and to transmit it by telegraph, also tomorrow, to the Ukrainian revolutionary committee."[111]

The interesting point in this document is that at the same time as the Borotbists were admitted to the Council of People's Commissars, and while the Bolsheviks of Ukraine were moving towards an amalgamation with the

Borotbists, the RCP was drafting plans and tactics for the complete annihilation of the Borotbists. In this document, the "nationalism" of the Borotbists is emphasized again, but for tactical reasons it is recommended that silence be maintained on this point, stressing instead the factors proving the "non-proletarian" character of the Borotbists. As Bertram Wolfe rightly remarks, the Bolsheviks were compelled by military considerations not only to continue their cooperation with the Borotbists in the Ukrainian government, but also to seek the aid of Makhno.[112] Wolfe concludes from this wavering policy that "first military decisions, then military-economic decisions, and finally pure economic and political decisions taken for their own sakes, gradually determined the future nationalities structure of the Soviet Union."[113]

The tactic of the RCP towards the Borotbists was regarded by Lenin as satisfactory. He did not agree with Bubnov, who accused the party of strengthening the Borotbists:

> This is a most complex and tremendous question, and I think in this most important problem, where intricate manoeuvring was needed, we came out the victors. In the central committee when we [i.e., Lenin] spoke of maximum concessions to the Borotbists, we were laughed at and told that we were not straight in our dealings with them. But one can attack one's adversary directly [only] when there is a straight line with him. Once the enemy decides to zigzag, we must pursue and catch him at every turn. We promised the Borotbists a maximum of concessions, but on condition that they pursue a Communist policy. In this way we proved that we are not guilty of the slightest intolerance. That our concessions were right was proved by the fact that all the better elements of the Borotbists have now joined our party. We have re-registered that party; instead of having a Borotbist uprising, which would have been inevitable, we have brought into our party, under our control and with our recognition, owing to the correct policy of the central committee superbly executed by comrade Rakovsky, all the best of the Borotbists, while the rest have vanished from the political scene. This victory is worth several good battles. To say, therefore, that the central committee was guilty of strengthening the Borotbists is not to understand the political line in the national problem.[114]

Lenin was implacable towards the Borotbists even before this. In his telegram to Rakovsky at the end of April 1919 he wrote: "The resolution of the Katerynoslavian SRs shows that they are scoundrels, defenders of kulaks. They must be attacked in the newspapers for defending the kulaks and for their slogan, 'resistance to centralization'; they must be required to unmask the kulaks and to struggle against the free sale of grain by the peasant. In the government they must be bound by the most precise directives, placed under the strictest supervision, and in the case of their slightest deviation from the line of the government in the questions of food, cooperatives, finance, and in the question of the closest *rapprochement* with Russia, their ignominious expulsion must be prepared."[115] It is unknown why Lenin had to make use of demagogy even in his correspondence with his collaborators. Both he and Rakovsky must have known that the Borotbists did not support the kulaks but leaned mainly on the rural proletariat, poorer peasantry, and to some extent the middle peasantry. Lenin himself advocated, at the eighth and ninth congresses of the party, an alliance with the middle peasantry. If there was a difference, then, between the attitudes of the Borotbists and the Bolsheviks towards the peasantry, it was that the Borotbists attempted to attract the peasantry to active soviet work, while the Bolsheviks put all the power into the hands of the proletariat, i.e., the Communist party. Moreover, the Borotbists were in favour of elected soviets, while the Bolsheviks admitted, where necessary, the appointment of the members of the soviets by the party. But the greatest sin of the Borotbists, with which neither Lenin nor the RCP wished to compromise at all, was their defence of an independent Ukraine.

In summing up, it may be said that the Ukrainian left socialist parties played a very important role both in the introduction and in the overthrow of Soviet power in Ukraine in its second period. The relationship between these pro-Soviet parties and the Bolsheviks has a special significance, for it illustrates the policy of the Bolsheviks towards the peasantry as well as their aim to split the Ukrainian socialist parties. On the other hand, this question is closely connected with the question of the hegemony of the proletariat over the peasantry and with the question of the hegemony of the Communist party in the revolution.

The RCP(B) adhered to the principle of a united Communist party for the whole of Russia, including the national Soviet republics, such as Ukraine. All the more merciless was the party's struggle against parties which stood on the Soviet platform, but which rejected the very principle of Communism: the dictatorship of the proletariat and its hegemony over the peasantry. That the RCP in some cases tolerated the existence of the Ukrainian social democrats (independentists) and the Ukrainian SRs (Borotbists) was the result of political circumstances. In the Russian republic the left SRs participated in Lenin's government only at the beginning of the revolution; by 1919 the Soviet government of Russia was purely Communist. In Ukraine the attitude towards the left "Soviet" socialist parties differed in some respects. This was partly because in Ukraine the Communist party for a long time did not have a separate centre but acted as a branch of the Russian party. Secondly, the Bolsheviks were weaker in Ukraine than in Russia. If it had not been for the military intervention of Soviet Russia, the role of the Ukrainian Bolsheviks would have been reduced to the role of the Bolsheviks in Russia during the Provisional Government.

The Ukrainian SRs were the most popular party in the Ukrainian countryside at the beginning of the revolution, particularly during the struggle of the Central Rada for the independence of Ukraine. This is borne out by the results of the elections to the all-Russian and the Ukrainian constituent assemblies at the end of 1917 and the beginning of 1918. From that time onwards, a strong trend to the left is noticeable among the Ukrainian SRs and Ukrainian social democrats, which was actually symptomatic of trends in the ranks of all socialist parties at that time, not only in Ukraine but throughout Europe. In spite of what has been said above concerning the amalgamation of the Ukrainian Communist parties—the Borotbists and the Ukapists—with the CP(B)U, numerically they were not of great importance for the party. According to data collected by Ravich-Cherkassky, in 1922 the CP(B)U had 4,746 members, who came from the parties listed in Table 34.

Table 34. Party Origin of CP(B)U Members, 1922

RSDWP	1,932
SRs, right and unclassified	771
Bund	715
SRs, left	462
Other Jewish parties	308
Borotbists	118
Anarchists	104
Borbists	45
Ukapists	34
Other parties	257
Total	4,746

SOURCE: M. Ravich-Cherkassky, *Istoriia Kommunisticheskoi partii (b-kov) Ukrainy* (Kharkiv, 1923), p. 241.

As may be seen, most of those who went over to the CP(B)U came from the Russian parties, the social democrats and the socialist revolutionaries, as well as from the Jewish parties, chiefly from the Bund. The Ukrainian parties supplied a very insignificant number. This may be explained not only by the Russian elements' gravitation towards the Bolsheviks, but also by the fact that the Communist party of Ukraine, being under the leadership of Russian and Jewish elements, did not admit to its ranks the so-called Ukrainian nationalists from the UCP and the UCP (Borotbists). Ravich-Cherkassky explains this small percentage of Ukrainian elements by the "lack of precision in the data supplied by the members of the party themselves."[116] It is quite possible that it was rather inopportune for a member of the party to call himself a former Borotbist or Ukapist. However, as has been pointed out, the main reason for Lenin's "tolerance" towards the Borotbists was that through them the Bolsheviks hoped to bring about a union between the proletariat and the poor peasantry.

Without doubt, thanks to the activity of the UCP independentists and Borotbists, Bolshevik policy in the twenties was marked by concessions to Ukrainian nationalism, at least in the cultural field. Without the activity of the UCP and the UCP (Borotbists) it is doubtful whether the Bolsheviks would have recognized even the formal existence of the Ukrainian Soviet republic. However, the formation of these parties hampered Ukrainian anti-Bolshevik forces in their struggle for an independent Ukraine, because they introduced an element of disintegration and doubt into the Ukrainian national movement, thus weakening its resistance.

Soviet Power and the Ukrainian Peasantry

The Disintegration of the Ukrainian Peasantry

On the eve of the revolution, Ukraine was a predominantly agrarian country with a typical individualist economy based on private ownership, in which, at least in the south, "agrarian capitalism of the peasant farmer type predominated."[117] There was a great difference between Ukraine and Great Russia in this respect.[118] Southern Ukraine, which comprised almost a third of Ukrainian territory, was a region in which agricultural capitalism of the American farming type predominated. At the time of the reform of 1861, serfdom had either not had time to become rooted there or was completely absent. Therefore, after the abolition of serfdom, the peasant of the southern provinces of Ukraine suffered relatively little from the shortage of land, from oppression by the landowners, from class attitudes, or from the other survivals of serfdom that oppressed the peasantry in agricultural central Russia. The most decisive factor in the economy of Left-Bank Ukraine was that "the predominant mass of the peasantry consisted of the Cossacks and other categories of state peasants, who were better provided with land after the reform than former landowners' peasants .... Their environment was constantly giving rise to farmers who pursued their farming on their own and on leased land, combining it with extensive manufacturing and trade activities."[119] The Right Bank of Ukraine, on the other hand, presented a completely different picture. Here the capitalist landownership of the nobility dominated, and the mass of the peasantry was subjected to a gradual expropriation and "long vegetation as land labourers, hired hands, and wage workers of various kinds."[120] The system of land ownership in Ukraine on the eve of the revolution did not differ from that in such other Central European countries as Hungary or Poland, where, on the one hand, there were great "magnates" with thousands of hectares of land, and on the other, peasants with few or no landed possessions. According to the 1905 census, landownership in Ukraine fell into the categories shown in Table 35.

Table 35. Categories of Land Ownership in Ukraine, 1905

	Thousands of desiatinas	Per cent	European Russia (%)
Privately owned land	20,625	46.7	25.8
Freed land[a]	20,127	46.6	35.1
Land owned by the state, church, institutions	3,375	7.7	39.1

SOURCE: M. A. Rubach, "Agrarnaia revoliutsiia na Ukraine v 1917 g.," *Letopis revoliutsii,* 1927, No. 5-6, p. 7.

[a]"Freed land" *(nadelnye zemli)* meant the system of peasant land ownership based on *"nadely."* After 1861 the peasants received from the landowners "allotted arable land *(zemelnye polevye nadely)* for permanent use" which had to be paid for by the peasants within a certain time (mostly within forty-nine years).

Apart from the 20,127,000 desiatinas of freed land, the peasantry also purchased an additional 5,674,000 desiatinas from the landowners between 1861 and 1905. After 1905 the landowners sold their land even more frequently, and by 1917 the peasantry had purchased another 2,300,000 desiatinas. Thus, peasant ownership of land on the eve of the February revolution amounted to approximately 28 million desiatinas, or 64 per cent of Ukraine's entire area.[121] The statistics on large estates in 1905 are shown in Table 36.

As Rubach points out, after 1905 the amount of land owned by landowners who had more than 1,000 desiatinas decreased by the 1.5

Table 36. Size of Land Holdings in Ukraine, 1905

Size of land holdings	Number of holdings	Land in thousands of desiatinas
Up to 100 desiatinas	192,661	2,160.3
From 100 to 1,000	17,793	5,959.6
Over 1,000	3,592	9,591.2

SOURCE: M. A. Rubach, "Agrarnaia revoliutsiia na Ukraine v 1917 g.," *Letopis revoliutsii,* 1927, No. 5-6, p. 8.

million they sold to the peasants. From this we can conclude that, on the eve of the revolution, 3,500 landowners owned some 8 million desiatinas of land, while 1.8 million farmsteads, possessing from one to seven desiatinas per farmstead, owned 7.5 million desiatinas of land.[122]

The above-mentioned 28 million desiatinas of freed land belonging to peasants were distributed among farms of various categories as shown in Table 37.

Table 37. Size of Peasant Holdings in Ukraine, 1917

Type of farm	Number of farms	Amount of land in desiatinas
Without land to 1 desiatina	80,630	39,400
From 1 to 2 desiatinas	132,942	215,600
" 2 to 5 "	1,083,051	3,817,900
" 5 to 7 "	579,503	3,457,900
" 7 to 10 "	602,887	5,017,000
" 10 to 15 "	363,454	4,380,000
Over 15	133,000	3,045,700

SOURCE: M. A. Rubach, "Agrarnaia revoliutsiia na Ukraine v 1917 g.," *Letopis revoliutsii,* 1927, No. 5-6, p. 10.

The first three groups of farms were regarded as small holdings, while the last type belonged to the well-to-do peasants, the so-called kulaks.[123] However, in the first period of the revolution, antagonism arose not between these two categories, but between these seven groups of peasants, on the one hand, and the so-called landowners, who owned over 100 desiatinas each, on the other. The first blows from the land-starved peasantry fell upon the large latifundias, which sometimes comprised 10–15,000 desiatinas, or even over 100,000 (for instance, the Falz-Fein family of German colonists owned over 200,000 desiatinas, Vassal had over 100,000, Count Mordvinov had 80,000).[124] Of course, this antagonism had nothing in common with the class antagonism upon which Marxism built its revolution. At most, this antagonism produced peasant unrest and a demand for agrarian reforms, which the Bolsheviks tried to utilize for their own purpose.

The Land Policy of the RCP(B) in Ukraine

According to the classical principle of Marxism, the peasantry is a reactionary stratum of society unsuitable for Communist revolution. There is a great difference between the political aims of the proletariat and the peasantry. While the proletariat, in the Marxist formula, strives towards the proletarian dictatorship with all its consequences, such as the nationalization of the means of production and the collectivization of agriculture, the peasantry strives to secure the possession of land. The middle and poor peasantry of Eastern Europe, and particularly of Russia, strove for the abolition of the feudal system, the expropriation of large landed properties, and the distribution of land among the peasants. These aims made the peasantry of Russia a revolutionary factor and impelled them to form a common front with the proletariat. Lenin quickly understood that without the aid of the peasant masses the revolution would fail, and therefore he formulated the land policy so as to gain the sympathy of the majority of the peasantry. In 1917 Lenin proposed—and this was distinct from the proposals of other parties—the immediate seizure of landowners' land by the peasants.

By the seizure of land the Bolsheviks understood "the nationalization of all land and the transfer of the ownership right to all land into the hands of the state," which in turn could transfer the right "of the disposal of land into the hands of local democratic institutions."[125] The Bolsheviks opposed the private ownership of land. In his speech at the first all-Russian congress of peasants' deputies, Lenin explained that the gratuitous transfer of the landowners' land into the hands of the local peasants did not mean the "seizure of these lands as property." The land became the property of the people in the sense that "everyone who takes land is taking it on lease from the whole people" and thus "takes land on lease from the state."[126] The peasantry was more impressed by the Bolsheviks' radical slogan, "An immediate seizure of landowners' land," than by their programme for the future of those lands. It must also be added that at that time the peasant party, the SRs, also preached the nationalization rather than the private appropriation of land. These differences of aim were bound to lead to a point at which the interests of the proletariat and the peasantry diverged. The Bolshevik revolution helped the peasantry seize the land of the landowners and the state, and in return the peasantry helped the proletariat overthrow the existing regime. Thus the peasantry of Russia attained, through the October revolution, its own class aim, the conquest of land. From that moment onwards, the peasantry abandoned its former ally, the proletariat, and, as a class organization, the Communist party. The peasants then undertook to secure the land and to cultivate it for themselves. On the basis of the distribution or, in contemporary terminology, the "equalizing division" (*uravnitelnyi delezh*) of land, a struggle began within the village itself between the wealthier peasants and the poorer and landless ones. However, the peasantry in its entirety stood in a common front against Soviet power, which waged a struggle with the landowners but at the same time expropriated grain from the peasants and prohibited free trade in grain. Furthermore, the policy of the Communist party was directed in principle towards the collectivization of agriculture or the nationalization of land, the ideal of which was the commune.

The main reason, however, for peasant antagonism towards Soviet power was the formation of *kombedy* (committees of the poor peasantry) in the villages. During the Civil War the *kombedy* functioned as a gendarmerie over the peasantry, though a rather weak one. As a speaker remarked at the eighth congress of the RCP in March 1919, the class differentiation of the countryside began with the creation of the *kombedy*.[127] Popov later pointed out that the policy of commandeering the peasantry and the creation of the *kombedy* "created in the village an extremely alarming and serious situation for our party."[128] The party's policy of banking upon the peasant, which Lenin forced through at the eighth congress of the RCP, was a constrained concession to the peasantry. However, even then the party did not retreat from its fundamental attitude on the land question.

What brought Lenin to revise the party's policy towards the middle peasantry? Why did the peasantry feel hostile towards Soviet rule? The causes of the change in peasant feeling were well analysed by Popov. He pointed out that from the summer of 1918 "an enormous number of risings" against Soviet rule took place. These were directed by the kulaks, but *the wide strata of the middle and even poor peasantry took part in them.* Popov explained these "waverings of the peasantry" by several factors. The Soviet regime, cut off from the great grain-supplying territories, was compelled to obtain grain from a very limited territory by means of coercion, by the creation of communes, Soviet state farms, and *kombedy*, without sufficiently taking into consideration the interests of the middle peasantry. The *kombedy* at the beginning had been "*an instrument in the hands of Soviet power for the expropriation of the surplus produce from the kulaks*; after completing this, their main task, they began to show tendencies hostile to *the middle peasantry*, thus furthering the alliance of the middle peasantry with the kulaks against Soviet power." The establishment of communes provoked the peasantry's hatred towards a regime that wished to force peasants into the commune.[129] Popov wrote that "*a considerable section of the Communists cherished a utopia about the speed and ease of the transformation of a small peasant economy into the Communist economy*. It was sufficient for the purpose to set up as many Soviet state farms and communes as possible, even by driving peasant small holdings into these communes, and so settling the business."[130] The Bolsheviks did not have to wait long for the result of such a policy: the armed struggle of the peasantry with the Bolsheviks.

In the borderlands the land question also had a national colouring. The masses of the peasantry there were often a reservoir of nationalism and therefore were in the fore of anti-Russian feeling. So it was in Finland, Poland, and the Baltic states; so it was, too, in Ukraine. The Russian Bolsheviks' purely agricultural measures in the borderlands were interpreted as Russification. In Ukraine the Bolshevik food policy gave rise to anti-Russian feeling among the peasantry, who bitterly opposed the appropriation of Ukrainian grain for Russia.

In Ukraine the peasantry were either partially pro-Soviet or neutral during the struggle of the Central Rada with the Bolsheviks, chiefly because the Bolsheviks had promised an immediate seizure of the landowners' land. But immediately after the establishment of the first Soviet regime in Ukraine the whole Soviet machinery was given the task of confiscating grain and transporting it to Russia, while the landowners' estates were organized into communes and Soviet state farms. The collectivization of agriculture began even more radically during the second Soviet regime, whose aims were to produce Soviet state farms and communes and to effect the communal cultivation of land. "Almost all of the landowners' land," wrote Popov, "was allotted for Soviet state farms and communes ... while the rest of the land was stolen by the kulaks."[131] This policy was determined by the third congress of the CP(B)U in March 1919:

> The chief task of the land policy is the transition from individual farming to communal. Soviet state farms, communes, the communal cultivation of land, and other means of communal agriculture are the best ways of achieving socialism in agriculture; hence individual agriculture must be regarded as

> temporary and as nearing the end of its life. The confiscated lands must therefore be used first for communal, social agriculture, and only then for the needs of individual users of land.[132]

Attempts to introduce collective agriculture into Ukraine met a common front of opposition in the countryside. Even the poorer peasantry would hear nothing of communes. In Ukraine, where individual farmstead agriculture was more widespread than in Russia, farmers were absolutely opposed to joining communes and Soviet state farms.[133] The social structure of the Ukrainian countryside was the chief obstacle to the sovietization of Ukraine. Here the wealthy peasantry was hegemonous, a result of the absence for several years of a firm and constant central state authority. The central governments, which changed kaleidoscopically after the February revolution, penetrated very little into the countryside. Central state power rarely extended beyond the walls of the large cities which, during the Civil War, were not equal partners of the countryside, since they did not have the kind of goods for which the countryside was willing to trade its produce. The countryside adopted a more and more isolationist attitude, cutting itself off from and defending itself against the cities, which, deprived of the means to buy the produce of the countryside, waged a war for grain. In addition, the national composition of the large cities of Ukraine played an important role; they were basically Russian and hostile to everything Ukrainian, including the Ukrainian countryside. The economic antagonism between the cities and the countryside was, then, at the same time a national antagonism.[134]

The many individual farmers—kulaks, according to Bolshevik terminology—gained almost total power in the countryside during the Civil War, both economically and politically. The Bolsheviks repeatedly stressed this fact and attempted to undermine the kulak's position. In the struggle between the Bolsheviks and the Directory and between the Bolsheviks and Denikin, the peasantry, in 1919–20, began to play the role of a significant third force. The fate of this or that power in Ukraine depended on the attitude of the peasantry, and the peasantry took whichever side seemed most likely to satisfy its economic and national interests. Thus during the introduction of the first Soviet regime the peasantry turned away from the Rada because the latter was unable to satisfy its economic interests, i.e., it did not permit an immediate and spontaneous seizure of the large estates. The same applies even more to the regime of the Hetmanate. The peasants tolerated the Soviet regime as long as it did not attack them. But as soon as the Bolsheviks began to confiscate grain, introduce communes, and, moreover, suppress Ukrainian national demands as the tsarist regime did, the peasantry turned away from the Bolsheviks.[135]

During the second Soviet regime the peasantry went even further towards independence and a struggle with Soviet power. The third congress of the CP(B)U, aware of the danger to Soviet power posed by the kulaks, decided to liquidate this stratum of the peasantry. But, as Ravich-Cherkassky pointed out later, "there were as many of these centres [of kulaks] as there were large kulak villages, and Soviet power was unable to defeat the Ukrainian kulak and to free Ukraine from the kulak centres."[136] The Soviets attempted to win over the middle peasantry, but the methods applied in the struggle against the kulaks provoked the hostility of the middle peasant as well. Particularly unpopular was the introduction of the *komnezamy* (Ukrainian equivalent of *kombedy*) in Ukraine; the party had successfully introduced them in Russia but had no success with them in Ukraine.[137]

The third Soviet regime broke temporarily with the land policy of the preceding year, with the introduction of communes and the spreading of *komnezamy*. The new policy was based on the principle of first satisfying the needs of the small and middle peasants. In accordance with the new land law, which was published by the all-Ukrainian revolutionary committee on 5 February 1920, all land formerly belonging to landowners, the state, and monasteries, and all freed land was handed over without charge for the use primarily of the landless peasantry and of the peasantry with small holdings. "All former non-working owners (landowners) and non-working leaseholders are subject to an immediate eviction from their farms." The distribution of land and implements was to be carried out within one month. Even part of the land that had been transferred in the previous year to the Soviet state farms was, in accordance with the new law, handed over to the peasants.[138] As a result of this law, the peasants received 15.5 million desiatinas of land, including 1.5 million desiatinas from Soviet state farms.[139] In another order concerning the land even greater stress was laid on the protection of the interests of the middle peasants: "The Soviet authorities will not adhere strictly to an equal allotment of land; certain deviation will be admitted in order not to injure the interests of the middle strata."[140] This policy aimed at undermining the hegemony of the wealthy peasantry; it was a policy of "divide and conquer" to facilitate the disintegration of the countryside as an anti-Soviet bloc. The idea was to isolate the wealthy peasants and gain the sympathies of the middle peasantry and of small farmers, who in the preceding years had opposed the Soviet authorities.

As a result of the new land policy, the number of Soviet state farms, compared with the preceding period, fell considerably. This is borne out by Table 38.

Table 38. Sovkhozes in Ukrainian Provinces, 1919-20

Provinces	1919 Number of Sovkhozes	1919 Desiatinas of land	1920 Number of Sovkhozes	1920 Desiatinas of land
Aleksandrovsk[a]	—	—	88	—
Chernihiv	95	32,750	34	8,019
Donets[a]	19	9,000	90	190,000
Katerynoslav	140	297,000	33	14,203
Kharkiv	196	110,000	99	24,589
Kiev	40	11,954	21	3,406
Kremenchuk[a]	—	—	25	6,625
Mykolaiv	250	350,000	76	66,875
Odessa[a]	—	—	73	16,586
Podillia	32	108,000	2	557
Poltava	219	85,896	79	7,572
Volhynia	194	100,000	20	2,327
Total	1,185	1,104,600	640	340,759

SOURCE: M. Kubanin, *Makhnovshchina. Krestianskoe dvizhenie v stepnoi Ukraine v gody grazhdanskoi voiny* (Leningrad, n.d.), p. 132.

a These provinces were first created in 1920; therefore there are no data for 1919. Their territory was often changed, and therefore they are not valid for comparison.

The number of Soviet state farms was reduced by one-half, and the amount of land owned by these farms decreased by one quarter. Only some farms were preserved to serve as model Soviet state farms and experimental stations.

The alpha and omega of party policy on the peasant question was disarming the Ukrainian kulaks, the wealthy peasants who even then showed no special liking for Soviet power. In his report on the attitude of the countryside to Soviet power, Rakovsky pointed out that the influence of the kulak elements in Ukraine was, even before the revolution, stronger than in any other part of the former Russian empire. "Having seized a part of the liquidated estates and estates which had belonged to the state, ... having grown insolent because of the prevailing lawlessness, possessing weapons, subsidizing the otamans, lording it over the ignorant, miserable, and hungry peasants whom he attracted to himself with the prospects of a share-out and of looting, and whom he incited against the cities, the kulak became the actual power on the territory of Ukraine." Rakovsky asserted that "the introduction of a genuine government of workers and peasants in the countryside and the liquidation of landowners' ownership are possible only when the dictatorship of the kulak is abolished."[141]

A general characterization of the peasantry's attitude to the land relationships in Ukraine was given in 1920 by the people's commissar for agriculture, Manuilsky, in his report at the fifth congress of soviets: "The mass of the peasantry attempted, by destroying former 'nests' of landowners, to abolish first the most glaring social inequality. The peasants were little concerned that, in sweeping away the capitalist shell of the landowner system, they were at the same time destroying the large agricultural industry which had every technical advantage over the small peasant economy. The laws of economics and the interests of the national economy as a whole retreated into the background before the elemental drive of the peasantry to the land. Here lay the root of the peasantry's lack of understanding of our policy in the preceding year (1919) with regard to the preservation of large farms in the form of Soviet state farms. In the eyes of the peasant masses, the Soviet state farm was a new form of 'serfdom,' in which the old owner was merely replaced by the new one in the person of the state. Therefore the land revolution of this year has not spared the Soviet state farms and has pursued in respect of them the same 'equalizing' policy of the peasants. But it has not created complete economic equality within the peasant mass itself."[142]

As we have seen, the second period of Soviet power did not satisfy the peasantry. On the contrary, holding back a considerable part of the landowners' implements and land, as well as the whole crop for 1919, it antagonized the peasantry, which continued to seize the landowners' land as before, thus actively opposing Soviet power and its state farms.

The CP(B)U adopted a resolution at its fourth conference, according to which the following measures were necessary to liquidate the "dictatorship of the kulaks": 1) the possession of sufficient armed force; 2) the systematic disarming of the kulaks; 3) the creation of satisfactory fighting machinery, both military and civil; 4) the creation of strong and actively functioning party, trade, and professional organizations. Without these measures, "any attempts by the Soviet authorities at the differentiation of the countryside or at the liberation of the poorer and middle peasantry from the dictatorship of the kulak by means of the land law and the law of grain *razverstka* are purely utopian."[143]

The party's main instrument against the Ukrainian countryside as a whole was the policy of fomenting class struggle among the peasantry, inciting the poor and middle peasants against the wealthier strata of the peasantry. A specialist on the land question, Iakovlev, proposed this very method in April 1920. In the first place, it was planned to alter the balance of power so that authority in the countryside would pass out of the hands of the kulaks into those of the poorer peasantry.[144] The role of the executors of the land and food policy of the party in the countryside was to be once again played by the *komnezamy*, the poor peasant committees. A decree of 19 May 1920 defined the tasks of these committees:

1) implementing the law for the allotment of land and implements to landless peasants and those with small holdings;

2) implementing the law dealing with the grain *razverstka*;

3) aiding the organs of Soviet power in their struggle with banditism and the sway of the kulaks, and also in the liquidation of illiteracy.[145]

The people's commissariat for internal affairs published instructions regarding the organization of these committees. The instructions admitted into the committees persons with no land as well as those who had not more than three desiatinas and were not subject to *razverstka*. The following were not to be admitted to the committees: persons using hired labour, those living on unearned income, speculators, traders, priests, makers of home-brewed brandy, persons who had served in a police force under the tsarist regime, under Skoropadsky, Petliura, or Denikin, and persons convicted of crimes against Soviet power.[146] These instructions gave the committees much wider and more varied tasks than the law of 19 May 1920. The committees now had to: 1) render all possible aid to the organs of Soviet power in the implementation of all laws and decisions, bearing in mind the interests of the poorer and middle peasantry; 2) preserve revolutionary order in the village and district; 3) register all kulaks and persons hostile to Soviet power and keep them under surveillance; 4) take part in meetings (of the district executive committees, in an advisory capacity); 5) organize the landless and small-holding peasants in the defence of the land law and in aid of a just and immediate distribution of land and implements among such peasants; 6) render aid to the food organs for a successful implementation of the grain *razverstka*, combat speculation, pay attention to supplying the poorer and middle peasant with the articles of prime necessity, supervise the correct distribution of 10–25 per cent of the collected quantity of grain; 7) aid in the implementation of all laws and orders of the central authorities concerning assistance to the families of Red Army men; 8) organize Sunday labour and food weeks [*sic*], attracting by their example the working peasantry; 9) conduct cultural and educational work; 10) register all the members with detailed data, and also register the participants in the Sunday work and other social measures.[147]

In accordance with this instruction, the committees were turned into a tool for the sovietization of the Ukrainian countryside, being given such vague terms of reference that they became at the same time the executive organs of the central authorities as well as the controllers of the local authorities and police organs. Whether "the working peasantry of Ukraine received the law ... for the organization of the committees of poor peasants with great enthusiasm"[148] is a question open to discussion. The report of the CP(B)U about the activity of the committees stated that the attitude of the peasants to the poor peasant committees in 393 districts was "sympathetic," in 257 "indifferent," and in 121 "hostile."[149]

The poor peasant committees began their activity against the kulaks by confiscating their land and grain. According to the data from the report of the CC CP(B)U, 348,622 desiatinas of land had been taken away from the kulaks, while the landowners lost only 24,650 desiatinas.[150] Gradually the committees, guided by party directives, began to take measures to ensure the liquidation of the kulaks as such. The line concerning the poor peasant committees was determined in principle by Lenin and the CC RCP. Thus, in his telegram "to the Soviet government of Ukraine and H. Q. of the southern front" of 16 October 1920, Lenin wrote: "In answer to your telegram concerning poor peasants I give my opinion. If they are really revolutionary, the following ought to be considered as a programme: 1) collective cultivation; 2) hire stations; 3) to take away money from the kulaks in excess of the working norm; 4) the surplus of grain to be collected in full, rewarding the poor peasants with grain; 5) the agricultural implements of the kulaks to be taken on hire; 6) all these measures to be implemented only on condition that collective cultivation is successful and under real control. The communes are to be placed last, for most dangerous of all are artificial pseudo-communes and the separation of individuals from the mass. [There should be] extreme caution towards innovations and triple checking of the actual accomplishment of the undertaking."[151] Soon after the victory over Piłsudski, Petliura, and Vrangel, and after the establishment of Soviet power, the tendency towards the creation of collective farms was revived. One resolution of the *komnezamy* presented a demand for collective farming: "The chief task of the whole land policy of Soviet power is the creation of conditions for a painless transition to the socialization of labour."[152] Beginning in 1920, the number of collective farms in Ukraine grew every year: in 1920 there were 300; in 1921—1,428; in 1922—3,778; in 1923—4,620; and in 1924—5,300.[153]

An important trump card in the Bolsheviks' hand was their new policy of the food *razverstka* which was likewise directed chiefly against the kulak and aimed at whipping up antagonism between the poor and rich peasantry. Guided by the instructions of the CC RCP(B), Rakovsky's government issued an order on 26 February 1920 dealing with the grain *razverstka*, to which all farms with more than three desiatinas of land were subject to the amount of one quarter of the total harvest.[154] Apart from the actual confiscation of grain for hungry cities and for Russia, it was intended to hand over a part of the collected grain to the poor peasants, thereby to enlist their support in the food *razverstka* and to incite them against the kulak.[155] On the other hand, the party intended to use the food *razverstka* to make the working class interested in the countryside, i.e., to incite the working class against the kulaks by suggesting to the former that the kulaks were the cause of its sufferings and hunger. By such means the party hoped to do away with the anomaly of the Ukrainian revolution, which was the hostility between the urban proletariat and the peasantry. It felt that the basic misfortune of the proletarian revolution in Ukraine was that the working class of the industrial regions on the Left Bank, "owing to a whole series of economic, political, and national causes, did not feel that it was organically connected with rural Ukraine." To make the uninterested worker develop an interest in this matter, the party proposed to "involve the worker in the civil war in the countryside on the question of food supplies, the most vital and sore one for him. Every worker must know that bread will not get to the worker by itself, that it must be conquered from the kulak ... and that this can be done only if the worker finds ways to achieve a permanent alliance of the proletarian of the city and the proletarian of the village."[156]

The food *razverstka* in Ukraine was designed to yield 160 million poods, of which about 20 million poods were to be given to the poor peasants. However, the regime was unable to collect even the latter quantity of grain. In fact only 9,721,000 poods were collected, and the collected produce often reached the wrong destination. On the whole, the food situation was very unfortunate. As Kubanin notes, "even these successes on the food front were gained at no small cost. During nine months of 1920 about one thousand food workers were killed by peasants, not to mention isolated skirmishes of Red Army detachments with partisan detachments. The party had to use all its strength and dispatch considerable cadres of its forces into the countryside ... but the party alone, with its own strength, leaning upon the urban proletariat, would not have been able to carry out the tremendous task of the extraction of grain surplus in the countryside. This work could have been carried out only in an alliance with the poor peasants." Kubanin acknowledges that the food *razverstka* failed in 1919 because the authorities had no support from the poorer peasants.[157] Comparing the attitude of the poor peasantry to Soviet power in 1919 and in 1920, Rakovsky has supplied interesting data concerning the participation of the poor peasantry in the uprising against Soviet power. He admitted that in 1921 about 10 per cent of the poor peasantry participated in anti-Soviet risings. Two years earlier, three quarters participated.[158]

It would be a mistake, however, to think that the Bolsheviks succeeded at one stroke in getting rid of the peasant antagonism or in achieving the political isolation of the wealthy peasants. As far as grain was concerned, the Bolsheviks suffered a complete defeat in Ukraine. "We are taking grain from Siberia," said Lenin in October 1920, "we are taking grain from the Kuban, but it was possible to take hardly anything from *razverstka*."[159] The committees of poor peasants on which the Bolsheviks were banking were powerless against the solid mass of middle and wealthy peasants. According to Kubanin: "The poor peasants of Ukraine, in spite of being well organized and in spite of the fierce class struggle that flared up in the countryside in 1920 and 1921, were unable to master the kulaks by themselves. Only after the kulak was routed by the Red Army, disarmed, and destroyed to the last shred, while the poor peasant was supplied at the cost of a part of the food *razverstka* which was taken from persons possessing over three desiatinas, only then was the kulak subdued."[160]

The attitude of the peasantry to the Soviet regime in Ukraine very much influenced the character of the *power and the functions of the local soviets*. The fourth conference of the CP(B)U adopted a resolution to the effect that, although the party stood in principle on the platform of the soviets as the basic cells of the Soviet form of power in the provinces, it could change the composition of the soviets if their political trend did not conform to the interests of the party. Point 8 of the resolution states:

> The soviets are the form of government inherent in the proletarian dictatorship, but since the proletariat itself is still under the influence of socially traitorous parties, and since in the countryside the proletarian masses and the working peasantry are not only under the actual dictatorship of the kulak, but also under a moral one, real enemies of the Soviet power often find their way into the rural soviets, entering them in order to destroy them

> from within. This phenomenon is particularly clear in the Ukrainian countryside, where many soviets, full of kulaks and speculators, were themselves the mainstay of the otamans, or at best adopted a passive attitude to the tasks imposed on them by the central authorities.

To prevent this, all province and district executive committees and party organs were ordered to ensure that at the election of soviets "not only the non-working elements, but also all counter-revolutionary elements, irrespective of which stratum of population they belong to, should be ruthlessly excluded." To facilitate the conquest of the countryside, it was planned to create militant class organizations uniting all proletarian and semi-proletarian elements in the countryside, i.e., "trade organizations of agricultural workers occupied in sugar refineries, as well as in other branches of agricultural industry and in Soviet state farms."[161] This summarized the ambivalence of party policy with regard to local Soviet power. The proletariat was to be in principle the bearer of power, but as soon as it became apparent that the proletariat did not carry out party orders, it too was ousted from power. This meant that the proletariat, in the party interpretation, was a section of society that originated from the working stratum of the population and, most important, was loyally devoted to the directives of the party centre. Thus the criterion of true revolutionary calibre was not the social origin of a given stratum of society but the degree of its devotion to party directives. All those countless decrees and declarations on the dictatorship of the proletariat and peasantry were nothing less than mass deception. Because of the almost completely negative attitude of the Ukrainian peasantry to Soviet power, it was eliminated from government participation almost to a man. Therefore Soviet power had in all its three periods an exclusively urban, i.e., purely proletarian, character. In this respect, the power of the soviets in Ukraine differed considerably from that in Russia. As Manuilsky wrote, in Russia Bolshevism was able to transfer the revolution into the countryside, where, as a result of the continuity of Soviet rule, the second period of the land revolution, the so-called period of the *kombedy,* began as early as 1918. As a result of the Brest Litovsk peace, masses of active soldiers returning from the front were faced with a new wealthy peasant stratum, which had seized the great bulk of the landowners' lands. There arose a common movement among the ex-soldiers and poorer peasants for a general "equalization" directed against the new wealthy peasants. Against this background the *kombedy* began to be organized spontaneously, "without any agitation on our part."[162]

In Ukraine the agrarian process and the sovietization of the countryside proceeded, as we have seen, along a somewhat different path. Manuilsky stressed that, in spite of Soviet power having come to Ukraine three times, the landowners' farms were not completely liquidated, and "the shrewd Ukrainian *diadko* (peasant)," having burned himself on the October revolution, "consciously delayed the agrarian revolution" during the period of the punitive expeditions of the Hetmanate and the German domination. The Soviet authorities therefore had to begin the social revolution each time from the same point as in the previous period. They occupied some premises for administrative offices in provincial and district centres and urgently issued a sheaf of decrees; but before the effect of these decrees could penetrate the peasant masses, they were swept away by the next attack of some new pretender to the hetman's mace or to the all-Russian crown.

> The power of our state and administrative machinery was limited by the boundaries of the provincial centre, beyond which was the turbulent free land (*volnitsa*) of the otamans, and where complete lawlessness reigned. The whole socialist revolution of ours did not go beyond the city boundaries . . . . All our measures floated on the surface and did not leave any deep trace in the Ukrainian countryside . . . . For peasants we have remained a new caste which desires to govern and exploit it, as it used to be exploited by the privileged classes. In the Ukrainian countryside the kulak and extortioner has not been forced on his knees as in the Great Russian countryside; he holds all the threads of administration in his hands even now and enjoys an unlimited influence in deciding peasant matters.

Manuilsky admitted that there was as yet no Soviet power in the countryside, and that in the past the Bolsheviks became bankrupt when it came to the implementation of the Soviet policy in the provinces. "We overflowed in disputations in various central commissions, we wrote mountains of all kinds of excellent projects, but we turned out to be unable to embrace the countryside organizationally."[163]

During the whole of 1920, 1921, 1922, and even 1923, the Ukrainian countryside waged an armed struggle against the land policy of the party. The peasant risings did not stop, although their number and scope diminished more and more. According to Soviet data, on 15 November 1921 nineteen "gangs" with a total number of 1,450 "bandits" operated on Ukrainian territory. In January 1922 there were fifteen "gangs" with approximately 400 "bandits." According to the data of the VUChK, by 1 September 1922 "there were registered 10,000 bandits and 200 otamans who surrendered voluntarily."[164]

The third attempt to sovietize Ukraine was also the final one. From the beginning of 1920 the continuity of Soviet power in Ukraine was uninterrupted, and only small parts of its territory were occupied, in May

1920 by the troops of Piłsudski and Petliura and in the autumn of the same year by the troops of Vrangel. It can be seen from the material quoted that the sovietization of Ukraine at the end of 1919 and the beginning of 1920 was carried out chiefly by military force. As soon as the Red Army relaxed its control over Ukraine, power passed into the hands of anti-Bolshevik forces, the Ukrainian Directory, and numerous insurgent centres: Makhno, Hryhoriiv, etc. However, the establishment of the Soviet power by military force was so ineffective that as late as the end of 1920 the countryside lived its own life or, in any case, was not subordinated to Soviet power. At that time Dzerzhinsky was sent to Ukraine "with a group of cheka men for the purpose of strengthening the internal front."[165] In October 1920 Lenin had to admit that Ukraine was Soviet only in form, while in fact the insurgents were the real masters there.[166] During the whole of 1921 the chief task of the Red Army in Ukraine was the suppression of peasant uprisings. The plenary meeting of the CC CP(B)U of 24 February 1921, the secretary of which was then Molotov, resolved to carry out "the most energetic struggle against nationalism, anti-Semitism, anarchist Makhnovism, and conciliatory parties that create a political atmosphere favourable to the development of banditism."[167] Mikhail Frunze, who in February became the deputy chairman of the Council of People's Commissars of Ukraine and at the same time the commander of the southern front, elaborated special tactics for the struggle with insurgents. As a result of continuous conflict, the insurgent ranks grew thinner. In August 1921 Makhno's movement was finally liquidated.[168] By the end of the same year the detachments of Petliura's otamans, among them Zabolotny, Orlyk, Mordalevych, and Tiutiunnyk, were liquidated. In Tiutiunnyk's detachment alone about 1,500 insurgents participated, armed with machine-guns, grenades, and cannons.[169] To liquidate the internal resistance completely, the party decided to grant an amnesty to all insurgents, which resulted in the surrender of over 10,000 insurgents in 1921 alone.[170]

Summing up this stage of party policy towards Ukraine and touching upon the question of the genesis of the Soviet regime in Ukraine, it may be asserted that the introduction of this regime was not a consequence of the internal political and social situation, but a result of an external intervention, of a military victory by the Red Army of Soviet Russia.[171]

The decisive importance of Russian intervention and its consequences for the sovietization of Ukraine is beyond any doubt. As a final argument supporting the main thesis of this work I will again quote Leon Trotsky, who more than any other Bolshevik leader was competent to testify, since he was in charge of the Soviet Russian Red Army engaged in operations.

In a coded letter to the members of the politburo (Lenin, Bukharin, Krestinsky, and Kamenev) on 2 November 1920, Trotsky wrote that "Soviet power in Ukraine has held its ground up to now (and it has not held it well) chiefly by the authority of Moscow, by the Great Russian Communists and by the Russian Red Army."[172] In view of the above, one wonders about the objectivity of E. H. Carr, who in his study of the Russian revolution and civil war represents the introduction of the Soviet power in Ukraine as lightly as if the Ukrainian Bolsheviks themselves had overthrown the Rada, and states that the Soviet armies "were greeted by the population with every show of enthusiasm."[173] Moreover, Carr goes on to allege that "the Soviet regime appeared to offer to the Ukrainian population not only the blessings of peace, but a government more tolerable than any which it had experienced in these turbulent years."[174] Furthermore, he writes that the ultimate disintegration of the anti-Bolshevik forces "showed that the Bolsheviks were at any rate accepted by the Ukrainian masses as the least of possible evils."[175] Thus Carr comes very close to the official Soviet interpretation of the revolution, which conceals the obviously forcible nature of the Soviet occupation of Ukraine as an aid "to the working class and the poorest peasantry of Ukraine."[176] Carr's interpretation, unfortunately, was readily accepted even by other Western historians.[177]

CHAPTER X

Relationships between the Russian SFSR and the Ukrainian SSR

A Relationship in Flux

Theoretically, the relationship between the Russian and the Ukrainian Soviet republics was based on the principles of Soviet federalism.[1] From the very beginning of the Soviet regime in Ukraine (December 1917–April 1918) the activity of its government was limited to assisting the Red Army in the expulsion of the Rada and later in the defence of the republic against the Central Powers and the Rada. The Ukrainian Soviet republic proclaimed itself to be a federative part of the Russian republic from its first days, recognizing the validity "on the territory of the Ukrainian republic of all decrees and orders of the Russian Soviet government."[2] The Council of People's Commissars of the RSFSR recognized, on 26 December 1917, the Soviet government of Ukraine in Kharkiv as "truly the people's Soviet power in Ukraine" and promised this government "full and omnifarious support."[3] Nothing was said about the recognition of this republic as an independent state, which cannot be explained as an oversight, since a few days later such express recognition was granted to Finland.[4] However, in the period of the first Soviet republic in

Ukraine no concrete forms of relations between the Ukrainian and the Russian republics were elaborated, although, according to a Soviet source, talks were begun on this subject.[5] By the terms of the Brest Litovsk peace Russia renounced Ukraine and recognized *de jure* its independence. The second congress of soviets of Ukraine in Katerynoslav (March 1918), proclaimed Ukraine an independent Soviet republic. It may thus be asserted that from the point of view of international law the Ukrainian Soviet republic in its first period began its existence as a federative part of the Russian republic and ended its existence as an independent state.

Summing up the relations between the RSFSR and the Soviet republics in the borderlands, the twelfth congress of the RCP stated in its resolution that in "the first period of the revolution when the working masses of the nationalities for the first time felt themselves to be independent national entities, while the threat of foreign intervention did not yet represent a real danger, the cooperation of peoples had as yet no completely definite, strictly settled forms."[6]

In the second period (December 1918–July 1919), Soviet Ukraine began its existence as a formally independent state, proclaiming in its declarations the independence of Soviet Ukraine and the readiness of its government "to establish regular diplomatic relations" with all states of the world.[7] The constitution of the Ukrainian SSR, adopted by the third congress of soviets of Ukraine, stressed the readiness of the Ukrainian SSR to enter "a single international socialist Soviet republic as soon as conditions for its founding are created."[8] Likewise, the declarations of the government of the Ukrainian SSR stated the readiness of the Ukrainian Soviet republic to enter into federative relations with other Soviet republics, including the RSFSR. The government of the Ukrainain SSR continued to act before other states as the sovereign government of an independent state. Rakovsky, as the head of the government and commissar for foreign affairs, repeatedly stressed the sovereign character of his government and the independence of the Ukrainian republic in his notes to the French, Polish, and Romanian governments.[9]

De facto, this independence was reduced to carrying out the policy of the RCP(B), which guided the state life of Ukraine through its agency, the CP(B)U. The Bolsheviks of Ukraine who stood at the head of the Soviet regime in Ukraine could not refuse to obey the instructions of the RCP, because their domination in Ukraine was based on the military force and party functionaries of Russia. At the beginning of 1919, the first federative organ functioning in Ukraine was the Red Army and its supreme command. The so-called Ukrainian front, under Antonov's command, was subordinated to the supreme commander-in-chief of the RSFSR, Vatsetis.

In June 1919 the Ukrainian front was completely liquidated, so that the Ukrainian SSR had no army of its own. In February 1919, through the initiative of the VTsIK the normative acts of the RSFSR in the field of military organization were introduced on the territory of the Ukrainian SSR.[10] At the same time, initial steps were taken towards the economic alignment of Ukraine with the RSFSR. On 13 March 1919 the all-Russian council of national economy issued the order "concerning the organization of the south Russian metallurgical state trust." The financing of the industry of Ukraine, especially of the Donets basin, was carried out at that time chiefly by the RSFSR and on the directive of the all-Russian council of national economy. At the same time the practice of the exchange of goods between the RSFSR and the Ukrainian SSR was abolished, in accordance with the declaration of the Ukrainian SSR of 29 November 1918.[11] The presidium of the all-Russian council of national economy resolved in March that the transport of goods from one republic into another must be carried out "not on the basis of the exchange of goods, but in the form of the realization of a single plan of supply. The totality of the supplies and produce of all republics will be the single fund for such supply."[12] The trend to federate the borderlands in the Bolshevik manner was manifested in May 1919 in the resolution of the CC RCP, entitled "Draft Directive of the CC on Military Unity," which resulted in the resolution of the all-Russian TsIK of 1 June 1919, "On the Uniting of the Soviet Republics." The all-Russian TsIK considered it necessary to unite: "1) military organization and military command, 2) the council of people's economy, 3) railway administration and management, 4) finance, 5) the commissariats for labour of the Soviet socialist republics of Russia, Ukraine, Latvia, Lithuania, Belorussia, and the Crimea, so that the management of these branches will be concentrated in the hands of single boards." This unification was to be carried out by means of agreement with the central executive committees and the Councils of People's Commissars of the above-mentioned Soviet republics. For this purpose, the all-Russian TsIK was to elect a commission to elaborate together with the TsIKs of the republics "the concrete norms of unification, while prior to the moment of the elaboration of the ultimate unification [the commission had to] prescribe immediately the forms of activity."[13] It is unknown whether such a commission ever met and whether it elaborated the concrete norms of unification. However, *Pravda* of 7 June 1919 declared that the all-Ukrainian TsIK at its next meeting would elect a commission "for the creation, together with other Soviet republics, of the concrete legislative form of the impending military union." Since the question of the elaboration of the federal constitution was a very complicated one and required lengthy deliberations, the commission would elaborate a provisional agreement and take up immediate practical work.[14]

Soviet power, of course, soon had to evacuate Ukraine for the second time, and nothing practical came of these measures. On the eve of the third offensive of the Red Army on Ukraine the seventh all-Russian congress of soviets affirmed, on 5 December 1919, that "at present the relations between the Ukrainian Socialist Soviet Republic and the RSFSR are determined by federative ties on the basis of the resolutions of the central executive committee of Ukraine of 18 May 1919 and of the all-Russian central executive committee of 1 June of the same year."[15] The same was said in the resolution of the fourth congress of soviets of the Ukrainian SSR of 20 May 1920. The same congress of soviets of the Ukrainian SSR ratified the agreement between the TsIK of Ukraine and the TsIK of the RSFSR concerning the unification of these commissariats—military, finance, railways, national economy, post and telegraph, and labour.[16] At the same time, it was resolved to propose that thirty representatives of Soviet Ukraine who had been elected at the fourth congress of soviets of Ukraine be included in the all-Russian TsIK.[17] This proposal was accepted by the all-Russian TsIK at its second session.[18] The all-Ukrainian TsIK resolved on 25 November 1920 that the soviets of the Ukrainian SSR should take part in the eighth all-Russian congress of soviets.[19] The all-Ukrainian revolutionary committee issued an order in January 1920 introducing on the territory of Ukraine the legislative acts of the RSFSR, "governing those branches of administration which were united by the decree of 1 June 1919."[20] From January 1920 the institute of the representatives of the united commissariats was introduced in Ukraine. These representatives were in charge of certain departments of the Ukrainian SSR and were in a position of twofold subordination. In this period of military union one could not speak of a real federation in the Western sense of the word, for the majority of the legal attributes of the state remained with the government of the Ukrainian Soviet republic. However, in actual fact the government of the RSFSR often spoke in the name of the Ukrainian SSR in diplomatic relations, perhaps without the agreement of the government of the Ukrainian SSR. Only on six occasions in the period from April to November 1920 did the RSFSR and the Ukrainian SSR appear together in the international arena.[21]

A step of considerable importance towards the realization of federation was the decree of the CPC of the RSFSR "concerning the Ukrainian council of the labour army." This Ukrainian council was to be a regional organ of the corresponding council of the RSFSR. In spite of the restriction of relations between the RSFSR and the Ukrainian SSR to the military sphere, the federation was actually being introduced by means of administrative orders and by the practice of individual economic organs. One must agree with Chistiakov who wrote in this connection that, under the conditions of the transition of peacetime construction, "the federative relations of the RSFSR and the Ukrainian SSR, which assumed during the period of intervention the form of a military alliance of Soviet republics, gradually became transformed into a military and economic union," and that the "union treaties" which were later concluded between the RSFSR and the Soviet republics merely "fixed the relations already formed between the RSFSR and the Soviet republics allied with it."[22] However, the above-mentioned resolution of the twelfth congress of the RCP defined this period as one of collaboration in the form of a military union, not a military and economic one.[23]

The Military and Economic Union

The union treaty between the RSFSR and the Ukrainian SSR, signed in Moscow on 28 December 1920, was a synthesis of the trends towards the federalization of the Ukrainian SSR during 1920, chiefly in the economic sphere. This treaty was actually one of a series of similar treaties concluded by the Russian republic with other Soviet republics during 1920–21. These treaties are rather inconsistent and characteristic of the whole activity of the Bolsheviks in this sphere. That the treaty with Ukraine was one of the most important is indicated, for instance, by the circumstance that its creator was none other than Lenin. This was, as Carr remarks, "the only one of these treaties to be signed by Lenin himself on behalf of the RSFSR."[24] Apart from Lenin, the treaty was signed by the people's commissar for foreign affairs, Chicherin, and on behalf of the Ukrainian SSR by the chairman of the Council of People's Commissars and the people's commissar for foreign affairs of the Ukrainian SSR, Rakovsky. The preamble of the treaty emphasized that both parties, the governments of the RSFSR and of the Ukrainian SSR, "taking as their point of departure the right of peoples to self-determination which was proclaimed by the great proletarian revolution, recognizing the independence and sovereignty of each of the parties to the treaty, and being conscious of the necessity of uniting their forces for the purposes of defence, as well as in the interests of their economic construction, have decided to conclude the present workers' and peasants' union treaty." Section 3 of the treaty said that all obligations which the two republics in future would take upon themselves in respect to other states "can be determined only by the common interests of the workers and peasants concluding the present union treaty of the republics. ... No obligations for the Ukrainian SSR towards anyone whatsoever issue from the mere fact of the former appurtenance of the territory of the Ukrainian SSR to the former Russian empire." For the realization of the aims defined in the first section, the governments of the RSFSR and of the Ukrainian SSR decided to unite the following commissariats: military and naval affairs, the supreme council of national economy, external trade, finance, labour, lines of communication, and post and telegraph.[25] These united commissariats "enter the Council of People's Commissars of the RSFSR and have in the Council of People's Commissars of the Ukrainian SSR their representatives, who are appointed and controlled by the Ukrainian TsIK and congress of soviets." "The order and form" of the internal "administration" of the united commissariats were to be established by a separate agreement of both governments. "The management and control" of the united commissariats "are realized through all-Russian congresses ... and also through the all-Russian central executive committee, to which the Ukrainian SSR sends its representatives on the basis of the resolution of the all-Russian congress of soviets." This treaty was subject to ratification by the appropriate supreme legislative bodies of both republics.[26] The original version of the treaty was composed and signed in Russian and in Ukrainian.

If this treaty is compared with the treaty concluded between the RSFSR and the Azerbaidzhan SSR of 30 September 1920, it can be seen that the Ukrainian model was edited with much greater formal precision than that of Azerbaidzhan, although this does not mean that it was perfect.[27] First, in the Azerbaidzhan treaty the mutual recognition of the parties to the treaty was not stressed; secondly, the subordination of the "representatives" of the united commissariats to the Azerbaidzhan TsIK and congress of soviets was not indicated; thirdly, this treaty was not subject to ratification, but "takes effect *ipso facto* and from the moment of its signing."[28] Carr characterizes the Azerbaidzhan model as "clumsy but direct," explaining this by the fact that Azerbaidzhan "was perhaps the poorest and weakest of the eight republics."[29] The same author writes that the Ukrainian treaty "had a certain solemnity and significance,"[30] because Ukraine "was certainly the strongest and the most insistent in her claim to formal independence and equality."[31] The Ukrainian model later served as a prototype for the treaties which the RSFSR concluded during 1921 with Georgia, Armenia, and Belorussia.

When analysing the Russo-Ukrainian treaty of 28 December 1920 from the constitutional aspect, it is possible to agree partially with Carr that it contains certain features of an alliance, a federation, and a purely unitarian state.[32] It was because of this inconsistency that the organs of the Ukrainian republic preserved enough legal attributes to qualify these relations with the RSFSR as confederative rather than federative. The Communists themselves at the time considered this treaty to be something like a convention. Stalin, for instance, called the treaties of 1920–21 "convention relations."[33] Soviet jurists of the early period unanimously regarded these treaties as confederative. In the textbook, *Soviet Federalism*, a prominent Soviet expert on international law, Reikhel, wrote that the treaty between the RSFSR and the Ukrainian SSR of 28 December 1920 resembled a "bourgeois confederation," a union of states. He remarked that

> the union treaties did not create any new state embracing the union republics; these treaties confirmed the independence and sovereignty of the republics and could be changed only by means of a treaty; separate republics continued to preserve the right to international diplomatic relations . . . ; each republic preserved its citizenship, had an incontestable right to leave the union, and independently established its constitution. Finally, the legislative and administrative acts of the government of the RSFSR which fulfilled the union functions were implemented in the majority of cases not directly, but through the governments of the union republics . . . (such was, at least, the prevalent practice of Ukraine and the Transcaucasian republics).[34]

Reikhel concluded from this that "all these features connect the form of the union of the independent Soviet republics prior to the formation of the USSR not with federation but with confederation, not with a union state but with a union of states."[35]

Analysing the international legal aspect of relations between the RSFSR and the Ukrainian SSR on the basis of that treaty, Reikhel pointed out further that:

> 1) The RSFSR and the Ukrainian SSR never acted as one state in international relations. Their people's commissariats for foreign affairs were organizationally completely separate, and they merely brought into line and coordinated their activity. Their diplomatic representations abroad, where they had such, were also created separately and acted each in the name of its republic. In the most important cases, as for instance in [the] Genoa and Lausanne [conferences], formally united representations (delegations) were also organized, but legally at the root of such united actions lay special agreements of the republics, while the mandates for representation were issued to each of the republics separately . . . .

2) There was no union citizenship, either separate or common, or absorbing the citizenship of the union republics, prior to the establishment of the USSR .... There existed no union citizenship; there were only citizens of separate Soviet republics which protected them where it was necessary to do so.

3) There were no supreme organs of the union in the real sense of this word .... There was only the participation of delegations of the union republics in the Russian supreme organs. These delegations were from the republics as such and not from the working masses directly ....

4) The supreme organs of the RSFSR which administered the people's commissariats united by treaty exercised no direct power over the territories and populations of the union republics, but [their authority was] only conditionally and relatively ... binding on their governments. The latter exercised the legislative and other authority on their territories exclusively in their own names.

5) The union association had no "competence of competences." The limits of the union association were established and could be changed only by means of a treaty.

6) Formally the union republics were completely sovereign (if the divisibility of sovereignty is admitted) or simply sovereign (if the viewpoint of indivisibility is adopted). The union treaty was without any time limit and could be abrogated by any party at any time.[36]

Reikhel's contemporary, Aleksandrenko, described this treaty as "an international legal act which was entered into by two subjects of international legal relations .... We have an association of two independent sovereign states in the form of a confederation, an international legal society." He, like Reikhel, regarded the independent management of foreign policy as the most important attribute of independence. Only with the creation of the USSR, in his opinion, did Ukraine enter the union on federative principles.[37] Reikhel is quite right in stressing that the treaty left certain things unsaid and did not answer the following questions: "a) Does it establish only the administrative unification of the commissariats, or also legislative unification? b) What is the force of the decrees of the all-Russian supreme organs, the congress of soviets and the TsIK, for the Ukrainian SSR? c) What is the procedure for settling conflicts between the supreme organs of the RSFSR and the Ukrainian SSR? etc."[38]

In practice, relations between the congresses of soviets of the RSFSR and the Ukrainian SSR showed that the all-Ukrainian legislative organ energetically defended its prerogatives as the supreme legislative organ of Ukraine. For instance, the fifth all-Ukrainian congress of soviets did not confirm the resolution of the eighth all-Russian congress of soviets, which said that "each of the sides to the treaty has the right to demand at a congress of soviets that the other side should act only in an advisory capacity with regard to non-united commissariats." As Reikhel remarked, the question in actual fact simply meant that the Ukrainian delegates were deprived of full voting powers at the all-Russian congress of soviets.[39]

The fifth all-Ukrainian congress of soviets, on the contrary, directed the TsIK "to develop and make concrete those points of the treaty which referred to the relations between the Ukrainian and all-Russian TsIKs, in particular the point concerning the internal order of the united commissariats *and their relations to both governments on the basis of full equality between both republics, as foreseen by the treaty*."[40] Commenting on this resolution, Reikhel stressed that this was already "an expansive tendency . . . towards equalization in administration and legislation."[41] The same congress resolved that: "a) all decrees referring to the general norms of political and economic life as well as all decrees introducing radical changes into the existing practice of state organs must be considered by the Ukrainian TsIK; b) legislative measures in military matters must be considered by the Ukrainian people's commissariat; c) no organs, apart from the all-Ukrainian congress of soviets and the Ukrainian TsIK, its presidium and the people's commissariat, have the right to promulgate legislative acts of state-wide importance."[42] The fifth congress of soviets of Ukraine likewise ignored the need for a change in the constitution of the Ukrainian SSR, which without doubt would have had to be changed if the treaty of 28 December 1920 had limited the sovereignty of the Ukrainian SSR on the legislative plane.

As the same writer stressed, "the Ukrainian SSR not only did not admit a direct extension of Russian laws upon its territory but also independently introduced into them changes and additions that were necessary from its point of view, and sometimes, although rarely, simply refused the 'registration' of some union legislative order."[43] It became established in practice that the representative of the united people's commissariats in the Ukrainian SSR "had a double line of subordination: to the government of the Ukrainian SSR and to his people's commissar with the formally dominating position of the former; in case of conflict the representative was obliged to carry out the order of the government of the Ukrainian SSR."[44]

Later works of the Stalin period revised the views on the relations between the RSFSR and other republics, putting them in rather confused language. Ronin termed the relations between the RSFSR and other Soviet republics "an extremely peculiar and complicated federative association."[45] Zlatopolsky wrote that the ties between the republics during 1919–22 had "not confederative forms ... but a federative form."[46] Iakubovskaia wrote, following Stalin, that "the government of the RSFSR in fact played the role of a common federative government in this period."[47] B. E. Chirkin and M. S. Akhmedov wrote in 1954 that the relations between the RSFSR and Ukraine before the formation of the USSR, "in spite of the assertions of some scholars, did not have an international legal character, but had a federative character from the very beginning of the creation of both states."[48]

Western scholarship dealing with this problem treats the Soviet republics as merely autonomous parts of the Russian federation, or even asserts that this treaty placed Ukraine in the same position as before the revolution. Such a view was represented by Batsell, who wrote that "in reality and practice from this time on she [Ukraine] was almost as closely bound to Moscow as before the revolution."[49] According to another Western expert on Soviet state law, the treaty had the character of a confederation.[50]

As has been pointed out, Lenin and Stalin did not agree concerning the classification of relations between the RSFSR and the Soviet republics. While Lenin differentiated between the type of federation based on treaties (Ukraine, Belorussia, etc.) and the type based on autonomous relations within the RSFSR, Stalin saw no such difference. In a letter of June 1920, Stalin argued with Lenin about this gradation of relationships. "In your theses," wrote Stalin, "you differentiate between the Bashkir and the Ukrainian types of federative ties, but in actual fact this difference does not exist, or it is so small that it equals zero."[51] Under Lenin's influence, Stalin soon changed his position on this question, and at the tenth congress of the RCP he differentiated between the various types of Soviet federation. Then he recognized federation "based on Soviet autonomy (Kirghizia, Bashkiria)" and "federation based on treaty relations with independent Soviet republics (Ukraine, Azerbaidzhan)."[52] Somewhat later Stalin qualified this whole period of relationships as "the phase of a diplomatic union of our republics."[53] The presidium of the TsIK of the USSR emphasized in its declarations that, although the Soviet republics constantly rendered mutual help, "for a long time they still remained, although tied by union treaties, separate states."[54] With the passing of time the significance of the treaty of 1920 has been more and more underrated by Soviet historians and constitutional experts, and the international legal status of these republics has been narrowed down to that of autonomous republics.

A final classification of the treaty is left to the competent legal experts. It is, however, necessary to review its practical consequences for the relations between the RSFSR and the Ukrainian SSR in subsequent years. As has been pointed out, the treaty was so framed that it left much leeway for interpretation and probably for conflict between the people's commissariats of the RSFSR and of Ukraine. As one historian of the post-Stalin period writes, the treaty created "a possibility of distorting this system in the spirit of bureaucratic centralization and imperialism." On the other hand, particularly in the rule concerning the "registration" of the decrees of the people's commissariats of the RSFSR by the republican organs, it "created the threat of the distortion of the policy of Soviet power by nationalist elements in separate Soviet republics." It often happened that the state organs of the RSFSR "attempted to diminish the rights of separate Soviet republics." For instance, the people's commissar for justice of the RSFSR demanded that all decrees and orders of the all-Russian TsIK that referred to the united people's commissariats should automatically extend to the territory of the Ukrainian SSR; the people's commissars of the Ukrainian SSR were to be notified of them for information purposes only.[55] Such an interpretation of the treaty caused protests from the government of the Ukrainian SSR.

Probably as a result of these protests, an agreement was reached between the TsIK of the RSFSR and the TsIK of the Ukrainian SSR on 10 October 1921. The agreement said: "In regard to the union treaty between the RSFSR and the Ukrainian SSR, it is to be suggested to all central people's commissariats of the RSFSR that they conduct all their relations with the local organs of Ukraine directly through the central organs of the Ukrainian SSR."[56] However, the administrative organs of the RSFSR continued to bypass the central organs of the government of Ukraine. This brought about an intervention through party channels. This violation of the competence of the republics found its reflection at the tenth congress of the RCP. The delegate from the CP(B)U, Zatonsky, pointed out that the relationships between the RSFSR and the Ukrainian SSR were so confused and undefined that he himself, as a member of the government and the CC CP(B)U, was unable to define with certainty the forms of the mutual relations of these republics. "With the conclusion of the last treaty," said Zatonsky, "we seem to be, and we seem not to be, in federation. The central institutions must understand this in order that there should not be such a muddle as is now observed always when certain comrades, when whole institutions, such as the CC, pursue one line, while the people's commissariats [pursue] another .... It is necessary to combat these Russian chauvinist tendencies. But it is necessary to define more precisely the mutual relations of the parts of the federation, not because it is necessary to increase or reduce the rights of these parts—this is not the point—but in order to do away with this muddle which we are in and which spoils an arrangement that has been working well."[57]

The question about the regulation of mutual relations between the RSFSR and Ukraine was discussed at a meeting of the politburo of the CC CP(B)U in March 1921. A resolution was passed to the effect that: "the CC CP(B)U regards as timely the necessity of defining the mutual relations between the RSFSR and the Ukrainian SSR in the sense of the determination and more precise definition of the rights and duties of the Ukrainian SSR, to which end it regards as necessary the establishment of a special commission composed of the members of the CC RCP(B) and the CC CP(B)U for the final and precise elaboration of the relations between the RSFSR and the Ukrainian SSR."[58] This proposition was tabled by Manuilsky, Frunze, and Iakov Ganetsky at the meeting of the politburo of the CC RCP(B) of 11 May 1922. The politburo of the CC RCP(B) adopted in this connection the following resolution: "Having heard the question and doubts of the members of the CC CP(B)U, the CC RCP affirms that no change has occurred in the attitude of the RSFSR towards the Ukrainian SSR, in the sense of the abolition or reduction of the independence of the Ukrainian republic, nor generally in the sense of the revision of the basic constitutional statutes of the Ukrainian republic."[59] At the same time, the politburo warned the people's commissar for foreign affairs of the RSFSR that it was inadmissible to act in the name of the Ukrainian SSR without the prior agreement of the people's commissar for foreign affairs of the Ukrainian SSR. To control relations between the RSFSR and the Ukrainian SSR and to elaborate statutes governing these relations, the politburo created a commission consisting of Manuilsky, Skrypnyk, Stalin, Frunze, and other representatives of the Ukrainian SSR and the RSFSR.[60] This commission elaborated the relationship between the RSFSR and the Soviet republics generally. Frunze, in his interview with a correspondent of *Kommunist*, said that the development of commercial connections demanded the establishment "of a single monetary unit for the whole Soviet federation, the abolition of customs barriers, of all restrictions in the calling of the ships of the union republics at union ports, etc.," and that it was decided "to suggest to all union republics that they should discuss the entire question of the mutual relations of the Soviet republics and draft corresponding resolutions."[61]

From the above it is clear that the central organs of the RSFSR tended towards the reduction of the competence of the Soviet republics, including the Ukrainian one, with the aim of reducing them to the status of ordinary administrative units. Such people's commissariats as that for foreign affairs tried to appropriate the competencies of the Ukrainian SSR, although in accordance with the treaty of 1920 foreign affairs remained the prerogative of the Ukrainian SSR. Subsequently, however, the people's commissar for foreign affairs of the RSFSR did not cease to exercise pressure in this direction on the Ukrainian people's commissariat for foreign affairs. The Ukrainian SSR, on its part, not only defended the prerogatives and sovereignty reserved for it by the treaty of 1920, but also tried to broaden them by practical moves. This tendency to expand the competence of the institutions of the Ukrainian SSR was emphasized by the head of its government, Rakovsky, in his report at the sixth conference of the CP(B)U on 10 October 1921. He stressed that "it has been necessary to give more independence to the Ukrainian organs, as far as the united commissariats are concerned, mainly because other organs of the commissariats are independent."[62] In the area of foreign trade particularly, considerable modifications of the treaty were achieved in the direction of allocating foreign trade to the Ukrainian commissariat. Rakovsky emphasized in the above-mentioned report that the Ukrainian commissariat for foreign trade was allocated 15 per cent or about 50 million gold roubles, and 20 per cent or about 60 million gold roubles was allocated for common federative needs. Both funds were at the disposal of the Ukrainian government. This was also a result of the division of spheres of activity in trade between the RSFSR and the Ukrainian SSR, so that for the latter Poland, Czechoslovakia, Bulgaria, Turkey, and Austria were reserved, while the remainder of countries belonged to the Russian sphere.[63] An agreement between the people's commissar for foreign trade of the RSFSR and the representative of the Ukrainian commissariat for foreign trade established the sphere of preferential influence of the Ukrainian SSR in regard to foreign trade with Poland, Czechoslovakia, Turkey, Romania, Bulgaria, and Greece. In these countries the trade representative of Ukraine occupied a leading position, with the trade representative of the RSFSR subordinate to him. Corresponding to this, the trade representative of the Ukrainian commissariat for foreign trade in Turkey was appointed the chairman of the united mission of the Ukrainian SSR and the RSFSR.[64]

The trend towards the unification (or rather the subordination) of the Soviet republics that were connected with the RSFSR by treaties was even more marked in the international field. For instance, Ukraine had independent diplomatic relations as late as the end of 1922, although this independence was rather relative in view of the relation between the RCP(B) and the CP(B)U examined earlier. During this short period of independent diplomatic relations, the Ukrainian Soviet republic, being bound by party directives, was unable to pursue a foreign policy independent and different from that of the RSFSR. It is quite possible that the whole campaign of the Ukrainian SSR on the external front was determined, as was admitted later by the acting Ukrainian commissar for foreign affairs, Iakovlev, by the struggle for recognition of the Soviet government of Ukraine to prevent thereby the recognition of Petliura's government, then in exile, as the legal government of Ukraine.[65] At that time Iakovlev openly declared:

> The foreign policy of Ukraine has not and cannot have any interests other than those common with Russia, which is just such a proletarian state as Ukraine. The heroic struggle of Russia, in complete alliance with Ukraine, on all fronts against domestic and foreign imperialists, is now giving way to an equally united diplomatic front. Ukraine is independent in its foreign policy where its own specific interests are concerned. But in questions that are of common political and economic interest to all Soviet republics, the Russian as well as the Ukrainian commissariats for foreign affairs act as the united federal power.[66]

The Comintern yearbook, referring to the treaty of 1920, spoke of "the first international action" of the Ukrainian republic which "served as a beginning to a whole series of agreements concluded by the government of the Ukrainian SSR with other foreign countries. ... An important task fell to the lot of the Ukrainian diplomatic mission in Moscow, as the first foreign representation of the Ukrainian SSR, to mediate in the matter of formulating and establishing the international position of the Ukrainain SSR by concluding a whole series of diplomatic agreements."[67]

The first diplomatic representative of the Ukrainian SSR abroad was M. Levytsky, appointed to Prague in April 1920. This is curious, since the Czechoslovak government at that time recognized neither Soviet Russia nor Soviet Ukraine. Such *de facto* recognition took place only as late as 1922, when a provisional treaty was signed between the Ukrainian Soviet republic and the Czechoslovak republic, in accordance with which both states established diplomatic relations.[68] Also in 1920, Vladimir Aussem was appointed the Ukrainian SSR's ambassador in Berlin. By the end of 1921 Shumsky arrived in Warsaw as the representative of the Ukrainian SSR.[69] These representatives of the Ukrainian SSR were separate, although it may be assumed that they worked in agreement with the Russian people's commissar for foreign affairs. It was only in 1923 that Ukrainian diplomatic missions ceased functioning, as a consequence of the creation of the Union of Soviet Socialist Republics.

The Ukrainian Soviet republic, during the period 1920–23, signed a series of political agreements whereby Ukraine was recognized as an independent state. The recognition of Ukraine as an independent state was expressly mentioned in the armistice and in the preliminary peace conditions between Russia and Ukraine, on the one hand, and Poland, on the other (signed on 12 October 1920 in Riga).[70] This recognition is also repeated in the text of the final peace treaty between the above-mentioned states in Riga on 18 March 1921.[71] In the provisional agreement with Austria of 7 December 1921, Ukraine was recognized *de facto* as an independent state; for, according to the agreement, there had to take place an exchange of diplomatic representatives between these countries.[72] "The heads of representations," the agreement said, "enjoy the privileges and prerogatives of the heads of accredited missions." The representatives received the following consular powers:

1) The protection of the interests of their citizens in accordance with the norms of international law.

2) The issue of passports, certificates of identity, and visas.

3) The drawing up of documents, including testaments, the witnessing of the signatures of institutions or private persons, the drawing up or testifying to the correctness of translations, and the authentication of copies from documents.[73]

The Ukrainian SSR was also recognized in a treaty it signed with the Lithuanian republic on 14 February 1921.[74] Similar recognition was accorded by Latvia in the treaty of 3 August 1921,[75] by Estonia in the treaty of 25 November 1921,[76] as well as by Czechoslovakia in the above-mentioned treaty of 6 June 1922.[77] On 21 January 1921 a treaty of friendship and brotherhood with Turkey was signed in Ankara; in it Turkey declared its "recognition of the Ukrainian Socialist Soviet Republic as an independent and sovereign state."[78] Apart from these states, Ukraine concluded agreements with Hungary—an agreement concerning the repatriation of prisoners of war (21 May 1920), a treaty about the exchange of prisoners of war and civilian internees (28 July 1921), and a protocol concerning the mutual exchange of prisoners of war (3 October 1921); with Germany—a treaty dealing with repatriation (23 April 1921) and an agreement concerning the extension of the treaty of 16 April 1922 to the union republics (5 November 1922); with Italy—a preliminary agreement (26 December 1921); with France—an agreement concerning the mutual evacuation of subjects (20 April 1920). On 10 May 1922 the Ukrainian SSR, together with the RSFSR and the Belorussian SSR, signed an agreement with the epidemics commission of the League of Nations concerning aid for the people's commissariats of health of the above-mentioned republics.[79] It must be noted that many of these treaties were signed by Ukraine together with the RSFSR and sometimes also with the Belorussian Soviet republic; this created an impression that Ukraine was merely an appendage of Russia. The peace treaty with Turkey and the treaties with Lithuania, Latvia, Estonia, and Czechoslovakia were signed by Ukraine independently.

The last independent international action of the Ukrainian republic was the signing in Kharkiv on 17 February 1923 of the additional protocol to the treaty between the Ukrainian and Estonian republics of 25 November 1921. This was followed on 27 October 1923 by the exchange of documents of ratification.[80] On 19 August 1923 the Ukrainian people's commissar for foreign affairs informed the representatives of foreign states in Ukraine that the international relations of the Ukrainian SSR had been transferred to the jurisdiction of the USSR.[81]

However, even earlier the people's commissariat for foreign affairs of the RSFSR was preparing to take over the republics' diplomatic functions. The first such steps were the measures of the government of the RSFSR to obtain the authorization of the Soviet republics to represent them at the Genoa conference. During January 1922 the politburo of the CC RCP(B) elaborated through its branches, the CCs of the Communist parties in the republics, the question of common action at the Genoa conference. On 22 February 1923 at a conference of the representatives of the republics in Moscow a protocol was signed, in accordance with which Azerbaidzhan, Armenia, Belorussia, Bukhara, Georgia, the Far East Republic,[82] Ukraine, and Khorezm authorized the delegation of the RSFSR to defend their interests in Genoa.[83] Although these authorizations referred to the Genoa conference only, they seemed to be a preparation for a further unification of the foreign policy of the republics in Moscow. In fact, the international activity of the Ukrainian SSR after the Genoa conference no longer had an independent character and was already moribund when it ended completely with the creation of the USSR.

CHAPTER XI

The Creation of the Union of Soviet Socialist Republics

A final step in the policy of the RCP(B) towards Ukraine and other nationalities of Russia was the creation of the USSR. From the moment of the creation of this multinational state, the national question ceased to extend beyond the internal political framework. Nonetheless, this did not solve the national question in the USSR, and it did not mean that this question was no longer discussed and exercised no influence on the policy of the Soviet government.

The main question which arises in the analysis of this act is whether this union was created from above, by a directive of the Communist party and thus of the Soviet government of Russia, or from below at the request of the non-Russian nationalities. How far did the Communists of the borderlands help in this process? Were they completely in favour of the RCP(B) line or did they oppose it and offer their own, different thesis of relations between the Russian and other Soviet republics?

The problem of the creation of the USSR and the nationality question has been treated by Soviet historians from the aspect of party expediency, taking into consideration in the first place the interest of the party and Soviet power. They have noted and emphasized only such manifestations among the nationalities of Russia as were favourable to the concept of union with Russia. On the other hand, separatist trends among the non-Russian peoples have been either passed over in silence or distorted. Historical facts have been twisted to suit the *a priori* premises of a struggle for unification. The Communist party of Russia is portrayed as the initiator and executor of the unifying trends among the non-Russian nationalities themselves. The will of the RCP has been identified with the will of the popular masses of the non-Russian peoples, and the creation of the USSR has been represented as being in fact only the expression of the people's will.[1]

After Stalin's death, and especially during the short period of the so-called de-Stalinization of historiography in 1955–57, several interesting, and in their way unique, articles were written concerning the creation of the USSR.[2] At the same time, several important documents were published,[3] which until then had not been mentioned and which shed much new light on this subject. They show that the union of the republics to form the USSR did not proceed as spontaneously and smoothly as had usually been claimed by Soviet historians. This event has also been investigated by Western scholars, who naturally arrived at different conclusions from Soviet historians.[4]

The RSFSR or the USSR?

Uniting the Soviet republics under the leadership of the Russian republic was an axiom of the party, and its whole policy on the national question was oriented towards that. The tenth congress of the RCP publicly buried the right of nations to self-determination, having proclaimed that the isolated existence of Soviet republics was unstable and insecure in view of the threat to their existence from the imperialist states. The chief protagonist of the unification of the republics, Stalin, began a campaign against their self-determination, publishing in *Pravda* a series of articles on the national question[5] and having his well known resolution against the self-determination and secession of the republics accepted at the tenth congress. The meaning of the campaign reduced itself, as Stalin said, to the fact that "the old treaty relationships—the convention relationships between the RSFSR and other Soviet republics—were exhausted, proved insufficient"; it was necessary "to change from the old treaty relationships to those of a closer association, to relationships which presuppose the creation of a single state with corresponding single executive and legislative organs."[6] The campaign for even closer ties between the Soviet republics and the RSFSR met with opposition among the Communists of the nationalities. Ukraine played the chief role in this respect. It has been pointed out elsewhere that within the CP(B)U itself there were certain elements which were strongly permeated by national patriotism and which struggled for a real national identity and demanded that relations with the RSFSR should be on the basis of equality. Within the RCP(B), on the other hand, there were many Great Russian chauvinists, who strove behind the screen of Soviet federalism towards one, indivisible Soviet Russia. It was during the formulation of the final pattern of relationships among the Soviet republics, in accordance with the resolution of the tenth congress of the party, that divergencies arose on the question whether the Soviet republics were to enter the RSFSR or whether they were to form a new state unit together with the RSFSR. While the predominant part of the RCP(B) held the first view, the Communist parties of the borderlands defended the second alternative. The non-Russian Communists demanded the creation of a new state edifice on the basis of equality, having the idea that in the future other Soviet republics outside the boundaries of the old tsarist empire would also join this union. On the basis of these national divergencies arose the dispute concerning the so-called "autonomization."

The first phase of the creation of the union began on 10 October 1922, when the politburo of the CC RCP(B) decided to form a commission comprising the representatives of the CC RCP(B) and of the CCs of the Communist parties of Azerbaidzhan, Armenia, Bukhara, Belorussia, Georgia, the Far East Republic, Ukraine, and Khorezm "for the elaboration of the question concerning the further mutual relations of the independent Soviet republics."[7] The first draft of the theses on unification was written by Stalin and presented by him to the above-mentioned commission under the title, "Draft Resolution Concerning the Mutual Relations of the RSFSR with the Independent Republics." In principle, the draft was dominated by the idea of the "autonomization" of the republics, i.e., the inclusion of the republics in the RSFSR on an autonomous basis. The first paragraph of Stalin's theses read: "To recognize as expedient the conclusion of a treaty between the Soviet republics of Ukraine, Belorussia, Azerbaidzhan, Georgia, Armenia, and the RSFSR concerning their formal entry into the RSFSR, leaving the question of Bukhara, Khorezm, and the Far East Republic open and limiting [ourselves] to the acceptance of a treaty with them concerning customs, foreign trade, foreign and military affairs, etc."[8] The commission of the CC RCP(B) adopted Stalin's draft "without substantial changes" and circulated it to the CCs CPs(B) of the union republics. It soon transpired that the CCs CPs(B) not only did not approve of the draft, but even launched a campaign against it. Thus the CC CP(B)U, in its resolution of 3 October 1922, opposed the "autonomization" of the Soviet republics, stressing that "the tactical centralized leadership of independent republics can be fully achieved through corresponding directives along party channels."[9] The leading personalities of the CC CP(B)U included supporters (e.g., Manuilsky and Frunze) of the autonomization of the republics.[10] The CC of the party of Georgia also rejected Stalin's draft, calling it "premature" and demanding in their counter-proposals "the preservation of all the attributes of independence" for the republics. The CC of the Communist party of Belorussia spoke in favour of the preservation of previous treaty relationships between the republics and the RSFSR.[11] The CCs of the Communist parties of Armenia and Azerbaidzhan, on the other hand, accepted autonomization.[12] However, as Pentkovskaia writes, "some Georgian, Bashkir, and Tatar functionaries suggested the liquidation of existing federal creations and the formation of a union of republics, in which all republics, including the autonomous ones, would be members as union republics. Suggestions were also made concerning the creation of a union of Soviet republics as a confederative state."[13]

The resistance of the Communist parties of the union republics, it seems, compelled Lenin to intervene against autonomization. Lenin was bedridden the whole summer and autumn of that year and was unable to take an active part in creating a new formula for unification of the republics. He hoped, he indicated to the politburo,[14] to be well again and to take part in the October and December plenary meetings of the CC RCP, and "to intervene in this question." He thought he could have intervened earlier in this question: "I, it seems, am very guilty before the workers of Russia for not having intervened energetically enough and sharply enough in the notorious question of autonomization." Only after the news reached him that autonomization was not a success, that the reaction of the CCs of the Communist parties in the borderlands was on the whole negative, and that Stalin, together with Ordzhonikidze and Dzerzhinsky, had begun to implement their idea by force, thus rousing even Communists in the borderlands (chiefly in Georgia) against them, did Lenin decide to intervene. On 27 September 1922 he sent a letter to Kamenev, with copies to all members of the politburo of the CC RCP(B), in which he condemned autonomization and proposed in principle another solution of the problem: "formal association together with the RSFSR into a Union of Soviet Republics of Europe and Asia. . . . The spirit of this concession," he wrote to Kamenev, "is, I hope, understandable: We acknowledge ourselves to have equal rights with the Ukr[ainian] SSR and other [republics] and form together with them and on an equal footing a new union, a new federation, 'the Union of Soviet Republics of Europe and Asia.'"[15] Lenin further proposed the creation of a "common federal VTsIK of the Union of

Soviet Republics," instead of subordinating the republics to the central organs of the RSFSR.

Stalin replied on the same day and also sent copies to the politburo members. He disagreed with Lenin on the creation of a separate VTsIK: "With reference to section 2, comrade Lenin's amendment concerning the creation of a federal VTsIK side by side with the VTsIK of the RSFSR, in my opinion, should not be adopted; the existence of two TsIKs in Moscow, one of which apparently will represent the lower house and the other the upper house, will produce nothing but friction and conflicts." He also attacked Lenin's proposal to unite the people's commissariats for finance, food, labour, and national economy into federal people's commissariats. "There can hardly be any doubt that this 'haste' 'will give food to independentists' to the detriment of Lenin's national liberalism."[16]

No less important was the question of the subjects of the union, which in point of fact determined the actual character of the relationships of the republics to the RSFSR and relationships among the republics themselves. For instance, the Georgian Communists insisted that all so-called union republics should be the subjects of the union and not the newly created artificial federations (e.g., the Transcaucasian Federation), on the one hand, and independent republics (the Ukrainian and Belorussian ones), on the other. The Georgians wished to get rid of the patchwork arrangement and to enter the union independently. Apparently it was proposed that the component parts of the RSFSR should also be separated from the latter, so that these parts would enter the USSR independently.[17] Stalin held that the integrity of the RSFSR and the Transcaucasian Federation should be preserved in any case. He regarded dividing the RSFSR into separate state units as unreasonable and useless, and as being "excluded by the very course of the campaign. . . . First, it would lead to a situation in which, side by side with a process leading to the uniting of the republics, we would have a process of separation of already existing federal formations, a process which would turn upside down the really revolutionary process of uniting the republics which has already started."[18] It would also lead automatically to the separation of the eight autonomous republics, and also to the separation from the RSFSR of a separate Russian TsIK and of the Council of People's Commissars, "which would cause a large organizational upheaval which is now completely unnecessary and harmful."[19] Only in 1936 did Georgia, Armenia, and Azerbaidzhan become independent component parts of the union, after the Transcaucasian Federation was liquidated.

After Lenin's intervention, the commission of the politburo redrafted the resolution proposed by Stalin on uniting the republics, and the October plenary meeting of the CC RCP(B) confirmed it. The draft no longer referred to the entry of the Ukrainian SSR, Belorussian SSR, and Transcaucasian Federation into the RSFSR, but to "the uniting of all Soviet socialist republics into the Union of Soviet Socialist Republics of Europe and Asia."[20] Thus the final formula adopted as its principle the creation of a new state formation instead of the old RSFSR, which many Russian patriots had seen as the basis of a future renewed, great, *one and indivisible* Russian republic. Lenin, as can be seen from his letters on the national question, waged an intensive struggle against all manifestations of Russian imperialist chauvinism. In a memorandum to the politburo of 6 October 1922, he wrote: "I challenge Great Russian chauvinism to mortal combat."[21] Having in view the same aim of eliminating the flourishing of Russian chauvinism, he proposed that in the union TsIK "the chair should be held in turn by a Russian, a Ukrainian, a Georgian, etc. Absolutely!"[22]

Stalin accepted Lenin's amendments as if he had never had anything against them. At the twelfth congress of the RCP, which took place several months later, Stalin spoke as the most faithful disciple and follower of Lenin. During Stalin's rule, his difference with Lenin was passed over in silence, and even if some short extracts from Lenin's attacks on Russian chauvinism were published, Stalin's approval was often added to them. This was the case with Lenin's memorandum of 6 October 1922, first published in 1937 with Stalin's added remark "Correct!"— which implied that Stalin was also in favour of the amendment.[23]

The correspondence between Lenin and Stalin shows that Lenin amended Stalin's autonomization plan under the immediate influence of Budu Mdivani, "a Georg[ian] Communist, suspected of separatism," and of other Communists of the republics.[24] In the correspondence, Stalin accused Lenin of liberalism towards the nationalities.[25] Subsequent events showed that Stalin was not to be tamed by "household remedies," at least not in respect to the Georgian question in which he was personally very much involved; and Lenin therefore decided to appeal to the party at the following congress. He resorted first to letters, which became the basis for a further discussion of the national question at the twelfth congress. In his first letter, dated 30 December 1922, he attacked Stalin directly for his project of autonomization and especially for his policy towards the Georgian Communists:

> From what I was told by comrade Dzerzhinsky, who headed the commission sent by the CC to "investigate" the Georgian incident, I could only draw the greatest apprehensions. If matters had come to such a pass that Ordzhonikidze could go to the extreme of applying physical violence, as

> comrade Dzerzhinsky informed me, we can imagine what a mess we have begot for ourselves. Obviously the whole business of "autonomization" was radically wrong and badly timed.
>
> It is said that a united apparatus was needed. Where did that assurance come from? Did it not come from that same Russian apparatus which, as I pointed out in one of the preceding sections of my diary, we took over from tsarism and slightly anointed with Soviet chrism?
>
> There is no doubt that that measure should have been delayed somewhat until we could say that we vouched for our apparatus as our own ....
>
> It is quite natural that in such circumstances the "freedom to secede from the union" by which we justify ourselves will be a mere scrap of paper, unable to defend the non-Russians from the onslaught of that really Russian man, the Great Russian chauvinist, in substance a rascal and a tyrant, such as is the typical Russian bureaucrat.

Lenin pointed further to the fact that the "fatal role" here was played by "Stalin's haste and his infatuation with pure administration, and also by his spite against the notorious 'nationalist-socialism.'" As to Dzerzhinsky, Lenin explained his role as a product of his "hundred-percent Russian attitude."[26]

In his next letter Lenin emphasized that it was necessary to make a distinction between the nationalism of great oppressing nations and the nationalism of small oppressed nations. Having been oppressed and wronged during their whole history, small nationalities were exceedingly sensitive to all restrictions and injustices. He stressed that "nothing so much delays the development and strengthening of proletarian class solidarity as national injustice, and there is nothing to which the offended nations are more sensitive than to the feeling of equality and to the violation of equality, even if due to negligence, even if in the form of a joke .... This is why in the given case it is better to stretch too much rather than too little in the direction of concessions and kindess towards the national minorities."[27]

In his subsequent notes Lenin proposed these main practical measures towards the solution of the urgent national problem: 1) the union of socialist republics had to be retained and strengthened; about this there could be no doubt; 2) the union of socialist republics in respect of the diplomatic machinery had to be retained; 3) exemplary punishment had to be meted out to comrade Ordzhonikidze, the inquiry had to be completed, and all the facts collected by Dzerzhinsky's commission had to be re-examined; Stalin and Dzerzhinsky had to be held responsible for this truly Great Russian nationalistic campaign; 4) the strictest rules concerning the use of national languages in the national republics entering the union had to be laid down, lest under the pretext of fiscal unity, the unity of the railway service, and so forth, a mass of abuses of a genuinely Russian character be allowed to arise.

In the end Lenin proposed the need for a detailed plan, which only the peoples in a given republic could formulate successfully. He stressed that, as a result, it was impossible to preclude future need for a reversal of policy at the next congress of soviets, the necessity, that is, to retain the Union of Soviet Socialist Republics only in the military and diplomatic spheres, restoring in all other respects the full independence of the separate republican commissariats. He affirmed that the decentralization of the commissariats and the lack of coordination between them and Moscow and other centres could be compensated for by party authority if it were applied with a modicum of circumspection and impartiality.

> The harm which can befall our government through the absence of unified national commissariats with Russian machinery will be incomparably smaller, infinitely smaller, than that harm which can befall, not only us, but also the hundreds of millions in Asia who in the near future are to enter upon the stage of history in our wake. It would be unforgivable opportunism, if on the eve of the emergence of the East and at the beginning of its awakening, we should undermine our prestige there with even the slightest rudeness or injustice to our own minorities. The necessity for solidarity of forces against the international West which defends the capitalist world is one thing. Of this there can be no doubt, and I need not say that I unconditionally approve all those measures. It is another thing when we ourselves fall into something like imperialistic relations with the oppressed nationalities.[28]

The following conclusions may be drawn from these letters of Lenin. Being remote from everyday practical nationality questions, unlike Stalin, who was actually applying Lenin's theory in Ukraine and later (through Ordzhonikidze) in his native Georgia, Lenin analysed these problems realistically, considering them from the point of view of the Communist revolution on the world scale. Knowing that it was the provocation of national feelings in the borderlands and the suspicion of everything Russian (as representing subjugation) which were to a great extent in the way of the development of that revolution, Lenin directed his attacks against the tactless treatment meted out to the borderlands by the Russian Bolsheviks, which treatment was at that time personified by Stalin and his followers from the commissariat for nationalities. In order not to frighten away from the Communist revolution the nationalities of Russia, on the one hand, and those of the colonial countries, on the other, Lenin was prepared for all possible compromises, except, of course, in the matter of "the strengthening of the union of socialist republics." At the twelfth congress of the RCP many opponents of Stalin, like Rakovsky, Mdivani, and Makharadze, referred to Lenin's letters and criticized Stalin and Ordzhonikidze. Avel Enukidze[29] replied that Lenin had written those letters under the influence of "incorrect information" from the "deviationists" who had exploited his illness. He asserted that Ordzhonikidze had in fact acted correctly, keeping to the directives of the CC, and that also Lenin himself, after "explanations" and "clarification," had "agreed with the policy that was being carried out there by comrade Ordzhonikidze."[30]

During the discussion about the new forms of the union the question of the name of the new formation also arose. This question had been touched upon previously, and beginning with the tenth congress of the RCP it reached the stage of concrete formulation. During the discussion of Stalin's report, the Ukrainian delegate, Zatonsky, maintained that the preservation of the old name of the RSFSR led to a deviation in favour of the *edinaia i nedelimaia* among a considerable section of the Communists, and he proposed the denationalization of the name. He emphasized that many Russian Bolsheviks were enthusiastic about "Red Russian patriotism," that they "proudly ... regard themselves as Russians, and sometimes even consider themselves to be Russians first and foremost," and that these Communists "do not value Soviet power and Soviet federation as much as they have a trend towards the '*edinaia i nedelimaia*.'"[31] "We must," continued Zatonsky, "extirpate from the minds of the comrades the idea of the Soviet federation as being necessarily a 'Russian' federation, for the point is not that it is Russian, but that it is Soviet. If, e.g., Romania is Soviet, if there is a Soviet Germany and another series of federations, will they also be called Russian? No. The fact that the federation is 'Russian' (*rossiiskaia*) causes enormous confusion in the minds of party comrades. This name ought simply to be removed, or simply the name 'Soviet federation' should be preserved, or some other name should be invented." In Zatonsky's theses, which he, in Stalin's words, "for some reason did not put forward for the attention of the congress," there was a proposal that the name of the "Russian" SFSR be changed to "East European," and the term *rossiiskaia* be replaced by the word *russkaia* or *velikorusskaia*.[32] This was an attempt to narrow down the old imperial name, *rossiskaia*, which had a meaning similar to that of "Great Britain" for England.

The question of the name was brought up by Frunze, who at that time was a Ukrainian delegate, at the tenth all-Russian congress of soviets on 26 December 1922. He said that the new name, proposed by Ukraine, aimed at "the abolition of all former proper national names. We have decided that you should renounce the name of the RSFSR." He continued that the name "RSFSR" was "much too narrow for that meaning which we intend giving it. It is not at the boundaries of the RSFSR, Ukraine, Georgia, and other Soviet republics, but at the boundaries of the whole world that our work of state building can be completed." For that reason Ukraine rejected the name "Federation of Europe and Asia" in the hope that the peoples of America, Australia, and "black-skinned Africa" would also join soon. "This is why the name proposed by us, 'the Union of Soviet Socialist Republics,' is the best one for this association of states which we are creating." The creation of this union, in Frunze's opinion, was only the first step towards the creation of "a Universal Soviet Republic of Labour."[33] At the fifth congress of soviets of Ukraine, one of the delegates went so far as to express the hope that the majority of the participants of the congress might live to see the time when the capital of the Soviet republics would not be Moscow but London.[34] Such airy prospects were pictured by some Communists.

It is impossible to establish with certainty who was the first to propose the name "USSR." According to Frunze's words, this name was "proposed by us," i.e., by Ukraine, in whose name he spoke. This name is found in documents for the first time in the declaration of the seventh congress of soviets of the Ukrainian SSR "concerning the creation of the Union of Soviet Socialist Republics" of 13 December 1922 and in the resolution of the same congress "concerning the principles of the constitution of the Union of Soviet Socialist Republics" of the same date.[35] However, this name appears also in the resolution of the first Transcaucasian congress of soviets of 13 December 1922.[36]

On the Bicameral Legislative System

In connection with the establishment of the union constitution the question of the distribution of the legislative and executive powers of the federal organs also arose. The majority of party leaders favoured a strong centralization of power and the concentration of both the executive and the legislative functions in one body. The party held the view that the legislative power had to be formally concentrated in the congress of soviets elected in general elections. However, while creating a union state, the party was compelled to reconcile this principle with the system of federation, i.e., the division of power between the federal organs and those of the union republics. In all federative states there usually exist two houses, one of which represents the interests and will of the units of the federation. Stalin, who was in a manner of speaking the mentor of uniting the Soviet republics with the RSFSR, rejected the idea of a bicameral system for the Soviet federation from the very beginning. He remarked in

1918 that the system to which the American and Swiss federations had given birth, "on the one hand, the parliament, elected on the principle of general elections; on the other, the federal council, formed by the states or cantons," was not going to come to life again. He emphasized that such a bicameral system normally led "to the usual bourgeois legislative dilatoriness. It goes without saying that the working masses of Russia will not acquiesce in such a bicameral system. We will not even mention the complete unsuitability of this system for the elementary requirements of socialism." Stalin expressed the hope that "the congress of soviets, elected by all the working masses of Russia, or the central executive committee which acts in its place, will be the supreme organ of power in the Russian federation."[37] He expressed the same opinion again in 1922. After the October plenary meeting of the CC RCP had accepted the project concerning the uniting of the republics, in November, in an interview with a *Pravda* correspondent, he declared that the supreme organs of power for the union should be the union TsIK, elected by "the republics comprising the union in proportion to the population represented by them," and the union Council of People's Commissars, elected by the union TsIK. He further stressed that the need had been voiced "for the creation, apart from the two union organs (the TsIK and the CPC), of a third union organ, intermediate between the two, so to speak, of an *upper* house with representation from the nationalities in equal numbers from each; but this opinion undoubtedly will not meet with sympathy in the national republics, if only because the bicameral system with the existence of an upper house is incompatible with socialist construction, at least at this given stage of its development."[38]

Stalin apparently defended this viewpoint stubbornly. The second chamber was mentioned neither at the tenth all-Russian congress of soviets at which were accepted the principles of a treaty among the republics concerning the creation of the union,[39] nor in Stalin's speech at the first congress of soviets of the USSR on 30 December 1922,[40] nor in the "declaration concerning the creation of the Union of Soviet Socialist Republics." However, Stalin had to capitulate before the demand of the national Communists, chiefly the Ukrainians, and recognize a second chamber, the soviet of nationalities.

The question of a second chamber was brought up prior to the congress by the representatives of the nationalities in the section devoted to the nationalities.[41] Since there are no minutes of the meetings of that section or of the plenary meetings of the CC of the party, it is impossible to establish precisely the course of discussion on the question. In the theses presented by Stalin at the plenary meeting of the CC of the party on

12–14 February 1923, there is already a reference to "a special organ for the representation of all national republics and national regions without exception [and] on the principles of equality." The creation of this organ was motivated by the consideration that the supreme organs of the union had to be constructed so as to "reflect fully not only the *general* needs and requirements of the whole proletariat, but also the *special* needs and requirements of separate nationalities."[42] Stalin admitted at the twelfth party congress in April 1923 that a stubborn struggle was being waged over the second chamber, chiefly its composition in the section dealing with nationalities.[43] Some non-Russian Communists, especially the Ukrainians, maintained that the second chamber, i.e., the soviet of nationalities, had to reflect the interests of the treaty republics, i.e., the members of the federation, as is customary in other federations.

It must be pointed out that the soviet of nationalities was not like the American Senate or the Council of the Cantons in Switzerland, which have the same, or even greater, prerogatives of a legislative character as the House of Representatives in the USA or the National Council in Switzerland, and in which the members of the federation are equally represented; nor was it like the corresponding organ in the Weimar republic, where the proportion of the population of the states was of importance, under the proviso that no member of the federation could have more than two-fifths of all the votes in the Reichsrat.

Stalin and the majority of Communists did not want the soviet of nationalities (the second chamber) to have equal rights with the congress of soviets; they wanted the interim legislative organ, the VTsIK, to be divided into two houses, the union soviet and the soviet of nationalities, which would be equal. When argument arose on the matter, it was primarily over whether the soviet of nationalities was to represent the treaty republics—the RSFSR, the Transcaucasian Federation, Ukraine, and Belorussia—or all nationalities without exception. Stalin held that in the soviet of nationalities "all republics (both the independent and the autonomous ones) and all national regions were to be represented."[44]

Stalin's opponents, whose spokesman at the twelfth congress was the chairman of the Soviet of People's Commissars of the Ukrainian republic, Rakovsky, maintained that such a system obviously favoured the RSFSR which, having within itself many nationalities with autonomous status, would obtain an overwhelming majority in the soviet of nationalities. In his declaration at the same congress, Rakovsky showed himself to be a staunch enemy of Russian chauvinism. Thus he proposed such a ratio of forces in the soviet of nationalities as would eliminate the domination of the RSFSR over other republics. Speaking "in the name of all Ukrainian comrades,"[45] he declared that the section dealing with nationalities had committed a great mistake by accepting Stalin's formula on the bicameral system. He remarked that the point of a bicameral system was the provision of guarantees for individual republics, while the system proposed by Stalin established an arrangement whereby out of 360 delegates of the union TsIK, 280 "and perhaps even more" would belong to the RSFSR, while the rest, 80 delegates, would belong to all the independent republics taken together. Stalin's system was accepted also in respect to the second chamber (the soviet of nationalities). The equality of nationalities actually meant the inequality of the treaty republics. In accordance with Stalin's system, fifteen autonomous republics and regions belonging to the RSFSR would have four votes each,[46] and Russia itself, Ukraine, the three Transcaucasian republics, and Belorussia also four votes each. "What then is the outcome?" asked Rakovsky. "The outcome," he himself answered, "is that in fact the RSFSR will have sixty-four or seventy votes, Ukraine will have four votes, Belorussia will have four votes." Rakovsky was ready to sign the most radical project if Stalin would permit Kirghizia, Turkestan, and all other autonomous republics to become independent republics, which would enter the second chamber separately and independently. He maintained that Stalin's proposal was a contrivance for establishing the supremacy of the RSFSR. He considered that the second chamber should not comprise "nationalities but state associations." He proposed that the RSFSR should be satisfied with not more than two-fifths of the votes in the second chamber and should divide them among various autonomous republics. "But if the RSFSR wishes to give an example of the liberalism and democratic nationalism which comrade Stalin wields against our bicameral system, let the RSFSR create a second chamber in its VTsIK to which these republics would be invited." He proposed that "none of the state associations comprising the second chamber can have more than two-fifths of all the votes."[47]

That Stalin accepted the bicameral system which he had been rejecting so stubbornly and began to stress the struggle against Russian chauvinism testifies to that chain of compromises which the secretary of the CC RCP(B) was compelled to make, apparently under pressure from Lenin and a part of the politburo and surely not without the influence of Communists like Rakovsky from the republics.[48] Stalin himself at the twelfth congress also noted those amendments which had been accepted by the nationalities section.[49] However, the acceptance of the principle of a second chamber did not mean that Stalin had abandoned his plans to secure a leading role for the RSFSR. On the contrary, he emphasized that it would have been dangerous for the proletarian revolution to show favour to the borderlands. He stressed that the political bases of the proletarian dictatorship were first and foremost the central industrial regions and not the borderlands, which were peasant countries. "If we overdo it in favour of the peasant borderlands, to the detriment of the proletarian regions, the result may be a crack in the system of the dictatorship of the proletariat. This is dangerous, comrades."[50] This was to a certain extent an attempt at self-justification in the face of the accusations of Lenin, who held that, on the contrary, in the policy towards the nationalities it was necessary rather to overdo it in favour of the borderlands.[51]

Stalin attacked Rakovsky in a rather demagogic fashion. He immediately remarked that by the acceptance of Rakovsky's amendments his theses were turned upside down. "Rakovsky proposes to construct the second chamber in such a way," Stalin said, "that it would be comprised of the representatives of state associations. He considers that Ukraine is a state association, while Bashkiria is not. Why? In fact, we are not abolishing the councils of people's commissars in the republics. Is the TsIK of Bashkiria not a state institution!? And why is Bashkiria not a state? Will Ukraine cease to be a state after entering the union?"[52] In a word, Stalin took up again the simplified qualification of autonomy that he had defended previously, according to which the autonomy of Bashkiria and of Ukraine was similar. For Stalin, Rakovsky's arguments were "state fetishism" and a passion "for the Prussian system of constructing a federation."[53] Stalin argued that all nationalities and chiefly the eastern ones had to be represented in the second chamber, for it was important with regard to the eastern nationalities' proximity to China and India and to the development of the revolution in the East. Stalin, if he had wished to be consistent, should have recognized actual—and not merely formal—equality for the nationalities of the East. In fact, an autonomous republic possessed much less sovereignty, even formally, than the union republics, not to mention the autonomous national regions which possessed even fewer rights than the autonomous republics. Stalin knew very well that the subjects of the USSR were not all the nationalities, but only "all the republics, including the four republics—Transcaucasia, Belorussia, Ukraine, and the RSFSR—which comprise the union [and] renounce to an equal degree some of their rights of independence in favour of the union"; nevertheless, he argued, they preserved the elements of independence "since each republic has the right of a unilateral secession from membership in the union. This is where the elements of independence are; this is the maximum of potential independence which remains with each of the republics comprising the union and which [each of them] can always realize." This was said by Stalin at the same twelfth congress.[54] The fact that the autonomous republics and regions enjoyed no such right was known to Stalin as well. It was because the union was formed by the four republics and not by all nationalities that Rakovsky's argument could withstand criticism.

The Prerogatives of the Union and the Union Republics

During the elaboration of the final form of the constitution of the new USSR the question was bound to arise concerning the powers of the union organs and of the organs of the union republics. A struggle was waged in the constitutional commission between the centralizing and the decentralizing trends; protagonists of the former were Stalin and his followers, while the latter was represented by the Ukrainian and other national Communists. Of course, this division not only had a national colouring, it reflected also the factional struggle within the party. Otherwise it is impossible to explain the defence of the subjugated nationalities at the twelfth congress of the RCP by such Russophiles and advocates of *edinaia i nedelimaia* as Bukharin, Radek, Rakovsky, Iakovlev, and Zinovev.[55] However, the opposition against Stalin was led not by these anti-Stalinists, but by the national oppositionists.

The formal uniting of the republics to form the Union of Soviet Socialist Republics was effected by the "treaty concerning the creation of the Union of Soviet Socialist Republics," signed on 30 December 1922 and adopted by the first congress of soviets of the USSR on the same day.[56] The treaty established the chief legal and political outlines of the new union and the relationships of the union with the union republics. The four republics: the RSFSR, Ukraine, Belorussia, and the Transcaucasian Federation, united "into one union state." The following powers were handed over to the supreme organs of the union: the representation of the union in international relations; the alteration of the external boundaries of the union; the conclusion of treaties concerning the admittance into the union of new republics; the declaration of war and the concluding of peace; the negotiation of external state loans; the ratification of international treaties; the establishment of the system of external and internal trade; the establishment of the principles and general plan of the whole national economy of the union, as well as the concluding of concessional treaties; the regulation of transport, postal, and telegraph affairs; the establishment of the principles of the organization of the armed forces of the Union of Soviet Socialist Republics; the ratification of a single state budget of the Union of Soviet Socialist Republics; the establishment of the system of coinage, money, and credit, as well as of the system of all-union, republican and local taxes; the establishment of the common principles of land order and agriculture, as well as of the use of subterranean riches, forests, and waters throughout the territory of the union; a common union legislation concerning migration; the establishment of the principles of the structure and administration of the judicature, as well as civil and criminal union legislation; the establishment of basic labour laws; the establishment of the general principles of popular education; the establishment of general measures in the domain of the protection of the people's health; the establishment of the system of weights and measures; the organization of all-union statistics; basic legislation in the domain of union citizenship in respect to the rights of foreigners; the right of general amnesty; the revoking of the decisions of the congresses of soviets, of central executive committees, and of councils of people's commissars of union republics contravening the union treaty.

It was further established that the supreme organ of power in the union was the congress of soviets, and in the period between the latter's sessions the central executive committee. The delegates to the congress of soviets were to be elected at district congresses of soviets.[57] The congress of soviets of the USSR was to elect the TsIK of the union, totalling 371 members, from the representatives of the union republics in proportion to the population of each republic.[58] The congresses of soviets and the sessions of the union TsIK were to be convoked in the capitals of the union republics according to a sequence established by the presidium of the union TsIK. This decision was never carried out in practice and was later deleted. The presidium of the union TsIK was to be elected, comprising nineteen members, from which the union TsIK was to elect four presidents of the union TsIK to correspond with the number of union republics. In the treaty the number of the people's commissariats of the union was set at five (foreign affairs, military and naval affairs, foreign trade, lines of communication, post and telegraph). The four people's commissariats (food, finance, labour, and worker's and peasants' inspectorate) and the supreme council of people's economy existed in the union as well as in the union republics, but they had to be guided by the orders of the corresponding commissariats of the union. The people's commissariats for agriculture, internal affairs, justice, education, health, social insurance, and national affairs belonged only to the union republics, and there were no corresponding union commissariats. The representatives of the union commissariats (foreign affairs, military and naval affairs, foreign trade, lines of communication, post and telegraph) belonged to the people's commissars of the union republics in a consultative capacity. A single union citizenship was established for the citizens of the union republics. The treaty guaranteed for the union republics the rights of free secession from the union.[59]

As will be seen, this treaty later underwent essential changes on many points during the elaboration of the constitution of the union, and was the subject of lively discussion. The party, personified by Stalin and his followers from the CC RCP, aimed at producing the most centralistic constitution possible and struggled with the opposition of the nationalities.

The elaboration of the constitution of the union was entrusted to an expanded commission composed of twenty-five members: fourteen members from the RSFSR, five from the Ukrainian SSR, three each from Belorussia and the Transcaucasian Federation.[60] If we consider the composition of this commission and of other commissions of a constitutional character generally (as for instance, the commission for the elaboration of regulations concerning the CPC, the council of labour and defence, and the people's commissariats of the union, which consisted of Kalinin, Sapronov, Aleksandr Cherviakov, Mdivani, Aleksei Rykov, Piatakov, Enukidze, Aleksandr Tsiurupa, Dmitrii Kursky, Andrei Andreev, Varlaam Avanesov, Aleksandr Beloborodov, Viktor Nogin, Rakovsky, and Manuilsky—with few exceptions, centralists of the *edinaia i nedelimaia* type),[61] and if, moreover, we consider that the CC RCP commission worked parallel with the TsIK commission and in fact dictated to it,[62] it may be imagined that the will of the union republics was not taken into serious consideration during the elaboration of the constitution.

The TsIKs of the union republics had to send in their considerations to the commission of the TsIK by 20 May.[63] Unfortunately, it has been impossible to obtain those considerations; however, those extracts that Stalin quoted in his speech at the fourth conference of the CC RCP(B) with the functionaries of the national republics and regions indicate that the considerations of the republics were often at cross purposes with the party line. It may be seen from the Ukrainian project that the TsIK of Ukraine adopted the platform of an extended federation or even a confederation. For instance, the phrase stating that the republics "unite into one union state" was deleted in this project. It proposed leaving the people's commissariats for foreign affairs and foreign trade in the category of directive commissariats, i.e., leaving them also in the union republics.[64] Stalin severely attacked the Ukrainian project:

> Is it by chance that the Ukrainian comrades, considering the known project of the constitution . . . , deleted from it the phrase stating that the republics 'unite into one union state'? . . . Why did they delete this phrase? Is it a coincidence that the Ukrainian comrades proposed in their counter-project not to merge the PCFTs [people's commissariats for foreign trade] and the

PCFAs [people's commissariats for foreign affairs] but to transfer them into the category of directive [commissariats]? Where is, then, the single union state, if every republic retains its own PCFT and PCFA? Is it a coincidence that the Ukrainians reduced to zero the power of the presidium of the TsIK in their counter-project, dividing it between the two presidiums of two houses?[65] ... I see in this insistence of certain Ukrainian comrades the desire to achieve in the definition of the character of the union something intermediate between a confederation and a federation, with a preference for a confederation. Meanwhile, it is clear that we are creating not a confederation, but a federation of republics, a single union state which unites the military, foreign affairs, foreign trade, and other affairs, a state whose existence does not reduce the sovereignty of separate republics.[66]

It can be seen from Stalin's declaration at the following day's session of the conference of the CC RCP(B) with the functionaries of the republics, that the Ukrainian Bolsheviks Rakovsky and Skrypnyk accused Stalin of Russian imperialism and of favouring *edinaia i nedelimaia.* They proposed to substitute for the phrase, "the republics *unite into one union state*," the phrase, "the republics form a *union of socialist republics*." It was in this phrase, as well as in the amendment concerning the PCFTs and the PCFAs, that Stalin discerned the separatism and confederalism of the Ukrainian Bolsheviks. Hence he concluded, not without grounds, that "some of the Ukrainian comrades underwent a certain evolution from federalism to confederalism during the period from the first congress of the union of republics to the twelfth congress of the party and the present conference."[67]

The Ukrainians manifested these "separatist," though actually merely decentralizing, tendencies also in their demands for the separation of the union council of people's commissars from the Russian one, and for the creation for this purpose of a separate council of people's commissars for the RSFSR. Rakovsky declared in his interview with the *Pravda* correspondent, Belogorsky, on 16 September 1922, that "for the sake of the complete authoritativeness of the union organs, they must be separated from the Russian central institutions."[68] The Ukrainian representatives in the commission of the union TsIK for the elaboration of the constitution had a somewhat different project with regard to the number of commissariats to be merged. They suggested that among the *merged* commissariats should be those for military affairs, lines of communication, and post and telegraph. Among the *directive* commissariats were to be those for foreign affairs, foreign trade, finance, food, labour, and the supreme council of national economy and that of the workers' and peasants' inspectorate. The remaining commissariats were to belong to the union republics only with completely autonomous rights.[69] To safeguard the interests of the republics, Rakovsky proposed that the union republics should have a guaranteed right of participation in the union government. He suggested that the republics ought to have their representatives on the boards of the merged commissariats with full members' rights. In foreign countries, whose economic or other ties with one of the union republics were stronger than with the others, the right of preponderance in the diplomatic representation had to be granted to that republic with the right of nominating the head of the union mission.[70] Rakovsky's intentions in this last proposal are open to speculation. It seems that he intended to secure priority for Ukraine, whose economic contacts with many European countries were more developed even than those of the RSFSR. On the other hand, in view of the subordinate position of the CP(B)U within the RCP(B), so that the latter in fact determined the whole foreign policy, Rakovsky's intentions are unclear.

Be that as it may, the proposal of the Ukrainians took away from the union, as Stalin pointed out, the right of acting before the outside world as a single state,[71] and the politburo of the CC RCP(B) rejected the Ukrainian proposal[72] and adopted as a basis for the constitution the proposal elaborated by the commission of the USSR's TsIK.[73]

In spite of the opposition of the Ukrainians and other "nationals,"[74] the centralistic line, defined by the commission of the CC RCP, won the day, except on certain minor points. The Ukrainian amendments suffered defeat both at the plenary meeting of the CC RCP(B) and at the extended commission of the union TsIK, and finally at the second session of the union TsIK on 6 June 1923, which adopted the constitution. It may be seen from comparison of the final version of the constitution with the treaty of the union of 30 December 1922 that the Ukrainians' amendments were unsuccessful. While the treaty refers to "the representation of the union in international relations," the constitution adds to this paragraph "the conduct of all diplomatic relations." While the treaty refers only to "the alteration of the external boundaries of the union," the constitution adds to this "also the settling of questions concerning changes of boundaries between the union republics." The section of the constitution referring to taxes is likewise characterized by the expansion of the competence of the union. On the whole, the constitution is permeated by the tendency to increase the powers of the union at the cost of the union republics, with the union being no longer satisfied with establishment of principles of policy and administration alone but claiming the actual leadership.

In this connection the following question arises: Why was it that, in spite of Lenin's apparent support of the nationalities and the apparently favourable attitude of the party twelfth congress to the national demands, the amendments of the representatives of the union republics did not find suitable recognition during the elaboration of the constitution? First, the success of the centralists and the partisans of the *edinaia i nedelimaia* can be attributed to the composition of the commission of the TsIK, and even more to that of the commission of the CC RCP(B), which as has been mentioned above consisted predominantly of Russian centralists. Secondly, the dependence of the delegates of the union republics on the CC RCP(B) in respect to both ideology and organization was important. Rakovsky, Skrypnyk, Makharadze, and other oppositionists could be dismissed from their party and government positions whenever the CC RCP(B) wished. It must also be added that the opposition representing the Soviet republics was numerically weak and was often outvoted by the purely Russian delegates. We may quote as an example the composition of the tenth all-Russian congress of soviets, which subsequently changed its name to the first congress of soviets of the USSR, and which adopted the treaty of the union of the republics. In accordance with the statistical data given in the appendix to the shorthand report of the congress, the territorial origin of the delegates was as is shown in Table 39.

Table 39. Delegates to the First Congress of Soviets of the USSR by Republic of Origin, 1922

		Percentage
RSFSR	1,694	77.7
Ukrainian SSR	377	16.9
Transcaucasian republics	93	4.1
Belorussia	27	1.3
Total	2,191	

SOURCE: *Desiatyi vserossiiskii sezd sovetov rabochikh, krestianskikh, krasnoarmeiskikh i kazachikh deputatov, 23-27 dekabria 1922 goda. Stenograficheskii otchet s prilozheniiami* (Moscow, 1923), diagrams.

By nationality the delegates were divided as in Table 40. Thus from the territorial point of view the delegates of the RSFSR dominated completely, and with regard to nationality the Russians also had a majority. If one takes into account that many non-Russian delegates, for instance the Jews and also the Georgians and even the Ukrainians, were Russified and more fervent Russian patriots than the Russians themselves, it may be imagined how small were the chances of a tiny handful of oppositionists.

Table 40. Delegates to the First Congress of Soviets of the USSR by Nationality, 1922

		Percentage
Russians	1,393	62.5
Jews	238	10.8
Ukrainians	176	8.0
Turkic nationalities	124	5.7
Caucasian nationalities	98	4.5
Latvians and Estonians	74	3.4
Belorussians	24	1.1
Others	87	4.0

SOURCE: *Desiatyi vserossiiskii sezd sovetov rabochikh, krestianskikh, krasnoarmeiskikh i kazachikh deputatov, 23-27 dekabria 1922 goda. Stenograficheskii otchet s prilozheniiami* (Moscow, 1923), diagrams.

The majority of the RSFSR at subsequent congresses of soviets of the USSR gradually decreased: at the second congress, the RSFSR had 69.2 per cent; at the third, 69 per cent; at the fourth, 68.3 per cent of delegates with full voting rights. The Ukrainian SSR had at the second congress 15.9 per cent; at the third, 18.8 per cent; at the fourth, 19.4 per cent. The same trend was noticeable with respect to the other nationalities. (The nationality of delegates to the fourth congress is shown in Table 41.)

However, it is impossible to deny the influence of the national opposition during the formulation of the union constitution of 1923. The struggle between the centralists and the decentralists just described is clear evidence of this. The fact is that it was thanks to this opposition that Stalin's plan for incorporation of the republics into the Russian federal republic on autonomous principles was rejected; it was also thanks to this opposition that the TsIK of the union was divided into two chambers, one of which became the soviet of nationalities. This chamber later became the arena of disputes between the centralists and the decentralists, chiefly over the delimitation of powers between the union organs and the organs of the union republics. It is not true, as is asserted by an expert on Soviet affairs, that "no continuous debates on matters of substance took place in either chamber."[75] The minutes of the meetings of both chambers between 1923 and 1926 bear witness to exactly the opposite. As will be seen below, the dispute over the powers of the union and of the union republics went on until the establishment of Stalin's regime. There is no doubt that, without the opposition of the representatives of the republics, the constitution of

Table 41. Delegates to the Fourth Congress of Soviets of the USSR by Nationality, 1927

		Percentage
Russians	905	56.6
Ukrainians	255	15.9
Jews	60	3.8
Belorussians	56	3.5
Kirghizians	53	3.3
Latvians	41	2.6
Uzbeks	31	1.9
Tatars	26	1.6
Georgians	25	1.5
Turkic nationalities	17	1.1
Armenians	14	0.9
Bashkirs	10	0.6
Germans	9	0.6
Mordvinians	7	0.4
Poles	7	0.4
Tadzhiks	7	0.4
Turkmens	6	0.4
Chuvashes	6	0.4
Various	67	4.0

SOURCE: *Chetvertyi sezd sovetov SSSR. Biuleten,* No. 18 (1927), pp. 6-8.

the union would have had a different aspect, and the republics would have been left with a minimum of rights. They would probably have become merely parts of the RSFSR as Stalin envisaged from the outset.

The chief spokesmen for the nationalities on the constitution were the Communist delegates from Ukraine, Skrypnyk and Rakovsky. The latter may be called a Ukrainian delegate only in the territorial sense, although by that time he had changed his attitude to the question of nationalities in general and to the Ukrainian question in particular. Now he defended the prerogatives of the union republics the same way that Skrypnyk did. It is difficult to explain Rakovsky's evolution towards republican separatism or at least particularism. Some authors attribute it to his antagonism towards Stalin, his adherence to the left opposition, and his sympathies towards Trotsky.[76] Others see in it some traces of Skrypnyk's influence.[77] It is quite possible that a rather important role in Rakovsky's attitude was also played by the personal motives characteristic of many careerists, e.g., his desire for the position of premier of a great state (the Ukrainian SSR had at that time a population of over thirty million and a territory of 443,000 square kilometres). It is possible that it was at that time that Rakovsky hesitated (or even made his choice) between the premiership in the Ukrainian SSR and a secondary and uncertain position in the union. After the establishment of the union, Rakovsky was appointed deputy people's commissar for foreign affairs and sent to Britain in the role of ambassador of the USSR.[78]

However, it was not Rakovsky but Skrypnyk who played first fiddle in the Ukrainian opposition against the *edinaia i nedelimaia* trend. Skrypnyk played this role from the very beginning of the establishment of Soviet rule in Ukraine and continued to struggle for the equality of the nationalities in the union until his suicide in 1933. Skrypnyk was a convinced Communist, but his national conscience apparently made him oppose the Russifying policy of the majority of the RCP. He demanded that the party implement the principles of Lenin's nationality policy.[79] Skrypnyk showed himself to be an indefatigable defender of the rights of small peoples, both during the discussions on the constitution[80] and later during the formulation of the competencies of the central organs and those of the union republics. The struggle of Skrypnyk and of other nationals in the commissions for the elaboration of the regulations concerning the competencies of the supreme organs of power show that the opponents of Stalin and his followers in this discussion were primarily the "national Communists"—Ukrainian, Georgian, and others—and not, as is asserted by Pipes, "the anti-Stalin opposition."[81] In fact, the anti-Stalin opposition was only in the process of formation in 1922–23, and its personal composition was changing during the twenties. Perhaps Rakovsky alone may be counted among the anti-Stalinists who spoke on the question of nationalities in 1923. However, the question is—did Rakovsky act in a common front with the national communist Skrypnyk only because of his sympathies with Trotsky? In fact, Rakovsky, being the head of the government of the Ukrainian SSR, had to obey directives of the all-Ukrainian TsIK.[82]

Ukrainian Opposition

No concrete regulations concerning the supreme organs of the union were established either by the treaty uniting the republics or by the constitution adopted on 6 July 1923 by the TsIK. They merely established the main principles of the administration and those of the mutual relationships between the union and the republics. The task of making concrete regulations was entrusted to the third session of the TsIK which was to meet on 6 November 1923.[83] However, these regulations went on being elaborated right through 1924–25.

The meeting of the TsIK on 6 November 1923 showed that there was profound disagreement on matters of principle between the national opposition and the centralists concerning the competencies of the central union organs and the organs of the union republics. The centralists, represented at this meeting by the secretary of the union TsIK, Enukidze, advocated the empirical approach to legislation, i.e., the introduction of changes and amendments in legislation on the basis of experience.[84] Skrypnyk, speaking with the approval of the representatives of the union republics, held the view that the powers of the central and republican organs had to be fixed in advance.[85]

The chief amendments introduced by Skrypnyk, who was a member of the constitutional commission representing the Ukrainian SSR, referred to the union TsIK and to the powers of the soviet of people's commissars. He insisted that "all decrees and decisions referring to substantial changes in the political and economic life of the union and introducing radical changes into the existing practice of the state organs of the union as well as all codes of laws should come up for confirmation by the TsIK of the union."[86] In accordance with this the constitutional commission adopted the decision that "the soviet of people's commissars issues decrees and decisions only as a development, and on the basis, of legislation issued by the central executive committee of the union." This formulation was rejected by the presidium of the TsIK. Another amendment, which was adopted and remained in the constitution, referred to the right of amnesty. Accordingly, it was said in article 1, point (c), that among the competencies of the union was "the right of amnesty extending over the whole territory of the union," while article 69 stated that "the right of amnesty as well as the right of reprieve and rehabilitation in respect of citizens sentenced by the juridical and administrative organs of the union republics is preserved for the TsIKs of these republics." Skrypnyk demanded that these principles be recorded also in the "regulations" concerning the council of people's commissars of the USSR.[87]

Skrypnyk attempted to introduce an amendment into the "regulations" concerning the council of people's commissars to the effect that on matters of disagreement between the council of people's commissars of the union, on the one hand, and the councils of people's commissars and the TsIKs of the union republics, on the other, the jurisdiction of the CPC of the union should be limited to the consideration of the matter only and should not extend to its solution. The solution of such a conflict was to belong to the competency of the presidium of the TsIK of the union. Skrypnyk emphasized that this question had a fundamental significance, and that to hand over to the CPC of the union the right to solve these conflicts was anti-constitutional because it "removes the dependence of the CPC of a union republic on the TsIK of a union republic" which was established by the constitution.[88] With reference to the right of "vetoing the decisions of the council of people's commissars of the union," Skrypnyk likewise proposed an amendment which amounted to the suggestion that this right was to belong not only to the people's commissars of the union republics, but also "to the plenipotentiary representatives of the union republics attached to the union." "This is a necessary safeguard for the interests of the union republics within the limits of the constitution."[89] Skrypnyk also demanded that the title as well as the character of the "plenipotentiary representative of the union republic" should be preserved, because the new title, that of a "representative of the union republic authorized especially to be present in the soviet of people's commissars," provided for the republics to have a whole series of "authorized representatives." This apparently abolished the principle in accordance with which each union republic authorized one appropriate functionary who represented its interests in all organs "and throughout the whole passage of legislative questions in all the organs of the union."[90] The centralists introduced into the "regulation concerning the council of people's commissars" a point (g) concerning the "conferences of the non-merged people's commissars of the union." Skrypnyk protested against this point as being anti-constitutional, for it turned these conferences into some special governing organ of the union. He stressed that these conferences were the forum "of the factual coordination of work," "but these conferences are not organs of the union, and we (the workers of the non-merged people's commissariats of the union republics) shall give an account of them, in accordance with the constitutions of our union republics, to the people's commissariats and to the TsIKs of the union republics." He also resisted granting the right of legislative initiative to these conferences.[91]

All these endeavours by Skrypnyk were in vain because the presidium of the union TsIK rejected all his amendments and introduced into the "regulations concerning the council of people's commissars" such principles as corresponded to the intentions of the CC RCP(B).

Nevertheless, opposition of the Ukrainian national Communists continued, as can be seen from some typical examples during discussion of the budgetary powers of the union and the union republics. Presenting the opinion of the all-Ukrainian TsIK, Skrypnyk declared that, from the constitutional point of view, the project concerning the budgetary rights of the USSR and the union republics "requires serious amendment." The last session of the all-Ukrainian TsIK, he declared, had considered all the projects submitted to the session of the TsIK of the union, and it had been established that "some of the articles submitted cannot be recognized as corresponding to the constitution of the USSR and to the regulations concerning the TsIK of the USSR, nor to the decisions of the TsIK of the USSR on budgetary questions which had been adopted previously."[92] He pointed out that the all-Ukrainian TsIK saw no reason why "*the income from direct taxes*, revenues, and customs" should be ceded exclusively to the income side of the common union budget. "We consider," Skrypnyk continued, "that the whole income deriving from the population of the union republics must be allotted in varying ratio for the satisfaction of the needs, both of the whole union and of each union republic."[93] In Skrypnyk's view, the project of the people's commissar for finance, Grigorii Sokolnikov, showed a trend towards making the union republics dependent on "the benevolence of comrade Sokolnikov and on deductions from the common union budget." He urged that the budgets of the union republics be constructed so "that every union republic would live according to its means and arrange the distribution of its means accordingly." "But comrade Sokolnikov constructs [them] according to a different rule: he who holds the purse, has influence [and] gives orders."[94] Skrypnyk admitted that the union, as represented by its supreme organ, must establish the basic principles of policy to be carried out throughout the territory of the union, but he emphasized that "daily life and daily activity in the sphere of cultural rights, in the sphere of the national culture of each people comprising our union are the inalienable possessions of the union republics of our union."[95] In the union soviet, the same remarks on the "regulations concerning the budgetary rights of the union and the union republics" were submitted by the Ukrainian delegates, N. Kuznetsov and Chubar.[96] The latter emphasized that the regulations contradicted the decisions of the party's twelfth congress, which had decided to broaden the budgetary rights of the republics. Yet the formulation of these rights by the people's commissar "tends to limit the rights [of the republics] rather than to broaden them."[97]

The most acute friction between the opposition and the centralists arose during discussion of the regulations concerning the structure of the judiciary at the second session of the TsIK of the union on 22 October 1924. Skrypnyk and Krylenko, both experts on the Soviet constitution, had to act in defence of the Soviet republics. Attention was again drawn to the violation of the principles of the constitution and the limitation of the sovereignty of the republics. For instance, Krylenko stressed that in the proposed "regulations concerning the structure and administration of the judicature, criminal legislation, and military crimes," not only were the principles of the structure of the judicature fixed, but also the details were elaborated. He felt that the project usurped the powers of the union republics in the spheres "of the social, political, cultural, and economic life of the republics, which were referred by the constitution, with the exception of their basic principles, entirely to the jurisdiction and the competency of the union republics, represented by their sovereign supreme organs."[98] Krylenko acknowledged that it was necessary to establish the principles of the functions of courts, but he said that "the concrete forms with which the content of these functions should be invested" were to be defined by the republics themselves on the basis of their political and national circumstances and their way of life.[99] Skrypnyk demanded a firm delimitation of the competencies to accord with the principle that "within the limits of the constitution, the union is sovereign; within the limits of the constitution, each republic is also sovereign." "We have no single and indivisible state (*edinoe nedelimoe gosudarstvo*)." However, Skrypnyk had his doubts on this point. "Tell [me], please, dear comrades," Skrypnyk asked, "is our union not becoming a single and indivisible state, if according to one of the drafts the union republics have no citizens (as in the original draft of the decree concerning union citizenship), according to another they have no territory?"[100] He believed that the supplementary points of the draft in fact led logically to the revision of the constitution. All this, in his opinion, was due to the influence of environment. Skrypnyk said that just as "Anteus, touching the earth, receives new strength from it, so also some persons, striving towards the *edinaia nedelimaia*, towards centralization to the point past endurance, touching the ground of bureaucracy and officialdom, gain new strength, and go in again and again to attack the line pursued by our Communist party and Soviet power."[101]

The centralist Vladimir Antonov-Saratovsky attacked Krylenko for his alleged formalism, for being hidebound, and for "sticking to the letter," saying that the result of Krylenko's reasoning was that actually there is no single union, there is no union state, but instead there "is arithmetic: one plus one, plus one, plus one [equals] four republics." "It is wrong," declared Antonov-Saratovsky, "we have the union." In his opinion, Krylenko and Skrypnyk were sinking the union, reducing its meaning to zero.[102] Another centralist, Kalinin, for many years chairman of the TsIK of the USSR, in a demagogic speech attacked Skrypnyk, Krylenko, and others for their formalism, calling Skrypnyk's argumentation "mere lyrical effusion." Discussing the sovereignty of the republic, he declared that "in our union every village, every soviet, is sovereign, but within the limits of rights allotted to it." He defended the "regulations," which established a unified system of courts throughout the union: the people's court, the district court, and the supreme court. Kalinin stressed that the union had to be able to use the local courts for political aims with common union ends in view, and that the courts had to become an instrument helping to build Soviet power. "The courts are for us one of the most serious means by which we must strengthen and unite the peoples of the union .... What are the ways for the peoples to draw nearer to each other? Among other things, both by the similarity of the judicial system ... and by the similarity of forms .... What do you think," Kalinin asked Krylenko, "is the court a bearer of the interest of the union or a bearer of the interest of a separate republic? ... Do you want the court, one of the mighty factors in uniting of peoples, serving the cohesion of the citizens, to bear the label of a union republic? No, comrades, we have not got so far yet."[103] In a word, centralists endeavoured to construct a system of courts that would favour the *rapprochement* of the republics. An original argument was used by the Georgian Mikhail Tskhakaia, who drew Krylenko's attention to "the proletarian world revolution," which was the "*suprema lex*." "This is the main thing, while the formalities are a partial, secondary thing."[104] The chairman of the supreme court of the union, Aleksandr Vinokurov, emphasized that it was necessary to bear in mind the interpretation of "federation" by the second congress of the Comintern as being a transitional stage toward complete unity, for which reason the integrating elements would more and more predominate over the autonomous elements.[105]

This discussion in the soviet of nationalities and in the soviet of the union shows that a stubborn conflict went on in these chambers between the centralists and the separatists concerning the delimitation of the powers of the union and of the union republics. It is difficult to establish how far this opposition influenced opinion within the party and within Soviet circles. However, it may be affirmed with certainty that, had it not been for that opposition, the "regulations" would have handed the union almost all powers. The importance of the Ukrainian opposition in these organs is expressed in the words of a staunch Russian centralist, Iu. Larin (Mikhail Lure), who said at the meeting of the union TsIK in April 1926:

> ... If it had not been for Ukraine, if it had not been for its energetic raising of questions about a complete, precise, hundred-per-cent implementation of our line in the question of nationalities, the life and work also of other, less considerable national republics would have been put into a more difficult situation in the national respect. I know that the attitude to Skrypnyk's

> frequent speeches at the sessions of the TsIK is sometimes somewhat sceptical .... And yet, comrade Skrypnyk by this activity of his in particular and the whole of Ukraine in general performs an extremely useful work, because they wage daily a persistent struggle for the full recognition of that equality of rights of all cultures situated on our territory, and this [equality of rights] constitutes one of the foundations of our order. But in order to realize such a state structure with equal national rights, it is necessary to overcome the internal and external Great Russian chauvinism which has come to us from the old [i.e., prerevolutionary] time. When discussing the activity of the Ukrainian government, this first feature, this first manifestation of a particular state role of Ukraine must be ... recognized and noted by us with gratitude.[106]

As far as Ukraine was concerned, this opposition and the opposition of the Ukrainian Bolsheviks had the effect that approximately from the middle of 1923 the so-called *korenizatsiia* or Ukrainianization of the state and party machinery and of cultural institutions was introduced. It was then that the official decree on Ukrainianization was issued.[107] Other, smaller nationalities found encouragement in the Ukrainian opposition and sought in it moral support.

CHAPTER XII

The Self-Determination of Nations after the Establishment of Soviet Power

The Methods of Implementation of the RCP's Nationality Policy

The disintegration of Russia which took place after the Bolshevik *coup d'état* influenced the position of the RCP in regard to the self-determination of nations. Having come face to face with the separatist aspiration of the national movements, representing nations which at the beginning of 1918 did in fact separate from Russia, the Bolsheviks modified their old positions and decided to recognize federation as a means of keeping "borderlands" in Russia. A policy of overt centralism and a Russia "one and indivisible" would have antagonized the national movements and led to a permanent disintegration of the Russian empire. It is obvious that this compromise was due to the strength of non-Russian nationalism in Russia. As Popov wrote later, "the broad scope of the national movements, the profound mistrust among the toiling masses of the oppressed nationalities towards any manifestations of centralism which were not directly dictated by their own interests (military alliance, etc.), demanded greater elasticity in establishing forms of contact and union between the

Soviet republics."[1] Stalin was outspoken about the causes of this turn towards federalism:

> This evolution of our party's views on the question of a state federation must be explained by three facts. First, at the time of the October revolution a number of the nationalities of Russia were found to be in fact in a state of complete separation and detachment from each other, in view of which federation turned out to be a step forward from the separation of the working masses of these nationalities to their *rapprochement*, to their uniting.
> Second, the forms of federation which were marked out in the course of the socialist construction turned out to be far from contradicting the aims of the economic *rapprochement* of the working masses of Russia's nationalities to such a degree as may have been anticipated earlier, and seemed even not to contradict these aims at all, as was shown subsequently in practice.
> Third, the relative importance of the nationalist movement turned out to be far more serious, and the way of uniting the nationalities far more complicated, than it could have seemed before, in the period before the war or in the period before the October revolution.[2]

Thus Stalin admitted, first, that the Bolsheviks merely recognized *de facto* the existing state of the disintegrated empire and that federation was not a concession by the party, but by the nationalities, who were dragged back from independence to federative dependence on Russia. Events showed that it was impossible to approach independent nationalities with the old principle of autonomy of 1903. Secondly, the form planned by the party in no way contradicted the economic centralization of the empire, for, as was seen in practice, it was the branches of the RCP(B) which governed not only the administration, but also the economic and cultural life of each of the component parts of the federation. The third admission seems to be the chief one, and it actually dictated the party's attitude. The party watched events from the October revolution until the party's eighth congress, hoping that, after all, the separatist nationalist movements were "a petty-bourgeois caprice" that would later disappear. Therefore the party vacillated between the old slogan of autonomy and the new one of federation. Therefore also the principle of federation, adopted by the eighth congress, was considered only "one of the transitional forms on the way to complete unity."[3]

The federative principle was officially adopted in January 1918 at the third all-Russian congress of soviets. The resolution of the congress said that "the Russian Socialist Soviet Republic is being established on the basis of a voluntary union of the peoples of Russia as a federation of the Soviet republics of these peoples." The mode of participation of Soviet republics and separate regions in the federal government, as well as the definition of the spheres of activity in the federal and regional institutions of the Russian republic "is being determined immediately after the creation of regional Soviet republics" by the all-Russian central executive committees and by the central executive committees of those republics. Elaboration of the principles of the federation was entrusted to the TsIK of the RSFSR, and they were to be ratified by the fourth congress of soviets.[4]

In connection with drafting the first constitution of the Russian Soviet republic in February 1918, the principles of the Soviet federation were defined. Two conceptions of the federation came up in the constitutional commission. One of them, proposed and defended by M. A. Reisner, consisted in the RSFSR's having to change into "a federation of local social and economic formations." Reisner emphasized that Soviet federalism "is not a union of territorial realms or states, but a federation of social and economic organizations." The Soviet republic was recognized "as a community of workers, united into unions; these unions organize themselves locally into federative communities called communes, headed by soviets formed from the delegates of the unions; the communes are united into a province, led by its congress, which is formed from the delegates of the communal soviets as well as from the representatives of the unions of the province; provincial federations form regional republics, and these latter form a union named the RSFSR."[5] This variant was rejected in the commission.

The other variant, submitted by Stalin, proceeded from the premise that the constitution which was being elaborated by the commission was to have only a temporary character, as it applied "to the period of transition from the bourgeois to the socialist regime." He stressed the need to take into consideration the demands of the nationalities "for autonomy on the basis of federation." The units of federation in Russia, in his opinion, were to be "not single towns which decide their own matters autonomously, and not any kind of region—the economic pecularities of which (if such exist) must be represented by the corresponding autonomous organizations of the supreme council of national economy—but fully defined regions which differ in their particular ways of life and national compositions."[6] Reisner and Stalin had different concepts of nationality and its role in history and the state. Reisner considered that the national factor played a secondary role also in contemporary bourgeois states. The only positive unifying element of the national factor was "the ideal of culture, particularly spiritual culture; language, science, art, education, press, etc." Hence Reisner deduced that "on the basis of the national principle it is possible to speak only of the cultural self-determination of nations, but never of the political." For a socialist state, the national principle could have an even smaller significance from the political point of view than for bourgeois democratic states, for a socialist state based its existence on the forms of economic reconstruction of its republic, on the principles of socialist economic production where primary importance is assigned not to state organizations but to economic ones.[7] Stalin, for his part, though not rejecting the importance of economic factors in the Soviet state, stressed at the same time that national motives could not be ignored during the period of transition. He felt that a combination of national and economic elements was necessary in the construction of the Russian federation.

In his interview with a *Pravda* correspondent, Stalin stated the official position of the party on the question of federation. He stressed that the characteristic feature in the creation of federations in Switzerland and the USA was that they were not created according to the national principle but because of an accidental seizure of one territory or another by one group or another of emigrant settlers or rural communities. The federation that was about to be created in Russia was completely different. First, the regions that had separated themselves from Russia represented completely definite units as regards their way of life and national composition. "Ukraine, the Crimea, Poland, Transcaucasia, Turkestan, the central Volga regions, the Kirghiz region, differ from the centre not only in their situation (borderlands!), but also in that they are compact economic territories with definite ways of life and ethnic composition of population." Secondly, these regions did not represent free and independent territories, but units that were forcibly pushed into the common Russian political organism, units that were now trying to obtain the necessary freedom of action in the shape of federative relations or full independence. "The history of the 'uniting' of these territories is a continuous picture of violence and oppression on the part of the old Russian authorities. The establishment in Russia of a federative order will mean the liberation of these territories and of the peoples living there from the old imperialist oppression." Thirdly, in the Western federations the state apparatus was controlled by an imperialist bourgeoisie, therefore the "uniting" could not have taken place without violence. In Russia the proletariat was in command politically, and therefore in Russia it was "possible and necessary to establish the federative order on the basis of a free union of peoples."[8]

Stalin even outlined some "general features" of the authority of the federal organs and of the organs of the constituent parts of the federation. "Military and naval affairs, external affairs, railways, post office and telegraph, money, trade agreements, general economic, financial, and banking policy—all this apparently would comprise the field of activity of the central council of people's commissars. All other matters, and primarily the forms of the implementations of common decrees, schools, justice, administration, etc., would go over to regional councils of people's commissars." As far as language was concerned, each region would choose the language of its main ethnic component.

The role of a federation in Russia was to be merely that of "a transitional stage towards socialist unitarianism." Stalin stressed that "many people are inclined to regard the federative order as the most stable and even ideal," referring to the example of America, Canada, and Switzerland. "But the enthusiasm for federalism is not justified by history." In Russia, in Stalin's opinion, "compulsory tsarist unitarianism is being replaced by voluntary federalism in order that, in the course of time, federalism should give way to a likewise voluntary and fraternal union of the working masses of all nations and races of Russia. Federalism in Russia is destined, just as in America and Switzerland, to play a transitional role; towards a future *socialist* unitarianism."[9]

These principles were fixed in the constitution of the RSFSR adopted by the fifth all-Russian congress of soviets on 10 July 1918. Its first chapter, point 2, stated that "the Russian Soviet republic is constituted on the basis of a free union of free nations as a federation of Soviet national republics."[10] The second chapter, point 11, declared that "the soviets of regions distinguished by a particular way of life and by their national composition may unite into autonomous regional unions" which "enter the Russian Socialist Federative Soviet Republic on federative principles."[11] Point 49 (g) also mentioned "regional soviet unions which enter the Russian Federative Soviet Republic."[12] In general, it must be stressed that the federative principle was defined very vaguely in this constitution; the vagueness corresponded to the spirit generally reigning in the party.

The eighth congress of the RCP(B) was very important for the party attitude to the national question. This congress produced a synthesis of previous policy on this and other questions. Regarding the national question, the party accepted federalism as the principle of relations among the nationalities of Russia.

The congress saw a continuation of the struggle between the two views of the party on the national question, that of Lenin and that of the so-called leftists represented by Piatakov and Bukharin. Here Lenin once more defended the view that the recognition of the right of nations to self-determination was the *conditio sine qua non* for the success of the Communist revolution. Piatakov and Bukharin insisted that the old slogan of the self-determination of nations should be replaced by the slogan, "the self-determination of the working classes of each nationality."[13] Bukharin declared that if Lenin's formula—"the right of nations to self-determination"—were accepted, the Bolsheviks in consequence would have to admit this right for the nation as "nation" is understood in its scholarly sense, as "the totality of all classes, which is not [either] the proletariat or the bourgeoisie, but is both the proletariat and the bourgeoisie." Further, this would mean that the Bolsheviks would have to recognize also "the fictitious so-called will of nations, which is normally embodied in nothing but a referendum of the so-called whole population, including also the ruling classes, or in a constituent assembly, a parliament assembled on the basis of universal, equal, and secret suffrage, which includes primarily the representatives of the ruling classes."[14]

On the other hand, he proposed accepting the slogan of the "right of nations to self-determination" for those countries "where the proletariat has not formed itself into a class, where it has not become conscious of the contradiction of its interests to those of the bourgeoisie, where it sees its bourgeoisie as 'its own people' (*svoi liudi*), where it does not pose as a task for itself the realization of its own, the workers' power, and of the proletarian dictatorship." By such "countries" Bukharin apparently meant colonies, but, it seems, not those of a European type. This is what he said: "If we proclaim the slogan 'the right of nations to self-determination' for colonies—for the Hottentots and Bushmen, Negroes, Hindus, etc.—we shall not lose anything by it. On the contrary, we [shall] win, because the whole national complex will be harmful to foreign imperialism, and its struggle will enter the common system of struggle against the imperialist regime."[15]

Criticizing Bukharin, Lenin correctly stressed that Bukharin—in his dreams about the differentiation within each nationality—took the desirable for the real and did not reckon with that which exists. Lenin, pointing to Germany as an example of an advanced capitalist state, emphasized that even there the proletariat had not differentiated from the bourgeoisie, and that the majority of the workers were against Scheidemann's party. In fact, the recognition of the right of nations to self-determination had in many countries speeded up the differentiation of the proletariat from the bourgeoisie. Among such countries Lenin claimed Finland, in which, thanks to the admission of its right to self-determination, the proletariat, in his opinion, had broken with the bourgeoisie. Further, Lenin quite rightly reproached Bukharin for having completely forgotten the nationalities in Russia, while enumerating the nationalities, which in his opinion could be granted the right to self-determination.[16] In a word, Lenin admitted the right of the party, i.e., of the Red Army, to intervene in the internal affairs of those countries where the proletariat had on the whole differentiated from the bourgeoisie, but he did not clarify what was to be done in those countries where the proletariat, after it had seized power, demanded self-determination. It seems that both Lenin and the party generally considered the proletariat to be under the influence of its bourgeoisie as soon as the proletariat defended self-determination, since this was contrary to the slogan, "Workers of the world, unite."

The question of what to do with a proletariat that claimed the right of nations to self-determination was answered at this congress by Piatakov. He proposed renouncing not only the "self-determination of nations" but also Bukharin's "self-determination of workers." The latter principle would mean that the party not only would not resist but would even "facilitate the political separation of some or other regions or countries," an alternative which Piatakov rejected. He said that "the party of the proletariat cannot admit in any case that a question which affects the interests, not only of the proletariat of these regions, but to a considerable extent also the interests of the proletariat of the whole capitalistically developed world, should be solved exclusively by the working class of that country."[17]

It was neither the degree of differentiation of the proletariat from the bourgeoisie nor the will of the proletariat that had to determine the application of self-determination; it was to be determined by the will or the interests of the proletarian revolution. If some country, for instance, Ukraine, was very important for economic, strategic, or other reasons for the success of this revolution, the proletariat of that country had no right to invoke the right to self-determination.

Piatakov also pointed out the inconsistency of Lenin's position that the party, on the one hand, defended the centralization of the economic life of all Soviet republics and, on the other hand, defended self-determination. "Since we unite economically," said Piatakov, "create one administrative machinery, one supreme council of national economy, one railway administration, one bank, etc., this whole celebrated 'self-determination' is not worth a fig. This is either simply a diplomatic game, which has to be played in some cases, or it is worse than a game if we take it seriously .... Where the proletariat has been victorious, an immediate uniting must take place, and we must pursue one line."[18] Lenin probably admitted to himself that Piatakov's criticism was right, but he could not in any case admit openly that self-determination was merely diplomacy and a ruse. Otherwise, what would the representatives of all those Bashkirs, Kirghiz, etc., have said, to say nothing of the Ukrainians, Georgians, and others? Lenin had to manoeuvre very skilfully between the centralists and the members of the nationalities in order to be followed by all the forces of the party. Replying to Piatakov, he pointed out that Russia needed economic unity, but it was neither necessary nor permissible to introduce it by force. He argued that it was necessary to take into consideration the historical stage of development of each nationality and to apply self-determination accordingly. The question was whether a given nationality was in the stage between the Middle Ages and bourgeois democracy, or between bourgeois democracy and proletarian democracy.[19] He very aptly remarked that "the decree that all countries must live according to the Bolshevik revolutionary calendar has not yet been published, and even if it had been published it would not have been carried out."[20] Lenin argued that it would have meant throwing the national question overboard, which, in his opinion, would have been possible "if there had been people without national characteristics. But there are no such people."[21]

The resolution the congress adopted reflected both positions on the national question. In it "self-determination" was replaced by "the recognition of the right to state secession for colonial nations and those having equal rights," while the question of who was the representative of the will of a nation to secession was dealt with by the RCP from the "class historical" point of view, "taking into account which stage of its historical development is occupied by a given nation." The first paragraph stressed that "the cornerstone is the policy of the *rapproachement* of the proletarians and semi-proletarians of various nationalities for their common revolutionary struggle for the overthrow of the landowners and bourgeoisie." With the same aim in view "the party proposes the federative union of states, organized according to the Soviet type, as one of the transitional forms on the way to complete unity." Then the resolution urged the proletariat of the oppressing nations to adopt a particularly considerate and attentive attitude towards the survival of national feelings in the workers of the oppressed nations and of those not having full rights.[22]

Having analysed and compared the positions of Lenin and his opponents, Bukharin and Piatakov, it may be asserted that there was no fundamental difference between them. There was only a verbal, tactical difference. While Bukharin and Piatakov approached the national question boldly and openly, Lenin and his followers used diplomacy, tactics, and word-play. Objectively, neither side was able to influence the course of events by its declarations, for events pursued their own irresistible course. The nationalities of the former Russian empire existed *de facto* independently from Russia. Poland, Finland, the Baltic states, Georgia, and Ukraine had entered upon the road of complete independence. The nationalities of the former Russian empire, which hoped to obtain the material and moral support of the Entente, did not lightly succumb to the vague and ambiguous resolution of the eighth congress of the RCP. The speeches of Piatakov and Bukharin were, for the anti-Bolshevik forces of the nationalities, a very welcome trump card in their anti-Communist propaganda. The Soviet historian Popov wrote, not without good reason, that "the attitude towards the national question, veiled by leftist phrases, did tremendous harm to the party and was of no less tremendous benefit to the forces of counter-revolution, which took every opportunity of playing upon the nationalist feeling to be met with among the formerly oppressed peoples."[23]

However, all talk about the self-determination of nations must be considered from the point of view of the total programme of the party, and chiefly from the point of view of the role of the RCP and its branches in the "borderlands." Elsewhere it has been mentioned that the Bolsheviks, led by Lenin, never wished to recognize even autonomy for the nationality parties, to say nothing of independence.[24]

Abandonment of Self-Determination

With the final victory over anti-Bolshevik forces, the RCP(B) began a new period in the history of the national question, marked by the abandonment of the slogan of the self-determination of nations. In his article, "The Policy of Soviet Power on the National Question in Russia," published in *Pravda* on 10 October 1920, Stalin rejected the self-determination of nations as the way to solve the national question in Russia. This question was now to be solved on the basis of an obligatory "union," which meant in fact the subordination of the "borderlands" to Russia. Since "Central Russia, this focal point of the world revolution," Stalin wrote, "cannot hold out for long without the assistance of the borderlands, which are rich in raw materials, fuel, and food produce," the purpose of party policy was "the establishment of definite relations, of definite connections, between the centre and the borderlands of Russia." For this reason, "the demand for the separation of the borderlands from Russia as a form of relation between the centre and the borderlands must be excluded." Stalin justified this not only by his assertion that the separation of the "borderlands ... would undermine the revolutionary might of Central Russia," but also by saying that, first of all, this "would contradict in principle the interests of the popular masses of the centre as well as the borderlands."[25] Independent states such as Poland, Finland, Armenia, and Georgia were, in Stalin's opinion, not independent states at all but vassals of the Entente or of other Great Powers. Stalin proposed these astonishing alternatives for the non-Russian nationalities: "*Either* together with

Russia, and then there is the liberation of the working masses of the borderlands from imperialist oppression; *or* together with the Entente, resulting in the inevitable imperialist yoke. There is no third way out."[26] It cannot be denied that, *de facto*, small states have always been to some degree dependent on their great neighbours, but the fact is that the second alternative, "together with the Entente," both offered and gave much more sovereignty to the nationalities than the prospect of being "together with Russia" which, as is known, reduced the nationalities to cultural and linguistic vegetation; Poland "together with the Entente" was much more sovereign, and its national interests were safeguarded much more, than Ukraine "together with Russia." But to Stalin the demand for the separation of the borderlands at this given stage of the revolution was "profoundly counter-revolutionary"[27]—such was the synthesis of his wisdom.

Stalin regarded "the *regional* autonomy of the borderlands, which differ by their special way of life and national composition," as the only way to solve the national question. In a word, it was the same autonomy which the Bolsheviks had espoused at the beginning of the century, and which had turned out to be such a weak propaganda slogan during the October revolution that it had to be abandoned. Now, after the establishment of the Soviet regime in Russia and its expansion to the borderlands, autonomy alone became acceptable to the party. In order to disperse the doubts of the nationalities, Stalin explained that Soviet autonomy was "elastic"; "it admitted of the most varied forms and stages in its development. . . . From a narrow administrative autonomy (the Volga Germans, Chuvash, Karelians) it passes over to a broader political autonomy (the Bashkirs, Volga Tatars, Kirghiz); from the broader political autonomy to its even more expanded form (Ukraine, Turkestan); finally, from the Ukrainian type of autonomy to the highest form of autonomy, to treaty relationships (Azerbaidzhan)."[28] This gradation of the relations between the RSFSR and the borderlands did not quite correspond to reality, for precisely at that time the RSFSR had concluded a series of "workers' and peasants' union treaties" with Ukraine, Khorezm, Belorussia, Armenia, Georgia, and Azerbaidzhan as with independent republics, expressly recognizing their independence. There was no difference between Azerbaidzhan and Ukraine from the legal point of view, although there was a *de facto* difference. Lenin seemed at that time to differentiate between federation based on the relations of the RSFSR with other Soviet republics, as for instance the Hungarian, Finnish, and Ukrainian, and the relations within the RSFSR itself towards the nationalities that formerly had "neither a state existence nor autonomy" (for instance, the Bashkir and Tatar republics).[29] Stalin, on the contrary, regarded all Soviet republics as parts of the RSFSR.

On the basis of these considerations of Stalin and, of course, also of Lenin's theses for the second congress of the Comintern,[30] the tenth congress of the RCP in March 1921 took final leave of the principle of the right of nations to self-determination. The national question in Russia was now reduced to the elimination of actual inequalities of a cultural, economic, and political character and to enabling the nationalities "to catch up with proletarian Central Russia, which was ahead of them."[31] But this was a question of practical measures and administrative arrangements and not one of theoretical premises.

The elimination of the idea of the separation of the Soviet republics was the dominating effect of the resolution adopted by this congress. The resolution made an *a priori* statement, that "while private ownership and capital inevitably separate people, ignite national strife, and increase national oppression, collective ownership and labour just as inevitably draw people closer, undermine national strife, and destroy national oppression." Here is an even better pearl from Stalin's aphorisms: "Chauvinism and national struggle are inevitable and unavoidable as long as the peasantry (and the petty bourgeoisie of state nations especially), full of nationalist prejudices, follows the bourgeoisie, and, on the contrary, national peace and national freedom can be regarded as secure if the peasantry follows the proletariat, i.e., if the dictatorship of the proletariat is secured."[32]

The resolution further asserted that the existence of the Soviet republics, although they are very insignificant in size, "presents a mortal threat to imperialism," because these republics were turning from colonies "into really independent states, and thus depriving the imperialists of another piece of territory and another [source] of income," and more importantly because the very existence of these republics "is the greatest agitation against capitalism and imperialism, agitation for the liberation of dependent countries from imperialist bondage." Hence the attempts of the great imperialist powers to destroy the republics at any price, the proof of which was to be the military intervention of the Entente, directed primarily against the borderlands. Having frightened these republics with the bogy of imperialism, the resolution goes on:

> Hence, in isolation, the existence of various Soviet republics is uncertain and unstable, because of the threat to their existence offered by the capitalist states. The joint interests of the Soviet republics—first, in the matter of defence, second, in the restoration of productive forces shattered during the war, and third, in the need for those Soviet republics which are rich in food to come to the aid of the Soviet republics which are poor in food—all imperatively dictate the political union of the various Soviet republics as the only means of escaping imperialist bondage and national oppression. Having

> liberated themselves from their own and foreign bourgeoisie, the national Soviet republics can defend their existence and defeat the combined forces of imperialism only by amalgamating themselves into a close political union.[33]

In the period of the tenth congress of the RCP (March 1921) the national question moved from the theoretical and ideological plane to the practical one and became a method for keeping the borderlands within the orbit of the Russian Soviet republic. This congress had the backing of the empirical achievements of the party in the national question, namely, the rendering of the Soviet national republics dependent on the Russian federative republic, which was legalized in the union treaties of 1920 and 1921. However, the party went further towards tying the borderlands closer to Russia. Until then, relations between the borderland republics and the RSFSR had been marked by rather indefinite forms—first military and then economic alliances. After the tenth congress, the party took the road of uniting the Soviet republics into one state as the only solution of the national question.

The twelfth congress of the RCP(B) of April 1923 brought no theoretical innovations in this question. It only set out in some detail the party's practical aspirations. It can be seen from the resolution adopted at this congress that the party was looking for a theoretical foundation for its centralist policy towards the nationalities, a foundation for its negative attitude towards the self-determination principle. The resolution stressed the progressiveness of capitalism, insofar as it led to the internationalization of the means of production and of the exchange of goods, to the abolition of national isolation, to the drawing together economically of peoples, and to the gradual uniting of large territories into one connected whole; and it prepared the *material* conditions for the future socialist economy. Why precisely for a socialist economy, the editors of the resolution did not explain, but only assumed *a priori*. It was also stressed in the resolution, but in a very hazy form, that the above-mentioned tendency to unite under capitalism had been carried out by violent means, by the oppression of some nations by others, by colonial slavery, by national injustice; but "inasmuch as the latter tendency implied a revolt of the oppressed masses against imperialist forms of amalgamation, inasmuch as it demanded the amalgamation of peoples on the basis of collaboration and voluntary union, it was and is a progressive tendency, for it is creating the psychological conditions for the future world socialist economic system."[34] The resolution comes to the conclusion that the experience of the disintegration of the old Russian empire, Austria-Hungary, and Turkey, and the history of such colonial powers as Great Britain and the old

Germany, and finally the great imperialist war and the growth of revolutionary movements among colonial and semi-colonial peoples—all this proves "the instability and insolidity of the multinational bourgeois states."[35] The resolution emphasized that Soviet power alone was able to solve the national question, and that the proletariat found in the Soviet order the key to the correct solution of the national question, "it discovered in it a way to the organization of a stable multinational state."[36] The establishment of the Soviet regime was to be a condition of the abolition of national oppression, the guarantee of national equality and of rights for national minorities. The subsequent history of the relations of Soviet Russia with the Soviet republics, and later also of the relations between the Soviet Union and the satellites (for instance, Hungary), obviously refute these categorical assertions. National antagonism is not eliminated merely by the establishment of a certain regime, for this antagonism possesses a much broader scale of causes than those which the Russian Communists were willing to admit.

However, the resolution had to admit that "to find the key to the correct solution of the national question still does not mean solving it fully and finally," and that there were in its way many "obstacles" inherited from the old regime. Those obstacles were the imperialist chauvinism of the Great Russians which manifested itself practically in "the presumptuously disdainful and callously bureaucratic attitude of Russian officials to the needs and requirements of the national republics"; the actual, i.e., economic and cultural, inequality of the nationalities of the union; and the survivals of nationalism among the peoples who had experienced the heavy yoke of national oppression and who had not yet freed themselves from the feeling of old national wrongs.[37]

Conclusions

The Russian Communists, guided by the empirical realities prevailing in Russia, were by no means dogmatic Marxists on the national question. Neither Marx nor Engels left for their disciples any clearly formulated system for the general solution of the national problem. Their attitude on the Irish and Polish questions was diffuse, and their negation of the national rights of the South Slavs and the Czechs could hardly serve as a pattern, much less as a directive for the Russian Communists. Lenin could not afford such sarcasm towards the nationalities of Russia as Marx and Engels could towards the Austrian Slavs during and after the revolution of 1848. He declared that the party was unable to continue the policy of Tsar Nicholas in the direction of the Russification of the non-Russian nationalities. Instead of Marx's straightforward dogmatic policy, Lenin proposed to apply a zigzag, dialectic one.

On the national question, Lenin achieved far more than his teachers. Having grasped the historical significance of the national question in Russia, he drew the party's attention to it from the first days of his career. However, the national prejudices and nationalistic feelings of the Russian proletariat, and even more those of the Russian radical intelligentsia, together with the conviction of the subjugated nationalities that they had been wronged, thwarted Lenin's intention to make use of the nationalities in the proletarian revolution. The difficulty the Bolsheviks faced in solving the nationalities problem was in correctly estimating the correlation between the liberation movements of the oppressed nations and the proletarian emancipation of the oppressing nation. Analysis of Lenin's theoretical premises shows how difficult it was to reconcile the two revolutionary currents of the century, nationalism and socialism. It is true that external circumstances often brought these two movements together, chiefly because their main antagonist was the same Russian tsarist regime. But this "alliance," so to speak, changed into open hostility as soon as the common enemy disappeared. Lenin made every effort to unite these two antipodes of the epoch by manoeuvering between the nationalist feelings of the subjugated nations and the imperialist tendencies of the Russian proletariat. But he only partly succeeded in this.

After examining the RCP(B)'s attitude to the self-determination of nations in the period between 1903 and 1917, we can assert that the party did not stand for the actual secession of the nationalities from the Russian state. On the contrary, Lenin and his adherents promoted the doctrine of the most centralistic and indivisible Russian state with the dictatorship of one, also indivisible, Communist party. Not only the independence of the nationalities in Russia but even autonomy and federalism were unacceptable to Lenin. The nationalities were offered territorial autonomy in which they had no political rights in legislation or administration; these powers were to be vested in the hands of the central government. The nationalities were to have neither their own political parties nor trade unions, nor their own cultural national policy (because they were not to have their own educational systems). What, then, was the self-determination of nationalities so patiently defended by Lenin during the ideological dispute with his opponents? It was, according to Lenin (and Piatakov and Bukharin), the self-determination of the proletariat of every nationality, on the assumption that the proletariat would not separate from a socialist Russia. If the national proletariat, e.g., Polish or Finnish, opted for separation, it should not be allowed to secede, because such a separation would run counter to the interests of the proletarian revolution. This meant that there was no guarantee for any nationality unless it acted according to the above-mentioned principles and in accordance with the Marxian doctrine of the proletarian revolution.

The Bolshevik doctrine of self-determination recognized that self-determination included the right of secession, but at the same time refused the nationalities the right to organize independent Communist parties. The Bolsheviks thus predetermined the shape of self-determination to the advantage of Russian centralism and in favour of the unity of the Russian empire. In practice the self-determination of nations as interpreted by Lenin was of very limited value for the nationalities in Russia. There was only an abstract conception of the right to self-determination. But the party lacked any positive attitude to the realization of this right. Any attempt to interpret Lenin's conception of self-determination as giving the nationalities the theoretical basis for secession from Russia must therefore be considered groundless.

After the October revolution the party began to combat self-determination in general, because it could be used in a way undesirable for the party. Prominent party leaders attempted to discredit the principle of national self-determination: "We must say directly and definitely," declared Kamenev in 1918, "that the slogan of the self-determination of nations turned in the course of the proletarian revolution in Russia into a weapon of the bourgeois counter-revolution against Soviet Russia."[1] The national movements lost their value for the Bolsheviks as an auxiliary factor in the struggle against tsarism, and later against the Provisional Government, from the moment of the Bolshevik coup. The national movements now stood in the way of the development of the revolution in the borderlands of Russia and subsequently began to slow down the expansion of the Communist revolution beyond Russia's boundaries. During their struggle with the White forces, the Bolsheviks pursued a twofold policy in respect to the nationalities. Where the power of the soviets was established, as in Ukraine during the Brest Litovsk negotiations, the Bolsheviks ignored the principle of self-determination and secession and pursued a policy of subordinating the borderlands to Russia; where, however, the borderlands were under the power of the White generals, Denikin and Kolchak, the Bolsheviks preached the right to self-determination and secession. The example of Ukraine shows that the Russian Bolsheviks declared war on the Central Rada not so much for being counter-revolutionary and supporting Kaledin, but mainly because the Rada began to carry out self-determination in earnest and proclaimed Ukraine an independent state.

The policy of the party towards Ukraine was determined by the conviction commonly held among the Russian parties that Ukraine was an integral part of Russia, and that retention of Ukraine was the basis of Russia's strength. From the territorial, strategic, and economic points of view, the separation of Ukraine was regarded by Russians of all political persuasions as a disaster. In this respect the Russian Communists did not differ from the Russian nationalists of the type of Purishkevich and Shulgin. For Lenin, the retention of Ukraine within Soviet Russia's orbit was the *conditio sine qua non* for the success of the world Communist revolution. In order to prevent the disintegration of the Russian empire, Lenin invoked Marx, who had likewise preached the usefulness for the proletariat of preserving large state formations with centralized national economies. To Lenin, the first premise for this was the preservation of proletarian unity over the whole of Russia, irrespective of nationality. Lenin sharply attacked the Ukrainian social democrats, accusing them of bourgeois nationalism and the like, because they demanded an independent Ukrainian social democratic party. Then after the creation of the Communist Party (Bolsheviks) of Ukraine, Lenin took great care to defend the hegemony of the Russian Communist party over the Ukrainian one. To disguise the obvious intentions of this policy, he proclaimed the right of the Ukrainian people to self-determination. This declared recognition of self-determination for the Ukrainian people assumed in Lenin's mind various tones and intensities according to the current political situation. At a time when the Ukrainian national movement showed no special energy and strength and when, under the pressure of the Russian reaction of Stolypin's government, national movements were being suppressed, Lenin began to advocate so-called autonomy for those nationalities willing to stay within the Russian empire. Protesting against the tsarist regime's Russifying policy towards Ukraine, Lenin at the same time advocated the idea of an alliance of the Russian and the Ukrainian peoples, which in actual fact meant the subordination of the latter to the former. Recognizing the rights to self-determination of the Ukrainian as well as other peoples, Lenin at the same time attacked all those who thought of applying this right. He tried to persuade the Ukrainian proletarians that only in a close alliance of both peoples would they be able to emancipate themselves nationally and socially. As is shown by the history of the Ukrainian national movement after the February revolution and during the Bolshevik revolution in Petrograd, the Ukrainians took a different road by separating themselves from the Russian "social-patriotic" Bolshevik imperialism.

An obstacle in the way of the Bolshevik revolution in Ukraine, as well as in the majority of Russia's borderlands, was the national movement and also the social and political circumstances. Ukraine did not offer a suitable terrain for the planting of the Bolshevik regime. Ukraine was predominantly an agricultural country with individualistic, farmer-type agriculture, with little developed industry and with a numerically weak proletariat belonging mainly to the Menshevik faction. However, the national movement must be regarded as the chief obstacle to the Bolshevik revolution in Ukraine. Both in Ukraine and in other borderlands the national trend seems to have been stronger than the social one. For the Ukrainians and particularly for their leaders, national emancipation was in the forefront. This to some extent alienated the Russified Ukrainian proletariat from the Central Rada, which led the Ukrainian national emancipation. The Rada's moderate policy towards the landowners made the poor peasants suspicious of it, and they began to pay attention to the enticing slogans of the Bolsheviks who preached immediate expropriation of the landowners' estates without compensation.

In Ukraine the Bolsheviks had to manoeuvre between the nationally minded Ukrainian masses and strong national minorities consisting of the Russians and the Jews who gravitated towards a united and indivisible Russia. Concentrated in large towns and having inherited from the old regime great political and economic power in Ukraine, the Russian and in part the Jewish national minorities occupied a key position *vis-à-vis* the introduction of any regime. Being politically heterogeneous, this force wavered between Kerensky's regime, the Ukrainian Central Rada, the Soviet regime, the hetman's government, Denikin, and the Directory, searching for a synthesis of its political and national desires. The only outcome of this was the disorganization of any stable rule in the country and the ultimate exploitation of this state of affairs by the Bolsheviks.

The first attempt at installing the Soviet regime in Russia took place under circumstances that were very favourable for the Bolsheviks. Kerensky's Provisional Government compromised itself by the policy of "war to a victorious end," which the Kadet party had tried to make popular at any price and which Kerensky, under Allied pressure (chiefly French), had begun to put into practice. The army, which consisted mainly of peasant masses, hard-pressed by hunger, cold, and death, and influenced to some extent by Bolshevik propaganda against the war, suddenly changed into a roaming mass of discontented seekers of the homeward road. The propaganda for the expropriation of land merely poured oil on this fire. Kerensky's regime fell, offering almost no resistance, and the Bolsheviks took power in Petrograd and then in other towns of Central Russia. In the borderlands power likewise passed without any noteworthy resistance into the hands of national governments, in Ukraine into the hands of the Central Rada. Soviet Russia suddenly found itself faced with the threat of encirclement by the anti-Bolshevik national borderlands which refused to recognize Lenin's government as a government of the whole of Russia. The Central Rada began to take measures to organize a truly representative all-Russian government on federative principles, which meant restricting Soviet power to Great Russia. On the Don old tsarist generals such as Alekseev and Kornilov gathered around Kaledin, nursing plans for the overthrow of the Soviet regime in Petrograd. The Bolsheviks, in turn, began an offensive against Kaledin, aimed at the destruction of their chief enemy and the occupation of the Black Sea littoral. The overthrow of the Ukrainian Central Rada was the next task, and the same instruments were to be employed: the Red Guards and the local Bolsheviks. The assertion of Soviet historians that the Soviet regime in Ukraine as well as in other borderlands was created by the local workers and peasants themselves is groundless and only serves the party's aim of representing itself as the spokesman of the workers and peasants.

After the downfall of the military and political force of the Central Powers in the autumn of 1918, an upsurge of leftist socialism took place in the West European countries. At the beginning of 1919 the Communists seized power in Hungary, proclaimed a soviet republic in Bavaria, attempted a revolution in Berlin, and made themselves felt in the Balkans and in the Scandinavian countries. The Russian Communist party made preparations for military intervention in Central and Western Europe. In a word, the prospects for a future world revolution seemed rosy.

It was at that moment of upsurge of world Communism that a crack appeared in its very centre. The anti-Communist forces gathered strength for the final overthrow of the Soviet regime in Moscow and undermined the strength of Bolshevism by internal rebellions. Just at that time the Soviet regime in Ukraine fell under the blows of the peasant rebellions organized by the Directory and by the anarchist Makhno, and partially by Hryhoriiv, a Ukrainian left SR. This prepared the ground for Denikin's military offensive from the south, from the Kuban and the Don, and for the attack of the Directory's troops, led by Petliura, from the west. The military situation changed abruptly, and instead of advancing against Europe the Communists were compelled to defend their capital, Moscow.

The Ukrainian countryside played a considerable role in the military and political balance of power in Ukraine in 1919. Therefore it is not surprising that Lenin paid particular attention to the peasantry. However, this happened only after the second overthrow of the Soviet regime in Ukraine. Both during the first and the second Bolshevik regimes the attitude towards the peasantry was negative or at least ignorant or indifferent. The party's chief concern in the Ukrainian countryside was its grain. The party needed this grain to save Central Russia from starvation, and later in 1919 Lenin tried to buy a truce with the Entente with the same Ukrainian grain. It was again this grain that became the bone of contention between the Bolsheviks and the peasantry. Another device by which the party thought to open the road into Western Europe was the national question. Declaring the right of nations to self-determination, even to secession, Lenin intended to gain the sympathies and cooperation of the subjugated nations of Russia, above all the Ukrainians. However, the practice of the Communists deviated markedly from their theory. The second Soviet regime in Ukraine under the leadership of Rakovsky, just like the first one under Piatakov, ignored the Ukrainian question and dragged Ukraine towards Moscow, leaving it with only a curtailed autonomy. Obviously this made the declarations of the party and the whole Soviet government suspect to the Ukrainian masses. It was no secret to anyone that the party made concessions to Ukrainian nationalism according to the degree of its need to placate the Ukrainian masses. As soon as world revolution became more plausible, the national question was pushed into the background. Proof of this is the revision of the right to self-determination of nations at the eighth congress of the RCP in March 1918, when this right was reserved only for the proletariat, and even then only in countries where the proletariat had broken with its bourgeoisie. In precisely which countries this breach had taken place was to be decided by the party.

The social bases of the Soviet regime in Ukraine were the Russian and Russified workers, pauperized rural workers, and the radical, predominantly non-Ukrainian, intelligentsia. The peasantry of Ukraine was in principle anti-Communist. In the first period of Soviet power in Ukraine the peasantry showed a favourable attitude towards the agrarian policy of the party which was based on the slogan "despoil the spoils" (*grab nagrablennoe*), i.e., the immediate expropriation of the landowners' lands. In the second period, the agrarian policy of the party began to be directed against the interests of the peasants. Now Rakovsky's government began preserving large landowners' estates for the state, christening them communes and compelling the peasants to join them along with their land and implements. This naturally aroused determined resistance on the part of the peasantry, which replied to the repressive measures of the cheka with similar armed and cruel reprisals against the Communists. Numerous peasant risings disorganized Soviet rule in the provinces, destroyed the communications of the army with the country, and diverted a considerable part of the Red Army from the front. Thus the Ukrainian peasantry played, if not a decisive role, at least a considerable one in the defeat of the Soviet regime in Ukraine in the summer of 1919.

Planning the counter-offensive for the conquest of Ukraine, Lenin summoned a special conference of the RCP in December 1919 to re-examine the past experience of party policy in Ukraine. The strong national feeling of the Ukrainian masses compelled the party to recognize the Ukrainian national movement as a force to be reckoned with in the future. This was a step towards the pacification of the Ukrainian anti-Bolshevik front, which, as can be seen from the existence of the UCP and the Borotbists, embraced not only the non-Communist parties, but also these two Communist parties of the nationalist type. The conflict of the

Ukapists (UCP) and the Borotbists with the RCP and its branch in Ukraine, the CP(B)U, had an exclusively national colouring. (It was this kind of national Communism that led in 1948 to the conflict between Tito and Stalin, the echoes of which reached the Polish Communist leaders, with Władysław Gomułka at their head, in 1956). Any domination by the Russian Communist party in Ukraine was interpreted by the Borotbists as a continuation of the old chauvinistic policy of the tsarist government, which had amounted to the assimilation of the non-Russian nationalities. Being powerless, the Ukrainian national Communists sought protection in the international forum of Communism, the Comintern, to which they apppealed for the recognition of a separate Communist party for Ukraine. Because of the dominant position of the Russian Communist party in the Comintern, the demand of the Ukrainian Communists was rejected. The uncompromising policy of the RCP towards the Ukrainian Communists was inspired by the stability of the Soviet government in Russia proper at the beginning of 1920. The Communist parties outside Soviet Russia, after their unsuccessful attempts at seizing power in their own countries, often existed by courtesy of the Russian Communist party.

The Communist party of Ukraine (the CP[B]U) in its totality adhered to the political line outlined by the leaders of the RCP(B). On the national question this meant paying lip-service to the principle of the right of nations to self-determination, but in practice it meant ignoring this same question and suppressing any national manifestations within the party. Many leaders of the CP(B)U, such as Piatakov, Bosh, Iakovlev, and Rakovsky, thought that the tsarist regime's two-hundred-year-old assimilatory policy had completely killed the national feelings of the Ukrainians. The emergence of the Central Rada and its actual victory over other claimants to sovereignty in Ukraine was explained by the Bolsheviks as an ephemeral upsurge. The Rada, having deceived the working masses and fanned their national feelings, had usurped power temporarily, until the masses should awaken and see its counter-revolutionary essence. The nationally conscious section of the CP(B)U, Shakhrai, Skrypnyk, and, to a point, Zatonsky, believed that Ukraine would liberate itself nationally and socially only under a Communist regime which had no interest in encroaching upon the national rights of small nations, including the Ukrainians. Some of these Communists became disillusioned by the party's national policy in Ukraine and broke with it (Shakhrai) or later committed suicide (Skrypnyk). However, had it not been for their opposition on the national question, it is anybody's guess what course party policy in Ukraine and in other republics would have taken. It can be clearly seen from the discussion about the competencies of the union organs and those of the union republics during the creation of the Soviet Union in 1923 that the national opposition against the centralists had considerable influence upon the formation of the party's policy in the republics. The retreat of the party from the so-called autonomism of the period before the revolution and the acceptance of a federalism modified in the Bolshevik manner seems to have been to a certain extent caused by national tendencies among the non-Russian Communists. Lenin's intervention during the forging of the relations between the RSFSR and other Soviet republics at the end of 1922 and the beginning of 1923 and his criticism of Stalin's proposal of the "autonomization" of the republics were a forced compromise with the national Communists, in whose van were the Ukrainians and Georgians.

Lenin and the party in general were most conciliatory towards Ukrainian nationalism during Denikin's offensive against Moscow, i.e., during the period of the peasantry's strongest resistance to Soviet rule. On the eve of the offensive on Ukraine Lenin broke with the policy of ignoring and underestimating the Ukrainian national movement and the national consciousness of the population. Not only were the Ukrainian language and culture recognized as having equal rights with the Russian, but he also agreed to the revision in Ukraine alone of the principle of the dictatorship of the proletariat, admitting the peasantry as well to power. The same fate also befell the policy towards the agricultural communes. Now Lenin was satisfied that it was impossible to introduce the communes by force, and that on the agrarian question, too, a zigzag policy had to be pursued.

As soon as their military fortunes changed, however, the party once more began tearing up resolutions and adopting the old tactics. The right to secession was now abolished and the separation of Ukraine was regarded as a crime, as counter-revolution. The Communists in Ukraine were issued with new directives. The national question and the interests of the peasantry were again ignored, and all the resources of the party were concentrated on the extraction of grain and other produce from Ukraine. The all-Ukrainian central executive committee and the whole Ukrainian government were reduced to the status of an agency of the RCP in Ukraine whose task was the execution of RCP directives.

To place the new policy of the party in Ukraine and elsewhere on theoretical foundations, a new theory was elaborated, the so-called Soviet federalism which was camouflage for a centralistic policy on the *edinaia i nedelimaia* pattern towards Ukraine. From the second half of 1920, a slow but resolute policy began of attracting Ukraine under the supreme party control. The CP(B)U underwent a thorough purge, and its whole central committee was elected anew in accordance with directives from Moscow.

Molotov was sent to Ukraine to be secretary of the local party. Considerable changes were introduced into the inter-state relations between the RSFSR and the Ukrainian SSR. The sovereignty of the Ukrainian Soviet government was gradually limited by various administrative measures. The chaotic intervention of the state organs of the RSFSR into Ukrainian affairs was stopped for a short time by the union treaty of 28 December 1920, but this had only propaganda value, for the party and administrative circles continued to pursue the policy of *edinaia i nedelimaia*. In the state and party organs of Ukraine a fierce struggle raged between the Russophiles and the Ukrainophiles. In spite of the directives from Moscow concerning the struggle against the imperialist and the local nationalist deviations, and according to which most attention was to be paid to the struggle against the former, in actual fact only the local nationalist deviations were persecuted, while the actions of the advocates of the *edinaia i nedelimaia* were not hindered. This pro-Russian trend of the party came clearly to the surface during the drafting of a constitution for the Union of the Soviet Socialist Republics. Stalin, followed by other mainstays of centralism, such as Zinovev, Rykov, Kamenev, Bukharin, Radek, Piatakov, Mikhail Tomsky, and Kalinin, tried by every means to neutralize the attempt of the representatives from the republics, Skrypnyk, Rakovsky, Mdivani, Makharadze, and M. Sultan-Galiev, to preserve national equality of rights within the union and to prevent the Russian federation's domination over the non-Russian republics. This opposition met with only limited success.

The process of the creation of the USSR and of the constitutional relationships between the RSFSR and the national republics confirms that the leaders of the RCP did not believe that Russia, dismembered into a series of independent national republics, could even maintain a Soviet regime at home, let alone lead the proletariat towards world revolution. Uniting the borderlands around the Russian republic was considered a prerequisite for the victory of the proletarian revolution. As Stalin admitted on one occasion, "Central Russia, this focal point of the world revolution, cannot hold out for long without the assistance of the borderlands which are rich in raw materials, fuel, food produce."[2] To keep these rich borderlands, the party applied all possible measures, of which military occupation was the most effective. One must agree with Pipes that "the establishment of the Soviet Union was in many respects an anticlimax, a mere legislation of conditions brought about by the Red Army, by the Communist Party and by the Government of the RSFSR between 1917 and 1922."[3]

In principle there was no disagreement among the leaders of the RCP on the necessity of preserving the territorial integrity of Russia. Both Lenin and Stalin, and even the so-called leftists led by Trotsky, were in favour of uniting the republics under the hegemony of Russia. The contradictions that arose between Lenin and Stalin at the end of 1922 were not ideological but tactical. It is interesting that the controversy between Lenin and Stalin originated at the time when Stalin's "administrative" methods towards his Georgian compatriots and others caused resistance not only among the "bourgeois nationalists," but also among orthodox national Bolsheviks. It was only then that Lenin began to doubt the success (but not the correctness) of the nationalities policy. Lenin correctly foresaw that to employ violence against the local Bolsheviks would sever the party from its last support in the borderlands. On the other hand, it may be assumed that Lenin was more realistic than Stalin, in whose hands, owing to Lenin's illness, the task of uniting the republics happened to be. But it must be remembered that Lenin was not fastidious in his own methods against the "bourgeois nationalists." His tactics towards the Ukrainian Communists (Borotbists) bear witness to his callous calculation.

There is no doubt that the form of the union was a synthesis of the desirable and the possible. From the very beginning the party aimed at a completely unitarian Republic of Soviets, admitting only a kind of cultural autonomy in local matters for the nationalties. However, the opposition of the nationalities happened to be stronger than expected; the party was therefore compelled to agree to a compromise. Owing to the energetic opposition of the national Bolsheviks, Stalin's project, in which the national republics would have been incorporated into the Russian republic and their status formally reduced to that of autonomous republics, was not accepted.

Abbreviations

ARR	*Arkhiv russkoi revoliutsii*
ASEER	*American Slavonic and East European Review*
BU	*Bilshovyk Ukrainy*
CC	Central committee
Cheka	Soviet secret police
CP(B)U	Communist Party (Bolsheviks) of Ukraine
CPC	Council of People's Commissars
GFM	German Foreign Ministry
KP(b)U	CP(B)U
LR	*Letopis revoliutsii*; *Litopys revoliutsii*
NKVD	People's commissariat for internal affairs
PCFA	People's commissariat for foreign affairs
PCFT	People's commissariat for foreign trade
PPS	Polish Socialist Party
RCP(B)	Russian Communist Party (Bolsheviks)
RKP(b)	RCP(B)
RPSR	Russian Party of Socialist Revolutionaries
RSDRP	RSDWP
RSDWP	Russian Social Democratic Workers' Party
RSFSR	Russian Soviet Federative Socialist Republic
RUP	Revolutionary Ukrainian Party
RVSR	Revolutionary military council of the republic

SD	Social democrat
SDPL	Social Democracy of Poland and Lithuania
SEER	*Slavonic and East European Review*
SF	Socialist federalist
SR	Social revolutionary
TsIK	Central executive committee
TsIKU	Central executive committee of Ukraine
TsVKU	TsIKU
TUP	Association of Ukrainian Progressists
UCP	Ukrainian Communist Party
UCP(B)	Ukrainian Communist Party (Borotbists)
UKP	UCP
UPSR	Ukrainian Party of Socialist Revolutionaries
URDP	Ukrainian Radical Democratic Party
USDRP	USDWP
USDWP	Ukrainian Social Democratic Workers' Party
VKP(b)	All-Union Communist Party (Bolsheviks)
VTsIK	All-Russian (all-union) central executive committee
VUChK	Ukrainian cheka
VUNR	*Vestnik Ukrainskoi narodnoi respubliki*
VUTsIK	All-Ukrainian central executive committee

NOTES

Introduction

1. A fact recognized even by Soviet historians (editorial, *Voprosy istorii*, 1958, No. 4). This trend was pointed out recently by Robert H. McNeal, "Soviet Historiography on the October Revolution: A Review of Forty Years," *The American Slavonic and East European Review* (ASEER), October 1958, No. 3, pp. 269–81; and in J. A. Armstrong, "Clues to the Soviet Political Archives," *The Russian Review*, 1957, No. 1, p. 47.
2. For further views on this problem, see pp. 11, 370.
3. The term "Bolshevik" originates from the second congress of the Russian Social Democratic Workers' Party (RSDWP) in 1903, at which the party was split into two factions: the Mensheviks (the minority) and the Bolsheviks (the majority). From this time the Russian social democrats of Lenin's faction called themselves the Bolsheviks. At the Prague conference (1912) the Bolsheviks organized a separate party, the RSDWP(B), which at the seventh congress in 1918 was renamed the Russian Communist Party (Bolsheviks). The terms Bolshevik and Communist are used synonymously. However, the term Bolshevik will be used in this work to refer to the Russian Communists during the Bolshevik revolution.
4. Some authors consider that the Soviet leaders have succeeded in eliminating national antagonism. See especially E. H. Carr, *Nationalism and After*, p. 36, and even C. A. Macartney, *National States and National Minorities*, pp. 459–64.
5. J. Lawrynenko, *Ukrainian Communism*, p. 141.
6. These letters were made public in *Kommunist*, 1956, No. 9, pp. 15–26, under the heading "Unpublished Documents of V. I. Lenin."
7. This fact was deplored by M. M. Popov in *Narys*, p. 212.
8. Here I am thinking chiefly of the following: *Velikaia oktiabrskaia sotsialisticheskaia revoliutsiia na Ukraine* and *Borba za vlast Sovetov na Kievshchine*.

9. A. L. Fraiman, in a review of *Podgotovka velikoi oktiabrskoi sotsialisticheskoi revoliutsii na Ukraine* (*Voprosy Istorii*, 1955, No. 11, pp. 129–33), finds that the book inadequately describes the special character of the revolution in Ukraine. Fraiman criticized the editor, Korolivsky, because he "tries to fit the whole course of the development of the revolution in Ukraine to the conditions of Central Russia, wishing to demonstrate that the processes of the revolutionary struggle of the working masses in Central Russia and in Ukraine were identical during the period of preparation for the October [revolution]." Another example of this tendency is the collection of documents *1917 god na Kievshchine*; its editor, Manilov, wrote: "As far as the selection of material characterizing the activity of petty-bourgeois parties and institutions, Ukrainian, Russian, and Jewish, is concerned, we have shown a definite Bolshevik tendentiousness, selecting our material in such a way as would show their anti-revolutionary and counter-revolutionary features with greatest clarity" (p. XI).
10. V. A. Antonov-Ovseenko, *Zapiski o grazhdanskoi voine*, Vols. I–IV.
11. Such was the accusation made by T. Skubitsky, in *Istorik-marksist* (Moscow, 1929, Vol. 12, p. 285) with regard to Iavorsky's *Istoriia Ukrainy v styslomu narysi*. Cf. also B. Krupnytsky, *Ukrainska istorychna nauka pid sovietamy*.
12. P. Gorin, "O roli proletariata v revoliutsionnom dvizhenii Ukrainy," *Bolshevik*, 1930, No. 1, p. 45.
13. P. Vershigora, in *Oktiabr*, 1954, No. 4, pp. 110–36.
14. Editorial, "For the profound scientific study of the history of the Ukrainian people," in *Voprosy istorii*, 1955, No. 7, p. 8.
15. Review of Likholat's book by Oslikovskaia and Snegov, in *Voprosy istorii*, 1956, No. 3, pp. 138–45.
16. F. E. Los, *Revoliutsiia 1905–1907 rokiv na Ukraini*.
17. See the review of Los' book by Shmorhun and Kravchuk in *Voprosy istorii*, 1956, No. 11, pp. 161–65.
18. E. H. Carr, *The Bolshevik Revolution*, Vol. I, pp. 410–18.
19. S. Page, "Lenin and Self-Determination," *The Slavonic and East European Review* (*SEER*) (London), 1950, Vol. XXVIII, No. 71, pp. 342–55.
20. B. Wolfe, *Three Who Made A Revolution*.
21. See especially W. E. D. Allen, *The Ukraine* (Cambridge, 1941); W. E. Chamberlin, *The Story of the Ukraine* (New York, 1949); W. Batsell, *Soviet Rule in Russia; The Bolshevik Revolution, 1917–1918*, ed. Bunyan and Fisher.
22. E. H. Carr, *The Future of Nations* (London, 1941), and also *Nationalism and After* (London, 1945).
23. G. Kennan, *Soviet-American Relations, 1917–1920*, Vol. I: *Russia Leaves the War* (Princeton, 1956), and Vol. II: *The Decision to Intervene* (Princeton, 1958).

Chapter I

1. Among the Western works on this problem, the following can be mentioned: B. D. Wolfe, *Three Who Made a Revolution*, pp. 568–77; R. Smal-Stocki, *The Nationality Problem of the Soviet Union and Russian Communist Imperialism*, pp. 43–52; E. H. Carr, *The Bolshevik Revolution*, Vol. I, pp. 410–18; S. Page, "Lenin and Self-Determination," *SEER*, 1950, No. 71, pp. 342–58; T. G. Masaryk, *Otâzka socialnî*, Vol. II, pp. 151 ff.; B. D. Wolfe, "Nationalism and Internationalism in Marx and Engels," *ASEER*, 1958, Vol. XVII, No. 4, pp. 403–17; Horace B. Davis, *Nationalism and Socialism*. Lenin, in his discussion with Rosa Luxemburg in 1914, wrote that "in general, the attitude of Marx and Engels to the national question was strictly critical, and they recognized its historically relative importance," and that Marx "had no doubt as to the subordinate position of the national question as compared with the labour question. But this theory is as far from ignoring the national question as heaven from earth." V. I. Lenin, *The Right of Nations to Self-Determination*, pp. 78–79. The Soviet historiography of the early period admits that "the problem of nationalities does not occupy an independent position in the works of Marx and Engels .... However, we find in Marx and Engels many cursory opinions concerning certain *concrete* national problems affecting the interests of the revolution, and those opinions referring to contemporary events present an excellent model of the way to approach national problems from the point of view of revolutionary Marxism." Velikovsky, *Natsionalnyi vopros*, p. 87. Cf. also G. Safarov, *Marks o natsionalno-kolnialnom voprose*.
2. In his early works ("Zur Judenfrage," Marx-Engels, *Historisch-kritische Gesamtausgabe*, Abt. I, Vol. I, pp. 576–606; "Die heilige Familie," ibid., Vol. III, pp. 259–300), Marx identified nationality with the state.
3. Carr, I, pp. 412–13.
4. For instance, Mill, while believing that "it is in general a necessary condition of free institutions that the boundaries of governments should coincide in the main with those of nationalities," nonetheless recommended the Irish not to secede from Britain for the sake of practical advantages. J. S. Mill, *Representative Government*, pp. 362, 365–66.
5. The Austrian constituent assembly in 1848 was convened in Kroměříž in Moravia. The most urgent question seemed to be that of nationalities. See R. Schlesinger, *Federalism*, p. 158.
6. K. Marx, *Revolution and Counter-Revolution in Germany in 1848*, pp. 99–101.
7. Bauer disagreed with Engels with regard to the question of "unhistorical peoples." He wrote: "Man hat solche Nationen als *geschichstlose Nationen* bezeichnet, und wir wollen diesen Ausdruck beibehalten; aber er bedeutet nicht, dass solche Nationen niemals eine Geschichte gehabt hätten ... auch nicht, dass solche Nationen, wie noch Friedrich Engels im Jahre 1848

geglaubt hat, zu geschichtlichem Leben überhaupt nicht fähig waren, geschichtliches Leben nie mehr erlangen könnten—denn diese Meinung ist durch die Geschichte des 19. Jahrhunderts endgültig wiederlegt." Otto Bauer, *Die Nationalitätenfrage und die Sozialdemokratie* (Vienna, 1924), pp. 190–91.

8. Marx and Engels, *Sochineniia*, XIII, I, pp. 154–57.
9. See *Neue Rheinische Zeitung*, 13 January and 15 and 16 February 1849.
10. *Aufruf an die Slaven*. Von einem russischen Patrioten Michael Bakunin, Mitglied des Slavenkongressens in Prag (Koethen: Selbstverlag des Verfassers, 1848). Russian translation by T. S. Z. in *Pisma M. A. Bakunina k A. I. Gertsenu i N. P. Ogarevu* (Geneva, 1896), pp. 372–74 ff.
11. *Neue Rheinische Zeitung*, 13 January and 15 and 16 February 1849. Cf. also *The Russian Menace to Europe by Karl Marx and Friedrich Engels*, ed. Paul W. Blackstock and Bert F. Hoselitz (Glencoe, 1952).
12. Quoted in Velikovsky, p. 107. Cf. also Engels' articles in *Neue Oder-Zeitung*, 21 and 24 April 1855. On Engels' attitude to "diese elenden Frümmerstücke ehemaliger Nationen," see his letter to Bebel (17 November 1885) in Friedrich Engels, *Briefe an Bebel*, p. 119. Cf. also *Arkhiv Marksa i Engelsa*, Vol. I (VI), pp. 314 ff., and Engels' letter to Kautsky of 7 February 1882, ibid., pp. 189–93. Almost a century before Engels, Herder gave a quite different appraisal of the Slav peoples. According to Kohn, *The Idea of Nationalism*, p. 437, Herder felt that "the Slavs fulfilled much better than the Germans the essential condition of a good and civilized people."
13. Ferdinand Lassalle, "Der italienische Krieg" (1859), *Gesamtwerke*, p. 379.
14. *Briefe von F. Lassalle an Karl Rodbertus-Jagetzow*, pp. 56–57.
15. Carr, I, p. 414.
16. For instance, the humanists Herder, Lessing, Klopstock, and others, including Bakunin, dealt with the problems of the small nationalities.
17. Carr, I, p. 414.
18. Smal-Stocki, p. 45. Cf. also V. Levynsky, *Sotsiialistychnyi Internatsional i ponevoleni narody*, pp. 7 ff., who asserts that between Marx's, Engels', and Lassalle's views and Hegel's historical theory there was "an organic connection." See also T. G. Masaryk, *Otâzka socialnî*, Vol. II, pp. 152–53, and B. Wolfe, "Nationalism and Internationalism," *ASEER*, pp. 406 ff.
19. For instance, in his article "Poles, Tschechs, and Germans" in the *New York Tribune* (1852), Marx wrote: "The Slavonians, and particularly the Western Slavonians (Poles and Tschechs), are essentially an agricultural race; trade and manufactures never were in great favour with them . . . . The production of all articles of manufacture fell into the hands of German immigrants, and the exchange of these commodities against agricultural produce became the exclusive monopoly of the Jews, who, if they belong to any nationality, are in these countries certainly rather Germans than Slavonians." *Revolution and Counter-Revolution*, p. 59. This was why

Marx regarded the demands of the Poles for their historical boundaries of 1772 as an anachronism.

20. Ibid., p. 63. Lenin in his article, "Sotsialisticheskaia revoliutsiia i samoopredelenie" (1916), *Soch.*, XXII, p. 139, justified Marx's attitude by political and historical motives; Marx in 1848 had the prerequisites for distinguishing between "reactionary" and revolutionary-democratic nations. In considering the Czechs reactionary, Marx's negative attitude was quite justified. Lenin himself also had the opportunity of encountering the national demands of the Czechs in a completely different historical situation. In 1913 Lenin attacked the Czech separatists because they broke up "the former unity of the Czech and German workers" in Austria. "Separatisty v Rossii i separatisty v Avstrii," *Soch.*, XIX, pp. 67–68. It is interesting to note that Velikovsky (p. 89) admitted that possibly Marx and Engels also committed some errors in "the concrete forecasts concerning the role and the prospects of development of this or that nationality."
21. These views were expressed by Marx and Engels in the *Neue Rheinische Zeitung* in the polemics with Wilhelm Jordan, who opposed the Poles' aspirations.
22. See Engels' articles "On the Eastern Question" published in full for the first time in *Gesammelte Schriften von Karl Marx and Fr. Engels, 1852–1862*, Vol. I, pp. 144–211, and particularly Engels' articles, "The Nationalities in Turkey" and "What Is To Happen to European Turkey?"
23. Velikovsky, p. 108.
24. See Kohn, *The Idea of Nationalism*, p. 431.
25. G. W. Hegel, *Vorlesungen über die Philosophie der Geschichte*, pp. 504–07.
26. Velikovsky and Levin, the compilers of the Soviet anthology on the national question, wrote that Marx's and Engels' negative attitude to the national movements of the Austrian Slavs was "determined by the *objective* counter-revolutionary role of these movements." Velikovsky, p. 89.
27. "I used to think the separation of Ireland from England impossible. I now think it inevitable, although after the separation there may come federation." Marx's letter to Engels, 2 November 1867, in Marx and Engels, *Historisch-kritische Gesamtausgabe*, Abt. III, Vol. III, p. 442; Lenin, *The Right of Nations to Self-Determination*, p. 81. Concerning Marx's *volte-face* in the Irish question, see the letter of the General Council of the International, written apparently by Marx, to the Romansh central committee in Geneva. G. Safarov, *Marks o natsionalno-kolonialnom voprose*, pp. 100–01.
28. Lenin, *The Right of Nations to Self-Determination*, pp. 84–85.
29. Ibid., p. 88.
30. Carr, Vol. I, p. 416.
31. For instance, Engels in his letter to Marx, 23 May 1851, gave a very negative evaluation of the historical role of Poland: "The Poles did nothing else in history but brave, impetuous acts of foolishness"; he thought that "everything possible must be taken away from the Poles in the western part;

their fortresses, particularly Poznań, must be occupied by the Germans under the pretext of defence; they must be kept busy, sent under fire; their lands must be taken away; they must be fed with the prospects of the capture of Riga and Odessa. And if it were possible to rouse the Russians, an alliance with them should be made, and the Poles compelled to surrender." Marx and Engels, *Historisch-kritische Gesamtausgabe*, Abt. III, Vol. I, p. 206. Cf. also Lenin, *The Right of Nations to Self-Determination*, pp. 78–79.

32. *Der Vorbote*, 1866, No. 11, p. 165. See also Marx's speech, read probably on 22 January 1867 in London and first printed in the magazine *Le Socialisme*, 15 March 1908, No. 18, quoted in Marx and Engels, *Soch.*, XIII, part I, pp. 190–94. Also Engels now went over to the Poles' side and supported the idea of the restoration of an independent Poland. See his letter to Kautsky, 7 February 1882, in *Arkhiv Marksa i Engelsa*, Vol. I (IV), pp. 189–93.
33. See the declaration of the Geneva delegate, Düpleir, in the report on the congress in *Der Vorbote*, 1866, No. 11, p. 166.
34. See the declaration of the French delegate Fribourg. Ibid., p. 165. There is no doubt that this position approached that of Proudhon, who opposed the restoration of the historical Poland of 1772 because it would have been unjust towards the small peoples who populated these regions and did not consider themselves Poles. "Mais les Lithuaniens ne sont pas des Polonais; les Ruthènes ne sont pas des Polonais," wrote Proudhon. And he propagated the idea of the liberation of all nationalities. "I declare that in my opinion all human races have an equal right to existence and an equal right to civilization." *Oeuvres complètes de P.-J. Proudhon*, pp. 395 ff., 420. On Marx's inconsistency, see also Wolfe, "Nationalism and Internationalism," *ASEER*, pp. 403–17.
35. *Der Vorbote*, 1866, No. 11, p. 167.
36. Ibid.
37. Marx and Engels, *Historisch-kritische Gesamtausgabe*, Abt. III, Vol. III, pp. 341–42.
38. Engels' letter to Kautsky, 7 February 1882, in *Arkhiv Marksa i Engelsa*, Vol. I, p. 192.
39. Ibid., pp. 189–90.
40. Ibid., p. 191.
41. Lenin, *Soch.*, XX, p. 412.
42. See Safarov, *Marks o natsionalno-kolonialnom voprose*, pp. 100–02.
43. Ibid.
44. See Engels' letter to Marx, 7 October 1858, in *Der Briefwechsel zwischen Friedrich Engels und Karl Marx*, Vol. II, pp. 289–91.
45. Safarov, *Marks o natsionalno-kolonialnom voprose*, pp. 100–02.
46. Ibid., p. 102.
47. Engels, in his letter to Marx, 15 August 1870, in *Der Briefwechsel zwischen Fr. Engels und K. Marx*, Vol. IV, pp. 318–20, wrote: "If Badinguet

[Napoleon III] is victorious [over Germany], then Bonapartism will take root for years, and Germany will go under for years, perhaps for whole generations. Then an independent German workers' movement will no longer be conceivable, the struggle to regain national existence will absorb everything, and, at best, the German workers will become the beasts of burden of the French workers. But if Germany is victorious, then in any case Bonapartism, the constant clamourer against the restoration of German unity, will have fallen, ... then the German workers will be able to organize in a different way from that hitherto possible, that is, nationally, and the French workers ... will surely have a freer field than under Bonapartism."

48. See, for instance, the resolution of the Brussels congress of 1891, which said that "the only way to liberation for the Jewish workers lies in their uniting with the workers' socialist parties of all countries where they live." Quoted in Velikovsky, p. 114.
49. The passivity of the International in this question may be explained by the fact that "no further troubles occurred in Poland or elsewhere to make it acute on the European continent." Carr, *The Bolshevik Revolution*, I, p. 417. However, it preserved its passive attitude also after the question of nationalities came to the fore in Russia in 1905–06 and in Austria. "But when at the Brno Congress in 1898 the Austrian Socialist Party had to decide its policy on the national question, the disintegration of the Austrian State had reached such a point that the Kremsier proposals were bound to prove inadequate." Rudolf Schlesinger, *Federalism in Central and Eastern Europe*, p. 209.
50. Quoted in Velikovsky, p. 114. Lenin, *Soch.*, XX, p. 203, gives a somewhat different Russian text of the resolution. Carr, I, p. 417, following an English source (*International Socialist Workers' and Trade Union Congress* [London, 1896] p. 31), uses the term "autonomy," explaining that the German version and the Russian version that followed it translated "autonomy" as *Selbstbestimmungsrecht* and *samoopredelenie* respectively.
51. See pp. 24, 28–31.
52. The nationality problem within the Russian Communist party in its early period has been treated by some Western historians; however, there is no monograph on the subject. See especially Carr, I, pp. 410–28; Page, pp. 342–58; Wolfe, *Three Who Made a Revolution*, pp. 478–90; Smal-Stocki, pp. 52–78; Pipes, *The Formation of the Soviet Union*, pp. 34–49.
53. At the RSDWP's second congress in 1903 Plekhanov was against tendencies that might endanger the unity of the future socialist Russia. *Leninskii sbornik*, II (1924), p. 144.
54. *Vsesoiuznaia kommunisticheskaia partiia (bolshevikov) v rezoliutsiiakh i resheniiakh sezdov*, Vol. I (1932), p. 4.
55. Popov, *Outline*, I, p. 52.
56. *Vsesoiuznaia kommunisticheskaia partiia*, I, p. 4.
57. The Jewish Bund was recognized by the RSDWP as "an organization which

is independent in questions affecting particularly the Jewish proletariat." Ibid., I, p. 3.

58. A. Kremer, "Osnovanie Bunda," *Proletarskaia revoliutsiia*, 1922, No. 11, p. 55.
59. N. Nedasek, *Bolshevizm v revoliutsionnom dvizhenii Belorussii*, p. 58.
60. The role of the Bund as the promoter of the discussion on self-determination was later stressed by Zinovev. See his *Istoriia Rossiiskoi kommunisticheskoi partii (bolshevikov)*, p. 96.
61. *Vtoroi sezd RSDRP*, p. 420.
62. Ibid., pp. 452–54. This proposition reflected the negative attitude of Rosa Luxemburg to the national question, which united her with such leftists as Piatakov, Radek, Bukharin, and Evgeniia Bosh.
63. See Koltsov's remark, ibid., p. 191.
64. See Martynov's remark, ibid., p. 184.
65. Lenin, *Soch.*, VII, pp. 83–85. The article originally appeared in *Iskra*, 1903, No. 51. Similar argumentation against the Jews as a nation was employed by Stalin in his polemics with Rudolf Springer and Otto Bauer. See Stalin, "Marxism and the National Question (1913)," *Marxism and the National and Colonial Question*, pp. 10–12.
66. Schwarz, p. 50.
67. Some writers, such as Smal-Stocki, argue that "Lenin, in his view of the Jews, was completely under the influence of Marx." Smal-Stocki, p. 58n.
68. Lenin, *Soch.*, VII, p. 85.
69. Page, p. 345.
70. Medem, *Sotsialdemokratiia i natsionalnyi vopros* (1905), quoted from Velikovsky, pp. 156–57. Goldblat stressed at the congress that self-determination did not at all eliminate national conflicts; he felt that either "self-determination or territorial self-government" could satisfy the right to national development of the minorities. The Bund's leader, Liber, noted that in Russia there were nationalities that did not want to separate and were satisfied with cultural autonomy. *Vtoroi sezd RSDRP*, pp. 190–91.
71. The Polish social democratic organization was organized as a counterweight to the Polish Socialist Party (PPS) founded by Limanowski in 1892 with the slogan of national independence for Poland. Under the leadership of Rosa Luxemburg, the internationalist elements formed in 1899 the Social Democracy of the Kingdom of Poland and Lithuania. For the history of this party, see V. Leder, "Natsionalnyi vopros v polskoi i russkoi sotsial-demokratii," *Proletarskaia revoliutsiia*, 1927, Nos. 2–3, pp. 148–208; B. Szmidt, *Socialdemokracja Królewstwa Polskiego i Litwy. Materiały i dokumenty 1914–1918* (Moscow, 1936); A. Warski, "Sotsial-demokratiia Polshi i Litvy i II sezd RSDRP," *Kommunisticheskii internatsional*, 5 April 1929, No. 14, pp. 30–41, and 26 April 1929, No. 16–17, pp. 24–36.
72. An abbreviated text of the manifesto is in Lenin, *Soch.*, VI, pp. 292–93.

73. *Soch.*, VI, p. 293. The article originally appeared in *Iskra*, 1 February 1903, No. 33. Armenian social democracy was also attacked by Stalin, who wrote in his article, "Kak ponimaiet s.-d. natsionalnyi vopros," that the Armenian social democrats probably unconsciously moved towards the unity of the national proletariat with its own national bourgeoisie and the creation of a homogeneous nation, while the proletariat was being divided according to nationality. Stalin placed two alternatives before the federalists: federalism, i.e., the strengthening of national barriers, or the rejection of federalism, i.e., the annihilation of national barriers and merging in a single camp—the Russian Social Democratic Workers' Party. Stalin, *Soch.*, I, pp. 33–55.
74. Lenin, *Soch.*, VI, pp. 412–20.
75. For Marx's and Engels' attitude on the Polish question, see above, pp. 19–20.
76. Lenin referred to Kautsky's article "Finis Poloniae" (1896), which argued that independence should not absorb the whole attention of the working masses, and that the proletarians could not strive towards independence under all conditions.
77. Lenin, *Soch.*, VI, p. 414, quoting Mehring.
78. Ibid., pp. 418–20.
79. In 1903 Lenin wrote to the representative of the oblast committee in Kiev to explain his attitude towards the PPS: "One must obtain from the PPS at least a small, but formal, paper [letter], and [one must] not tell them: 'we are antinationalists' (why frighten people unnecessarily?), but gently persuade them that our programme (the recognition of the right to national self-determination) is sufficient for them as well .... Our chief trump card against the PPS is that we recognize in principle national self-determination, but within *reasonable* limits, determined by the unity of the proletarian class struggle." *Leninskii sbornik*, VII, p. 356. Emphasis added.
80. See the resolution of the congress in *Tretii sezd RSDRP*, pp. 16–17. Cf. also *Tretii ocherednoi sezd RSDRP*, p. xxii.
81. Popov, *Ocherk*, p. 129. Apart from these organizations, present at the congress as guests were the Latvian, Ukrainian, and Armenian social democratic organizations, which did not unite with the RSDWP.
82. *Chetvertyi sezd RSDRP*, p. 22.
83. Morev's remark, ibid., p. 23. Popov later admitted that "the local party organizations had hitherto not paid the national question the attention it deserved, and as a consequence were not always able to counteract successfully the influence of the bourgeois nationalists who made great capital out of their national demands among the workers and toilers of the oppressed nationalities." Popov, *Outline History*, Vol. I, p. 285.
84. *Chetvertyi sezd RSDRP*, p. 24.
85. *Piatyi sezd RSDRP*, pp. 286–87. Popov, *Narys*, p. 83, wrote that the nationality question was postponed because it had not been properly

prepared before the congress.

86. *Piatyi sezd RSDRP*, pp. 312–13.
87. Ibid., p. 645.
88. Popov, *Ocherk*, p. 144.
89. Lenin, *Soch.*, XXXI, p. 11. Cf. also Popov, *Ocherk*, pp. 143–53.
90. Lenin, "Tezisy po natsionalnomu voprosu," *Soch.*, XIX, pp. 213–21.
91. Popov, *Ocherk*, p. 181.
92. The most important of Lenin's studies on this question were "Tezisy po natsionalnomu voprosu" (June 1913); "O natsionalnoi programme RSDRP" (December 1913); "Kriticheskie zametki po natsionalnomu voprosu" (December 1913); "O prave natsii na samoopredelenie" (February–June 1914); "O natsionalnoi gordosti velikorossov" (1914); "Sotsialisticheskaia revoliutsiia i pravo natsii na samoopredelenie" (1916); "Itogi diskussii o samoopredelenii" (1916); "O karikature na marksizm" (1916).
93. Popov, *Ocherk*, p. 183.
94. Lenin, *Soch.*, XIX, pp. 71–72.
95. See the resolution of the August conference in Poronin in 1913 in *VKP(b) v rezoliutsiiakh*, Vol. I, pp. 238–40.
96. Lenin said that social democracy should "demand that a decision on the question of such separation should depend exclusively on general, direct, equal, and secret ballot of the population of the given territory." *Soch.*, XIX, p. 214.
97. *VKP(b) v rezoliutsiiakh*, Vol. I, pp. 238–40.
98. Ibid.
99. For the Austrian attitude on the national question, see Otto Bauer, *Die Nationalitätenfrage und die Sozialdemokratie* (Vienna, 1924) and *Die österreichische Revolution* (Vienna, 1923); Karl Renner, *Das Selbstbestimmungsrecht der Nationen in besonderer Anwendung auf Österreich* (Leipzig-Vienna, 1918). An English summary of their views is in R. Schlesinger, *Federalism in Central and Eastern Europe*, pp. 209–32.
100. Quoted in Velikovsky, p. 163.
101. "Kriticheskie zametki po natsionalnomu voprosu," *Soch.*, XX, pp. 17–18.
102. Ibid., p. 12.
103. Ibid., p. 19.
104. Ibid., p. 20. A still stronger argument against the separation of education from the state was employed by Lenin in his speech, "K voprosu o natsionalnoi politike," published for the first time in 1924 in *Proletarskaia revoliutsiia*, No. 3, reprinted in *Soch.*, XX, pp. 197–204. The speech was written for the Bolshevik deputy in the Duma, Petrovsky. It was never read because of the expulsion of the social democratic deputies. Here Lenin also wrote that "to take educational matters out of the hands of the state and to divide them among nationalities organized separately into national unions is a harmful measure both from the point of view of democracy and even more so from the point of view of the proletariat .... This would lead to the

growth of chauvinism, while we must move towards the closest union of the workers of all nations."

105. Lenin, *Soch.*, XX, pp. 28–34.
106. Ibid., pp. 381–82.
107. Ibid., p. 382.
108. Ibid., pp. 384–85.
109. Lenin, *Soch.*, XXI, p. 377.
110. Lenin, *Soch.*, XIX, pp. 453–54. First published in *Leninskii sbornik*, III (1925), pp. 470–73.
111. Nedasek, pp. 138–39.
112. Lenin, *Soch.*, XIX, pp. 453–54. For the correspondence between Lenin and Shaumian, see also G. S. Akopian, "Perepiska V. I. Lenina i S. G. Shaumiana po natsionalnomu voprosu," *Voprosy istorii*, 1956, No. 8, pp. 3–14.
113. Lenin, *Soch.*, XXII, pp. 135–36.
114. Page, pp. 353–54, stated that Lenin's position enabled the Bolsheviks "to gain the confidence of various minority national groups . . . during one or another phase of the Civil War period." This confidence was gained fully only among very small strata of the population on the territories of various nationalities. As is known, all national governments in the borderlands were at war with the Bolsheviks during all phases of the Civil War, a fact stressed also by Page.
115. See below, pp. 125–29.
116. R. Luxemburg, *Die russische Revolution*, pp. 40–41.
117. Lenin, *Soch.*, XIX, p. 453.
118. See especially S. W. Page, "Lenin, National Self-Determination and the Baltic States, 1917–19," *ASEER*, 1948, Vol. VII, pp. 15–31; B. Kalnins, *De baltiska staternas fribetskamp* (Stockholm, 1950); Pipes; A. Shwabe, *A History of Latvia* (Stockholm, 1950); F. W. Pick, *The Baltic Nations* (London, 1945).
119. There are many accounts of the position of the socialists during the war, among them: Gankin and Fisher, *The Bolsheviks and the World War*, pp. 133 ff.; C. Grünberg, *Die Internationale und der Weltkrieg* (Leipzig, 1916); M. Fainsod, *International Socialism and the World War* (Cambridge, Mass., 1935).
120. Lenin expressed disgust in connection with the news that the German socialists voted for war aims; he called them "patriots, chauvinists." *Soch.*, XXI, p. 5.
121. H. Cunow, *Partei: Zusammenbruch*, pp. 26 ff.
122. E. David, *Socialdemokratie und Vaterlandsverteidigung*, pp. 25 ff.
123. Cf. P. Lensch, "Die Selbstbestimmungsklause," *Die Glocke*, 1915–16, pp. 465–76.
124. Ibid., p. 465.
125. P. Lensch, "Socialismus and Annexionen in der Vergangenheit," *Die Glocke*, 1915–16, p. 494.

126. Lenin's theses on the war are in *Soch.*, XXI, pp. 1–4; cf. also the revised version, "Voina i rossiiskaia sotsial-demokratiia," ibid., pp. 11–18.
127. Lenin, *Soch.*, XXI, pp. 12–13.
128. Ibid., p. 17.
129. Ibid.
130. Ibid., p. 16.
131. Gankin and Fisher, pp. 214–15.
132. "Theses and Resolution of the Editorial Board of *Gazeta Robotnicza*, Organ of the Regional Presidium of the Social Democracy of Poland and Lithuania," in [K. Radek], "Thesen über Imperialismus und nationale Unterdrückung," *Der Vorbote*, April 1916, No. 2, pp. 44–51, quoted in Gankin and Fisher, pp. 507–18.
133. D. Baevsky, *Ocherki po istorii oktiabrskoi revoliutsii*, Vol. I, pp. 516–18, quoted in Gankin and Fisher, pp. 219–21. Cf. also Dimanshtein, pp. xxix–xxxi, and Velikovsky, pp. 358–60.
134. Lenin, "Sotsialisticheskaia revoliutsiia i pravo natsii na samoopredelenie," *Soch.*, XXII, p. 144.
135. Lenin, "Otvet P. Kievskomu," written in 1916, published in *Proletarskaia revoliutsiia*, 1929, No. 7 (90), pp. 3–14. Lenin, *Soch.*, XXIII, pp. 10–15, quoted in Gankin and Fisher, p. 227.
136. D. Baevsky, "Bolsheviki v borbe za III Internatsional," *Istorik-marksist*, 1929, No. 11, p. 36.
137. Lenin, "Itogi diskussii o samoopredelenii," *Soch.*, XXII, p. 326.
138. Ibid., pp. 330–31.
139. Ibid., p. 332.
140. Velikovsky, p. 377.
141. Ibid., pp. 377–78.
142. Stalin, *Marxism and the National and Colonial Question*, p. 63.
143. Ibid., pp. 64–65.
144. Lenin, *Soch.*, XXIV, pp. 264–65.
145. Dimanshtein, p. 11.
146. Ibid., pp. 12–13.
147. Lenin, *Soch.*, XXIV, p. 267.
148. According to Stalin, "a nation is a historically evolved stable community of people with common language, territory, economic life, and psychological make-up manifested in a community of culture." Stalin, *Marxism and the National and Colonial Question*, p. 8.
149. Schlesinger, *Federalism in Central and East Europe*, p. 329.
150. The resolution was adopted by fifty-six votes to sixteen, with eighteen abstentions. *VKP(b) v rezoliutsiiakh i resheniiakh*, Vol. I, p. 272. The text of the resolution is on pp. 271–72.
151. This article was rewritten in May 1917 from a series of articles in *Nashe slovo* and published in L. Trotsky, *Voina i revoliutsiia*, Vol. II, pp. 485–509.
152. Ibid., pp. 496–99.

153. Lenin, *Soch.*, XXII, pp. 343–44.
154. Ibid., XX, p. 425. In his draft of the resolution for the August conference, Lenin warned particularly the proletarians of Poland and Finland, where the landowners and the bourgeoisie in 1905 "gave up the revolutionary struggle for freedom and sought reconciliation with the tsarist monarchy and ruling classes in Russia." Ibid., XIX, p. 214.
155. Ibid., V, pp. 442–50; *Vtoroi sezd RSDRP*, p. 87.
156. Ibid., p. 98. The democratic principles were rejected by Plekhanov more unequivocally than by Lenin. Plekhanov said at the congress: "The success of the revolution is the supreme law; and if the success of the revolution should demand the temporary limitation of any one or another democratic principle it would be criminal to refrain from such limitations." Popov, *Ocherk*, p. 71n.
157. *Vtoroi sezd RSDRP*, pp. 87–88.
158. Lenin, *Soch.*, V, p. 248.
159. *Vtoroi sezd RSDRP*, pp. 48–49n.
160. Ibid., pp. 89–90.
161. See the remark of Karsky, ibid., p. 47. Among the centralists were Lenin, Plekhanov, Trotsky, Martov, Egorov, and Knuniants. Ibid., pp. 47–194. The position of the Bund was strengthened, curiously, by the demands of the Polish social democrats for the "complete independence of Polish social democracy in all internal activities concerning agitation and organization, . . . [their] own congresses, committees, and literature." Ibid., pp. 141, 452–54.
162. Ibid., p. 337.
163. During the congress and afterwards, Knuniants went by the name of Rusov. He was a devoted "Iskrist" Bolshevik who died in prison in 1910.
164. Ibid., pp. 337, 343.
165. Ibid., p. 118.
166. Paragraph 8 of the statutes stated: "All organizations entering the party shall deal independently with all affairs belonging especially and exclusively to the field of activity for the management of which they were created." Ibid., p. 424. This formulation was presented by L. Martov and accepted by forty-six votes (among them Lenin, Plekhanov, Trotsky, Martov) to five (Goldblat, Iudin, V. Hoffman, Liber, K. Abramson—all Bundists). Ibid., p. 107n.
167. For the further and detailed argumentation of the Bund's delegates, see: "Declaration of the Bund Delegation of the Second RSDWP Congress," ibid., pp. 454–56.
168. N. N. Zhordaniia, using the name Kostrov at the congress, was the leader of the Georgian social democrats (Mensheviks). In 1906 he was a member of the first Duma; at the London congress of the RSDWP he was elected a member of the central committee; during the revolution he was in opposition to the Bolsheviks and from 1918–20 he was president of the Georgian republic. In 1921 he escaped to France after his democratic

government was overthrown by Bolshevik troops.

169. *Vtoroi sezd RSDRP*, pp. 336–37. Topuridze ("Karsky" at the congress), representative of the Tiflis committee, gave the following circumstances as preventing the CC RSDWP from fulfilling its work in the Caucasus: language, remoteness, peculiar customs of life. Ibid., p. 339.
170. Ibid., p. 340.
171. Ibid., p. 339.
172. Ibid., pp. 339–40.
173. This resolution, as stressed by the editor of the proceedings of this congress, was written in the hand of Lenin and signed by Isary (Karsky) and Dzhordzh (Kostrov). Ibid., p. 343.
174. *Tretii sezd RSDRP*, pp. 16–17.
175. See, for example, the Bolshevik draft of a resolution written by Lenin according to which the nationalist organizations were permitted to send their representatives to the CC. *Chetvertyi sezd RSDRP*, pp. 515–16.
176. *Shestaia (prazhskaia) vserossiiskaia konferentsiia RSDRP*, p. 221.
177. This resolution stressed that the separate existence of the "nationalities" and their separate activity "would result in a very bad type of federation" and that the Russian organizations were therefore not able to put into action "the most necessary and most important party undertakings." The resolution entrusted the CC RSDWP "to strive unceasingly for the unity and attainment of normal relations between the national organizations entering the RSDWP." *VKP(b) v rezoliutsiiakh*, Vol. I, p. 199.
178. In the resolution of this conference, the leadership of the Bund was condemned for "extreme opportunism" and for "liquidatorship." The Latvian CC was condemned because it "tended to support the anti-party actions of the liquidators." *VKP(b) v rezoliutsiiakh*, Vol. I, pp. 224–25. At the same time, in a series of articles, Lenin attacked the Bund and the Czech social democrats for separatism. See Lenin's article, "Separatisty v Rossii i separatisty v Avstrii," *Pravda*, 8 May 1913, No. 104, *Soch.*, XIX, pp. 67–68. Lenin also attacked the projected platform for the fourth congress of the Latvian social democrats. *Soch.*, XIX, pp. 87–94.
179. This fact is indicated by Wolfe, *Three Who Made a Revolution*, p. 581, who noted that the "August bloc" (the parties that met at the conference in Vienna in August 1912) adopted a resolution in which the demand for cultural autonomy was declared not to be incompatible with the party's programme concerning the right of nations to self-determination. See also Page, pp. 348–57. This fact is completely omitted by Carr, *The Bolshevik Revolution*, cf. Vol. I, pp. 65, 418–38, and, of course, by the Bolshevik historian Leder, "Natsionalnyi vopros v polskoi i russkoi sotsialdemokratii," in *Proletarskaia revoliutsiia*, 1927, No. 2–3, pp. 151–58. N. Popov, *Outline History*, Vol. I, p. 280, commenting on the Mensheviks' compromise with national and cultural autonomy, called it a plain attempt to adapt socialism to nationalism.
180. Stalin, *Marxism and the National and Colonial Question*, p. 270.

181. Ibid., p. 66.
182. Popov, *Ocherk*, p. 174.
183. *Shestoi sezd RSDRP(b)*, pp. 166–71. Among the opponents to this amendment were Molotov and Latsis. For biographical information on Angaretis and Kapsukas, see ibid., pp. 323, 340.
184. *Vosmoi sezd Rossiiskoi kommunisticheskoi partii (bolshevikov)*, p. 367; also *Zhizn natsionalnostei*, 1919, No. 21, p. 2.
185. *Vosmoi sezd RKP(b)*, pp. 246–47.
186. Similar ideas on Bolshevik party centralism were stressed by Smal-Stocki, *The Nationality Problem of the Soviet Union*, p. 57.

Chapter II

1. An illustration of this is the well-known declaration of the Russian nationalist, Savenko, vice-president of the Nationalist Union in Kiev, who warned Russia against Ukrainian separatism and its consequences. In the conservative daily, *Kievlianin*, 17 November 1911, No. 318, Savenko wrote that "the Polish, Armenian, Finnish, and other problems are all peripheral, i.e., secondary problems. The Mazepist [Ukrainian separatist] problem injures Russia at the origin of its existence as a great power. Poland, Finland, and other borderlands did not give Russia its greatness."
2. *Bolshaia sovetskaia entsiklopediia* (Moscow, 1947), col. 1809; *Entsyklopediia ukrainoznavstva*, Vol. I, p. 25.
3. *Pravda*, 27 February 1954, No. 58.
4. *Entsyklopediia ukrainoznavstva*, I, p. 25. According to Russian sources, Ukrainian territory in Russia at the end of the nineteenth century came to 400,427 square versts (one verst is 1,138 metres) or 455,000 square kilometres. *Entsiklopedicheskii slovar* (St. Petersburg, 1899), Vol. XXVII, pp. 76–77. Another Russian source states that the national territory of Ukraine before the revolution was about 750,000 square kilometres, with about 664,000 square kilometres in Russia. Stankevich, *Sudby narodov Rossii*, p. 50.
5. Dmytryshyn, pp. 183–214, provides a more exhaustive treatment.
6. Iavorsky, *Ukraina v epokhu kapitalizmu*, p. 33. According to B. L. Lychkov, *Rudnye i nerudnye bogatstva Ukrainy*, Vol. I, p. 14, the share of Ukraine in 1913 was 72 per cent of Russia's total production.
7. *Ukraine and Its People*, p. 134.
8. Stalin, *Soch.*, IV, p. 351. Kh. Rakovsky, "Khoziaistvennye posledstviia interventsii 1918–19 gg.," in *Chernaia kniga* (Katerynoslav, 1925), pp. 28–30. The same was stressed by Popov, *Outline History*, Vol. II, pp. 22–23, 32–33. Cf. also the introduction to *Sovetskaia Ukraina i Polsha*; V. P. Miliutin, *Istoriia ekonomicheskogo razvitiia SSSR*, pp. 141 ff.
9. See, e.g., Mazepa, I, p. 13, and Khrystiuk, I, pp. 5–8.
10. Lenin, "Razvitie kapitalizma v Rossii," *Soch.*, III, pp. 218–19.

11. D. Naumov, "Marks, dyktatura proletariiatu i sotsiialistychne budivnytstvo URSR," *Bilshovyk Ukrainy*, 1933, No. 5–6, p. 51.
12. M. Iavorsky, *Ukraina v epokhu kapitalizmu*, pp. 18–19.
13. Ibid., pp. 17–18. See also Popov, *Narys*, p. 12, who described Ukraine as a country "that produced and exported food." Left-Bank Ukraine is the region situated to the east of the Dnieper.
14. Iavorsky, pp. 17–18. Cf. also V. M. Kuritsyn, *Gosudarstvennoe sotrudnichestvo mezhdu Ukrainskoi SSR i RSFSR v 1917–1922 gg.*, pp. 5–10.
15. M. I. Suprunenko, *Rozhrom kontrrevoliutsiinoi Tsentralnoi rady i vstanovlennia radianskoi vlady na Ukraini*, p. 3.
16. In this connection the following works may be mentioned: P. I. Liashchenko, *Istoriia narodnogo khoziaistva SSSR*, Vol. III: *Ocherki istorii proletariata' SSSR*; V. I. Nevsky, *Istoriia VKP(b)*; N. Popov, *Ocherki istorii Vsesoiuznoi kommunisticheskoi partii (bolshevikov)*; A. A. Nestorenko, *Ocherk istorii promyshlennosti i razvitie proletariata na Ukraine*.
17. I. Mazepa, *Bolshevyzm i okupatsiia Ukrainy*, quoted in Ravich-Cherkassky, *Istoriia Kommunisticheskoi partii (b-kov) Ukrainy*, p. 3.
18. *Istoriia Ukrainskoi RSR*, Vol. I, p. 511.
19. Pankratova, p. 65. Later Soviet works admitted that "in 1870–1890 in the metallurgical and mining industries of Ukraine there was a tremendous influx of workers from the Russian provinces." L. M. Ivanov, "K voprosu ob formirovanii proletariata Ukrainy," *Voprosy istorii*, 1957, No. 6, p. 146. A Bolshevik admitted that "in Ukraine capitalism developed not on a Ukrainian basis and not gradually .... Capital came there immediately as concessional capital, which at the same time brought over an instrument, i.e., skilled workmen, from abroad." V. Zatonsky, "Pro pidsumky ukrainizatsii," *Budivnytstvo radianskoi Ukrainy*, Vol. I, p. 7. Cf. Lenin, "Razvitie kapitalizma v Rossii," *Soch.*, III, p. 292; also "Kriticheskie zametki po natsionalnomu voprosu," *Soch.*, XX, p. 15; and B. S. Itenberg, "Vozniknovenie 'Iuzhnorossiiskogo soiuza rabochikh,'" *Istoricheskie zapiski*, Akademiia nauk SSSR (Moscow, 1953), Vol. 44, pp. 94–129.
20. This figure is almost certainly exaggerated.
21. F. E. Los, *Formirovanie rabochego klassa na Ukraine*, p. 95.
22. Ibid., p. 158.
23. I. O. Hurzhii, *Zarodzhennia robitnychoho klasu Ukrainy* (Kiev, 1958), pp. 90–95.
24. Iurii Larin, "Ob izvrashcheniiakh pri provedenii natsionalnoi politiki," *Bolshevik*, 1926, No. 23–24, p. 53. In the manufacturing industry in Kharkiv province, 33.1 per cent of the workers were Russian and 61.4 per cent Ukrainian, while in the city of Kharkiv itself, of 26,996 workers, 14,619 (56 per cent) were Russian and only 7,410 (28 per cent) were Ukrainian. Los, *Formirovanie rabochego klassa na Ukraine*, p. 95.

25. *Natsionalnaia politika VKP(b) v tsifrakh*, p. 47.
26. M. Rafes, one of the leaders of the Bund, wrote that "in actual fact, the genuinely revolutionary proletarian elements in the same Ukraine must be sought in the mass of the proletariat of national minorities—Russian and Jewish workers—who played such a great role in the struggle for the establishment of Soviet rule." M. Rafes, *Natsionalnye voprosy* (Moscow, 1921), p. 22. This was stressed, too, by the central bureau of the Jewish sections of the RCP in its memorandum to the RCP and the CPU of 20 December 1919. It stated that "the Jewish industrial workers often form here (in Lithuania, Belorussia, Kiev province, Volhynia, and Podillia) the only proletarian stratum for the Soviet regime to rely upon." Ibid., p. 63.

Chapter III

1. This chapter is a reprint, with minor alterations, of my contribution to *The Ukraine, 1917–1921: A Study in Revolution,* ed. Taras Hunczak (Cambridge, Mass., 1977), pp. 128–58. A fuller treatment of the political parties in Ukraine is in the first edition of Jurij Borys, *The Russian Communist Party and the Sovietization of Ukraine: A Study in the Communist Doctrine of the Self-Determination of Nations* (Stockholm, 1960), pp. 67–99.
2. S. Iefremov, *Z hromadskoho zhyttia* (St. Petersburg, 1909), pp. 34–35; also the Ukrainian Marxist historian, M. Iavorsky, *Korotka istoriia Ukrainy* (Kharkiv, 1927), pp. 90–91.
3. Iefremov, p. 42; Ie. Chykalenko, *Spohady (1861–1907)*, Vol. III (Lviv, 1925–26), pp. 6 ff.; D. Doroshenko, *Ievhen Chykalenko, ioho zhyttia i hromadska diialnist* (Prague, 1934), pp. 34 ff.
4. M. Drahamanov, *Volnyi soiuz—Vilna spilka. Opyt ukrainskoi politiko-sotsialnoi programmy* (Geneva, 1884), pp. 7 ff.; D. Doroshenko, "Mykhajlo Drahomanov and the Ukrainian Movement," *Slavonic and East European Review,* No. 48 (London, 1938), pp. 662 ff.
5. H. Lototsky, *Storinky mynuloho,* Vol. III (Warsaw, 1932–34), p. 91; Chykalenko, Vol. III, p. 30.
6. N. Romanovych-Tkachenko, "Na dorozi do revoliutsii," *Ukraina,* Book 4, p. 108.
7. Borys (first ed.), p. 72.
8. Ibid., pp. 70–71.
9. M. Popov, *Narys istorii Kommunistychnoi partii (bilshovykiv) Ukrainy* (5th ed.; Kharkiv, 1931), p. 61; also Borys (first ed.), p. 75.
10. M. Ravich-Cherkassky, *Istoriia Kommunisticheskoi partii (b-kov) Ukrainy* (Kharkiv, 1923), p. 40; Lev Iurkevych [L. Rybalka], "Rosiiski marksysty i ukrainskyi robitnychyi rukh," *Dzvin,* Nos. 7–8, 1913, p. 89.
11. Popov, p. 76; Ravich-Cherkassky, p. 40.
12. I. Mazepa, *Ukraina v ohni i buri revoliutsii,* Vol. I (Prague, 1942), p. 10.

13. Borys (first ed.), p. 74, n. 30.
14. Ibid.
15. Iurkevych, p. 93.
16. V. I. Lenin, *Soch.*, Vol. XXXV, pp. 100–01.
17. *L'Ukraine et la Guerre: Lettre ouverte adressée à la 2ème conférence socialiste internationale tenue en Hollande en mai 1916* (Lausanne, 1916). See also K. Zalevsky, "Natsionalnye partii v Rossii," in L. Martov *et al.* eds., *Obshchestvennoe dvizhenie v Rossii*, Vol. III, bk. 5 (St. Petersburg, 1914), pp. 297–98.
18. Mazepa, Vol. II, pp. 123–35.
19. P. Fedenko, *Sotsializm davnii i novochasnyi* (London, 1968), pp. 202–04.
20. For the election results, see pp. 165–70.
21. For the history of this party, see A. Zhyvotko, "Do istorii Ukrainskoi partii sotsialistiv revolutsioneriv," *Vilna spilka,* No. 3 (Prague-Lviv, 1927–29), pp. 128–32; V. Andriievsky, *Z mynuloho,* 3 vols. (Berlin, 1921–23); *Le parti socialiste revolutionnaire ukrainien* (Prague, 1919); P. Khrystiuk, *Zamitky i materialy do istorii ukrainskoi revolutsii, 1917–1920 rr.*, Vol. III (Vienna, 1921–22), pp. 19 ff.
22. On factionalism in this party, see pp. 263–78. Iwan Majstrenko, *Borotbism: A Chapter in the History of Ukrainian Communism* (New York, 1954); Khrystiuk, Vol. III, pp. 23–24.
23. Popov, p. 192.
24. *Deviatyi sezd RKP(b), mart-aprel 1920 g.* (Moscow, 1934), pp. 96–97, 142–43.
25. *Kommunisticheskii internatsional,* Nos. 7–8 (Moscow, 1920), cols. 1125–26; see also Majstrenko, pp. 184–86.
26. See p. 273.
27. Ravich-Cherkassky, pp. 148–49.
28. For the history of this party, see Mazepa, Vol. I; V. Vynnychenko, *Vidrodzhennia natsii,* Vol. III (Vienna, 1920); Khrystiuk, Vol. III, pp. 19 ff.
29. Vynnychenko, Vol. III, pp. 82 ff.
30. On Vynnychenko's Canossa, see his "Povorot tov. Vynnychenka z Ukrainy," *Nova doba,* No. 34 (Vienna, 1920).
31. On this split, see A. Butsenko, "O raskole U.S.-D.R.P. 1917–18 god," *Letopis revoliutsii,* No. 4 (Kharkiv, 1922–23), pp. 121–22.
32. Mazepa, Vol. I, pp. 76–78.
33. Khrystiuk, Vol. IV, pp. 50–52.
34. Popov, p. 274.
35. D. Doroshenko, *Istoriia Ukrainy 1917–1923,* Vol. I (Uzhhorod, 1930–32), pp. 11 ff.; P. Haidalemivsky, *Ukrainski politychni partii, ikh rozvytok i prohramy* (Salzwedel, Germany, 1923); Andriievsky, *Z mynuloho.*
36. Doroshenko, Vol. I; Haidalemivsky, *Ukrainski politychni partii.*
37. S. Shemet, "Do istorii Ukrainskoi demokratychno-khliborobskoi partii," *Khliborobska Ukraina,* Vol. II (Vienna, 1920), pp. 56 ff.; V. Andriievsky,

Do kharakterystyky ukrainskykh pravykh partii (Berlin, 1921), pp. 13 ff.
38. Shemet, p. 13.
39. Lenin, *Soch.*, XXXV, pp. 100–02.
40. *Vosmoi sezd RKP(b)* (Moscow, 1919), p. 367.
41. *Protokoly Tsentralnogo komiteta RSDRP, august 1917–fevral 1918* (Moscow, 1929), p. 39.
42. U. Riadnina, *Pershyi zizd KP(b)U* (Kiev, 1958), p. 136.
43. *Istoriia KP(b)U v materiialakh ta dokumentakh, 1917–1920 rr.* (2nd ed.; Kharkiv, 1934), pp. 29–30 note 1, p. 356; Popov, p. 165.
44. See pp. 150–60.
45. Ravich-Cherkassky, p. 43.
46. *Shestoi sezd RSDRP(b). Avgust, 1917 g.* (Moscow, 1934), pp. 194–95.
47. O. H. Radkey, *The Agrarian Foes of Bolshevism* (New York, 1958), pp. 269–70; Doroshenko, Vol. I, p. 120; Popov, pp. 142 ff.
48. Popov, *Narys,* pp. 142 ff.; Khrystiuk, I, pp. 45 ff.; Doroshenko, I, p. 120; Radkey, pp. 269–70.
49. Khrystiuk, Vol. I, pp. 145 ff., and Vol. II, p. 118; Doroshenko, Vol. I, pp. 120 ff.,
50. Rafes, pp. 74–75. See also S. Goldelman, *Lysty zhydivskoho sotsial-demokrata pro Ukrainu* (Vienna, 1921), pp. 3–4.
51. A. Margolin, *Ukraina i politika Antanty. Zapiski ievreia i grazhdanina* (Berlin, 1922), pp. 40 ff.
52. P. Miliukov, *Istoriia vtoroi russkoi revoliutsii,* Vol. I (Sofia, 1921) and his *Rossiia na perelome,* Vol. II (Paris, 1927); Khrystiuk, Vol. III, pp. 26 ff.
53. A. Denikin, *Ocherki russkoi smuty,* Vol. I (Berlin, 1924–25), pp. 179 ff.
54. Denikin, *Ocherki russkoi smuty,* I, pp. 179–84 ff.; Stankevich, *Vospominaniia* (Berlin, 1920), pp. 321 ff.
55. B. Wolfe, *Three Who Made a Revolution*, p. 183.
56. Ibid.
57. S. Schwarz, *The Jews in the Soviet Union* (Syracuse, N.Y., 1951), p. 49.
58. The representative of the Bund and three Mensheviks were the only votes put against the Fourth Universal.
59. Borys (first ed.), pp. 97–98; M. Rafes, *Natsionalnye voprosy* (Moscow, 1921) and his *Dva goda revoliutsii na Ukraine. Evoliutsiia i raskol Bunda* (Moscow, 1920), pp. 74 ff.
60. Rafes, *Dva goda,* pp. 9 ff.
61. Ibid., pp. 10 ff.; Doroshenko, Vol. I, p. 120.
62. Rafes, *Dva goda,* pp. 10 ff.; Doroshenko, Vol. I, p. 120.
63. Margolin, pp. 44 ff.; Khrystiuk, Vol. II, pp. 143 ff.
64. H. Jabłoński, *Polska autonomia narodowa na Ukrainie, 1917–1918* (Warsaw, 1948), pp. 25 ff.
65. Ibid.
66. Ibid.
67. Ibid.; Doroshenko, Vol. I.

Chapter IV

1. This chapter deals with the attempt in 1917–18 to restore Ukrainian statehood. This is a short summary of a complicated period already well analysed by John Reshetar and others.
2. Vynnychenko, I, pp. 41–42. See also Andriievsky, *Z mynuloho*, I, p. 5. For the development of Ukrainian national demands during this period, see Reshetar, *The Ukrainian Revolution*, pp. 47 ff.
3. Vynnychenko, I, p. 79.
4. Khrystiuk, I, p. 16. Cf. also M. Hrushevsky, *Ukrainska Tsentralna rada i ii universaly*, pp. 2–5.
5. Vynnychenko, I, p. 80.
6. Ibid., p. 84.
7. Ibid., p. 80.
8. Ibid., pp. 82 ff. One of the opponents of the Central Rada wrote: "The Ukrainian social democrats hesitated in participating in it [the Central Rada], being afraid of allying themselves with the bourgeoisie; but finally they did so, to achieve one aim—an autonomous Ukraine." V. Shakhrai [Skorovstansky], *Revoliutsiia na Ukraine*, p. 20.
9. Vynnychenko, I, pp. 81–82.
10. Ibid., p. 45. Cf. also Mykola Porsh, *Avtonomiia Ukrainy i sotsiial-demokratiia*, 2nd ed., pp. 78–79.
11. Vynnychenko, I, p. 43.
12. Khrystiuk, I, p. 36
13. *1917 god na Kievshchine*, p. 28.
14. Lototsky, III, pp. 339 ff.
15. Khrystiuk, I, pp. 38 ff., and Vynnychenko, I, pp. 87 ff.
16. Doroshenko, I, pp. 74–75.
17. Shakhrai-Skorovstansky, p. 28. For more on *Spilka*, see Khrystiuk, I, pp. 44 ff.; Doroshenko, I, p. 52; and Lypynsky, *Lysty do brativ khliborobiv*, pp. 165 ff.
18. Shakhrai-Skorovstansky, pp. 51–53.
19. Doroshenko, I, p. 108.
20. Khrystiuk, I, pp. 48–49; M. M. Oberuchev, *Den stora ryska revolutionen, 1917*, pp. 108 ff.
21. Ibid., p. 111. Cf. also Denikin, p. 250.
22. Khrystiuk, I, pp. 50–51.
23. Ibid. Cf. also Hrushevsky, *Ukrainska Tsentralna rada*, p. 6.
24. For the text of the memorandum, see Dimanshtein, pp. 143–49. For more on the delegation, see Khrystiuk, I, pp. 55 ff., and Vynnychenko, I, pp. 159 ff.
25. Vynnychenko, I, p. 170.
26. Doroshenko, I, pp. 86–87.
27. Ibid., p. 88.
28. Dimanshtein, p. 58.

29. Khrystiuk, I, pp. 70–71.
30. Ibid., pp. 65 ff.
31. Shakhrai-Skorovstansky, pp. 37–38.
32. For the text of the First Universal, see Khrystiuk, I, pp. 72 ff.; Vynnychenko, I, pp. 219 ff.
33. Khrystiuk, I, pp. 132 ff., quotes (from Ukrainian and Russian newspapers) telegrams of greeting from local authorities and other organizations to the Rada; in the telegrams the Rada was ascribed governmental competence.
34. Ibid., I, pp. 77 ff.; Doroshenko, I, pp. 95 ff. Vynnychenko, I, p. 259, rightly insists that the General Secretariat was not a government in the ordinary sense because it had "neither officials nor clerks nor caretakers."
35. Khrystiuk, I, p. 78.
36. *1917 god na Kievshchine*, pp. 109, 118.
37. Vynnychenko, I, pp. 240–41.
38. Khrystiuk, I, pp. 86–87.
39. Rafes, pp. 38–39.
40. Doroshenko, I, p. 104.
41. Khrystiuk, I, p. 135.
42. Doroshenko, I, p. 104. Shulhyn's opinion, however, was not representative.
43. For the text of the declaration, see Doroshenko, I, pp. 104 ff., and Vynnychenko, I, pp. 260 ff.
44. The Provisional Government's decision finally to open negotiations with Ukraine was undoubtedly due in part to the pressure of the Bolsheviks, who used the Ukrainian question as a weapon against the Provisional Government. They described the policy of the government toward the Ukrainians as "counter-revolutionary and shamefully anti-democratic" and asserted that the Ukrainians should be assured the right not only of autonomy but also of independence. Doroshenko, p. 110. On the negotiations cf. also A. Choulgine, *L'Ukraine contre Moscou 1917*, pp. 122 ff.
45. Doroshenko, I, pp. 112–13.
46. P. N. Miliukov, *Istoriia vtoroi russkoi revoliutsii*, I, pp. 236–37. Ten members of the government voted for the agreement (the socialists together with Prince Lvov and V. N. Lvov), and the five Kadet ministers voted against it.
47. Ibid., pp. 236 ff. Miliukov writes that the decision of the government delegation in Kiev on the Ukrainian question "undermined the foundations of the coalition and provided a particularly clear and typical proof of the impossibility of maintaining the coalition in the future."
48. Khrystiuk, I, pp. 93 ff. *1917 god na Kievshchine*, pp. 481–82.
49. For the text of the Second Universal see Khrystiuk, I, pp. 93–94; Vynnychenko, I, pp. 278 ff.
50. Doroshenko, I, p. 115.
51. Ibid., I, p. 116.
52. Khrystiuk, I, p. 118; Miliukov, *Istoriia vtoroi russkoi revoliutsii*, I, p. 233,

gives incorrect figures.

53. Khrystiuk, I, p. 137.
54. Doroshenko, I, pp. 119–20.
55. Vynnychenko, I, pp. 302–03.
56. Ibid., pp. 298 ff.; Choulgine, pp. 125 ff.
57. Doroshenko, I, p. 124.
58. For the text of the instruction see Vynnychenko, I, pp. 315 ff.; Dimanshtein, pp. 63–64.
59. Vynnychenko, I, pp. 313–14.
60. Khrystiuk, I, pp. 143–44.
61. Ibid., I, pp. 145–47.
62. Ibid., pp. 145 ff.
63. Vynnychenko, I, pp. 335 ff.
64. Khrystiuk, I, pp. 148–49.
65. Ibid., pp. 143–44.
66. Ibid., pp. 147–48. Cf. Vynnychenko, I, p. 337.
67. Khrystiuk, I, p. 145.
68. Ibid., p. 151.
69. For the text of the resolution, see Khrystiuk, I, pp. 118–19.
70. Shulhyn, *Polityka*, p. 10.
71. The Russian historian Miliukov in his work, *Rossiia na perelome*, I, pp. 88 ff., gives an apt analysis of the situation in the country after the February revolution. On the question of the border regions, he says (p. 91) that Russia "was faced with a network of independent republics, which took no account of each other and within their territorial areas exercised all the functions of sovereign power."
72. Ibid., pp. 112–13.
73. Ibid., pp. 88 ff.; Doroshenko, I, pp. 141 ff.
74. Miliukov, *Istoriia vtoroi russkoi revolutsii*, I, p. 162–63, calls attention to this fact and explains the successes of the Rada as the result of the Ukrainian population's fear of the general process of disintegration in Russia and "the all-Russian socialist experiment." In this he sees the healthy instinct of self-preservation.
75. Doroshenko, I, pp. 147–48.
76. Khrystiuk, II, p. 18.
77. Ibid. Cf. also Rafes, pp. 40 ff.
78. Khrystiuk, II, p. 18.
79. Ibid., p. 19.
80. Ibid.
81. Doroshenko, I, p. 155.
82. Ibid., I, p. 157; Dimanshtein, p. 66; Rafes, p. 41.
83. Doroshenko, I, p. 157.
84. Rafes, p. 41. In this connection the Bund representative gave a joint explanation, in the name of the Bund, the Mensheviks, and the Russian socialist revolutionaries, stating that the attitude of the minorities had been

determined by a desire to "bring about the unity of the Ukrainian and non-Ukrainian democratic forces" and by the "violent campaign of the counter-revolutionary elements against the Ukrainian movement." Ibid.

85. The Bund also intervened in Petrograd when the Provisional Government tried to apply reprisals against the General Secretariat. Rafes, p. 41.
86. Khrystiuk, II, pp. 39–40; Doroshenko, I, p. 159, says there were 965 delegates.
87. Khrystiuk, II, p. 40.
88. Doroshenko, I, pp. 164–65.
89. Khrystiuk, II, p. 41. With this last phrase Vynnychenko was probably recalling the resolution adopted by the Congress of Nationalities at Kiev. This congress had been held on the initiative of the Rada on 21–28 September 1917. Ninety-three delegates took part: six Belorussians, two Georgians, four Estonians, ten Jews, eleven Cossacks, ten Lithuanians, ten Tatars, six Poles, six Romanians, three Russian socialist revolutionaries, five Turkomans, and nine Ukrainians. The congress worked out the guiding principles for the transformation of Russia into a federation of free democratic republics. See Dimanshtein, pp. 443 ff., and Khrystiuk, II, pp. 20 ff.
90. Doroshenko, I, pp. 160–61.
91. Ibid., I, p. 163.
92. Rafes, p. 53, points out that "this transfer of power ... took place with the collaboration of all political parties except the extreme Right (Shulgin's group) and the extreme Left."
93. For the text of the Third Universal see Khrystiuk, II, pp. 51 ff.; Vynnychenko, II, pp. 74 ff. What Dimanshtein quotes as the Third Universal of the Rada is in reality a Russian translation of the declaration of the General Secretariat of 19 October 1917. Cf. also *Kievskaia mysl*, 1917, No. 267.
94. Rafes, p. 56.
95. In the Little Rada forty-two votes were cast for the Universal, and there were four abstentions (one Menshevik, two Russian socialist revolutionaries, and one representative of the Polish Democratic Centre). Ibid., p. 58; Doroshenko, I, pp. 181–82.
96. Rafes, p. 57.
97. Ibid., p. 58.
98. Jabłoński, *Polska autonomia*, pp. 68–72, maintains that the Polish Democratic Centre cooperated with the Rada on account of a shared anti-Russian attitude. "The action taken towards the disintegration of the Russian empire and the desire to acquire in this way an ally in the struggle for the independence of Poland was the decisive motive."
99. Khrystiuk, II, pp. 61 ff.
100. Doroshenko, I, pp. 185–86.
101. Ibid., pp. 186–87.
102. Ibid., pp. 187–88. Later even the Ukrainian Bolsheviks admitted that the

"proclamation of the Ukrainian People's Republic was received with great manifestations all over Ukraine." Shakhrai-Skorovstansky, p. 74; and Mazlakh, "Oktiabrskaia revoliutsiia na poltavshchine," *LR*, 1922, No. 1, pp. 126 ff.

103. Vynnychenko, II, p. 81.
104. Trotsky, *Den Ryska arbetarrevolutionen*, p. 88.
105. Khrystiuk, II, p. 93.
106. Ibid.
107. Ibid., pp. 93–94.
108. Ibid., pp. 94 ff.
109. Doroshenko, I, p. 227.
110. For the text of the note, see Khrystiuk, III, pp. 95–96.
111. For the text of the official notes exchanged between the representatives of the Entente and the General Secretariat, see Arnold Margolin, *Ukraina i politika Antanty*, pp. 365 ff.; Doroshenko, I, pp. 233–37; Choulgine, pp. 163 ff.
112. For the text of the Fourth Universal, see Khrystiuk, II, pp. 103 ff.; Vynnychenko, II, pp. 244–45; Mazepa, III, pp. 158 ff. The text in Vynnychenko deviates somewhat in style, but not in content.
113. Vynnychenko, II, pp. 230–31.
114. Doroshenko, I, p. 269.
115. Ibid., p. 263.
116. Ibid., pp. 261–62.
117. Ibid., p. 263.
118. Doroshenko, I, pp. 262–63.
119. Chykalenko, *Uryvok iz moikh spomyniv*, p. 27.
120. Rafes, pp. 74–75.
121. Doroshenko, I, p. 268.
122. Solomon Goldelman, a well-known Jewish social democrat, wrote of the Jewish parties that emigrated to Vienna: "The Zionists and *Paolei-Zion* work for the creation of a national home for the Jews in Palestine, ... where the Jews constitute a minority of the population, ... but are hostile to the strivings of the Ukrainian people to create a national home of their own in Ukraine, where they constitute 76 per cent of the population." S. Goldelman, *Lysty zhydivskoho sotsiial-demokrata pro Ukrainu*, pp. 3–4.

Chapter V

1. In spite of the clear evidence of the national demands of the Ukrainian movement, some Russian historians have denied their existence. M. N. Pokrovsky, *Russkaia revoliutsiia v samom szhatom ocherke*, p. 264, asserted that "the national slogans did not play any role in the Ukrainian movement of 1905."

2. P. Miliukov, *Rossiia na perelome,* Vol. I, p. 8.
3. For discussions on the Ukrainian question, see *Gosudarstvennaia Duma. Stenograficheskie otchety,* 1906, Vol. II, pp. 994–95, 1043–48; 1907, Vol. I, pp. 704–890, 1310–30.
4. See Reshetar, p. 35; Chykalenko, *Spohady,* III, p. 66.
5. See the address by Volodymyr Shemet delivered on 5 June 1906. *Gosudarstvennaia Duma. Stenograficheskie otchety,* 1906, II, pp. 994–95.
6. Cf. *Vtoraia gosudarstvennaia Duma. Stenograficheskie otchety,* II, pp. 542 ff.
7. Lototsky, *Z mynuloho*, pp. 422–23.
8. Popov, for example, praises Lenin because he drew attention to the national question at a time when "there were still no manifestations of a mass national movement in Russia." Popov ignores the existence of the national social democratic movements in the borderlands; Lenin had opposed these at the second RSDWP congress and also later.
9. It is difficult to agree with Sadovsky, who held that Lenin, like all Russian radicals, "neglected" the Ukrainian problem and approached it this time only "incidentally." V. Sadovsky, *Natsionalna polityka Sovitiv na Ukraini,* p. 27. As will become evident when we discuss Lenin's policy towards the Ukrainian social democrats, especially Iurkevych, Lenin prepared his Ukrainian politics with some care. Cf. pp. 125–29.
10. See the editors' remark in Lenin, *Stati i rechi ob Ukraine,* p. 213, note 1. Cf. also Ie. Hirchak, "Lenin i ukrainske pytannia," *BU,* 1929, No. 1, p. 25.
11. Lenin, "Sotsialisticheskaia revoliutsiia i pravo natsii na samoopredelenie," *Soch.,* XXII, p. 142; "O prave natsii na samoopredelenie," ibid., XX, pp. 379–80.
12. Ibid., XXI, p. 86.
13. Petrovsky's address is to be found in Lenin, *Stati i rechi ob Ukraine,* pp. 213–20.
14. Bishop Nikon proposed a motion to the Duma demanding freedom to teach Ukrainian in the primary schools and freedom for Ukrainian associations. See ibid., pp. 224–25.
15. Ibid., p. 225.
16. Lenin, "Kadety ob ukrainskom voprose," *Soch.,* XIX, pp. 236–37.
17. Lenin, *The Right of Nations to Self-Determination,* pp. 38–39.
18. "Mazepists" was the epithet given by the Russian nationalists to all Ukrainian patriots who defended the right of their people to a distinct national identity. Ivan Mazepa, a Ukrainian hetman, tried to sever Ukraine from the Muscovite state during the war between Peter the Great and Charles XII of Sweden.
19. Ibid., pp. 52–53.
20. Lenin, "Kriticheskie zametki po natsionalnomu voprosu," *Soch.,* XX, pp. 13–14.
21. Ibid., p. 16.
22. Ibid., pp. 16–17.

23. Lenin in an article, "O natsionalnoi gordosti velikorossov," wrote: "Let us assume that history should decide the question in favour of Great Russian state capitalism against the hundred and one small nations, and this is not improbable, as all history is a record of violation and robbery, blood and dirt. We are by no means necessarily the champions of small nations; we are unconditionally, other conditions being equal, in favour of centralization and against the bourgeois ideal of federal relations." *Soch.*, XXI, p. 87.
24. In this connection Lenin wrote that even if the Russian social democrats were against small national states and against the federal principle, "it is not our business, not the business of democrats (to say nothing of socialists), to help Romanov, Bobrinsky, and Purishkevich to strangle Ukraine, etc." Ibid.
25. Lev Iurkevych, "Rosiiski marksysty i ukrainskyi robitnychyi rukh," *Dzvin,* 1913, No. 7–8, p. 83.
26. Ibid., pp. 83–84.
27. Ibid., pp. 85–86.
28. Martov, *Istoriia RSDRP,* p. 157; Popov, *Narys,* p. 60.
29. Iurkevych, "V spravi ukrainskoi robitnychoi hazety," *Dzvin,* 1913, No. 4, pp. 277–78.
30. Iurkevych, "Kooperatsiia i robitnychyi rukh," *Dzvin,* 1913, No. 9, pp. 208–09. "The national revival of the workers of the subjugated nation is inevitable, as is the revival of the nation itself," wrote Iurkevych in 1913. *Natsionalna sprava i robitnytstvo,* pp. 14–15.
31. Iurkevych, "Rosiiski marksysty i ukrainskyi robitnychyi rukh," *Dzvin,* 1913, No. 7–8, p. 92.
32. Ibid., pp. 92–93. Iurkevych was referring here to Stalin's article in *Prosveshchenie,* 1913, No. 4. Cf. Stalin, *Marxism and the National and Colonial Question,* pp. 3–61.
33. Iurkevych, "Rosiiski marksysty," p. 91.
34. Iurkevych, *Natsionalna sprava i robitnytstvo,* p. 16.
35. Iurkevych, "Rosiiski marksysty," p. 93.
36. Iurkevych, "Paky i paky," *Dzvin,* 1914, No. 6, pp. 542–50. Cf. also Iurkevych [L. Rybalka], *Russkie sotsial-demokraty i natsionalnyi vopros* (Geneva, 1917).
37. Chiefly "Kriticheskie zametki po natsionalnomu voprosu," in *Prosveshchenie,* 1913, No. 10–12, under the signature V. Ilin (in *Soch.*, XX, pp. 1–34), and "O prave natsii na samoopredelenie," in *Prosveshchenie,* 1914, Nos. 4–6 (in *Soch.*, XX, pp. 365–424), published in English as *The Right of Nations to Self-Determination.*
38. Inessa Armand (Elisaveta Fedorovna Petrova) (1875–1920) was a member of the Bolshevik faction of the RSDWP. During the world war, she was a close associate of Lenin's. She attended the Zimmerwald and Kienthal conferences and in 1912–13 worked in St. Petersburg. She was active in the women's and socialist youth international movements. After the October revolution she held responsible party posts. She was a president of the First

International Conference of Communist Women. See *Shestoi sezd RSDRP* p. 324; also *Slavnye bolshevichki* (Moscow, 1958), pp. 75–88.

39. These letters are included in Lenin's *Soch.*, XXXV, pp. 100–03, and belong to the group "of twenty-three documents published for the first time" in 1950. Ibid.
40. This address was published in *Trudovaia pravda,* 29 June 1914, No. 28, and was signed Oksen Lola. Cf. Lenin, *Soch.*, XX, p. 551, note 131.
41. Lenin, *Soch.*, XX, p. 462.
42. Lenin, *Soch.*, XXXV, pp. 100–02.
43. Lenin, *Soch.*, XXIV, pp. 267–68.
44. Ibid., p. 304.
45. Ibid., pp. 527–28.
46. *Pravda,* 28 June 1917, No. 82. Lenin, *Soch.*, XXV, pp. 73–74.
47. Ibid., pp. 81–83; *Pravda,* 30 June 1917, No. 84. See also Lenin's article, "Ruling and Responsible Parties," *Pravda,* July 1917, No. 85, in *Soch.*, XXV, pp. 86–88, in which he accused the SRs and SDs of imperialism and annexationist policy towards Finland and Ukraine.
48. Popov, *Narys,* p. 116.
49. *Pervyi vserossiiskii sezd sovetov r. i s.d.*, Vol. II, pp. 78–81.
50. Ibid., p. 182.
51. Ibid., p. 236. Cf. also Kollontai's argument, ibid., p. 172. The position of the Bolsheviks was interpreted in this way also by the participants of the congress. See, e.g., the declaration of the SR Berg, ibid., p. 237.
52. Ibid., pp. 463–64.
53. "Da zdravstvuiet avtonomnaia Ukraina," *Edinstvo,* 2 June 1917, No. 54, in G. V. Plekhanov, *God na rodine,* Vol. I, pp. 167–70.
54. Ibid., pp. 210–13.
55. *Protokoly Tsentralnogo komiteta RSDRP,* p. 22.
56. Ibid., pp. 47–48.
57. Ibid., pp. 60–63.
58. Until the thirties, i.e., until the stabilization of Stalin's regime, these movements were considered progressive in Soviet historiography. See, e.g., Popov, *Narys,* pp. 112–20. Thereafter the nationalist movements were declared reactionary and counter-revolutionary. See Likholat, *Razgrom,* and also—on Iavorsky's deviation in Ukrainian Soviet historiography—*LR,* 1930, No. 1–2.
59. The term "Ukrainian Bolsheviks" is used in this work in the territorial, not national, sense.
60. Ravich, p. 43. Lapchynsky writes in his memoirs that there was then no organizational contact with the CC RCP: "Instead of direct party instructions, [the Bolsheviks in Ukraine] were guided by the Petersburg party press." Lapchynsky, "Z pershykh dniv," *LR,* 1927, No. 5–6, p. 47.
61. In the first months of the so-called democratic revolution, February-June, Bolshevik declarations completely ignored the question of nationalities. See *1917 god na Kievshchine,* pp. 1–80, 467–90.

62. Lapchynsky, *LR,* 1927, No. 5–6, p. 48.
63. Popov,*Narys,* p. 118; Kulik, "Kievskaia organizatsiia," *LR,* 1927, No. 5–6, p. 225.
64. Bosh, *God borby,* pp. 35 ff. Kulik, *LR,* 1927, No. 5–6, pp. 224–28, wrote that the Kievan Bolsheviks had completely disregarded the alternative of an armed conflict with the Central Rada.
65. E. Bosh, *Natsionalnoe pravitelstvo,* p. 23.
66. See pp. 160–64.
67. Popov, *Narys,* p. 119.
68. Soviet historiography always condemned Piatakov's position. Hirchak, "Lenin i ukrainske pytannia," *BU,* 1929, Nos. 1–2, p. 33, argued that Piatakov was tailing after the Russian petty bourgeoisie, and that Piatakov's policy had made the Bolshevik revolution in Ukraine more complicated and difficult. See also Likholat, *Razgrom,* pp. 639–40.
69. Kulik, *LR,* 1927, no. 5–6, p. 225.
70. *1917 god na Kievshchine,* pp. 104–07.
71. Ibid.
72. Ibid., p. 104. Cf. also *Golos sotsial-demokrata,* 23 July 1917, No. 78.
73. *1917 god na Kievshchine,* pp. 149–50.
74. The declaration of Chekerul-Kush, ibid.
75. Zarnytsin's declaration, ibid.. Kreisberg also demanded a "plebiscite." Ibid., pp. 121–22. Elsewhere, Zarnytsin declared that "it is not the all-Russian constituent assembly, but only the peoples themselves of a given territory (Ukraine, the Baltic territories, the Caucasus, Lithuania), who have the right to decide their own fate." Zarnytsin's article in *Golos sotsial-demokrata,* 23 May 1917, No. 25. *1917 god na Kievshchine,* p. 72. Kulik, however, asserts that the Kiev Bolsheviks "did not even find it necessary to react to the First Universal of the Central Rada." Kulik, *LR,* 1927, No. 5–6, pp. 229–30.
76. Kreisberg's declaration, *1917 god na Kievshchine,* pp. 121–22.
77. Ibid., pp. 113–14.
78. Ibid. With the aim of disrupting the national front, the Bolsheviks entered the Central Rada. As early as 22 July 1917, the Bolshevik faction declared at a Rada meeting: "Entering the Central Rada, we shall conduct here a steadfast struggle with the bourgeoisie and the bourgeois nationalists." Ibid., p. 504.

Chapter VI

1. Popov, *Narys*, pp. 5–6.
2. The following works may be included in this period: M. Iavorsky, "K istorii KP(b)U"; M. Ravich-Cherkassky, *Istoriia KP(b)U*; M. Popov, *Narys*; M. Skrypnyk, "Istoriia proletarskoi revoliutsii na Ukraini"; P. Samsonov, *Kak postroena VKP(b) i KP(b)U.* To this period belong also the following

editions of documents from the history of the CP(B)U: *Pervyi sezd KP(b)U; Vtoroi sezd KP(b)U; 1917 god na Kievshchine.*

3. During Pavel Postyshev's regime not a single work on the CP(B)U appeared. The history of the CP(B)U disappeared into the history of the RCP, and even this was not written after 1934, apart from the official *Istoriia Vsesoiuznoi kommunisticheskoi partii (bolshevikov). Kratkii kurs.* At that time a very tendentious collection of documentary material was published, *Istoriia KP(b)U v materialakh ta dokumentakh.*
4. During this brief period many articles and short monographs about the CP(B)U appeared, mainly on the occasion of the fortieth anniversary of the creation of the CP(B)U. See: Ivan Shevchenko, "Chetverta konferentsiia KP(b)U"; U. Riadnina, *Pershyi zizd KP(b)U*; M. Pohrebinsky, *Druhyi zizd KP(b)U*; V. Chyrko, *Piata konferentsiia KP(b)U.* N. Podgorny, "Kommunisticheskaia partiia Ukrainy—boevoi otriad velikoi KPSS"; N. R. Dony, "Obrazovanie Kommunisticheskoi partii Ukrainy." See also several articles in the July 1958 issues of *Radianska Ukraina* (Kiev) and *Literaturna hazeta* (Kiev). All these works and articles represent the origin of the CP(B)U as the result of the strivings of the Ukrainian proletariat in alliance with the Russian proletariat. The real role of the RCP is not mentioned. These works are, in the main, propaganda.
5. Popov, *Narys*, p. 5.
6. M. Skrypnyk, "Do spravy ukrainizatsii," *LR*, 1930, No. 1, pp. x–xi, wrote that Ravich-Cherkassky had written the history of the CP(B)U on the basis of "an incorrect and erroneous theory of the two roots of the CP(B)U." Later this theory was attributed to "bourgeois nationalist elements" and was regarded as a "nationalist distortion of the history of the CP(B)U." Riadnina, pp. 51–52.
7. Iavorsky, justifying his paper, "K istorii KP(B)U," wrote that although the CP(B)U "is a regional organization of the RCP, although its history is a part of the whole history of the RCP, a part of the whole proletarian revolution within the borders of the former empire, *yet it has its own past, its peculiar features of development which so vividly correspond to the distinguishing peculiarities of the revolution in Ukraine from 1917.*" But in order to mitigate the impression left by his heresy, Iavorsky added that "the imprint of particular Ukrainian byways of the common Russian revolutionary road shows up on it [the history of the CP(B)U] in relief." M. Iavorsky, p. 93.
8. Lapchynsky, *LR*, 1927, Nos. 5–6, p. 47; see also Riadnina, pp. 22–23.
9. Popov, *Narys*, p. 119.
10. Lapchynsky, p. 48.
11. M. Iavorsky, pp. 94–95.
12. *Golos sotsial-demokrata*, No. 74; *1917 god na Kievshchine*, pp. 493–95; Iavorsky, p. 95.
13. The following, among others, were elected to the committee: Tarnogrodsky, A. Grinevich, Tsirlin, Bosh, Nerovny, and Gishvaliner. *1917 god na*

Kievshchine, pp. 161–63.

14. Riadnina, pp. 28–30.
15. As N. R. Dony remarks ("Obrazovanie Kommunisticheskoi partii Ukrainy," *Voprosy istorii KPSS*, 1958, No. 3, p. 36), these two regional party centres were created "in accordance with a directive of the CC RSDWP(B)."
16. According to the statistical data of the sixth congress of the RSDWP(B), of the total number of party members in Ukraine (22,402), the organization of the Donets basin had about 16,000. *Shestoi sezd RSDRP(b)*, p. 195.
17. *Proletarskaia mysl*, 9 November 1917, No. 4.
18. This document, from the Archives of the Institute of Marxism-Leninism of the CC CPSU, was first published in Riadnina, pp. 37–38.
19. *Protokoly Tsentralnogo komiteta RSDRP*, p. 188.
20. Ibid., pp. 181–89; Riadnina, p. 39, for obvious reasons, did not mention Trotsky.
21. Ibid., p. 39. Italics mine.
22. Reference is made here to the letter of 12 December 1917 from the Poltava committee of the party to the CC RSDWP(B); the letter said that "in connection with the proclamation of the Ukrainian People's Republic" it was necessary "to convoke a congress of all party organizations of the Ukrainian republic." Dony, p. 39. The Poltava organization seems to have recognized the Ukrainian People's Republic proclaimed by the Central Rada in its Third Universal; this probably reflected the influence of Shakhrai and Mazlakh, who belonged to the Poltava committee. See Sergei Mazlakh, "Oktiabrskaia revoliutsiia na Poltavshchine," *LR*, 1922, No. 1, pp. 126 ff.
23. Riadnina, p. 40 (italics mine). Mazlakh, pp. 126–27, points out that the attitude of the CC in Petrograd to the proposal of the Poltava committee expressed in the reply of the CC was "not quite approbatory," and as far as the policy of the party in Ukraine was concerned, they "received no answer."
24. Dony, p. 40. My italics.
25. Ibid.
26. "Oblastnoi sezd RSDRP (b-kov). Protokoly," *LR*, 1926, No. 5, pp. 65–66.
27. Ravich, pp. 45–46.
28. *LR*, 1926, No. 5, pp. 79–82.
29. Ibid., p. 82. The members of the committee are arranged according to the number of votes each of them obtained at the election. For instance, Aussem and Shakhrai each received twenty-six votes, Lapchynsky twenty-five, Bosh twenty-four, Zatonsky twenty-one, etc. L. Piatakov obtained only ten votes.
30. The resolution itself caused disagreements, since the Katerynoslavians questioned the competence of the conference. See Ia[kovlev] E[pshtein], "O sozdanii samostoiatelnoi kommunisticheskoi partii Ukrainy," *Pravda*, 30 June 1918, No. 132. The conference itself also spoke in the same terms on this subject. See the minutes of the conference in *Istoriia KP(b)U*,

p. 283; cf. also Dony, p. 44.

31. According to Dony, p. 43, there were sixty-nine participants, while Riadnina, p. 74, quotes the figure seventy-one.
32. Ravich, pp. 51–52.
33. Erde wrote the article, "Taganrogskoe soveshchanie i obrazovanie KP(b)U," which was unavailable to me.
34. Ravich, pp. 51–52.
35. Iavorsky, pp. 97–98.
36. Ia[kovlev], *Pravda*, 30 June 1918, No. 132. The leader of the Katerynoslavians, Kviring, later wrote that, by the time the trends towards an independent party in Ukraine "became quite clear at the Taganrog conference, the Katerynoslavians (perhaps not all of them) had left Taganrog." Kviring, "Nashi raznoglasiia," p. 6.
37. *Istoriia KP(b)U*, p. 283; Shakhrai, *Do khvyli*, p. 15; Popov, *Narys*, p. 150.
38. Ravich, pp. 56–57. He called this motion "Russophile." Iavorsky, p. 98, likewise wrote that it was "inspired by the spirit of Russophilism."
39. *Istoriia KP(b)U*, p. 281; Shakhrai, *Do khvyli*, p. 19. This proposal was later condemned as "a deviation towards Ukrainian nationalism." Iavorsky, p. 98.
40. *KP(b)U v rezoliutsiiakh*, p. 7.
41. Ravich, p. 56.
42. Kviring, p. 6. The editors of *Istoriia KP(b)U*, p. 281, ascribed the same motives to the Kievans.
43. The editors of *Istoriia KP(b)U*, p. 283, note 2, wrote that Skrypnyk's attitude was "a manifestation of separatist trends, of a deviation towards local nationalism among a number of delegates." Cf. also later Soviet works on the subject: Dony, p. 44, and Riadnina, p. 76.
44. Skrypnyk stressed in his polemics with Lenin and others that "the CC RCP on 18 May 1918 ... resolved that it recognized the independence of the Communist party of Ukraine and its independent membership in the Third International, since Ukraine was an independent state." *Odinnadtsatyi sezd RKP(b)*, pp. 78–79. The post-Stalin historiography considered the creation of an independent CP(B)U "a serious error, a concession to the separatist moods." Dony, p. 44.
45. *Istoriia KP(b)U*, p. 285, note 1; Ravich, p. 62; Iavorsky, p. 98.
46. The "defeatist" mood among the Bolsheviks of Ukraine is mentioned by Zatonsky, a participant at the congress. He wrote that the atmosphere of the congress was determined by the Bolshevik failure in Ukraine: "the defeat of the proletarian movement, the lack of faith in their own strength among the working masses, side by side with an intensive growth of the revolutionary mood of the peasantry." Zatonsky, "K piatiletiiu KP(b)U," p. 14.
47. *Istoriia KP(b)U*, p. 356, note 1.
48. Ibid.
49. *KP(b)U v rezoliutsiiakh*, pp. 29–30.
50. Popov, *Narys*, p. 165.

51. Kviring, "Nashi raznoglasiia," p. 7. Cf. Ia. E., "O sozdanii . . . ," *Pravda*, 30 June 1918, No. 132.
52. Riadnina, pp. 54–63.
53. Zatonsky, "K piatiletiiu KP(b)U," p. 14.
54. *Pervyi sezd KP(b)U*, p. 37.
55. Zatonsky, "K piatiletiiu KP(b)U," p. 16.
56. Popov, *Narys*, p. 162.
57. Iavorsky, p. 104; Ravich, p. 81; Riadnina, p. 126; Popov, *Narys*, p. 166, note 1.
58. Popov, *Narys*, p. 164, remarks only that Skrypnyk did not play such a prominent mediatory role at this congress as he played at the Taganrog conference. This was possibly the result of Skrypnyk's attitude to the independence of Soviet Ukraine and the CP(B)U, about which Lenin and the RCP were very well informed. The isolation of the Ukrainian separatists is borne out also by the fact that, apart from the opportunist Zatonsky, there were no nationally conscious Ukrainians in the CC CP(B)U.
59. At the plenary meeting of the CC CP(B)U in September 1918, Piatakov was replaced by Kviring. *Vtoroi sezd KP(b)U*, p. 183.
60. Ravich, p. 81.
61. For further information on this rising, see "Iz deiatelnosti TsK KP(b)U i TsV RK," *LR*, 1927, No. 1, pp. 124–73.
62. *Vtoroi sezd KP(b)U*, p. v.
63. Ibid., p. 194; Ravich, p. 90.
64. Kamenev's speech at the second congress. *Vtoroi sezd KP(b)U*, pp. 125–27. Rakovsky took a similar line in his speech. Ibid., pp. 14–19. Zatonsky commented that at a dangerous moment for Soviet Russia, when "the liberated forces of the imperialism of the Entente could descend with all their weight on the RSFSR, which was still weak, the CC RCP was most of all afraid of the independentist (*samostiinicheskii*) actions on the part of the Ukrainian organizations, and therefore the CC supported the Ukrainian rightists at the congress itself." Ibid., p. vi.
65. Popov, *Narys*, p. 167.
66. Popov later admitted that "any danger could have threatened the CP(B)U at that time, but, of course, not the danger of Ukrainian nationalism. Such a danger could exist at the most for individual members of the party. The tactics of holding on to the leadership of the movement out of a fear of being contaminated by Ukrainian chauvinism was the pinnacle of political myopia for the person proposing it." Ibid., p. 167.
67. M. Pohrebinsky, p. 153.
68. Popov, *Narys*, p. 168.
69. *Vtoroi sezd KP(b)U*, pp. 174–75.
70. Ibid., p. 181; *Istoriia KP(b)U*, pp. 327–29. Commenting on the programme of the new CC, Iavorsky remarked that it had broken with the insurgent enthusiasm of the Kievans, but instead "it sinned . . . to a certain degree by ignoring the local peculiarities of the class struggle." Iavorsky, p. 107.

71. Iavorsky, pp. 107–08.
72. *Vtoroi sezd KP(b)U*, pp. 113–14.
73. *Istoriia KP(b)U*, pp. 330–31.
74. Ravich, p. 108. Khristian Rakovsky spoke for the first time at the congress of the CP(B)U, where he was elected to the CC. He was put in charge of the newly created Ukrainian Soviet government to replace Piatakov, because Rakovsky was considered more "neutral" in Ukrainian affairs and in the factional struggle. Popov, *Ocherki*, p. 419; *Narys*, p. 186.
75. See pp. 50–51.
76. Popov, *Narys*, p. 189, note 1; Ravich, p. 117.
77. This applies chiefly to Slynko, a Ukrainian SD independentist, who during the second Soviet regime in Ukraine broke with the official policy of the party and accepted independentist principles. See H. Lapchynsky, "Pismo v redaktsiiu gazety *Chervonyi prapor*," in *Revoliutsiia v nebezpetsi*, pp. 73–82. Skrypnyk also came out, even at the eighth congress of the RCP, with a sharp criticism of the restorers of Russia, *edinaia i nedelimaia*. See *Vosmoi sezd RKP*, p. 151.
78. For instance, Kharechko, a member of the CC, was sent to Viatka, Skrypnyk to Penza, Antonov-Ovseenko to Tambov, Iakovlev to Vladimir. Ravich, p. 136.
79. Lapchynsky, "Gomelskoe soveshchanie," *LR*, 1926, pp. 36–37. These memoirs are the main source on this conference. The editors of the journal *LR* reprove Lapchynsky for having a bad memory and frequently distorting facts. Ibid., pp. 48–50.
80. Ibid., pp. 38–39; cf. also Lapchynsky, "Pismo v redaktsiiu gazety 'Chervonyi prapor.'"
81. The latter two were sent by the CC RCP to dissolve the conference as illegal. Lapchynsky, "Gomelskoe soveshchanie," p. 44.
82. Ibid.; Popov, *Narys*, p. 202.
83. Lapchynsky, "Gomelskoe soveshchanie," pp. 47–48; also his letter to *Chervonyi prapor*.
84. This will be dealt with elsewhere (see pp. 249–53).
85. Ravich, pp. 149–50.
86. Ibid., p. 150.
87. See Byk's speech, ibid., pp. 150–51.
88. Laponin's declaration, ibid.
89. Ibid.
90. Kosior apparently had in mind Lapchynsky's declaration at the Homel conference.
91. Ravich, p. 152. The last words of this quotation read in Popov, *Narys*, p. 218, as follows: " . . . which is afraid to go to the front."
92. Ravich, p. 158; Popov, *Narys*, p. 226.
93. Trotsky wrote afterwards that Stalin had been a "plenipotentiary representative of the central committee [of the RCP], armed with the explicit resolution of that body on the Ukrainian question." Leon Trotsky,

Stalin, p. 265.

94. Ravich, pp. 155–56. According to Trotsky's own testimony, he wrote these theses in accordance with a directive of the politburo. Trotsky, *Stalin*, pp. 265–66.
95. Ravich, pp. 155–56.
96. Ibid., p. 158; Popov, *Narys*, p. 223; Iavorsky, p. 122.
97. Popov, *Narys*, p. 223.
98. Ravich, p. 162. Later the CC RCP asserted that the fourth conference had been unable to elect a new CC at all. A protest against this was made by the delegates of the CP(B)U at the ninth congress of the RCP, who stressed that the elections to the CC CP(B)U had taken place under the chairmanship of a member of the politburo of the CC RCP, Stalin, who neither during the elections nor after had made any remarks about the incorrectness of the elections. *Deviatyi sezd RKP*, pp. 222–23.
99. Ibid., pp. 62–65.
100. Ibid., pp. 94–95. Lenin was informed by Shvarts (Semen) about "Rakovsky's baiting by the Ukrainian semi-Makhnovites." See Trotsky's Archives, "Delo 'Direktivy i pr.,' papka No. 1, za 1919–20 gg.," p. 504.
101. Lenin's telegram to Shumsky (23 March 1920), copies to the new CC CPU and to Rakovsky, Trotsky's Archives, "Delo 'Iskhod. shifr. telegr.' ch. I za 1920 g., Sekr. Zam. Pred. R.V.S.R.," p. 139; cf. also *Deviatyi sezd RKP*, p. 94.
102. Appeal of the CC RCP to all organizations of the Communist party of Ukraine. *Kommunist* (Kharkiv), 20 May 1920, No. 1, p. 3; Ravich, pp. 235–36. On the appointment of the new CC, see also *Deviatyi sezd RKP*, p. 572, note 88.
103. Appeal of the CC RCP, *Kommunist*, (Kharkiv), 1920, No. 1.
104. Likholat, *Razgrom*, p. 443.
105. Ibid.
106. *Kommunist*, 20 May 1920. From the end of the ninth congress of the RCP, i.e., from 5 April 1920, until September 1920 alone, the CC RCP sent to Ukraine "about a thousand comrades with long party and Soviet experience to replace the "local functionaries 'with partisan habits' and 'local psychology' who have been recalled from Ukraine." *Desiatyi sezd RKP(b)*, p. 850.
107. *Kommunist*, 20 May 1920, pp. 6–9; Ravich, pp. 166–67; Popov, *Narys*, p. 225. Popov remarks that the dissolution of the CC and the appointment of the new one was regarded as the greatest breach of intra-party democracy in the whole history of the party.
108. Iavorsky, p. 114.
109. See Antonov's speech in Ravich, pp. 237–38.
110. Ravich, p. 178.
111. Ibid., pp. 172–75.
112. At this conference 203 delegates from local organizations and 175 delegates from military units represented 39,229 party members in Ukraine and

35,881 members of the military organizations of the party. Ravich, p. 171. Popov, *Narys*, p. 228, remarks that "more than half of the delegates of the fifth conference (there were 318 delegates representing over 73,000 party members) were the representatives of the *Red Army*, and the greater part of the *Red Army* consisted of divisions that came from Soviet Russia, not, of course, as invaders and conquerors, but as *friends and helpers of the working masses of Ukraine*." Cf. also A. Gilinsky, "Sostoianie KP(b)U k piatiletiiu oktiabrskoi revoliutsii," *Oktiabrskaia revoliutsiia*, p. 167.

113. This CC comprised Petrovsky, Rakovsky, Manuilsky, Zatonsky, Mikhail Frunze, Kin, N. Ivanov, Chubar, Piatakov, Voroshilov, Kon, A. Ivanov, Shumsky, Dmitrii Lebed, Molotov, Nikolaenko, and Minin. The candidates were Drobnis, Kharechko, and Averin. Popov, *Narys*, p. 246, note 1; Iavorsky, p. 126.
114. If one does not count the episode when, after the fall of the second Soviet regime in Ukraine, the federalists created a separate Ukrainian section of the CP(B)U within the Moscow organization of the RCP, led by Lapchynsky, which submitted memorandum to the CC RCP in the autumn of 1919 criticizing party policy in Ukraine. Ravich, p. 138.
115. Cf. *Desiatyi sezd RKP(b)*, pp. 749–64, 809–10.
116. *Korenizatsiia* meant the recruiting of the local nationalities into the Communist party and Soviet administration.
117. The Secretary of the CC CP(B)U, Postyshev, later admitted that the Borotbists' amalgamation with the party had been of great value. "The joining of the Borotbists to the CP(B)U made easier our task of strengthening our ties with the countryside, our task of increasing the proletarian influence on the Ukrainian countryside." P. P. Postyshev, "Itogi proverki partiinykh dokumentov v KP(b)U i zadachi partiinoi raboty," *Bolshevik* (Moscow), 1936, No. 5, p. 10.
118. Ravich, pp. 5–6. Rish held a similar position on this question. See *LR*, 1930, No. 1–2, pp. 330–32; also M. Volin, *Istoriia KP(b)U u styslomu narysi*.
119. See, for instance, Popov, *Ocherki*; also *Istoriia Vsesoiuznoi kommunisticheskoi partii (bolshevikov). Kratkii kurs*.
120. M. Skrypnyk, "Do spravy ukrainizatsii," *LR*, No. 1, 1930, pp. x–xi; D. Frid, "Pro deiaki pytannia z istorii KP(b) na Ukraini," *LR*, 1930, No. 3–4, pp. 238–56.
121. A. Khvylia, "KP(b)U v borotbi za leninsku natsionalnu polityku," *BU*, 1932, pp. 80–81.
122. Ravich, p. 43.
123. *1917 god na Kievshchine*, p. 38.
124. Popov, *Narys*, p. 101.
125. Ibid., p. 107.
126. *Shestoi sezd RSDRP(b)*, p. 195. Popov, *Narys*, p. 107, says there were 22,000 members.
127. *Shestoi sezd RSDRP(b)*, p. 194.

128. O. H. Radkey, *The Election to the Russian Constituent Assembly of 1917*, p. 2; *Dekrety oktiabrskoi revoliutsii*, Vol. I, p. 18.
129. Radkey, *The Election to the Russian Constituent Assembly*, p. 40.
130. Ibid., Appendix.
131. Lenin, "Vybory v uchreditelnoe sobranie i diktatura proletariata," *Soch.* XXX, pp. 246–47.
132. Radkey, *The Election to the Russian Constituent Assembly*. Cf. also Lenin, *Soch.*, XXX, p. 246, who points out that the Ukrainian SRs received 3.9 million votes out of 7.6 million.
133. Lenin, *Soch.*, XXX, pp. 232–33.

Chapter VII

1. The text of the resolution is in Dimanshtein, pp. 443–49.
2. The Ukrainian government sent notes to the Southeastern Union of the Highland Cossacks and the Peoples of the Free Steppes, to the governments of the Caucasus, Siberia, autonomous Moldavia, Crimea, Bashkiria, and to other organized regions. Doroshenko, I, p. 205. As can be seen from the meetings of the Little Rada, the General Secretariat's efforts to create an all-Russian government were supported by the Russian SRs and Mensheviks and by the Bund. *Kievskaia mysl,* No. 284, cited in *1917 god na Kievshchine,* p. 411.
3. Doroshenko, I, p. 205.
4. On this occasion, Moscow's *Pravda,* in an article entitled, "Pochemu nadvigaetsia stolknovenie s Radoi?" argued that the conflict with the Rada resulted, among other reasons, because the Rada "wishes to establish in the whole of Russia a regime of bourgeois power." In the same issue, in the article, "Sut dela," it explained that "the Rada demands the creation for the whole of Russia of a new government on principles different from those on which the Council of People's Commissars is now formed. Both Kaledin and the Rada pursue an all-Russian policy, and by no means a Ukrainian or a Cossack one." *Pravda,* 22 December 1917.
5. See the report of the people's commissar for foreign affairs, Trotsky, in the soviet of workers' and soldiers' deputies on 6 December, where he expressed his anxiety that "our bourgeoisie wants, under the Rada's protection against the Bolshevik danger, to convene the constituent assembly in Kiev." *Pravda,* 21 December 1917; cf. also Margolin, *Ukraina i politika Antanty,* p. 48.
6. *Pravda,* 9 December 1917, No. 200.
7. Hereafter referred to only as Antonov.
8. Antonov, *Zapiski,* I, pp. 23–24.
9. Stalin's article "The General Secretariat of the Rada and the Kadets' and Kaledin's Counter-revolution," *Pravda,* 21 December 1917, No. 209.
10. *Pravda,* 18 December 1917.
11. Popov, *Narys,* pp. 111 ff.

12. The text of the ultimatum and its draft, with Lenin's corrections, is in *Dekrety oktiabrskoi revoliutsii,* I (Moscow, 1933), pp. 227–36; also *Pravda,* 18 December 1917, No. 206.
13. There are several opinions on the authorship of the ultimatum: Lenin was its author, though Stalin made corrections (*Dekrety oktiabrskoi revoliutsii,* I, pp. 227–36; Lenin wrote the first part of the ultimatum and Trotsky the second (the editors of L. Trotsky, *Sochineniia,* Vol. III, part 2, p. 142 n.); Lenin wrote the first part, while Stalin wrote the second part along with the points of the ultimatum proper (V. Sadovsky, *Natsionalna polityka sovitiv na Ukraini,* p. 79).
14. *Dekrety oktiabrskoi revoliutsii,* I, pp. 232–35.
15. Ibid., pp. 228–29.
16. Ibid., p. 229.
17. Ibid., p. 231.
18. *Pravda,* 9 December 1917, No. 200. Italics mine.
19. *Pravda,* 28 December 1917, No. 215.
20. Rosa Luxemburg categorically denied the Ukrainian right to independence. She wrote that "Ukrainian nationalism was ... nothing else than simply an invention, a pastime, simply the clamouring of some couple of dozen petty-bourgeois intellectuals, without the slightest roots in the economic, political, or spiritual conditions in the country, without any historical tradition, for Ukraine never had been a nation or a state, having no national culture except the reactionary romantic verses of Shevchenko." R. Luxemburg, *Die russische Revolution,* pp. 41–42.
21. *LR,* 1926, No. 5, p. 76, minutes of the conference. Shortly before the congress, Bosh even expressed the view that "it is enough to withdraw from the southwestern front the second corps of the Guards, which has been under the influence of the Bolsheviks, to order it to disperse the Central Rada, and this will be the end of Ukrainian nationalism." Popov, *Narys,* p. 131. See also S. Sh[reiberg], "Iz istorii sovvlasti na Ukraine," *LR,* 1924, No. 4, p. 166.
22. "Oblastnoi sezd RSDRP (b-kov)," *LR,* 1926, No. 5, p. 77.
23. Ibid., p. 78.
24. Vasyl Shakhrai was one of the most prominent Bolshevik personalities in Ukraine. He was one of those exceptions among the Bolsheviks who was of Ukrainian origin. Shakhrai approached the Ukrainian problem and the question of nationalities most realistically, for which he was expelled from the CP(B)U. He was killed in the Kuban in 1919 during Denikin's rout of the Kuban Rada (which resisted the inclusion of the Kuban in the White Army's sphere of influence and strove towards making the Kuban independent). See Lapchynsky, "Z pershykh dniv," *LR,* 1927, No. 5–6, p. 59.
25. "Oblastnoi sezd RSDRP (b-kov)," *LR,* 1926, No. 5, pp. 65–92.
26. Ibid., p. 79.
27. Lapchynsky said that the ultimatum "placed us in a very difficult position,

for we did not yet know the text of the telegrams, nor were we at all prepared for such a step on the part of our Petrograd comrades." H. Lapchynsky, "Z pershykh dniv," *LR,* 1927, No. 5–6, pp. 63, 65.

28. Shakhrai so qualified the ultimatum at the congress of soviets. See Khrystiuk, II, p. 70.
29. "Oblastnoi sezd RSDRP (b-kov)," *LR,* 1926, No. 5, pp. 83–84.
30. This aspect of Piatakov's activities emerges clearly from Bakynsky's talk with Stalin. To Bakynsky's question whether Piatakov was in Petrograd and "whether he informed you to a sufficient degree about the state of affairs," Stalin replied: "I learned from him everything about Kiev." *1917 god na Kievshchine,* pp. 531–33.
31. "Oblastnoi sezd RSDRP (b-kov)," *LR,* 1926, No. 5, p. 84.
32. Ibid., p. 85.
33. See *Proletarskaia mysl* and *Donetskii proletarii,* December 1917.
34. The resolution of the congress of the organizations of the RSDWP(B) of the southwestern region concerning their attitude towards the Central Rada, 18 December 1917. *Borba za vlast sovetov na Kievshchine,* pp. 480–81.
35. Ibid., pp. 484–86.
36. Stalin's declaration at the third all-Russian congress of soviets; *Soch.,* IV, pp. 31–32.
37. On these events, see Doroshenko, pp. 158–83, and Popov, *Narys,* pp. 122–23.
38. Serhii Bakynsky was a second-rank Bolshevik in Ukraine. He was to become the commissar for nationalities and foreign affairs in the first Soviet government in Ukraine.
39. *Pravda,* 7 December 1917, No. 198; Stalin, *Stati,* pp. 16–17.
40. Later Soviet historiography interpreted every step of the RCP in relation to Ukraine as a directive to the local Bolsheviks. Baby, *Vozziednannia Zakhidnoi Ukrainy z Ukrainskoiu RSR,* p. 9.
41. The quotas are described in *Borba za vlast sovetov na Kievshchine,* pp. 440–42.
42. Stalin, *Stati,* p. 27.
43. D. Petrovsky, *Revoliutsiia i kontrrevoliutsiia na Ukraine,* p. 15.
44. Khrystiuk, II, p. 69.
45. Likholat, *Razgrom,* p. 64; Doroshenko, I, p. 219, quotes the figure 150.
46. The peasants' union representative, Stasiuk, remarked that the Bolshevik regional committee of the soviets of workers' and soldiers' deputies, by granting the majority not to the peasants, but to the (in the main, non-Ukrainian) workers and soldiers, was attempting to falsify the will of the Ukrainian people, and that therefore the central committee of the peasants' union took care to increase the peasant representation at the congress. Doroshenko, I, pp. 220–21.
47. Likholat wrote that absent from the congress were "the delegates from the soviets of the Donets basin, of the Kharkiv and Katerynoslav regions, who at that time attended the congress of soviets of the Donets and Kryvyi Rih

basins." *Razgrom*, p. 64n.

48. Popov, *Narys*, p. 133; also Iavorsky, pp. 96–97; S. Sh., "Iz istorii sovvlasti na Ukraine," *LR*, 1924, No. 4, pp. 167–69; M. Skrypnyk, in *Chervonyi shliakh*, 1924, No. 2, pp. 80–81.
49. The Stalinist historian, Likholat, in *Razgrom*, pp. 64–65.
50. Khrystiuk, I, p. 69.
51. S. Sh., "Iz istorii sovvlasti na Ukraine," *LR*, No. 4, 1924, p. 170.
52. Lapchynsky, "Z pershykh dniv," *LR*, 1927, No. 5–6, p. 66.
53. M. Skrypnyk, "Donbass i Ukraina," *Kommunist* (Kharkiv), 1920, No. 4, in *Statti i promovy*, II, i, p. 25.
54. V. Zatonsky, "Shkola revoliutsii," pp. 93–95.
55. Popov, *Narys*, pp. 120–22.
56. It must, however, be remembered that even the working masses were not all under Bolshevik influence. This is borne out, for instance, by the composition of the Kharkiv soviet of workers' and soldiers' deputies and its executive committee, where the Bolsheviks were in the minority. At the elections to the executive committee on 25 August 1917, of 324 votes cast, the Bolsheviks polled 101, the socialist revolutionaries—122, the Mensheviks—48, the Ukrainian socialists—34, the USDWP independentists—13, and the anarchists—6. Thus elected to the executive committee of the soviet of workers' and soldiers' deputies were fifteen socialist revolutionaries, twelve Bolsheviks, six Mensheviks, four Ukrainians, two independentists, and one anarchist. *Velikaia oktiabrskaia sotsialisticheskaia revoluliutsiia na Ukraine*, I, p. 561.
57. Popov, *Narys*, p. 124.
58. Ibid., p. 139.
59. Ibid., p. 125.
60. Ibid., p. 123. Cf. also A. Ivanov, "Tsentralna rada . . . ," *LR*, 1922–23, No. 1, pp. 9–15.
61. Kulyk, *LR*, 1927, No. 5–6, pp. 226–27.
62. Trotsky, *Stalin*, p. 264.
63. For instance, S. M. Drabkina, "Krakh," *Istoricheskie zapiski*, 1949, No. 28, pp. 69–77. During Stalin's dictatorship the party gradually re-evaluated the relations of forces in Ukraine during the October revolution, and as early as the thirties the Soviet historians broke all records by arriving at the conclusion that the leader of both the so-called bourgeois (February) and the October revolutions was the proletariat under the guidance of the Communist party. See the discussion on Iavorsky's deviations, the hegemony of the proletariat, and the scheme of Ukrainian history in *Litopys revoliutsii*, 1929–31.
64. *Dekrety oktiabrskoi revoliutsii*, p. 236.
65. Lenin, *Soch.*, XXVI, p. 359.
66. "Why the Bolsheviks Fight the Rada," in *Petrogradskii golos*, 27 January 1918, No. 8, p. 3.
67. Doroshenko, I, p. 216.

68. Antonov, I, p. 51.
69. Ibid., p. 46.
70. Ibid., p. 52.
71. Ibid., p. 36.
72. Ibid., pp. 28–32. That Ukrainian soldiers in the Red Army ranks went unwillingly, or even refused, to fight against the Rada is confirmed elsewhere by Antonov. Ibid., pp. 35, 52–53. The same was also asserted by Shakhrai, the first secretary for military affairs of the Soviet Ukrainian government. He said then to his colleague, Lapchynsky: "What kind of a 'Ukrainian Military Minister' am I, when all Ukrainianized units in Kharkiv throw down their arms because they do not wish to follow me to defend Soviet power." H. Lapchynsky, "Pershyi period radianskoi vlady na Ukraini," *LR,* 1928, I, p. 171.
73. Antonov, I, p. 34.
74. Ibid., pp. 53–59.
75. Popov, *Narys,* p. 136.
76. Or, as Antonov wrote (I, p. 108), "a certain lull in the operations against Kaledin" occurred.
77. Ibid., p. 121.
78. See pp. 195–99.
79. Antonov, I, p. 86.
80. Ibid., pp. 130–31. The aim of the southwestern front was, according to Antonov, "the distraction of the Central Rada's attention westwards."
81. Ibid.
82. Doroshenko, I, pp. 278–84.
83. The aim of this action was, according to Antonov (I, p. 161), "the liquidation of the Romanian oligarchy."
84. Ibid., pp. 146–47.
85. Ibid., p. 158.
86. *Dokumenty po istorii grazhdanskoi voiny v SSSR,* I, p. 79.
87. *Pravda,* 7 February 1918, No. 19.
88. Popov, *Narys,* pp. 134 ff.; cf. also *Ocherki razvitiia narodnogo khoziaistva Ukrainskoi SSR,* p. 151.
89. This has been admitted *post factum* by Soviet historians. V. Meluichenko, for instance, mentions that "the armies of the Central Rada were defeated on several occasions by the battalions of Kikvidze." *Radianska Ukraina,* 12 March 1975.
90. Popov, *Narys,* p. 133. However, as a Soviet source points out, the composition of the TsIKU had already been planned in Kiev. S. Sh., *LR,* 1924, No. 4, p. 171.
91. Ravich-Cherkassky, p. 48.
92. S. Sh., *LR,* 1924, No. 4, p. 173; and pp. 176–77: "Obiavlenie Narodnogo sekretaria po vnutrennim delam Ukrainskoi narodnoi respubliki."
93. Another Soviet source asserts that Skrypnyk was the chairman of the People's Secretariat, as well as the people's secretary of foreign affairs.

"Piat let borby za priznanie sovetskoi vlasti," *Oktiabrskaia revoliutsiia,* p. 280.

94. Popov, pp. 133–34. As S. Sh. points out, Bosh, Aussem, Skrypnyk, Liuksemburg, Shakhrai, and Lapchynsky worked most actively, while others, like Artem, took no part in the meetings of the People's Secretariat. Zatonsky was in Petrograd, while Bakynsky constantly travelled. *LR,* 1924, No. 3, pp. 174–75.
95. Khrystiuk, II, pp. 147–49.
96. S. Sh., *LR,* 1924, No. 4, p. 174, note 1. See also I. Kulyk, *LR,* 1927, No. 5–6, p. 226.
97. S. Sh., *LR,* 1924, No. 4, p. 175.
98. Skrypnyk, *Narys istorii proletarskoi revoliutsii na Ukraini,* p. 158. On the attitude of the first group, see Bosh, *God borby,* p. 45. Kviring wrote that the main cause for the anti-Ukrainian attitude among the Katerynoslavians was their proximity to the Don and the character of the war, which attracted them to Kharkiv and Moscow since from there they sometimes received "arms and reinforcements at the time of the encounter with the *haidamaky* in December." Generally, "the workers of the Left-Bank regions then understood Ukraine as Petliura's enterprise, and the slogan of 'Soviet Ukraine' was incomprehensible to their hearts." "Nashi raznoglasiia," p. 5. *Haidamaky* were Ukrainian rebels from the eighteenth century. In 1917–19 some Ukrainian forces bore this name.
99. Antonov, I, pp. 135–42.
100. Ibid., pp. 87, 154. On 5 February Lenin sent a telegram in the CPC's name addressed "to all" (*"vsem, vsem, vsem"*). The telegram announced that the Soviet troops that took Kiev "were led by the deputy people's secretary for military affairs, Iurii Kotsiubynsky." *Leninskii sbornik,* XI, p. 24. But the announcement was contrary to the facts, and Muravev had every right to be indignant about it. As Antonov remarks, the People's Secretariat appointed Kotsiubynsky the commander-in-chief of all units "in order to mitigate the impression of a number of Muravev's tactless actions," especially because Muravev "was, in the eyes of many Kievans, an 'occupier,' an invader from the Soviet north." Antonov, I, p. 154.
101. Ibid., p. 140.
102. Ibid.
103. Ibid., p. 182.
104. Antonov himself admits that, owing to the shortage of manpower, he used to send to "the posts of commissars at stations" "those boys [*rebiata*] who happened to be handy." "And they used to be mostly newcomers from Petrograd or valiant seamen, . . . but sometimes they were also drunkards and thick-headed thugs." Ibid., pp. 174 ff.
105. Ibid., pp. 180–82.
106. Lenin, *Stati,* p. 283; also Antonov, I, p. 182.
107. See the message of greeting to this government, dated 29 December 1917, *Dekrety oktiabrskoi revoliutsii,* I, p. 327.

108. Antonov, I, pp. 184–86.
109. Ibid., p. 187.
110. Ibid., p. 160.
111. *VUNR*, No. 44, 19 March 1918; Antonov, II, pp. 79–80, note 2.
112. Mazepa, I, p. 47.
113. Ibid.
114. *VUNR*, No. 46, 21 March 1918.
115. Ievhen Neronovych, who shortly before taking office had belonged to the Ukrainian social democratic party, was a convinced *samostiinyk* ("independentist") before the revolution. At the beginning of the revolution he studied at the Institute of Electrical Technology in Petrograd, where he belonged to an organization of the USDWP. Later he was elected a member of the Central Rada from the Ukrainian colony in Petrograd. At the beginning of 1918 he embraced the Soviet platform and left the Rada together with the Ukrainian left SRs. Several weeks after the Katerynoslav congress he was shot by a Ukrainian military detachment in Sorochyntsi in the Poltava region, through which he was passing in order to see his wife on his way abroad. Mazepa, I, pp. 48–49; Khrystiuk, II, p. 152.
116. Antonov, II, pp. 78–79.
117. Ibid., p. 79; Khrystiuk, II, p. 152.
118. Khrystiuk, II, p. 152. According to Mazepa, I, p. 50, a similar motion was also put forward by Medvedev, the chairman of the TsIKU.
119. Mazepa, I, pp. 48–49.
120. Ibid., p. 51; Antonov, II, p. 80.
121. *VUNR*, No. 45, 20 March 1918; Mazepa, I, p. 51.
122. Khrystiuk, II, p. 152. It is interesting that Skrypnyk still considered Ukraine independent after the liquidation of the TsIKU and the PS. He therefore issued a decree from the TsIKU and the PS that troops of the Ukrainian republic crossing the Russian border "enjoy the rights of civilians of the Ukrainian republic ... inasmuch, of course, as they themselves will not express the wish to be accepted and will not be accepted into the citizenship of the Russian Soviet federation." Antonov, II, pp. 263–64.
123. Kulyk, *Ohliad revoliutsii na Ukraini*, p. 38.
124. According to recent Soviet sources, Skrypnyk became a president of the *"deviatka."* V. M. Kuritsyn, *Gosudarstvennoe sotrudnichestvo*, p. 33, note 3.
125. Ravich, p. 51.
126. The text of the manifesto is in Ravich, pp. 191–92.
127. Ia[kovlev] E[pshtein], "O sozdanii 'samostiinoi' Kommunisticheskoi partii Ukrainy," *Pravda*, 30 June 1918, No. 132; cf. also Shakhrai, *Do khvyli*.
128. Bosh, *Natsionalnoe pravitelstvo*, pp. 35–36.
129. Antonov, II, p. 11.
130. Ibid., pp. 12–13. *Pravda*, 25 June 1918, No. 127, wrote after the event that the masses of Ukraine had "lightly given up" the Soviet government; Rakovsky also complained later that "the greater part of the workers were

indifferent to the appeals of the Communists for struggle and resistance." *Pravda,* 17 October 1918, No. 224. Cf. also Shakhrai-Skorovstansky, *Revoliutsiia na Ukraine,* pp. 116–19, who admitted that the Ukrainian masses expressed their enthusiasm over the return of the Ukrainian Rada accompanied by German armies. Some Western experts on the Bolshevik revolution emphasize that in Ukraine "the people, especially the peasants, were putting up a desperate resistance to the occupying forces and their Ukrainian tools." I. Deutscher, *The Prophet Armed,* p. 394.

131. Lenin, *Soch.,* XXVI, p. 409.
132. Ibid., pp. 401–08.
133. M. Rubach, "K istorii ukrainskoi revoliutsii," *LR,* 1926, No. 6, pp. 20–21.
134. Bukharin spoke about it very characteristically at the seventh congress of the RCP in March 1918 when he opposed Lenin's arguments on the need for a respite, since a peace with Germany deprived Soviet Russia of the prerequisites for a respite and for the organization of forces. "It is just these conditions which the treaty deprives us of. We are being cut off from Ukraine, separated from the Donets basin, i.e., the centres feeding Russian industry; we are cut off from grain, coal .... For, after all, we must not hide the fact from ourselves that we remain, even in numbers of population, almost at half strength." *Sedmoi sezd RKP(b)* (Moscow, 1928), pp. 32–33. The food shortage in Soviet Russia was widely known in Entente diplomatic circles. See e.g., the cable of Secretary of State Lansing to Ambassador Francis, 31 May 1918, *Russian-American Relations, March 1918–March 1920,* p. 22.
135. *Pravda,* 7 February 1918, No. 19.
136. Antonov, I, p. 133. This fact was emphasized even by official Soviet sources. *Grazhdanskaia voina 1918–1921,* III, p. 48.
137. Resolution of the TsIKU in *LR,* 1924, No. 4, pp. 182–83.
138. According to Doroshenko, I, p. 306.
139. "Materialy o brest-litovskikh peregovorakh za 18–19 god iz arkhiva NKID," Trotsky's Archives. This declaration was contradictory to Kamenev's arguments presented at the special commission on political questions in January 1918: "From the fact that the occupied territories belonged to the former Russian empire the Russian government draws no conclusions that would impose any constitutional obligations on the population of these regions in relation to the Russian republic .... The old frontiers of the former Russian empire ... have vanished with tsarism." *Mirnye peregovory v Brest-Litovske, s 22 dekabria 1917 g. po 3 marta 1918 g.,* I, pp. 92–94.
140. Lenin, *Soch.,* XXVI, p. 382.
141. Ibid., p. 464.
142. Ibid., p. 465. Cf. also Brest Litovsk talks, *GFM Friedenspärliminarien zu Brest-Litowsk,* D 820792–D 820818.
143. Stalin telegraphed to Antonov in Kharkiv and told him that Trotsky was not being kept up to date by the Kharkiv and Kiev Bolsheviks. Stalin stressed that if the People's Secretariat did not officially inform the

delegation in Brest Litovsk about the course of affairs, the Germans would sign a treaty with the Rada. Antonov, I, p. 273. On the telegraph and telephone messages of the CPC and the Rada, see *GFM*, D 820491–D 820625.

144. Stalin, *Soch.*, IV, pp. 42–44. For this purpose, the chairman of the Soviet Ukrainian peace delegation, V. Zatonsky, sent the following telegram on 27 February 1918 to Count Ottokar Czernin, Richard von Kühlmann, General Max Hoffman, and the chairman of the Russian peace delegation: "Die Delegation des Volkssekretariats der Ukrainischen Volksrepublik ... befindet sich auf dem Wege von Kiew nach Brest-Litowsk, um den Friedensvertrag, der mit der ehemaligen Kiewer Rada abgeschlossen wurde, zu unterzeichnen." *GFM,* 6, D 820718. Later, Soviet historiography thought that the Bolsheviks would have been able to prevent the signing of peace between the Central Powers and the Rada if they had made use of the antagonism between the German and Austro-Hungarian delegations over the Polish question. M. Rubach, "K istorii ukrainskoi revoliutsii," *LR,* 1926, No. 6, pp. 22–23.

145. This opinion predominated even among the military leaders of the Red Guards. The commander-in-chief, Antonov, wrote in this connection: "All of us in Ukraine were then uninformed about the Germans' policy towards the Ukrainian Rada. We imagined that with the capture of Kiev and with our establishment in Right-Bank Ukraine, our military operations against the Rada were on the whole concluded." Antonov, I, pp. 158–59.

146. Ibid., pp. 295–96.

147. For the text of the treaty, see *Sedmoi sezd RKP(b),* pp. 249–53.

148. Ibid., pp. 44–45.

149. Ibid., pp. 32–33.

150. Ibid., pp. 73–75.

151. Ibid., p. 116.

152. See Wolfe, *Three who Made a Revolution,* p. 183.

153. In his theses on foreign policy Lenin wrote that the foreign policy of the Soviet government was unchanging. "Our military preparations are not yet complete, and therefore our general slogan still remains: to manoeuvre, retreat, and wait, while continuing these preparations with all our might. Never renouncing any military agreements with one of the imperialist coalitions against the other in those cases when such an agreement, without infringing on the foundations of Soviet power, could strengthen its position and paralyse the pressure upon it of any imperialist power." Lenin, "Tezisy o sovremennom politicheskom polozhenii," *Soch.,* XXVII, p. 325.

154. Antonov, II, p. 150. The question of the peace talks between Soviet Russia and Ukraine is treated in Ukrainian scholarship mainly by Doroshenko, *Istoriia Ukrainy,* II, pp. 162–87.

155. Antonov, II, p. 252.

156. Lenin, *Stati,* p. 290. Apart from Stalin, the delegation also comprised D. Z. Manuilsky and Kh. Rakovsky. This delegation held a conference in

Moscow on 27 April at which Lenin, Chicherin, and Lev Karakhan were also present. Ibid., p. 290, note 1.

157. Doroshenko, II, p. 163.
158. Antonov, II, pp. 293–94.
159. Ibid., p. 294.
160. Doroshenko, II, pp. 164–65n.
161. As a result, Ukraine established consulates-general in Moscow and Petrograd and consulates in another nineteen Russian cities. Ibid., p. 167.
162. The coal problem and the importance of the Donets basin were generally discussed in the Russian press. Thus A. Lomov, in his article on "the problem of the Donets coal at the peace talks with Ukraine" (*Pravda,* 13 August 1918, No. 170) wrote that "it depends on the solution of the question of the Russo-Ukrainian border how far Soviet Russia will be supplied with coal in the immediate future. . . . Therefore it is understandable why it was around this question in Kiev that impassioned debates developed in the Russian-Ukrainian commission."
163. Lenin, *Stati,* pp. 299–300.
164. *Pravda,* 26 June 1918, No. 128.
165. I. Kulyk, in *Zhizn natsionalnostei,* 1919, No. 4. Rakovsky afterwards admitted that "the Russian delegation used their stay in Ukraine to intensify the struggle that had already been waged by the Ukrainian workers and peasants." Kh. Rakovsky, "Mezhdunarodnoe polozhenie sovetskoi respubliki," p. 33. Zatonsky later wrote that Manuilsky sent from Moscow a coded telegram from the CC RCP asking Piatakov and Zatonsky to come to direct the revolution in Ukraine; the telegram said that Bubnov and Kosior were already illegally in Kiev. "K voprosu ob organizatsii Vremennogo r.-k. pravitelstva Ukrainy," *LR,* 1925, no. 1, p. 140. These intentions of the Russian delegation were also no secret to the Ukrainian delegation. See Doroshenko, II, pp. 172–74.
166. *Piatyi sozyv Vserossiiskogo tsentralnogo ispolnitelnogo komiteta,* p. 93.
167. This was discussed also at the second congress of the CP(B)U. Rakovsky declared there that Ukraine would be of "immense importance" to the Russian revolution. "When there is Soviet power in Ukraine, we shall obtain for our Red Army the richest reserves of human materials, . . . the richest resources of grain and food, the richest resources of weapons, equipment, and artillery, and moreover we shall obtain an invulnerable line of defence of the Black Sea shore." *Vtoroi sezd KP(b)U,* p. 15.

Chapter VIII

1. *Piatyi sozyv Vserossiiskogo TsIK*, pp. 257–66. Also Lenin, *Soch.*, XXVIII, pp. 94–107.
2. One of the leading figures of Soviet diplomacy, Rakovsky, wrote: "The German revolution was for the Russian revolution an immense help and at

the same time the beginning of a new period of struggle. The end of the war meant that now we had to face the Entente. While the war lasted and both camps mutually destroyed each other, this presented us with a period of respite." The task of the Soviet government from the Versailles to the Genoa conferences was "carefully to direct our ship between the Scylla and Charybdis of capitalist discord, steering clear of the whirlpool of one or the other of these groups." "Mezhdunarodnoe polozhenie sovetskoi respubliki," pp. 33–36.

3. The fear of the Entente was then great among the Russian Bolsheviks, mainly because nobody knew what proportions the intervention of the Entente in Russia would assume. See the speeches of Rakovsky, Radek, and Kamenev at the second congress of the CP(B)U, *Vtoroi sezd KP(b)U*, pp. 12 ff.
4. Lenin, *Soch.*, XXVIII, pp. 108–09. The Bolsheviks also tried to persuade the German command not to withdraw its troops from Ukraine until it was occupied by the Bolsheviks, after which they guaranteed the German troops an undisturbed passage home. M. Rubach, "K istorii grazhdanskoi voiny na Ukraine," *LR*, 1924, No. 4, pp. 156–57. Meshcheriakov in *Petrogradskaia pravda*, 12 November 1918, No. 274, wrote that "in this struggle for the takeover of power by workers and peasants, the force of revolutionary Austrian and German soldiers who are in Ukraine may, and must, be made use of." Further, in a lead article of *Pravda*, "The German Revolution and Russian Grain" (19 November 1918, No. 250), attempts were made to influence the German army with the grain of Ukraine. The article said that the German soldiers were "committing a serious error," since they "do not assist the Ukrainian insurgents to strengthen their power.... The revolutionary German soldiers must not go home from Ukraine, but they should give all their strength in order to secure these regions, rich in grain, for Soviet Russia." Cf. also *Pravda*, 26 November 1918, No. 256; also "Iz istorii grazhdanskoi voiny na Ukraine v 1918 g.," *Krasnyi arkhiv* (Moscow), 1939, No. 4, p. 94.
5. Lenin's article, "Proletarskaia revoliutsiia i renegat Kautsky," *Soch.*, XXVIII, p. 92.
6. Ibid., pp. 101–02.
7. The fact that the "national" governments of the borderlands were unable to resist for long the offensive "on the part of the Soviet power of Russia" and on the part of "their own" workers and peasants is dealt with by Stalin in *Pravda*, November 1918 (Stalin, *Soch.*, IV, p. 162).
8. *Vtoroi sezd KP(b)U*, pp. 94–95.
9. Ibid.
10. *Piatyi sozyv Vserossiiskogo TsIK*, pp. 248–49.
11. *Vtoroi sezd KP(b)U*, p. 96.
12. The problem of the invasion of Ukraine was very often discussed in the Soviet Russian press. See *Pravda,* October 1918, and *Petrogradskaia pravda*, 8 October 1918, No. 219. The party also arranged numerous

meetings to discuss this. Thus on 18 December 1918 the Moscow committee of the RCP arranged "large meetings" on "Ukraine and the imperialists' new conspiracy" with the following among the speakers: Kamenev, Bukharin, Sverdlov, Iurii Steklov, Emelian Iaroslavsky, Krylenko, and Petrovsky. *Pravda*, 17 October 1918, No. 224.

13. Lenin, *Soch.*, XXVIII, p. 205.
14. Antonov, III, p. 11.
15. Ibid., pp. 11–12.
16. They apparently had in view the declarations of the well-known "consul" E. Hennot who bombarded Kiev with his telegrams from Jassy, Romania, saying that the Allies were against the Directory and supported Skoropadsky. See Doroshenko, II, pp. 409–10; Mazepa, I, pp. 66–70; Reshetar, p. 201.
17. These attempts are described in detail in Fischer, *The Soviets in World Affairs*, Vol. I, pp. 128–30, and A. Fredborg, *Storbritannien och den ryska frågan*, pp. 20 ff.; they are based on the memoirs of the German ambassador in Moscow, K. Hellferich, *Der Weltkrieg*, Vol. III.
18. Antonov, III, p. 12.
19. Soon after, Stalin was recalled from that post to Moscow. This, however, did not prevent the historiography of the Stalin period from giving him full credit for the creation of the Soviet regime in Ukraine. For instance, Likholat, *Razgrom burzhuazno-natsionalisticheskoi Direktorii*, p. 128, says that "comrade Stalin was at the head of the struggle of the Ukrainian workers for the establishment of Soviet power," and that he was the head of the revolutionary military council.
20. Antonov, III, pp. 12 ff.
21. Ibid. The controversy between Vatsetis and Antonov-Ovseenko was recently dealt with in the article by A. Adams, "The Bolsheviks and the Ukrainian Front in 1918–1919," *SEER*, 1958, Vol. XXXVI, No. 87, pp. 396–417. The article would have had greater value if the author had made use of Trotsky's recently discovered archives.
22. Antonov, III, pp. 25–26.
23. Ibid., p. 27.
24. Ibid., p. 27.
25. Vatsetis' telegram is published in Antonov, III, pp. 111–14.
26. Zatonsky, "K voprosu ob organizatsii Vrem. R.-K. pravitelstva Ukrainy," *LR*, 1925, No. 1, pp. 139–40. The Bolsheviks used to call the whole Ukrainian movement "Petliurite," after the general secretary for military affairs in the Central Rada government, Symon Petliura. During the Hetmanate, Petliura was one of the leaders of the nationalist opposition against the hetman's pro-Russian trend; under the Directory, he became the leader of the anti-Bolshevik Ukrainian troops and later the president of the Directory.
27. The Bolsheviks admitted this. See *Istoriia KP(b)U*, pp. 387–91.
28. Zatonsky, p. 141.

29. Ibid.
30. Zatonsky says that Stalin in his talk with him reported that Lenin was angry with the Ukrainian Bolsheviks for their rashness. Ibid., p. 142.
31. Arthur Adams, p. 404, refers to Rubach (*LR*, 1924, No. 4, p. 164) who, however, does not mention the matter at all.
32. This unity is mentioned by Zatonsky and confirmed by the editors of *LR*. Zatonsky, p. 141.
33. "Dela iskhodiashchie bum. No. 1, s No. 1 po 500 za 1919 g. ch. 2. kants. poezda Predsed. R.V.S.R.," Trotsky's Archives.
34. See pp. 148–52.
35. The report of the Ukrainian Bolsheviks was probably signed by Piatakov and Zatonsky and addressed "To I. V. Dzhugashvili-Stalin." Zatonsky, pp. 142–46.
36. Ibid., pp. 145–46. Cf. also the telegrams, signed by Piatakov (23 November 1918) and by Piatakov and Zatonsky (27 November 1918). M. Rubach, "K istorii grazhdanskoi voiny na Ukraine," *LR*, 1924, No. 4, p. 151.
37. Zatonsky, pp. 146–47. Cf. also Rubach, pp. 160–62, who quotes another version of what seems to be the same report, in which it is said that "the Soviet centre had to come into existence at the earliest opportunity, but this has not been done up to the present moment, which is our serious omission. Your prohibiting the publication of the manifesto we regard as a considerable political error, which has made it much more difficult to concentrate the forces for Soviet power and against the hetman and the Rada."
38. Zatonsky, "K voprosu ob organizatsii," p. 147.
39. Ibid., p. 148.
40. Zatonsky's answer to Stalin in a direct telegram: "Pardon me, but this is some sort of mockery. For I have said three times, the last time today, that there are no disagreements among us. The whole trouble lies in the fact that the centre confuses the issue with its contradictory directives and by that indefiniteness which seems to be created on purpose. In the name of the CC [CP(B)U], I ask you directly: will you give us the possibility of acting? This concerns both the publishing of document No. 2 and the creation of a single command and leadership. The policy pursued up to now has compelled me and Iurii [Piatakov], to ask you a straightforward question about the attitude towards the Petliurite movement, since some directives can be explained only by an attempt to bank on Petliura, unless they are caused by a complete ignorance of the situation and by unwillingness to know it. In reply to all our requests you speak of sending functionaries, which is very well .... By the way, you throw out the phrase that all rights are in our hands. If this is no mockery, the conclusion from it is the immediate publishing of document No. 2 and then an order in our name about the creation of a single front and a single command. If a venture, so be it a venture. Please reply and reply in a more enlightened way." Ibid., p. 149.
41. Ibid., p. 148. This admission is confirmed by Antonov's letter to Stalin of

18 December 1918, which said that Piatakov and Artem "have come to you in order to solve the question of the creation of an RVS of the Ukrainian army, a question that arose spontaneously (in connection with the proclamation of the Ukrainian Workers' and Peasants' Government), in accordance with your instructions. After the arrival of comrade Piatakov and after his statement that you agreed to it, the RVS of the Ukrainian front was announced. The directives of the C. in C. were not contravened either before this or after." Antonov, III, p. 41. The minutes of the "government" meeting of 28 November 1919 are in Rubach, pp. 162–65.

42. See *Zhizn natsionalnostei*, 1 December 1918, No. 4.
43. "Bumagi Trotskogo, Iz del 'Iskhodiashchie bumagi Pol[evoi] Kants[eliarii], No. 1-za 1919 god No. 2,'" Trotsky's Archives.
44. Ibid., coded with the code JUA and sent as No. 001 of 3 January 1918, $22^{h}20^{m}$.
45. "Iz del 'Sekretn. iskhodiashch. bumagi s I/I–17/IX–1919 g. s No. 1 po No. 400,' ch. I," ibid., pp. 10–12. It is not true that Trotsky's letter "contains no proposal to consult the Ukrainian partisans, the Ukrainian Communists or any other Ukrainian body," as Wolfe stated in "The Influence of Early Military Decisions," *ASEER*, 1950, Vol. IX, pp. 171–72. In fact, Trotsky proposed to conclude a formal agreement with the Provisional Soviet Ukrainian Government.
46. See Antonov's reports. Antonov, III, pp. 58–61, 104–05, 114–15.
47. *Politika*, p. 111; Popov, *Narys*, p. 177. That this government was formed in Moscow by order of the CC RCP did not prevent Stalin from asserting in his propagandist works that this government was born "on the tide of the revolution." *Zhizn natsionalnostei*, 1 December 1918, No. 4. It is even more curious that the new historiography, governed by the instructions of the CC, purged from the history of Soviet power in Ukraine all the names of people who were to be later excluded from the party or liquidated. Thus B. M. Baby, "Utvorennia i rozkvit ukrainskoi radianskoi derzhavy," p. 80, mentions only that the Provisional Workers' and Peasants' Government of Soviet Ukraine "comprised comrades Voroshilov, Artem (Sergeev), and others."
48. Zatonsky, "K piatiletiiu KP(b)U," p. 16.
49. Shlikhter, a member of several governments of Soviet Ukraine, wrote about it with a great deal of irony in a letter to the editor of *Litopys revoliutsii*, 1931, No. 1–2, pp. 300–01.
50. The text of this declaration is in *Politika*, pp. 111–12.
51. Ibid., p. 112.
52. Khristiian Grigorevich Rakovsky was born in Bulgaria in 1873. His political career started in 1889 when he began participating in the social democratic movement in Bulgaria. From 1890 to 1896 he took part in the workers' movements in Switzerland, Germany, and France, and between 1896 and 1903 he was active in Romania and Russia. In 1907 Rakovsky was expelled from Romania and deprived of political rights. In 1917 he was freed by

Russian troops from the Jassy prison (in Romania). In January–March 1918 he was head of the Supreme Commission (*kollegiia*) for Combatting Counter-Revolution in Ukraine, and in May–September 1918 he led the Russian peace delegation in Kiev. He was premier of the Soviet government in Ukraine (1919–23) and the USSR's ambassador to Great Britain (1923–25) and to France (1925–27). He became a member of the CC RCP(B) in 1919, and later belonged to the Trotskyist opposition. At the fifteenth congress of the RCP(B) in 1927 he was expelled from the party. *Malaia sovetskaia entsiklopediia*, Vol. VII (Moscow, 1930), col. 168. Rakovsky's close friend Trotsky thus characterized him: "Khristiu Rakovsky is one of the most international figures in the European movement. A Bulgarian by descent, but a Romanian subject; a French doctor by education, but a Russian intellectual by connections, sympathies, and literary work." Trotsky, *Voina i revolutsiia*, II, pp. 32, 35, 316.

53. This is how Rakovsky is characterized by Goldenveizer, "Iz kievskikh vospominanii," *ARR*, Vol. VI, pp. 249–50.
54. In his article "Beznadezhnoe delo" in *Izvestiia VTsIKS*, 3 January 1919, No. 2, Rakovsky wrote that from the ethnographic as well as socio-economic standpoint there was no Ukrainian nation. "Ethnographic differences between Ukrainians and Russians are in themselves insignificant .... More important is the fact that among the Ukrainian peasantry there is a lack of what is generally called 'national consciousness' .... The Ukrainian proletariat is completely Russian in origin .... It is also well known that three-quarters of the urban population of Kiev is non-Ukrainian, while Odessa is only 10 per cent Ukrainian. It is also well known that within the boundaries of Ukraine, of that Ukraine which was imagined by the authors of the Third Universal, i.e., within the boundaries of eight provinces, and with the Taurida province as the ninth, without Crimea, there lived, according to the 1897 statistics, over two million Great Russians .... Finally, ... it is well known that the industrial bourgeoisie and the greater part of the landowning class is of Russian, Polish, or Jewish origin." Khrystiuk, IV, p. 173n.
55. Popov, *Narys*, p. 184.
56. Ibid. Quoting Rakovsky's statement in an article in *Kommunist* (Kharkiv), 1921, that "the domination of the Ukrainian language had to mean the domination of the Ukrainian bourgeois intelligentsia and the kulak," Hirchak felt that Rakovsky had inclined "towards imperialist chauvinism." Hirchak, *Na dva fronta*, pp. 19–20.
57. Kotsiubynsky and Zatonsky were the Ukrainians in this government. Sergeev, Voroshilov, Piatakov, Kviring, Mogilev, and Averin were all Russians by origin and conviction. Mezhlauk was a Latvian and Rukhimovich a Jew. As Carr, I, p. 301, note 6, rightly remarked, some of these persons were, just as Trotsky and Zinovev, born in Ukraine, "but hardly regarded themselves as Ukrainians."
58. *Politika*, p. 113.

59. The chief of the supreme military inspectorate, Podvoisky, appointed Genrikh Iagoda, Vladimir Iudovsky, Ioffe, Smenov, Nikolaev, Kulikov, and Mazurkevich to posts in Ukraine. Antonov, III, p. 120.
60. *Politika*, pp. 112–13.
61. There were 106 Ukrainian left SRs, 97 Ukrainian SRs, 107 representatives of other parties, 42 independentists. Likholat, *Razgrom burzhuazno-natsionalisticheskoi Direktorii*, p. 176. The same author, in another work, *Razgrom natsionalisticheskoi kontrrevoliutsii*, p. 276, quotes different figures: the total number as 1,719, comprising 1,435 Communists, 100 Ukrainian left SRs, 150 Borotbists, 22 representatives of other parties, and 70 non-party.
62. V. Stakhiv, *Druha sovietska respublika v Ukraini*, p. 180, apparently went too far in his statement that this government "had under its control only approximately one-third of the Ukrainian territory" at that time (i.e., by 10 April).
63. See Khmelnytsky's report at the third congress of the CP(B)U concerning the constitution of the Ukrainian Soviet republic. Ravich, p. 111.
64. Ibid.
65. For the text of the constitution, see *Politika*, pp. 113–16.
66. Cf. the constitution of the Russian Soviet republic adopted on 10 July 1918 in *Sezdy sovetov RSFSR v postanovleniiakh i rezoliutsiiakh*, pp. 91–104.
67. These powers of the VTsIKS made this constitution differ from the constitution of the RSFSR, in which the powers of the VTsIKS were limited to a congress of soviets. Thus the Russian TsIK was unable to decide in questions of the ratification of a peace.
68. The organs of local government were empowered to lower the established age limit (article 20, note 1).
69. In this respect, the Ukrainian constitution copied the corresponding article from the Russian constitution practically word for word; cf. article 64 of the constitution of the RSFSR.
70. The expert on the constitution, Khmelnytsky, declared at the third congress of the CP(B)U that the question of federative ties with the RSFSR could not be solved on the constitutional plane, since it was a political matter. See Ravich, p. 111.
71. Stalin's apologist, Likholat, wrote that against "borrowing the experience of Soviet Russia and [against] the fraternal union of the Ukrainian people with the great Russian people there spoke at the congress only a handful of despicable traitors who falsely called themselves Ukrainian 'socialists' (the factions of the Ukrainian SRs, Borotbists, and Bundists)." *Razgrom*, pp. 276–77.
72. *Politika*, pp. 109–11.
73. Ibid., pp. 111–12.
74. Likholat, *Razgrom*, p. 276.
75. Ravich, p. 119.
76. *Pravda*, 1 January 1919, No. 287, p. 3.

77. Ibid., 4 January 1919, No. 3, the leading article "Direktoriia ili sovety."
78. Vynnychenko, III, pp. 158–59. Participants in these talks were Iu. Mazurenko, S. Mazurenko, V. Mazurenko, and Vynnychenko. Khrystiuk, IV, p. 29.
79. Khrystiuk, IV, p. 35; Vynnychenko, III, pp. 205–22.
80. For the text of the note, see Khrystiuk, IV, pp. 35–36.
81. Ibid., pp. 37–38; also *Pravda*, 12 January 1919, No. 7.
82. Khrystiuk, IV, pp. 38–39; also *Pravda*, 12 January 1919, No. 7.
83. Khrystiuk, IV, p. 39. *Pravda*, 4 January 1919, No. 3, wrote with reference to the talks that "the Ukrainian national conciliators 'became more clever.'"
84. *Pravda*, 29 January 1919, No. 20.
85. Vynnychenko, *Pered novym etapom*, quoted in I. Mazepa, p. 74, note 25; see also Khrystiuk, IV, pp. 34–36.
86. Vynnychenko, III, pp. 222–25. He had in mind that addition to the note of the Council of People's Commissars to the Directory in which it was said that "on the condition of the recognition by the Directory of the Workers' and Peasants' Government in Ukraine, we undertake to guarantee the personal safety of the members of the Directory's government, as well as the free activity of the parties comprising the same." Ibid.
87. Ibid., pp. 227–29. Vynnychenko accused "otamanism" of intentionally obstructing the contact of the Ukrainian delegation in Moscow with the Directory in order to prevent any agreement. Ibid., pp. 228–30.
88. Ibid., pp. 223–30; Khrystiuk, IV, pp. 36–40.
89. Concerning the leftist trend in the Ukrainian socialist parties (SDs and SRs), see pp. 257–78.
90. See pp. 212–14.
91. *V zashchitu sovetskoi Ukrainy*, p. 19.
92. Antonov, III, p. 126.
93. Ibid.
94. Ibid.
95. I. Mazepa, I, pp. 97–98. On the subject of the first talks of the Ukrainian delegation, comprising Serhii Ostapenko and Osyp Nazaruk, with Colonel Freydenberg (chief of staff of General Philippe d'Anselme), see O. Nazaruk, *Rik na Velykii Ukraini*, pp. 119 ff., and Ostapenko's article, "Direktoriia i okupatsiia Ukrainy," pp. 260–82; cf. also Reshetar, pp. 239–49, and Kutschabsky, *Die Westukraine*, pp. 202–08.
96. Some time before that, in Odessa, the military mission of the Directory, led by General M. Grekov, was faced with very burdensome conditions from the Entente, which the Bolsheviks later used in a propagandistic way against the Directory and France. Soviet intelligence in Odessa "procured" and sent to the Kievan Bolsheviks an obviously falsified text of the "treaty" between the Directory and the Entente, the authenticity of which "seemed to be very doubtful" even to the Bolsheviks themselves. Antonov, III, p. 145. For the Bolshevik version of this "treaty," see *Istoriia KP(b)U*, pp. 385–86.
97. This mission, consisting of the minister for economic affairs, Ostapenko, the

minister for military affairs, General Grekov, and the members of the labour congress, S. Bachynsky and I. Mazepa, met with Freydenberg on 3 March 1919 on the initiative of the French command. Mazepa, I, pp. 99–103.

98. Ibid., pp. 99–100.
99. Ibid., p. 99.
100. Jean Xydias, *L'Intervention française en Russie, 1918–1919*, p. 163.
101. Reshetar, p. 239.
102. See Sevriuk, "L'Intervention française en Ukraine, en Janvier et Fevrier 1919," GFP, 6, 100, *S.A. Ukraine nr 1*, Vol. 34. This did not stop later Soviet writers from calling the Ukrainian bourgeois nationalists the hirelings of the Anglo-French imperialists. B. M. Baby, "Utvorennia i rozkvit ukrainskoi radianskoi derzhavy," p. 81.
103. Mazepa's (I, p. 103) version said "the recognition by the Directory of the Soviet power in Ukraine"; Antonov, III, p. 251; *Pravda*, 5 February 1919, No. 26. Antonov's version seems to be more nearly identical.
104. I. Mazepa, p. 103. Italics mine. A complete but distorted text of this telegram is in Antonov, III, pp. 251–52.
105. I. Mazepa, p. 104.
106. On the war between Hryhoriiv's detachments and the French expeditionary force, see Antonov, III, pp. 218–59.
107. As Reshetar rightly remarked (p. 244), the humiliating talks with the French had no result and "succeeded only in antagonizing most of the population."
108. The text of this declaration is in Antonov, III, p. 254.
109. For the text of the manifesto, see Vynnychenko, III, pp. 271–76.
110. *V zashchitu sovetskoi Ukrainy*, p. 12.
111. Ibid., pp. 13–14.
112. Ibid., pp. 15–16.
113. The note from the chairman of the Ukrainian Soviet government, Rakovsky, to the government of Western Ukraine, read (in part):

"Having freed the territory of the Ukrainian Socialist Soviet Republic from the forces of the Directory which attempted to establish here bourgeois power against the will of the workers and peasants of Ukraine, the Red Ukrainian forces have approached the borders of Eastern Galicia, offering their fraternal hand to the workers and peasants of Eastern Galicia, with whose liberation from all bourgeois oppression we sympathize ardently. I find it necessary to declare in the name of the Workers' and Peasants' Government of Ukraine that the problem of the political organization of Eastern Galicia is a matter for the Galician workers and peasants themselves. Considering that they themselves, having learned from the experience of the Russian and Ukrainian revolutions, and filled with class consciousness, will bring into existence Soviet power through their own organizational struggle, the Ukrainian Socialist Soviet Republic declares its firm intention to refrain from any military activities on the territory of

Eastern Galicia on the condition that the government of the Eastern Galician People's Republic, which has declared its respect for the will of the working masses, cease hostile actions against the Ukrainian Socialist Soviet Republic and agree both to the conclusion of a truce and to the establishment of a demarcation line and a border between both republics. It is entirely up to it [the government of the Eastern Galician People's Republic] to put an end to the fratricidal war which furthers the realization of the policy of imperialist annexation by the Romanian monarchy and by the Polish landowners." Antonov, IV, p. 185.

114. Ibid., p. 283.
115. Ibid., pp. 289–90.
116. Ibid., p. 290.
117. Lozynsky, pp. 102–03. Béla Kun wanted very much for Ukraine and Russia to arrive at an understanding, since Ukraine stood in the way of military aid from Soviet Russia to Soviet Hungary. Vynnychenko, former president of the Directory, writes in his memoirs that the government of Béla Kun had talks with him in Budapest concerning the possibility of a union of the Russian, Ukrainian, and Hungarian Soviet republics and the attraction to it of Western Ukraine. Béla Kun made a *dêmarche* in Moscow on this matter, but found no response there. Vynnychenko, III, pp. 322–23; Lozynsky, pp. 102–03; Kutschabsky, pp. 141–44.
118. Lozynsky, p. 103.
119. Antonov, IV, p. 292. A somewhat different text of this offer has been given by O. Nazaruk, pp. 187–91.
120. Ibid.
121. Concerning Denikin's policy towards Ukraine, see Denikin, *Ocherki*, V, pp. 255 ff.
122. Paneiko's point of view is given in his book, *Ziedyneni derzhavy Skhidnoi Evropy* (Vienna 1922). Concerning his influence on Petrushevych's policy, see Lozynsky, pp. 174 ff.
123. See his article "Kudy doroha?" in the semi-official organ of the West Ukrainian embassy in Vienna, *Ukrainskyi prapor*, 1919, No. 4 , quoted in Lozynsky, pp. 174–75.
124. The Entente's attitude in this question is well documented in *Documents on British Foreign Policy*, Series I, Vol. III, pp. 308 ff.
125. Antonov, IV, p. 291.
126. Lenin's article "Vse na rabotu po prodovolstviiu i transportu," *Pravda*, 28 January 1919, No. 19, in Lenin, *Soch.*, XXVIII, pp. 417–20.
127. Lenin, *Soch.*, XXIX, p. 234. *Razverstka* (allotment) meant the requisitioning of grain by the state; the peasants were given receipts in return.
128. Lenin's speech at the extraordinary plenary meeting of the Moscow soviet of workers' and Red Army deputies on 3 April 1919, *Soch.*, XXIX, pp. 234–35.
129. Lenin, "Uspekhi i trudnosti sovetskoi vlasti," *Soch.*, XXIX, pp. 64–65.

130. Ibid., p. 66. A lead article in *Pravda* said that "the whole of Soviet Russia writhes in the torment of hunger," but that "the Ukrainian Soviet troops have occupied the whole of the Left Bank of Ukraine." Here "a faithful warrior of the international proletariat, comrade Rakovsky" was in command; he would be "the best friend of Soviet Russia." "Now they offer to export to us grain, sugar, raw materials. For us here, where every bit of bread, every crystal of sugar, is precious, it is necessary to bring, *at any price*, everything which is offered to us by our Ukrainian brethren." "Za khlebom i uglem!" *Pravda*, 1 February 1919, No. 23.
131. L. Trotsky, *Stalinskaia shkola falsifikatsii*, p. 66. In only four months of 1919 (until June) 1,766,505 poods of various produce were taken out of Ukraine and sent to Russia: meat—109,372 poods; pork fat—48,417 poods; meat products—97,498 poods; fish—11,517 poods; butter—7,599 poods; eggs—29,739 poods. *Ekonomicheskaia zhizn*, 14 July 1919, No. 179.
132. Ravich, p. 123.
133. Antonov, IV, p. 148.
134. Ibid., III, p. 325.
135. Ibid., p. 338.
136. Popov, *Narys*, p. 188.
137. *Deviatyi sezd RKP(b)*, pp. 63–64.
138. *Vosmoi sezd RKP(b)*, p. 91.
139. The commander of the Ukrainian front, Antonov, said in his instructions to the commander of the Kiev group that "the general idea is to cut off the Allies from Galicia. It is necessary to incite strife between the Poles and the Galicians. This aim requires written and spoken agitation, to which all available party forces must be enlisted." Antonov, III, p. 262.
140. After the capitulation of the Central Powers, the Ukrainians of Eastern Galicia proclaimed the independence of their country, calling it the "Western Ukrainian People's Republic." Later, on 22 January 1919, this republic united with the Ukrainian People's Republic by an act signed in Kiev and adopted the name "Western Region of the Ukrainian People's Republic." In diplomatic circles this republic was usually referred to simply as Eastern Galicia or "the Ukrainian republic." On the creation of this republic and its relations to the Bolsheviks, see Lozynsky, *Halychchyna v rr. 1918–1920*, pp. 95 ff.
141. See Chicherin's note to the delegate extraordinary of the government of the Polish Republic in Moscow, Więckowski, of 15 April 1919, in Antonov, IV, p. 182.
142. The plans for an offensive on Romania were, according to Antonov's testimony, approved by Rakovsky. This attitude of Rakovsky apparently had an admixture of the settling of personal accounts with the boyar regime of Romania, which had imprisoned him more than once. Ibid., pp. 29–30.
143. Ibid., pp. 30–33.
144. Ibid., pp. 34–35.
145. Ibid., pp. 40–41.

146. Ibid., p. 45.
147. Concerning this anomaly, A. Skachko, the commander of the army, wrote to Antonov very much to the point on 18 April 1919. Ibid., pp. 61–63.
148. Partially published in Wolfe, "Early Military Decisions," *ASEER*, 1950, No. 9, pp. 169–79; the papers are kept in the International Institute for Social History in Amsterdam and at Harvard College Library.
149. "Iz arkhiva t. Sklianskogo," Trotsky's Archives; cf. also Wolfe, "Early Military Decisions," p. 173.
150. "Dela iskhod. 'shifrovannye telegrammy za 1919 g.' Sekretariata Zam. Pred. R.V.S.R.," Trotsky's Archives, p. 19.
151. "Iz arkhiva t. Sklianskogo." This directive is mentioned also by Antonov, IV, pp. 120–21.
152. "Iz arkhiva t. Sklianskogo."
153. Ibid.
154. Ibid. Cf. also Wolfe, "Early Military Decisions," pp. 174–76.
155. See Antonov, IV, p. 145. This project was also rejected by Podvoisky himself.
156. "Iz arkhiva t. Sklianskogo." A somewhat different version is given by Antonov, IV, p. 59.
157. "Iz del 'Sekretnye iskhod. bumagi s 1/I–17/IX–1919 g. s No. I po No. 400,' chast I," Trotsky's Archives, pp. 78–81.
158. Telegram of 17 May 1919, "Iskhod. bumagi, chast I," Trotsky's Archives, p. 133.
159. Lenin, in his telegram to Trotsky of 22 May, insisted on the "immediate removal of Podvoisky and his collaborators," making them responsible for the "misdeeds" in Ukraine. "Rasshifr. telegrammy papka No. I, za 1918 g.," Trotsky's Archives, p. 371. Trotsky replied that "the trouble lay in the fact that there is no other organization in Ukraine except the military one." "Iz del 'Sekretnye iskhod. bumagi,' chast I," Trotsky's Archives, p. 87.
160. "Iz arkhiva t. Sklianskogo."
161. Antonov, IV, p. 310.
162. Ibid., p. 263.
163. Ibid., p. 311. After the event, the author of this telegram himself thought that the tone at the end of the telegram was "egoistically hysterical" and that it bore witness to the "nervous bankruptcy" of the author. Ibid., p. 311, note 1.
164. *Karbovantsi* were Ukrainian currency issued by the Rada and later by the hetman's government and the Directory.
165. "Dela iskhod. shifrovan. telegrammy za 1919 god, Sekretariat zam. pred. R.V.S.R.," Trotsky's Archives, p. 63.
166. "Our army, which consists almost exclusively of peasants, is being disrupted by the policy which confuses the middle peasant with the 'kulak,' . . . which carries out a 'food supply dictatorship,' supported by the Moscow food supply army men, while the Soviet power is almost completely absent locally (in the villages). The work of the *chrezvychaiki* [cheka] and of the

food expeditionists all over the Right Bank of Ukraine, in which they are assisted by 'international' detachments, excites nationalism, rousing the whole population without any distinctions to the struggle with the 'invaders.' The land policy being carried out by Meshcheriakov does not take any local peculiarities into account; the clumsy wording of the land decrees and of Meshcheriakov's articles furthers the hatred towards the Communists which is diligently sown by our numerous enemies. The Ukrainian army, which was created not by the Communists alone but also by the Ukrainian SRs, the left SRs, and the anarchists, is very little amenable to discipline, not by any means having banished the partisan-insurgent spirit, and cannot at all be considered in its mass as completely reliable support for us." Antonov, IV, pp. 147–48.

167. Ibid., p. 148.
168. Ibid., pp. 152–54.
169. Lenin, *Soch.*, XXIX, pp. 373–74. This directive was first published in 1942.
170. Lenin to Trotsky and Skliansky, Trotsky's Archives.
171. "Rasshifrovannye telegrammy chast 1-ia za 1918–19 g.," ibid., p. 312.
172. "Iz del 'Sekretnye iskhod. bumagi' chast I," ibid., p. 124.
173. Ibid., p. 141.
174. Antonov, IV, pp. 320–21.
175. Ibid., pp. 325–26.
176. "Dela 'iskhod. shifrovannye telegrammy za 1919 god,' Sekretariata zam. pred. R.V.S.R.," Trotsky's Archives, p. 216.
177. Ravich, p. 131.
178. *LR*, 1925, No. 1, pp. 58–62.
179. Lapchynsky, *LR*, 1926, No. 6, p. 37. Rakovsky, defending himself against the criticism of ingratiating himself with the RCP, said later that the CC CP(B)U and the government "went into liquidation" because both he and his colleagues admitted that "the problems of Ukraine could be solved only by the Red Army and by a rising of the workers and peasants of Ukraine." *Kommunist*, 1920, No. 1, pp. 27–28.
180. Popov, *Narys*, pp. 182–84.
181. Ibid., p. 184.
182. Ibid., p. 184, note 1.

Chapter IX

1. In spite of the fact that Denikin, Poland, and the Directory were all opposed to Bolshevism, they were unable to overcome the contradictions in their political aims, and a struggle among them was soon to begin. See Denikin, *Ocherki,* V, pp. 175 ff.; D. Kin, *Denikinshchina,* pp. 229–73; G. Pokrovsky, *Denikinshchina*; A. I. Egorov, *Razgrom Denikina,* pp. 44–45, 114–15.
2. Numerous works have been written on the subject of the relations between the Entente and Soviet Russia during this period. Among the main ones are

A. Fredborg, *Storbritannien och den ryska frågan. 1918–1920*; Carr, III; *Documents on British Foreign Policy, 1919–1939,* Vol. III; *Russian-American Relations: Papers Relating to the Foreign Relations of the United States;* B. Stein, *"Russkii vopros" na parizhskoi mirovoi konferentsii.*

3. This passage from the memorandum is taken from Popov, *Narys,* p. 203. Popov's authorship is confirmed by Lapchynsky, "Gomelskoe soveshchanie," *LR,* 1926, No. 6, p. 41. This memorandum was later reprinted in Zhytomyr as a pamphlet in Ukrainian: *Nasha suchasna polityka,* with an introduction signed: "The organizational bureau of the group of federalists, members of the CP(B)U." Ibid., p. 41, note 1.
4. Ibid.
5. Popov wrote:

   "On the whole one must recognize that the government of the Directory and the circles supporting it ... have no clearly defined political line of their own. The only thing they stand firmly on is the national question. In all other respects they 'agree' with anybody. They hold their ground exclusively because the petty-bourgeois mass of the Ukrainian population (the majority of the peasantry, the intelligentsia) is afraid of both the Communists and Denikin. A peace with the former or the latter will be the final act in the history of the Directory. From the moment that a peace is concluded, its existence will lose any sense whatsoever. And the one with whom it concludes a peace will be its heir ....

   The idea of Soviet power is very popular among the masses. But they are afraid of the arrival of the 'Muscovite army' which they imagine as an invasion of foreigners. This is exploited by the Ukrainian counter-revolution which itself partially created such ideas.

   An attempt to conquer Ukraine will provoke a new rallying of all Ukrainian groups and new risings. A peace with Ukraine and a war against Denikin in alliance with it will help in the process of that differentiation which is already proceeding among the Ukrainian peasantry and which is hampered by two causes: by the economic backwardness of Ukraine and by the national movement in the shade of which the whole counter-revolution is hiding. They must be unmasked, the forces of the Directory must be used for the struggle with Denikin, the idea that national freedom is being carried by Petliura alone must be eradicated among the masses, the inability of the Directory to solve social questions ... must be shown in practice, and the Directory will die a natural death, and we will come forward as its heirs." "Doklad tov. P. Popova v zafrontbiuro TsK KP(b)U," *LR,* 1926, No. 2, pp. 43–49.
6. Ibid., pp. 49–50.
7. Lapchynsky, "Gomelskoe soveshchanie," p. 45.
8. Ibid., pp. 47–48.
9. About the same time Manuilsky, too, opposed the policy of the party and refused to go to Moscow. He wrote in an article in the party organ,

Kommunist, that "every spring we [the RCP] equip another troupe for Ukraine, which, having toured there, returns to Moscow by the autumn." In the same issue of the journal he expressed himself ironically about the "Ukrainians" whom the party included in its governmental combinations, comparing them with "notables" whom a colonial administration usually attracted from among the prominent aborigines for participation in local administration and who played in it a purely decorative role. Ibid., p. 40.

10. Majstrenko writes that the party changed its policy because "the Borotbists now emerged as a dangerous rival to the CP(B)U." *Borotbism,* p. 162.
11. F. K. Ordzhonikidze, *Stati i rechi,* Vol. I, pp. 106–07.
12. The question of who were the initiators and the editors of this resolution was for a long time unclear to the Bolshevik leaders themselves. Some asserted that the resolution had been tabled and defended by the delegate of the Vladimir organization, comrade Iakovlev (Epshtein), who by that time had not worked in Ukraine for over a year. The Ukrainian Bosheviks, without exception, "bluntly refused to come forward with a report and proposals." Lapchynsky, pp. 41–42. The editors of *LR* asserted, however, that Lapchynsky's "memory failed him again" and that the resolution was elaborated by the CC RCP *together with* the CC CP(B)U and was tabled at the all-Russian conference "at the *insistence* of the CC CP(B)U." *LR,* 1926, No. 6, p. 42, note 1.
13. *Draft Resolution of the CC RCP(B) on Soviet power in Ukraine:*

"1) Having discussed the question of the relations with the working people of Ukraine which is liberating itself from a temporary occupation by Denikin's gangs, the CC RCP(B), inflexibly applying the principles of the self-determination of nations, deems it necessary to emphasize once again that the RCP inflexibly holds to the point of view of the recognition of the independence of the Ukrainian SSR.

"2) The RCP will strive towards the establishment of federative ties between the RSFSR and the Ukrainian SSR on the basis of the decisions of the VTsIK of 1 June 1919 and of the TsIKU of 18 May 1919 (resolution appended).

"3) In view of the fact that Ukrainian culture (language, schooling, etc.) has been suppressed for centuries by tsarism and the exploiting classes of Russia, the CC RCP imposes upon all members of the party the duty of facilitating in every way the removal of all obstacles to the free development of the Ukrainian language and culture. Inasmuch as nationalist tendencies are observable among the backward section of the Ukrainian masses as a result of the oppression of many centuries, members of the RCP are obliged to treat them with the utmost patience and tact, counteracting them with a word of comradely explanation of the identity of interests of the toiling masses of Ukraine and Russia. Members of the RCP on the territory of Ukraine must in practice implement the right of the toiling masses to study and speak in their native language in all Soviet institutions, in every way opposing Russifying attempts to reduce the Ukrainian language to a secondary plane, striving [on the contrary] to transform it into a weapon of Communist education of the toiling masses. Steps should be taken immediately so that all Soviet institutions will have a sufficient number of employees conversant in the Ukrainian language and so that in the future all employees will be able to make themselves understood in Ukrainian.

"4) It is essential to guarantee the closest contact of Soviet institutions with the indigenous peasant population of the country; to do this it should be the rule that, even at the beginning, during the very formation of the revolutionary committees and soviets, the majority in them must be secured for the working peasantry, while securing a decisive influence for the poor peasantry.

"5) In view of the fact that in Ukraine, to an even larger extent than in Russia, the peasantry makes up the overwhelming mass of the population, the task of the Soviet government in Ukraine is to gain the confidence not only of the poor peasant, but of the wide strata of the middle peasantry, whose real interests tie them most closely to Soviet rule. In particular, in preserving the principles of our food policy (state grain purchases at fixed prices), the methods of implementation of this policy must be modified.

The next task of our food policy in Ukraine should be to extract grain surpluses only on a rigidly limited scale, [in an amount] necessary to feed the Ukrainian poor peasants, the workers, and the Red Army. In extracting surpluses special attention must be given to the interests of the middle peasantry, strictly distinguishing them from the 'kulak' elements. Counter-revolutionary demagoguery which instills in the Ukrainian peasantry the idea that the aim of Soviet Russia is to extract grain and other food products from Ukraine to Russia must be unmasked.

The enrolment on the broadest scale of the poor and middle peasantry into administrative rule should be made a duty of the agents of the central governmental authority, all party workers, instructors, etc.

With the same aim in view, establishing genuine rule by the toilers, steps must be taken immediately to prevent the inundation of Soviet institutions by elements of the Ukrainian urban petty bourgeoisie [*meshchanstvo*], who are devoid of any understanding of the conditions of life of the broad peasant masses and who frequently masquerade under the name of Communists.

The conditions under which such elements can be admitted to both party ranks and Soviet institutions must be the preliminary verification of their efficiency and devotion to the interests of the toilers in action, above all at the front, in the ranks of the army. Everywhere and under all conditions such elements must be placed under the rigid class control of the proletariat.

Because a large quantity of the arms in the hands of the rural population in Ukraine is—as experience has shown—inevitably concentrated in the hands of the kulak and counter-revolutionary elements because of the lack of organization of the poor, and because this leads to the actual domination of the bandit kulaks instead of the dictatorship of the toilers, the very first task of Soviet construction in Ukraine is the removal of all arms and their concentration in the hands of the workers' and peasants' Red Army.

"6) Agrarian policy must be conducted with special attention to the interest of the land economy of the poor and middle peasantry. The goal of agrarian policy in Ukraine should be:

a) Complete liquidation of proprietor landownership, re-established by Denikin, with the transfer of landowners' land to those without land and poor in land.

b) State farms are only to be established with strict limits to their scale and numbers, conformable to the vital interests of the local peasants.

c) In respect to the amalgamation of peasants into communes, cartels, etc., party policy, which rejects all compulsion in this respect, is to be rigidly applied, leaving [amalgamation] exclusively to the free decision of the peasants themselves and rigorously punishing any and all attempts to introduce the principle of compulsion into this matter." Lenin, *Soch.,* XXX, pp. 142–44.

14. After the occupation of Ukraine, Lenin wrote in a telegram to Stalin on 22 February 1920 that it was necessary "to introduce immediately interpreters in all headquarters and military establishments, imposing upon everybody the unconditional duty of accepting applications and papers in Ukrainian. With regard to language, every concession and a maximum of equality is absolutely necessary." Lenin, *Soch.,* XXX, p. 348.
15. Even Ravich-Cherkassky, p. 139, who could hardly be accused of sympathies towards the Ukrainian movement, admitted that "the whole resolution is permeated by the spirit of conciliation with the 'Ukrainian revolutionary force,' although it must be said that the points referring to the national question are distinguished by a certain haziness."

16. "Zakliuchitelnoe slovo po voprosu o sovetskoi vlasti na Ukraine 3 dekabria 1919 g.," Lenin, *Soch.,* XXX, pp. 171–72; also *Vosmaia konferentsiia RKP(B),* pp. 109–10.
17. Ibid., p. 172.
18. Lenin, *Soch.,* XXX, pp. 246–47.
19. Ibid., pp. 267–73.
20. Likholat, *Razgrom,* p. 414. Another source states that 801 party workers were sent to Ukraine. *Deviatyi sezd RKP,* p. 482.
21. N. R. Prokopenko, "Borba za vozrozhdenie ugolnogo Donbassa v 1920 godu," *Istoricheskie zapiski,* 1948, No. 25, pp. 29–30.
22. Ibid., p. 30.
23. Ibid.
24. Lenin's report to the first session of the VTsIK of the seventh convocation about the work of the VTsIK and the Council of People's Commissars, 2 February 1920, *Soch.,* XXX, pp. 291–312.
25. *Zhizn natsionalnostei,* 21 December 1919, No. 48.
26. *Izvestiia VTsIK,* 21 February 1920, No. 39.
27. Here were meant apparently the Russian left SRs (Borbists) whom Terletsky also represented in the first People's Secretariat.
28. *Izvestiia VTsIK,* 21 February 1920, No. 39.
29. Vynnychenko, II, pp. 221–23.
30. Popov, *Narys,* p. 142, note 1; Ravich, pp. 47–48.
31. Popov, P. 161. On this group's entry into the CP(B)U, see the speeches of Skrypnyk and Slynko at the first congress of the CP(B)U, *Pervyi sezd KP(b)U,* pp. 24 ff.
32. Ravich, p. 88.
33. "1) It is an anti-Ukrainian party. Being against the national and political rights of the Ukrainian people, it is a party hostile to the Ukrainian state. It is a party in the service of the Russian imperialist Bolshevik government . . . .

    "2) It is a party which strives, not towards a dictatorship of the proletariat and the revolutionary peasantry, but towards the dictatorship of a part of the proletariat and its party, and therefore it is a party full of violence, and it introduces, instead of the compulsion of a proletarian dictatorship over the bourgeois order, the compulsion of a small clique.

    "3) This party spoils and ruins the economy of Russia by its rash and disorderly way of introducing socialist reforms, and intends to do the same with the economy of Ukraine.

    "4) It is a double-dealing party which always breaks its own principles. Having acknowledged the principle of the self-determination of nations, it has nevertheless involved Ukraine in the war with Russia for the conquest of Ukraine. Having recognized at the Katernynoslav congress the independence of the Ukrainian workers' and peasants' republic, a miserable second voice to the Petrograd Bolsheviks, it has again taken the side of the reactionary demand for a federation, for a union of former Russia.

In view of this, the party cannot be trusted, even if it happened to change sides again and to recognize the independence of Ukraine and the right of the Ukrainian people to self-determination, until it changes organically and adopts the interests of the Ukrainian working people. Therefore any actions, agreements, candidatures, etc., in common with it are inadmissible." Khrystiuk, IV, pp. 55–56.

34. Mazepa, I, pp. 76–81.
35. See Pisotsky's arguments, ibid., p. 77.
36. See P. Fedenko, *Isaak Mazepa,* p. 53.
37. Mazepa, I, p. 80. There were also Chinese who joined the Red Army.
38. Ibid., pp. 78–79.
39. *Robitnycha hazeta,* 17 January 1919, No. 434, after Khrystiuk, IV, pp. 50–52.
40. *Chervonyi prapor,* 6 February 1919, No. 5; Khrystiuk, IV, p. 82.
41. Ibid.
42. Declaration of the Bolshevik Cheskis, a member of the executive committee of the Kiev soviet of workers' deputies, *Chervonyi prapor,* 9 February 1919, No. 9; Khrystiuk, IV, p. 83.
43. Ibid. Rakovsky's attitude has been mentioned above.
44. *Chervonyi prapor,* 9 March 1919, No. 28; Khrystiuk, IV, p. 90: "If in exchange for our grain and sugar we were given the possibility of a free existence and development of the creative forces of the masses of the people, the hungry 'brother' would be welcome to that grain and sugar. But worst of all is the fact that this 'brotherly' attitude is much too unceremonious and *encroaches not only upon grain and sugar but also upon the soul of the people.* We have not known *such a mad and infamous Russification as that which now rolls over the whole of Ukraine in a tidal wave* even during the rule of the Hetmanate in its last 'federative' phase. *Not a single leaflet in Ukrainian for the Ukrainian peasant, not a single pamphlet, not a single newspaper of the Soviet power in Ukrainian! Ukrainian is being driven out from everywhere, wherever it might be.*"
45. See, e.g., the letter of 27 December 1919 from the chief otaman of the insurgent forces, Iurii Mazurenko, to Rakovsky and Manuilsky. Khrystiuk, IV, p. 179.
46. For the text of the agreement, see Khrystiuk, IV, pp. 131–33; see also Antonov, IV, pp. 160–61; Mazepa, I, pp. 203–05.
47. Mazepa, I, p. 204, says that the agreement failed because the CC USDWP rejected the proposal that this agreement should be signed on behalf of the party by those members of the CC USDWP who stayed in Kiev.
48. For the text of the ultimatum, see Khrystiuk, IV, p. 134, note 2.
49. Soviet historiography calls these insurgents "bandits." To prove that this is

not in complete agreement with the truth here are extracts from a report of Soviet Intelligence about Zeleny: "Zeleny, ... real name Terpylo, Danylo Illich. During the tsarist period he was exiled for Ukrainophilism into the Archangel region, where he spent about four years .... During the war ... he served with the H.Q. of the 35th corps. A member of the party of independentist USDs, ... Zeleny is fully educated politically and is a good orator." During the Hetmanate he was persecuted by the police, and in accordance with the instructions of his party he agitated against the hetman, "having thus gained popularity." He took the side of the Directory against the hetman. Petliura appointed him otaman of the first division. Antonov, IV, pp. 170–71.

50. Popov, *Narys,* p. 194.
51. See pp. 269–70.
52. Ravich, p. 139.
53. M. Tkachenko was one of the best-educated Ukrainian Marxists. In 1902–05 he belonged to the RUP, and after its split he went over to the *Spilka.* In the Central Rada he was minister for internal affairs. He was the main ideologue of the USDWP, and after having moved to the left he became the ideologue of the UCP. Tkachenko died in Moscow during the talks on the legalization of the UCP.
54. Popov, *Narys,* p. 197; Ravich, p. 143.
55. Popov, *Narys,* p. 273.
56. For some passages of the letter of the UCP, see A. Khvylia, "KP(b)U v borotbi za leninsku natsionalnu polityku," *BU,* 1932, No. 17–18, p. 115, and also Pylypenko, "Ukrainskaia intelligentsiia i sovetskaia vlast," pp. 273–77.
57. Pylypenko, pp. 273–77, wrote that the UCP "knocked ... even at the Comintern's door but the nationalism which has not yet been overcome and which does not allow the Ukapists to consider Ukraine otherwise than as a colony of Moscow ... keeps the doors of the Comintern closed for them even now."

    The resolution of the executive committee of the Comintern concerning the letter of the UCP said, among other things:

    "The formation at the beginning of 1920 of the so-called UCP out of former Ukrainian social democrats (independentists), who a year ago conducted an armed struggle against Soviet power, was the continuation of the same process of the gradual transition of a group of the Ukrainian socialists, who under the influence of Communist criticism and struggle came to realize the lessons of the revolution, from the camp of conciliation and alliance with the bourgeoisie into the camp of Communism.

    But accepting the general principles of the Communist programme, the UCP committed its distortions on the national and colonial questions, treating contemporary Soviet Ukraine as [a state] which leans on external forces, demanding a form of interstate relations between the Ukrainian SSR and other Soviet republics such as would not only not have been justified by the experience of the eight years of war and economic struggle of these republics, but would in fact have opposed to one another their working masses, in whose close union lies the foundation of the strengthening of the whole USSR and further successes of the international revolution. These distortions of the Communist programme in the practice of the UCP were the consequence of the remnants of those socialist-chauvinist views which used to be held by its members . . . .

The UCP worked against the RCP(B) and CP(B)U, making propaganda for such a separation of the Ukrainian state machinery, the Ukrainian army, and Ukrainian workers' movement, which in fact leads to its opposition to other Soviet republics, [and] thus the UCP worked objectively in the direction of a national fragmentation of the forces of the proletarian dictatorship in Ukraine, independently of the aim which it put before itself." Popov, *Narys,* p. 274.

58. According to unverified documents which were used by the secretary of the CP(B)U, Postyshev. P. P. Postyshev, "Itogi proverki partiinych dokumentov v KP(b)U i zadachi partiinoi raboty," *Bolshevik,* 1936, No. 5, p. 16.
59. A short history of the split of the UPSR is given in the declaration of the "central stream" of the party in the summer of 1918 in Khrystiuk, III, pp. 23–24.
60. Vynnychenko, II, pp. 220–21; Popov, *Narys,* p. 142; Khrystiuk, II, p. 125.
61. Popov, *Narys,* p. 153.
62. Ibid.
63. See the resolution of the right faction which was adopted by the congress. Khrystiuk, III, pp. 21–22.
64. The declaration of the provisional committee of the central faction, in Khrystiuk, III, pp. 23–24.
65. This CC comprised: Levko Kovaliv, Andrii Zalyvchy, Hnat Mykhailychenko, Lashkevych, Antin Prykhodko, and Shrah. Khrystiuk, III, pp. 22–23.
66. The text of the "platform of the central committee of the Ukrainian Party of Socialist Revolutionaries" is in Khrystiuk, III, pp. 91–94.
67. Later Soviet historians pointed out that the left Ukrainian SRs were at that time still very far from Bolshevism (Popov, Ravich, Iavorsky).
68. Majstrenko, *Borotbism,* p. 74.
69. Ibid., p. 92.
70. Ibid., p. 94.
71. See Khrystiuk, IV, pp. 45–46.
72. Majstrenko, p. 102.
73. For Trotsky's view, see pp. 441–42.
74. Rafes, *Dva goda,* p. 154.
75. Ibid.
76. Ravich, p. 102.
77. Rafes, p. 154.
78. The text of the telegram is in Majstrenko, p. 118.
79. Antonov, III, p. 247. This was also asserted by Hryhoriiv in his telegram to

Rakovsky. Ibid., IV, p. 73.

80. Ibid., III, p. 249, and IV, pp. 73–74.
81. Ibid., III, p. 249.
82. Rafes, p. 163. An English version of this resolution is in Majstrenko, pp. 124–25.
83. Antonov, in his letter to A. Skachko of 8 April (Antonov, IV, p. 64), and in his letter to Lenin and to the RVS (pp. 147–48), where he wrote that "it is necessary . . . to introduce into the Ukrainian government some representatives of the parties connected with the middle and small peasantry (independentist SDs and Ukrainian SRs.)"
84. Kubanin, p. 73.
85. There are no reliable data about this connection. It was affirmed as a fact by Antonov in his telegram to Rakovsky after his talk with Hryhoriiv. Antonov, IV, p. 83. See also Kubanin, p. 73, who asserts that Hryhoriiv was at that time supported only by the active left SRs and by the active SDs (independentists).
86. The text of Hryhoriiv's universal is in Antonov, IV, pp. 203–05.
87. Antonov's conversation with Hryhoriiv in ibid., pp. 203–08.
88. Ibid., pp. 208–09.
89. Ibid., pp. 209–10.
90. Popov, *Narys,* p. 192.
91. *Deviatyi sezd RKP(b),* p. 566, note 39.
92. "V Ispolnitelnyi komitet III Kommunisticheskogo internatsionala," *Kommunisticheskii internatsional* (Petrograd) November–December 1919, Nos. 7–8, cols. 1111–12; an English version of this letter is in Majstrenko, pp. 136–38; cf. also Ravich, p. 145. In this covering letter of a memorandum the following motives are given for the creation of a new united Communist party:

    "The act of merging into a single Communist party two detachments of Ukrainian Communism, which until now have participated separately in the proletarian revolution in Ukraine, is a great, crowning moment in the development of the Ukrainian Communist movement, which accurately expresses a real command of local social reality and at the same time is a new point of departure in the future organizational and ideological consolidation of Communist forces in the towns and villages of Ukraine . . . .

    In the heat of this struggle for the greatest ideal of our age, the struggle in the name of rule by soviets, the last threads are being cut, the last traces of former contacts with the compromising parties are vanishing, and the intrinsic nature of the organizational and ideological centre of Ukrainian Communist forces, which has been strengthened in battle, is outgrowing the bounds of old party names.

    The struggle against the Hetmanate and the Directory was conducted shoulder to shoulder with the Communists-Bolsheviks of Ukraine. The deep realization of all the dangers [arising out] of the existence of two

Communist centres in Ukraine forced the organizational and ideological core of Ukrainian Communist forces (the Communists-Borotbists) to call, in March 1919, for the formation of an interparty soviet centre at the moment of uprising and for an organizational merger with the Communists-Bolsheviks.

The urgent need for the creation of a single Communist centre in Ukraine has not been understood and evaluated by the Communist-Bolsheviks of Ukraine.

The experience of the subsequent development of the proletarian revolution in Ukraine, the practical participation [of the Borotbists] in the formation of the Soviet government and its fateful outcome, have sharpened awareness among the ranks of Ukrainian Communists of the urgent need to create a single Communist centre, which will grow organically out of the aggregate of social and economic conditions and peculiarities of Ukraine.

A consideration of this experience and the increased understanding of the next and most important task in the development of the revolution in Ukraine have led to the merger of two detachments of Ukrainian Communist forces into one Ukrainian Communist Party (Borotbists), which has assumed the leadership of the Ukrainian Communist movement and its representation in the ranks of the Third International.

Facing the eclipse of the second proletarian revolution in Ukraine, entering a period of the fiercest reaction in Ukraine, leading the entire party, and, together with it, going underground [in preparation] for a new struggle, the central committee of the Ukrainian Communist Party (Borotbists) announces the entry of the party into the ranks of the Third International and sends warm greetings to the leaders of the proletarian revolution, assuring them that the hour is at hand when, forged together by one Communist centre, the workers and peasants of Ukraine will start a new uprising in the name of rule by soviets, and a regenerated Ukrainian Soviet republic once again will engage in open battle with the enemies of international Communism.

Kiev, 28 August 1919.

Central committee of the Ukrainian Communist Party (Borotbists)."

93. *Memorandum Ukrainskoi komunistychnoi partii (borotbistiv) do Vykonavchoho komitetu III Internatsionalu,* pp. 7–22; English text in Majstrenko, pp. 277–86.
94. Ibid., p. 285.
95. *LR,* 1925, No. 1, pp. 67–68; an English version is in Majstrenko, pp. 172–73:

    "1) The directives drafted at the conference of the RCP, upon the proposal of the delegation of the CP[(B)]U are accepted as the basis of collaboration.

    "2) The Ukrainian Communist Party (Borotbists) endorses unconditionally the manifesto of the all-Ukrainian revolutionary committee and, together with the representatives of the CP(B)U in the revolutionary committee, will carry out the programme outlined in the manifesto.

"3) Inasmuch as all work of the all-Ukrainian revolutionary committee is subordinated to the main task of the struggle against the united forces of Russian and international counter-revolution, represented at this moment by Denikin, Kolchak, Petliura, and all other enemies of the workers' and peasants' government, both sides signatory to this agreement pledge themselves to support with all their efforts the Russo-Ukrainian Red Army in the execution of its task of annihilating once and for all the forces of imperialist world reaction.

Therefore we pledge ourselves to eradicate all attempts to disperse the forces of the united revolutionary front against the White Guard army, especially condemning all agitation which advocates the organization in Ukrainian territory of separate military formations of former partisans and disbanded Petliurist army men and the separation of Ukrainian troops from the Russian Red armies. We pledge ourselves to fight mercilessly any agitation which disorganizes the front and aids counter-revolution.

Signed: Kh. Rakovsky, D. Manuilsky, G. Petrovsky, and S. Kosior for the central committee of the Communist Party of Ukraine (Bolsheviks); L. Kovaliv and H. Hrynko for the central committee of the Ukrainian Communist Party (Borotbists).

Moscow, 17 December 1919."

96. Majstrenko, p. 174.
97. Majstrenko (pp. 182–83) asserts that this paper was not Borotbist but Bolshevik.
98. Ravich, p. 146.
99. *Kommunisticheskii internatsional,* 30 Janaury 1920, Nos. 7–8, cols. 1125–26; English text in Majstrenko, pp. 184–86.
100. Majstrenko, pp. 186–87.
101. Popov, p. 216. The number of members of the UCP (Borotbists) at the time of their merger with the CP(B)U was about 4,000; however, as Skrypnyk stated at the twelfth congress of the RCP, there were only 118 Borotbists in the CP(B)U in 1923. The others went to Russia, left the CP(B)U, or—and this applied to the majority of them—were excluded from the CP(B)U during the purge, allegedly because "they preserved nationalist survivals." *Dvenadtsatyi sezd Rossiiskoi kommunisticheskoi partii (bolshevikov),* p. 524.
102. Majstrenko, pp. 189–90.
103. Lenin, *Stati i rechi,* p. 344.
104. A. Khvylia, "KP(b)U v borotbi za leninsku natsionalnu polityku," *BU,*

1932, Nos. 17–8, pp. 19–20. Blakytny's critique of the CP(B)U:

"Full of petty-bourgeois elements and clever fellow travellers, the party was unable to master the revolutionary tide, lost touch with the working class, and did not get into touch with the rural semi-proletariat, was unable to fulfill the main tasks of the political extermination of Petliurism and otamanism, and of the formation of a firm basis in the village, because of its stratification into classes; and it began finally to disintegrate, literally before our eyes. A characteristic sign of this disintegration was that another Communist organization, the UCP (Borotbists), began to grow at the cost of the CP(B)U; the trend towards self-liquidation within the UCP (Borotbists) ceases, and finally within the CP(B)U a separate organizational trend developed (the so-called federalist group). It is quite clear that the party was unable to be an organized factor, and Soviet power in Ukraine fell once more under outside pressure. Meanwhile, in Russia, to which the mass of the doubtful elements emigrated, the words 'a Ukrainian Communist' became a symbol of being petty-bourgeois, philistine, disorderly, and unworthy ....

The CP(B)U returned to Ukrainian territory, having got rid of a considerable part of its speculative element, leaning upon strong military forces and upon an organized military and party machinery, reinforced by new Bolshevik proletarian elements from the RCP(B) .... Uniting with the Borotbists gave the party considerable cadres from the revolutionary rural proletariat, land workers, poorer peasantry, rural intelligentsia, and the nationally conscious Ukrainian proletariat, who, having strayed on the bypaths of the national revolution, tore themselves away from it as soon as the signs of its becoming the bourgeois counter-revolution became noticeable .... But while this was a positive factor for the party, a great negative one was that the elements sent from the RCP(B) for the purposes of aid were, though proletarian, yet tired out, with shattered nerves, irrepressibly oppositionist to the centre, with marks of corruption .... This group brought about a catastrophe in the party which ended in the split of the party conference, repressive measures against the leaders of this group, the introduction of a strict regime, of an iron, actually military discipline."

Blakytny thus characterizes the "colonial" position of Ukraine:

"This tendency, which we call colonialist, having its foundations in the national affinity of the majority of the urban proletariat of Ukraine with the proletariat, semi-proletariat, and petty bourgeoisie of Russia, and in the weakness of the industrial proletariat of Ukraine, calls for the creation of an economic system within the framework of the RSFSR, within the restored framework of the old empire of which Ukraine was a component part, and strives towards a complete levelling of the CP(B)U in the RCP(B), and towards the dissolving in the national Russian section of the Comintern of all young proletarian forces of non-historic nations."

The leader of the "colonialist" plans in Ukraine, in Blakytny's opinion, "quite naturally, is the part of the urban and industrial workers that has not assimilated in Ukrainian surroundings, and most of all the mass of the urban Russian and Russified petty bourgeoisie which comprised the whole machinery of the domination of the Russian bourgeoisie in Ukraine .... "

Vrona spoke even more sharply at the Volhynian district party conference:

"The CP(B)U, having originated in the depths of non-Ukrainian elements—from the RSDWP (Bolsheviks) and from the urban proletariat—for which there has never been any national oppression, developing a Communist revolution within the framework of the old united Russia, considering themselves, too, only an inalienable and indivisible part of the all-Russian revolutionary stream, unconnected organically with the Ukrainian masses and their national revolution, took from the very beginning a disastrous course ....

Having made such disastrous policy in the approach to the social revolution, the CP(B)U had necessarily to lose touch with the social and economic basis, with the daily life of the Ukrainian masses, and to develop more and more its strictly colonizing and occupying policy, which mercilessly centralizes the whole party and Soviet machinery, subordinating it to the Great Russian centre and destroying all its initiative and independence ....

The imperialist and colonizing policy which now dominates in Ukraine is profoundly injurious to the interests of the Communist revolution. Since it ignores the natural and lawful national aspirations of the Ukrainian working masses which up to now have been subjugated in the national respect, it is completely reactionary and counter-revolutionary, it is a manifestation of the old Great Russian imperialist chauvinism which has not yet disappeared, and it is being pursued by the representatives of an oppressing nation against an oppressed nation, such as the Ukrainian nation has been." Popov, *Narys,* pp. 238–45.

105. Ravich, pp. 148–49.
106. Quoted after Postyshev, "Itogi proverki partiinykh dokumentov KP(b)U i zadachi partiinoi raboty," *Bolshevik,* 1936, No. 5, p. 11.
107. Ibid.
108. The historiography of the Stalin period regarded the Borotbists as belonging entirely to the anti-Communist camp, not having anything in them which would remind one of Communism. See, for instance, M. Zahretsky, "V borotbi z iakymy dribnoburzhuaznymy ukrainskymy natsionalistychnymy partiiamy KP(b)U zabezpechyla peremohu proletarskoii revoliutsii na Ukraini," *BU,* 1933, No. 78, pp. 73–81.
109. *Deviatyi sezd RKP(b),* pp. 142–43.
110. The full text of the draft resolution is in "Iz dela 'Papka No. 1, PART' za vremia s 31 ianvaria 1919 goda po 11-e noiabria 1920 goda," Trotsky's Archives; also Wolfe in *ASEER,* 1950, No. 9, pp. 177–78.

Trotsky's resolution on the Borotbists, in part:

"1) The bloc of our party with the Borotbists had as its aim to attract to a sustained Communist policy a young political party in the socialist structure of Ukraine, still so poor in experience.

"2) In conducting this experiment, our party clearly had in mind that it might have directly opposite results, namely, that it might hasten the degeneration of the Borotbists into a militant party of counter-revolution, with the splitting off from it of its most honest and conscious socialist elements.

"3) In either case, drawing the party of Borotbists into governmental responsibility—by hastening the political evolution of the party—would have a progressive significance, since it shortened the period of indefiniteness and formlessness of political groupings and relationships.

"4) At the present time it can be confirmed with full conviction that the party of Borotbists has evolved to the right, i.e., to the side of degeneration into an intellectual political group, basing itself mainly on kulak elements of the villages and on swindler-scoundrelly elements of the city, including also the greater part of the working class [*sic*] ....

"11) It is incumbent upon the leading elements of our party and of Soviet power in Ukraine to open a most serious, attentive, and energetic campaign against the party of the Borotbists, exposing its intelligentsia-careerist, chauvinist, and exploiter-kulakist character.

"12) Attention must especially be paid to all those cases where Borotbists directly or indirectly support corrupted partisans and undermine the authority and strength of the Russo-Ukrainian Red Army ....

"13) It is incumbent upon the corresponding Soviet organizations not to leave unanswered even one single chauvinist, anarcho-kulakist declaration of the Borotbists. It is necessary by means of merciless exposure to make the genuinely alert section of the toilers who follow the Borotbists aware that the road of this party is the road to inevitable ruin for Soviet Ukraine.

"14) It is necessary to take into account that a certain number of pure socialist elements have so far remained in the ranks of the Borotbists because of the official Communist banner of the party and its external revolutionary phraseology ....

"15) By means of all the measures indicated above, i.e., by means of a broad and energetic exposure of the chauvinistic politics of the Borotbists, by means of the attraction into our own ranks of its best elements and the merciless dispersion of the Makhnovist and Petliurist elements in the ranks of the Borotbists, our party must in a short time prepare the conditions for driving the Borotbists out of the ranks of the government, and for the complete liquidation of the Borotbists as a recognized Soviet party."

111. "Iz dela 'Papka No. 1, PART' za vremia s 31 ianvaria 1919 goda po 11-e noiabria 1920 goda," Trotsky's Archives.
112. Wolfe, "The Influence of Early Military Decisions," p. 178. Makhno was a leader of the anarchist uprising in Ukraine.
113. Ibid., p. 179.
114. *Deviatyi sezd RKP(b),* pp. 96–97.
115. The telegram to the chairman of the Council of People's Commissars of Ukraine was published for the first time in 1950 in Lenin, *Soch.,* XXIX, p. 300.
116. Ravich, p. 241.
117. V. T. Gorbatiuk, T. D. Ionkina, "Razvitie kapitalizma v zemledelii," *Voprosy istorii,* 1956, No. 9, p. 111.
118. An American historian also pointed out that in Ukraine after 1861 there "emerged a prosperous class of independent farmers, without parallel in Russia proper. On the whole the Ukrainian peasantry knew neither the communal type of land ownership nor the service relationship between peasant and landlord *(barshchina).* Its soil was individually owned, and paid for by money, not by personal labor." Pipes, *The Formation of the Soviet Union,* p. 9.
119. Gorbatiuk, "Razvitie kapitalizma." Concerning the difference between the Right Bank and Left Bank of Ukraine in this respect, see M. Kubanin, *Makhnovshchina,* pp. 9–22.
120. Gorbatiuk, "Razvitie kapitalizma."
121. Rubach, p. 8; Vobly, *Ekonomicheskaia geografiia Ukrainy,* pp. 50–51.
122. Rubach, p. 8.
123. There were great disagreements concerning the quotas of the "poor peasants" and the "kulaks." Thus the Central Rada established in its land law the quota of a "working farm property" at forty desiatinas, while the Ukrainian SRs and particularly the Peasants' Union regarded twenty desiatinas as the "working quota" (a "working farm property" was meant to be a farm worked by the owner's labour or by the labour of his own family).
124. Liashchenko, *Istoriiia narodnogo khoziaistva SSSR,* Vol. II, p. 477; cf. also *Ocherki razvitiia narodnogo khoziaistva Ukrainskoi SSR,* p. 45.
125. See the resolution on the land question at the seventh conference of the RSDWP(B), April 1917, in Lenin, *Soch.,* XXIV, pp. 257–60.
126. Lenin, *Soch.,* XXIV, p. 60.
127. *Vosmoi sezd RKP(b),* p. 221.
128. Popov, *Ocherki* (1928), p. 260.
129. Ibid., pp. 260–65; cf. also D. Kin, *Denikinshchina,* p. 38, who wrote that "when the proletarian dictatorship manifested its socialist essence, a differentiation took place among the insurgents. Among their wealthy part

there began a wavering and a disintegration, which later took the form of a rebellion against Soviet power."

130. Popov, *Ocherki,* p. 268.
131. Popov, *Narys,* p. 183.
132. *KP(b)U v rezoliutsiiakh ee sezdov i konferentsii,* pp. 50–51. Khrystiuk, IV, p. 130, note 2, gives the information that during the spring and summer of 1919 up to one million desiatinas of land were taken for Soviet state farms, about 800,000 desiatinas of land formerly belonging to sugar-beet farms were nationalized by the council of national economy; about 2,800,000, or perhaps even 3,000,000 desiatinas of land not tilled by the owner's labour, i.e., 25 per cent of the land not tilled by the owner's labour, was nationalized. The remaining 75 per cent the Soviet government was unable to distribute among the peasants with few or no landed possessions, and this land was appropriated by the law of seizure.
133. Post-Stalin historiography also points out that "the practice of compulsory organization of communes and associations acquired in Ukraine a particularly widespread and monstrous character .... The Soviet power in Ukraine in 1919 was unable to carry out such a land policy as would have closely and organically linked it with the broad masses of the peasantry." P. M. Ponomarenko, "O politike partii v ukrainskoi derevne v 1919–1920 gg.," p. 106.
134. Skrypnyk mentioned this peculiarity of Ukraine in his article "Donbas i Ukraina," *Statti i promovy,* II, 1, pp. 22–23. "The countryside in Ukraine is almost exclusively Ukrainian in its national composition. The towns consist of elements which are by nationality Russian or semi-Russified, Jewish, and partially, on the Right Bank, Polish." The urban proletariat, he continues, is still under the influence of petty-bourgeois ideology and superstitions, considering the Ukrainian language and culture to be third rate. Historical circumstances thus drive a wedge between the proletariat and the countryside, so that the latter "has a mistrustful and cautious attitude to all things Russian or Muscovite."
135. Trotsky, who grew up in a Ukrainian village, characterized the situation of Soviet power in Ukraine and the attitude of the peasantry to it during the offensive of Denikin and the Directory as follows: "The extraordinarily rapid tempo of our failures in Ukraine is explained by the same causes as the tempo of our successes: the extreme instability of the Ukrainian terrain. The numerous changes of regime in Ukraine dislocated their social relationships and psychology and for a long period turned broad masses of the peasantry into human material for whom it is extremely difficult to settle down into a crystallized social whole. This applies, however, also to the lack of consciousness of a part of the Ukrainian working class. Various regimes came and went during two years, and it was only the Ukrainian kulak who stood firm under these regimes and who was always on the alert under all regimes. A regime stands and a regime falls, but the Ukrainian kulak stays put as the master of the village. This Ukrainian kulak took a

rifle into his hands, for he is as yet firmer and more determined than the middle peasant, and even more so than the poor peasant. The Ukrainian kulak, having become insolent, having seen all the regimes which there are in the world, and armed to the teeth, is the element of anarchy and of the general destruction of all the foundations of human existence in Ukraine. It can be said with conviction that no regime in Ukraine will exist and stand firmly on its feet until the Ukrainian kulak is disarmed. This is the first task of those Ukrainian troops which enter Ukraine." Trotsky's speech at the seventh all-Russian congress of soviets, *Sedmoi vserossiiskii sezd sovetov,* pp. 98–99.

136. Ravich, p. 123.
137. Criticizing the policy of the party concerning the *komnezamy,* Ravich wrote (p. 125) that "the policy of *komnezamy,* which represented in Ukraine a banking upon a semi-mythical quantity, was the very factor which created this almost united front of the middle peasant and the kulak. The poor peasantry which was being organized by the Soviet government ... did not manage to become a revolutionary factor of any importance or a leader of the idea of proletarian dictatorship in the countryside." On the role of *komnezamy,* cf. Timoshenko, "Soviet Agricultural Policy," pp. 33 ff.
138. *Kommunist,* 8 February 1920, No. 32.
139. The law, "O nadelenii krestian zemlei," in *Kommunist,* 18 May 1920, No. 110.
140. *Kommunist,* 2 April 1920, No. 72. Rakovsky later stressed that this new land law had been drawn up "under the immediate guidance and supervision of Ilich" (Lenin). Rakovsky, "Ilich i Ukraina," *LR,* 1925, No. 2, p. 9.
141. Popov, *Narys,* pp. 221–22.
142. Kubanin, p. 133.
143. *Kommunist,* No. 2, pp. 35–36.
144. *Kommunist,* No. 1, p. 6.
145. *Rezoliutsii vseukrainskykh zizdiv rad,* p. 77.
146. As far as the composition of the committees of poor peasants is concerned, we can agree with a Soviet source that they were by no means peasantry "in the narrow meaning of the word." "Many of them worked in cities and factories, and therefore it was in the cities that they acquired their cultural development and proletarian solidarity." Further, it is said that the "poor peasants" were nationally of a Russophile character, which is borne out by the fact that at the first congress of the poor peasants 23 per cent of the speakers spoke in Ukrainian, at the second congress 24 per cent, and at the third congress 36 per cent. But, "having found themselves in a real Ukrainian village, they had to assimilate themselves without noticing it," i.e., to Ukrainianize. G. Petrovsky, "Nezamozhne selianstvo," *Izvestiia TsIK Soiuza SSR,* 7 December 1923, No. 280, p. 3.
147. *Instruktsiia pro orhanizatsiiu komitetiv nezamozhnykh selian,* pp. 2–7, after LIkholat, pp. 471–72. Cf. also G. Kh. Rakovsky, *Komitety*

nezamozhnykh selian i nova ekonomichna polityka, pp. 10–11.
148. Likholat, p. 472.
149. "Otchet TsK KP(b)U," supplement to *Kommunist* (Kharkiv), 15 November 1920, No. 5.
150. *Kommunist*, 1920, No. 5, supplement.
151. Lenin, *Soch.*, XXXI, p. 313.
152. *Obzor deiatelnosti komitetov nezamozhnikh selian so dnia ikh osnovaniia po 1 dekabr*, ed. by the NKVD of the Ukrainian SSR, p. 49, after Kubanin, p. 141.
153. Terletsky, "Differentsiatsiia ukrainskogo krestianstva i kolkhozy," *Na agrarnom fronte*, 1925, No. 5, p. 59.
154. *Kommunist*, 29 February 1920.
155. In his orders to Stalin, who was then working in Ukraine, Lenin stressed the necessity of "an obligatory distribution of a part of the collected grain to the poor peasants as a priority. The poor peasantry must be made interested first of all." Lenin, *Soch.*, XXX, p. 338. In another telegram to Stalin, he wrote that he approved of "a moderate *razverstka:* 158 [million poods], and you leave 10 per cent for the poor peasantry .... The food *razverstka* is to be implemented in full, while rewarding the poor peasantry with grain and salt." Lenin, *Soch.*, XXX, p. 339.
156. Iakovlev, "Zadachi partii v blizhaishii period," *Kommunist* (Kharkiv), 1920, No. 1, p. 6.
157. Kubanin, p. 130.
158. Rakovsky, *Doklad na kharkovskoi gub. partiinoi krasnoarmeiskoi konferentsii 15/II–1921 g.*, p. 21, after Kubanin, pp. 135–36.
159. Lenin, *Soch.*, XXXI, pp. 310–11.
160. Kubanin, p. 114.
161. *Kommunist*, 1920, No. 2, pp. 35–36. Ravich, pp. 233–34.
162. Manuilsky, "O nashei politike v derevne," *Kommunist*, 1920, No. 2, pp. 5–6. Cf. also *Rezoliutsii vseukrainskykh zizdiv rad*, pp. 77–78.
163. Manuilsky, "O nashei politike," pp. 6–7.
164. "Krasnaia armiia na Ukraine," *Oktiabrskaia revoliutsiia*, pp. 420–24.
165. N. F. Kuzmin, *Krushenie poslednego pokhoda Antanty*, p. 132.
166. Lenin, *Soch.*, XXXI, pp. 310–12.
167. *KP(b)U v rezoliutsiiakh*, p. 147.
168. On the last phase of the struggle of Makhno's insurgents with the Red Army, see P. Arshinov, *Istoriia makhnovskogo dvizheniia*, pp. 167–203; Kubanin, *Makhnovshchina*, pp. 153–66; N. Makhno, *Ukrainskaia revoliutsiia*.
169. Likholat, p. 594; Mazepa, III, pp. 96–111.
170. Likholat, p. 593.
171. Cf. the declaration of the president of the Ukrainian Soviet government, Rakovsky, at the eighth conference of the RCP(B) in December 1919. He stated that "in this year [1919] [Ukraine] will be liberated, not by the sporadic insurgent regiments, ... but by a Russian Red Army." *Vosmaia*

konferentsiia RKP(b), p. 96.

172. "Iz del Sekretnye iskhodiashch. bumagi za 1920 g. s No. 901 po No. 1032, chast 4," Trotsky's Archives, p. 56. Cf. also Arshinov, pp. 40–41. Kviring admitted that the victory of Soviet power in Ukraine was due only to the assistance of Soviet Russia. Kviring, "Nashi raznoglasiia," in *Pervyi sezd Kommunisticheskoi partii (bolshevikov) Ukrainy* (Gos. izd. Ukrainy, 1923), p. 131.
173. Carr, I, p. 301. Carr misinterpreted Vynnychenko's statement that "the clear social policy of the Russian Communists in Ukraine won all the sympathies of the working masses." Ibid., pp. 304–05.
174. Ibid., p. 304.
175. Ibid., p. 305.
176. A. V. Likholat, "Borba ukrainskogo naroda protiv inostrannykh interventov," p. 39.
177. Schlesinger, *Federalism*, p. 404, wrote that the role of the Red Army in Ukraine consisted in its participation "in local civil wars decided by essentially local forces in favour of the Soviet." Deutscher wrote that "the Bolshevik guerillas in the Ukraine proved, after all, strong enough to defeat Petliura, to seize Kharkov and to carry the revolution into most of the country." I. Deutscher, *The Prophet Armed*, pp. 428–29.

Chapter X

1. See pp. 342–46.
2. *Istoriia sovetskoi konstitutsii*, pp. 86–87.
3. Ibid., p. 90.
4. Ibid., p. 91.
5. Chistiakov in *Sovetskoe gosudarstvo i pravo*, 1954, No. 2, p. 17.
6. *Dvenadtsatyi sezd RKP(b)*, p. 645.
7. *Politika*, p. 113.
8. Ibid.
9. See *V zashchitu sovetskoi Ukrainy*, pp. 12–16.
10. Chistiakov, "Razvitie federativnykh otnoshenii," p. 19.
11. Ibid. *Politika*, pp. 111–12.
12. *Pravda*, 11 March 1919.
13. *Istoriia sovetskoi konstitutsii*, pp. 207–08 (see also p. 149).
14. *Pravda*, 7 June 1919.
15. *Istoriia sovetskoi konstitutsii*, pp. 215–16.
16. Ibid., pp. 233–34.
17. Ibid., p. 234.
18. Ibid.
19. Ibid., p. 247.
20. Chistiakov, p. 20.
21. Ibid., p. 22.

22. Ibid.
23. *Dvenadtsatyi sezd RKP(b)*, p. 465.
24. Carr, I, p. 386.
25. F. Pigido, *Ukraina pid bolshevytskoiu okupatsiieiu*, p. 11, incorrectly states that by this treaty the commissariat for "foreign policy" was also united and that in accordance with this treaty "Ukraine preserved the right to its own army, as well as the right to maintain its diplomatic representation in Poland, Germany, and Austria." Nothing of the kind was determined in the treaty. The Ukrainian SSR had diplomatic relations with the above-mentioned states for the precise reason that a separate commissariat for foreign affairs was kept by the Ukrainian republic.
26. The text of the treaty is in *Sbornik deistvuiushchikh dogovorov, soglashenii i konventsii*, I, No. 8, pp. 15–16; for its English text, not quite correctly translated, see W. R. Batsell, *Soviet Rule in Russia*, pp. 246–47. He erroneously calls this treaty a "treaty of alliance between the workers and peasants of the Russian . . . republic," while the treaty was called in Russian "*Soiuznyi raboche-krestianskii dogovor mezhdu Rossiiskoi . . . respublikoi . . . .* "
27. A Soviet expert on state law rightly stressed that this treaty, too, "was very laconic and in many respects very incomplete and unclear." Reikhel, *Soiuz sovetskikh sotsialisticheskikh respublik*, p. 43.
28. *Istoriia sovetskoi konstitutsii*, pp. 240–41.
29. Carr, I, pp. 385–86.
30. Ibid.
31. Ibid.
32. Ibid., p. 389.
33. Stalin, *Soch.*, V, p. 145.
34. *Sovetskii federalizm*, pp. 27–28. An illustration of this is the "statute concerning the mutual relations of the representative of the people's commissariat for finance at the Council of People's Commissars of the Ukrainian SSR with the people's commissariat for finance of the RSFSR" of 25 August 1922, which said that "in their relationships with Ukraine in the financial sphere, the people's commissariat for finance of the RSFSR and all its other people's commissariats and central institutions act exclusively through the administration of the people's commissariat for finance of Ukraine and do not in any case permit any direct dealings with the provincial and district finance organs situated on the territory of Ukraine. Likewise, these latter and all people's commissariats and other central institutions of Ukraine communicate with the people's commissariat for finance of the RSFSR only through the representative of the people's commissariat for finance or through its administration." *Istoriia sovetskoi konstitutsii*, pp. 372–73.
35. *Sovetskii federalizm*, p. 28.
36. Ibid., pp. 49–51.
37. Aleksandrenko, *Avtonomni respubliky ta avtonomni oblasti v Soiuzi RSR*,

pp. 78–79. The chairman of the Council of People's Commissars, Rakovsky, likewise stressed this fact; see his speech at the sixth all-Ukrainian conference of the CP(B)U in 1921: *Biuleten VI vseukrainskoi konferentsii KP(b)U*, No. 1, 1921, pp. 9–10.
38. Reikhel, p. 43.
39. Ibid., p. 44.
40. Ibid.
41. Ibid.
42. Ibid., pp. 44–45.
43. Ibid., p. 45.
44. Ibid., p. 47.
45. Ronin, *K istorii konstitutsii SSSR 1924 goda*, p. 60.
46. Zlatopolsky, *Obrazovanie i razvitie SSSR kak soiuznogo gosudarstva*, p. 97.
47. Iakubovskaia, *Obedinitelnoe dvizhenie za obrazovanie SSSR*, pp. 129–30.
48. *Sovetskoe gosudarstvo i pravo*, 1954, No. 3, p. 125.
49. Batsell, p. 215. Pigido, p. 11, holds almost the same extreme view concerning this treaty.
50. Iurchenko, *Pryroda i funktsiia sovietskykh federatyvnykh form*, pp. 50–53. Cf. also Mazepa, "Ukrainia under Bolshevik Rule," *SEER*, 1934, Vol. XII, pp. 323 ff.
51. Iakubovskaia, "Rol V. I. Lenina v sozdanii SSSR," *Kommunist*, 1956, No. 10, p. 31.
52. *Desiatyi sezd RKP*, p. 638.
53. *Pravda*, 18 September 1922, No. 261.
54. *Vestnik Tsentralnogo ispolnitelnogo komiteta* (Moscow), 1923, No. 1, p. 3.
55. Pentkovskaia, "Rol V. I. Lenina v obrazovanii SSSR," *Voprosy istorii*, 1956, No. 3, p. 14. Iakubovskaia in her work published at the height of the Stalin cult, in 1947, emphasized only the second factor, [illegible] the stri[illegible]g of the "chauvinists and separatists" "to violate the treaties and agreements concluded among the Soviet republics." Iakubovskaia, *Obedinitelnoe dvizhenie*, p. 132.
56. Iakubovskaia, *Obedinitelnoe dvizhenie*, p. 131.
57. *Desiatyi sezd RKP*, pp. 208–09.
58. Pentkovskaia, pp. 14–15.
59. Ibid.
60. Ibid., p. 15.
61. Ibid.
62. *Biuleten VI vseukrainskoi konferentsii KP(b)U*, 1921, No. 1, p. 12.
63. Ibid., p. 13.
64. *Deiatelnost ukrvneshtorga za pervuiu chetvert 1922 g.*, p. 11. In the first half of 1922, trade representations of the Ukrainian SSR existed in Poland, Czechoslovakia, Germany, Latvia, Turkey, and Austria. Ibid., p. 12.
65. Dennis, *The Foreign Policies of Soviet Russia*, pp. 188–89.
66. Ibid., p. 189.

67. *Ezhegodnik Kominterna*, 1923, p. 468.
68. *Sbornik deistvuiushchikh dogovorov i soglashenii*, issue 1–2, Moscow, 1935, 3d ed., pp. 209–14.
69. Allen, pp. 338–39.
70. *Peremirie i preliminarnye usloviia mira mezhdu Rossiei i Ukrainoi s odnoi storony i Polshei s drugoi (Offitsialnyi tekst)* (Moscow, 1920).
71. *Sbornik*, pp. 119–46.
72. Ibid., pp. 5–11.
73. Ibid., pp. 6–7.
74. Ibid., pp. 101–07.
75. Ibid., pp. 72–84.
76. Ibid., pp. 234–41.
77. Ibid., pp. 209–14.
78. Ibid., pp. 176–81.
79. Ibid., pp. 465–73.
80. Ibid., pp. 242–43, 473.
81. *U. S. S. R. A Concise Handbook*, p. 116.
82. The Far East Republic was proclaimed an independent state on 6 April 1920 in Verkhneudinsk. It comprised the Trans-Baikal, Amur, and the maritime provinces of Kamchatka and Sakhalin. The declaration of the constituent assembly of the Far East Republic to the governments of the U. S. A., Great Britain, France, Japan, China, Italy, and the RSFSR, and to all governments and peoples of the world said that the creation of an independent Far East Republic had been the result of "their [the provinces of the republic] economic and geographical position, the large extent of their boundaries and their remoteness from the centre of the Russian republic." *Vneshniaia politika SSSR. 1917–1944*, Vol. I, pp. 422–23. This was a provisional state creation, which was not destined to exist for long. By the decision of the parliament of the Far East Republic of 14 November 1922 this republic was incorporated into the RSFSR as an inalienable part. *Bolshaia sovetskaia entsiklopediia*, XIII (1952), pp. 314–16 and Vol. XX (1930), pp. 216–22.
83. *Istoriia sovetskoi konstitutsii*, pp. 337–38.

Chapter XI

1. See Trainin, *Sovetskoe mnogonatsionalnoe gosudarstvo*, (Moscow, 1947); E. B. Genkina, *Obrazovanie SSSR* (Moscow, 1947); S. I. Iakubovskaia, *Obedinitelnoe dvizhenie za obrazovanie SSSR (1917–1922)* (Moscow, 1947); I. S. Chigarev, *Partiia bolshevikov—organizator Soiuza SSR, 1917–1922* (Moscow, 1949); *Obrazovanie SSSR. Sbornik dokumentov. 1917–1924*, ed. E. B. Genkina (Moscow, 1949); A. Chugaev, *Obrazovanie Soiuza sovetskikh sotsialisticheskikh respublik* (Moscow, 1951); O. I. Chistiakov, "Razvitie federativnykh otnoshenii mezhdu USSR i

RSFSR (1917–1922)," *Sovetskoe gosudarstvo i pravo*, 1954, No. 2, pp. 14–25; V. M. Kuritsyn, *Gosudarstvennoe sotrudnichestvo mezhdu Ukrainskoi SSR i RSFSR*, IV: *1918–1922* (Moscow, 1957).

2. Iakubovskaia, "Rol V. I. Lenina v sozdanii Soiuza sovetskikh sotsialisticheskikh respublik," *Kommunist*, July 1956, No. 10, pp. 26–41; Pentkovskaia, "Rol V. I. Lenina v obrazovanii SSSR," *Voprosy istorii*, March 1956, No. 3, pp. 13–24.
3. "Neopublikovannye dokumenty V. I. Lenina," *Kommunist*, June 1956, No. 9, pp. 15–26.
4. For modern non-Soviet description of this issue, see especially: Pipes, pp. 240–86; Schlesinger, pp. 357–69; Carr, I, pp. 381–409; Iurchenko, pp. 53–59.
5. See pp. 350–54.
6. Stalin's declaration at the tenth congress of soviets of the RSFSR, *Desiatyi vserossiiskii sezd sovetov*, p. 185.
7. Pentkovskaia, "Rol V. I. Lenina," p. 17.
8. Ibid.
9. Ibid., pp. 17–18.
10. See Manuilsky's article in *Izvestiia*, 17 November 1922.
11. Pentkovskaia, p. 17; Iakubovskaia, "Rol V. I. Lenina," p. 36.
12. Ibid.
13. Pentkovskaia, p. 16.
14. "Neopublikovannye dokumenty V. I. Lenina," *Kommunist*, 1956, No. 9, pp. 22–23. During his illness Lenin expressed his views in letters which he sent to the members of the politburo, and which, thanks to the intrigues of Stalin and his followers, were not published in the Soviet Union during Stalin's lifetime. Some of these letters were distributed among the participants of the twelfth congress of the RCP in April 1923 and were partially published by Trotsky in his *Stalinskaia shkola falsifikatsii* and by *Sotsialisticheskii vestnik*, December 1923, pp. 13–15. Copies of these letters are in Trotsky's papers in the Harvard College Library, and they are published in English in Pipes, pp. 273–77. Three years after Stalin's death they were published in *Kommunist*.
15. Trotsky, *Stalinskaia shkola falsifikatsii*, pp. 77–78. Iakubovskaia, "Rol V. I. Lenina," pp. 36–37, and the editors of *Kommunist*, quoted the letter in abbreviated form, so that there is no mention of "the Union of Soviet Republics of Europe and Asia"; the same applies also to the *Istoriia sovetskoi konstitutsii*, p. 399, note 1.
16. Trotsky, *Stalinskaia shkola falsifikatsii*, pp. 78–79.
17. This question was also raised by Rakovsky at the twelfth congress of the RCP. *Dvenadtsatyi sezd RKP(b)*, pp. 603–04. A stubborn struggle was waged over this in the section for nationality problems of the RCP. Ibid., p. 599.
18. *Desiatyi vserossiiskii sezd*, p. 187.
19. Ibid.

20. Pentkovskaia, p. 19. Pentkovskaia rightly emphasizes that the words "of Europe and Asia" were deleted in the process of subsequent work on the treaty of union. It must be noted that they were not mere words which had somehow found their way there by chance, but that they stood for a widely popular idea, especially among the Communists in the borderlands. For instance, the Ukrainian Communist, Zatonsky, spoke at the tenth congress of the RCP(B) of an "East European" Soviet republic. *Desiatyi sezd RKP(b)*, p. 215. See also Frunze's declaration at the tenth all-Russian congress of soviets. *Desiatyi vserossiiskii sezd sovetov*, p. 192.
21. Lenin, *Soch.*, XXXIII, p. 335.
22. Ibid. This principle was subsequently incorporated into the constitution of the USSR (see section 27) and is also found in section 6 of the "principles of the constitution of the USSR" adopted by the eighth congress of soviets of the Ukrainian SSR. *Istoriia sovetskoi konstitutsii*, p. 386.
23. Lenin, *Soch.*, XXXIII, p. 335.
24. Trotsky, *Stalinskaia shkola falsifikatsii*, p. 78. Lenin wrote in fact: "On the basis of talks with Mdivani and other comrades, I shall also demand other changes."
25. Ibid., p. 79.
26. *Kommunist*, 1956, No. 9, p. 23. For an English translation of Lenin's letters, see Pipes, pp. 273–74.
27. *Kommunist*, 1956, No. 9, p. 23.
28. Ibid., pp. 24–25.
29. Enukidze, a Georgian Bolshevik, Stalin's follower, became the secretary of the presidium of the supreme soviet.
30. *Dvenadtsatyi sezd RKP(b)*, pp. 537–43.
31. *Desiatyi sezd RKP(b)*, p. 209.
32. Ibid., p. 215. There are two words in Russian which are both rendered in English by the same word, "Russian." The word *russkii* pertains specifically to the Great Russian people, which is only one of the peoples (nationalities) inhabiting the country referred to in English as "Russia." An adjective referring to Russia as an imperial state is *rossiiskii*. Thus the RSFSR should rightly be read as *Rossiiskaia Soviet Federative Socialist Republic.*
33. *Desiatyi vserossiiskii sezd sovetov*, p. 192.
34. Ibid., p. 191. As Skrypnyk later remarked, many Communists "were painfully touched when our congress accepted the name of the Union of Soviet Socialist Republics and not the Russian Soviet Socialist Republic. They considered it an insult to, and a digression from, tradition, when some argued that the Russian Communist Party be changed into the Communist Party of the Union of Soviet Socialist Republics." Skrypnyk, *Statti i promovy*, II, 1, p. 11. It can be seen from the minutes of the twelfth congress of the RCP that this change of the party name was proposed by Skrypnyk himself. *Dvenadtsatyi sezd RKP(b)*, pp. 606–07.
35. *Istoriia sovetskoi konstitutsii*, pp. 384–88.
36. Ibid., pp. 383–84.

37. From Stalin's interview with a *Pravda* correspondent; see Stalin, *Soch.*, IV, pp. 70–71.
38. *Pravda*, 18 November 1922, No. 261, in *Soch.*, V, p. 143.
39. *Desiatyi vserossiiskii sezd sovetov*, pp. 184–89.
40. Stalin, *Soch.*, V, pp. 156–59.
41. Sapronov said at the session of the all-Russian TsIK of 29 June 1923 that after the first congress of soviets of the union "the national question began to be discussed in autonomous and union republics and in autonomous regions, and from a whole series of discussions there emerged a wish to organize a central executive committee of the union consisting of two parts or, as was said, of two houses." *Vtoraia sessiia Vserossiiskogo tsentralnogo ispolnitelnogo komiteta* (Moscow, 1923), p. 9.
42. *Dvenadtsatyi sezd RKP(b)*, p. 452.
43. Ibid., p. 599.
44. Ibid., pp. 599–600.
45. Kviring, a member of the CC CP(B)U, at this point explained that he had voted for Rakovsky's amendments in the CC CP(B)U, but that now he was convinced that Rakovsky's amendment to admit to the soviet of nationalities only the four union republics "may be interpreted by the national autonomous republics as an attempt to impair the interests of these national republics." He therefore voted against Rakovsky and for Stalin's theses. Ibid., p. 607.
46. A different principle of representation in the second chamber was ultimately established in the constitution of the USSR, i.e., that the union and autonomous republics should have five representatives each and autonomous regions one representative each (the constitution of the USSR, chapter 4, section 15).
47. *Dvenadtsatyi sezd RKP(b)*, pp. 603–05. This principle was propounded by Rakovsky prior to the congress in the Ukrainian Communist journal, *Chervonyi shliakh* (Kharkiv), 1923, No. 1, pp. 88–89.
48. It seems that Deutscher, *Stalin*, p. 279, exaggerates when he says that Stalin's projected policy towards small nationalities reflected to a much lighter degree Trotsky's style rather than his own.
49. *Dvenadtsatyi sezd RKP(b)*, pp. 599–602.
50. Ibid., p. 596.
51. *Kommunist*, 1956, No. 9, p. 25.
52. *Dvenadtsatyi sezd RKP(b)*, p. 605.
53. Ibid.
54. Ibid., p. 443.
55. *Dvenadtsatyi sezd RKP(b)*, pp. 545–66.
56. Iurchenko, p. 59, erroneously asserts that this treaty was adopted by the tenth all-Russian congress of soviets on 26 December 1922. In actual fact, this congress merely resolved "to authorize a delegation ... to conclude a treaty of the RSFSR with the Soviet socialist republics ... concerning the creation of a union of Soviet socialist republics." *Desiatyi vserossiiskii sezd*

sovetov, postanovleniia desiatogo vserossiiskogo sezda sovetov, p. 4.

57. In this point the treaty differed from the Ukrainian project, according to which the union congress of soviets was to be composed of deputies "elected by the national congresses of soviets in proportion to the population." The resolution of the seventh congress of soviets of the Ukrainian SSR of 13 December 1922, *Istoriia sovetskoi konstitutsii*, p. 386.
58. Later, in the final version of the constitution of the USSR, this figure was fixed at 414. Ibid., p. 463.
59. For the text of the treaty, see *Istoriia sovetskoi konstitutsii*, pp. 394–98.
60. *Vtoraia sessiia Tsentralnogo ispolnitelnogo komiteta SSSR (1923)*, pp. 11–12.
61. *Vestnik Tsentralnogo ispolnitelnogo komiteta*, 1923, No. 1, pp. 1–5.
62. See Enukidze's declaration, *Tretia sessiia Tsentralnogo ispolnitelnogo komiteta Soiuza sovetskikh sotsialisticheskikh respublik, Biuleten*, 1923, No. 1, pp. 7–8.
63. Genkina, p. 135.
64. Stalin, *Soch.*, V, pp. 335–36.
65. The "Ukrainians" proposed, instead of a common presidium for both houses (as Stalin proposed), separate presidiums for either house with equal legislative functions. Stalin objected to this, saying that the creation of two presidiums would have meant "splitting the supreme power, which is bound to create great difficulties in work." He conceded instead separate presidiums for both houses, but such as would not possess legislative functions. Stalin, *Soch.*, V, pp. 295–96.
66. Ibid., pp. 335–36.
67. Ibid. pp. 340–41. Later works of the Stalin period drew a conclusion from this that well suited the demands of the time; these works called both Skrypnyk and Rakovsky "enemies of the people" and "bourgeois nationalists." Genkina, *Obrazovanie SSSR*, p. 136; A. Alimov, "SSSR i soiuznaia konstitutsiia." After Stalin's death, this exaggerated evaluation of Skrypnyk began to be revised. *Voprosy istorii*, 1956.
68. *Pravda*, 16 September 1922, No. 259.
69. Stalin, *Soch.*, V, p. 296. Another source states that the Ukrainian project also excluded from the number of merged commissariats the people's commissariat for food and the workers' and peasants' inspectorate. Alimov, "SSSR i soiuznaia konstitutsiia."
70. *Chervonyi shliakh*, 1923, No. 1, p. 88.
71. Stalin, *Soch.*, V, p. 336.
72. Ibid., p. 325.
73. Genkina, *Obrazovanie SSSR*, pp. 140–41. She says that at the first meeting of the commission of the TsIK the question arose whether it was the treaty concerning the creation of the union of 30 December 1922 or the project of the constitution elaborated by the commission of the CC RCP(B) that was to be taken as the basis for the commission's work. The treaty was favoured by "the small Mdivani-Skrypnyk-Rakovsky group," while Kalinin and the

rest of the commission were in favour of the project.

74. This opposition was later represented by Soviet historiography in a simplified manner as sabotaging the commission. Genkina wrote that "the Rakovskys and Skrypnyks attempted till the end, till the last meeting of the commission [of the union TsIK], to break up its work, but they always met with a concerted repulse." Ibid., p. 140.
75. Carr, I, p. 408.
76. Pipes, p. 278. Sadovsky, p. 89, supposed "that this change of [Rakovsky's] views was caused not so much by the realization of the importance of the Ukrainian national cause as by the result of relationships between factions within the Bolshevik party itself," and that Rakovsky was connected with the anti-Stalin opposition which aimed at making the Ukrainian SSR its outpost and at concentrating its forces there.
77. Panas Fedenko, "Mykola Skrypnyk," p. 60. Walter Kolarz in *Russia and Her Colonies*, pp. 128–29, also writes about Rakovsky's defence of the "statehood of the Ukraine."
78. Skrypnyk spoke openly against the *edinaia i nedelimaia* trends in the party at the eighth congress of the RCP (*Vosmoi sezd RKP[b]*, pp. 150–51), at the eleventh congress (*Odinnadtsatyi sezd RKP[b]*, pp. 77–78), and at the twelfth congress (*Dvenadtsatyi sezd RKP[b]*, pp. 522–26).
79. Skrypnyk was delegated by the government of the Ukrainian SSR to the constitutional commission. *Biuleten VI vseukrainskoi konferentsii KP(b)U*, 1921, No. 1, p. 12.
80. See pp. 335–41.
81. Pipes, p. 278.
82. This is confirmed by the resolution of the all-Ukrainian TsIK of 1 April 1923, which approved the position of Skrypnyk and Rakovsky in the commission and, apart from this, instructed them to pursue a line "in the same direction as before." *Pravda*, 13 April 1923, No. 80.
83. The TsIK received the authority to exercise supreme power until that moment when the new congress of soviets created an elected soviet of the union and confirmed the composition of the soviet of nationalities.
84. Enukidze's declaration at the session. *Tretia sessiia Tsentralnogo ispolnitelnogo komiteta Soiuza sovetskikh sotsialisticheskikh respublik. Biuleten*, 1923, No. 1, p. 3.
85. Ibid., p. 16.
86. Ibid., p. 17.
87. Ibid., pp. 15–16.
88. Ibid.
89. Ibid., pp. 17–18.
90. Ibid., p. 18.
91. Ibid., pp. 18–19.
92. *Vtoraia sessiia Tsentralnogo ispolnitelnogo komiteta Soiuza SSR, Sovet natsionalnostei. Zasedanie 21 oktiabria 1924 g. Biuleten*, No. 6 (Moscow, 1924), p. 258.

93. Ibid., p. 259.
94. Ibid., p. 261.
95. Ibid., p. 262.
96. *Vtoraia sessiia TsIK, Soiuznyi sovet. Biuleten,* No. 7 (1924), pp. 310–13. Chubar was then head of the Soviet government in Ukraine.
97. Ibid., pp. 332–37.
98. *Vtoraia sessiia Tsentralnogo ispolnitelnogo komiteta. Zasedaniia TsIK Soiuza SSR. 22 oktiabria 1924 g. Biuleten,* No. 13, pp. 395 ff.
99. Ibid., pp. 394–97.
100. Ibid., pp. 413–15.
101. Ibid., p. 416. Krylenko and Skrypnyk were supported in the discussion by the following representatives of the republics: Kaplan (Ukrainian SSR), Alibek Takho-Godi (Daghestan ASSR), Blakytny (Ukrainian SSR), and Samed Aga Agamaly-Ogly (Azerbaidzhan).
102. Ibid., pp. 403–05.
103. Ibid., pp. 417–22.
104. Ibid., p. 433.
105. Ibid., *Biuleten,* No. 12, pp. 461–67.
106. *Vtoraia sessiia Tsentralnogo ispolnitelnogo komiteta Soiuza SSR 3-go sozyva, Biuleten,* No. 13 (Moscow, 16 April 1926), pp. 12–13. Schwarz very correctly stressed that "the pertinacity of the Ukrainians (demanding the federal principle) made the Soviet government give way, though reluctantly, to the idea of a federal union." S. Schwarz, *The Jews in the Soviet Union,* p. 61.
107. Pigido, pp. 32–33; Luckyj, pp. 43–44.

Chapter XII

1. Popov, *Outline,* II, p. 72.
2. Stalin, *Soch.,* III, pp. 30–31.
3. *Vosmoi sezd RKP(b),* pp. 343–44.
4. *Istoriia sovetskoi konstitutsii,* pp. 105–06.
5. Gurvich, *Istoriia sovetskoi konstitutsii,* p. 29.
6. Ibid., pp. 146–47.
7. Ibid., pp. 128–30.
8. Stalin, *Soch.,* IV, pp. 66–69.
9. Ibid., pp. 70–73.
10. *Istoriia sovetskoi konstitutsii,* p. 143.
11. Ibid., p. 145.
12. Ibid., p. 151.
13. *Vosmoi sezd RKP(b),* p. 41.
14. Ibid., p. 40–41.
15. Ibid., p. 41.
16. Ibid., pp. 45–47.

17. Ibid., pp. 67–69. Piatakov was also supported at the congress by Sunytsia, who stressed that the conference of the Orenburg region and the conference of the first revolutionary army adopted the thesis that "the principle of the right of nations to self–determination must be rejected in the most decisive manner, not only in respect to the bourgeois nations, but also in respect to the proletariats of separate nations. Not the self-determination of the workers of one or another nation, but the subordination of the interests of the proletariat of any nation to the interests of the worldwide (*vsemirnaia*) militant organization of the proletariat." Ibid., p. 75.
18. Ibid., p. 70.
19. Ibid., p. 47.
20. Ibid., p. 48.
21. Ibid., p. 92.
22. For the resolution, see ibid., pp. 343–44.
23. Popov, *Outline History,* II, p. 72.
24. See pp. 46–51.
25. Stalin, *Soch.,* IV, pp. 351–52.
26. Ibid., p. 353.
27. Ibid., p. 354.
28. Ibid., p. 355.
29. Lenin, "Theses on the National Question for the Second Congress of the Comintern," in *Soch.,* XXXI, pp. 122–24.
30. Ibid., pp. 122–28.
31. *Desiatyi sezd RKP(b),* pp. 188, 579.
32. Ibid., p. 576.
33. Ibid., p. 577. Cf. also Stalin, *Marxism and the National and Colonial Question,* pp. 92–93.
34. For the text of the resolution, see *Dvenadtsatyi sezd RKP(b),* pp. 642–50. Cf. also Stalin, *Marxism and the National and Colonial Question,* pp. 137–38.
35. *Dvenadtsatyi sezd RKP(b),* p. 643.
36. Ibid., p. 645.
37. Ibid., pp. 645–48.

Conclusions

1. *Vtoroi sezd KP(b)U,* p. 165.
2. See p. 350.
3. Pipes, p. 265.

Bibliography

Relevant literature published after the appearance of the first edition of this book is marked by an asterisk.

UNPUBLISHED SOURCES

German Foreign Ministry [GFM] (Public Record Office—London).

Abteilung A. *Akten betreffend: allgemeine Angelegenheiten der Ukraine.*

—*Die Ukraine,* No. 1. Vom 1 Januar 1918 bis 31 Juli 1919. 36 Vols.

—*Friedenpräliminarien zu Brest-Litowsk.* (Frames: D 820302—D 820965 Vol. I, vom 15.XII.1917 bis 31.I.1918).

Trotsky's Archives, Harvard College Library and International Institute for Social History—Amsterdam.

"Dela 'iskhodiashchie shifrovannye telegrammy za 1919 g.' Sekretariata Zam[estitelia] Pred[sedatelia] R.S.V.R."

"Iz del 'Sekretnye iskhodiashchie bumagi' s 1/I - 17/IX 1919 g. s No. 1 po No. 400."

"Iz arkhiva t. Sklianskogo."

"Rasshifrovannye telegrammy chast 1-ia za 1918–19 gg."

"Iz dela 'PART Papka' No. 1, za vremia s 31 ianvaria 1919 goda po 11-e noiabria 1920 goda."
"Iz arkhiva t. Aralova."
"Delo: sekret. iskhod. bumagi poezda Pred. RVSR za 1919 g. M."

PUBLISHED SOURCES

Arkhiv Marksa i Engelsa, ed. Adoratsky. Vol. I. Moscow, 1932.

Bakunin, M. "Aufruf an die Slaven," in *Pisma M. A. Bakunina k A. I. Gertsenu i N. P. Ogarevu.* Geneva, 1896.

Biuleten VI vseukrainskoi konferentsii Kommunisticheskoi partii (bolshevikov) Ukrainy, No. 2. (Kharkiv, 1922).

The Bolshevik Revolution, 1917–1918: Documents and Materials, ed. J. Bunyan and H. H. Fisher. Stanford, 1934.

The Bolsheviks and the World War: The Origin of the Third International, ed. O. H. Gankin and H. H. Fisher. Stanford, 1940.

* *Bolshevitskie organizatsii Ukrainy v period ustanovleniia i ukrepleniia sovetskoi vlasti. Sbornik dokumentov i materialov.* Kiev, 1962.

Borba za vlast sovetov na Kievshchine (mart 1917 g.—fevral 1918 g.) Sbornik dokumentov i materialov. Kiev, 1957.

Briefe von F. Lassalle an Karl Rodbertus-Jagetzow. Berlin, 1878.

Der Briefwechsel zwischen Friedrich Engels und Karl Marx, 1844 bis 1883. 4 vols. Stuttgart, 1913.

Chernaia kniga. Sbornik statei i materialov ob interventsii Antanty na Ukraine v 1918–1919 gg., ed. Shlikhter. Katerynoslav, 1925.

Chetvertyi (obedinitelnyi) sezd RSDRP. Moscow, 1934.

Chetveryi sezd sovetov SSSR. Biuleten, No. 18, 1927.

Cunow, H. *Partei—Zusammenbruch? Ein offenes Wort zum innern Parteistreit.* Berlin, 1915.

David, E. *Socialdemokratie und Vaterlandsverteidigung.* Rede des Reichstagsabgeordneten Dr. Eduard David-Beril gehalten den 6 Mars 1915 in Bielefeld.

Deiatelnost Ukrvneshtorga za pervuiu chetvert 1922 g. Informatsionnyi biuleten, Nos. 32–33, Statistichesko-ekonomicheskii otdel UpNKVT (Kharkiv, 1922).

Deistvuiushchie dogovory, soglasheniia i konventsii vstupivshie v silu do 1 ianvaria 1921 goda. 2nd ed. 2 vols. Moscow, 1928.

Dekrety oktiabrskoi revoliutsii (Pravitelstvennye akty podpisannye i utverzhdennye Leninym, kak predsedatelem Sovnarkoma), ed. V. G. Sorin. Moscow, 1933.

10 let konstitutsii SSSR. Moscow, 1933.

Desiatyi sezd RKP(b). Mart 1921. Moscow, 1933.

Desiatyi vserossiiskii sezd sovetov rabochikh, krestianskikh, krasnoarmeiskikh i kazachikh deputatov, 23–27 dekabria 1922 goda. Stenograficheskii otchet s prilozheniiami. Moscow, 1923.

Deviatyi sezd RKP(b). Mart–aprel 1920 g. Moscow, 1934.

Dimanshtein [See *Revoliutsiia i natsionalnyi vopros*].

Documents on British Foreign Policy, 1919–1939, ed. E. L. Woodward and R. Butler. First Series. Vol. III: *1919*. London, 1949.

"Doklad tov. Popova P. v Zafrontbiuro TsK KP(b)U o poezdke v Ukrainskuiu narodnuiu respubliku." *LR*, 1926, No. 2, pp. 43–50.

Dokumenty po istorii grazhdanskoi voiny v SSSR. Pervyi etap grazhdanskoi voiny. Vol. I, ed. I. I. Mints and E. N. Gorodetsky. Moscow, 1940.

Dragomanov, M. *Volnyi soiuz—Vilna spilka. Opyt ukrainskoi politikosotsialnoi programmy*. Geneva, 1884.

Dvenadtsatyi sezd Rossiikoi kommunistcheskoi partii (bolshevikov). Stenograficheskii otchet. 17–25 aprelia 1923 g. Moscow, 1923.

Engels, Friedrich. *Briefe an Bebel*. Berlin, 1958.

Gankin and Fisher [See *The Bolsheviks and the World War*].

Gosudarstvennaia Duma. Stenograficheskie otchety. St. Petersburg, 1906, Vols. I–II; 1907, Vol. II; 1914, Vol. II.

Hegel, G. W. Fr. *Vorlesungen über die Philosophie der Geschichte*. 3rd ed. Berlin, 1848.

Hermaize, O. "Materiialy do istorii ukrainskoho rukhu za svitovoi viiny," in *Ukrainskyi arkheografichnyi zbirnyk* Vol. I (Kiev, 1925), pp. 271–354.

Instruktsiia pro organizatsiiu komitetiv nezamozhnykh selian. Kiev, 1920.

Istoriia KP(b)U v materiialakh ta dokumentakh. 1917–1920 rr., ed. S. Barannyk. 2nd ed. Kharkiv, 1934.

Istoriia sovetskoi konstitutsii (v dokumentakh), 1917–1956. Moscow, 1957.

Itogi desiatiletiia sovetskoi vlasti v tsifrakh, 1917–1927. Moscow, 1928.

Iurkevych, L. [Rybalka]. "Kooperatsiia i robitnychyi rukh." *Dzvin*, 1913, No. 9.

—*Natsionalna sprava i robitnytstvo*. Kiev, 1913.
—"Paky i paky." *Dzvin,* 1914, No. 6.
—"Rosiiski marksysty i ukrainskyi robitnychyi rukh." *Dzvin,* 1913, No. 7–8.
—"V spravi ukrainskoi robitnychoi hazety." *Dzvin,* 1913, No. 4.
"Iz deiatelnosti TsK KP(b)U i TsVRK v period mezhdu I–II sezdami KP(b)U." *LR,* 1927, No. 1, pp. 121–73.
Kak i pochemu Ispolkom Kominterna raspustil UKP. Kharkiv, 1925.
Kautsky, K. *Nationalität und Internationalität*. Stuttgart, 1908.
Kommunisticheskaia partiia Ukrainy v rezoliutsiiakh i resheniiakh sezdov i konferentsii (1918–1956). Kiev, 1958.
"Ko vsem organizatsiiam Kommunisticheskoi partii Ukrainy." *Kommunist* (Kharkiv), 20 May 1920, No. 1.
Lapchynsky, G. "Pismo v redaktsiiu gazety 'Chervonyi prapor.'" *Revoliutsiia v nebezpetsi* (Vienna-Kiev, 1920), pp. 73–82; *Nova doba* (Vienna, 1920), No. 38.
Lassalle, Ferdinand. *Gesamtwerke,* ed. E. Blum. Leipzig, n.d.
Lenin, V. I. *The Right of Nations to Self-Determination.* Moscow, 1951.
—*Sochineniia*. 4th ed. 35 vols. Moscow, 1941–50. [Lenin, *Soch.]*
—*Stati i rechi ob Ukraine*. Kharkiv, 1936. [Lenin, *Stati.]*
Leninskii sbornik (Moscow-Leningrad), ed. L. B. Kamenev. Vol. II (1924), Vol. III (1925), Vol. IX (1926).
Lensch, P. "Die Selbstbestimmungsklause." *Die Glocke,* 1915–16, pp. 465–76.
Listovki bolshevikov Ukrainy perioda pervoi russkoi revoliutsii (1905–1907 gg.). Kiev, 1955.
Marx, K. *Revolution and Counter-Revolution or Germany in 1848,* ed. E. Marx-Aveling. London, 1896.
Marx, Karl, and Friedrich Engels. *Gesammelte Schriften, 1852–1862,* ed. Riazanov. Stuttgart, 1920.
—*Historisch-kritische Gesamtausgabe.* I Abt. Vol. I (Frankfurt A. M., 1927); Vols. 2–6 (Berlin, 1929–32); Vol. 7 (Moscow 1935); III Abt. Vols. 1–4 (Berlin, 1929–31).
—*Sochineniia*. 29 vols. Moscow, 1928-.
Materiialy do problemy, taktyky i organizatsii Ukrainskoi narodnoi partii. Kiev–Vienna, 1920.
Memorandum Ukrainskoi komunistychnoi partii (borotbistiv) do Vykonavchoho komitetu III Komunistychnoho internatsionalu. Vienna–Kiev, 1920.
Mirnye peregovory v Brest-Litovske, s 22 dekabria 1917 g. po 3

marta 1918 g. Vol. I. Moscow, 1920.
Narodnost i rodnoi iazyk naseleniia SSSR. Moscow, 1928.
The Nationalities Problem and Soviet Administration: Selected Readings on the Development of Soviet Nationalities Policies, ed. R. Schlesinger. London, 1956.
Natsionalnaia politika VKP(b) v tsifrakh, ed. S. M. Velikovsky and I. Levin. Moscow, 1931. [Velikovsky.]
"Neopublikovannye dokumenty V. I. Lenina." *Kommunist,* 1956, No. 9, pp. 15–26.
"Oblastnoi sezd RSDRP(b-kov). (Pervoe vseukrainskoe soveshchanie bolshevikov)." *LR,* 1926, No. 5, pp. 55–92.
Obshchestvennoe dvizhenie v Rossii v nachale XX-go veka, ed. L. Martov, P. Maslov, and A. Potresov. Book. III. Vol. IV. St. Petersburg, 1911.
Odinnadtsatyi sezd RKP(b). Mart–aprel 1922. Moscow, 1936.
Ordzhonikidze, F. K. *Stati i rechi.* Vol. I. Moscow, 1956.
Otchet o deiatelnosti Ts. I. K. SSSR i ego prezidiuma. Moscow, 1925.
Papers Relating to the Foreign Relations of the United States.
—*1918. Russia,* 1–2. Washington, 1931–32.
—*1919. Russia.* Washington, 1937.
—*1919. The Paris Peace Conference 1919,* 1–3. Washington, 1942–47.
Le parti socialiste rêvolutionaire ukrainien. Prague, 1919.
Peremiriia i preliminarnye usloviia mira mezhdu Rossiei i Ukrainoi s odnoi storony i Polshei s drugoi (Ofitsialnyi tekst). Moscow, 1920.
Pervyi sezd Kommunisticheskoi partii (bolshevikov) Ukrainy. Stati i protokoly sezda, ed. M. Ravich-Cherkassky. Kharkiv, 1923. *[Pervyi sezd KP(b)U.]*
Pervyi vserossiiskii sezd sovetov r. i s. d., ed. V. N. Rakhmetov. Moscow-Leningrad, 1931.
Piatyi sezd RSDRP. Mai–iiul 1907 g. 2nd ed. Moscow, 1935.
Piatyi sozyv Vserossiiskogo tsentralnogo ispolnitelnogo komiteta. Stenograficheskii otchet. Moscow, 1919.
Plekhanov, G. V. *God na rodine. Polnoe sobranie statei i rechei 1917–1918 g.* Vol. II. Paris, 1921.
Politika sovetskoi vlasti po natsionalnomu voprosu za tri goda. 1917–XI–1920. Moscow, 1920. [*Politika.]*
Postanovleniia desiatogo vserossiiskogo sezda sovetov. Moscow, 1924.
Protokoly shestogo sezda RSDRP(b). Moscow, 1934.
Protokoly Tsentralnogo komiteta RSDRP, avgust 1917–fevral 1918,

ed. M. A. Savelev. Moscow, 1929.
Radek, K. "Thesen über Imperialismus und nationale Unterdrückung." *Der Vorbote,* 1916, No. 2, pp. 44–51.
Revoliutsiia i natsionalnyi vopros. Dokumenty i materialy po istorii natsionalnogo voprosa v Rossii i SSSR v XX veke, ed. S. M. Dimanshtein. Vol. III: *Fevral–oktiabr 1917.* Moscow, 1930. [Dimanshtein.]
Revoliutsiia na Ukraine v 1905–1907 gg. Sbornik dokumentov i materialov. Vols. I–II. Kiev, 1955.
Revoliutsiia v nebezpetsi (Lyst zakordonnoi hrupy UKP do kommunistiv i revoliutsiinykh sotsiialistiv Evropy ta Ameryky). Vienna–Kiev, 1920.
Rezoliutsii vseukrainskykh zizdiv rad, ed. Kyrychenko. Kharkiv, 1932.
Rubach, M. A. "K istorii grazhdanskoi voiny na Ukraine (Perekhod Grigorieva k sovetskoi vlasti)." *LR,* 1924, No. 3, pp. 175–88.
—"K istorii grazhdanskoi borby na Ukraine (K voprosu ob organizatsii vremennogo raboche-krestianskogo pravitelstva Ukrainy. Dokumenty i materialy)." *LR,* 1924, No. 4, pp. 154–65.
Russian–American Relations, March 1917–March 1920. New York, 1920.
The Russian Menace to Europe by Karl Marx and Friedrich Engels, ed. Paul W. Blackstock and Bert F. Hoselitz. Glencoe, 1956.
Sbornik deistvuiushchikh dogovorov, soglashenii i konventsii, zakluchennykh RSFSR s inostrannymi gosudarstvami. Vol. I. Petrograd, 1921.
—3rd ed. Moscow, 1935.
Sedmoi sezd RKP(b), mart 1918 goda. Moscow, 1928.
Sedmoi vserossiiskii sezd sovetov rabochikh, krestianskikh, krasnoarmeiskikh i kazachikh deputatov. Moscow, 1920.
Sevriuk, O. "L'Intervention Francaise en Ukraine en Janvier et Fevrier 1919." *GFM–6, Ukraine,* No. I, Vol. 33, A 13367.
Sezdy sovetov RSFSR v postanovleniiakh i rezoliutsiiakh, ed. A. I. Vishinsky. Moscow, 1939.
* Shakhrai, V., and S. Mazlakh, *On the Current Situation in the Ukraine,* ed. P. Potichnyj. Ann Arbor, 1970.
Shestaia (prazhskaia) vserossiiskaia konferentsiia RSDRP. 18–30 (5–17) ianvaria 1912 g. Sbornik statei i dokumentov. Moscow, 1952.
Shestoi sezd RSDRP(b). Avgust 1917 g. Moscow, 1934.
Skrypnyk, M. *Statti i promovy.* Vol. II: *Natsionalne pytannia.*

Kharkiv, 1931. [Skrypnyk, *Statti.*]

Sotsialisticheskoe stroitelstvo Soiuza SSR (1933–1938 gg.) Moscow–Leningrad, 1939.

Sovetskaia Rossiia–Ukraina i Rumyniia. Sbornik diplomaticheskikh dokumentov i istoricheskikh materialov. Kharkiv, 1930.

Sovetskaia Ukraina i Polsha. Kharkiv, 1921.

Stalin, I. V. *Marxism and the National and Colonial Question.* London, 1936.

—*Sochineniia.* 13 Vols. Moscow, 1946–53. [Stalin, *Soch.*]

—*Stati i rechi ob Ukraine.* Kharkiv, 1936. [Stalin, *Stati.*]

Statisticheskii ezhegodnik na 1914 g. St. Petersburg, 1914.

Statisticheskii spravochnik SSSR, za 1928 god. Moscow, 1929.

Tretia sessiia Tsentralnogo ispolnitelnogo komiteta Soiuza sovetskikh respublik. Biuleten. Nos. 1, 4. Moscow, 1923.

Tretii ocherednoi sezd Ross.-sots.-dem. rabochei partii. Polnyi tekst protoklov. Geneva, 1905.

Tretii sezd RSDRP. Sbornik dokumentov i materialov. Moscow, 1955.

Tretii vserossiiskii sezd sovetov rabochikh, soldatskikh i krestianskikh deputatov. Moscow, 1918

Trinadtsatyi sezd Rossiiskoi kommunisticheskoi partii (bolshevikov). Stenograficheskii otchet. 23–31 maia 1924 g. Moscow, 1924.

Trotsky, L. *Sochineniia.* Vol. III: *1917,* Part I: *Ot fevralia do oktiabria. Voina i revolutsiia. Krushenie Vtorogo internatsionala i podgotovka Tretego.* Petrograd, 1922 (Vol. I–II). Moscow, 1924; Part 2: *Ot oktiabria do Bresta.* Moscow, 1925.

Trudy pervoi vserossiiskoi konferentsii istorikov marksistov. Vol. I. Moscow, 1930.

1917 god na Kievshchine. Khronika sobytii, ed. V. Manilov. Kiev, 1928.

L'Ukraine et la Guerre. Lettre ouverte adressée a la 2me conférence socialiste internationale tenue en Holland en mai 1916. Lausanne, 1916.

Ukraine and Its People: A Handbook with Maps, Statistical Tables and Diagrams, ed. I. Mirchuk. Munich, 1949.

Velikaia sotsialisticheskaia revoliutsiia na Ukraine. Fevral 1917–Aprel 1918. Sbornik dokumentov i materialov. Vols. I–III, ed. S. M. Korolovsky. Kiev, 1957.

Velikovsky. [See *Natsionalnaia politika.*]

Vestnik Tsentralnogo ispolnitelnogo komiteta, Soveta narodnykh

komissarov i Soveta oborony Soiuza sovetskikh sotsialisticheskikh respublik. Moscow. Nos. 1–13. (1923); 7 (1924).
VKP(b) v tsifrakh. 5th ed. Moscow, 1926.
Vosmaia konferentsiia RKP(b). Dekabr 1919 g., ed. N. N. Popov. Moscow, 1934.
Vosmoi sezd Rossiiskoi kommunisticheskoi partii (bolshevikov). 18–23 marta 1919 goda. Stenograficheskii otchet. Moscow, 1919.
Vsesoiuznaia kommunisticheskaia partiia (bolshevikov) v rezoliutsiiakh i resheniiakh sezdov, konferentsii i plenumov TsK (1898–1933). Vol I: *(1898–1924)*. Moscow, 1932; Vol. II: *(1924–1933)*. Moscow, 1933. *[VKP(b) v rezoliutsiiakh.]*
"Vseukrainskaia konferentsiia KP(b)U. Materialy iz deiatelnosti Tsentralnogo komiteta KP(b)U. Iz protokolov sezda." *Kommunist* (Kharkiv), 1920, No. 1, pp. 27–33.
Vtoraia sessiia Tsentralnogo ispolnitelnogo komiteta Soiuza SSR. Sovet natsionalnostei. (21 October 1924). *Biuleten*, No. 6.
—*Soiuznyi Sovet*. (21 October 1924). *Biuleten*, No. 7.
—*Zasedanie TsIK Soiuza SSR*. (22 October 1924). *Biuleten*, No. 11. *3 Sozyva*. (16 April 1926). *Biuleten*, No. 13.
Vtoraia sessiia Vserossiiskogo tsentralnogo ispolnitelnogo komiteta X sozyva. Stenograficheskii otchet. Moscow, 1923.
Vtoroi ocherednoi sezd Ross. sots.-dem. rabochei partii. Polnyi tekst protokolov. Geneva, n.d.
Vtoroi sezd KP(b)U. Protokoly. 2nd ed., ed. V. Zatonsky. Kharkiv, 1927.
Vtoroi sezd RSDRP. Iiul–avgust 1903 g. Moscow, 1932.
V zashchitu sovetskoi Ukrainy. Sbornik diplomaticheskikh dokumentov i istoricheskikh materialov. Kharkiv, 1922.
Za sto lit. Materialy z hromadskoho i literaturnoho zhyttia Ukrainy XIX i pochatkiv XX stolittia. Books 1, 2, 4. Kiev, 1928.
Zinger, L. *Natsionalnyi sostav proletariata SSSR*. Moscow, 1934.

CONTEMPORARY NEWSPAPERS AND JOURNALS

Chervonyi prapor. Kiev, 1919–20. (Organ of the CC of the UCP.)
Donetskii proletarii. Kharkiv, 1918. (Bolshevik publication.)
Dzvin. Kiev, 1913–14. (Publication of the USDWP.)
Ekonomicheskaia zhizn. Kharkiv, 1919.

Ezhegodnik Kominterna. Moscow, 1919.
Die Glocke: Socialistische Wochenschrift. Berlin, 1915–25.
Golos sotsial-demokrata. Kiev, 1917. (Organ of the RSDWP[B].)
Izvestiia. Moscow, 1917. (Organ of the Soviet government.)
Izvestiia V. Ts. I. K. S. Moscow, 1919–20. (Organ of the all-Russian central executive committee.)
Kievskaia mysl. Kiev, 1900–18. (Liberal daily.)
Kievskaia starina. Kiev, 1906. (Literary and historical journal.)
Kommunist. Kharkiv, 1920–21. (Journal of the CC of the CP[B]U.)
Kommunisticheskii internatsional. Moscow, 1919. (Organ of the executive committee of the Communist International.)
Krasnyi arkhiv. Moscow, 1922. (Bimonthly journal of the main archival administration of the NKVD.)
Neue Rheinische Zeitung. Cologne, 1848–49.
New York Tribune. 1852.
Nova doba. Vienna, 1920–21. (Organ of the foreign group and foreign committe of the UCP.)
Petrogradskaia pravda. Petrograd, 1918. (Organ of the Petrograd committee of the RCP[B].)
Pravda. Petrograd, later Moscow, 1917. (Central organ of the CC of the RCP[B].)
Proletarskaia mysl. Kiev, 1917. (Organ of the RSDWP[B] in the Kiev district.)
Robitnycha hazeta. Kiev, 1917–19. (Daily of the CC of the USDWP.)
Ukrainskaia zhizn. Moscow, 1915. (Ukrainian political and literary journal.)
Ukraina. Kiev, 1914, 1917–18, 1924–32. (Bimonthly of the historical section of the All-Ukrainian Academy of Sciences.)
Vestnik Ukrainskoi narodnoi respubliki. Kharkiv-Kiev-Taganrog, 1918. (Publication of the Ukrainian Soviet government.)
Vilna spilka. Prague-Lviv, 1921–29. (Organ of the UPSR in exile.)
Der Vorbote. Geneva, 1866–71. (Organ of the International Workingmen's Association.)
Vorbote: Internationale Marxistische Rundschau. Berne, 1916.
Zhizn natsionalnostei. Moscow, 1918–24. (Organ of the people's commissariat for the nationalities.)

MEMOIRS

Andriievsky, V. *Z mynuloho.* 2 vols. Berlin, 1921–23.

Antonov-Ovseenko, V. A. *Zapiski o grazhadansoi voine.* Moscow, Vol. I (1924); II (1928); III (1932); IV (1932). [Antonov.]

Chykalenko, E. *Spohady (1861–1907).* 3 vols. Lviv, 1925–26.

—*Shchodennyk (1907–1917).* Lviv, 1939.

Denikin, A. I. *Ocherki russkoi smuty.* Berlin, 1924–25. Vols. III–V.

Doroshenko, D. *Moi spomyny pro nedavne-mynule (1914–1918).* 4 vols. Lviv, 1923–24.

Goldenvaiser, A. N. "Iz kievskikh vospominanii." *ARR* (Berlin), 1922, Vol. VI, pp. 161–303.

* Halahan, M. *Z moikh spomyniv.* 4 vols. Lviv, 1930.

Konovalets, E. *Prychynky do istorii ukrainskoi revoliutsii.* 2nd ed. N. p., 1948.

Kirov, A. "Rumcherod i Radnarkom odeskoi oblasty v borotbi za Zhovten." *LR,* 1927, No. 5–6, pp. 235–41.

Kotsiubynsky, I. "Chernigovskaia organizatsiia bolshevikov vo vremia voiny." *LR,* 1927, No. 2, pp. 189–99.

* Kovalevsky, M. *Pry dzherelakh borotby. Spomyny, vrazhennia, refleksii.* Innsbruck, 1960.

Kulik, I. IU. "Kievskaia organizatsiia bolshevikov v oktiabrskie dni." *LR,* 1927, No. 5–6, pp. 219–34.

Lapchynsky, G. "Gomelskoe soveshchanie (Vospominaniia)." *LR,* 1926, No. 6, pp. 36–50.

—"Pershyi period radianskoi vlady na Ukraini. TsVKU ta narodnyi sekretariiat (Spohady)." *LR,* 1928, No. 1, pp. 160–75.

—"Z pershykh dniv vseukrainskoi radianskoi vlady." *LR,* 1927, No. 5–6. pp. 46–66.

Lototsky, O. *Storinky mynuloho.* Vols. I–II. Warsaw, 1923–34.

Makhno, N. *Ukrainskaia revoliutsiia.* Paris, 1937.

Margolin, A. *Ukraina i politika Antanty. (Zapiski evreia i grazhdanina).* Berlin, 1922.

Mazepa, I. *Ukraina v ohni i buri revoliutsii.* Vols. I–II (Prague, 1942); III (n.p., n.d.). [Mazepa.]

Mazlakh, S. "Oktiabrskaia revoliutsiia na Poltavshchine." *LR*, 1922, No. 1, pp. 126–42.

Nazaruk, O. *Rik na Velykii Ukraini.* Vienna, 1920.

Oberuchev, K. *Den stora Ryska Revolutionen.* Stockholm, 1919.

Rafes, M. *Dva goda revoliutsii na Ukraine. Evoliutsiia i raskol Bunda.* Moscow, 1920. [Rafes.]

Romanovych-Tkachenko, N. "Na dorozi do revoliutsii." *Ukraina*

(Kiev), 1925, book 4.
Stankevich, M. B. *Vospominaniia, 1914–1919 gg.* Berlin, 1920.
Vynnychenko, V. *Vidrodzheniia natsii.* 3 vols. Vienna, 1920. [Vynnychenko.]

BIOGRAPHIES, GENERAL WORKS, PAMPHLETS, AND ARTICLES

Adams, A. E. "The Bolsheviks and the Ukrainian Front in 1918–1919." *SEER,* January 1958, Vol. XXXVI, No. 87, pp. 396–417.
* —*Bolsheviks in the Ukraine: The Second Campaign 1918–1919.* New Haven and London, 1963.
Akopian, G. S. "Perepiska V. I. Lenina i S. G. Shaumiana po natsionalnomu voprosu." *Voprosy istorii,* 1956, No. 8, pp. 3–14.
Aleksandrenko, H. V. *Avtonomni respublyky ta avtonomni oblasti v Soiuzi R. S. R.* Kharkiv, 1928.
Aleksynsky. "Chy zaderzhala revoliutsiia rozvytok kapitalizmu na Ukraini?" *Dzvin,* 1913, No. 1, pp. 31–36.
Allen, W. E. *The Ukraine: A History.* Cambridge, 1940.
Alimov, A. "SSSR i soiuznaia konstitutsiia," in *Desiat let konstitutsii SSSR.* Moscow, 1933.
Andriievsky, V. *Do kharakterystyky ukrainskykh pravykh partii.* Berlin, 1921.
Anishev, A. *Ocherki istorii grazhdanskoi voiny, 1917–1920.* Leningrad, 1925.
Antonovych, D. "Karl Marks i ukraintsi." *Dzvin,* 1913, No. 3, pp. 188–90.
Arshinov, P. *Istoriia makhnovskogo dvizheniia, 1918–1921.* Berlin, 1923.
Baby, B. M. "Utvorennia i rozkvit ukrainskoi radianskoi derzhavy, torzhestvo leninsko-stalinskoi natsionalnoi polityky," in *Pytannia istorii derzhavy i prava Ukrainskoi R. S. R.* Kiev, 1953, pp. 55–103.
Bachynsky, Iu. *Ukraina irredenta.* 2nd ed. Lviv, 1900.
Baevsky, D. "Bolsheviki v borbe za III Internatsional." *Istorik marksist,* 1929, No. 11, pp. 12–48.
Bahalii, D. I. *Shevchenko i kyrylometodiievtsi.* Kharkiv, 1925.
* Baron, S. *The Russian Jew under the Tsars and Soviets.* New York, 1964–74.

Batsell, W. R. *Soviet Rule in Russia.* New York, 1929.
Bauer, Otto. *Die Nationalitätenfrage und die Sozialdemokratie.* Vienna, 1924.
—*Die österreichische Revolution.* Vienna, 1923.
Blakytny, V. Ellan. "Komunistychna partiia Ukrainy i ii znachinnia." *Kommunist* (Kharkiv), 17 November 1920.
Bolshaia sovetskaia entsiklopediia. Moscow. Vols. 1–65 (1926–31); 1–50 (1949–58).
Bosh, Evgeniia. *God borby.* Moscow, 1925.
—*Natsionalnoe pravitelstvo i sovetskaia vlast na Ukraine.* Moscow, 1919. [Bosh, *Natsionalnoe pravitelstvo.]*
Butsenko, A. "O raskole USDRP (1917–1918 gg.)" *LR,* 1922, No. 4, pp. 121–22.
Budivnytstvo radianskoi Ukrainy. Zbirnyk. Kharkiv, 1929.
Burnatovych, O. *Ukrainska ideologiia revoliutsiinoi doby.* Lviv-Vienna, 1922.
Carr, E. H. *The Bolshevik Revolution, 1917–1923.* 3 vols. London, 1950. [Carr.]
—*The Future of Nations: Independence or Interdependence.* London, 1941.
—*Nationalism and After.* London. 1945.
Chigarev, I. S. *Partiia bolshevikov—organizator Soiuza SSR, 1917–1922.* Moscow, 1949.
Chistiakov, O. I. "Razvitie federativnykh otnoshenii mezhdu USSR I RSFSR (1917–1922 gg.)." *Sovetskoe gosudarstvo i pravo,* 1954, No. 2, pp. 14–25.
Choulgine, A. [Shulhyn]. *L'Ukraine contre Moscou (1917).* Paris, 1935.
Chugaev, A. *Obrazovanie Soiuza sovetskikh sotsialisticheskikh respublik.* Moscow, 1951.
Chyrko, V. *Piata konferentsiia KP(b)U.* Kiev, 1958.
Dennis, A. *The Foreign Policies of Soviet Russia.* New York, 1924.
Deutscher, I. *Stalin: A Political Biography.* London-New York-Toronto, 1949.
—*The Prophet Armed, Trotsky: 1879–1921.* London-New York-Toronto, 1954.
Dmytryshyn, B. *Moscow and the Ukraine, 1918–1953: A Study of Russian Bolshevik Nationality Policy.* New York, 1956.
Dony, N. R. "Obrazovanie Kommunisticheskoi partii Ukrainy." *Voprosy istorii KPSS* (Moscow), 1958, No. 3, pp. 34–49. [Dony.]

Doroshenko, D. *Evhen Chykalenko, ioho zhyttia i hromadska diialnist*. Prague, 1934.
—*Istoriia Ukrainy, 1917–1923 rr.* 2 vols. Uzhhorod, 1930–32. [Doroshenko.]
—"Mykhailo Dragomanov and the Ukrainian National Movement." *SEER,* 1938, Vol. XVI, No. 48, pp. 654–66.
—*Z istorii ukrainskoi politychnoi dumky za chasiv svitovoi viiny*. Prague, 1934.
Doroshenko, V. *Revoliutsiina ukrainska partiia (1900–1905)*. Lviv, 1921.
Drabkina, A. M. "Krakh prodovolstvennoi politiki germanskikh imperialistov na Ukraine (fevral–iiul 1918 goda)." *Istoricheskie zapiski* (Moscow), 1949, No. 28, pp. 69–110.
Dubnow, S. M. *History of the Jews in Russia and Poland*. Philadelphia, 1928.
* Dzyuba, Ivan, *Internationalism or Russification? A Study in the Soviet Nationalities Problem*. London, 1968.
Egorov, A. I. *Razgrom Denikina, 1919*. Moscow, 1931.
Entsiklopedicheskii slovar. Vol. XXVII. St. Petersburg: Brokgauz-Efron, 1899.
Entsykopediia ukrainoznavstva. Vol. I. Part 3. Munich-New York, 1949.
Erde, D. *Revoliutsiia na Ukraini. Vid kerenshchyny do nimetskoi okupatsii*. Kharkiv, 1927.
Fainsod, M. *How Russia Is Ruled*. Cambridge, Mass., 1953.
Fedenko, P. *Isaak Mazepa. Borets za voliu Ukrainy*. London, 1954.
—"Mykola Skrypnyk: His National Policy, Conviction and Rehabilitation." *Ukrainian Review* (Munich), 1957, No. 5, pp. 56–72.
* Fedyshyn, Oleh S. *Germany's Drive to the East and the Ukrainian Revolution, 1917–1918*. New Brunswick, N.J., 1971.
Fischer, L. *The Soviets in World Affairs: 1917–1929*. 2 Vols. Princeton, 1951.
Fraiman, A. L. "Retsenzii." *Voprosy istorii,* 1955, No. 11, pp. 129–33.
Fredborg, A. *Storbritannien och den Ryska Frågan, 1918–1920*. Stockholm, 1951.
* Frenkin, M. *Russkaia armiia i revoliutsiia 1917–1918*. Munich, 1978.
Frid, D. "Pro deiaki pytannia z istorii KP(b) na Ukraini." *LR,* 1930, No. 3–4, pp. 238–56.
Genkina, E. B. *Obrazovanie SSSR*. Moscow, 1947.
Gilinsky, A. "Sostoianie KP(b)U k piatiletiiu oktiabrskoi revoliutsii,"

in *Oktiabrskaia revoliutsiia,* pp. 167–84.
* Gitelman, Z. *Jewish Nationality and Soviet Politics.* Princeton, 1972.
Goldelman, S. *Lysty zhydivskoho sotsiial-demokrata pro Ukrainu.* Vienna, 1921.
Gorbatiuk, V. T., and T. D. Ionkina. "Razvitie kapitalizma v zemledelii i razlozhenie krestianstva na Ukraine vo vtoroi polovine XIX veka." *Voprosy istorii,* 1956, No. 9, pp. 110–19.
Gorin, P. "O roli proletariata v revoliutsionnom dvizhenii Ukrainy." *Bolshevik,* 1930, No. 1, pp. 43–52.
Grazhdanskaia voina, 1918–1921, ed. A. S. Bubnov, S. S. Kamenev, and R. P. Eideman. Vol. I–II (Moscow, 1928); Vol. III (Moscow, 1930).
Gurvich, G. S. *Istoriia sovetskoi konstitutsii.* Moscow, 1923.
Haidalemivsky, R. *Ukrainski politychni partii, ikh rozvytok i prohamy.* Salzwedel, 1923.
Halii, M., and B. Novytsky. *Het masku! Natsionalna polityka na radianskii Ukraini v svitli dokumentiv.* Prague, 1934.
Hekhtman, I. "Do pytannia pro sotsiialni korinnia ukrainskoho natsionalizmu." *BU,* 1929, No. 2, pp. 83–84.
Hellferich, K. *Der Weltkrieg.* Vol. III. Berlin, 1919.
Hermaize, O. *Narysy z istorii revoliutsiinoho rukhu na Ukraini.* Kiev, 1926.
Hirchak, Ie. F. "Lenin i ukrainske pytannia." *BU,* 1929, No. 1–2.
—*Na dva fronta v borbe s natsionalizmom.* 2nd ed. Moscow, 1931.
Hrushevsky, M. "Iak tvorylas ukrainska derzhava." *Vistnyk polityky i literatury.* Vienna, 1918–19.
—*Ukrainskii vopros. Stati.* Moscow, 1917.
—*Ukrainstvo v Rossii, ego zaprosy i nuzhdy.* St. Petersburg, 1907.
—*Ukrainska Tsentralna rada i ii universaly, pershyi i druhyi.* Kiev. 1917.
* Hunczak, Taras, ed. *The Ukraine, 1917–1921: A Study in Revolution.* Cambridge, Mass., 1977.
Hurzhii, I. O. *Rozklad feodalno-kriposnychoi systemy v silskomu hospodarstvi Ukrainy pershoi polovyny XIX st.* Kiev, 1954.
—*Zarodzhennia robitnychoho klasu Ukrainy.* Kiev, 1958.
Ia[kovlev] E[pshtein]. "Natsionalnyi vopros v programme Kommunisticheskoi partii Ukrainy." *Pravda,* 30 June 1918, No. 132.
—"O sozdanii samostoiatelnoi kommunisticheskoi partii Ukrainy." *Pravda,* 30 June 1918, No. 132.
—"Zadachi partii v blizhaishii period." *Kommunist* (Kharkiv), 1920,

No. 1.
Iakubovskaia, S. I. *Obedinitelnoe dvizhenie za obrazovanie SSSR*. Moscow, 1947.
—"Rol V. I. Lenina v sozdanii Soiuza sovetskikh sotsialisticheskikh respublik." *Kommunist* (Moscow), 1956, No. 10, pp. 26–41.
Iavorsky, M. *Istoriia Ukrainy v styslomu narysi*. Kharkiv, 1928.
—"K istorii KP(b)U," in *Oktiabrskaia revoliutsiia* (Kharkiv, 1922), pp. 93–130.
—*Korotka istoriia Ukrainy*. Kharkiv, 1927.
—*Narys z istorii revoliutsiinoi borotby na Ukraini*. 2 vols. Kharkiv, 1927–28.
—*Revoliutsiia na Ukraini v ii holovnishykh etapakh*. Kharkiv, 1923.
—*Ukraina v epokhu kapitalizmu*. Kharkiv, 1924. [Iavorsky.]
Iefremov, S. *Z hromadskoho zhyttia*. St. Petersburg, 1909.
Istoriia Ukrainskoi RSR. 2 vols. Kiev, 1953–58.
Istoriia Ukrainy. Korotkyi kurs. Kiev, 1943.
Istoriia VKP(b), ed. Iaroslavsky. Vol. I (1926); II (1930); IV (1929).
Istoriia Vsesoiuznoi kommunisticheskoi partii (bolshevikov). Kratkii kurs. Moscow, 1938.
Itenberg, B. S. "Vozniknovenie Iuzhnorusskogo soiuza rabochikh." *Istorichieskie zapiski* (Moscow), 1953, Vol. 44, pp. 94–129.
Iurchenko, O. *Pryroda i funktsiia sovietskykh federatyvnyh form*. Munich, 1956.
Iurkevych, L. [Rybalka]. *Russkie sotsialdemokraty i natsionalnyi vopros*. Geneva, 1917.
Ivanov, M. K. "K voprosu ob formirovanii proletariata Ukrainy." *Voprosy istorii*, 1957, No. 6, pp. 137–47.
Jabłoński, H. *Polska autonomia narodowa na Ukrainie, 1917–1918*. Warsaw, 1948.
* Kenez, P. *Civil War in South Russia, 1919–1920: The Defeat of the Whites*. Berkeley, 1977.
Kennan, G. F. *Soviet-Russian Relations, 1917–1920*. Vol. I: *Russia Leaves the War* (Princeton, 1956); Vol. II: *The Decision to Intervene* (Princeton, 1958).
Khrystiuk, P. *Zamitky i materiialy do istorii ukrainskoi revoliutsii, 1917–1920 rr.* 4 vols. Vienna, 1921–22. [Khrystiuk.]
Khvylia, A. "KP(b)U v borotbi za leninsku natsionalnu polityku." *BU*, 1932, No. 17–18.
Kin, D. *Denikinshchina*. Leningrad, n.d.
Kohn, H. I. *The Idea of Nationalism: A Study in Its Origin and Background*. New York, 1946.

Kolarz, W. *Russia and Her Colonies*. 3rd ed. New York, 1953.
* Koshelivets, Ivan. *Mykola Skrypnyk*. Munich, 1972.
Kovalevsky, M. *Ukraina pid chervonym iarmom. Dokumenty i fakty*. Warsaw-Lviv, 1936.
Kremer, A. "Osnovanie Bunda." *Proletarskaia revoliutsiia,* 1922, No. 11, pp. 55–56.
Krupnytsky, B. *Geschichte der Ukraine*. Leipzig, 1939.
—*Ukrainska istorychna nauka pid sovietamy*. Munich, 1957.
Kubanin, M. *Makhnovshchina. Krestianskoe dvizhenie v stepnoi Ukraine v gody grazhdanskoi voiny*. Leningrad, n.d.
Kulyk, I. I. *Ohliad revoliutsii na Ukraini*. Kharkiv, 1921.
—"Revoliutsionnoe dvizhenie na Ukraine." *Zhizn natsionalnostei,* 1919, Nos. 2–4.
Kuritsyn, V. M. *Gosudarstvennoe sotrudnichestvo mezhdu Ukrainskoi SSR i RSFSR v 1917–1922 gg*. Moscow, 1957.
Kutschabsky, W. *Die Westukraine im Kampfe mit Polen und dem Bolschevismus in den Jahren 1918–1923*. Berlin, 1934.
Kuzmin, N. F. *Krushenie poslednego pokhoda Antanty*. Moscow, 1958.
Kviring, E. "Nashi raznoglasiia," in *Pervyi sezd KP(b)U,* pp. 6–7.
Larin, I. "Ob izvrashcheniiakh pri provedenii natsionalnoi politiki," *Bolshevik,* 1926, No. 23–24; 1927, No. 1, pp. 59–69.
Lawrynenko, J. *Ukrainian Communism and Soviet Russian Policy towards the Ukraine: An Annotated Bibliography*. New York, 1953.
Lebed, D. *Sovetskaia Ukraina i natsionalnyi vopros za piat let*. Kharkiv-Moscow, 1924.
Leder, V. "Natsionalnyi vopros v polskoi i russkoi sotsial-demokratii." *Proletarskaia revoliutsiia,* 1927, No. 2–3, pp. 148–208.
Levynsky, V. "Narys rozvytku ukrainskoho robitnychoho rukhu v Halychyni." *Dzvin,* 1913, No. 7–8.
—*Sotsiialistychnyi internatsional i ponevoleni narody*. Vienna, 1920.
Liashchenko, P. I. *Istoriia narodnogo khoziaistva SSSR*. 2 vols. Moscow, 1956.
—*Istoriia russkogo narodnogo khoziaistva*. Moscow, 1927.
Likholat, A. V. "Borba ukrainskogo naroda protiv inostrannykh interventov i vnutrennoi kontrrevoliutsii v pervye gody sovetskoi vlasti," in *Doklady i soobshcheniia Instituta istorii. Akademiia nauk SSSR* (Moscow, 1954).
—*Razgrom burzhuazno-natsionalisticheskoi Direktorii na Ukraine*. Moscow, 1949.

—*Razgrom natsionalisticheskoi kontrrevoliutsii na Ukraine (1917–1922)*. Moscow, 1954. [Likholat, *Razgrom*.]
Los, F. E. *Formirovanie rabochego klassa na Ukraine i ego revoliutsionnaia borba*. Kiev, 1955.
—*Revoliutsiia 1905–1907 rokiv na Ukraini*. Kiev, 1955.
Lozynsky, M. *Halychchyna v rokakh 1918–1920*. Vienna, 1922. [Lozynsky.]
Luckyj, G. *Literary Politics in the Soviet Ukraine, 1917–1934*. New York, 1956.
Luxemburg, R. *Die russische Revolution*. Hamburg, 1948.
Lychkov, B. L. *Rudnye i nerudnye bogatstva Ukrainy*. Vol. I. Kiev, 1926.
Lypynsky, V. *Lysty do brativ khliborobiv*. Vienna, 1926.
Macartney, C. A. *National States and National Minorities*. London, 1934.
McNeal, R. H. "Soviet Historiography on the October Revolution: A Review of Forty Years." *ASEER,* October 1958, No. 3, pp. 261–81.
Magidov, B. "Donetsko-krivorozhskaia respublika," in *Oktiabrskaia revoliutsiia* (Kharkiv, 1922), pp. 569–73.
Maiorov, M. *Z istorii revoliutsiinoi borotby na Ukraini*. Kharkiv, 1928.
Majstrenko, I. *Borotbism: A Chapter in the History of Ukrainian Communism*. New York, 1954.
* —*Natsionalnaia politika KPSS*. Munich, 1978.
Malaia sovetskaia entsiklopediia. 10 vols. Moscow, 1928–31.
Manuilsky, D. Z. "O nashei politike v derevne." *Kommunist* (Kharkiv), 1920, No. 2.
* Markus, V. *L'Ukraine Sovietique dans les Relations Internationales 1918–1923*. Paris, 1959.
Martel, R. *La France et la Pologne. Realites de l'Est Europeen*. Paris, 1931.
Martov, L. *Istoriia rossiiskoi sotsial-demokratii. Period 1898–1907 g.* 3rd ed. Petrograd-Moscow, 1923.
Masaryk, T. G. *Otâzka sociâlnî. Zaklady marxismu filosofickê a sociologickê* 2 vols. Prague, 1948.
—*Zur russische Geschichts- und Religionsphilosophie: Sociologische Skizzen,* 2 vols. Jena, 1913.
Mazepa, I. *Pidstavy nashoho vidrodzhennia*. N. p., 1946.
—"Ukrainia under Bolshevik Rule." *SEER,* 1934, Vol. XII, No. 35, pp. 323-46.

Mikhels. "Promyshlennye raiony Ukrainy," in *Materialy po raionirovaniiu Ukrainy* (Kharkiv: Gosplan SSSR, 1923).
Miliukov, P. N. *Istoriia vtoroi russkoi revoliutsii*. Sofia, 1921.
—*Rossiia na perelome*. 2 vols. Paris, 1927.
Miliutin, V. P. *Istoriia ekonomicheskogo razvitiia SSSR (1917–1927)*. Moscow, 1928.
Myrhorodsky, K. "Z robitnychoho zhyttia." *Dzvin,* 1913, No. 2, pp. 129–30.
* Nahorna, L. O. *Proty suchasnoi burzhuaznoi i burhuazno-natsionalistychnoi falsyfikatsii istorii zhovtnia na Ukraini*. Kyiv, 1971.
Naumov, D. "Marks, dyktatura proletariiatu i sotsiialistychne budivnytstvo URSR." *BU,* 1933, No. 5–6, pp. 51–52.
Nedasek, N. *Bolshevizm v revoliutsionnom dvizhenii Belorussii*. Munich, 1956.
Nestorenko, A. A. *Ocherki istorii promyshlennosti i razvitie proletariata na Ukraine*. Moscow, 1954.
Nevsky, V. I. *Istoriia VKP(b). Kratkii ocherk*. Leningrad, 1926.
Ocherki po istorii filosofskoi i obshchestvenno-politicheskoi mysli narodov SSSR. Vol. II. Moscow, 1956.
Ocherki razvitiia narodnogo khoziaistva Ukrainskoi SSR, ed. A. A. Nestorenko, I. N. Romanenko, and D. F. Virnyk. Moscow, 1954.
Odintsev, P. "K voprosu ob ukrainskom narodnichestve." *Kievskaia starina,* 1906.
Oktiabrskaia revoliutsiia. Pervoe piatiletie. Kharkiv, 1922.
Oslikovskaia, E. S., and A. V. Snegov. "Za pravilnoe osveshchenie istorii proletarskoi revoliutsii." *Voprosy istorii,* 1956, No. 3, pp. 138–45.
Page, S. "Lenin and Self-Determination." *SEER,* 1950, Vol. XXVIII, No. 71, pp. 342–55.
Paneiko, V. *Ziedyneni derzhavy Skhidnoi Evropy. Halychchyna i Ukraina suproty Polshchi i Rosii*. Vienna, 1922.
* Palij, M. *The Anarchism of Nestor Makhno, 1917–1921: An Aspect of the Ukrainian Revolution*. Seattle, 1976.
Pankratova, A. M. "Proletariat v revoliutsii 1905–1907 gg.," in *Ocherki istorii proletariata SSSR* (Moscow, 1931), pp. 146–217.
Pentkovskaia, V. V. "Rol V.I. Lenina v obrazovanii SSSR." *Voprosy istorii,* 1956, No. 3, pp. 13–24.
Petrovsky, G. "Nezamozhne seliansto." *Izvestiia TsIK Soiuza SSR,*

1923, No. 280.
—*Revoliutsiia i kontr-revoliutsiia na Ukraine.* Moscow, 1920.
"Piat let borby za sovetskuiu vlast," in *Oktiabrskaia revoliutsiia* (Kharkiv, 1922), pp. 280–81.
* Pidhainy, O. S. *The Ukrainian Republic in the Great East–European Revolution.* Toronto, 1966–71.
Pigido, G. *Ukraina pid bolshevytskoiu okupatsiieiu.* Munich, 1956.
Pipes, R. *The Formation of the Soviet Union: Communism and Nationalism, 1917–1923.* Cambridge, Mass., 1954.
Podgorny, N. "Kommunisticheskaia partiia Ukrainy—boevoi otriad velikoi KPSS." *Kommunist,* 1958, No. 8, pp. 11–26.
Pohrebinsky, M. *Druhyi zizd KP(b)U.* Kiev, 1958. [Pohrebinsky.]
Pokrovsky, G. *Denikinshchina. God politiki i ekonomiki na Kubani (1918–1919 gg.).* Kharkiv, 1926.
Pokrovsky, M. N. *Russkaia revoliutsiia v samom szhatom ocherke.* Moscow, 1928.
Ponomarenko, P. M. "O politike partii v ukrainskoi derevne v 1919–1920 gg." *Voprosy istorii,* 1956, No. 8, pp. 105–07.
Popov, N. *Narys istorii Komunistychnoi partii (bilshovykiv) Ukrainy.* 5th ed. Kharkiv, 1931. [Popov, *Narys.*]
—*Ocherk istorii Vsesoiuznoi kommunisticheskoi partii (bolshevikov).* Moscow, 1928. [Popov, *Ocherk.*]
—*Outline History of the Communist Party of the Soviet Union.* 2 vols. New York, 1934. [Popov, *Outline.*]
Porsh, M. *Avtonomiia Ukrainy i sotsiialdemokratiia.* 2nd ed. Kiev, 1917.
Postyshev, P. P. "Itogi proverki partiinykh dokumentov v KP(b)U i zadachi partiinoi raboty." *Bolshevik,* 1936, No. 5, pp. 8–28.
* Pritsak, O., and J. Reshetar. "The Ukraine and the Dialectics of Nation-Building," *Slavic Review,* 1963, Vol. XXII, No. 2, pp. 224–55.
Prokopenko, N. R. "Borba za vozrozhdenie ugolnogo Donbassa v 1920 godu." *Istoricheskie zapiski,* 1948, No. 25, pp. 8–28.
Proudhon, P J. "Si les traités de 1815 ont cessé d'exister?" in *Oeuvres Complètes de P. J. Proudhon.* Paris, 1952.
Pylypenko. "Ukrainskaia intelligentsiia i sovetskaia vlast," in *Oktiabrskaia revoliutsiia* (Kharkiv, 1922), pp. 273–77.
Radkey, O. H. *The Agrarian Foes of Bolshevism: Promise and Default of the Russian Socialist Revolutionaries, February to October 1917.* New York, 1958.
—*The Election to the Russian Constituent Assembly of 1917.*

Cambridge, Mass., 1950.
Rafes, M. *Natsionalnye voprosy*. Moscow, 1921.
Rakovsky, Kh. "Ilich i Ukraina." *LR*, 1925, No. 2, pp. 5–10.
—"Khoziaistvennye posledstviia interventsii 1918–1919 gg," in *Chernaia kniga* (Katerynoslav, 1925), pp. 28–30.
—*Komitety nezamozhnykh selian i nova ekonomichna polityka*. Kharkiv, 1923.
—"Mezhdunarodnoe polozhenie sovetskoi respubliki," in *Oktiabrskaia revoliutsiia* (Kharkiv, 1922), pp. 33–34.
—"Rossiia i Ukraina." *Kommunisticheskii internatsional,* 1920, No. 12, pp. 2197–202.
Ravich-Cherkassky, M. *Istoriia Kommunisticheskoi partii (b-kov) Ukrainy*. Kharkiv, 1923. [Ravich.]
Reikhel, M. *Soiuz sovetskikh sotsialisticheskikh respublik. Ocherk konstitutsionnykh vzaimootnoshenii sovetskikh respublik*. Kharkiv, 1925.
Reshetar, J. S. *The Ukrainian Revolution, 1917–1920: A Study in Nationalism*. Princeton, 1952.
Riadnina, U. *Pershyi zizd KP(b)U*. Kiev, 1958. [Riadnina.]
Ronin, S. L. *K istorii konstitutsii SSSR 1924 goda*. Moscow, 1954.
Rubach, M. A. "Agrarnaia revoliutsiia na Ukraine v 1917 g." *LR*, 1927, No. 5–6, pp. 7–45.
—"K istorii ukrainskoi revoliutsii." *LR*, 1926, No. 1, pp. 41–85; No. 6, pp. 7–50.
Rubinshtein, N. *Bolsheviki i uchreditelnoe sobranie*. Moscow, 1938.
* Rudnytsky, Ivan L. "The Role of the Ukraine in Modern History." *Slavic Review*, 1963, Vol. XXII, No. 2, pp. 199–216, 256–62.
Sadovsky, V. *Natsionalna polityka sovitiv na Ukraini*. Warsaw, 1937.
Safarov, G. *Marks o natsionalno-kolonialnom voprose*. Moscow, 1954.
—*Natsionalnyi vopros i proletariat*. Petrograd, 1922.
Samsonov, P. *Kak postroena VKP(b)U*. Kharkiv, 1928.
Schlesinger, R. *Federalism in Central and Eastern Europe*. London, 1945.
Schwarz, S. M. *The Jews in the Soviet Union,* Syracuse, 1951.
Seton-Watson, H. *The Decline of Imperial Russia, 1855–1914*. London, 1952.
—*The Pattern of Communist Revolution*. London, 1953.
Shakhrai, V. [Skorovstansky]. *Revoliutsiia na Ukraine*. Saratov, 1919. [Skorovstansky.]
Shakhrai, V., and S. Mazlakh. *Do khvyli (Shcho diietsia na Ukraini i z Ukrainoiu)*. Saratov, 1919.

Shemet, S. "Do istorii Ukrainskoi demokratychno-khliborobskoi partii." *Khliborobska Ukraina* (Vienna), 1920, Vol. I, pp. 56–57.

Shevchenko, I. "Chetverta konferentsiia KP(b)U." *Vitchyzna* (Kiev), 1958, No. 7, pp. 121–40.

Shlosberg, D. "Profesiinyi rukh 1905–1907 rr. na Ukraini." *LR,* 1930, No. 6.

Shmorgun, P. M., and M. I. Kravchuk. Review of Los' book. *Voprosy istorii,* 1956, No. 11, pp. 161–65.

Sh[reiberg], S. "Iz istorii sovvlasti na Ukraine. O pervom vseukrainskom sezde sovetov i pervom sovetskom pravitelstve Ukrainy." *LR,* 1924, No. 4, pp. 66–185.

—"K protokolam pervogo vseukrainskogo soveshchaniia bolshevikov." *LR,* 1926, No. 5, pp. 55–63.

Shtein, B. *Russkii vopros na parizhskoi mirnoi konferentsii (1919–1920).* Moscow, 1949.

Shulhyn, O. *Polityka.* Kiev, 1918.

Skabichevsky, A. M. *Ocherki istorii russkoi tsenzury 1700–1863 gg.* St. Petersburg, 1892.

Skrypnyk, M. "Donbass i Ukraina." *Kommunist,* 1920, No. 4, pp. 52–54.

—"Do spravy ukrainizatsii 'Litopysu revoliutsii.'" *LR,* 1930, No. 1, pp. x–xi.

—*Istoriia proletarskoi revoliutsii na Ukraini.* Kharkiv, 1923.

—"Pomylky ta vypravlennia akademika M. Iavorskoho." *BU,* 1930, No. 2.

Slavnye bolshevichki. Moscow, 1958.

Smal-Stocki, R. *The Nationality Problem of the Soviet Union and Russian Communist Imperialism.* Milwaukee, 1952.

* Smolynchuk, A. I. *Bolsheviki Ukrainy v borbe za sovety (mart 1917–ianvar 1918).* Lviv, 1969.

Sovetskii federalizm. Sbornik, ed M. O. Reikhel. Moscow-Leningrad, 1930.

Spiridovich, A. I. *Istoriia bolshevizma v Rossii ot vozniknoveniia do zakhvata vlasti, 1883–1903–1917.* Paris, 1922.

—*Revoliutsionnoe dvizhenie v Rossii.* St. Petersburg, 1914.

* Stakhiv, M., P. G. Stercho, and N. I. Chirovsky. *Ukraine and the European Turmoil, 1917-1919.* New York, 1973.

Stakhiv, V. *Druha sovietska respublika v Ukraini.* New York-Detroit-Scranton, 1957.

—*Persha sovietska respublika na Ukraini.* New

York-Detroit-Scranton, 1956.
—*Zvidky vzialasia sovietska vlada v Ukraini ta khto ii buduvav?* New York-Detroit-Scranton, 1955.
Stankevich, V. *Sudby narodov Rossii.* Berlin, 1921.
* Sullivant, R. S. *Soviet Politics and the Ukraine, 1917–1957.* New York, 1962.
* Suprunenko, M. I. *Ocherki istorii grazhdanskoi voiny i inostrannoi voennoi interventsii na Ukraine.* Moscow, 1966.
—"Rozhrom kontrrevoliutsiinoi Tsentralnoi rady i vstanovlennia radianskoi vlady na Ukraini," in *Z istorii borotby za vstanovlennia radianskoi vlady na Ukraini* (Kiev, 1957), pp. 3–35.
Terletsky. "Diferentsiatsiia ukrainskogo krestianstva i kolkhozy." *Na agrarnom fronte*, 1925, No. 5, pp. 59–60.
Timoshenko, V. P. "Soviet Agricultural Policy and the Nationalities Problem in the USSR." *Report on the Soviet Union in 1956: A Symposium of the Institute for the Study of the USSR.* Conference at the Carnegie International Center, New York, 28–29 April 1956. Munich, 1956,
Trainin, I. P. *Sovetskoe mnogonatsionalnoe gosudarstvo.* Moscow, 1947.
Trotsky, L. D. *Den Ryska arbetarrevolutionen.* Stockholm, 1918.
—*Stalin: An Appraisal of the Man and His Influence.* New York-London, 1946. [Trotsky, *Stalin.*]
—*Stalinskaia shkola falsifikatsii. Popravki i dopolneniia k literature epigonov.* Berlin, 1932.
—*1905.* Moscow, 1922.
Tuchapsky, P. L. "Rolia Drahomanova v suspilnomu rukhu Rosii i Ukrainy." *Ukraina,* 1926, Book 2–3, pp. 100–24.
Ukraine. A Short Sketch of Economical, Cultural and Social Constructive Work of the Ukrainian Socialist Republic. Kharkiv, 1929.
Ukrainska zahalna entsyklopediia. Lviv-Stanyslaviv-Kolomyia, n.d.
Ukrainskii narod v ego proshlom i nastoiashchem. St. Petersburg, 1916.
U. S. S. R.: A Concise Handbook, ed E. J. Simons. New York, 1947.
Verhan, V. M. "Rolia Ivana Franka v ukrainskomu robitnychomu rusi." *Narodna volia* (Scranton), 1957, No. 11.
Vershigora, P. Review of the History of the Ukrainian SSR in *Oktiabr* (Moscow), 1954, No. 4, pp. 110–36.
Vikul, I. "Liudnist mista Kyiva," in *Demografichnyi zbirnyk*, ed.

Ptukha. Kiev, 1930.
Vobly, K. G. *Ekonomicheskaia geografiia Ukrainy*. Kiev, 1948.
Volin, M. *Istorii KP(b)U v styslomu narysi*. Kharkiv, 1931.
Vozniak, M. *Kyrylo-metodiievske bratstvo*. Lviv, 1921.
Vynnychenko, V. "Povorot t. Vynnychenka z Ukrainy." *Nova doba* (Vienna), 1920, No. 34.
Warski, A. "Sotsial-demokratiia Polshi i Latvii i II sezd RSDRP." *Kommunisticheskii internatsional,* 1929, No. 16–17, pp. 24–36.
Wolfe, B. D. "The Influence of Early Military Decisions upon the National Structure of the Soviet Union." *ASEER,* 1950, Vol. IX, No. 3, pp. 169–79.
—"Nationalism and Internationalism in Marx and Engels." *ASEER,* 1958, Vol. XVII, No. 4, pp. 403–17
—*Three Who Made a Revolution*. New York, 1948.
Xidias, J. *L'Intervention française en Russie, 1918–1919. Souvenirs d'un têmoin*. Paris, 1927.
Zalevsky, K. "Natsionalnye partii v Rossii," in *Obshchestvennoe dvizhenie v Rossii,* ed. L. Martov, P. Maslov, and A. Potresov. St. Petersburg, 1914. Vol. III, book 5, pp. 227–344.
Zaslavksy, D. *Mikhail Petrovich Dragomanov. Kritiko-biograficheskii ocherk*. Kiev, 1924.
Zatonsky, V. "K piatiletiiu KP(b)U," in *Pervyi sezd KP(b)U,* pp. 14–16.
—"K voprosu ob organizatsii vremennogo r.-k. pravitelstva Ukrainy." *LR,* 1925, No. 1, pp. 139–49.
—"Materialy do ukrainskoho natsionalnoho pytannia." *BU,* 1927, No. 5, pp. 9–32.
—"Pro pidsumky ukrainizatsii," in *Budivnytsvo radianskoi Ukrainy,* pp. 7–24.
—"Shkola revoliutsii," in *Oktiabrskaia revoliutsiia* (Kharkiv, 1922), pp. 93–95.
Zhyvotko, A. "Do istorii Ukrainskoi partii sotsiialistiv revoliutsioneriv." *Vilna spilka* (Prague-Lviv), 1927–29, No. 3, pp. 128–32.
Zinovev, G. *Istoriia Rossiiskoi kommunisticheskoi partii (bolshevikov)*. Leningrad, 1926.
Zlatopolsky, D. L. *Obrazovanie i razvitie SSSR kak soiuznogo gosudarstva*. Moscow, 1954.

Index